VISIBLE ENGLISH

UTRECHT STUDIES IN MEDIEVAL LITERACY

54

UTRECHT STUDIES IN MEDIEVAL LITERACY

General Editor

Marco Mostert (Universiteit Utrecht)

Editorial Board

Gerd Althoff (Westfälische-Wilhelms-Universität Münster)
Pierre Chastang (Université Versailles St-Quentin-en-Yvelines)
Erik Kwakkel (University of British Columbia)
Mayke de Jong (Universiteit Utrecht)
Rosamond McKitterick (University of Cambridge)
Arpád Orbán (Universiteit Utrecht)
Francesco Stella (Università degli studi di Siena)
Richard H. Rouse (UCLA)

VISIBLE ENGLISH

GRAPHIC CULTURE, SCRIBAL PRACTICE, AND IDENTITY, C. 700-C. 1550

Wendy Scase

BREPOLS

British Library Cataloguing in Publication Data

A catalogue record for this book is available from the British Library

© 2022 – Brepols Publishers n.v., Turnhout, Belgium
All rights reserved. No part of this publication may be reproduced, stored in a retrieval system, or transmitted, in any form or by any means, electronic, mechanical, photocopying, recording, or otherwise, without the prior permission of the publisher.

D/2022/0095/259

ISBN 978-2-503-59842-0

e-ISBN 978-2-503-59843-7

DOI 10.1484/M.USML-EB.5.127374

ISSN 2034-9416

e-ISNN 2294-8317

Printed in the EU on acid-free paper

For Rosie

Contents

Acknowledgements	ix
Notes on the Text	xiii
Abbreviations	xv
List of Figures	xvii

Introduction: Visible English: *Littera*, Identity, and Communities
of Practice 1

The Pedagogy of *Littera*	6
Identity and Communities of Practice	14
Visible English: Argument, Scope, and Organisation	21

1. Graphs, Alphabets, and Scripts 29

Grammar, Alphabets, and the Primer	43
The *Anglice littere* Tradition	61
Roman and Runic Scripts	86
Conclusion	99

2. Graphic Models 101

Imitation, Pedagogy, and Identity	103
Copy-Texts beyond the Classroom	120
Pattern Books	139
Conclusion	155

viii   *Contents*

3. Graphic Play   157

    Pedagogy and Graphic Puzzles   162
    Alphabet Games, Acrostics, and Riddles   168
    Signature Playfulness   201
    Conclusion   216

4. Graphic Display   217

    The Medieval Parish Church   223
    Domestic and Civic Spaces   244
    The Pre-Conquest Epigraphic Landscape   275
    Conclusion   281

5. Reprographics   283

    Littera and the Copying of Verse   290
    Littera and the Copying of Prose   317
    Littera and the Copying of Indexes   331
    Conclusion   348

Conclusion: Medieval English Literacy   351

Bibliography   359

    Primary Sources: Printed and Electronic   359
    Secondary Sources: Printed and Electronic   364

Indexes   395

    Index of Medieval Manuscripts   395
    General Index   399

Acknowledgements

During the preparation of this book I have incurred many debts of gratitude. The award of a Leverhulme Trust Major Research Fellowship gave me three years of uninterrupted research and writing and also provided funds for travel to libraries and conferences and for the purchase of images and copyright permissions. I am deeply grateful to the Trust for this enormous privilege. I am also indebted to the University of Birmingham for allowing me to take up the Fellowship and for facilitating my release from teaching and administrative duties. My thanks also go to Marco Mostert of Utrecht Studies in Medieval Literacy and to Guy Carney of Brepols Publishers for welcoming a typescript containing so many words and images (and for even inviting more), and for their efficient and generous support with the publication process. Grateful thanks are due also to the many scholars who have supported and advised on my work – while any remaining shortcomings are my full responsibility. Two stalwarts, Professor Matti Peikola and Professor Jeremy Smith, valiantly read and commented on the entire typescript in its first draft; Jeremy read the second draft also (and would, I am sure, have offered to read the third, but there are times when one has to save the extremely generous from themselves). During the course of the project, I benefited from the advice of many on specific points and on the project in general, and from the willingness of colleagues to share materials when libraries and archives were closed owing to the Covid-19 pandemic. They include Laura Ashe, Margaret Connolly, James Freeman, Catherine Karkov, Takako Kato, Stuart Lee, Nicola McDonald, Bella Millett, Linne Mooney, Ryan Perry, David Rundle, Merja Stenroos, Jacob Thaisen, Kjetil Thengs, Elaine Treharne, Daniel Wakelin, and Veronica West-Harling. This project has involved consultation of a large number and huge range of medieval materials and I am enormously grateful to the many librarians and curators who made this possible. Alan Cole of the University of

London Museum of Writing and Meriel Jeater of the Museum of London generously advised me about styli when their collections were closed owing to the pandemic; Richard Edgcombe of the Victoria and Albert Museum provided help with the Studley Alphabet Bowl; and Pernille Richards of Maidstone Museum provided me with reference images of MS Maidstone, Museum, A.13. While libraries and archives were closed, I benefited from the resourcefulness and generosity of staff who provided advice and in some cases mediated copying. My special thanks go to Frank Bowles, Cambridge University Library Department of Archives and Modern Manuscripts, for information about and mediated copying of Cambridge, UL, Hh.3.15; to Adam Goodwin, Archivist at the Record Office for Leicestershire, Leicester, and Rutland, for images of MS 18 D 59; and to staff of the Bodleian Libraries Special Collections Mediated Copying Service, and especially to Oliver House, Superintendent of the Special Collections Reading Rooms, who promptly came to my aid on many occasions. A large debt of thanks is also due to those who generously helped me navigate the sometimes tricky processes of obtaining publication-quality images and copyright permissions and frequently shared materials without charge; they include: Ann Barwood, Emeritus Canon Librarian of Exeter Cathedral and Gary Stringer of Exeter University who helped me to obtain images of the Exeter Book and permission to publish; Pippa Brook, of Stratford Town Trust; Matthew Champion of the Norfolk Graffiti Survey; Derek Craig of the Corpus of Anglo-Saxon Stone Sculpture; Tony Grant, British Library Customer Services, who supplied an image from MS Cotton Titus D.xviii; Angie McCarthy of the Imaging Department at the John Rylands Library; Fergus Wilde, Librarian, Chetham's Library, Manchester, who supplied images of their manuscript of the *Polychronicon*; and Linda Wilson and Anthea Hawdon of Raking Light who shared their images of the *ABC of Aristotle* graffito at Great Bardfield. I am also grateful to the many persons and institutions that have provided permissions to publish images. I am also hugely indebted to the digitisation programmes, their staff and funders, that made much of the manuscript material used in this book accessible online. It proved impractical to include URLs for digital surrogates used in this book but the material can readily be found. The availability of this material facilitated much of the research in this book and became even more crucial when the pandemic hit. Over the course of this project I have benefited from opportunities to present papers on work in progress at seminars and conferences and have received valuable from feedback from audiences. These include events hosted at the University of Bangor, the Uni-

Acknowledgements xi

versity of Birmingham, the University of Cambridge, Trinity College Dublin, Durham University, the University of Edinburgh, the University of Glasgow, the University of Kent, the University of Leiden, the University of Liverpool, the University of Newcastle, the University of Oslo, the University of Pennsylvania, the University of Stavanger, the University of Toronto, the University of Turku, the University of Warwick, and the University of York. My greatest debts, as ever, are to Elizabeth Scase and Roger Scase for their support and encouragement. Finally, this book is dedicated to Rosie Hobday-Scase, wishing her joyful discovery of reading and writing.

Notes on the Text

In line with the practice of *Utrecht Studies in Medieval Literacy*, all words in this book in any language other than modern English are printed in italics. This includes all material in Old and Middle English, even in cases where a word is the same in medieval and modern English. This policy also means that italicisation is applied uniformly to quotations that mix medieval languages, i.e. reverse italics are not used to indicate shifts in language in quotations that combine medieval languages. In addition, this policy on typeface sometimes entails that the punctuation of quotations from printed editions must be further lightly edited; normally no mention is made of this editing in individual references. The one exception to this policy of italicisation of text that is not in modern English is the printing of runes, which are not italicised.

In quotations of medieval material from manuscripts, editorial expansions of abbreviations are printed in superscript. Corrections supplied by scribes above the line are printed within back and forward oblique strokes. Scribal corrections made by erasure and overwriting are printed within angle brackets. Editorial matter is placed in square brackets.

Phonetic symbols are printed within forward oblique strokes. Italics (and reverse italics where appropriate) are used to indicate letters of the alphabet. In line with the remit of the series, it is hoped that this book will attract readers from various disciplinary backgrounds and to try to facilitate this quotations in all languages other than modern English are glossed. A range of methods is used from loose translation to paraphrase to sporadic glossing. The method chosen in any particular instance depends on what seems necessary to facilitate a grasp of the meaning rather than to offer exact translation. All translations are my own unless explicitly indicated and credited as quotations.

Unless otherwise indicated, all web-based resources for which a URL is provided in the footnotes, list of Abbreviations, or Bibliography, were last accessed on 12 May 2022. Should hyperlinks embedded in certain URLs not work for users of the e-book, this may be because extra spaces or codes have been introduced for layout purposes; a remedy is to input these URLs into a search engine manually.

Abbreviations

AND   *The Anglo-Norman Dictionary*, gen. ed. W. ROTHWELL, first edn. (London, 1977-1992), <http://www.anglo-norman.net>.

AND²   *The Anglo-Norman Dictionary*, gen. ed. W. ROTHWELL, second edn. (London, 2000-2012), <http://www.anglo-norman.net>.

BL   British Library

BnF   Paris, Bibliothèque nationale de France

Bod. Lib.   Oxford, Bodleian Library

CCCC   Cambridge, Corpus Christi College

DIMEV   *The DIMEV: An Open-Access, Digital Edition of the "Index of Middle English Verse"*, ed. L.R. MOONEY, D.W. MOSSER, and E. SOLOPOVA, with D. THORPE, D.H. RADCLIFFE, and L. HATFIELD (n.d.), <http://www.dimev.net>.

DMLBS   *Dictionary of Medieval Latin from British Sources Online*, ed. R. ASHDOWNE, D. HOWLETT, and R.E. LATHAM (Turnhout, 2015), <http://clt.brepolis.net/dmlbs/Default.aspx>.

DOE   *Dictionary of Old English: A to H online*, ed. A. CAMERON, A.C. AMOS, A. DI PAOLO HEALEY, *et al.* (Toronto, 2016), <http://doe.utoronto.ca/pages/index.html>.

EETS   *Early English Text Society*

    o.s.   Original Series

    s.s.   Supplementary Series

LAEME   *A Linguistic Atlas of Early Middle English, 1150-1325, Version 3.2*, ed. M. LAING (Edinburgh, 2008, 2013), <http://www.lel.ed.ac.uk/ihd/laeme2/laeme2.html>.

LALME   *An Electronic Version of "A Linguistic Atlas of Late Mediaeval English"*, ed. M. BENSKIN, M. LAING, V. KARAISKOS, and K. WILLIAMSON (Edinburgh, 2013), rev. online edn. of *A Linguistic Atlas*

	of Late Mediaeval English, ed. A. MCINTOSH, M.L. SAMUELS, and M. BENSKIN (Aberdeen, 1986), <http://www.lel.ed.ac.uk/ihd/elalme/elalme.html>.
LP	Linguistic Profile (in *LALME, q. v.*)
MED	*Middle English Dictionary*, ed. H. KURATH, S.M. KUHN, and R.E. LEWIS (Ann Arbor, 1954-2001), <https://quod.lib.umich.edu/m/middle-english-dictionary/dictionary>.
MELD	*A Corpus of Middle English Local Documents, 2017.1*, ed. M. STENROOS, K.V. THENGS, and G. BERGSTRØM (Stavanger, 2017-2020), <https://www.uis.no/en/meld-corpus-files>.
MLGB3	*Medieval Libraries of Great Britain, Version 3*, ed. R. SHARPE and J. WILLOUGHBY, with D. MAIRHOFER and P. KIDD (Oxford, 2015-), <http://mlgb3.bodleian.ox.ac.uk/>.
n.d.	no date given
n.p.	no page numbers
n.s.	new series
OED	*Oxford English Dictionary,* 3rd edn. (Oxford, 2000-), <http://oed.com>.
PL	*Patrologia Latina*, 217 vols., ed. J.P. MIGNE (Paris, 1844-1855).
RS	*Rolls Series*
STC	*The English Short Title Catalogue*, <http://estc.bl.uk>.
TNA	The National Archives
UL	University Library

List of Figures

Cover   Master-scribe and the *ABC of Aristotle*, MS London, BL, Addit. 37049, f. 86v (detail). Photo: © The British Library Board, MS British Library, Addit. 37049, f. 86v.

Fig. 1   Practice alphabet, MS London, BL, Harley 208, f. 87v (detail). Photo: © The British Library Board, MS British Library, Harley 208, f. 87v.   44

Fig. 2   Practice alphabet, MS London, BL, Harley 208, f. 88r (detail). Photo: © The British Library Board, MS British Library, Harley 208, f. 88r.   45

Fig. 3   Primer alphabet, MS Manchester, John Rylands Library, Eng. 85, f. 2r. Imaging: Copyright of the University of Manchester.   56

Fig. 4   *Anglice littere* table, MS London, BL, Cotton Titus D.xviii, f. 8v. Photo: © The British Library Board, MS British Library, Cotton Titus D.xviii, f. 8v.   68

Fig. 5   Runes and Roman script in *Juliana*, in the Exeter Book, MS Exeter, Cathedral Library, 3501, f. 76r (detail). Image reproduced with permission of the University of Exeter Digital Humanities and the Dean and Chapter, Exeter Cathedral.   91

Fig. 6   Script-language specialisation, MS Oxford, Corpus Christi College, 197, f. 90v. Photo: © Corpus Christi College, Oxford. By permission of the President and Fellows of Corpus Christi College, Oxford, MS 197, f. 90v.   93

Fig. 7   Female name *Osgyth* in both runes and Roman script on Lindisfarne 24 grave marker. © Corpus of Anglo-Saxon Stone Sculpture, photographer T. Middlemass.   95

Fig. 8   Practice writing in a school-book, MS London, BL, Harley 1002, f. 187v. © The British Library Board, MS British Library, Harley 1002, f. 187v.   115

xviii *List of Figures*

Fig. 9 Practice writing in a *Canterbury Tales* manuscript, MS Manchester, John Rylands Library, Eng. 113, f. 195v (detail). Imaging: Copyright of the University of Manchester. 130

Fig. 10 Page from a model writing book, MS Oxford, Bod. Lib., Ashmole 789, f. 4v. Photo: © Bodleian Libraries, University of Oxford. Creative Commons licence CC-BY-NC 4.0. 142

Fig. 11 Practice writing based on models in Humphrey Newton's manuscript, MS Oxford, Bod. Lib., Lat. Misc. c. 66, f. 98r. Photo: © Bodleian Libraries, University of Oxford. Creative Commons licence CC-BY-NC 4.0. 145

Fig. 12 Practice writing and drawing in Humphrey Newton's manuscript, MS Oxford, Bod. Lib., Lat. Misc. c. 66, f. 95v. Photo: © Bodleian Libraries, University of Oxford. Creative Commons licence CC-BY-NC 4.0. 148

Fig. 13 Master-scribe and the *ABC of Aristotle*, MS London, BL, Addit. 37049, f. 86v (detail). © The British Library Board, MS British Library, Addit. 37049, f. 86v. 176

Fig. 14 Chaucer's *ABC* with embellished initials and imitation, MS London, BL, Addit. 36983, f. 176r. © The British Library Board, MS British Library, Addit. 36983, f. 176r. 185

Fig. 15 Exuberant ascenders in the *Pilgrimage of the Life of Manhood*, MS Oxford, Bod. Lib., Laud Misc. 740, f. 18r (detail). Photo: © Bodleian Libraries, University of Oxford. Creative Commons licence CC-BY-NC 4.0. 187

Fig. 16 John Benet's '*quod*' signature (above, right); below, encrypted prophecy game with dice and glosses, MS Dublin, Trinity College, 516, f. 118r (detail). The Board of Trinity College Dublin. Image may not be further reproduced from software. For reproduction application must be made to the Head of Digital Resources and Imaging Services, by post to Trinity College, College Street, Dublin 2, Ireland; or by email at digitalresources@tcd.ie. 214

Fig. 17 Poem related to the *Dream of the Rood*, inscribed in runes around decorative panel, Ruthwell Cross, east side (detail). © Corpus of Anglo-Saxon Stone Sculpture, photographer T. Middlemass. 219

Fig. 18 *B* line from the *ABC of Aristotle*, graffito on pillar in north arcade, Great Bardfield Church, Essex. Photo: Anthea Hawdon of Raking Light (<www.rakinglight.co.uk>). 226

Fig. 19 Graffito, "*Well fare my lady Cateryne*", encrypted with a die and musical notation, Lidgate Church, Suffolk. Photo: M.J. Champion. 228

List of Figures xix

Fig. 20 Alphabets on the Studley Bowl, London, Victoria and Albert Museum, M.1:1, 2-1914. Photo: © Victoria and Albert Museum, London. 245

Fig. 21 Drinking bowl with moralising inscription, New York, Metropolitan Museum of Art, Cloister Collection, 55.25. Photo: © New York, Metropolitan Museum of Art. Creative Commons Zero (CC0). 248

Fig. 22 *Erthe upon erthe* and *Who-so him bethought* murals, Stratford-upon-Avon, Holy Cross Guild Chapel. Photo: © Stratford Town Trust. 261

Fig. 23 Orthography and hand of the *Ormulum*, MS Oxford, Bod. Lib., Junius 1, f. 10ra (detail). Photo: © Bodleian Libraries, University of Oxford. Creative Commons licence CC-BY-NC 4.0. 294

Fig. 24 Graphic rhyme in the *Prick of Conscience*, MS Leeds, UL, Brotherton 500, f. 43v. Reproduced with the permission of Special Collections, Leeds University Library. 307

Fig. 25 Intertwined *SI* or *IS* in the hand of the Amherst scribe, in "*Sequitur*", line 1, and in top right corner, MS London, BL, Addit. 37790, f. 226r (detail). © The British Library Board, MS British Library, Addit. 37790, f. 226r. 319

Fig. 26 The distinctive majuscule *I* in the hand of the Amherst scribe, e.g., "*as I was sclepande*", line 6, MS Cambridge, St. John's College, 189 (G.21), f. 1v. By permission of the Master and Fellows of St. John's College, Cambridge. 320

Fig. 27 The letter *3* (for 'Zoroastes' etc.) in the English index to the *Polychronicon*, MS Manchester, Chetham's Library, 11379 (Mun.A.6.90), f. 33v. Photo: Chetham's Library. 338

Fig. 28 The letter *3* (for 'York' etc.) in the English index to the *Polychronicon*, MS Manchester, Chetham's Library, 11379 (Mun.A.6.90), f. 34r. Photo: Chetham's Library. 339

Introduction: Visible English:
Littera, Identity, and Communities of Practice

[King Alfred] remained ignorant of letters until his twelfth year, or even longer. However, he was a careful listener, by day and night, to English poems, most frequently hearing them recited by others, and he readily retained them in his memory. [...] One day, therefore, when his mother was showing him and his brothers a book of English poetry which she held in her hand, she said: "I shall give this book to whichever one of you can learn it the fastest". Spurred on by these words, or rather by divine inspiration, and attracted by the beauty of the initial letter [...] he immediately took the book from her hand, and went to his teacher and learnt it. When it was learnt, he took it back to his mother and recited it.

(Asser, *Life of King Alfred*)[1]

Visible writings help to define, orient, and express our identities as diverse peoples who create and respond to these writings collectively in ever-changing, historically determined ways.

(Marija Dalbello, *Visible Writings*)[2]

Writing English makes the language visible. In Asser's *Life of King Alfred* (893), seeing English poems written in a book stimulates the young king's desire to learn to read. The *visibility* of English poetry – not just *hearing* the poetry – is a formative event for the future king and for his realm. Asser's story neatly illustrates sociolinguist Florian Coulmas's ob-

---

[1] Asser, *Life of King Alfred*, in: *Alfred the Great: Asser's* Life of King Alfred *and Other Contemporary Sources*, trans. S. KEYNES and M. LAPIDGE (Harmondsworth, 1983), pp. 66-110, at p. 75.

[2] M. DALBELLO, "Introduction", in: *Visible Writings: Cultures, Forms, Readings*, ed. M. DALBELLO and M. SHAW (New Brunswick, 2011), pp. 3-11, at p. 6.

2   *Introduction*

servation that the visibility of a language has functions beyond communicating information: "The visibility of a language is strongly indicative of its status and, therefore, subject to political decision".[3] We know this from our own modern experience. A few well-known examples of the many communities and nation states today where language visibility is a live issue illustrate the point. There are, of course, many languages and language varieties for which there is no visible presence, languages without writing (for example, some of the languages of the North American First Nations). Many multilingual communities legislate for official status for two or more of their languages in speech and writing (for example, French and English in Canada), or for protection of certain minority languages through measures that include public visibility (for example, bilingual Welsh-English road signs and official documents). Sectarian differences in Northern Ireland are expressed in ongoing disputes over the status of the Irish language and support for its use in speech and in writing.[4] Language visibility is perceived by both policy-makers and citizens as crucial to social identity. The Scottish government's current language policy explicitly aims to increase the visibility of Scots, "*tae encourage the increased yiss o Scots as a valid an visible means o communication in aw aspects o Scottish life*", quoting a curriculum statement that the Scots language is "a rich resource for children and young people to learn about Scotland's culture, identity and language".[5]

Visible language may communicate identity in its smallest details: for example, we are familiar with the associations that scripts, letters, and fonts may acquire. Anglophones educated in Britain will perceive 'honor' and 'pro-

[3] F. COULMAS, *Sociolinguistics: The Study of Speakers' Choices*, 2nd edn. (Cambridge, 2013), p. 207.

[4] For a list of over thirty multilingual states and regions with language laws in the 1990s see R. LANDRY and R.Y. BOURHIS, "Linguistic landscape and ethnolinguistic vitality: An empirical study", *Journal of Language and Social Psychology*, 16.1 (1997), pp. 23-49, at pp. 24-25.

[5] "To encourage the increased use of Scots as a valid and visible means of communication in all aspects of Scottish life" (SCOTTISH GOVERNMENT and EDUCATION SCOTLAND, *Scots Language Policy* (2015), <https://www.gov.scot/binaries/content/documents/govscot/publications/factsheet/2015/09/scots-language-policy-scots-version/documents/scots-language-policy-scots-pdf/scots-language-policy-scots-pdf/govscot%3Adocument/scots%2Blanguage%2Bpolicy%2B%2Bscots.pdf>. The curriculum statement quoted by the document is *Literacy and English: Principles and Practice Document* (2009). Tabouret-Keller observes that "[m]embers of a group that feel their political or cultural identity threatened are likely to make particularly assertive claims about the social importance of maintaining or resurrecting *their language*" (A. TABOURET-KELLER, "Language and identity", in: *The Handbook of Sociolinguistics*, ed. F. COULMAS (Oxford, 1997), pp. 315-26, at pp. 319-20, italics in original).

Introduction 3

gram' as American spellings. For users of the Latin alphabet, particular scripts, letters, and diacritics may iconify non-English languages, for example the Greek and Cyrillic alphabets, *ø* in Danish, and *ü* in German. Anglophones in New York recognise when they are in Chinatown even if they cannot read Chinese characters. The shapes and designs of letters may signify a brand. Coca-Cola has recently adopted a bespoke font, TCCC Unity, to communicate the brand's identity: for example, the letter *Q* is said to resemble a glass with a drinking straw.[6] The Reith typeface recently commissioned for the British Broadcasting Corporation (named for the founder John Reith) references classic British typefaces such as Gill Sans to express the heritage and national identity of the Corporation, while aiming for functional and aesthetic letterforms that promote legibility and accessibility to maximise audiences worldwide.[7] All of these examples testify to Marija Dalbello's statement, quoted in the epigraph to this chapter, that "visible writings help to define, orient, and express our identities". Visible language – writing – can make, and manifest, boundaries between identity and difference.

Although the contribution of visible language to identity formation is a familiar part of experience in many contemporary societies, and the "Uniformitarian Principle", "the idea that languages varied in the same patterned way in the past as they have been observed to do today", suggests that the same *could* have been true in the past, it does not follow that it *was* the case.[8] Nor, if it *was* the case in the past, is it obvious in what ways writing was experienced as a vehicle for identity formation and how experiences of writing as a vehicle for social identity differed in different times and societies. As Dalbello points out, engagement with visible language – writing – is "historically determined". The present study investigates the question of whether and in what ways visible language contributed to identity formation in the past by making a case study of visible English *c.* 700-*c.* 1550, when literate practice

---

[6] L. WOODHOUSE, "After 130 years, Coca-Cola has the typeface it deserves", *Campaign*, 16 Jan. 2018, <https://www.campaignlive.co.uk/article/130-years-coca-cola-typeface-deserves/1454619>.

[7] D. BAILEY, "Introducing Reith – the new face of the BBC", *GEL: Global Experience Language* (16 Jan. 2018), <http://www.bbc.co.uk/gel/articles/introducing-bbc-reith>.

[8] J.C. CONDE-SILVESTRE and J. HERNÁNDEZ-CAMPOY, "A sociolinguistic approach to the diffusion of chancery written practices in late fifteenth-century private correspondence", *Neuphilologische Mitteilungen* 105.2 (2004), pp. 133-152, at p. 135; cf. A. BERGS, "The uniformitarian principle and the risk of anachronisms in language and social history", in: *The Handbook of Historical Sociolinguistics*, ed. J.C. CONDE-SILVESTRE and J. HERNÁNDEZ-CAMPOY (Malden, 2012), pp. 80-99.

4 *Introduction*

was predominantly in Latin and all texts were – save for the final few decades – produced individually by hand.[9]

Previous work on medieval English language and social identity has mainly focused on the discursive representation of regional dialect sounds in Middle English and the emergence of socially-prestigious orthographies in the fifteenth century. The evidence that spoken varieties of medieval English indexed regional, cultural, and social identities (as of course did multilingual competence, for example in varieties of French, in Latin, in Welsh, in Flemish, in Gaelic, and so on) is well known.[10] In an often-cited example, the Miller in Chaucer's *Reeve's Tale* smiles at the northernisms of the students; Aleyn and John may be university scholars but their classroom learning is (he thinks) no match for his guile.[11] Mak in the Towneley *Second Shepherds' Play* is identifiable as a representative of the king by his "*sothren tothe*" ("southern speech").[12] Language-bending Covetousness in *Piers Plowman* is familiar with the "*Frenssh*" ("French") of the farthest end of Norfolk but not the language of penitence.[13] Medieval written English, however, is often seen as a distorting, murky lens on the social semiotics of speech rather than as a set of resources for identity formation. Tim Machan reminds us that "our access to [...] sociolinguistic markers is only through discursive representations of them"

---

[9] The present study of the medieval English corpus is offered in the hope that it might provide case-material for future comparative, cross-cultural, and cross-period studies of literacy practices of the kinds envisaged by Malachi Beit-Arié for book history: "immersed as we are in the particularities of each script and in the history of book production, we should nevertheless embark on a quest for a 'general' or 'universal' grammar of the codex [...] and add further common structure and texture to cultural multiplicity" (M. BEIT-ARIE, "Why comparative codicology?", *Gazette du livre médiévale* 23 (1993), pp. 1-5, at p. 5). For an excellent comparative essay collection on vernacular book history see *Vernacular Manuscript Culture 1000-1500*, ed. E. KWAKKEL (Leiden, 2018).

[10] A. PUTTER, "The linguistic repertoire of medieval England, 1100-1500", in: *Imagining Medieval English: Language Structures and Theories, 500-1500*, ed. T.W. MACHAN (Cambridge, 2016), pp. 126-144, at p. 126; T.W. MACHAN, *English in the Middle Ages* (Oxford, 2003), pp. 76, 80.

[11] Geoffrey Chaucer, *Canterbury Tales*, in: *The Riverside Chaucer*, ed. L.D. BENSON, 3rd edn. (Oxford, 1988), lines I.4022-4047; cf. W. SCASE, "Tolkien, philology, and the *Reeve's Tale*: Towards the cultural move in Middle English studies", *Studies in the Age of Chaucer* 24 (2002), pp. 325-334.

[12] *The Shepherds (2)*, in: *The Towneley Plays*, ed. G.P.J. EPP (Kalamazoo, MI, 2018), line 311.

[13] William Langland, The Vision of Piers Plowman: *A Complete Edition of the B-Text*, ed. A.V.C. SCHMIDT, new edn. (London, 1987), v.235.

Introduction   5

which cannot be taken at face value.[14] Lexis is sometimes seen as important to identity construction; for example, Timofeeva suggests that vocabulary used by the ecclesiastical elite in the highest written register of Old English and in Latin was associated with "how the Anglo-Saxon ecclesiastical community saw its own history in relation to the broader Christian history and constructed itself in relation to the bigger community of all Christians".[15] However, *graphic* variation in written English language – what the language looks like – is not usually recognised as capable of performing identity-work until a standardised, or focused, written variety emerges in the fifteenth century, when prestige and non-prestige categories of English writing emerge.[16] To date, variations in scribal outputs have usually been studied in relation to questions of language change and the emergence of standard orthography.[17] This research tradition builds on the seminal work of Angus McIntosh and the Middle English Dialect Project which reoriented attitudes towards the value of written texts in historical linguistics. The present study is greatly indebted to and engages with this tradition, although it develops a very different, socio-cultural, approach to the material.[18]

---

[14]   MACHAN, *English in the Middle Ages*, p. 80. Cf. R. Anthony Lodge's regret that written sources are limited evidence for the spoken language, "[a]s soon as we come near the vernacular, it slips away, leaving only the faintest traces of its passage" (R.A. LODGE, *A Sociolinguistic History of Parisian French* (Cambridge, 2004), p. 22).

[15]   O. TIMOFEEVA, "'*Of Ledene bocum to Engliscum gereorde*': Bilingual communities of practice in Anglo-Saxon England", in: *Communities of Practice in the History of English*, ed. J. KOPACZYK and A.H. JUCKER (Amsterdam, 2013), pp. 201-223, at p. 217.

[16]   CONDE-SILVESTRE and HERNÁNDEZ-CAMPOY, "A sociolinguistic approach". Cf. Jeremy Smith's studies of Gower, J.J. SMITH, "Spelling and tradition in fifteenth-century copies of Gower's *Confessio Amantis*", in: *The English of Chaucer and his Contemporaries*, ed. J.J. SMITH (Aberdeen, 1989), pp. 96-113; and ID., "John Gower and London English", in: *A Companion to Gower*, ed. S. ECHARD (Cambridge, 2004), pp. 61-72.

[17]   Cf. "most historical sociolinguistic studies on orthographic variants deal with aspects of standardization", H. RUTKOWSKA and P. RÖSSLER, "Orthographic variables", in: *The Handbook of Historical Sociolinguistics*, ed. J. HERNÁNDEZ-CAMPOY and J.C. CONDE-SILVESTRE (Oxford, 2012), pp. 213-236, at p. 214.

[18]   From the 1950s, McIntosh opposed the view then prevailing in sociolinguistics that "[a] spoken manifestation of language is felt to be 'the real thing', a corresponding written manifestation [...] no more than a dim and distorted reflection or derivative" (A. MCINTOSH, "The analysis of written Middle English" [1956], repr. in: *Middle English Dialectology: Essays on Some Principles and Problems by Angus McIntosh, M.L. Samuels, and M. Laing*, ed. M. LAING (Aberdeen, 1989), pp. 1-21, at p. 6. He called for closer collaboration between linguists and palaeographers to investigate "the true significance of the graphic data" and for a "reorientation" of approaches to written language (p. 8). Writing should, he argued, be analysed on "graphematic" lines (pp. 7-8), by which he meant that graphic features – letters and other graphs – should

6   *Introduction*

The Pedagogy of Littera

Visible English argues that elementary Latin grammar pedagogy transmitted an understanding and experience of graphic practice as a set of resources available for the definition of identity, difference, and belonging. This study investigates for the first time the experience of Anglophone literacy (by which I mean literate practice in the English language) in relation to this framework, proposing that it gives insight into the ways in which communities that read and wrote English understood and experienced their literate practices. To illustrate this claim, *Visible English* identifies and analyses inflections of basic literacy pedagogy from across the corpus of medieval English and offers diverse case studies of this discourse's identity-forming potential. Of course, we do not know nearly as much as we would like about how people in the past learned to read and write, and we lack granular accounts of how practices varied in different periods and communities.[19] Asser's story about Alfred's re-

---

be analysed to discover the basic graphic elements and their functions in any written system. Both disciplines of palaeography and linguistic study, he argued, had a vital contribution to make to this endeavour. The present study takes up McIntosh's challenge to enhance our understanding of the ways in which medieval English was capable of communicating and functioning graphically.

[19] Valuable studies with relevance to Insular medieval literacy education include G.H. BROWN, "The dynamics of literacy in Anglo-Saxon England", *Bulletin of the John Rylands Library* 77.1 (1995), pp. 109-142; M. CAMARGO and M. CURRY WOODS, "Writing instruction in late medieval Europe", in: *A Short History of Writing Instruction: From Ancient Greece to Modern America*, ed. J.J. MURPHY, 3rd edn. (New York, 2012), pp. 114-147; C. CANNON, *From Literacy to Literature: England, 1300-1400* (Oxford, 2016); M.T. CLANCHY, *From Memory to Written Record: England 1066-1307*, 3rd edn. (Malden, Oxford, and Chichester, 2013); J. CRICK, "The art of writing: Scripts and scribal production", in: *The Cambridge History of Early Medieval English Literature*, ed. C. LEES (Cambridge, 2012), pp. 50-72, and "English vernacular script", in: *The Cambridge History of the Book in Britain: Volume I: c. 400-1100*, ed. R. GAMESON (Cambridge, 2011), pp. 174-186; M. DENLEY, "Elementary teaching techniques and Middle English religious didactic writing", in: *Langland, The Mystics, and the Medieval English Religious Tradition: Essays in Honour of S.S. Hussey*, ed. H. PHILLIPS (Cambridge, 1990), pp. 223-241; I. DUMITRESCU, *The Experience of Education in Anglo-Saxon England* (Cambridge, 2018); H. GNEUSS, "The study of language in Anglo-Saxon England", in: *Textual and Material Culture in Anglo-Saxon England: Thomas Northcote Toller and the Toller Memorial Lectures*, ed. D. SCRAGG (Cambridge, 2003), pp. 75-105; M. GODDEN, "King Alfred's *Preface* and the teaching of Latin in Anglo-Saxon England", *English Historical Review* 117 (2002), pp. 596-604; M. GRETSCH, "Literacy and the uses of the vernacular", in: *The Cambridge Companion to Old English Literature*, ed. M. GODDEN and M. LAPIDGE (Cambridge, 2013), pp. 273-294; S. GWARA, "Anglo-Saxon schoolbooks", in: *The Cambridge History of the Book in Britain: Volume I: c. 400-1100*, ed. R. GAMESON (Cambridge, 2011), pp. 507-524; J. HILL, "Learning Latin in Anglo-Saxon

Introduction 7

sponse to seeing a book of English poetry is a narrative about literacy pedagogy, but Asser does not provide the kind of detail we might like about *how*
Alfred's tutor taught the twelve-year old prince to read English.[20] Yet, we do
know that the broad basics of grammar teaching were widespread and long-
lived: alongside rhetoric, write Copeland and Sluiter, the art of grammar, "con-

---

England: Traditions, texts, and techniques", in: *Learning and Literacy in Medieval England and
Abroad*, ed. S. REES JONES (Turnhout, 2003: *Utrecht Studies in Medieval Literacy* 3), pp. 7-30,
and "Ælfric's grammatical triad", in: *Form and Content of Instruction in Anglo-Saxon England
in the Light of Contemporary Manuscript Evidence*, ed. P. LENDINARA, L. LAZZARI, and M.A.
D'ARONCO (Turnhout, 2007: *Fédération Internationale des Instituts d'Etudes Médiévales, Textes
et Etudes du Moyen Age* 39), pp. 285-307; R.W. HUNT, "Oxford grammar masters in the Middle
Ages", repr. in: R.W. HUNT, *The History of Grammar in the Middle Ages: Collected Papers*, ed.
G.L. BURSILL-HALL (Amsterdam, 1980: *Studies in the History of the Language Sciences* 5), pp.
167-197; T. HUNT, *Teaching and Learning Latin in Thirteenth-Century England*, 3 vols.
(Cambridge, 1991); M. IRVINE, "Bede the grammarian and the scope of grammatical studies in
eighth-century Northumbria", *Anglo-Saxon England* 15 (1986), pp. 15-44, and *The Making of
Textual Culture: 'Grammatica' and Literary Theory, 350-1100* (Cambridge, 1994); M. IRVINE
and D. THOMSON, "*Grammatica* and literary theory", in: *The Cambridge History of Literary
Criticism, Vol. 2, The Middle Ages*, ed. A. MINNIS and I. JOHNSON (Cambridge, 2005), pp. 13-41;
C.D. LANHAM, "Writing instruction from late Antiquity to the twelfth century", in: *A Short
History of Writing Instruction: From Ancient Greece to Modern America*, ed. J.J. MURPHY, 3rd
edn. (New York, 2012), pp. 77-113; V. LAW, *The Insular Latin Grammarians in the Early Middle
Ages* (Woodbridge, 1982), and "The study of grammar in eighth-century Southumbria", *Anglo-
Saxon England* 12 (1983), pp. 43-71; J.A.H. MORAN, *The Growth of English Schooling:
Learning, Literacy, and Laicization in Pre-Reformation York Diocese* (Princeton, 1985); M.
MOSTERT, "Some thoughts on urban schools, urban literacy, and the development of western
civilisation", in: *Writing and the Administration of Medieval Towns: Medieval Urban Literacy
I*, ed. M. MOSTERT and A. ADAMSKA (Turnhout, 2014: *Utrecht Studies in Medieval Literacy* 27),
pp. 337-348; N. ORME, *English School Exercises, 1420-1530* (Toronto, 2013: *Pontifical Institute
of Mediaeval Studies, Studies and Texts* 181), "Games and education in medieval England", in:
Games and Gaming in Medieval Literature, ed. S. PATTERSON (New York, 2015), pp. 45-60,
Medieval Children (New Haven, 2001), and *Medieval Schools: From Roman Britain to
Renaissance England* (New Haven, 2006); M.B. PARKES, "*Rædan, areccan, smeagan*: How the
Anglo-Saxons read", *Anglo-Saxon England* 26 (1997), pp. 1-22; S. REYNOLDS, *Medieval
Reading: Grammar, Rhetoric and the Classical Text* (Cambridge, 1996); and the essays in
*Teaching Writing, Learning to Write: Proceedings of the XVIth Colloquium of the Comité
Internationale de Paléographie Latine*, ed. P.R. ROBINSON (London, 2010). Much of the work
on Old and Middle English literacy investigates ideas that informed Old and Middle English
literary *composition*, for example, ideas drawn from scholastic theories of authorship and
authority, from rhetoric, and from poetics, rather than graphic education or practice. For English
literacy and formal schooling see further below.

[20] Asser goes on to record that Alfred's desire to learn was frustrated by lack of teachers and
it seems that the king did not become literate until he was almost forty (C.P. WORMALD, "The
uses of literacy in Anglo-Saxon England and its neighbours", *Transactions of the Royal
Historical Society* 27 (1977), pp. 95-114, at p. 105.

8   *Introduction*

stituted the abiding theoretical toolbox for anyone engaged in a life of letters"
from late antiquity to the fifteenth century.[21] The basics comprise a theory of
the letter (*littera*) that is set out in the first few pages of the most influential
classical and medieval grammars and widely informs medieval discourse about
language. Ancient grammarians and their medieval followers taught that the
littera was the smallest linguistic unit. Whereas the modern word 'letter' usually refers to a written character, rather than to a speech-sound, the *littera* has
three attributes or properties: a shape (*figura*), a name (*nomen*), and a sound
value (*potestas*). For example, the fourth-century grammarian Donatus in his
chapter "*De Littera*" in his *Ars maior*, states that the *littera* is the smallest part
of articulate speech, it is *vox* that can be written separately and it has three
properties, name, shape, and sound:

> [*l*]*ittera est pars minima vocis articulatae* [...] *littera est vox, quae scribi potest*
> *individua* [...] *accidunt cuique littera tria, nomen figura potestas, quaeritur enim,*
> *quid vocatur littera, qua figura sit, qua possit.*[22]

Donatus's work was widely known, studied, and imitated in the medieval period.[23] Priscian's *Institutiones grammaticae*, which follows and is broadly
structured like Donatus's *Ars maior*, is however a much amplified account of
grammar. Priscian opens the first book of the *Institutiones* with a chapter on
vox (broadly, sound), showing there are four kinds of sound, two of which are
"*literata*", that is, they can be written.[24] The second chapter of Book 1, "*De*
Litera", explains that a letter is the smallest unit of *vox* that can be written

---

[21] *Medieval Grammar and Rhetoric: Language Arts and Literary Theory, AD 300-1475*, ed.
R. COPELAND and I. SLUITER (Oxford, 2009), p. 1. For the origins of grammar and its history in
the ancient world see V. LAW, *The History of Linguistics in Europe: From Plato to 1600* (Cambridge, 2003), pp. 52-93, and IRVINE and THOMSON, "*Grammatica* and literary theory", who note
that "[t]he elementary grammar-school curriculum was remarkably consistent throughout the
Middle Ages" (p. 37) but "[e]xactly how the classical grammatical heritage was transmitted to the
monasteries of Ireland and England remains a matter of debate" (p. 19).

[22] Donatus, *Ars maior*, in: "*Donati* Ars grammatica", ed. H. KEIL, in: *Grammatici Latini*,
ed. H. KEIL, 8 vols. (Leipzig, 1864), 4, pp. 367-402, at pp. 367-368. For Donatus and the *Ars*
maior see LAW, *The Insular Latin Grammarians*, pp. 14-16.

[23] S. GWARA, "Anglo-Saxon schoolbooks", pp. 512-513.

[24] Priscian, *Institutiones grammaticae*: "*Prisciani* Institutionum grammaticarum *Libri I-XII*",
ed. M. HERTZIUS, in: *Grammatici Latini*, ed. H. KEIL, 8 vols. (Leipzig, 1855), 2, p. 5 (Book 2,
ch. 5). For Priscian (fl. *c*. 500) see LAW, *The History of Linguistics in Europe*, pp. 86-91 and for
Priscian's theory of *vox* and its reception by early Christian grammarians see M. IRVINE, *The*
Making of Textual Culture, pp. 94-97.

Introduction 9

separately, "[*l*]*itera est vox, quae scribi potest individua*".[25] The letter is an image of a literate sound and may be recognised by its form: a letter therefore has a name, a shape, and a sound-value ("[*l*]*itera igitur est nota elementi et velut imago quaedam vocis literatae quae cognoscitur ex qualitate et quantitatae figurae linearum* [...] [*a*]*ccidit igitur literae nomen, figura, potestas*").[26] From the point of view of traditional grammar, therefore, the *littera* is a broader concept than that connoted by the modern word 'letter'.[27] These basics introduce the study of 'orthography', etymologically, 'correct graphisation' in English, as the homilist and grammarian Ælfric (*c.* 950-*c.* 1010) writes in his grammar (which is based on excerpts from Priscian), "*'ortographia' on Grecisc, þæt is on Leden 'recta scriptura' and on Englisc 'riht gewrit'*".[28] Many grammarians follow the analysis of *littera* with discussion of alphabets, after which they often proceed to discuss the syllable. The syllable is basic to the doctrine of how letters may be written and read in combination to produce words. Priscian, for example, explains that the syllable is "*comprehensio literarum consequens sub uno accentu et uno spiritu prolata* [...] *vox literalis*" ("a cluster of consecutive letters that can be pronounced in one breath and under one accent [...] sound in letters").[29] The verb '*spellen*' (*MED, spellen,* v.2) is used in Middle English to denote this skill of combining letters into sounds.[30] The syllable is also taught as the essential building block of poetic metre and the foundation of study of how poetry should be read aloud. Combinations of syllables of different kinds (long and short for example) produce metrical feet that in turn combine to produce the lines of the standard metres. Therefore, in the theory of *littera*, language was not considered to be a phenomenon prior to or potentially independent from writing. Language could not be thought about independently of its *figurae* and their relationships with *potestates*. In this way, the doctrine of *littera* was a theory of reading and writing, of how language was made visible.[31]

---

[25] Priscian, *Institutiones grammaticae*, p. 6 (Book 1, ch. 2).

[26] Priscian, *Institutiones grammaticae*, pp. 6-7.

[27] D. ABERCROMBIE, "What is a 'letter'?", *Lingua* 2 (1949), pp. 54-63; LAW, *The History of Linguistics in Europe*, p. 61.

[28] Ælfric, *Ælfrics Grammatik und Glossar*, ed. J. ZUPITZA (Berlin, 1880), p. 291. For Ælfric's grammar see LAW, *The History of Linguistics in Europe*, pp. 193-197. See further in Chapter Five.

[29] Priscian, *Institutiones grammaticae*, p. 44 (Book 2, ch. 1).

[30] See Chapter Five, p. 297.

[31] "The stream of *litterae* in writing is represented by a sequence of *figurae*; indeed this is the way the *littera* becomes visible" (*LAEME*, 2.3.1). Irvine comments, "[t]he theory of letters [i.e.

10 *Introduction*

This perspective on language as *littera* may be illustrated with the story of the shibboleth from the Old Testament Book of Judges as it appears in the Wycliffite Bible translation (late fourteenth century). The people of Gilead are at war with the people of Ephraim. The Gileadites take control of the fords over the River Jordan to prevent their enemies from crossing. When a man arrives at one of the fords, the Gileads ask him if he is an Ephraimite. If he says that he is not an Ephraimite, they test his claim by asking him to pronounce 'shibboleth'. If he pronounces the word with a sibilant rather than a fricative, they identify him as an Ephraimite and kill him. By pronouncing the word in a different way from the Gileads, fugitives are identified as Ephraimites, denied passage across the border, and killed. So 42,000 Ephraimites are slaughtered. The story of shibboleth is recounted in the Wycliffite Bible in this way:

> *Wh^{a}n a man of the nou^{m}bre of Eff^{a}im fleende* [when a fleeing Ephraimite] *was comen to þe forþ^s* [fords] *^{and} hadde seid, "Y p^{re}ȝe þ^{at} ȝee lete me passe", Galadites seiden to him, "wheþ^{er} art þ^u an Effrate?", þe whiche seiende, "Y am not", þei askeden him, "sei þa^{n}ne 'sebolech'" (þ^{at} is to menen 'an er'* [that is to mean an ear of corn]*), þe whiche answerde "shebolech", by the same lettre an 'er' not myȝti to b^{ri}ngen out* [these letters *sh* lacking the *potestas* to express 'ear' (of corn)] *^{and} anoen take þe kutteden his þrote* [they cut his throat] *in þ^{at} going ou^{er} Iordan ^{and} þer fellen i^n þ^{at} time of Effraim xlii thousend.*

> (Judges 12:6, Wycliffite Bible, Early Version, MS Oxford, Christ Church, 145, f. 81v).[32]

The Wycliffite translator uses the language of *littera* to describe the moment of linguistic boundary-drawing in the Judges story of 'shibboleth'. The *Latin Vulgate Bible* reads, *"Dic ergo 'Scibboleth', quod interpretatur 'Spica'. Qui respondebat, 'Sibboleth': eadem littera 'spicam' exprimere non valens"* ("the same letter [*s*] not having the power to express '*spica*'"). The Wycliffite translator's word *"lettre"* translates *"littera"*, the super-ordinate category '*letter*'. MED glosses *"myȝti"* here as "able (to do something)" (*"mighti"*, adj., 2b), but arguably *"not myȝti to b^{ri}ngen out"* suggests that the translator reads *"non valens"*

---

litterae] is thus part of the larger network of discourse that frames the theory of language and discloses that *grammatica* was primarily a body of theory about writing and texts" (M. IRVINE, *The Making of Textual Culture*, p. 97).

[32] My punctuation. Anne Hudson regards this manuscript as the most reliable one of the early version of the translation (*Selections from English Wycliffite Writings*, ed. A. HUDSON (Cambridge, 1978), p. 163).

Introduction 11

in grammatical terms, as *non habens potestatem*, not having the *potestas*. The translator thinks of the pronunciation test in terms of *littera*: the Ephraimite uses the wrong letters, not just the wrong sound. The scribe too thinks in terms of *littera*: he represents the difference in sound in his choice of letters to spell the initial sound of 'shibboleth', "*sebolech*" contrasting with "*shebolech*".

In the story of 'shibboleth', pronunciation difference becomes a boundary between peoples and a lethal identity marker. It is not hard to think of further examples of linguistic variants that became associated with social identity and demarcated boundaries between belonging and difference. Chillingly echoing the story from Judges in its violence is that of the distinguishing of Flemings in fourteenth-century London during the Peasants' Revolt: according to one of the London chronicles, Flemings were identified because they said "*Case and Brode*" and could not say "*Breede and Chese*" and were then executed; their variant pronunciation of these cognate words was a marker of difference.[33] Frenchmen who could not say 'shield' and 'friend' in Dutch were murdered in Bruges in 1302, and Germans who could not say 'lentil', 'wheel', and 'mill' in Polish were murdered in Cracow in 1312.[34] Stories about shibboleths are not always so violent, though they are always about social belonging and difference, inclusion and exclusion. Reynard the Fox, in the continental French poem the *Roman de Renart*, adopts a disguise as the minstrel Galopin. 'Galopin' makes many comical errors, including using the verb '*foutre*' ('to fuck') where the verbs '*être*', '*avoir*', and '*pouvoir*' ('to be', 'to have', 'to be able') would normally be used, and mixes French with English; for example, when addressing Isengrin the wolf, "*Godehelpe [...] bele sire [...] Ya, ge fot molt bon jogler*" ("may God help, fine sir, yes, I *fot* very well entertain").[35] Reynard cunningly exploits boundary-drawing features of language as part of his assumption of the false identity of Galopin: for those who used Parisian French, these linguistic habits distinguished their variety from the French used in England. These are stories about spoken language, but, as we have seen with the

---

[33] *Chronicles of London*, ed. C.L. KINGSFORD (Cambridge, 1905), p. 15.

[34] L. SCALES, "Bread, cheese, and genocide: Imagining the destruction of peoples in western medieval Europe", *History* 92.3 (2007), pp. 284-300, at p. 286; E. SPINDLER, "Flemings in the Peasants' Revolt", in: *Contact and Exchange in Later Medieval Europe: Essays in Honour of Malcolm Vale*, ed. H. SKODA, P. LANTSCHNER, and R.L.J. SHAW (Cambridge, 2012), pp. 59-78, at pp. 69-70.

[35] *Le Roman de Reynard*, ed. E. MARTIN, 4 vols. (Strasbourg, 1882-1887), 1, 1b lines 2351, 2370; M. LAWRENCE, "The story-teller's verbal *Jonglerie* in '*Reynard Jongleur*'", in: *Telling the Story in the Middle Ages: Essays in Honor of Evelyn Birge Vitz*, ed. K.A. DUYS, E. EMERY, and L. POSTLETHWAITE (Cambridge, 2015), pp. 31-46, at pp. 34-36, and see references at n. 8.

12 *Introduction*

example from the Wycliffite Bible, the theory of *littera* meant that such varia-tion was thought about in terms of written forms: the *potestas* or sound of speech was discussed as an aspect of a letter.[36]

Literate practice *enlarged* the possibilities for linguistic variation – the look of language, and not just the sound of language, could vary – while the *pedagogy of littera*, the present study argues, made graphic variation socially meaningful. The theory of *littera* was transmitted by elementary pedagogic texts and institutions and its framing in a pedagogic discourse is intrinsic, the present study argues, to its identity-forming potential. While the discourse of *littera* provided a way of thinking about variation and narrating stories of shib-boleths, the pedagogy of *littera* produced understanding of *and experiences of* identity and difference. Grammar pedagogy is an 'us and them' discourse: the grammarians of antiquity prescribed practice and drew dividing lines between 'our' graphic practices and 'theirs'. As the present study will demonstrate, something as basic as the alphabet could manifest social boundaries. The basic modes of teaching this knowledge and instruction in its application in reading and writing instantiated this 'us and them' discourse. Learning through imita-tion of model letters and writing is an example of how pedagogic practice produced identity and difference. Activities that were set to promote skills of letter and syllable recognition and analysis, for example, solving letter and word puzzles such as riddles and acrostics, and encoding and decoding lan-guage in cryptographs, also instantiated 'us and them' discourse and produced identity and difference. Drawing boundaries between 'our' practice and 'theirs', *Visible English* argues, basic grammatical pedagogy transmitted liter-ate practice as a way of entering into and inhabiting a social identity.

Anyone in a post-conversion Anglophone society (by which I mean a soci-ety that used English as one of its spoken languages) who learned to read or write to any degree, by whatever processes, however informal, *Visible English* argues and illustrates, must have come into contact with the basics of this peda-gogy. This pedagogic tradition provided the foundation for what *Visible English* calls 'graphic culture', the set of theories and practices that reside where the visible, hand-made mark meets language. As this basic graphic culture was transmitted through Christian grammar pedagogy it made graphic practices

---

[36] Cf. IRVINE and THOMSON, "*Grammatica* and literary theory", p. 30: "[i]n medieval grammatical theory, language is unthinkable outside writing, and even the theory of speech was modelled on the properties of writing [...] articulate speech was understood to bear the marks of writing".

Introduction 13

resources for identity formation among medieval literate communities. *Visible English* argues that this graphic culture framed the graphisation of English, that the basic elements of grammar pedagogy were transferred and adapted to English. Of course, literacy in English does not often seem to have been the target of *formal* schooling in medieval Anglophone communities. Furthermore, it seems likely that formal, institutional attention to the acquisition of literacy in English, where it existed, varied considerably. At one extreme we have evidence for substantial projects to promote literacy in English, for example, the Alfredian project to teach boys to read English before they learned Latin, Æthelwold's school at Winchester, Ælfric's pedagogy, and Lollard schools.[37] At the other extreme we have late medieval grammar schools, for which the evidence for formal literacy education in written English is ambiguous. Cannon has argued convincingly that "English competence [was] not essential" in the later medieval grammar classroom.[38] However, it is sometimes claimed that late medieval grammar schools were a focus for teaching English-language reading and writing. Michael Samuels posits that a growth in grammar schools in the fifteenth century might explain the perceived diffusion of scribal output that is sometimes described as 'colourless', that is, less marked than earlier texts by distinctive dialect forms, when he claims that "the growth of *centres* of education (especially grammar schools) caused the breakdown of minute regional variations of spelling which are found earlier in Middle English and which had presumably been based on the parish".[39] Jeremy Smith builds on this view: "a process of orthographic divergence may be expected given what we know about the evolution of vernacular literacy in the area [the South-West Midlands], a shift from the restricted literacy of the Anglo-Saxon period, focused on a few provincial and monastic centres, to a parish-based literacy asso-

---

[37] See GODDEN, "King Alfred's *Preface*"; H. GNEUSS, "The origin of standard Old English and Æthelwold's school at Winchester", *Anglo-Saxon England* 1 (1972), pp. 63-83 (for Æthelwold's school at Winchester); J. HILL, "Learning Latin in Anglo-Saxon England" (for Ælfric's pedagogy); and for Lollard schools see A. HUDSON, *The Premature Reformation: Wycliffite Texts and Lollard History* (Oxford, 1988), pp. 180-194 and R. COPELAND, *Pedagogy, Intellectuals, and Dissent in the Later Middle Ages: Lollardy and Ideas of Learning* (Cambridge, 2004), pp. 15, 134-135.

[38] CANNON, *From Literacy to Literature*, p. 38.

[39] M.L. SAMUELS, "Spelling and dialect in the Late- and Post-Middle-English periods", in: *So Meny People Longages and Tonges: Philological Essays in Scots and Mediaeval English Presented to Angus McIntosh*, ed. M. BENSKIN and M.L. SAMUELS (Edinburgh, 1981), pp. 43-54, at p. 48 (italics in original). Cf. ID., "Langland's dialect", repr. in: *The English of Chaucer and his Contemporaries*, ed. J.J. Smith (Aberdeen, 1988), pp. 70-85, at p. 75, "[p]eople learned the dialect spelling of the place in which they were brought up".

14   *Introduction*

ciated with the rise of characteristic twelfth-century institutions, such as grammar schools".[40] The two views may perhaps be reconciled by inferring that the
late medieval grammar schools, while they taught Latin, were often informally
centres for the formation of Anglophone literate practice. Alongside this apparent spectrum of formal Anglophone literacy teaching in educational institutions, informal modes of acquisition of Anglophone literacy must often have
been the norm. However, at whatever point on the spectrum of formality
Anglophone literacy was acquired, the pedagogy of *littera*, this 'us and them'
discourse, made engaging with visible English an experience freighted with
social identity, belonging, and difference.

Identity and Communities of Practice

'Identity' is, of course, a term with many meanings, to the extent that its
utility as an analytical category in social sciences has been questioned.[41] *Visible English* is concerned with identity as experienced by individuals when they
feel that they belong or are different. May defines identity as "produced
through a process of categorization, that is, the drawing of boundaries between
'us' and 'them'" and argues that to understand how categories operate requires
"a focus on belonging".[42] A statement, actual or implied, about 'us', about what
'we' do or who 'we' are is amenable to many appropriations and applications.
In grammatical pedagogic discourse, 'we' and 'they' were therefore infinitely
open to redeployment and redefinition, and graphic practices became resources
for generating and indexing infinite forms of belonging and difference. Such
identities are, therefore, fleeting and myriad. They may partake of, but will
never be limited to, the broad, socially-ascribed, and modern identity categories of which Caroline Walker Bynum writes: "my identity is that which signals group affiliation – often race or biological sex but sometimes statuses

[40]   J.J. SMITH, "Standard language in Early Middle English", in: *Placing Middle English in
Context*, ed. I. TAAVITSAINEN, T. NEVALAINEN, P. PAHTA, and M. RISSANEN (Berlin, 2000:
Topics in English Linguistics 35), pp. 125-139, at p. 131.
[41]   R. BRUBAKER and F. COOPER, "Beyond 'identity'", *Theory and Society* 29.1 (2000), pp.
1-47; S. HALL, "Who needs 'identity'?", in: *Questions of Cultural Identity*, ed. S. HALL and P.
DU GAY (London, 1996), pp. 1-17.
[42]   V. MAY, *Connecting Self to Society: Belonging in a Changing World* (Basingstoke,
2013), p. 79. For a useful survey of approaches to and theories of belonging in philosophical,
psychological, and sociological literature see pp. 78-93.

Introduction 15

generally understood as more socially shaped, such as class, language group, or religion".[43] In his discussion of language and identity, Tabouret-Keller summarises the alternative view of identities as fleeting and myriad as follows, "social groups need not be defined beforehand [...] [g]roups or communities and the linguistic attributes of such groups have no existential locus other than in the minds of individuals, and such groups or communities inhere only in the way individuals behave towards each other". In his view, identity is therefore *both* a social construct and a subjective construct and he defines identification as "a process on which rests the operation of bringing together identities as social constructs and identities as subjective constructs".[44] *Visible English* combines this model of identity with the paradigm of how identity is shaped in language and how social meanings are ascribed to linguistic features as part of pedagogic processes that is associated with the sociolinguistic concept of the 'community of practice'.

The concept of the community of practice, developed by education theorist Etienne Wenger, models how learning may take place in informal and not even specifically educational structures. For Wenger, a community of practice is any group that is engaged in a shared enterprise, has common rules, and a shared repertoire of resources. Wenger studied the learning that takes place informally in communities of practice such as workplace teams or families or even virtual communities sustained by the internet, investigating how learning happens "in the context of our lived experience of participation in the world".[45] In sociolinguistics, the concept of the community of practice has been further developed to describe and explain the processes involved in the construction of identity in language. Sociolinguists hold that variation and choice are fundamental objects for study of how linguistic communication works as a social transaction and much work in variationist sociolinguistics is concerned with language as a medium for identity construction. In the words of John E. Joseph, "it is through variation that the identity of individuals is indexed and interpreted".[46] Indexicality is a key concept in contemporary sociolinguistic theories of how language is associated with identity construction, "the social positioning of self

---

[43] C.W. BYNUM, *Metamorphosis and Identity* (New York, 2001), p. 163.

[44] A. TABOURET-KELLER, "Language and identity", in: *The Handbook of Sociolinguistics*, ed. F. COULMAS (Oxford, 1997), pp. 315-326, at pp. 323, 324.

[45] E. WENGER, *Communities of Practice: Learning, Meaning, and Identity* (Cambridge, 1998), p. 3.

[46] J.E. JOSEPH, "Historical perspectives on language and identity", in: *The Routledge Handbook of Language and Identity*, ed. S. PREECE (London, 2016), pp. 19-33, at p. 19.

16   *Introduction*

and other", in a dynamic and shifting process that is located in language.[47] Citing the example of the variant pronunciation of the present participle, "where '-ing' can express intelligence and articulateness whereas '-in' expresses casualness", Drummond and Schleef define the phenomenon of indexing as follows: "[i]ndexicality is a mechanism by which semiotic links are created between linguistic forms and social meanings".[48] The community of practice provides a model of the processes involved in the ascription of social meanings to linguistic forms and helps us to recognise that those meanings and identities are in constant flux. The work of Penelope Eckert is particularly important here. Eckert built on Wenger's work in a study of how variation in spoken language was given meaning and constructed identity within a Michigan high school, illuminating the "process of constructing meaning in variation".[49] Meyerhoff and Strycharz stress that the process of identity formation is lifelong and not confined to formal pedagogic institutions, "[t]hroughout adulthood, we continue to participate in a variety of communities of practice (both as expert, core members and peripheral, neophyte members). These present the possibility of strengthening existing identifications and redefining ourselves with new ones as [...] workplace studies so clearly demonstrate".[50] In short, the community of practice models how 'shibboleth' becomes a shibboleth.

    In linguistics, the community of practice framework has largely been applied to the *spoken* language recorded in *contemporary* communities. However, recently attempts have been made to apply the framework to historical communities only known from written records. In English historical linguistics the community of practice paradigm has been used recently to address questions about where language change originates and to identify communities who

---

[47]   K. BUCHOLTZ and K. HALL, "Locating identity in language", in: *Language and Identities,* ed. C. LLAMAS and D. WATT (Edinburgh, 2010), pp. 18-28, at p. 18. Cf. K. BUCHOLTZ and K. HALL, "Identity and interaction: A sociocultural linguistic approach", *Discourse Studies* 7.4 (2005), pp. 585-614, at pp. 593-594.

[48]   R. DRUMMOND and E. SCHLEEF, "Identity in variationist sociolinguistics", in: *The Routledge Handbook of Language and Identity*, ed. S. PREECE (London, 2016), pp. 50-65, at p. 55.

[49]   P. ECKERT, *Language Variation as Social Practice: The Linguistic Construction of Identity in Belten High* (Oxford, 1999), p. 38; cf. P. ECKERT and E. WENGER, "Dialogue: Communities of practice in sociolinguistics", *Journal of Sociolinguistics* 9.4 (2005), pp. 582-589.

[50]   M. MEYERHOFF and A. STRYCHARZ, "Communities of practice", in: *The Handbook of Language Variation and Change*, ed. J.K. CHAMBERS, P. TRUDGILL, and N. SCHILLING-ESTES (Oxford, 2002), pp. 525-548, at p. 536.

Introduction 17

initiate change.[51] Timofeeva examines monks and clerics as communities of practice as defined by Wenger.[52] Rogos argues that scribes who copied a particular recension of the *Canterbury Tales* (the manuscripts of the *d* group) are developing orthographies and "assign[ing] new functions to old forms [of abbreviations]" so constituting a community of practice. The tradition of Latin literacy is their shared repertoire of resources. Rogos concludes that orthographic practice is one of the most important ways in which scribes of the *Canterbury Tales* "construe themselves as members of a distinct community of practice".[53] Tyrkkö proposes extending the concept of the community of practice to "publishing communities [...] to producers of media, that is, to the professionals who, in interaction and cooperation with the primary authors, produce communicative artifacts such as texts".[54] Jeremy Smith, in *Transforming Early English*, adopts the concept of the community of practice in his investi-

---

[51] A.H. JUCKER and J. KOPACZYK, "Communities of practice as a locus of language change", in: *Communities of Practice in the History of English*, ed. J. KOPACZYK and A.H. JUCKER (Amsterdam, 2013), pp. 1-16.

[52] O. TIMOFEEVA, "'Of Ledene bocum to Engliscum gereorde': Bilingual communities of practice in Anglo-Saxon England", in: *Communities of Practice in the History of English*, pp. 201-223.

[53] J. ROGOS, "Crafting text languages: Spelling systems in manuscripts of the 'Man of Law's Tale' as a means of construing scribal community of practice", in: *Communities of Practice in the History of English*, pp. 105-121, both quotations at p. 118.

[54] J. TYRKKÖ, "Printing houses as communities of practice: Orthography in early modern medical books", in: *Communities of Practice in the History of English*, pp. 151-176, at pp. 152-153. This study finds a remarkable degree of conformity across the outputs of the printing houses over the early modern period, suggesting that they formed a "robust community of practice [...] within a fairly confined area in London [of printers who] knew each other both commercially and socially" and the purpose of the study is to "make the case that printers as well as authors or networks of correspondents also formed communities that had rules and universally acknowledged ways of doing things" (p. 170). Tyrkkö argues that standardisation and codification processes carried out by the printing houses meet Wenger's three criteria for a community of practice because they involve shared rules, a "jointly negotiated enterprise", and a "shared repertoire of resources" (p. 153). Meyerhoff and Strycharz stress that "mediated communication" has not yet (in 2002) been analysed in the community of practice framework: to date the community has been defined as involving face-to-face contact (MEYERHOFF and STRYCHARZ, "Communities of practice", p. 526). Both Rogos and Tyrkkö, extending the paradigm to "producers of media" as the latter terms printers, do not explicitly argue for extending the framework to communities whose practice is mediated textually rather than – or as well as – face-to-face, but this is what they in fact do. Schiegg questions how far the communities discussed in the Kopaczyk and Jucker essay collection conform to the three criteria for a community of practice (M. SCHIEGG, "[Review of] *Communities of Practice in the History of English* (Pragmatics & Beyond New Series 235), edited by Joanna Kopaczyk and Andreas H. Jucker", *Journal of Historical Sociolinguistics* 1.1 (2015), pp. 135-138).

18 *Introduction*

gation of changes in accidentals such as fonts and punctuation in editions of medieval texts dating from the sixteenth to the nineteenth centuries.[55] *Visible English* benefits from these experiments with the application of the community of practice paradigm to medieval, early modern, and later Anglophone societies, though the present study differs from these in its fundamental research question. Whereas these studies focus on language change over time, *Visible English* investigates graphic practice as a vehicle for social identity. *Visible English* harnesses the concept of the community of practice to theorise applications of grammar pedagogy in medieval Anglophone literacy. The concept of the community of practice provides a model for explaining how basic Latin literacy pedagogic discourse enabled identity-formation and the drawing of boundaries between belonging and difference as members of communities learned – whether formally or informally or even outside of educational structures – to read and write English and to make sense of their Anglophone literate experience. This study refers to such communities as 'communities of Anglophone literate practice'. It is important to note that this study does not find that such communities ever solely use Anglophone literacy. Using English within the framework of basic *littera* pedagogy, they are distinguished by their use of English for the purposes of reading and writing within the Latin grammatical framework, and, it follows, never by *only* using English. In many cases, as we shall see, these communities are additionally literate in at least one other vernacular. Using English for literate purposes distinguishes them from communities that do not use visible English. Their ways of using English as a visible language provide additional opportunities for identity-making.

The present study has elements in common with other recent studies of medieval literate practice that invoke the category of community. Claire Jones argues for the adaptation of the methods of network theory to understand groups of medieval medical texts as evidence for "discourse communities".[56] Merja Stenroos proposes the concept of the "text community" as a framework for understanding variation in scribal outputs: we cannot normally know much about the actual social groupings to which scribes belonged but we can examine their practice in relation to groupings of texts, for example medical texts or manuscript witnesses of a particular text. In this framework, text types and

---

[55] J.J. SMITH, *Transforming Early English: The Reinvention of Early English and Older Scots* (Cambridge, 2020).

[56] C. JONES, "Discourse communities and medical texts", in: *Medical and Scientific Writing in Late Medieval English*, ed. I. TAAVITSAINEN and P. PAHTA (Cambridge, 2004), pp. 22-36.

Introduction 19

families (stemmatically-related texts) stand in for the scribe's community. Stenroos's "text community" is similar in some ways to the concept of the community of practice adopted in the present study.[57]

Studies grounded in social history also develop an understanding of graphic activity as a social practice focused in communities. Butcher emphasises that scribal activity, even in relation to pragmatic texts such as historical records, is an example of a social practice. He illustrates with reference to the archives of Hythe, Kent, speculating on their social functions and elucidating the role of the scribes who created the documents within a complex "'speech / text' community". Butcher infers "the work of the clerks themselves" from the surviving records: it must have involved "copying, editing, clarification and conversion [English into Latin ...] checking and verification [...] making of the fair copy", gathering, sewing, binding, and curating. These activities imply "specialist training", knowledge of the community, and "calligraphic skill".[58] This approach is a step in the direction that the present study takes, but Butcher does not reflect on how members of this community might have identified themselves or been identified by means of their graphic choices.

An approach somewhat similar to Butcher's lies behind the concept of the "*communauté graphique*" ("graphic community") developed by Paul Bertrand in his sociology of documentary culture ("*les écritures ordinaires*") between the Rhine and the Escaut (an area straddling modern Belgium and the Netherlands), 1250-1350. Bertrand's graphic communities use graphic means to administer and to distinguish themselves. Bertrand defines the graphic community as one that identifies itself through its graphic practices and resources ("*qui se reconnaît aux outils et aux attributs graphiques qu'elle maîtrise et développe*"). The distinctive choices that define a community can go beyond the strictly graphic, encompassing, for example, a preference for imitating certain documentary models and a preference for rolls over codices: "[c]*ette communauté graphique s'ouvre largement à toutes les formes et pratiques de connaissances de l'écrit et de l'écriture*". Bertrand's investigation concerns itself with the ways in which documentary literacy functions in a given society in relation to communication, validation, memory, and understanding and or-

---

[57] M. STENROOS, "From scribal repertoire to text community: The challenge of variable writing systems", in: *Scribal Repertoires in Egypt from the New Kingdom to the Early Islamic Period*, ed. J. CROMWELL and E. GROSSMAN (Oxford, 2017), pp. 20-46.

[58] A. BUTCHER, "The functions of script in the speech community of a late medieval town, *c.* 1300-1550", in: *The Uses of Script and Print, 1300-1700*, ed. J. CRICK and A. WALSHAM (Cambridge, 2004), pp. 157-170, quotations at pp. 162, 166, 166-167.

20   *Introduction*

ganising the world, building on Brian Stock's concept of the "textual community" that structures its group identity in relation to certain texts.[59] Serge Lusignan's investigation of Picard French of the thirteenth to fifteenth centuries as a *'scripta'* – a writing practice whose distinctive forms bear particular social associations – is also aligned to the approach of the present study.[60] Some work in Old English studies is moving in a similar direction. Eric Weiskott observes that recent work on the poetry "broaches the possibility of transregional communities organised around text and language".[61]

Although theories of community may not always be explicitly invoked, correlations between graphic outputs and particular social groups and individuals play a major part in palaeographic study. Some monastic houses developed house-styles of script and decoration; this kind of evidence helps to identify scriptoria and relations between them. Rodney Thomson has shown that examples of houses with distinctive styles of decorated initial include Cirencester, Worcester, Winchcombe, and Hereford. Worcester books have a "home-made" appearance though output is varied. Likewise books made at St. Peter's Abbey, Gloucester, are "humble". The manuscripts made at Winchcombe Abbey may have "set the bench-mark for the 'west country' style": decoration of initials is distinctive and the work of different scribes hard to distinguish.[62] David Dumville associates different varieties of the Anglo-Caroline script with particular centres, such as St. Augustine's Abbey, Canterbury.[63] The manuscripts associated with monastic scriptoria on grounds of script idiosyncrasies are mainly Latin. However, some correlations have been proposed between some English-language corpora with distinctive scripts and particular communities. For example, Lollards appear to have favoured a uniform Textura script for the Wycliffite Bible.[64] Script has also featured in the attribution of scribal work in the

---

[59] P. BERTRAND, *Les Ecritures Ordinaires: Sociologie d'un temps de révolution documentaire (entre royaume de France et empire, 1250-1350)* (Paris, 2015), at pp. 307-309, 316.

[60] S. LUSIGNAN, *Essai d'histoire sociolinguistique: Le français picard au Moyen Age* (Paris, 2012: *Recherches littéraires médiévales* 13). For this study, see further in the Conclusion, pp. 354-355, n. 8.

[61] E. WEISKOTT, "Puns and poetic style in Old English", in: *Etymology and Wordplay in Medieval Literature*, ed. M. MALES (Turnhout, 2018), pp. 191-211, at p. 196.

[62] R.M. THOMSON, "Monastic and cathedral book production", in: *The Cambridge History of the Book in Britain: Volume II: 1000-1400*, ed. N. MORGAN and R.M. THOMSON (Cambridge, 2008), pp. 136-167, quotations at pp. 150, 151, 152.

[63] D.N. DUMVILLE, *English Caroline Script and Monastic History: Studies in Benedictinism, AD 950-1030* (Woodbridge, 1993).

[64] A. HUDSON, "Observations on the 'Wycliffite orthography'", in: *Pursuing Middle English Manuscripts and their Texts: Essays in Honour of Ralph Hanna*, ed. S. HOROBIN and A. NAFDE

Introduction 21

English language. Handwriting in an intentionally recognisable and distinctive style associated with a particular person is not often found either in medieval book hands or in document hands, but minute idiosyncrasies of letter-form and ductus have been used to attribute unsigned English-language outputs to individual scribes. McIntosh's proposal that linguistic forms could be allied with palaeographical analysis to create scribal profiles has gained some traction, particularly in work on the scribes of the *Canterbury Tales* and other Middle English canonical writings which seeks to identify scribes and locate them in late medieval places and institutions.[65] Work in this tradition analyses graphic variation in order to determine provenance, rather than to consider its possible social functions. But the fact that script- style variation can be used today as a diagnostic tool to identify individual scribes and their communities suggests that it is possible that some aspects at least of variation also served as identity markers for the scribes and their communities.

Visible English: *Argument, Scope, and Organisation*

Visible English argues that grammar pedagogy provided ways of understanding graphic practice in English, of thinking about its special characteristics and challenges, and understanding them in relation to identity. One form of variation that could be deployed as a marker of identity, the present study argues, was the selection or avoidance of graphs special to English such as thorn, yogh, and eth. Another potentially significant variation was the composition and order of the alphabet used for English. Models used for imitation when learning to read and write in English also functioned to create boundaries between social belonging and difference. Elementary literacy training encouraged and advertised the value of graphic ingenuity and this value was trans-

---

(Turnhout, 2017), pp. 77-98, at p. 94; cf. M. PEIKOLA, "The Wycliffite Bible and 'Central Midland standard': Assessing the manuscript evidence", *Nordic Journal of English Studies* 2.1 (2003), pp. 29-51, at p. 33.

[65] A. MCINTOSH, "Scribal profiles from Middle English texts", repr. in: *Middle English Dialectology: Essays on some Principles and Problems by Angus McIntosh, M.L. Samuels, and M. Laing*, ed. M. LAING (Aberdeen, 1989), pp. 32-45, and "Towards an inventory of Middle English scribes", repr. in: *Middle English Dialectology*, pp. 46-63. Examples of influence include L.R. MOONEY, S. HOROBIN, and E. STUBBS, *Late Medieval English Scribes, Version 1.0* (2011), <http://www.medievalscribes.com> and L.R. MOONEY and E. STUBBS, *Scribes and the City: London Guildhall Clerks and the Dissemination of Middle English Literature 1375-1425* (York, 2013).

22   *Introduction*

ferred to English. Playful and creative engagement with the graphic properties of English informed understanding of specialised literate practices such as copying across dialects or encoding new vernacular metres in writing. The public display of written English within particular locations both amplified and particularised the reach of graphic culture, animating its resources for identity-formation among the people who used those spaces. Variations in and changes to practices of copying English texts from exemplars were generated, understood, and transmitted within the pedagogic frameworks of graphic culture and were ascribed social meanings.

Visible English proposes that this understanding of graphic culture may be used to frame analysis of all medieval English of the manuscript era that comes from societies in contact with basic Latin grammatical pedagogic traditions, whether written with a quill, a knife, a chisel, a stylus, or a fingernail and whatever the surface written on: whether parchment, paper, plaster, metal, glass, wood, or stone. All kinds of writing materials, therefore, fall within the scope of this study. Considered alongside English-inscribed parchment and paper codices and wax tablets are objects made of materials such as stone, metal, wood, and bone. Some bear coloured writing made with ink or paint and some carry deformational writing made with sharp objects such as styluses and chisels. This study also includes in its scope the most numerous category of textual survivals: documents.

Visible English proposes that graphic variation *always* had the potential to form identity and in consequence it draws its examples from across the corpus of medieval English writing that was informed by Latin pedagogic traditions, that is to say, all writing produced after the conversion to Christianity. It investigates the writing of what we now call English from very early records of this period to the later medieval period and the beginnings of print. In date, the English materials discussed in relation to Latin pedagogy range from grave-markers of *c*. 700 to poetry manuscripts of c. 1550, by which time English-language texts had been printed for nearly eighty years. An inscribed object of *c*. 450, the period of our earliest vernacular (Germanic) writing of Insular provenance, is used to consider the problems raised by the mysterious early scraps that cannot safely be related to Latin pedagogy. Of course, handwriting continues down to the present day. Twenty-first century electronic styluses and tablets may even be restoring the tracings of the hand to their earlier primacy. The age of the digital is also the age of the hand. However, since *c*. 1472 when Caxton printed his first English-language book in Bruges, typography has of-

Introduction   23

fered a new set of choices and models for the encoding of English visibly. The present volume focuses on the graphic choices and meanings available to writers and readers of English before typography made handwriting itself a matter of choice.

Each chapter in this study focuses on an aspect of Latin grammar pedagogy and examines its inflections in several examples of English-language texts and literate practice. Pedagogic traditions and sources are examined within frameworks provided by sociolinguistics and literacy studies. This aspect of the present study benefits from the turn in recent linguistics from attention to spoken language towards a focus on writing.[66] Identities and belonging are a key theme of work in this tradition. The journal *Writing Systems Research*, founded and first issued in 2009, provides a forum for interdisciplinary work in this area, while a survey of the field to that date provided by Mark Sebba in the first issue of this journal summarises "how writing systems can function as markers of difference and belonging, and be involved in the creation of identities at different levels of social organisation".[67] Theresa Lillis's book *The Sociolinguistics of Writing* explores "writing as a social semiotic and social practice" that performs "identity-work".[68]

[66] For the founders of twentieth-century linguistics such as Ferdinand de Saussure († 1913) and Leonard Bloomfield († 1949), the conservative properties of writing concealed the processes of language change in speech which were the proper focus of linguistic enquiry (COULMAS, *Sociolinguistics*, pp. 2-3; cf. R. HARRIS, *Rethinking Writing* (London, 2000), pp. 15-16). Insights in social philosophy, for example in the work of Jacques Derrida and Pierre Bourdieu, have more latterly led to the view that writing is a "social practice" that uses "symbolic resources" in ways quite different from speech (Coulmas, *Sociolinguistics*, p. 11).

[67] M. SEBBA, "Sociolinguistic approaches to writing systems research", *Writing Systems Research* 1.1 (2009), pp. 35-49, at p. 36.

[68] T. LILLIS, *Sociolinguistics of Writing* (Edinburgh, 2013), at pp. 18, 25. The present volume also benefits from – and seeks to contribute a new dimension to – recent work in various disciplines beyond linguistics that engage with visuality and writing. There is room here to mention only a small selection. Malcolm Parkes has traced the classical and medieval history of the idea of writing as "visible language" (M.B. PARKES, "Reading, copying, and interpreting a text in the early Middle Ages", in: *A History of Reading in the West*, ed. G. CAVALLO and R. CHARTIER, trans. L.G. COCHRANE (Cambridge, 1999), pp. 90-102, at p. 93; cf. M.B. PARKES, *Pause and Effect: An Introduction to the History of Punctuation in the West* (Aldershot, 1992), p. 23). Ben C. Tilghman provides evidence that despite the classical theory that letters were no more than signs encoding spoken words, it was nonetheless understood that letters could bear iconographic meaning (B.C. TILGHMAN, "The shape of the word: Extralinguistic meaning in Insular display lettering", *Word & Image*, 27.3 (2011), pp. 292-308). David Ganz has reflected on the capacity of the graphic traces that make up display letters in pre-ninth-century Latin manuscripts to bear symbolic meanings (D. GANZ, "Early medieval display scripts and the problems of how we see them", in: *Graphic Signs of Identity, Faith, and Power in Late Antiquity*

24 *Introduction*

Visible English is organised thematically rather than chronologically. The examples within each chapter of the present study are selected and ordered according to the aspect of the pedagogy of *littera* and its applications that forms its topic. This study does not offer a history of Anglophone medieval literacy, but rather a framework for analysing examples of visible English across the corpus and for investigating the experience of applying the pedagogy

and the Early Middle Ages, ed. I. GARIPZANOV, C. GOODSON, and H. MAGUIRE (Turnhout, 2017), pp. 125-143). Garipzanov has proposed that the modern propensity for graphic visualisation of data is anticipated by a culture of "graphicacy" in the antique and early medieval worlds, where signs are much more than an equivalent of verbal shorthand (I. GARIPZANOV, "The rise of graphicacy in late Antiquity and the early Middle Ages", *Viator* 46.2 (2015), pp. 1-21 and ID., "Introduction", in: *Graphic Signs of Identity, Faith, and Power in Late Antiquity and the Early Middle Ages*, pp. 1-22). A conference at Dumbarton Oaks and a related publication *Sign and Design* explored "script as image" from 300-1600 across western, Byzantine, and Latin American civilisations (B.M. BEDOS-REZAK and J. HAMBURGER, "Introduction", in: *Sign and Design: Script as Image in Cross-Cultural Perspective (300-1600 CE)*, ed. B.M. BEDOS-REZAK and J. HAMBURGER (Washington, 2016), pp. 1-16, at p. 1). Jeffrey Hamburger argues that for early monastic scribes, "seeing formed an essential part of the process of reading" (J. HAMBURGER, "The iconicity of script", *Word & Image* 27.3 (2011), pp. 249-261, at p. 255). Michael Camille shows that writing could function as a visual image, impressing the illiterate (M. CAMILLE, "Seeing as reading: Some visual implications of medieval literacy and illiteracy", *Art History* 8.1 (1985), pp. 26-49, at pp. 32-37). Cynthia Hahn associates scribes' and artists' strategies for engaging the eye with a model of the reading process as spiritual (C. HAHN, "Letter and spirit: The power of the letter, the enlivenment of the word in medieval art", in: *Visible Writings: Cultures, Forms, Readings*, ed. M. DALBELLO and M. SHAW (New Brunswick, NJ, 2011), pp. 55-76). Reflexes of the visual turn are also abundant and diverse in scholarship on medieval English. The Bodleian Library's 2017-2018 exhibition *Designing English: Graphics on the Medieval Page* and associated catalogue (D. WAKELIN, *Designing English: Early Literature on the Page* (Oxford, 2017)), is a recent example of interest in visuality that has a focus on medieval English. Discussing the Eadwine or Canterbury Psalter of *c.* 1160, Elaine Treharne analyses its multimedia design as an "emphasis on seeing" (E. TREHARNE, *Living Through Conquest: The Politics of Early English, 1020-1220* (Oxford, 2012), p. 173). In her work on Old English poetry manuscripts, Katherine O'Brien O'Keeffe demonstrates the persistence of orality as a component of "visible song" (K. O'BRIEN O'KEEFFE, *Visible Song: Transitional Literacy in Old English Verse* (Cambridge, 1990), p. 22). Sonja Drimmer studies illustrated manuscripts as evidence for "the emergence of England's literary canon as a *visual* and literary event" (S. DRIMMER, *The Art of Allusion: Illuminators and the Making of English Literature, 1403-1476* (Philadelphia, 2019), p. 3, my italics). Important studies that follow Parkes's seminal work on graphic means of displaying text structure (M.B. PARKES, "The influence of the concepts of *ordinatio* and *compilatio* on the development of the book", repr. in: M.B. PARKES, *Scribes, Scripts, and Readers: Studies in the Communication, Presentation, and Dissemination of Medieval Texts* (London, 1991), pp. 55-74), include R. CARROLL, M. PEIKOLA, H. SALMI, M.-L. VARILA, J. SKAFFARI, and R. HILTUNEN, "Pragmatics on the page", *European Journal of English Studies* 17.1 (2013), pp. 54-71, and A. NAFDE, "Hoccleve's hands: The *mise-en-page* of the autograph and non-autograph manuscripts", *Journal of the Early Book Society* 16 (2013), pp. 53-83.

Introduction 25

of *littera* in Anglophone literate environments. The case studies and the communities of practice that hove into view across this study collectively suggest that a history of Anglophone medieval literacy would not be possible: there are many histories and none because each community of Anglophone literate practice inflects and applies the pedagogy of *littera* to make English visible in its own ways.

Chapter One, "Graphs, Alphabets, and Scripts", examines variations in letters, alphabets, and orthographies that were available for writing English in relation to *littera* pedagogy. Study of medieval English orthography has to date typically focused on the degree to which spelling encodes the sounds of the spoken language, often in the context of research on dialect and standardisation. This chapter adopts perspectives offered by the recent sociolinguistics of orthography which analyses how letters, scripts, spellings, and even diacritics may express identity and perform social functions. To date, sociolinguistic approaches to orthography have mainly focused on contemporary examples, or examples from the recent past. By means of case studies of alphabets, *Anglice littere* texts (texts about 'English' letters), and relations between runic and Roman script in pre-Conquest codices and on monuments, the chapter argues that such features were important in processes of identity formation and the production of belonging and difference.

Chapter Two, "Graphic Models", considers the use of models in medieval literacy pedagogy, investigating the use of the model as a practice of literacy socialisation. It argues that as they acquired graphic proficiency by imitating models, learners participated in a process that invested their practices and outputs with value for identity-work. It proposes that the classroom pedagogy of imitation of models has left traces in certain so-called 'pen-trials' found on margins and flyleaves of Old and Middle English literary manuscripts and that many examples of micro-texts such as colophons, ownership inscriptions, and dictaminal formulas are better thought of as 'copy-texts' for writing practice. It also brings together for the first time the evidence for pattern books of English provenance. Pen-trials, micro-texts, and pattern books are all used to explore how imitation pedagogy informs literate practice and identity formation in communities of Anglophone literate practice.

Chapter Three, "Graphic Play", focuses on the medieval pedagogic tradition that developed and challenged pupils' graphic skills and knowledge through activities involving codes, acrostics, and other kinds of letter puzzles and play. At the same time that it facilitated elementary literacy training, play with graphic puzzles resourced and transmitted identity formation, dividing those who could solve them from those who could not. The chapter draws on approaches to language play in linguistics and literacy studies, where play is seen as an important component of language learning that involves heightened attention to the graphic properties of text. Chapter Three argues that vernacular genres such alphabet poems, acrostics, and cryptographics are informed by this pedagogic tradition and contribute to the construction of belonging and difference.

Chapter Four, "Graphic Display", examines graphic practice when English writing is displayed to view in chosen locations. The chapter contributes to the present study's arguments for links between graphic culture and identity by arguing that the display of writing in English in particular spaces amplified graphic pedagogies and the potential of writing to create belonging and social difference. Display spaces were galleries where the reader – and in some cases the writer – viewed writing collectively, and display both broadened exposure to and participation in graphic culture and sharpened its potential to create social boundaries. Chapter Four is informed by recent work in epigraphy that views the public display of written texts as a significant variable in a semiotic system. The chapter brings epigraphy together with the sociolinguistic concept of 'linguistic landscape' which holds that social relations and identities may be expressed and negotiated through publicly displayed signs, billboards, advertisements, and place-names in a given space, the usual focus being on contemporary, usually urban, spaces. Displayed writing investigated in this chapter includes pre-Conquest epigraphy (with special reference to the runic poem on the Ruthwell Cross); graffiti and other graphic display in the later medieval parish church (with special reference to St. Mary's Church, Ashwell, Hertfordshire and St. Mary's, Great Bardfield, Essex); the late medieval fashion for the display in domestic and civic buildings of literary texts such as proverbs and precepts, verses on social order, and mortality poems; and the role of inscribed objects as media for the collective experience of graphic culture.

Chapter Five, "Reprographics", uses the term 'reprographics' to signal this chapter's focus on scribes' practices of and thinking about the reproduction of text. Taking as a starting-point ideas of the copy developed in cultural theory and histories of print, the chapter argues that elementary literacy pedagogy informed the varied copying practices of medieval scribes of English-language texts and provided a framework within which they understood their practice in relation to social identity. This framework, the chapter suggests, complicates

Introduction   27

the prevailing modern typology of medieval Anglophone scribal practice associated with the Middle English Dialect Project. The case studies offered examine scribal practices in the *Ormulum*; in copies of popular didactic rhymed verse texts such as the *Prick of Conscience* and the *South English Legendary*; in Carthusian literary manuscripts and other prose traditions; and in manuscripts of John Trevisa's translation of the *Polychronicon*.

The Conclusion, "Medieval English Literacy", reflects on some of the implications and further ramifications of the material and arguments presented in the foregoing chapters. Current assumptions about medieval English literacy and its relationship with Latinity, it is argued, require review and refinement in the light of *Visible English*. In addition, vernacular multilingual literacies and the emergence of print culture add further dimensions to the graphic culture described in *Visible English* that would repay further study.

It is hoped that by offering a new perspective on the graphic dimensions of English writing by many hands from the earliest surviving materials until it became possible to print the language, some of the mysteriousness of medieval English will be dispelled and a new facet of its interest revealed. Every teacher of medieval English knows that it is medieval writing systems that present the biggest barrier to comprehension by beginners. Old and Middle English *look* so strange and vary so much. This strangeness is what makes it difficult to recognise continuities with the modern language of even the most everyday words: '*rad*' ('road'), '*paŏ*' ('path'), '*hus*' ('house'), '*scip*' ('ship'), '*cicen*' ('chicken'), '*cokkou*' ('cuckoo'), '*buterfliʒe*' ('butterfly'). The barriers are there in print, and even more so in the original manuscripts: literate competence in medieval English is itself a kind of shibboleth in contemporary English Studies. *Visible English* proposes new ways of understanding what differences in practices and outputs could mean to writers and readers. The story of writing told in these pages offers new perspectives on the choices made by persons not so different from ourselves to negotiate identity using graphic resources in ways still familiar today. *Visible English* aims to offer a bold new proposition about medieval English and new ways of seeing its manuscripts and other material records.

Chapter 1: Graphs, Alphabets, and Scripts

Sumtyme þe same word & þe self þat is writen of sum man in oo manere is writen of a-noþir man in a-noþir manere. As, wher summe writen þese wordis 'thyng' & 'theef' wiþ t.h., opire vsen to writen þoo same wordis wiþ þis figure þ.

Sometimes the same word and the self-same that is written by one man in one way is written by another man in another manner. As, where some write these words 'thing' and 'thief' with *th*, others write those same words with this letter-shape *þ*.

(*Preface to the Wycliffite Biblical Concordance*)[1]

[W]hile from a linguistic point of view, scripts, orthographic conventions, and diacritics are often seen as socially neutral items which can be evaluated, if they are evaluated at all, in terms of their efficiency in providing a system of notation, this is not how their users typically see them. On the contrary, they are an integral part of a culture, endowed with a powerful symbolism of identity.

(Mark Sebba, "Sociolinguistic approaches to writing systems research")[2]

T he author of the *Preface* to the early fifteenth-century *Wycliffite Biblical Concordance*, quoted in the epigraph to this chapter, recognises that the graph thorn and the digraph *th* are alternatives in the written English of his day. As the passage quoted continues it becomes clear that he is aware, too,

---

[1] *Preface to the Wycliffite Biblical Concordance*, ed. S.M. KUHN, in: "The preface to a fifteenth-century concordance", *Speculum*, 43 (1968), pp. 258-273, at p. 272. I have lightly edited Kuhn's text.

[2] M. SEBBA, "Sociolinguistic approaches to writing systems research", *Writing Systems Research* 1.1 (2009), pp. 35-49, at p. 40.

30   *Chapter 1*

of other alternatives. The graph yogh is an alternative to the digraph *gh*, and *h* or a vowel are alternative initial letters in certain words:

> *Summe writen* g.h. *in summe wordis, whiche wordis ben writen of summe oþire with a yogh, þat is figured þus:* ʒ. *As, sum man writeþ þus þese termes 'doughter', 'thought', where anoþir writiþ hem þus: 'douʒter', 'thouʒt' [...] Also, sum man writeþ sum word wiþ an* h, *which saame word anoþir man writiþ wiþouten an* h. *As is of þe Englisch word which þis Latyn word 'heres' signyfieþ, which terme summe writen wiþ* h, *þus: 'here', & summe þus: 'eir' wiþouten* h. *Þese diuerse maneris of writyng ben to be considerid in þis concordaunce.*

> Some write *gh* in some words, words that are written by others with a yogh that is shaped thus: ʒ. As where one man writes in this way the terms '*doughter*' ['daughter'], '*thought*', where another writes them thus, '*douʒter*', '*thouʒt*' ['thought', ...]. Also, one man may write a word with an *h*, and another man may write the same word without an *h*. As with the English word that corresponds with the Latin word '*heres*' ['heir'], which some write with an *h*, thus, '*here*', and some thus, '*eir*', without an *h*. These differences in ways of writing are relevant to this concordance.[3]

All of these "*diuerse maneris of writyng*", he notes, make it difficult to arrange his material in alphabetical order. He describes and explains the practices he has adopted. He has used *th* at the beginning of all words that begin with thorn and has placed them in the correct place under the letter *t*. And because yogh looks like the letter zed he has grouped words beginning with yogh under zed, at the end of the alphabet:

> *Wher-fore alle þe wordis of þis concordaunce of which þe firste carecte is þis figure* þ *bigynnen in þis table wiþ* t.h. *And in* T *þei stonden aftir þat here ordre axiþ* [...] *But for as miche as þe carect yogh, þat is to seie,* ʒ, *is figurid lijk a zed; þerfore alle þe wordis of þis table þat biginnen wiþ þat carect ben set in zed, which is þe laste lettre of þe* a, b, c.

> Wherefore all of the words of this concordance whose first letter is this shape þ begin in this table with *th*. And they are placed in the correct order under the letter *t*. But because the character yogh, that is to say ʒ, is shaped like a zed, all of the words that begin with that letter are positioned under zed, which is the last letter of the *ABC*.[4]

---

[3] *Preface to the Wycliffite Biblical Concordance*, p. 272.
[4] *Preface to the Wycliffite Biblical Concordance*, p. 272.

Graphs, Alphabets, and Scripts   31

Should his practice not conform with that of any future scribes of the *Preface*, he invites them to adapt the text (carefully) to their own "*manere of writyng*"; future scribes are not expected to follow the Wycliffite author, but if they do not they must amend the text with good care ("*good avisement*").[5]

The Wycliffite author expects that scribes will be capable of paying close attention to variation in choice of letters and there are plenty of examples that bear this out. Good evidence for systematic attention to thorn / *th* variation in later Middle English legal documents comes from cases where we can compare an exemplar with its copy. An example is offered by the original petition of Thomas Scargill, formerly usher of the king's chamber, to be exempted from the Act of Resumption (1455) and its copy in the Parliament Rolls.[6] The scribe of the roll makes twenty changes in copying 114 words and 572 characters meaning that he changes 3.5 percent of characters. He also makes one correction (deleting "*the*").[7] He is, therefore, a close and careful copyist. One of the few changes he makes is to substitute *th* for thorn. The original uses both *th* and thorn ("*other*", "*therupon*", "*þe*", "*the*"). The scribe of the roll consistently uses *th*. A preference for *th* over thorn is also exhibited by the enrolling scribe in the Roll of Parliament for 1424 when he copies a Common Petition concerning non-residence.[8] The enrolling scribe makes several changes, preferring "*this*" to "*þys*" (line 6 up), and also "*your*" to "*ʒoure*" (line 1) and "*gode*" to "*gude*" (line 8), for example.[9]

Ricardus Franciscus, a fine fifteenth-century professional scribe, is an example of a literary scribe who also pays close attention to his set of characters. His copy of an English translation of the *Golden Legend* in MS London, BL, Harley 4775 gives us an excellent opportunity to investigate his copying,

---

[5]   This advice to scribes is discussed more fully in Chapter Five.

[6]   Scargill's original is MS Kew, TNA SC8/28/1373 and the copy in the Parliament Roll is MS Kew, TNA C65/103/47, mem.8.

[7]   Counting word spaces and abbreviations as one; not counting bars on double ell, strokes on final letters, or points. Cf. *Rotuli Parliamentorum; Ut Et Petitiones, Et Placita in Parliamento Tempore Edwardi R.I.*, 7 vols. (London, 1767-1777), 5, p. 314.

[8]   The original Common Petition concerning non-residence is MS Kew, TNA, SC8/135/6716 and the copy in the Parliament Roll is MS Kew, TNA C65/86, mem. 13, No. 38.

[9]   Commenting on the pairs of exemplar and copy, Fisher *et al.* infer that "the principle was, obviously, to represent the original exactly [...] substantive words are rarely changed, no matter how eccentric the spelling" (*An Anthology of Chancery English*, ed. J.H. FISHER, M. RICHARD-SON, and J.L. FISHER (Knoxville, 1984), p. 24). They also describe the scribes as "trying to eliminate [...] orthographic inconsistency" (p. 27). However, they neither record substitutions for thorn, yogh and so on in their collations (pp. 63-66) nor comment on litteral substitution in their discussion of orthography (pp. 26-33).

32   *Chapter 1*

because its exemplar has been identified: it is MS Oxford, Bod. Lib., Douce 372.[10] MS Douce 372 is in the hands of four scribes whose spelling practices vary from one another and whose practices are internally inconsistent also. Ricardus copies over the spellings of the various scribes and on this basis, *LALME* categorises MS Harley 4775 as a "near-literatim" copy of MS Douce 372. Despite following his exemplar slavishly, Ricardus does, however, systematically replace thorn with *th*.[11] Another scribe who carries out a similar graphic 'search-and-replace' is the scribe of MS London, BL, Addit. 37790, a fifteenth-century manuscript that includes the short text of the *Revelations of Divine Love* by Julian of Norwich and other mystic texts. Laing and Williamson observe that this scribe fairly slavishly copies the variable language of the scribes of his exemplar, concluding that he is copying letter-by-letter.[12] He does, however, make 'macro' changes, notably replacing thorn with *th* and initial yogh with *y*.[13] Clearly, the Wycliffite author recognises that the graphic options available at the turn of the fourteenth / fifteenth centuries pose a *practical* problem when scholastic practices of visual text organisation such as alphabetical order are adopted in English.[14] But the Wycliffite author's expectation that future scribes may not wish to adopt his alphabetical practice and the close attention to graphs paid by the scribes of the rolls and by Ricardus Franciscus and the scribe of BL, Addit. 37790 suggest that there may be more at stake with the selection among variants than simple practicality.

The long history of change and variation in written English lies behind the alphabetical practices in the manuscripts and a brief summary of this history may be useful at this point. English before the Conquest was recorded in two scripts: in runes and in Roman script, both of them scripts within the alphabetic

[10] R.F.S. HAMER, "Spellings of the fifteenth-century scribe Ricardus Franciscus", in: *Five Hundred Years of Words and Sounds*, ed. E.G. STANLEY and D. GRAY (Cambridge, 1983), pp. 353-365.

[11] For example, a collation of the rubric and first six lines of *The Exaltation of the Cross* from MS Oxford, Bod. Lib., Douce 372, f. 107ra and Ricardus's copy (MS London, BL, Harley 4775, f. 169ra), reveals that Ricardus makes the following changes (Ricardus's reading is the second of each pair of variants): [Rubric], line 2: *biginnith*] *bigynnith*; *Exaltaciou^n*] *exaltaciou^n*; line 3: *þᵉ*] *the*; *cros*] *Cros*; *Cap^{itulo}*] *Capitulo*; [Text], line 1: *cros*] *Cros*; line 2: *þᵃᵗ*] *that*; line 4: *þᵃᵗ*] *that*; *þᵉ*] *the*; line 5: *c^{ris}te*] *Crist*; *þᵉ*] *the*; *þᵉ cros*] *the Cros*; line 6: *cros*] *Cros*; *þᵃᵗ*] *that*.

[12] M. LAING and K. WILLIAMSON, "The archaeology of medieval texts", in: *Categorization in the History of English*, ed. C.J. KAY and J.J. SMITH (Amsterdam, 2004), pp. 85-145, at p. 92.

[13] See LAING and WILLIAMSON, "The archaeology of medieval texts", p. 94. For further discussion of this scribe (the Amherst scribe) see Chapter Five.

[14] For further discussion of pressures on graphic practice associated with indexing and other modes of scholastic text organisation see Chapter Five.

Graphs, Alphabets, and Scripts   33

writing system. Roman script was learned from Irish and Roman missionaries to Northumbria (from 635) and Kent (from 597) respectively in the form of the alphabet used for writing Latin. According to Bede (*c.* 673-735), King Æthelberht of Kent had laws of his kingdom recorded in the script, so its use for English must have begun around the end of the sixth century.[15] However, a runic alphabet was brought by settlers in Britain in the fifth century.[16] There were different versions of the Germanic runic alphabet (the futhark). The settlers' runes became distinctive, the futhark or rune-row developing into the futhorc, with its distinctive character set and some variation in different areas.[17] Also to be found in pre-Conquest England were examples of Scandinavian runes, used to encode Scandinavian languages.[18] In later Old English writings in Roman script new letters appear: the runic letters and letter-names *p*, 'wynn' ('joy'), *þ*, thorn, the ligature *æ*, from Latin, today named 'ash' after its runic equivalent ᚠ, but named '*diptongon*' in Old English (*DOE*, *diptongon*) and later '*diptonge*' or '*dipton*' (*MED*, '*diptonge*', n.), and *ð*, a modification of Roman *d* that is now called 'eth' but was then called '*ðæt*' ('that').[19] Thorn and eth appear towards the end of the seventh century, providing alternatives to the *th* and *d* found in very early manuscripts from the north of England,[20] *th* being the spelling of Greek theta (*θ*).[21] Wynn provided an alternative to *u/v* and *uu/vv*.

---

[15]   A. SEILER, "The scripting of Old English: An analysis of Anglo-Saxon spellings for *w* and *þ*", *Sprachwissenschaft* 33.2 (2008), pp. 139-172, at pp. 142-143. Seiler provides an extremely detailed analysis of how scribes addressed the problem of encoding Germanic sounds in the Latin alphabet.

[16]   See J. CRICK, "English vernacular script", in: *The Cambridge History of the Book in Britain: Volume I: c. 400-1100*, ed. R. GAMESON (Cambridge, 2011), pp. 174-186, at p. 175; R. DEROLEZ, "Runic literacy among the Anglo-Saxons", in: *Britain 400-600: Language and History*, ed. A. BAMMESBERGER and A. WOLLMANN (Heidelberg, 1990), pp. 397-436; P. ORTON, *Writing in a Speaking World: The Pragmatics of Literacy in Anglo-Saxon Inscriptions and Old English Poetry* (Tempe, AZ, 2014), p. 60; and A. SEILER, *The Scripting of the Germanic Languages: A Comparative Study of 'Spelling Difficulties' in Old English, Old High German, and Old Saxon* (Zurich, 2014), p. 28.

[17]   R. DEROLEZ, "Runic literacy among the Anglo-Saxons", pp. 411-415.

[18]   R.I. PAGE, *An Introduction to English Runes*, 2nd edn. (Woodbridge, 1999), pp. 200-207.

[19]   M. STENROOS, "A Middle English mess of fricative spellings: Reflections on thorn, yogh, and their rivals", in: *To Make his Englissh Sweete upon his Tonge*, ed. M. KRYGIER and L. SIKORSKA (Frankfurt am Main, 2007), pp. 9-35, at p. 12.

[20]   R.M. HOGG, "Phonology and morphology", in: *The Cambridge History of the English Language: Volume I: The Beginnings to 1066*, ed. R.M. HOGG (Cambridge, 1992), pp. 67-167, at p. 76.

[21]   M. STENROOS, "A Middle English mess of fricative spellings", p. 12.

34   *Chapter 1*

Eth and wynn fell into disuse at the end of the thirteenth century.[22] Ash is found in English writing as late as the second half of the thirteenth century, in copies of writs of Edward I to the abbey at Bury St. Edmunds (MS Cambridge, UL, Ff.2.33, ff. 22r-23v), though the archaising tradition at Bury may be at play here.[23]

In the eleventh century the special, Insular shape of *g* was sometimes replaced by the Caroline *g* whose shape is still familiar in modern roman type, a shape derived from continental script and whose importation was associated with the Benedictine Reform.[24] The Caroline letter shape can be seen in its alphabetical place in MS London, BL, Harley 208, f. 87v (see Figure 1), alongside something closer in shape to the Insular form in "*reg*[...]" at the end of the sequence (f. 88r, see Figure 2). The Insular shape of *g* was adapted and became the new letter *ȝ* in Middle English, now called 'yogh'. In early examples it still has the shape of the Insular *g*, but it is named '*iye*' and is used in places that yogh was later to be used for /j/ and /χ/ while Caroline *g* was used, by contrast, for /g/.[25] As the *Preface to the Wycliffite Biblical Concordance* records, yogh was an alternative to the digraph *gh* (as well as consonantal *y*, while the same form was also used for *z*) and thorn was now an alternative to *th*.

The existence of letters that were not part of the Latin alphabet as alternatives to letters found there gave scribes and their communities a set of variants, and linguists have provided various kinds of explanation for the factors that drove preferences.[26] Some variation in representations of the sounds /θ/ and /ð/

[22]   S. HOROBIN, *Does Spelling Matter?* (Oxford, 2013), p. 85.

[23]   For the date see the entry in P. SAWYER, S. KELLY, and R. RUSHFORTH, *The Electronic Sawyer: Online Catalogue of Anglo-Saxon Charters* (2016), <http://www.esawyer.org.uk/about/index.html>. For archaising hands and late copies of charters at Bury see J. CRICK, "Historical literacy in the archive: Post-Conquest imitative copies of pre-Conquest charters and some French comparanda", in: *The Long Twelfth-Century View of the Anglo-Saxon Past*, ed. M. BRETT and D. WOODMAN (Aldershot, 2015), pp. 159-190; and K. LOWE, "Bury St. Edmunds and its liberty: A charter-text and its afterlife", in: *English Manuscripts Before 1400,* ed. A.S.G. EDWARDS and O. DA ROLD (London, 2012: *English Manuscript Studies 1100-1700* 17), pp. 155-172.

[24]   CRICK, "English vernacular script", p. 180.

[25]   In contexts where the difference between yogh and Insular *g* is indeterminable, I transcribe *ȝ*/Insular *g*. I indicate all other conceptual fluidities similarly, for example, later, yogh sometimes potentially merges conceptually with *z* and I indicate this as *ȝ*/*z*. See further below.

[26]   A note about my terms. The 'Latin alphabet' here refers to the alphabet used for Latin and defined by the early grammarians. The terms 'modified Latin alphabet' and 'Latin-based alphabet' refer to alphabets (i.e. full repertoires or rows of symbols) that include letters such as wynn and thorn that are not found in the standard Latin alphabets. This is a convenient distinction; however it does not map onto a hard-and-fast, empirical reality: we will see that the composition of the Latin alphabet and the relationships between the letter sets used for English and those used for

Graphs, Alphabets, and Scripts 35

has been explained in terms of both cultural meanings and communicative systems. In early pre-Conquest administrative texts, the digraphs *th* and *uu* were preferred to characters not found in the Latin alphabet, such as ash, eth, wynn, and thorn, even when these characters continued to be used in writing the vernacular.[27] According to Gregory of Tours, the Merovingian king Chilperic I (561-584) ordered that these digraphs be used to spell Frankish personal names.[28] Seiler hypothesises that Merovingian Latin orthography influenced the adoption of these graphs in the vernaculars, concluding, "it seems likely that the digraphs were considered 'Latin' rather than 'vernacular' spellings and were transmitted as part of Latin orthography".[29] The letters thorn and eth are not found in many pre-Conquest (and later) texts and administrative documents where the matrix language is Latin (administrative documents that include English names date as far back as the seventh century).[30] Cultural determinants for selection among graphic variants are also suggested by the quantitative analysis of eth / thorn variation in certain Old English poetic texts carried out by Drout and Chauvet. They argue that their data points to the distribution of thorn and eth being attributable to respect for the exemplar rather than having any systematic or phonemic significance.[31] A similar situation to that in the

Latin were matters for anxiety and debate. 'Roman script' and 'Roman letters' here are used here to contrast with other scripts such as runic, Greek, and Hebrew, 'script' being used with the sense of a "distinct graphical system" (S. GRIVELET, "Introduction", in: *Digraphia: Writing Systems and Society* (= *International Journal of the Sociology of Language* 150 (2001)), pp. 1-10, at p. 2). Cf. Unseth, "'script' [... means] whole sets of symbols, such as Roman, Arabic, Cyrillic, Hangul (Korean), Ethiopic, Devanagari (India), Hiragana (Japanese)" (P. UNSETH, "Sociolinguistic parallels between choosing scripts and languages", *Written Language & Literacy* 8.1 (2005), pp. 19-42, at p. 21). 'Roman script' in the present study means the same as lower-cased 'roman script' (e.g., as used in E. OKASHA, "Vernacular or Latin? The languages of Insular inscriptions, AD 500-1100", in: *Epigrafik 1988: Fachtagung für mittelalterliche und neuzeitliche Epigrafik, Graz, Mai 1988*, ed. W. KOCH (Vienna, 1990), pp. 139-150), but I have used the capitalised variant to avoid any confusion with the typographic term that distinguishes a kind of type from 'italic' type and 'blackletter' type. When there might be confusion between this kind of higher order of 'script' and 'script' as a distinctive way of writing the symbols of a given script (e.g., Insular script), I term the latter 'script-style' (cf. UNSETH, "Sociolinguistic parallels between choosing scripts and languages", p. 21).

[27] A. SEILER, "Writing the Germanic languages: The early history of the digraphs *th*, *ch*, and *uu*", in: *Writing Europe, 500-1450*, ed. A. CONTI, O. DA ROLD, and P. SHAW (Cambridge, 2015: *Essays and Studies collected on behalf of the English Association* 68), pp. 101-121, at p. 120.

[28] SEILER, "Writing the Germanic languages", pp. 114-115.

[29] SEILER, "Writing the Germanic languages", pp. 120-121; quotation at p. 120.

[30] CRICK, "English vernacular script", p. 175.

[31] M.D.C. DROUT and E. CHAUVET, "Tracking the moving ratio of *þ* to *ð* in Anglo-Saxon texts: A new method, and evidence for a lost Old English version of the 'Song of the Three

36   *Chapter 1*

documents pertains in post-Conquest administrative writing. According to Clark, Domesday Book scribes, working from *c.* 1086, "adopted Latin conventions ill-suited to the English sound system" for place- and personal names, disregarding Old English spelling traditions.[32] For example, Clark concludes that since "a Latin-based orthography did not provide for the distinction between /θ/ and /t/ or between /ð/ and /d/", spellings such as *t* and *d* for /θ/ and /ð/ "may reasonably be taken as being, like the associated use of Latin inflections, matters of graphic decorum".[33]

It has been suggested that in some Middle English cases, which were perhaps regionally distributed, the digraph *th* was used to represent the unvoiced sound /θ/ (the sound, for example, in modern English 'thin') while thorn was reserved for the voiced sound /ð/ (for example, in modern English 'the').[34] In the case of *th*/ thorn variation, non-phonemic forms of systemic variation have also been suggested. In the second continuation of the *Peterborough Chronicle*, written *c.* 1155, word class may be a factor in the selection between thorn and *th*: there appears to be a preference for *th* in lexical words and thorn in grammatical words, while position in the word may also be a factor as *th* appears more commonly in word-initial and final position than in the middle of words.[35] Analysis of later Middle English texts localised to Yorkshire confirms the general rule that thorn is used for grammatical words and *th* for lexical words, with the exception of Middle English spellings of 'through'.[36] It has also been suggested that genre and social or professional background may sometimes be factors in the selection of graph. Examining incidences of *th* and

Youths'", *Anglia* 133.2 (2015), pp. 278-319.

[32] C. CLARK, "Onomastics", in: *The Cambridge History of the English Language: Volume Two: 1066-1476*, ed. N. BLAKE (Cambridge, 1992), pp. 542-606, at p. 544.

[33] CLARK, "Onomastics", p. 549.

[34] M. STENROOS, "Regional dialects and spelling conventions in late Middle English: Searches for *th* in the LALME data", in: *Methods and Data in English Historical Dialectology*, ed. M. DOSSENA and R. LASS (Bern, 2004), pp. 257-285.

[35] A. BERGS, "Writing, reading, language change – a sociohistorical perspective on scribes, readers, and networks in medieval Britain", in: *Scribes as Agents of Language Change*, ed. E.-M. WAGNER, B. OUTHWAITE, and B. BEINHOFF (Berlin, 2013: *Studies in Language Change* 10), pp. 241-258, at p. 254.

[36] V. JENSEN, "The consonantal element *th* in some late Middle English Yorkshire texts", in: *Studies in Variation, Contacts and Change in English, Volume 10, Outposts of Historical Corpus Linguistics: From the Helsinki Corpus to a Proliferation of Resources*, ed. J. TYRKKÖ, M. KILPIÖ, T. NEVALAINEN, and M. RISSANEN (Helsinki, 2012: *Research Unit for Variation, Contacts and Change in English (VARIENG)*), n.p., <https://varieng.helsinki.fi/series/volumes/10/jensen/>.

Graphs, Alphabets, and Scripts 37

thorn recorded by *LALME*, Stenroos concludes that preference for *th*, "is first adopted by a limited class of people with legal training into texts of a particular type".[37] The particular type of text in which *th* is preferred is the legal document. Stenroos hypothesises that the training received by lawyers and legal scribes at the Inns of Court explains the adoption of *th* and its gradual spread into texts of other types, such as literary texts.[38] Late medieval thorn / *th* variation is, therefore, potentially conditioned by social factors. Stenroos proposes that the decline in the use of both yogh and thorn in the fifteenth century is systemic and inter-related, that the use of thorn and yogh and of *th* and *y* in character sets "indicate[s] that spellings tend to be adopted in clusters rather than individually".[39] Alongside suggestions for systemic and phonological explanations for variation in graph choice, we find suggestions for aesthetic motivations. Thaisen mentions that position in a line of verse may be a factor affecting letter-choice, stating that "scribes of late medieval English manuscripts regularly disfavour[ ] this letter [thorn] in line-initial position, perhaps for aesthetic reasons".[40] Aesthetic reasons have also been suggested as an explanation for variation between thorn and *th* in the late fourteenth-century manuscript of *Patience* (MS London, BL, Cotton Nero A.x), where Bergs finds, "spelling for purely aesthetic (one might almost say calligraphic) purposes: it contains alternating lines that show '*thay ar*' and '*for þay*'".[41]

---

[37] STENROOS, "Regional dialects and spelling conventions", p. 281.

[38] STENROOS, "Regional dialects and spelling conventions", pp. 280-281.

[39] STENROOS, "A Middle English mess of fricative spellings", p. 28.

[40] J. THAISEN, "Initial position in the Middle English verse line", *English Studies* 95.5 (2014), pp. 1-14, at p. 4, n. 9.

[41] BERGS, "Writing, reading, language change", p. 225. There has long been recognition that not all graphic variation can be attributed to variations in the sounds of the spoken language. In 1956, Angus McIntosh identified the phenomenon of "orthographic variation", which he exemplified with alternative spellings such as '*erþe*' / '*erthe*' ('earth'), '*him*' / '*hym*', '*noȝt*' / '*noght*' ('not'), and '*up*' / '*vp*' (A. MCINTOSH, "The analysis of written Middle English", repr. in: *Middle English Dialectology: Essays on some Principles and Problems by Angus McIntosh, M.L. Samuels, and M. Laing*, ed. M. LAING (Aberdeen, 1989), pp. 1-21, at pp. 4-5). These variants cannot have conveyed any difference in pronunciation. Such alternatives, he supposed, were neither related to the hand of the scribe nor to the spoken language; they "manifest other new distinctions of their own, distinctions which are in no sense a reflection of, or correlated with, anything in the spoken language" (p. 4). Regretting that the topic of such orthographic variation had "scarcely attracted the attention it deserve[d]", he hypothesised that such variations might have "demonstrably regional" distribution, "a possible correlation with places", and with the circumstances in which a scribe was trained (pp. 4-5). Later linguists have also recognised the possibility of non-phonetic orthographic variation. With early Middle English, which draws on orthographies of Latin, Old English, and French, Milroy admits, "the varying spellings in some cases indicate no

38   *Chapter 1*

The present chapter seeks to add a new dimension to these accounts of graph selection practices in the writing of English. It will argue that the grammar pedagogy of *littera* framed medieval knowledge and understanding of alphabets and graph selection and that this discourse, which was fundamental to the acquisition of literacy, provides a lens through which we may interpret the practices of writers and readers of English. In this chapter, we shall see that along with this basic theory of the letter was transmitted an understanding that sets of graphs and other aspects of alphabetical practice provided resources that erected boundaries between belonging and difference. For writers of English, this provided a way of thinking about variations in graphic practices. The author of the Wycliffite *Preface* draws on basic Latin literacy pedagogy to analyse his graphical problem and his solutions to it. The Wycliffite author proposes an alphabetical order that is based on *figura* (yogh is *"figurid lijk a zed"*, so words that begin with yogh are listed under zed), and on *potestas* (thorn represents the same sound as *th*, so words that begin with thorn are listed under *th*). This chapter will argue that, when they were viewed through the lens of basic Latin literacy training, variations in graph selection and the variant alphabets they are associated with provided resources for the construction and signalling of social identity. Framed with the basic pedagogy of *littera*, these choices, it will be argued, could, as Mark Sebba claims for modern orthography in the passage quoted in the epigraph to this chapter, "carry a powerful symbolism of identity". This chapter will seek to demonstrate that the identity-work shown to apply to modern graphic variation also applies to visible English in the medieval past.

Mark Sebba gives some examples of symbolic graphic variation in late early modern and modern languages in his important monograph, *Spelling and Society*.[42] He argues that variation in letter choice and spellings such as orthographic differences between British English 'vulcanising a tyre' and American

---

more than graphic differences"; variations in the hand of a single scribe probably do not mean that he pronounced a given word in different ways, simply that he did not have standard spelling (J. MILROY, "Middle English dialectology", in: *The Cambridge History of the English Language, Volume 2, 1066-1476*, ed. N. BLAKE (Cambridge, 1992), pp. 156-206, at p. 164). Megginson proposes that the spellings of the scribes of Old English poetry were often "purely written variations" that were "independent of phonetic history" (D. MEGGINSON, "The written language of Old English poetry" (unpublished PhD thesis, University of Toronto, 1993), at pp. 38, 130; cf. D. MEGGINSON, "The case against a 'general Old English poetic dialect'", in: *Prosody and Poetics: Essays in Honour of C.B. Hieatt*, ed. M.J. TOSWELL (Toronto, 1995), pp. 117-132).

[42] M. SEBBA, *Spelling and Society: The Culture and Politics of Orthography around the World* (Cambridge, 2007).

Graphs, Alphabets, and Scripts 39

English 'vulcanizing a tire', or the choice between *ss* and the Eszett in some varieties of modern written German can symbolise belonging, identity, and difference. Such work provides us with new approaches to the analysis of orthographic variation. Sebba aims to create a "sociolinguistics of orthography" to provide a framework for "accounting for orthographic choices in their social context".[43] Orthography "touches on matters of social identity, national identity, cultural politics, representation and voice".[44] Orthography has been overlooked by sociolinguistics because the discipline has concentrated on "studying spoken language".[45] Graphic signs, Sebba claims, carry not only linguistic meaning, but also social meaning at the same time. He distinguishes two models of orthography: an autonomous model and a socio-cultural model. Autonomous models view orthography as a neutral technology. The sociocultural model, preferred by Sebba, views these practices as "ideological and therefore culturally embedded".[46] Orthography is, according to Sebba, a "social practice".[47] When an orthography is selected to encode or re-encode a language, "the new orthography [...] may be designed to enhance the *difference*, rather than the similarity, between itself and one or more of the potential models".[48] The selection of orthography, from this point of view, is a means of encoding visually the relations between languages and their users: "orthographies can provide a useful way of creating a sense of difference".[49] Sebba gives the example of Manx, which is visually unlike Scottish and Irish Gaelic even though these languages are very closely related: "[h]ad Manx shared its orthography with Scots or Irish Gaelic it may well have come under pressure from these near relations, losing its claim to linguistic independence".[50] The selection of an English orthographic model in the eighteenth century meant that written

[43] SEBBA, *Spelling and Society*, pp. 1-7.
[44] SEBBA, *Spelling and Society*, p. 6.
[45] SEBBA, *Spelling and Society*, p. 7.
[46] SEBBA, *Spelling and Society*, p. 14.
[47] SEBBA, *Spelling and Society*, p. 9; cf. M. SEBBA, "Orthography and ideology: Issues in Sranan spelling", *Linguistics* 38.5 (2000), pp. 925-948, at pp. 925-926.
[48] M. SEBBA, "Orthography as literacy: How Manx was 'reduced to writing'", in: *Orthography as Social Action: Scripts, Spelling, Identity, and Power*, ed. A.M. JAFFE, J. ANDROUTSOPOULOS, S. JOHNSON, and M. SEBBA (Berlin, 2012), pp. 161-175, at p. 163. The late Middle English *Hymn to the Virgin* is an astonishing case of the adoption of a model that has marked political and cultural meaning: the Middle English is encoded in Welsh orthography in the sixteenth-century and later manuscripts. See M. THUILLIER, "The Welsh *Hymn to the Virgin*: Contexts and reception" (unpublished M. Phil. thesis, University of Glasgow, 2018).
[49] SEBBA, "Orthography as literacy", p. 171.
[50] *Ibid.*

40   *Chapter 1*

Manx was visually very different from its cognates, reflecting the importance of English in the cultural formation of the clergy and other readers for whom English was the medium of literacy training.[51] A twentieth-century example of the use of orthography to create an impression of difference between languages is offered by the written creole of British speakers of Caribbean heritage also studied by Sebba. Sebba gives examples of spellings that differ visually from Standard English even though they signify no phonological distinction, such as 'kool' for 'cool' and 'pitty' for 'pity'. His research suggests that users of the creole orthography intended to make a distinction from Standard English plain, though they were not necessarily aware that they were "making Creole *look* different from English".[52] Orthography can also create a sense of *similarity* between languages: "minimizing orthographic distance can help to create 'language unity'", states Sebba, giving the example of Bahasa Indonesian and Bahasa Malaysian.[53]

Choices *within* a script system may also be powerfully associated with social identities and political valencies. Sebba points out that particular graphic choices can take on ideological and social meaning: "[w]ithin a single script system, such as the Roman one, there exist many possibilities for iconising particular font styles, characters, and diacritics".[54] Florian Coulmas gives a twenty-first- century example of the sensitivity of character choice within an alphabet: "[t]he Turkish government passed a law in 2002 enabling the use of Kurdish on the air, but it steadfastly refused to augment the official Turkish alphabet with the letters *Q, W* and *X*".[55] According to Sebba, the combination *zh* in Breton is "a perennial source of dispute and division" because it "characterises an orthography introduced in 1941 during the period of the Nazi occu-

---

[51] SEBBA, "Orthography as literacy", p. 164.

[52] M. SEBBA, "Phonology meets ideology: The meaning of orthographic practices in British Creole", *Language Problems and Language Planning* 22.1 (1998), pp. 19-47, at pp. 33-35; quotation at p. 35.

[53] SEBBA, "Orthography as literacy", p. 171.

[54] SEBBA, "Sociolinguistic approaches to writing systems research", p. 39; for 'iconisation' as a process in the formation of linguistic ideologies see J.T. IRVINE and S. GAL, "Language ideology and linguistic differentiation", in: *Regimes of Language: Ideologies, Polities, and Identities*, ed. P. KROSKRITY (Santa Fe, 2000), pp. 35-83, at pp. 36-37. Cf. "linguistic features that index social groups or activities appear to be iconic representations of them" (R. VOSTERS, G. RUTTEN, M. VAN DER WAL, and W. WANDENBUSSCHE, "Spelling and identity in the southern Netherlands (1750-1830)", in: *Orthography as Social Action: Scripts, Spelling, Identity, and Power*, ed. A.M. JAFFE, J. ANDROUTSOPOULOS, S. JOHNSON, and M. SEBBA (Berlin, 2012), pp. 135-159, at p. 142.

[55] COULMAS, *Sociolinguistics*, p. 207.

Graphs, Alphabets, and Scripts 41

pation of France" and "the 'deviant' *k* of the Spanish anarchists" which in the twentieth century replaced *c* or *qu*, became an icon of the anarchists as a group: "an icon of the anarchists' rejection not just of spelling rules, but of rules more generally".[56]

The selection of one *script* rather than another has also been shown to be powerfully capable of expressing boundaries between belonging and difference in the modern world. Unseth suggests that four factors affect choice of script: "clan identity", "national identity", "political movements", and "religion". Relatedly, few scripts are created from scratch; most are borrowed and choices are "made with a conscious awareness of [...] neighbours".[57] Calvet gives an example when he describes *"une campagne d'arabisation de l'environnement"* ("a campaign to make the environment Arabic"): over a period of months in 1976, Roman script was replaced with Arabic on car number plates, road names, and commercial signs and remaining inscriptions in Roman script on the walls of Algiers were covered with tar.[58] Coulmas gives the example of Moldovan, the Romanian language scripted in the Cyrillic alphabet. The use of Cyrillic promoted visual similarities between Romanian and Russian. With the collapse of the USSR in 1989, the Moldavian Soviet Socialist Republic called for Roman script to be used, "thereby eliminating the visual differences between Moldovan and Romanian" formerly promoted by USSR to strengthen relations with Cyrillic languages; the motive for the substitution being "primarily ideological rather than practical".[59] Sebba explains that attitudes towards script change may be associated with beliefs that it facilitates loanwords and therefore cultural influence: "[t]he large-scale importation of vocabulary can amount to the transmission of a culture, and script can have – or at least is perceived to have – a significant role in facilitating vocabulary transfer", giving the examples of the adoption of Roman script for Malay, and the adoption of Cyrillic for the Turkic languages of Central Asia.[60]

But how far are the models developed in the linguistics of modern languages applicable to language visibility in the medieval past? Sebba gives rather conflicted messages about the application of his approach to languages without standard orthography. On the one hand, he argues that "the view of

---

[56] SEBBA, *Spelling and Society*, p. 83.
[57] UNSETH, "Sociolinguistic parallels between choosing scripts and languages", pp. 21, 33.
[58] J.-L. CALVET, *Les voix de la ville: Introduction à la sociolinguistique urbaine* (Paris, 1994), pp. 172-173.
[59] F. COULMAS, *Writing and Society* (Cambridge, 2013), p. 115.
[60] SEBBA, *Spelling and Society*, pp. 96-97, quotation at p. 97.

42   *Chapter 1*

orthography as social practice holds for all languages".[61] On the other hand, in a completely phonetic system, no meaningful variation would be possible, he argues: variation would have "little or no social meaning, since everyone [would be] free to spell as they cho[]se".[62] Sebba believes that variation in English spelling before the seventeenth century exemplifies this state of affairs. He therefore shares the view common in traditional study of medieval English, where it is assumed that meaningful variation in orthography only becomes possible with the beginnings of spelling standardisation.[63] This chapter seeks to provide evidence that orthographic variation in medieval English *always* had the potential to mark identity for its scribes and their communities.

Although sociolinguistic work on orthographies is often focused on contemporary examples, the relevance of the approach to earlier written material has on occasion been demonstrated. Vosters *et al.* focus on a case study in historical linguistics: orthography in southern Dutch of the eighteenth and nineteenth centuries. In the nineteenth century a few minimal differences in orthography such as *ae* as opposed to *aa*, *ey* as opposed to *ei*, and *den* as opposed to *de* acquired salience; the differences in spelling, they argue, did not represent pronunciation differences but "served as tools for indexing different social identities".[64] Sebba also takes a historical subject, in his treatment of the orthography of Manx mentioned above. Spitzmüller uses historical examples to illustrate what he terms graphic "ideologies", sets of beliefs articulated by users to rationalise or justify graphic choices.[65] The meaning of graphic features, he shows, is ascribed by users and is "floating" and can change across time. He demonstrates that German vowels that carry umlauts, the Eszett letter, and black-letter type, are variously ascribed with meanings of Germanness. A key point is that these features have no intrinsic or necessarily enduring mean-

---

[61] SEBBA, "Orthography and ideology", p. 926.

[62] SEBBA, *Spelling and Society*, p. 33.

[63] See, for example, *An Anthology of Chancery English*, ed. J.H. FISHER, M. RICHARDSON, and J.L. FISHER; J. HERNÁNDEZ-CAMPOY, "Overt and covert prestige in late Middle English: A case study in East Anglia", *Folia Linguistica Historica* 42 (2009), pp. 1-26; the studies in J. KOPACZYK and A.H. JUCKER (ed.), *Communities of Practice in the History of English* (Amsterdam, 2013); and J.J. SMITH, "Spelling and tradition in fifteenth-century copies of Gower's *Confessio Amantis*", in: *The English of Chaucer and his Contemporaries*, ed. J.J. SMITH (Aberdeen, 1989), pp. 96-113.

[64] VOSTERS *et al.*, "Spelling and identity", p. 140.

[65] J. SPITZMÜLLER, "Floating ideologies: Metamorphoses of graphic 'Germanness'", in: *Orthography as Social Action: Scripts, Spelling, Identity, and Power*, ed. A.M. JAFFE, J. ANDROUTSOPOULOS, S. JOHNSON, and M. SEBBA (Berlin, 2012), pp. 255-288.

Graphs, Alphabets, and Scripts 43

ing; they are features that can be *ascribed* with meaning in given communities and times.

This chapter will apply some of these approaches to the letters, orthography, and scripts of medieval English. It will include discussion of various scripts, and most crucially, variation between runic and Roman script in the representation of English. In the next section of this chapter we will consider variations in medieval understandings of the alphabet and their applications in writing. Evidence that these variations could acquire valency with respect to identity will be drawn from grammatical treatises widely used in the medieval teaching of literacy. These pedagogic traditions will provide a framework for the analysis of alphabets in pre-Conquest manuscripts and in later medieval primers. The second section will examine a series of micro-texts about *Anglice littere* (letters that are thought of as 'English') that also have clear pedagogic associations. The third section will examine variation between runic and Roman script, offering case studies of inscriptions on pre-Conquest stone monuments and of the use of runes in manuscripts of Old English poetry. This section will argue that, even though these materials are not explicitly pedagogic, they repay analysis through the lens of traditional grammatical texts and their teaching on scriptal variation. These case studies will illustrate the claim that variations in letter choice, the alphabet, and script were resources for marking belonging and difference. They will also demonstrate an important and hitherto insufficiently recognised point that for readers and writers of medieval English, the very identification and analysis of graphs and understanding of the available repertoire varied and could signify belonging and difference. Even if 'their' alphabet has the same *figurae* as 'ours', the *nomina* and *potestates* that 'we' associate with the *figurae* may not be the same in 'their' analysis. For example, 'we' may count four *figurae* but five *different* letters in the Middle English word '*boȝeȝ*' ('boughs'), 'they' may count four *figurae* and only four letters, for one is seen as repeated.

Grammar, Alphabets, and the Primer

Alphabet rows or sequences provide us with evidence that letters not found in the alphabet used for Latin were sometimes viewed as having a different status from the graphs of the character set used for Latin and that decisions about this matter could acquire social meanings beyond or apart from any pho-

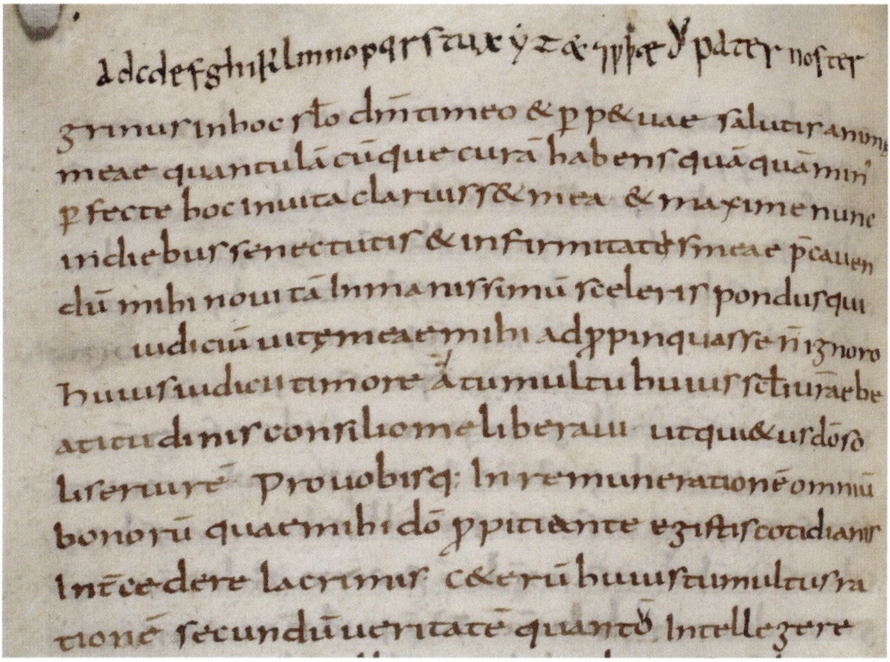

44   *Chapter 1*

Fig. 1   Practice alphabet, MS London, BL, Harley 208, f. 87v (detail). Photo: © The British Library Board, MS British Library, Harley 208, f. 87v.

nemic significations. In some Old English alphabet rows, the letters not found in the Latin alphabet were added at the end of the sequence, along with various other symbols, such as abbreviations. This positioning perhaps suggests that the non-Latin letters were felt to be somehow peripheral to the main alphabet. The earliest alphabetical sequence in a pre-Conquest manuscript occurs in MS London, BL, Harley 208, ff. 87v-88r, where it has been entered in the top margin of Alcuin's epistles, followed by the beginning of the *Pater noster* (see Figure 1 and Figure 2). The main text is thought to have been copied in France in the ninth century, but the alphabet is a later, Insular addition which dates to the turn of the tenth and eleventh centuries.[66] The alphabet in MS Harley 208 is an example of the Latin alphabet modified with additional letters. It begins

---

[66] F.C. ROBINSON, "Syntactical glosses in Latin manuscripts of Anglo-Saxon provenance", *Speculum* 48.3 (1973), pp. 443-479, p. 449; D. SCRAGG, *A Conspectus of Scribal Hands Writing English, 960-1100* (Cambridge, 2012: *Publications of the Manchester Centre for Anglo-Saxon Studies* 11), No. 635.

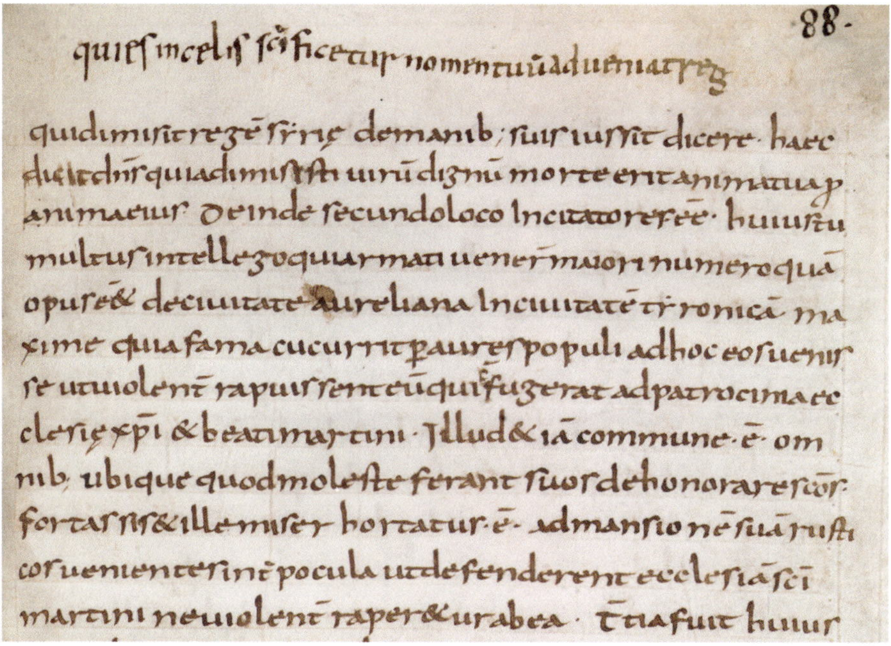

Graphs, Alphabets, and Scripts 45

Fig. 2 Practice alphabet, MS London, BL, Harley 208, f. 88r (detail). Photo: © The British Library Board, MS British Library, Harey 208, f. 88r.

with the usual Latin graphs and then adds the ampersand and the Tironian *et*, and then the non-Latin graphs, the rune wynn, the rune thorn, ash, and eth. Around the same time, *c.* 1010-1012, Byrhtferth, master of the school at Ramsey Abbey, inserted a similar modified Latin alphabet in his Old English *Enchiridion* alongside the Latin alphabet. The two alphabets run parallel, until the end of the English alphabet which concludes with Tironian *et*, wynn, thorn, eth, and ash.[67] The purpose of this part of his book is to explain the alphabet for the benefit of "*uplendiscum preostum*" ("rustic priests").[68] The placing of the non-Latin letters at the end of these alphabetical sequences suggests that they were viewed as somehow different from the basic Latin alphabet. Ælfric, by contrast, in the alphabet in his Old English *Grammar* (probably composed 993-

[67] Byrhtferth, *Byrhtferth's* Enchiridion, ed. P. BAKER and M. LAPIDGE (Oxford, 1995: *EETS*, s.s. 15), p. 184; for the date and Byrhtferth's career see Byrhtferth, *Byrhtferth's* Enchiridion, pp. XXXIII-XXXIV.
[68] Byrhtferth, *Byrhtferth's* Enchiridion, p. 184.

46   *Chapter 1*

995 for young boys), omits wynn, thorn, and eth, and categorises ash as a diphthong.[69]

Doubt about the status of the non-Latin letters in the alphabet evident in these examples is arguably a response to the grammar texts used in pre-Conquest England.[70] In his highly influential *Ars maior*, the fourth-century grammarian Donatus discusses the Latin alphabet in the chapter *"De Littera"*.[71] According to some people, the Latin alphabet has only seventeen letters (*"ut quidam putant, Latinas litteras non plures esse quam decem et septem"*).[72] However, Donatus explains, it actually has twenty-three letters. The letters of the alphabet consist of five vowels (save that *i* and *u* can be consonants when combined with other vowels in words such as '*Iuno*' and '*uates*'). Added to these are seven consonants that are semi-vowels (*f l m n r s x*, letters which do not produce a syllable when pronounced; *x* however is double, i.e. /ks/). There are nine mute consonants (*b c d g h k p q t*, letters that cannot be pronounced alone). Donatus notes that some people dispute whether *h*, *k* and *q* should be included in the alphabet, for *q* and *k* are duplicated by *c*, while *h* is the sign of a breathing. Donatus defends *q* and *k*: these letters are properly used when *u* and *a* follow. Finally, Donatus states that *y* and *z* are part of the alphabet; they are actually Greek letters but "we have admitted" them because they are required for spelling Greek names (*"quas litteras propter Graeca nomina admisimus"*).[73] In his fifth-century *De Nuptiis Philologiae et Mercurii*, Martianus Capella too numbers twenty-three letters in the alphabet, noting that *y* was

---

[69] Ælfric, *Grammar: Ælfrics* Grammatik *und* Glossar, ed. J. ZUPITZA (Berlin, 1880), pp. 5, 7. Ælfric's *Grammar* is based on that used in Æthelwold's (his teacher's) school, which was probably a Carolingian work consisting of excerpts from Priscian whose import into England was associated with the Benedictine Reform (J. HILL, "Ælfric's grammatical triad", in: *Form and Content of Instruction in Anglo-Saxon England in the Light of Contemporary Manuscript Evidence*, ed. P. LENDINARA, L. LAZZARI, and M.A. D'ARONCO (Turnhout, 2007: *Fédération Internationale des Instituts d'Etudes Médiévales, Textes et Etudes du Moyen Age* 39), pp. 285-307, at p. 296). See also T. HUNT, *Teaching and Learning Latin in Thirteenth-Century England*, 3 vols. (Cambridge, 1991), 1, pp. 99-119, for the sources of and later glosses on the *Grammar*.

[70] For knowledge of ancient and early medieval grammatical works in pre-Conquest England, including Donatus and Donatus commentaries, Priscian, Cassiodorus, Isidore of Seville, and of course Bede and Alcuin, see H. GNEUSS, "The study of language in Anglo-Saxon England", in: *Textual and Material Culture in Anglo-Saxon England: Thomas Northcote Toller and the Toller Memorial Lectures*, ed. D. SCRAGG (Cambridge, 2003), pp. 75-105, at pp. 78-80, 82-83.

[71] Donatus, *Ars maior*, in: "*Donati* Ars grammatica", ed. H. KEIL, in: *Grammatici Latini*, ed. H. KEIL, 8 vols. (Leipzig, 1864), 4, pp. 367-402, at pp. 367-368.

[72] Donatus, *Ars maior*, p. 368.

[73] Donatus, *Ars maior*, p. 368.

Graphs, Alphabets, and Scripts   47

not recognised in early Latin because it was "a Greek letter", but he includes it for the sake of writing Greek names.[74] Likewise he includes *z* despite the fact that Roman orthographer Appius Claudius despised the letter because when it is pronounced the speaker's teeth look like a corpse's teeth ("Z *vero Appius Claudius detestatur, quod dentes mortui, dum exprimitur, imitatur*").[75] Priscian (fl. *c.* 500) follows, stating "we use" twenty-three letter-forms ("[*s*]*unt igitur figurae literarum quibus nos utimur viginti tres*").[76] These treatises, which were to remain important to the teaching of grammar throughout the Middle Ages, presented the alphabet not only as variable, but also as something whose variants distinguished social groups. Some letters are recognised as Greek rather than Latin; nonetheless "*we*" admit them, writes Donatus, while Priscian states that "*we* use" an alphabet of twenty-three letters.

Early Christian writers continued to recognise that alphabetical analysis and practice could mark identity and difference, inflecting this tradition with their desire to Christianise their pedagogy. In his *Etymologiae*, Isidore of Seville (*c.* 560-636) followed Donatus and Priscian in his account of the composition of the Latin alphabet, but he added Christianising legitimations for the alphabet he used. He explains that the letter *x* only came into use in the time of Augustus, which was proper because Christ became renowned at that time and the letter *x* is the sign of the cross ("X *littera usque ad Augustini tempus nondum apud Latinos erat,* [*et digne hoc tempore, quo Christi nomen innotuit, quod per eam, quae crucis signum figurat, scriptitatur*]").[77] The Greek letter *y* stands for the life of a human; the lower stem of the letter is upright but the upper part of the letter is divided into two paths, a virtuous path branching steeply to the right, and an easier but morally disreputable path branching to the left.[78] Like Isidore, Bede adapts the classical grammatical teaching on the alphabet, creating an account that provides an alphabet for his community that is marked with Christian identity.[79] In the first chapter of his *De Arte metrica*

---

[74] Martianus Capella, *De Nuptiis Philologiae et Mercurii*, ed. J. WILLIS (Leipzig, 1983: *Bibliothecae Teubnerianae Scriptorum Graecorum et Romanorum*), p. 63.

[75] Martianus Capella, *De Nuptiis Philologiae et Mercurii*, pp. 68-69.

[76] Priscian, *Institutiones grammaticae*: "*Prisciani*, Institutionum grammaticarum *Libri I-XII*", ed. M. HERTZIUS, in: *Grammatici Latini*, ed. H. KEIL, 8 vols. (Leipzig, 1855), 2, p. 7.

[77] Isidore of Seville, *Etymologiae: Isidori Hispalensis Episcopi,* Etymologiarum *sive* Originum, ed. W.M. LINDSAY, 2 vols. (Oxford, 1911), 1, Book 1, ch. 4, section 14. The square brackets are Lindsay's and indicate that the matter within them is not attested in all manuscript traditions.

[78] Isidore of Seville, *Etymologiae*, 1, Book 1, ch. 3, section 7.

[79] Law believes that orthography did not much interest Insular teachers (V. LAW, *The In-*

48   *Chapter 1*

(*c.* 710), Bede states that "we use" twenty-seven letters ("*Itaque omnes littere quibus utimur sunt XXVII*"), for although the Latin alphabet consists of twenty-one letters, plus *y* and *z*, since becoming Christian, Latin-speaking peoples have used the Greek letters found in the Bible (eta, chi, rho, and omega and alpha).[80] However, these Greek letters have not been admitted into the order of the alphabet, with the exception of "alpha [which] differs only in name; otherwise it is equivalent both in form and value to our *A*"; "and so we use twenty-seven letters in all" ("*Qui etiam post perceptionem dominice fidei* H *et* X *et* P *et* Ω *cum* A *Grecas litteras, etsi non in alfabeti ordinem recipiunt, divinis tamen paginis inditas continent* [...] *Itaque omnes litterae quibus utimur sunt XX et VII*").[81] Arguably, the addition of the non-Latin letters at the end of the Latin alphabet in MS Harley 208 and in Byrhtferth's *Enchiridion* follows a conception of the alphabet similar to Bede's. Perhaps eth was positioned at the end with the other dubious letters because it was considered to be an abbreviation like barred thorn, on account of its name '*þæt*'; abbreviations, as we have seen, were also placed at the end of the row. Perhaps ash was also grouped there because it was recognised as a diphthong. Indeed, arguably the use of the names '*þæt*' and '*diptongon*' or '*diptonge*' for eth and ash indicate a desire to analyse these graphs as an abbreviation and a digraph respectively rather than to consider them as distinct and unprecedented letters of the alphabet. This treatment of the graphs by resourcefully applying the doctrine of *littera* – naming them in ways that indicate their relation to Latin letters and placing them at the end of the row – implies that these are letters that 'we use', even though they are not quite admitted into the order of the alphabet, as Bede puts it. There was, however, a limit to the utility of the precedent established by Bede, and perhaps for this reason not everyone followed this model. Greek additions to

---

sular Latin Grammarians in the Early Middle Ages (Woodbridge, 1982), p. 41, n. 56), but Porter shows the importance of Isidore's *Etymologiae* to pre-Conquest development of vernacular literacy: the text existed in epitome form in seventh-century Canterbury and "gave thousands of English words their first written form" (D. PORTER, "Isidore's *Etymologiae* at the school of Canterbury", *Anglo-Saxon England* 43 (2014), pp. 7-44 at p. 7), while Barney *et al.* describe Isidore's huge influence for which the evidence includes nearly 1,000 surviving manuscripts from across Europe and the importance of Isidore to Bede (Isidore of Seville, *The* Etymologies *of Isidore of Seville*, trans. S. BARNEY, W. LEWIS, J. BEACH, and O. BERGHOF (Cambridge, 2006), pp. 24-25). For Bede's sources in the "*De Littera*" section see R. PALMER, "Bede as a textbook writer: A study of his *De Arte metrica*", *Speculum* 34.4 (1959), pp. 573-584.

[80]   Bede, *De Arte metrica*, in: *Bede, Libri II* De Arte metrica *et* De Schematibus et tropis, ed. and trans. C.B. KENDALL (Saarbrücken, 1991), pp. 38-39.

[81]   Bede, *De Arte metrica*, pp. 36-37; cf. Isidore of Seville, *Etymologiae*, 1, Book 1, ch. 3.

Graphs, Alphabets, and Scripts   49

the Latin alphabet were legitimised by Bede on the grounds that these letters
had particular meaning in the Bible. Thorn and wynn, derived from runic script
and bearing runic names, had no such legitimacy. It is perhaps because of this
that Ælfric follows the grammarians' tradition strictly, not acknowledging
thorn and wynn at all when he enumerates and lists the letters of the alphabet.[82]
By following the ancient grammars in enumerating twenty-three letters and
omitting any mention of wynn, thorn, and eth, he implies that these are not
letters that may be aligned with the alphabets of the Bible, even though they
appear in manuscripts of his own text. He only mentions English orthography
when it aligns with that taught by the Latin grammars. For example, repeating
the traditional justification for including *y* in the alphabet to spell Greek names,
he adds the comment that *y* is very usual in English writing ("*se ylca* y *is on
engliscum gewritum swiðe gewunelic*").[83] Ælfric frames his grammar as a beginning text for both languages, but in his view, graphic practice in English can
only be understood in relation to the model of Latin.[84] This, he implies, is what
"*we*" find when we analyse text into its component parts, down to the indivisi-
ble components of letters ("*we todælad þa boc to cwydum and syððan ða cwy-
das to dælum, eft ða dælas to stæfgefegum and syððan þa stæfgefu to sta-
fum*").[85] 'Our' grammatical analysis, implies Ælfric, does not include wynn,
thorn, and eth.

As the special letters eth and wynn fell into disuse at the end of the thirteenth century and the letter yogh was recognised as a new letter, the alphabet
was sometimes modified again and new treatments of the alphabetical sequence convey attitudes towards the letters thorn and yogh. Powerful evidence
that alphabetical practice continued to acquire significance as an identity
marker is provided by discussions of it. John Trevisa's later fourteenth-century

---

[82]   Ælfric, *Grammar*, p. 5.

[83]   Ælfric, *Grammar*, p. 5.

[84]   Menzer discusses the extent to which Ælfric's grammar is a grammar of English, though
does not mention the alphabet (M.J. MENZER, "Ælfric's English 'Grammar'", *Journal of English
and Germanic Philology* 103.1 (2004), pp. 106-124). Joyce Hill notes that outside Romance-
speaking areas, "some innovations [to the ancient grammatical pedagogy] were needed in the
organisation and presentation of grammatical texts in order to teach those whose native language
was Germanic, not Latinate" (J. HILL, "Ælfric's grammatical triad", in: *Form and Content of Instruction in Anglo-Saxon England in the Light of Contemporary Manuscript Evidence*, ed. P.
LENDINARA, L. LAZZARI, and M.A. D'ARONCO (Turnhout, 2007: *Fédération Internationale des
Instituts d'Etudes Médiévales, Textes et Etudes du Moyen Age* 39), pp. 285-307, at p. 287).
However, it appears that changing the alphabet was a step too far for Ælfric.

[85]   Ælfric, *Grammar*, p. 5.

50   *Chapter 1*

translation of *De Proprietatibus rerum* by Bartholomaeus Anglicus († 1272)
notes that the alphabet has twenty-two letters: "*two and twenty lettres of* a. b.
c, *by þe whiche al þe lore of Goddes lawe is y write*".[86] Bartholomaeus stresses
that the number twenty-two has biblical significance. God carried out twenty-
two works in the first six days after creation; there were twenty-two generations from Adam to Jacob; and there are twenty-two books of the Old Testament.[87] This indicates that any letters other than those of the Latin alphabet
(such as thorn and yogh) are considered not to be of equal status to Latin letters, because not sanctioned by divine providence and exemplified in scripture.
The fourteenth-century *Mandeville's Travels* offers a more positive view of the
non-Latin letters: "*wee in Englond haue in oure langage and speche II lettres
mo þan þei haue in hire* abc, *and þat is* þ *&* 3, *the whiche ben clept thorn &
yogh*" ("we in England have in our language and speech two more letters than
they have in their *ABC*, and that is *þ* and *3*, which are called 'thorn' and
'yogh'").[88] This gives legitimacy to the augmented alphabet, and suggests that
the non-Latin letters are identity markers, signifying belonging and difference:
"*wee in Englond haue*" these letters in "*oure langage*". Likewise, as we saw
above, the author of the *Preface to the Wycliffite Biblical Concordance* shows
awareness of the power of alphabetical variation to signify identity. He notes
the doubt about whether *h* should be represented at all in words such as '*eir*',
showing his knowledge of debates that were current when Donatus wrote, as
we have seen, and were still the subject of learned discussion in pedagogic
contexts. He is aware that other scribes have their "*own manere of writyng*"; he
recognises that some do not use thorn and yogh and that there is a problem
concerning where words that begin with these graphs should be placed in the
alphabetical order of his concordance. Just as Bede argued that Greek alpha
was really the same letter as "our" Latin *a* on grounds of its shape and sound
value ("*Alfa etenim tantum nomine discrepat, ceterum et figura et potestate
nostrum* A *equiperat*"),[89] so the Wycliffite author makes a case for listing
words that begin with yogh under *z*, because it "*is figurid lijk a zed*". Words
that begin with thorn are listed under *t*, perhaps following the precedent that

---

[86] Bartholomaeus Anglicus, *On the Properties of Things: John Trevisa's Translation of
Bartholomaeus Anglicus* De Proprietatibus rerum, ed. M.C. SEYMOUR *et al.*, 3 vols. (Oxford,
1975-1988), 2, p. 1374.
[87] Bartholomaeus Anglicus, *On the Properties of Things*, 2, pp. 1373-1374.
[88] *Mandeville's Travels*, ed. M.C. SEYMOUR (Oxford, 1967), p. 104.
[89] Bede, *De Arte metrica*, pp. 38-39.

Graphs, Alphabets, and Scripts 51

Greek names beginning with theta were spelled in Latin with initial *th*.[90] An allusion to Greek precedent would provide an elegant solution to the problem of thorn. While yogh was descended from an English form of *g* and also looked legitimate in that it had the same shape as *z*, thorn was problematic in that it had no precedent in a biblical script. This kind of discussion resonates with that in the grammatical texts of the period.[91] MS London, BL, Harley 1277, a fifteenth-century collection of grammatical materials, begins with an ortho-graphic treatise that starts by enumerating the letters that "we use": "*Sunt eni^m figure litt^er ar^um quib^us nos vtim^ur 23*", a statement attributed to Priscian (f. 1r). The vowels are *A E I O V*, the semi-vowels are *L M N R S X*, there are nine consonants, *B C D F G K P Q T*. '*Zizannia*' is an example of "*vocabula barbara*" where *z* is used. Debates about the use of *h*, *k*, and *q*, are discussed in an orthographic treatise in MS London, BL, Harley 1002, ff. 31r-81r (scc ff. 39r-42r, 46r-47r, 71r-v). Another collection of school-texts in MS London, BL, Addit. 12195, a composite later fifteenth-century paper manuscript that seems to have been partly copied by one John Leke of North Creake, Norfolk, in-cludes a treatise on versification that begins "*Aput latines viginti sunt littere*" ("among the Latins there are twenty letters"; ff. 91r-96v).

Late Medieval Primers

Late medieval English primers provide an intriguing set of data that evi-dences considerable variation in analysis of the alphabet on the part of scribes of Middle English and perhaps also on the part of the readers of their books. The primer, a first prayer book, often commenced with an alphabet.[92] It has

---

[90] For examples see Chapter Five, p. 340, n. 133. According to Isidore, theta signifies death because the Greek word θάνατος ('death') begins with that letter ("*id est mortis signum*", Isidore of Seville, *Etymologiae*, 1, Book 1, ch. 3, section 8), while Roman *T* signifies the cross of Christ because Hebrew tau is cross-shaped, "T *figuram demonstrans Dominicae crucis, unde Hebraice signum interpretatur*" (Ezechiel 9:4; 1, Book 1, ch. 3, section 9).

[91] For teaching of grammar in fourteenth-century Oxford see R.W. HUNT, "Oxford grammar masters in the Middle Ages", repr. in: ID. *The History of Grammar in the Middle Ages: Collected Papers*, ed. G.L. BURSILL-HALL (Amsterdam, 1980: *Studies in the History of the Language Sciences* 5), pp. 167-97. MSS Worcester, Cathedral Library, F. 61 and F. 123, London, BL, Addit. 43797, and MS Cambridge, UL, Hh.1.5 are examples of fourteenth-century grammar books. MS Worcester, Cathedral Library, F. 61 contains extracts from Bede, Donatus, and Priscian with later commentary and there is some overlap with material in MS F. 123.

[92] Orme notes, "rather confusingly, it [the word 'primer'] seems to have been applied both to books of basic prayers and to Books of Hours" (N. ORME, *Medieval Children* (New Haven,

52   *Chapter 1*

often been pointed out that, by beginning with the alphabet, and following it
with the *Pater noster*, *Ave*, and other basic prayers, primers represent the learning of letters as foundational and intrinsic to Christian faith. The tradition of
preceding the alphabet with a cross and marking its close with '*amen*' presents
learning the alphabet itself part of a devotional act.[93] But the symbolism of the
alphabet does not stop there. We may first tease out its sensitivities in English-
language contexts by comparing the treatment of the alphabet in Latin and
English primers. A Latin primer of the first half of the fifteenth century survives in the Bolton Hours, MS York, Minster Library, Add. 2, f. 13r.[94] The
alphabet (f. 13r), runs: + *a* [two shapes] *b c d e f g h i k l m n o p q r* [two
shapes] *s* [two shapes] *t u* [two shapes, *u* and *v*] *x y z 7 con* [abbreviation] ≡
[three-bar tittle].[95] It is revealing to compare this example with English-language primers. A late fourteenth-century Middle English primer, MS Glasgow,
UL, Hunter 472 (V.6.22), begins with a very similar alphabet; except for the
form of the tittle, at first glance these alphabets are identical.[96] The alphabet in
MS Hunter 472 (f. 1r) runs: + *a* [two shapes] *b c d e f g h i k l m n o p q r* [two
shapes] *s* [two shapes] *t u* [two shapes, *u* and *v*] *x p/y 3/z 7* ⋮ [three-dot tittle] *est*

2001), at p. 264). He notes that the "Carthusian priory of Hinton (Som.) owned two books called
'primers of children' in 1343". The term continues to be used for both kinds of book. K.E.
KENNEDY, "Reintroducing the English Books of Hours or 'English Primers'", *Speculum* 89.3
(2014), pp. 693-723, builds on Orme's discussion of the terminology (pp. 695-696). Copeland
helpfully distinguishes between "catechetical" primers and "liturgical primers" (R. COPELAND,
Pedagogy, Intellectuals, and Dissent in the Later Middle Ages: Lollardy and Ideas of Learning
(Cambridge, 2004), p. 16). Clanchy distinguishes the "*ABC* Primer", "a booklet for instructing
children in the elements of literacy and doctrine" from the "Primer", "a full-sized prayer book or
Book of Hours designed for adult use" (M.T. CLANCHY, *Looking Back from the Invention of
Printing: Mothers and the Teaching of Reading in the Middle Ages* (Turnhout, 2018: *Utrecht
Studies in Medieval Literacy* 40), p. 137, n. 3). Some of the volumes discussed in the present
chapter combine materials like those that Clanchy calls the "*ABC* Primer" with material probably
intended for adult use.

[93] See for example M. DENLEY, "Elementary teaching techniques and Middle English religious didactic writing", in: *Langland, The Mystics, and the Medieval English Religious Tradition: Essays in Honour of S.S. Hussey*, ed. H. PHILLIPS (Cambridge, 1990), pp. 223-241; M.D.
RUST, *Imaginary Worlds in Medieval Books: Exploring the Manuscript Matrix* (Basingstoke,
2007), p. 44; and N. MCDONALD, "A York primer and its alphabet: Reading women in a lay
household", in: *The Oxford Handbook of Medieval Literature in English*, ed. E. TREHARNE and
G. WALKER with W. GREEN (Oxford, 2010), pp. 181-199.

[94] On this manuscript see MCDONALD, "A York primer and its alphabet". I am grateful to
Nicola McDonald for showing me an image of the Bolton Hours alphabet page.

[95] Cf. *OED, tittle*, n., 1 c.

[96] Dated second quarter of the fourteenth century in the Glasgow Special Collections
Catalogue. The alphabet is followed by the *Pater noster*, *Ave Maria*, and *Creed*.

Graphs, Alphabets, and Scripts 53

amen.[97] The letter *w* is omitted, probably because it was regarded as a digraph of *vv* or *uu*.[98] At first sight, in addition, neither thorn nor yogh is included in either alphabet. Generally, this alphabet has been seen by modern scholars as that of Latin. Stating that the MS Hunter 472 alphabet omits "the Anglo-Saxon letters later used in the prayers", Wolpe takes the view that it follows the "black-letter *ABC* of the earlier Latin tradition".[99] Wolpe's view aligns with other interpretations of the medieval educational alphabet. It has been claimed that the alphabet studied by the child in medieval Britain was "not the alphabet of the mother-tongue – French or English – but the alphabet of Latin".[100] Orme tells us that the pre-Conquest alphabet was designed to support "reading and writing in English as well as Latin" whereas the alphabet taught "from the twelfth to the sixteenth centuries ... [was] directed to learning Latin, rather than English and Latin together".[101] Clanchy too stresses that "it is Latin letters which are being taught and not an English alphabet" in such cases.[102] However, the situation may be more complex than this suggests. Above, it was argued that ash and eth were analysed as part of the Latin alphabet by means of their naming and grouping as a diphthong and as an abbreviation. We might think of this kind of analysis as *conceptual assimilation*. The alphabet in MS Hunter 472 and others like it may suggest that either or both thorn and yogh have been *assimilated conceptually* to the twenty-two letter Latin alphabet, with yogh

[97] I have transcribed the two graphs before Tironian *et* as þ/y ȝ/z because, as I shall argue below, yogh and thorn are *assimilated conceptually* to the *y* and *z* graphs. Henceforth, to discuss graphs in alphabets where conceptual assimilation has occurred, I use this manner of representing them. I refrain from extending this convention to all transcription, only using it where it is necessary to indicate probable assimilation.

[98] For sequences in which *w* becomes part of the alphabet see Chapter Five and for the early history of the double *u* digraph see SEILER, "The scripting of Old English".

[99] B. WOLPE, "Florilegium alphabeticum", in: *Calligraphy and Palaeography: Essays Presented to Alfred Fairbank on his 70th Birthday*, ed. O.S. OSLEY (London, 1965), pp. 69-75, at p. 70.

[100] S. REYNOLDS, *Medieval Reading: Grammar, Rhetoric and the Classical Text* (Cambridge, 1996), p. 8. Cf. DENLEY, "Elementary teaching techniques", p. 226, "the alphabet was first learnt to acquire passive literacy in Latin, that is, the ability to read out loud (without comprehension) the sounds of the Latin psalms and other service book material". Rust states that "no primer alphabet produced in England that I know of includes the letter-forms then in use for recording the sounds the English language does not share with Latin, þ and ȝ" (RUST, *Imaginary Worlds*, p. 41).

[101] N. ORME, *Medieval Schools: From Roman Britain to Renaissance England* (New Haven, 2006), p. 56.

[102] CLANCHY, *Looking back from the Invention of Printing*, p. 143. Clanchy makes the rather different suggestion that *ABC* primers, though they taught the Latin alphabet, may have been commonly written in English (pp. 155-157, 162).

54   *Chapter 1*

being assimilated to *z*, whose shape it shares, and perhaps thorn being mentally assimilated to *th* on the basis of their shared *potestas* or to *y*, on the basis of their shared *figura* in some hands (the figural assimilation of thorn to *y* is especially found in manuscripts of northern provenance).[103] Conceiving of yogh as the same letter as *z* and thorn as the same letter as *y* on grounds of shape cleverly exploits the theory of *littera* and such resourcefulness was, arguably, legitimated by the identification of aleph, alpha and *A* as the same letter by early grammarians on account of their similarities in shape, as in the example from Bede mentioned above.[104]

Support for this interpretation of the status of these graphs is given by comparing the alphabet in MS Hunter 472 with the repertoire of characters used for the text. Evidence for the conceptual assimilation of thorn with *y* in the alphabet is that the shape of *y* in the alphabet is identical with the shape of thorn in the text (compare the alphabet *y* with thorn in "*þat*" and "*þi*"; "that", "thy", f. 1r). But the digraph *th* is also used in the text, sometimes in display positions, and sometimes elsewhere ("*The ferthe hest is þis*", "the fourth commandment is this", f. 74r). The graph *y/þ* in the alphabet is upright and has a short vertical descender in the alphabet whereas when used in the text it sometimes has a hairline angled descender (for example, "*almyȝtti*", "*day*"; "almighty", "day", lines 8 up, 2 up). I have not located an example of *z* in the text, but evidence for assimilation of yogh to *z* (yogh is used for both /j/ ("*ȝife*", "*forȝeue*"; "give", "forgive") and /χ/ ("*noȝt*", "*almyȝtti*"; "not", "almighty")) is provided by the use of the 2-shaped form of *z* used in the alphabet as the majuscule form of yogh used in the blue initial letter of "*Ȝong*" ("young"), "*Ȝife*" ("give"), and "*Ȝif*" ("if") (ff. 21v, line 4 up, 28v, line 3, 70v, line 13). Therefore, the scribe of MS Hunter 472 does not *completely* follow the alphabet as a model for his practice when copying the vernacular texts. But his merging of thorn and *y*, in the face of his evident knowledge of traditional distinctions in form between the two letters, and perhaps the form of majuscule yogh, if executed by him or under his direction, suggest that he views these letters as part of the Latin alphabet.

This analysis of thorn and yogh was presumably transmitted by pedagogic communities as part of the practice of Anglophone literacy. It may have become a feature that indexed 'what we do' in the communities of practice asso-

---

[103] See M. BENSKIN, "The letters *þ* and *y* in later Middle English, and some related matters", *Journal of the Society of Archivists* 1 (1982), pp. 13-30.

[104] Bede, *De Arte metrica*, p. 38.

Graphs, Alphabets, and Scripts 55

ciated with MS Hunter 472 and similar primers. Some of the texts in the Hunter volume are resonant with Lollardy, for example, a treatise on the Ten Commandments complains about those who bequeath their goods to "*auerous prestes ᵃⁿᵈ namliche to sotil flateringe idel ᵃⁿᵈ myȝtty freres*" ("avaricious priests and especially to subtle, flattering, idle, and mighty friars", f. 80r).[105] Many are harmed: the dead for hanging onto ill-gotten gains, executors who divert bequests to themselves, and priests, whom excessive wealth makes evil as taught in "*godes lawe*" ("God's law", f. 80r). Possibly the attempt to align the alphabet with the alphabet of the text here is linked with Lollardy and the resonances of the scribe's practice with the policy of the Wycliffite *Preface* writer may be more than coincidental.

Another later medieval English primer alphabet row occurs in MS New York, Columbia University, Plimpton 258, a manuscript dated third quarter of the fifteenth century. The alphabet occurs in an independent quire of eight leaves which Acker describes as "a primer for elementary education".[106] The

---

[105] Rubric: "*Þe commaundmentys of god*", inc. "*Almyȝty god seith in his law on þis wise who so seiþ þat he loueþ me ᵃⁿᵈ kepiþ not myn hestis he is a lier*" ("Almighty God says in his law in this way whoever says he loves me and does not keep my commandments, he is a liar", f. 72r); expl. "*us drenched depe in synne*" ("us drowned deeply in sin", f. 80v); the text is linked with a text on the seven gifts of the Holy Ghost and an explicit for both texts occurs on f. 81v. The text has been neglected. Young and Aitken do not list the full contents of the manuscript (J. YOUNG and P.H. AITKEN, *A Catalogue of the Manuscripts in the Library of the Hunterian Museum in the University of Glasgow* (Glasgow, 1908), pp. 392-393). Jefferson classifies this commentary on the Ten Commandments as type DVII; this group includes MS Glasgow, UL, Hunter 472; MS Oxford, Bod. Lib., Bodley 85, 110r-122r; MS Cambridge, UL, Nn.4.12, 3r-7v; and MS London, BL, Addit. 27592, 42r-45v ("An edition of the Ten Commandments commentary in BL Harley 2398 and the related version in Trinity College Dublin 245, York Minster XVI.L.12, and Harvard English 738, together with discussion of related commentaries", ed. J.A. JEFFERSON (unpublished Ph.D. thesis, University of Bristol, 1995), p. CXXXIV). The Hunter manuscript is not mentioned in the classifications of the Ten Commandments texts in A.L. KELLOGG and E.W. TALBERT, "The Wycliffite *Pater noster* and Ten Commandments, with special reference to English MSS 85 and 90 in the John Rylands Library", *Bulletin of the John Rylands Library* 42.2 (1960), pp. 345-377, or in C.A. MARTIN, "The Middle English versions of The Ten Commandments, with special reference to Rylands English MS 85", *Bulletin of the John Rylands Library* 64.1 (1981), pp. 191-217. For discussions of MS Hunter 472 and reproductions of f. 1r see RUST, *Imaginary Worlds*, pp. 41-42, and J. GARDHAM, *The World of Chaucer: Medieval Books and Manuscripts* (Glasgow, 2004), <https://www.gla.ac.uk/myglasgow/library/files/special/exhibns/chaucer/index.html>, case 5.

[106] P. ACKER, "A schoolchild's primer (Plimpton MS 258)", in: *Medieval Literature for Children*, ed. D.T. KLINE (London, 2003), pp. 143-154 at p. 146. Clanchy suggests that such *ABC* primers must have been the "commonest of all manuscript books", being made in many thousands of copies; intended for children's education, they would mostly have been used to destruction (*Looking back from the Invention of Printing*, pp. 81, 129, 137-139; quotation at p. 81).

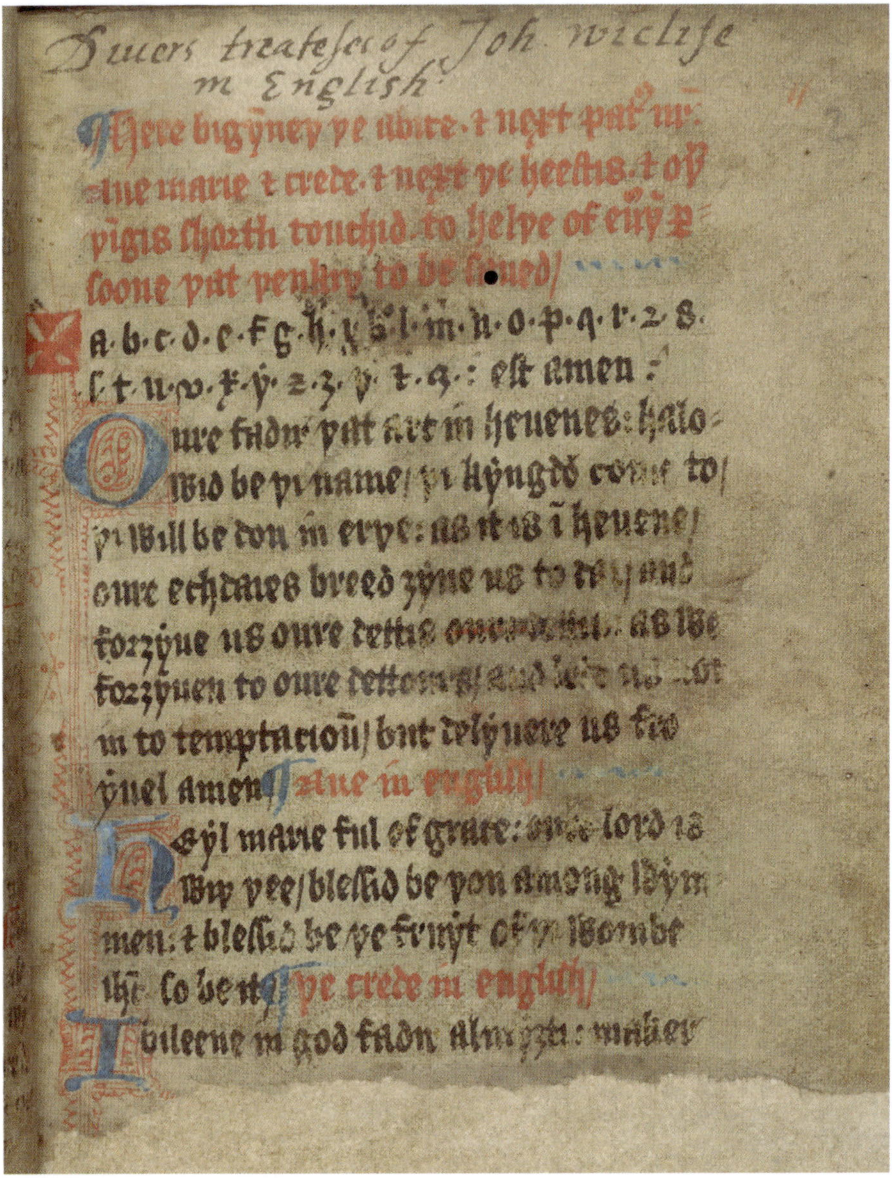

Fig. 3. Primer alphabet, MS Manchester, John Rylands Library, Eng. 85, f. 2r. Imaging: Copyright of the University of Manchester.

Graphs, Alphabets, and Scripts 57

alphabet is similar to those in the Bolton Hours (Add. 2) and MS Hunter 472. The alphabet is preceded by a cross and finishes with a three-dot tittle and the words "*est amen*": + *a* [two shapes] *b c d e f g h i k l m n o p q r* [two shapes] *s* [two shapes] *t u* [two shapes, *u* and *v*] *x y ʒ/z ⁊ con* ⸫ [three-dot tittle] *est amen*. Compared with MS Hunter 472, the alphabet row in MS Plimpton 258 conforms a little more closely with the character set used in the texts, though there are notable discrepancies. In MS Plimpton, the letter *y* is used for /j/ ("*yeue*", "give"), and *th* is used throughout for unvoiced and voiced sounds /θ/ ("*erthe*", "earth") and /ð/ ("*the*", "*with*"). The use of *th* and initial *y* mean that the alphabet and the text align and also that *y* is not assimilated conceptually with thorn. Yogh is used for /χ/ ("*almyʒti*", "almighty"). Evidence that yogh is aligned conceptually with *z* in MS Plimpton is provided by the unusual form of *z* in the alphabet row, where the character merges the crossed 2-shaped and the 3-shaped forms. Possibly this is an innovation: with other allographs (such as *u* / *v*) this alphabet follows the convention of displaying the two forms side by side. Somewhat similar to MS Plimpton 258 is MS Oxford, Bod. Lib., Rawl. C. 209, a fifteenth-century English-language primer that contains an alphabet, the *Pater noster*, *Ave Maria*, and *Creed* followed by basic didactic materials, all in Middle English prose. MS Rawl. C. 209, however, is smaller and more ornate than MS Plimpton 258, its alphabet beginning with a fine decorated initial with a spray and an illuminated cross (f. 1r). Unlike in MS Plimpton also, thorn appears in the text and it and *y* have a similar *figurae*. The letter *y* is occasionally distinguished from thorn with the addition of a tittle (for example, "*dayly*", "daily", f. 1r), but possibly the scribe and his community would have regarded this as the addition of a diacritic rather than the use of a different letter.

Powerful evidence that supports my suggestion that choice and arrangement of graphs in the alphabet row and the set used in the text are social markers associated with particular communities of practice where Anglophone literacy was promoted comes from an earlier English-language primer found in the first section of MS Manchester, John Rylands Library, Eng. 85, a manuscript dated fourteenth- / early fifteenth century in the John Rylands Library catalogue (see Figure 3). The alphabet here (f. 2r) departs from the other examples we have examined in its treatment of the non-Latin letters: after *x y z* come yogh / 3-shaped *z* and thorn, before the usual row resumes with the abbreviations Tironian *et*, and the symbol for *con*-: + *a b c d e f g h i k l m n o p q r* [two shapes] *s* [two shapes] *t u* [two shapes] *x y z* [two shapes, *z* and ʒ] *þ ⁊ con* ⸫ [three-dot tittle] *est amen*. The alphabet row in MS John Rylands Library, Eng.

58   *Chapter 1*

85 differs from those in the Bolton Hours (Add. 2), MS Hunter 472, and MS Plimpton 258 in subtle but important ways. It clearly provides both the 2-shaped and the 3-shaped forms of *z*, leaving open the interpretation of these characters. They could be read as allographs, simply different forms of the same letter *z*. Or the 3-shaped character could be read as a different letter from *z*; in this reading, yogh would have the status of a letter in its own right and a position in the Latin alphabet. Thorn is unambiguously given the status of a letter in its own right, being clearly distinguished in form from *y* (*y* is dotted, thorn is not) and is given its own position at the end of the letter sequence and before the abbreviations. There is a close correspondence between the alphabet and the text. The text in this manuscript clearly follows the model of the alphabet and demonstrates its implementation. As in the alphabet row, so in the text thorn and *y* are clearly distinguished in form, *y* being distinguished by a dot. Thorn is used consistently for the voiced and unvoiced consonant throughout the volume. In the text, yogh / 3-shaped *z* is used consistently for both for /j/ and for /χ/ ("*forȝyue*", "*almyȝti*", "forgive", "almighty", f. 2r).

The close attention paid by the scribe to the alphabet row and character sets in the primer section of MS John Rylands Library, Eng. 85 is shared by the author of the *Preface to the Wycliffite Biblical Concordance* who, as we have seen, is explicitly interested in orthographic practices and has worked out a clear policy with regards to the non-Latin letters. MS John Rylands Library, Eng. 85 aligns with the Wycliffite *Preface* author's observation that yogh is "*figurid lijk a zed*" and therefore belongs with *z* in the alphabetical sequence. MS John Rylands Library, Eng. 85 perhaps shares the Wycliffite *Preface*'s insistence that yogh is a separate letter that is positioned with *z*. The correspondence between the alphabetic policy in Eng. 85 with that of the Wycliffite *Preface* may be no coincidence. The unusual alphabet and repertoire of characters in the text in MS John Rylands Library, Eng. 85 may be associated with the religious affiliations of the textual content, for the alphabet row and English texts of the basic prayers *Pater noster*, *Ave Maria*, and *Creed* are followed by texts associated with Lollardy. In common with MS Hunter 472, MS John Rylands Library, Eng. 85 includes a treatise on the Ten Commandments (ff. 2v-9r) that has been associated with Lollardy (though the text in MS Hunter 472 is not the same one).[107] Notably, among the texts that follow the primer unit in

---

[107] For an edition of this text and the argument that it is associated with Lollardy see KELLOGG and TALBERT, "The Wycliffite *Pater noster* and Ten Commandments". The text was certainly acceptable to the scribe of the Lollard material that follows this unit; see below.

Graphs, Alphabets, and Scripts 59

MS John Rylands Library, Eng. 85 is a *Declaration of the* Pater noster. This text justifies its exposition of the *Pater noster* in English on the grounds that truth is not the property of any one language: "*siþ truþe of god stondiþ \not/ in oo langage more þan in anoþer*" ("since God's truth stands not in one language more than in another", f. 37r). Noting that Christ wished for the prayer to be preached to the people so that they might learn and emulate it, the author asks "*whi may we not þa^{n}ne writen in englisch þe gospel and oþ^{er}e þingis*" ("why may we not then write the gospel and other things in English", f. 37v). This Lollard defence of English may be associated with the clear graphic policy employed by the scribe of the primer unit. The scribe of the *Declaration of the* Pater noster is different from that of the primer unit, but his alphabetical practice is very similar (save that he does not dot *y*). He takes care to integrate the material he adds into the visual layout of the first unit, supplying similarly worded rubrics, and adding running headers in the former unit as in his own parts of the manuscript, and he inserts some corrections in the earlier unit.[108]

The *scribe* of the Wycliffite *Preface* manuscript, MS London, BL, Royal 17. B.i, is also highly alert to graphic policy.[109] His treatment of *z* and yogh in the text conforms with the rules set out in the *Preface*: "*þerfore alle þe wordis of þis table þat biginnen wiþ þat carect ben set in zed, which is þe laste lettre of þe a, b, c*".[110] In the text of the *Concordance*, *z* is used for the first letter of words that begin with the voiced sound /z/ (for example, "*Zebedee*", "*Zeele*" ("zeal"), f. 168v), while yogh is used for words that begin with the sound /j/ (for example, "*ȝeelde*", "*ȝerde*", "*ȝeer*"; "yield", "yard", "year", f. 169r). Again, in the entry for "*Thouȝt*" ("thought"), the headword is spelt with *th* whilst the quotations given spell the word with thorn. The entries for "*Thirst*", "*Thorne*" ("thorn"), "*Thousynde*" ("thousand") and other *th* words follow suit.

---

[108] For the contents, layout, and organisation of the first section see M. CONNOLLY, "Books for the '*helpe of euery persoone þat þenkiþ to be saued*': Six devotional anthologies from fifteenth-century London", *The Yearbook of English Studies* 33 (2003), pp. 170-181 at pp. 172-175. Connolly argues that the first part of MS John Rylands Library, Eng. 85 is one of a group of London manuscripts that share access to a common set of basic catechetical texts.

[109] According to the *LALME* profile for this hand (LP 518), the scribe uses only thorn and yogh, eschewing the alternatives *th*, *y*, and *gh*. *LALME* used only the *Preface* when profiling this scribe, but it is worth observing that this policy is carried over to the text of the Concordance. Cf. McIntosh: the manuscript of the *Preface* is written "in a highly consistent language and with a remarkable degree of orthographic uniformity" (A. MCINTOSH, "Some linguistic reflections of a Wycliffite", in: *Franciplegius: Medieval and Linguistic Studies in honor of Francis Peabody Magoun,* ed. J.B. BESSINGER and R.P. CREED (London, 1965), pp. 290-293, at p. 290).

[110] *Preface to the Wycliffite Biblical Concordance*, p. 272.

60   *Chapter 1*

An exception to this strict implementation of the principles and orthography of the *Preface*, however, is in the entry for "*theef*" ("thief"). Despite normally using thorn, the scribe retains variation between thorn and *th* in the entry for "*Theef*" (f. 147r-v), for example, "*Theef In what our þe þeef were \to\ come. m^{at}t. Foure and twentiþe ^{capitulo}. As to a theef ȝe ha^n gon out m^{at}t. sixte ^{and} twentiþe c^{apitulo}. Þeeues weren crucyfied* [...]" ("Thief: In what hour the thief were to come, Matt 24. You have gone out as to a thief, Matt 26. Thieves were crucified [...]", f. 147r). Perhaps he has been trained to copy letter for letter and is following an exemplar closely and uncritically. But it may be no coincidence that variation in the spelling of "*Theef*" is one of the examples discussed in the *Preface*, "*As, wher su^mme write^n þese wordis 'Thyng' ^{and} 'theef' wiþ t. h. oþ^{er}e vsen to writen þoo same wordis wiþ þis figure .þ.*" (MS London, BL, Royal 17. B.i, f. 4v).[111] Perhaps the scribe retains the orthographic variation in the "*Theef*" entry because it is an example of what was discussed in the *Preface* and therefore he judges it legitimate to vary the orthography here. On balance, it seems that the scribe is alert to and understands the orthographic policy set out in the *Preface*.

The Middle English primers provide us with intriguing and suggestive traces of the development of variant forms of alphabet analysis and implementation and their use in identity formation. Similarities between the graph set and alphabet sequence found in MS John Rylands Library, Eng. 85 and the orthographic policy of *Preface to the Wycliffite Biblical Concordance* may suggest that they were characteristic of Wycliffite authors and their scribes and that they became recognised as iconic of Lollardy and the movement's defence of English, at least among some of their users. But the development of such practices and their ascription with identity significances could have taken place in any kind of community of practice in which English literacy was promoted and transmitted within the framework of *littera* pedagogy. As much is suggested by the distinctive and variant practices in the orthodox primers. The scribes and users of orthodox primers too must have been aware, through encounters with the pedagogy of *littera* and the grammar of the alphabet, that letter choice signalled identity. The alphabet rows and other texts in the primers, with their various subtly different analyses and implementations of the letters of the alphabet, demonstrate how communities of practice adapted the grammar of *littera* to the writing of English and how their practices acquired

---

[111] Given my focus on the scribe's practice here, I have provided my own transcription rather than using Kuhn's edition.

Graphs, Alphabets, and Scripts 61

the potential to become iconic of group identity. The Old English alphabet rows and practices associated with Ælfric, Bryhtferth, and the learner whose hand appears in MS Harley 208 are likewise subtly variant and it seems reasonable to assume that these variant practices also contributed to the formation of boundaries between belonging and difference among early communities of Anglophone literate practice.

The Anglice littere *Tradition*

Texts that illustrate engagement with the relationships among scripts and letters and the implications of variant practices for identity-construction particularly well are the texts in what I shall call the '*Anglice littere*' ('English letters') tradition. My name for this tradition of brief (and sometimes micro-) texts is based on the rubrics associated with these materials. This tradition has not previously been identified as such and the relations between its texts and the grammarians' treatment of alphabets has not previously been noticed. Rooted in the pedagogy of *littera*, the study of the shapes, names, and sounds of letters of the alphabet, these texts invoke grammarians' attempts to account for, defend, and rationalise practice through narratives concerning the relationship of the Latin alphabet with other alphabets. Examples of this tradition in this section will be drawn from Jerome, Bede, and Isidore, grammars in the *computus* tradition, and the later grammar of Hugh of St. Victor. *Anglice littere* texts in MS London, BL, Stowe 57 (twelfth century) and MS London, BL, Cotton Titus D.xviii (late fourteenth century) provide the fullest examples of the analysis of so-called English letters in relation to the grammarians' comparative alphabets. This tradition also frames micro-texts found in MS London, BL, Harley 3763, MS Cambridge, Trinity College, B.14.39-40, MS Maidstone, Museum, A.13, MS Cambridge, Fitzwilliam Museum, McClean 123, and MS London, BL, Cotton Cleopatra C.vi, all dated to the thirteenth century. Taken together, these texts are very revealing about the shifting and contested cultural status of the non-Latin letters sometimes used for writing English and it is by no means a coincidence that they offer most of our few dictionary attestations of the names for ȝ and þ. Although rooted in the pedagogy of *littera*, we shall see, the shapes, names, and sounds of these graphs are highly unstable in this tradition, perhaps reflecting an ongoing process of analysing these letters in relation to the Latin alphabet and working out and transmitting orthographic

62   *Chapter 1*

policy and practice in pedagogic environments, most of them probably informal. The *Anglice littere* texts in Stowe 57 and Cotton Titus D.xviii display learned reflection on many alphabets while the micro-texts appear to have had practical functions but they all provide traces of the processes of applying the comparison of alphabets associated with the theory of *littera* to the reading and writing of English and of the ways in which this experience contributed to identity formation.

A framework for the *Anglice littere* texts is arguably provided by the work of the early Christian grammatical texts. According to Isidore, both Greek and Latin scripts derived from Hebrew ("*[l]itterae Latinae et Graecae ab Hebraeis videntur exortae*").[112] The first text was the law handed to Moses and the scripts of the Syrians, Chaldeans, Phoenicians, and Egyptians were all related to this originary Hebrew script ("*Hebraeorum litteras a Lege coepisse per Moysen: Syrorum autem et Chaldaeorum per Abraham*").[113] Bede, as we have already seen, argued that Christians legitimately used both Latin and Greek letters. Bede followed Isidore in noting that the Greek letters chi and rho (frequently written as a logogram for '*Christus*') were used "*propter nomen Xpisti*" ("on the authority of the name of Christ").[114] The use of Greek omega and alpha was justified by the biblical text "I am the Alpha and the Omega" (Rev. 21.8).[115]

In somewhat later medieval grammars the relationship of the Latin alphabet with other alphabets is expressed visually in tabular form. In a manuscript of the *De Grammatica* by Hugh of St. Victor († 1141) for example, Hebrew letters are arranged with their *figurae* and names and Latin equivalents in the first column. In the next column section, Greek letters are treated in a similar way. Over the page, the Latin alphabet is set out in a column from *a* to *z*, and then the alphabet is rearranged in letter categories (vowels, semi-vowels, mutes and so on) and letters in the Latin alphabet that are derived from Greek are also grouped (MS Paris, Bibliothèque Mazarine, latin 717, f. 55r-v).[116] In grammars that are associated with the teaching of *computus* even more elaborate sets of

---

[112] Isidore of Seville, *Etymologiae*, 1, Book 1, ch. 3, section 4.

[113] Isidore of Seville, *Etymologiae*, 1, Book 1, ch. 3, section 5.

[114] Bede, *De Arte metrica*, pp. 36-37; cf. Isidore of Seville, *Etymologiae*, 1, Book 1, ch. 3, section 14.

[115] Bede, *De Arte metrica*, pp. 36-37; cf. Isidore of Seville, *Etymologiae*, 1, Book 1, ch. 3, section 9.

[116] For an edition see Hugh of St.Victor, *De Grammatica*, in: *Hugonis de Sancto Victore Opera Propaedeutica*, ed. R. BARON (Notre Dame, IN, 1966), pp. 67-163.

Graphs, Alphabets, and Scripts 63

alphabetical tables appear. In this tradition the alphabets treated by ancient grammarians are supplemented with alphabets of which they give no account, some of them fanciful or even invented.[117] MS Oxford, St. John's College, 17, dated 1102-1113 and associated with Thorney Abbey, for example, provides various runic futharks along with exotic and invented alphabets in parallel in a table (f. 5v).[118] This table, which will be discussed in more detail below, provides *figurae*, Latin letter equivalents, and in some cases names of the letters.

MSS *London, BL, Stowe 57 and Cotton Titus D.xviii*

In MS London, BL, Stowe 57, a manuscript collected and probably copied by one Geoffrey de Ufford (according to an inscription on f. 1r in the hand of the scribe) and dated *c.* 1154, *Anglice littere* material occurs in the context of several alphabets.[119] Hebrew letters and their names are laid out in a table, below which occurs a table with the letters of the Greek alphabet and their names (f. 3r). Over the page is a table setting out the Latin alphabet, with twenty-three letters "*Abecedarivm Latinorum*" with their names. Also included in this table, in the lower portion of the third column, after "*Am^{en} Am^{en}*", occurs the *Anglice littere* text (f. 3v), where the *Anglice littere* occur along with their names. Below this table, a table of "*lettere normor^{um} que dicuntur 'rune stafas'*" ("letters of Norsemen which are called 'runes'") appears. This table includes runes with their equivalents in the augmented alphabet in the upper table, some variant forms, and some Ogham letters, some of them with equivalents and names.

The paralleling of English, runic, and other scripts in Stowe 57 in juxtaposed tables clearly builds on the teaching about and comparisons of alphabets

---

[117] Mary Carruthers proposes that these exotic alphabets were used as memory aids (M. CARRUTHERS, *The Book of Memory: A Study of Memory in Medieval Culture* (Cambridge, 1990), pp. 109-111).

[118] For the date and extensive discussion of the manuscript and its tradition see *The Calendar and the Cloister: Oxford, St. John's College, MS 17*, ed. F. WALLIS (n.d.), <https://digital.library.mcgill.ca/ms-17/index.htm>.

[119] For the date see N.R. KER, *Catalogue of Manuscripts Containing Anglo-Saxon*, reissued with supplement (Oxford, 1990), p. 337, No. 272; the entry in O. DA ROLD, T. KATO, M. SWAN, and E. TREHARNE, *The Production and Use of English Manuscripts 1060 to 1220* (Stanford, 2018), <https://em1060.stanford.edu/>; and V.P. MCCARREN and R.N. MORY, "The *Abecedarium* from British Museum Cotton Titus D.18", *Modern Philology* 87 (1990), pp. 266-271, at p. 266.

64 *Chapter 1*

of Isidore, Bede, and other Christian grammarians. Bede's chapter on the letter in *De Arte metrica* compares and contrasts letters in Greek and Latin to help the student of metre. Alpha and *a* have a different name in the Greek and Latin alphabets but have the same shape and sound value. Latin *e* and *o* may be metrically long or short but in Greek eta and omega are always long. Isidore includes some of this material in Book 1, chapter 3 of the *Etymologiae*, where he also discusses alphabets from comparative and historical perspectives. He proposes that Hebrew is the original source of Greek and Latin letters, for the first letter of the alphabet of each is related. The alphabets of the Syrians and Chaldeans agree with that of Hebrew in the sounds and numbers of their letters, though their shapes are different. Each has twenty-two letters, reflecting the origin of Hebrew letters with Moses and of the latter two alphabets with Abraham and the twenty-two books of the Old Testament. Geoffrey de Ufford's immediate source for the parallel alphabets in Stowe 57 is the *De Grammatica* by Hugh of St. Victor which is in turn based on Book 1 of Isidore's *Etymologiae*.[120]

The alphabet tables in Stowe 57 are followed by extracts that are furnished with marginal and linear glosses and that are related to Isidore's *Etymologiae* (from f. 4v). The compiler builds on this material and extends it to alphabets of which the Christian grammarians give no account. One extract that is related to Isidore in Stowe 57 notes the omission of the alphabets of barbarous peoples: "*hiⁿc omissis alphabetis Barbaru^m gentiu^m*" (f. 4v). The following extract announces its subject as alphabets of various peoples, "*Annotatis quarunda^m gentiu^m quib^{us}da^m alphabetis in scripturaru^m notulis* [...]" (f. 5r). The text goes on to list the twenty-one Latin letters, adding *y* and *z*: "*Litt^{er}e enim Latine XX sunt ^{et} una ^{scilicet}* A B C D E F G H I K L M N O P Q R S T U X Y *eni^m ^{et}* Z" (f. 5r). The text continues with the sounds of the letters. Explicitly adding to the early grammarians' accounts of the Latin alphabet letters and alphabets not mentioned by them – runes, Ogham, and the *Anglice littere* – and paralleling these alphabets with Latin, Hebrew, and Greek, the tabulation of the alphabets in Stowe 57 suggests a consideration of relationships and equivalences among them culturally as well as orthographically.

---

[120] Hugh of St. Victor, *De Grammatica*; E. STEINOVÁ, "*Notam superponere studui*: The use of technical signs in the early Middle Ages" (unpublished PhD thesis, Utrecht University, 2016), p. 263.

Graphs, Alphabets, and Scripts   65

The naming of the English letters in the table is an additional way that the compiler suggests that non-Latin letters are acceptable forms rather than barbarous symbols:

Anglice litt^{er}e
p *pen*
ð *ðet*
þ *þorn*
⁊ *and*
(Stowe 57, f. 3v)

Whereas the names for the Latin alphabet letters are given in Latin, here the names of the *Anglice littere* are given in English.[121] Wynn and thorn are given the names that persist to this day. The letter that is today called 'eth' is named "*ðet*" ("that"); Tironian *et* is treated as an English letter named "*and*".[122] The naming of the letters in English suggests that the target audience of the text will identify with the compiler as English-reading. The spelling of the names also subtly indicates the expected literacy practice of the audience: wynn, thorn, and eth are used to spell the names of the letters suggesting that 'we' not only read English but also 'we use these letters'. This is borne out by material elsewhere in the volume. In the English glosses to the *Libellus de nominibus naturalium rerum* (ff. 156r-160r), a list of names of animals, birds, insects and so on, both wynn and *w* are used, for example, "*Cignus*" is glossed "*Span*" ("swan", f. 158r) while "*Catuli*" is glossed "*id est 'whelpes'*" ("that is, 'of a puppy'", f. 156v). Thorn is also used, for example, "*Merula*" is glossed "'*merle*' *i^{d est} 'þrostle*'" ("'*merle*', that is 'thrush'", f. 158v).[123] The alphabetical

---

[121] The names of the Latin letters are provided in two spellings. The name of the letter *b* is "'*be*' *vel* '*bei*'", for *c* is "'*ce*' *vel* '*cei*'", for *d* is "'*de*' *vel* '*dei*'", for *g* is "'*ge*' *vel* '*gei*'", and for *h* is "'*hah*' *vel* '*hake*'". Some of the spellings could be construed as French (see *AND*, *b*, *be*, *bei*; *AND²*, *c*, *cei*; *AND²*, *dey*), but the Latin conjunction '*vel*' suggests that Latin is used. The forms '*ge*', '*gei*', '*hah*', and '*hake*' do not occur as letter-names in *AND*.

[122] In the table of runes the thorn appears with the name "*þurs*" while the Ogham symbol for *æ* is glossed "*dyptong*" (f. 3v).

[123] As this example demonstrates, some items are glossed in both English and French. Some glossed items have only an English gloss, perhaps suggesting that the glossator's competence in English is greater than his competence in French. For example, "'*Hinnulus*', '*hindcalf*' ['young female deer'] *id est*", "'*Vulpes*' *id est* '*fox*'", and "'*Canis*' *id est* '*hund*' ['dog']" (f. 156v) have no French gloss. The disparity in the amount of French and English glossing might also be related to the fact that the glossing is sporadic and presumably the work of creating it was incomplete. For further reflections on vernacular multilingual literacy see the Conclusion.

66 *Chapter 1*

material and the ongoing glossing of the *Libellus de nominibus* both perform the interest in the relations of English with other languages including French of which the compiler and his audience presumably also had a reading and speaking knowledge. Here, English is incorporated into a multilingual reading and writing environment.

Although the contents of Stowe 57 are learned, a pedagogical frame for the volume is established by the opening pages as well as by what we know of its scribe. The alphabetical material is part of a compilation titled the *"Scutum Bede"* (ff. 1v-5r). This is an explicitly pedagogic compilation. After a table of virtues that represents the shield of Bede (f. 1v), it opens with a warning from a teacher to a pupil:

> *Noli mi fili :*
> *Monitum mispendere vili.*
> *Cipus erit lavdis :*
> *Si que pater edocet audis.*

My son, do not hold my advice in low regard. Your legacy will be one of esteem if you listen to what the father teaches.[124]

The text is attributed to Cato and it appears to be a paraphrase of lines from the staple text of grammar teaching, the *Disticha Catonis*. The teacher and the pupil (the 'father' and 'son' who are the imagined author and addressee of the *Disticha*) are depicted in roundels on either side of the verse. The teacher is depicted as a bearded, finely-dressed man who wears an academic's skull cap and wags his finger at the figure in the opposite roundel.[125] The figure opposite him is depicted as a respectful young male scholar, unbearded and bare-headed. His left hand is raised and open-palmed in a gesture of submissive acceptance, while in his right hand he holds aloft what I take to be a pair of wax tablets opened back on their hinge to reveal stylised representations of graphs on the wax. Stowe 57 has been associated with the Benedictine house at Peterborough on grounds of its contents and the abbey's ownership of the village of Ufford and Geoffrey de Ufford was apparently at work as a master-scribe at Peter-

---

[124] F. 2r. A gloss in the manuscript explains that *"cipus"* refers to a monument.

[125] For other examples of a skull cap as headgear that typifies a teacher see the image of Cato in MS Aberystwyth, National Library of Wales, Peniarth 481, f. 1r, where Cato is depicted wearing a skull cap and dictating his *Disticha* to the Middle English translator Benedict Burgh (who also sports a skull cap) who in turn teaches a boy; and MS New York, Pierpont Morgan Library, M.537, f. 62v, an image of a teacher and pupils.

Graphs, Alphabets, and Scripts 67

borough Abbey in 1147.[126] This suggests a monastic, multilingual community of practice within which Geoffrey's *Anglice littere* text performed its identity work.

A later *Anglice littere* text that is very similar in many ways to that in Stowe 57 appears in later fourteenth-century manuscript MS London, BL, Cotton Titus D.xviii, f. 8v. Here an "*Alphabetum Anglicum*" (f. 8v) is included along with Hebrew, Greek, Gothic, runic, and other alphabets (ff. 1v-8v) in an independent booklet of twelve leaves (ff. 1r-12v). Like Stowe 57, this text lays out the alphabets in tabular form. It provides both Latin letter equivalents and letter-names. The tables are glossed and commented on with material drawn from early grammatical texts. As in Stowe 57, the compilation expands traditional teaching on alphabets by incorporating alphabets not found in the early grammars. Unlike the alphabet material in Stowe 57, however, the compilation in Cotton Titus D.xviii teaches that 'we' use the Latin alphabet; 'others' use non-Latin letters.

Discursive commentary on the tables is drawn from several grammatical sources. The first passage, introducing the Hebrew alphabet, selects and rearranges material from Isidore's *Etymologiae*, Book 1, chapter 3. This passage follows Isidore in recording that Greek and Latin letters derive from Hebrew ("[*l*]*ittere eni^m grece ^et latine ab hebreis vident^ur exorte*", f. 1v), and that on account of the debt of Greek alpha and Latin *A* to the Hebrew letter aleph, Hebrew is the mother of all languages and literatures.[127] Further commentary on Hebrew letters is attributed to Jerome. This passage is drawn ultimately from Jerome's preface to his commentary on the Old Testament, where he begins by noting that the Hebrew alphabet has twenty-two letters.[128] Various forms of the Greek alphabet with commentary follow. The compiler turns back to Isidore for discussion of Greek letters derived from the Phoenician alphabet and an account of the source of *y* (f. 4v). Next, the compiler turns to the Latin alphabet (f. 5v), prefacing a table of majuscule and minuscule Latin letters with

---

[126] For the abbey see KER, *Catalogue of Manuscripts containing Anglo-Saxon*, p. 337, No. 272 and for the scribe see STEINOVÁ, "*Notam superponere studui*", p. 89.

[127] "*Apud illos eni^m prius dictu^m est Aleph. Deinde ex simili enuntiatione apud g^recos tractu^m e^st Alpha. Inde apud Latinos .A. Translator eni^m de simili sono alterius li^ngue l^itteram condid^it vt nosc^ere possim^us lingua^m hebraica^m om^n i^um linguar^um ^et l^itterar^um esse matre^m*" (f. 1v).

[128] Jerome, "Praefatio Hieronymi Presbiteri de omnibus libris de Veteris Testamenti", in: *Sancti Eusebii Hieronymi Stridonensis Presbyteri Divina Bibliotheca antehac inedita, studio et labore monachorum ordinis S. Benedicti è Congregatione S. Mauri*, ed. CONGREGATION OF ST. MAUR (Paris, 1693), cols. 318-322, at col. 318.

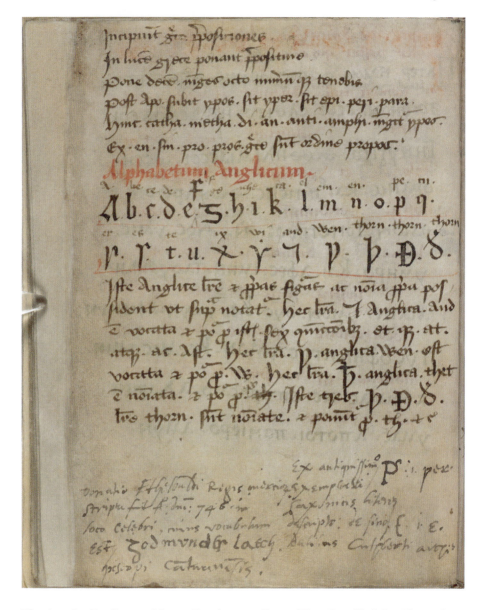

Fig. 4. *Anglice littere* table, MS London, BL, Cotton Titus D.xviii, f. 8v. Photo: © The British Library Board, MS British Library, Cotton Titus D.xviii, f. 8v.

Graphs, Alphabets, and Scripts 69

commentary based on Isidore, Book 1, chapter 4. The Greek origins of *y* and *z* are noted: *y* is followed by Greek upsilon (Y) and *z* by the name "*zeta*" (f. 5v). Following a table of syllables come tables of Gothic letters, Persian letters, and a table of runes (f. 6v).

The alphabet material in Cotton Titus D.xviii is framed in various ways that present the Latin alphabet as 'ours'. The runes on f. 6v are set out in the order of the Latin alphabet with their equivalents in that alphabet, from *a* to '*amen*'. There is no thorn and no wynn. The table would permit one to transliterate from Latin letters to runes but not from runes to Latin letters. After a table of letters of "*aethicus philosophus*" similar to that in Stowe 57 (f. 4r), which, the compiler notes, 'we' do not use in 'our' writing *("[n]o^n vt illos imitem in scripturis n^{ost}ris"*), follows a table of more runic letters allegedly found in Norse *("l^{itte}rar^{um} figure in gente Normannor^{um} feruuntur p^{ri}mitus i^{n}uente"*, f. 7r). The table gives the names of these "*runstafas*", which are again arranged in the order of the Latin alphabet; again there is no thorn or wynn and some inaccuracy (for example, the ᛖ rune is called "*eth*" rather than '*eh*', f. 6v). Ordered in this way, this table is also clearly designed to map runes onto the Latin alphabet rather than to support study of the futhark.

A table headed "*Alphabetum Anglicum*" (f. 8v) is the final one in the booklet, appearing after a text of the *Pater noster* in Greek with Latin glosses (f. 8r) and a list of Greek-derived prepositions (see Figure 4). Similar to the other alphabets, the "*Alphabetum Anglicum*" is framed in a Latin script centred way. It lists twenty-two letters from the Latin alphabet, *a* to *y*, giving the shapes of the letters *g*, *r*, and *s* as written in Insular Minuscule. To this list are added ꝛ, *p*, *þ*, Ð, and *ð*. The letters are all named; Tironian *et* is named "*and*", wynn is "*wen*", and thorn, and minuscule and majuscule eth, are all labelled "thorn". Beneath the glossed alphabet appears a note about *Anglice littere*:

> *Iste Anglice l^{itte}re ^{et} prop^{ri}as fig^{ur}as ac no^{m}i^{n}a p^{ro}p^{ri}a possident vt sup^{ra} notat^{ur}. Hec l^{itte}ra ꝛ Anglica 'and' est vocata ^{et} po^{nitur} p^{ro} ist^{is} sex co^{n}iu^{n}cc^{i}o^{n}ib^{us} 'et'. 'q^{ue}'. 'at'. 'atq^{ue}'. 'ac'. 'Ast'. Hec l^{itte}ra . p . anglica .'wen'. est vocata ^{et} po^{nitur} p^{ro} .w. Hec l^{itte}ra .þ. anglica .'thet'. est no^{m}i^{n}ata. ^{et} po^{nitur} p^{ro} 'q^{uo}d' [.th. crossed through]. Iste tres .þ. Ð. ð. l^{itte}re 'thorn'. su^{n}t no^{m}i^{n}ate. ^{et} ponu^{n}tur p^{ro} .th. $^{et\ cetera}$.*

These English letters have their own forms and names as noted above. This letter ꝛ in English is called 'and' and is put in place of these six [Latin] conjunctions '*et*', '*que*', '*at*', '*atque*', '*ac*', '*ast*'. This letter *p* is called 'wynn' in English and is used

70   *Chapter 1*

for *w*. This letter þ is called 'that' in English and is used for [Latin] '*quod*'. These three letters þ Ð ð are called 'thorn' and they are used for *th*, and so on.

The booklet finishes with some geographical material and some brief transliterated Greek liturgical texts. McCarren and Mory describe the *Alphabetum Anglicum* text in Cotton Titus D.xviii as "a fifteenth-century antiquarian's attempt to construct a long obsolete alphabet".[129] But the text is not just concerned with recovering ancient graphic practice: it also indicates orthographic preferences and subtly recommends them to the reader in the course of providing the shapes, names, and *potestates* of the letters of the 'English' alphabet. For example, "*wen*" is spelled with *w* rather than wynn, and its familiar equivalent is given as *w*. The commentary text does not mention yogh, and in the alphabet row it is not included (the letter in sixth place is shaped like Insular *g* or early yogh but is named "*ge*"). Perhaps this omission implies that yogh is considered to be the same letter as zed. The treatment of thorn is particularly revealing of the practice expected of the compiler's community: the letter-name 'thorn' is spelled with *th* rather than the letter thorn, and this name is applied to minuscule thorn, and majuscule and minuscule eth, while the commentary explains that these three letters are used for *th*. We would not expect wynn and eth to be recognised at this date, perhaps, but it is at first sight odd that a later fourteenth-century English author should identify thorn and explain its sound value. This implies that the author expects the reader to be aware of the digraph *th* and its value in English but not to be aware of thorn. It gives the message that thorn is an exotic letter and somewhat foreign and that it is not a letter that an educated (Latin-reading) target reader in later fourteenth-century England is expected to use, or perhaps even to know. This seems to suggest that thorn is iconic of groups other than the author and his target readers. Perhaps it also suggests that thorn is socially stigmatised in the author's community, whoever they were: unfortunately the booklet bears no contemporary provenance evidence.[130]

[129] McCarren and Mory, "The *Abecedarium*", p. 271.

[130] "Andreas Dauidsonus" occurs in a blank space on f. 1v. Possibly this is the Andreas Davidsonus of the first half of the sixteenth century whose name occurs twice in MS Oxford, Bod. Lib., Digby 62, ff. 93v and 94v, a fifteenth-century copy of Alanus de Insulis, *Anticlaudianus*, and in MS Glasgow UL, p.e.6, a Bible printed in Venice (for the latter two signatures see the entry for MS Digby 62 in W.D. Macray, *Bodleian Library Quarto Catalogues IX: Digby Manuscripts*, repr. with addenda by R.W. Hunt and A.G. Watson (Oxford, 1999) and the Addenda, p. 31. The booklet is now bound with texts from the Katherine Group and later material.

Graphs, Alphabets, and Scripts 71

Dating from the twelfth and fourteenth centuries respectively, these texts in Stowe 57 and Cotton Titus D.xviii are late examples of the elaborate alphabetical tables found in *computus* manuscripts, innovating in that tradition to take account of 'English' letters. For example, unlike in Stowe 57 and Cotton Titus D.xviii, in the various runic futharks provided in MS Oxford, St. John's College, 17, 'English' letters are not identified or given a table, even though they are used to a limited extent in the text where names of the runes are provided in English. The thorn is given various names spelt with thorn: "*þurs*" and "*þors*", and "*þorn*". Eth appears in "*reð*", the name given for the rune ᛀ, and Insular *g* in "*dæʒ*" ("day", the name given for the rune ᛗ), but wynn is transliterated as *uu* and not used in the text. However, the aim of the tables in MS Oxford, St. John's College, 17 seems to be to enable a user to encode and decode Latin in exotic alphabets rather than English, for the transliterations of the alphabets do not include thorn, eth, wynn, or Tironian *et*. One could not, therefore, encode an English-language text spelt with 'English' letters in most of the alphabets provided. The text suggests that while 'we' can read English, 'we' would only use special runic script, like the other exotic scripts, to read and write Latin. With access to this alphabet table, 'we' are able to exchange Latin messages in cryptic forms and this shared, specialised graphic skill helps to identify 'us'. But a set of runic alphabets in MS London, BL, Cotton Vitellius A.xii (late eleventh to late twelfth century) provides a suggestive model for the *Anglice littere* additions in Stowe 57 and Cotton Titus D.xviii. Following two of the rows of runes in the order of the Latin alphabet, additional sets of letters are grouped, "*super sunt iste*" and "*sup^er s^unt littere iste .iiii.*", below which are written *h*/Insular *g* ᛉ *þ* ᚠ (f. 65r). These additional sets of four letters are not given names or Latin equivalents with the exception of the second instance of ᚠ which has a superscript *æ*. But the principle for their grouping at the end of the rune rows as sets of four seems clear. The rune-rows are organised in the order of the Latin alphabet, arranged from *a* to *z*. The additional sets of four letters correspond to the letters grouped after the alphabet row in modified alphabetical sequences such as that in Byrhtferth's *Enchiridion*: *ʒ*/Insular *g* ᛉ *þ* ᚠ are presumably treated as sounds with no *figurae* in the Latin alphabet, i.e. *ʒ*/Insular *g* [/ŋ/] *þ æ* (f. 65r).[131]

---

[131] The first instance of *ʒ*/Insular *g* is written as *Z*. The leaf is a fragment; the verso bears the beginning of a calendar.

72   *Chapter 1*

MS *London, BL, Harley 3763*

Five further texts belong with the tradition of attempting to align alphabets
and to position 'English' letters in relation to them within the framework of
littera. None of these texts has previously been recognised to be part of this
grammatical tradition, perhaps because these texts are much briefer, less
learned, and more practical than those in Stowe 57 and Cotton Titus D.xviii.
All date from the thirteenth century and several are associated with other basic
pedagogic material. All repay analysis in terms of informal application of the
theory of *littera* and teaching on alphabets in communities of practice where
Anglophone literacy was cultivated.

One of these micro-texts about the *Anglice littere* is found in MS London,
BL, Harley 3763, f. 81v, the Cartulary and Register of Evesham Abbey. It occurs below a Latin entry about tithes in 'Salforth' and is written in a different,
somewhat later hand than that of the entry, arguably of the later thirteenth
century.[132] The text, headed "*Hec suⁿt lⁱᵗᵗᵉre anglⁱᶜᵉ*" ("these are English letters")
in the left margin, extends across the page in two lines. The bottom of the two
lines displays letters separated by some paraph marks and points:

  Ð . þ . ð . ¶ ᵽ . ¶ ӡ . ¶ ⁊ . ¶ ꝥ . ¶ ꞃ . ¶ ſ . ¶ ꝼ . ¶ æ .

Above the row of letters, in the upper line, occur glosses, one for each division of the
row, "*thorn wen eie ant thet ant thet* r s f *diptong*ᵒⁿ/ᵉ". The side heading labels the non-
Latin characters as "English" letters, while the glosses give names for them in English:
majuscule and minuscule eth and thorn are all grouped under the name "*thorn*", wynn
is named "*wen*", Tironian *et* is named "*ant*", thorn with a line crossing its ascender is
named "*that*", *ӡ* is named "*eie*", while *æ* is named "*diptong*ᵒⁿ" or "*diptong*". This text
also includes distinctive Insular letter-forms in the list of English letters, offering alternative Insular and more modern forms for the letters *r*, *s*, and *f*.

In applying basic *littera* pedagogy to 'English' letters, the *Anglice littere*
text in Harley 3763 ascribes identity to graphic practices. It establishes that the

---

[132] The manuscript is dated by the British Library Catalogue last quarter of the twelfth and first half
of the thirteenth centuries. Laing dates all of the English in the manuscript last quarter of the twelfth
century (M. LAING, *Catalogue of Sources for a Linguistic Atlas of Early Medieval English* (Cambridge,
1993), p. 97). My own view is that the forked ascender on *h*, the two-compartment *a* that protrudes
above *x*-height, and the forms of *r*, *s*, and *f* in the hand of the *Anglice littere* text point to a date in the late
thirteenth century, if not somewhat later. The manuscript attracted additions up to the fourteenth century,
with an index and some further material being added in the seventeenth century.

Graphs, Alphabets, and Scripts 73

letters thorn, eth, wynn, and *ȝ*, the abbreviations for 'and' and 'that', and the Insular shapes of *r*, *s*, and *f* are 'English'. The glosses – the names and letters in the upper row – could be seen as offering alternatives or equivalents *preferred* in the language of the text's author and his community. The *w* spellings in "*wen*" and *th* in "*thorn*" indicate preferences for those graphs over wynn and thorn. The *g* spelling in "*diptong^on / diptong^e*" demonstrates that 'we' use modern *g* in place of Insular *g* where it has the value of the velar plosive. If we assume that *ȝ*, named "*eie*", refers to a letter for /j/ (compare the formation of the letter-names "*em*", "*en*" and "*iye*" in MS Cambridge, Trinity College, B.14.39, f. 85r, discussed below), then, the note may imply, 'we' use thorn, *w*, *i* and *g*, 'and', 'that', and the modern shapes of *r*, *s*, *f*, while ash is now regarded as the diphthong discussed in Latin grammars. The text expresses identification with a modern orthography and script that is differentiated from but still provides access to the 'English' letters and letter-forms. This text is a brief note unaccompanied by the kind of additional grammatical material found in Stowe 57 and Cotton Titus D.xviii. Nonetheless, it appears to belong to a similar tradition concerned with working out an acceptable graphic practice within the frame of *littera* pedagogy. This *Anglice littere* micro-text could have been produced by someone interested in the letters of the Old English charter bounds found earlier in the volume, perhaps as an aid for study of the practice of its scribe, for the featured graphs in this text all occur in the bounds copied earlier in the volume in an archaising hand of the twelfth century (for example, f. 65v), while eth occurs in the heading for the entry above, the place-name "*Salforð*".[133] It provides a trace of the process of changing graphic practice and the ascription of meaning to it in a community of Anglophone scribal practice. Like Stowe 57, Harley 3763 testifies to applications of *littera* pedagogy in a male religious house, but in this case *littera* pedagogy is applied in the context of the cultivation of a tradition of continuing to read and write early English texts.

MS Cambridge, Trinity College, B.14.39-40

Similar texts concerned with non-Latin letters do not label them *Anglice littere* explicitly, but they share with the texts discussed above the functions of

---

[133] For the bounds at f. 65v see SAWYER, KELLY, and RUSHFORTH, *The Electronic Sawyer*, S1565.

74   *Chapter 1*

reviewing and offering graphic alternatives and implying a preference by applying the frame of *littera* pedagogy. In the bottom margin of a page of a copy of the *Proverbs of Alfred*, in the thirteenth-century portion of MS Cambridge, Trinity College, B.14.39-40, f. 85r, a two-line micro-text exhibits, on the bottom line, three letters from the modified alphabet, Insular *g*, wynn, thorn, and Tironian *et*. The top line glosses the lower row of letters with three names and one transliteration:

> *iye . w ant iyorn .*
> . ʒ . p . 7 . þ .

The first graph of the row of letters has the shape of the Insular *g*, but it is named "*iye*" (compare "*eie*" in Harley 3763) and is used in the text in values that yogh was later to be used; Caroline *g* is used for a different sound value in the text ("*god* [...] *ʒiuen*", "God [...] give").[134] The fourth graph, *þ*, is named, perhaps significantly, "*iyorn*". Wynn is not named but is provided with a letter gloss, *w*. Tironian *et* is named "*ant*" ("and"). Scahill sees this *Anglice littere* text as practical, suggesting that its purpose is to help the scribe to "distinguish the shapes of the letters" wynn from thorn, and thorn from yogh.[135] But there are two factors that do not quite square with this interpretation. First, the two lines of the micro-text are in two different shades of ink, and look to be the work of two different hands. The scribe that wrote the main text of the *Proverbs* seems to have provided the upper line, or glosses, judging from the letter-shapes, and someone else, who forms wynn and thorn quite differently from the main scribe, wrote the row of English letters below.[136] Second, the *main text* uses *all* of the graphs in the *Anglice littere* text, both those named in the glosses and the letters in the row beneath. Had someone listed the graphs that would be encountered in the *exemplar* that the scribe was given to copy, and

---

[134] For names of yogh, see A. PAUES, "The name of the letter *ʒ*", *The Modern Language Review* 6.4 (1911), pp. 441-454.

[135] J. SCAHILL, "Prodigal early Middle English orthographies: Minds and manuscripts", in: *Language Change and Variation from Old English to Late Modern English: A Festschrift for Minoji Akimoto*, ed. M. KYTOE, J. SCAHILL, and H. TANABE (Berne, 2011), pp. 239-252, at p. 245.

[136] The scribe that wrote the row of English letters beneath could be Hand D who corrects the work of Hand C (I follow the naming of hands in *LAEME*; however, *LAEME* attributes *all* of the micro-text *and* the *Proverbs* to Hand D): see the form of thorn in "*heþe*", f. 30r, line 15, with its straight and upright first stroke that ascends high above the bowl of the letter and compare the thorn in the row of letters in the lower line of the micro-text on f. 85r. Perhaps this correcting scribe – whose hand does not appear extensively in the manuscript – was operating in some kind of supervisory capacity.

Graphs, Alphabets, and Scripts 75

has the scribe been instructed to look out for these letters while copying and to work out their equivalents and values in the written English of his community? Or has he perhaps been instructed to transliterate the older letters when he finds them into letters that 'we' use (and often failed to spot them)? For, his glosses suggest, 'we' use "*iye*" for Insular *g*, *w* for *p*, and "*ant*" for Tironian *et*, while his spelling of 'thorn' as "*iyorn*", with a dotted *y*, suggests that 'we' do not prefer thorn, or even that 'we' do not distinguish thorn from *y*. In these ways, this *Anglice littere* micro-text may reflect the application of the pedagogy of *littera* in some kind of community of practice.[137]

There is no firm early provenance evidence for MS Cambridge, Trinity College, B.14.39-40. The *Proverbs* is on the last three leaves of the thirteenth-century part of the manuscript and it is possible that these leaves did not originally belong with the rest of the material in this part of the volume. They have a larger writing space than the other leaves and have been cropped to fit the volume.[138] It is not possible to say whether the corrections to the *Proverbs* text are in one of the hands found earlier in the volume, although the hand that fills space at the end of the text with some Latin could be one of those hands. Yet, the contents of the whole volume are clearly pedagogic and there are many

---

[137] My proposal that this *Anglice littere* text points to a pedagogic process differs from those of previous commentators. Earlier commentators viewed the scribe (designated Hand D in *LAEME*) as an incompetent or confused 'Anglo-Norman', e.g., The Proverbs of Alfred *Re-edited from the Manuscripts*, ed. W.W. SKEAT (Oxford, 1907), p. XIV (on the *Anglice littere* text); W.W. GREG, "The troubles of a Norman scribe", *The Modern Language Review* 5.3 (1910), pp. 282-285; and PAUES, "The name of the letter ȝ". Following C. CLARK, "The myth of the Anglo-Norman scribe", in: *History of Englishes: New Methods and Interpretations in Historical Linguistics*, ed. M. RISSANEN, O. IHALAINEN, T. NEVALAINEN, and I. TAAVITSAINEN (Berlin, 1992: *Topics in English Linguistics* 10), pp. 117-129), Laing proposes by contrast that this scribe and another in the manuscript (Hand A) are pioneering linguists who "were English speaking, competent in the writing of French and Latin, and were using the available mixture of spelling conventions to reinvent ways of writing their mother tongue" (M. LAING, "Confusion *wrs* confounded: Litteral substitution sets in early Middle English writing systems", *Neuphilologische Mitteilungen* 100 (1999), pp. 251-269, at p. 261). Laing does not mention the *Anglice littere* text in her discussion of the manuscript. Cf. Laing's and Lass's suggestion that the scribe is working within a "litteral substitution set" (M. LAING and R. LASS, "Tales of the 1001 nists: The phonological implications of litteral substitution sets in thirteenth-century South-West-Midland texts", *English Language and Linguistics* 7.2 (2003), pp. 257-278, at pp. 259-260. Cf. also STENROOS, "A Middle English mess of fricative spellings".

[138] Cf. a pencil note in the Trinity College copy of the James catalogue that suggests that "ff. 85-87 might have been part of a dismantled quire" (M.R. JAMES, *A Descriptive Catalogue of the Western Manuscripts in the Library of Trinity College Cambridge*, 4 vols. (Cambridge, 1900-1904), 1, p. 439, entry for James 323-324).

76   *Chapter 1*

signs of learners at work in both the thirteenth- and indeed in the fifteenth-century parts of the volume.[139] It is particularly significant that the graph-naming micro-text occurs with the *Proverbs of Alfred*. Proverbs were a basic staple of elementary writing exercises, involving writing in Latin and in English and parallel Latin and English proverbs occur in several school-books.[140] Two different hands have written the English equivalent for some Latin admonitory verses that have been entered in a blank space at the end of *De Ordine creaturum*:

> *Oti de te munio v^{er}bo scripto t^{ibi} monstro*
> *transsit^{is} ab hoc s^{e}c^{u}lo larg^{us} paup^{er}ibus esto*
> *Debita solue tua p^{e}cc^{at}i pond^{e}re pe^{n}sa*
> *Tu^{n}c absolueris ^{et} habebis gaudia lucis*
> *Vid word ^{and} wrid ic warne þe sire ode*
> *Dele al þi goid pouere þad habbit neode*
> *Q^{ui}te dettes ^{and} scrive of sinful deode*
> *Þu salt ben idemet i^n þisse þridde nicste*
> *Þi goid þi^n evel idemit sul ben riste*
> *Do nu so wel þat þu þe^{n}ne come to liste*

With word and writing I warn you Sir Ode, give your goods to those who have need, pay your debts and be absolved for your sins, you shall be judged three nights hence, your good and evil deeds shall be judged rightly, do well now so that you shall come to the light.

(Cambridge, Trinity College, B.14.39, f. 19r)[141]

[139] For pedagogy and the hands of learners in the later part of the manuscript see Chapter Two.

[140] For an edition of the *Proverbs of Alfred* see *The Proverbs of Alfred Re-edited* and for school-books with proverbs see the following. "A collection of proverbs in Rawlinson MS D. 328", ed. S.B. MEECH, in: *Modern Philology* 38 (1940-1941), pp. 113-132 includes proverbs from MS Oxford, Bod. Lib. Rawl. D. 328, ff. 140-144 with a list of other manuscripts that contain proverb collections. N. ORME, "An English grammar school, *c.* 1450: Latin exercises from Exeter (Caius College MS 417/447, folios 16v-24v)", *Traditio* 50 (1995), pp. 261-294 discusses MS Cambridge, Gonville and Caius College, 417/447, ff. 16v-24v. J. BELLIS and V. BRIDGES, "'What shalt thou do when thou hast an English to make into Latin?': The proverb collection of Cambridge, St. John's College F.26", *Studies in Philology* 112 (2015), pp. 68-92, discusses MS Cambridge, St. John's College, 163 (F.26). C. CANNON, *From Literacy to Literature: England, 1300-1400* (Oxford, 2016), p. 73, gives examples of school exercises that use proverbs from MSS London, BL, Harley 5751 and Addit. 37075. For further examples and discussion of the role of proverbs and other moral precepts in literacy education see Chapters Two, Three, and Four.

[141] My transcription differs in a few substantive particulars from those of Brown (*English*

Graphs, Alphabets, and Scripts   77

Clearly the Latin quatrain is paraphrased in the English verses that follow. That this is something of a pedagogic exercise is suggested not only by the cramming in of the text in a blank space and the badly formed letters but also by the occurrence of another attempt at writing an English version a little later in the volume, in another, even less practised hand:

> *Bisete* [bestow] *þi"ne ponevis* [your pennies] *sire eode*
> *Þeng* [think] *on poremo"nins* [*sic*, poor men's] *neode* [need]
> *Betere þe were of god mede* [better for you to have good reward]
> *Þe"ne i" helle and veinde breden* [than be in hell and fiends' bread (?)]

(MS Cambridge, Trinity College, B.14.39-40, f. 25rb)[142]

There are many other examples in the manuscript of the pedagogic staple of moral and admonitory verses in English, French, and Latin (e.g., ff. 28v-29r, 46r, 47v, 57r, 83v). The engagement of various unpractised hands in the work of writing this material suggests a multilingual pedagogic environment, perhaps quite informal.[143]

MS *Maidstone, Museum, A.13*

A similar set of graphs and letter-names, also associated with the *Proverbs of Alfred*, occurs in MS Maidstone, Museum, A.13, f. 93r, dated first half of the thirteenth century in *LAEME*.[144] Here, a two-line *Anglice littere* micro-text occurs in the top margin of the first page of the *Proverbs*. The graphs *þ, 7,* Insu-

---

Lyrics of the XIIIth Century, ed. C.F. BROWN (Oxford, 1932), p. 20, No. 14) and *LAEME*. In line 1, where they read "*Otide*", I read "*Oti de*", seeing a point between the two words, and viewing the first word as an attempt at the name 'Oto' (cf. "*Eode*" in the English version and Brown's identification of Sir Eode as the legendary avaricious cleric Odo or Udo and, perhaps related, Eudo, a profligate noble in Walter Map's *De Nugis curialium* (pp. 175-177). In line 7, Brown reads "*scripe*" and *LAEME* reads "*scrif*", but the *v* in "*evel*" below is similar to that in "*scrive*". *LAEME* attributes this text to Hand A.

[142] For "*ponevis*" cf. the spelling "*ponewes*" attested *c*. 1300 in MS Oxford, Bod. Lib., Digby 86; see *MED*, peni, n.. *LAEME* attributes this text to Hand B.

[143] Laing finds that at least four hands are responsible for writing the English texts (*LAEME*).

[144] I am grateful to Pernille Richards of Maidstone Museum for providing me with photographs of this manuscript. For an edition of the *Proverbs* in MS Maidstone, Museum, A. 13 see C.F. BROWN, "The Maidstone text of the *Proverbs of Alfred*", *Modern Language Review* 21.3 (1926), pp. 249-260.

78   *Chapter 1*

lar *g*/ʒ, *p* , *þ*, and a possible sixth character, now very indistinct, are recorded on the lower line, and on the upper line these letters are labelled respectively "*þorn*" ("thorn"), "*andt*" ("and"), "*ye*" (see below), "*wen*" ("wynn"),   and "*þath*" ("that").[145] Faint lines join three of the letter-names to the *figurae*. Two attempts have been made at writing the graphs Insular *g*/ʒ and Tironian *et*. As in MS Cambridge, Trinity College, B.14.39, all of the graphs of the *Anglice littere* text occur in the main text. Notably, the scribe uses *w* liberally alongside wynn (which is sometimes dotted – thus looking like *y*). Insular *g*/ʒ is used for /j/ ("*seʒe*"; cf. "*seie*", "say") and Caroline *g* is distinguished in value from it ("*þinge*", "thing"). Scahill sees this micro-text as being "for the scribe's bene-fit, to deal with unfamiliar characters in his exemplar", but we may go further: there is much evidence that the context is pedagogic.[146] The text of the *Prov-erbs* has been described by Brown as "selections";[147] selection, revision, and rearrangement are associated with pedagogic uses of such texts.[148] Other evi-dence for a pedagogic environment for the Maidstone manuscript where prov-erbs are being used as material for elementary reading and writing exercises is the cautionary couplet from the twelfth-century *Poema morale* at the foot of the page written in a different hand, one of similar date to the main text; the same couplet also occurs on ff. 46v and 253r: the meat of swine and venison is very delicious, warns the couplet, but it's not worth hanging for. Further prov-erbs in English occur on ff. 54r-55v.[149] In addition to the associations of pro-verbial material with grammar pedagogy, further evidence that the scribe of the micro-text and the *Proverbs of Alfred* is a learner is given by the great many blots, errors, crossings out and corrections in the main text. Along with learn-ing to copy, the scribe is acquiring – or being taught – preferences and under-standing of what these preferences mark. Although he has both wynn and *w* in his repertoire, he favours *w* over wynn in the text and uses *w* to spell the name "*wen*".[150] He has been given the name "*ye*" for Insular *g*/ʒ, but he executes the letter *y* poorly, scarcely distinguishing it from thorn. His preference is to use Insular *g*/ʒ for /j/. Here again, perhaps, we have a glimpse of how graphic pref-

---

[145] Brown recorded "*yod*" also but I do not see this word and Laing did not see the letter yogh or this name (BROWN, "The Maidstone text of the *Proverbs of Alfred*", p. 249; *LAEME*).

[146] SCAHILL, "Prodigal early Middle English orthographies", p. 246.

[147] BROWN, "The Maidstone text of the *Proverbs of Alfred*", p. 250.

[148] For this argument and further examples see Chapters Three and Four.

[149] See *LAEME*.

[150] Brown notes that the scribe sometimes writes *w* for ʒ (BROWN, "The Maidstone text of the *Proverbs of Alfred*", p. 250).

Graphs, Alphabets, and Scripts 79

erences were transmitted, learned, and acquired meaning. The verso of the *Proverbs* bears a poem in English with music (*DIMEV* 3370), a note in Latin about allegory, and a French poem in praise of the Virgin Mary. The leaf serves as the first half of a bifolium which encloses a ten-leaf quire that bears Latin miracle tales. The history of the quire, and its relation with the rest of the codex remain to be fully elucidated.[151] Nonetheless it is clear that when the *Anglice littere* micro-text names the 'English' letters it brings them into relation with different alphabets and orthographies within the context of a multilingual pedagogy.

The *Proverbs of Alfred* scribe is not the only hand responsible for contributing brief English proverbial and moral texts to MS Maidstone, Museum, A.13; *LAEME* finds that perhaps three different hands are responsible for the English, and there is a larger (but still uncertain) number of hands at work if one includes those of the French and Latin material.[152] The presence of these multiple hands suggests a community of practice engaged in reading and writing English, French, and Latin and understanding the relations among these written languages and their own place in relation to them within the framework of grammar pedagogy. A set of accounts entered in blank spaces beneath an alphabetical table (ff. 6v-7r) suggests that the volume was owned by the hospital of St. John the Baptist and St. John the Evangelist, Northampton, in the thirteenth and fourteenth centuries.[153] The hospital, served by a master and brethren, provided for the elderly and infirm, including retainers from the royal household.[154] That hospitals could host communities of literate pedagogy is evidenced by such things as their ownership of books, and their association with resident scribes such as John Cok and John Shirley at St. Bartholomew's

---

[151] Ker provides a codicological analysis and maps it onto the manuscript's contents (N.R. KER, *Medieval Manuscripts in British Libraries, II: Abbotsford to Keele* (Oxford, 1976), pp. 317-321).

[152] Ker's account of the number and distribution of scribal hands requires further elaboration (KER, *Medieval Manuscripts in British Libraries, II*, pp. 317-321).

[153] For the Northampton provenance see KER, *Medieval Manuscripts in British Libraries, II*, p. 320. According to Ker, before entering Maidstone Museum, the volume appears to have been part of the parish library, All Saints Church, Maidstone (p. 317). C.F. Brown, who edited the accounts, proposed that the volume was originally at the Cluniac priory of St. Andrew, Northampton (C.F. BROWN, "A thirteenth-century manuscript at Maidstone", *Modern Language Review* 21.1 (1926), pp. 1-12) but Ker rejects this suggested provenance.

[154] R.M. SERJEANTSON and W.R.D. ADKINS, "Hospitals: St. John Baptist and St. John Evangelist, Northampton", in: *A History of the County of Northampton: Volume 2* (London, 1906: *Victoria History of the Counties of England*), pp. 156-159.

80   *Chapter 1*

Hospital in London in the fifteenth century.[155] The Maidstone manuscript appears to have been owned and partly compiled by one or more persons who were collecting sermons and other material useful for preaching, and some of the sermon content includes brief pieces of English verse. Possibly the *Proverbs of Alfred* was collected and the *Anglice littere* memorandum made with such a use in view. But the compilation of the volume by several hands could in addition be part of the formation and training of new brethren at the hospital. In 1345, Bishop Bokyngham issued an injunction stating that no novice should be admitted there unless he "excelled in reading and was otherwise suitable", suggesting that in the past some of the brethren had not been as accomplished in literacy as they should have been and that communities of literate practice at the hospital may have felt pressurised to adopt an explicitly pedagogic role.[156]

MS Cambridge, Fitzwilliam Museum, McClean 123

A brief *Anglice littere* text similar to that in MS Maidstone, Museum, A.13 in the Nuneaton Codex, MS Cambridge, Fitzwilliam Museum, McClean 123, dated *c.* 1300 in *LAEME*, occurs on a specially ruled page that faces a full text of the *Poema morale* (ff. 115r-120r), the only English text in the volume (most of the other material is in French). The graphs thorn, wynn, yogh, and 7 are displayed, named, and provided with examples of their use:

> . þorn .
> . þ . þanne . þo . þider . þe . þu . haueþ . naueþ . teþ . goþ .
> . wen .
> . ƿ . ƿimman . ƿepman . ƿonie . ƿende . ƿele . ƿope[157] .
> . yoȝ.

---

[155] For hospital libraries see N. RAMSAY and J.M.W. WILLOUGHBY, *Corpus of British Medieval Library Catalogues XIV: Hospitals, Towns and the Professions* (London, 2009). For Shirley see M. CONNOLLY, *John Shirley: Book Production and the Noble Household in Fifteenth-Century England* (Aldershot, 1998). For Cok see J. ETHERTON, "Cok [Coke], John (*c.* 1393-*c.* 1468), Augustinian canon and compiler of the cartulary of St. Bartholomew's Hospital, London", *Oxford Dictionary of National Biography* (Oxford, 2004), <https://www.oxforddnb.com/>. For Cok and Shirley see further in Chapter Three.

[156] For the injunction see SERJEANTSON and ADKINS, "Hospitals", pp. 156-159.

[157] "Woman, man, live, go, well, woo"; for "*ƿope*", Scahill misreads "*powe*" (SCAHILL, "Prodigal early Middle English orthographies", p. 248).

Graphs, Alphabets, and Scripts 81

. 3 . *ʒef* . *ʒus* . *ʒer* . *ʒender* . *draʒ* . *sclaʒ* . *arʒ* . *marʒ* .
And
. 7 . *Williame* . 7 . *Ion* . 7 . *thomas* . 7 . *symun* . 7 . *þu* . 7 . *ich* .

(MS Cambridge, Fitzwilliam Museum, McClean 123, f. 114v)

Following the pedagogy of *littera*, this *Anglice littere* text provides examples of the graph shapes with their multiple sounds (*potestates*) and their names. The examples for thorn illustrate, perhaps, both its voiced *potestas* (the examples where thorn occurs in initial position: "*þanne . þo . þider . þe . þu*" ("than, those, thither, ye, you") and its unvoiced sound (those where it occurs in final position: "*haueþ . naueþ . teþ . goþ*", "has, hasn't, teeth, goes"). At least two values of yogh are exemplified: /j/ in initial position: "*ʒef . ʒus . ʒer . ʒender*" ("if, yes, year, yonder"), and in final position: "*draʒ . sclaʒ . arʒ . marʒ .*" ("draw, slew(?), timid, marrow"), perhaps exemplifying the use of the letter for /χ/. Conventionally, a distinction is made between personal names of English and non-English origin: thorn ("*þu*") appears alongside *th* in "*thomas*" ("Thomas"; the scribe follows the guidance of the grammarians that words spelled with Greek theta should be spelled with *th* in Latin) and *w* rather than wynn is used initially in "*Williame*" ("William"; this common practice of spelling French *g-* with *w* perhaps extrapolates from the guidance of the grammarians with regards to theta). As with the texts discussed above, preferences are subtly communicated by the table. The name of *ʒ* is "*yoʒ*", suggesting that, despite the examples given for yogh as initial /j/, the preference of the scribe is for *y* in this value.

The text of the facing *Poema* broadly – though not completely – follows the orthography modelled by the table: on the page that faces the table (f. 115r) occur "*þane*" (line 3), "*þe*" (line 4), "*teþ*" (line 12 up), "*þel*" (line 3 up), "*ʒef*" (line 15) "*arʒ*" (line 19), 7 (line 1), "*ich*" (line 2). Over the leaf, on f. 115v, occur "*draʒ*" (line 15), "*þider*" (line 12), and "*haueþ*" (line 6). On f. 116r "*pende*" appears (line 16). There are, however, differences between the practice of the table and that of the text; in the *Poema* text, initial wynn in 'when', 'what', and 'while' is followed with an *h* ("*phane*", f. 116r, line 11 up; "*phile*", line 12 up, "*phat*", line 9). 'Such' is spelt with a *u* rather than wynn ("*suike*", f. 116v, line 3), 'we' with *w* rather than wynn (f. 117r, line 6 up), and 'while' is spelt "*huile*" (f. 118v, line 2). Both text and table are inconsistent in different ways; both seem to represent incomplete attempts to establish a pedagogic analysis of

82   *Chapter 1*

how the English letters function in the alphabet and a model for what 'we' –
". *þu* . *7*. *ich* ." ("you and I") in the table – do.

"*Þu 7 ich*" could be inhabited by any reader and teacher, of course, and
within the context of any community of practice. However, the examples con-
joined with "you and I" are male names: *William, John, Thomas, Simon.* Lacking honorific titles or family names or patronymics, and in English spelling, the
names perhaps suggest young male intimates, such as junior members of a
family, household, or classroom, in other words, an informal community of
Anglophone literate practice to which "you and I" belong. In this way, the
names grow out of and reflect back on the pedagogic framework of the discourse of *littera.* Yet, we know from an inscription in the volume (f. 9r) that at
least within a century, perhaps less, of its copying, MS Fitzwilliam Museum,
McClean 123 belonged to Margaret Selman, Prioress of Nuneaton Convent
1367-1386, and "*discip^u las suas*" ("her disciples").[158] Here, "disciples" may
mean young women of the kind entrusted to Margaret's charge in 1373-1374
by the convent's patron John of Gaunt[159] or young women such as the daughter
of the founder, evidently placed in the convent for her education.[160] Female
community ownership evidently continued into the following century, for a
fifteenth-century inscription on the same page records that it then belonged to
Alice Shenton and her convent.[161] This suggests that male-gendered pedagogic
discourse must have been appropriated by a female learning community (and,
perhaps, by their chaplains). So when Scahill, alluding to the nunnery provenance of the volume, suggests that the micro-text "reminds the user [of the
manuscript] of the value of the graphs by means of everyday examples – from
the spoken English with which *she* was no doubt familiar",[162] we must remember that it also reminds the user that this is an 'us and them' discourse and "you
and I" are by implication male. If this text is the trace of an attempt to establish
an acceptable system of graphs, a menu of acceptable letters in, and distinctive

---

[158] B. HILL, "A manuscript from Nuneaton: Cambridge Fitzwilliam Museum MS McClean
123", *Transactions of the Cambridge Bibliographical Society* 12.3 (2002), pp. 191-205, at p. 201;
cf. B. HILL, "Cambridge, Fitzwilliam Museum, MS McClean 123", *Notes and Queries* n.s. 12.3
(1965), pp. 87-90. Hill suggests that the manuscript was initially made for a wealthy laywoman
who was entering the novitiate, before it was gifted to Nuneaton (HILL, "A manuscript from
Nuneaton", p. 201), but advances no firm evidence for this.
[159] HILL, "A manuscript from Nuneaton", p. 202.
[160] W. PAGE, *A History of the County of Warwick: Volume 2* (London, 1908: *Victoria History
of the Counties of England*), pp. 66-70.
[161] HILL, "A manuscript from Nuneaton", p. 201.
[162] SCAHILL, "Prodigal early Middle English orthographies", p. 248, my italics.

Graphs, Alphabets, and Scripts 83

of, the scribe's and readers' community by applying the pedagogy of *littera* to English letters, its provenance here suggests the appropriation of this discourse in diverse and informal communities of Anglophone literate practice. The volume's female readers were invited to identify as members of a grammar class.

MS London, BL, Cotton Cleopatra C.vi

Our final example of an *Anglice littere* micro-text is also found in the ownership of a woman donor and then of a female religious community. MS London, BL, Cotton Cleopatra C.vi includes an *Anglice littere* note in the margin of the text of *Ancrene Wisse*. The note, which occurs in the bottom left of f. 8v, in the quadrant formed where the frames for the left and lower margins intersect, provides an account in Latin of thorn, yogh, and wynn:

> *Hec su^{n}t sig^{na} po^{n}ita i^n hoc libro anglico . þ . ʒ . þ p p et istud ponit^{ur} pro duplici . v . þ ꞉ sicut þorn . hec ʒ pro i .*
>
> These signs are used in this English book: *þ, ʒ, þ, p*. And this *p* is used for double-*u*. *þ* is used as thorn. This letter *ʒ* is used for *i*.[163]

These are the signs used in this English book, the annotator explains, giving the *figurae* of the letters and then their equivalent letters in his alphabet and that of his audience. This letter *p* ("p *et istud*") is used for double-*u*, thorn is used as thorn, and this *ʒ* in place of *i*. The equivalents in the annotator's and users' alphabet are referred to by their names, while the letters being explained are identified only by their *figurae*. This lack of names and *potestates* suggests that the glossed letters are not found in the alphabet that 'we' have learned. The *figurae*, too, are treated as exotic. The appearance of thorn twice in the list of letters ("þ . ʒ . þ p") and the prominent and rather awkward ductus of these letters may perhaps be explained as an attempt to imitate the actual shapes of

---

[163] I see two thorns and two wynns in the initial list of letters; in this way my transcription differs slightly from that of Dobson, who reads "*hec sunt signa posita in hoc / libro anglico.* p . ʒ . p / p p *et istud ponitur pro* ʒ *duplici .*v. þ*; sicut þorn. / hec* ʒ*; pro* i." (*Ancrene Wisse: The English Text of the* Ancrene Riwle*: BM MS Cotton Cleopatra C.vi*, ed. E.J. DOBSON (London, 1972: EETS, o.s. 267, p. 14, n. 35) and from that of Wirtjes, whose transcription is close to Dobson's, "*Hec sunt signa posita in hoc libro anglico.* p . ʒ . p . p . p *et istud ponitur pro duplici .* v. þ*; sicut þorn. Hec* ʒ*; pro* i" (*The Middle English* Physiologus, ed. H. WIRTJES (Oxford, 1991: EETS, o.s. 299), p. XLIV).

84   *Chapter 1*

the thorns in the main text where the first stroke leans to the left and the majuscule form is composed of very thick strokes.

The hand of the main text of the *Ancrene Wisse* in MS London, BL, Cotton Cleopatra C.vi has been dated to the first half of the thirteenth century and the hand of the annotator who wrote the *Anglice littere* note to the second half of the thirteenth century.[164] By *c.* 1289-*c.* 1300, the volume was at the house of Augustinian Canonesses at Canonsleigh, Devon, to whom it had been donated by the nunnery's founder and first Abbess, Maud de Lacy, Duchess of Gloucester († 1289).[165] The annotator *may* have been working at Canonsleigh though there is evidence against it.[166] Informal material in the volume suggests that it was used in a multilingual pedagogic environment, perhaps associated with its novices, the tightening of whose discipline was enjoined by Bishop Stapledon in 1320.[167] For example, the numbers 1-1,000,000 in Arabic and Roman numerals and their names appear on f. 200v. Facing, on f. 201r, a ruled, originally blank page, an elementary Latin text about numbers has been entered in a cramped and wobbly hand and below, in a different, spidery, and uneven hand a fourteen-line poem in Insular French about love of Christ slopes across the page, spilling beyond the writing frame and the ruling, beginning: "*Ky uuoet* [*sic*] *amer saunz pesaunce*" ("whoever wishes to love without pain").[168] Over the page, an extremely uneven and wobbly hand has written a French and Latin text about prayers. A variant of the first two lines of the "*Ky uuoet*" poem occurs on the next leaf, where it is laid out as one line in a space beneath a fair copy of some Latin prayers on f. 202v, in another(?) unpractised hand: "*kar ce* [?] *ky ueot amer saunz dotaunce un amy ky ueil*". To the left of this text, a partial alphabet appears in a different hand. Above the line of French verse, the same hand has written "*Ieo pense et ieo ne di rein Ieo vodreie mes ieo ne pus bein*" ("I think and I say nothing, I would but I cannot well"). At the foot of the

---

[164] See the *LAEME* entries 1 and 3 for the manuscript.

[165] For the donation inscription of *c.* 1300, see f. 3r; for the endowment of the abbey see F.T. ELWORTHY, "Canonsleigh", *Reports and Transactions of the Devonshire Association* 24 (1892), pp. 359-376, at p. 368.

[166] The scribe of the *Anglice littere* note has also been attributed with copying MS Cambridge, Trinity College, B.1.45 (James 43); if Malcolm Parkes's dating of his hand there to 1250-1265 is correct then he cannot himself have been at work in Canonsleigh (for Parkes's dating and this point see the *LAEME* entry for MS Cambridge, Trinity College B.1.45, entry 1).

[167] ELWORTHY, "Canonsleigh", p. 371.

[168] For an edition see A. LÅNGFORS, "*Ky voet amer saunz pesaunce*: Musée Britannique Cotton Cleopatra C.v [*sic,* for C.vi]", *Romania* 55 (1929), pp. 551-552.

Graphs, Alphabets, and Scripts 85

same page yet another hand (very faint, probably later), has attempted an English translation of the "*Ieo pense*" text:

> *I þ* [false starts]
> *III þynke & say noȝt I wolde & I may* [???] *for i am desesyd*
> [????] *a byd* [?]

These little texts, in various unpractised hands, appear to be those of learners. The pedagogy-inspired *Anglice littere* text sits among traces of informal, multilingual writing practice in this manuscript.

Discussion

We have seen that the *Anglice littere* texts belong with an ancient grammatical tradition which taught that letters and alphabets provided resources for marking identity, relations with others, and 'what we do'. This tradition of alphabetical comparison frames the primer and practice alphabets discussed in the previous section, as well as the micro-texts that analyse 'English' letters that we have examined here. Analysing the relations of 'English' letters to the Latin alphabet was an ongoing process that gave rise to different versions of practice and understanding of how that practice signified social and cultural identity. The examples discussed above provide traces of the application of this grammar pedagogy to the reading and writing of English among various different communities of practice, in male and female religious houses as well as in a hospital. *Littera* pedagogy and the study of the alphabet, these examples demonstrate, provided a flexible set of resources for understanding graphic practice and drawing boundaries between belonging and difference across gender, period, degrees and kinds of multilingualism, and levels and practices of literate culture. There are also important implications for our modern analysis of the medieval alphabets used for English. All of these texts, from the basic alphabets in the primers to the most learned *Anglice littere* texts, challenge our modern assumption that the alphabet and the graphs thorn, yogh, wynn, and eth had ontological status: they demonstrate that this was not so.

86   *Chapter 1*

Roman and Runic Scripts

The final section of this chapter offers some remarks about runes and their use in relation to Roman script for reading and writing texts in English. The history and cultural significance of runic literacy and its implications for identity are of course huge and difficult topics. There has been much discussion of how runic script intersects with literacy practices.[169] The geographical and chronological distribution of runic literacy has also attracted much attention. Regional distributions and changes over time may be driven by technological necessity and change as well as different literacies.[170] Runes have frequently

---

[169] Drawing on Brian Stock's concept of a 'textual community', Spurkland proposes that with Scandinavian rune use, "we are dealing with script communities of different kinds [...] [t]hese two scripts [Roman and runic] represented different ideologies of self-definition and manifested dissimilar conceptual relationships between the oral and the written" (T. SPURKLAND, "Literacy and 'runacy' in medieval Scandinavia", in: *Scandinavia and Europe 800-1350: Contact, Conflict, and Coexistence*, ed. J. ADAMS and K. HOLMAN (Turnhout, 2004: *Medieval Texts and Culture of Northern Europe* 4), pp. 333-344, at pp. 343-344). He suggests that we should confine the term 'literacy' to Latin training and use 'runacy' for the formation of competence in runic scripts. Hogg suggests that runes were "used for inscriptions and dedicatory formulae rather than for the purposes of communication" (R.M. HOGG, "Phonology and morphology", in: *The Cambridge History of the English Language: Volume 1: The Beginnings to 1066*, ed. R.M. HOGG (Cambridge, 1992), pp. 67-167, at p. 72). Other suggestions include the view that runes may have had a magical or ritualistic purpose, though Lerer stresses that "Christian literates effectively 'invent' the idea of a runic mysticism" (S. LERER, *Literacy and Power in Anglo-Saxon Literature* (Lincoln, NE, 1991), p. 16) and Page too is sceptical that runes were ever directly associated with magic: "I am prepared to accept that runes were sometimes used to enhance magical activities [...] without wanting to think them essentially magical during the Anglo-Saxon era" (R.I. PAGE, *An Introduction to English Runes*, 2nd edn. (Woodbridge, 1999), pp. 13-14).

[170] Page hypothesises that the distribution of runes may be explained by an uneven spread of runic literacy (PAGE, *An Introduction to English Runes*, p. 218). Discussing the coexistence of runic and Roman script in medieval Scandinavia, Spurkland suggests that "Scandinavia in the Middle Ages was a two-script community, where the two script systems mutually excluded each other, not completely, but to a great extent" (SPURKLAND, "Literacy and 'runacy' in medieval Scandinavia", p. 342). He suggests that the availability of materials may have been the deciding factor, "wooden sticks and a knife were more accessible than parchment, pen, and ink"; accordingly there is a "rather sharp social and functional divide" between the two scripts while angular marks were easier than curves to inscribe on stone, wood, and other hard surfaces (p. 334). Observing a decline in runic inscriptions towards the end of the ninth century, Orton suggests that "competition from the Roman alphabet; technical advances enabling the Roman alphabet to be used more easily than before for inscriptions on hard surfaces", may explain their decline, though he acknowledges that cultural associations may also be at play (P. ORTON, *Writing in a Speaking World: The Pragmatics of Literacy in Anglo-Saxon Inscriptions and Old English Poetry* (Tempe, AZ, 2014), p. 85). However, Conner's dating of the inscription on the Ruthwell Cross to the tenth or eleventh centuries complicates the picture (P.W. CONNER, "The Ruthwell monument runic

Graphs, Alphabets, and Scripts 87

been discussed in relation to religious and cultural identities.[171] Here the aim will be very specific: to reflect on how the framework of *littera* pedagogy may have informed the understanding of the relations between runic and Roman script as vehicles for reading and writing English. We saw in the previous section that MSS London, BL, Stowe 57 and Cotton Titus D.xviii include runes among their alphabet tables when they supplement the alphabetical teaching of the ancient grammarians with additional scripts not mentioned by them. MS Stowe 57 includes "*lettere normor^{um}* [letters of Norsemen] *que dicuntur rune stafas*" (f. 3v) while MS Cotton Titus D.xviii gives the *figurae* ("*l^{itte}rar^{um}* figure*", f. 7r) and the names of "*runstafas*", arranging them in the order of the Latin alphabet. Paralleling the futhark with other alphabets and analysing runes in terms of their *figurae*, *nomina*, and *potestates*, these texts apply grammar pedagogy to the futhark. This section will consider what this framework offers to the analysis of the uses of runes for writing English in two kinds of material: in Old English poetry codices and in pre-Conquest monumental inscriptions.[172]

The Exeter and Vercelli Books

An example which illustrates variation in practice and, arguably, understanding of practice, within poetry texts is provided by the two manuscripts of the four poems where the ninth-century poet Cynewulf / Cynwulf signs his name: *Christ II* and *Juliana* in the Exeter Book (*c.* 970; MS Exeter Cathedral Library, 3501, ff. 8r-32r and 65v-76r) and *Elene* and the *Fates of the Apostles* in the Vercelli Book, also of the second half of the tenth century (MS Vercelli, Biblioteca Capitolare, CXVII, ff. 121r-133v and 52v-54r).[173] In each of these

poem in a tenth-century context", *Review of English Studies* 59 (2008), pp. 25-51; see further in Chapter Four in the present study).

[171] Seiler writes, "[t]he Roman alphabet functions as a bearer of Late Antique and Christian culture whereas runes point to the Germanic heritage" (SEILER, *The Scripting of the Germanic Languages*, p. 25). Cf. Orton, who suggests that a decline in the use of runes may be explained by their having become "tainted by early associations with paganism or minor superstitious practices condemned by the Church" (ORTON, *Writing in a Speaking World*, p. 85). Noting the appearance of runic names in graffiti left by Insular travellers or pilgrims in Italy, R.I. Page speculates that in this context, perhaps runes were regarded as characteristically "English" (PAGE, *An Introduction to English Runes*, p. 224) alongside the other names that are inscribed in Roman.

[172] For examples of runes in codices see PAGE, *An Introduction to English Runes*, pp. 186-199 and ORTON, *Writing in a Speaking World*, pp. 232-235.

[173] See *The Vercelli Book: A Late Tenth-century Manuscript containing Prose and Verse, Vercelli Biblioteca Capitolare CXVII*, ed. C. SISAM (Copenhagen, 1976: *Early English Manu-*

88   *Chapter 1*

cases the poet signs his name (or pseudonym) in runes in the context of poems that are in the modified Latin alphabet in the manuscripts.[174] Analysis of these materials suggests that the scribes of these texts display variation in their practices, providing evidence that different scribes positioned themselves differently with respect to their understanding of relations between runes and Roman script.

In the *Fates of the Apostles* the poet distributes the runic letters of his name at a rate of one or two in each line.[175] As the reader reads each line he or she is required to name the rune to make sense of the text, for example, the rune ᚹ must be identified and named as '*wynn*' ('joy') to make the phrase "ᚹ *sceal gedreosan*" meaningful ("joy must fade away", line 100). Arguably, used in this way, the runes are not a rescripting of English in another script: they are logographic, referring to their names, rather than purely graphic. But the riddles on the seven runes of the name *Cynwulf* are followed by a further challenge to the reader where the runes must be read as graphs, "*nu ðu cunnon miht / hwa on þam wordum wæs werum oncyðig*" ("now you may know who in these words was unknown to humans", lines 105-106). This cues the reader to return to all of the runes to work out the poet's name by reading the letters to spell out an English word. At this point, the reader confronts a further challenge, for the runes are an anagram, '*fwulcyn*'. The reader must play with the letters until the name is revealed. This anagrammatic acrostic engages with biscriptality, with the shape and names of letters, and with their arrangement on the page.[176]

In *Elene*, Cynewulf's name is embedded as a runic acrostic across thirteen lines of the poem in Gradon's edition, and across seven lines of the poem as laid out in the Vercelli Book (f. 133r).[177] The runes spell out the poet's name: this time it is spelt with eight runes and the runes are arranged in order rather than anagrammatically. Here the reader confronts two challenges. First, he or she must name the runes in order to find the subjects of the lines, for example, "ᚹ *is gespiðrad / gomen æfter gearum*" ("joy [i.e., 'wynn', the name of the rune

---

scripts in Facsimile 19).

[174] On the Cynewulf signatures see ORTON, *Writing in a Speaking World*, pp. 121-132.

[175] Andreas *and the* Fates of the Apostles, ed. K.R. BROOKS (Oxford, 1961), p. 59, lines 98-106.

[176] For work towards creating a sociolinguistic typology and terminology for modes of biscriptality see D. BUNČIĆ *et al.*, *Biscriptality* (n.d.), <http://biscriptality.org>.

[177] Cynewulf, *Elene*, ed. P.O.E. GRADON (Exeter, 1977), lines 1257-1269; the final rune is not reproduced in the edition. F. 133r is reproduced as the frontispiece to this edition.

Graphs, Alphabets, and Scripts 89

ᛈ] has diminished, games after the years").[178] Then the reader must assemble the runes and read the word they spell to discover the name of the "*secg*" ("poet") who is describing how the story of the finding of the cross gave him the gift of composing the poem.[179]

In *Christ II*, the name *Cynwulf* is spelled in seven runes, in the order that they occur in the word, over eleven lines of verse that describe the Last Judgement and terror at the end of the world when all joy and prosperity will have passed away.[180] The runes require to be named to fit into the grammar and the alliterative metre of the Roman script text. The rune ᚹ (i.e., the 'joy') is that of the "*eorþan frætwa*" (line 805), the joy in earthly treasures that will have faded. The rune ᚢ, '*ur*' ('our'), modifies "*lifwynna dæl*" (line 806, "our portion of life-joys"), our ᚠ, '*feoh*', "*on foldan*" (line 807, 'worldly wealth') which will have been overwhelmed by ᛚ, '*lagu*' ('water'). When the king of heaven speaks angrily, the ᚳ, '*cen*' ('torch') will quake (perhaps the breath emitted with the angry speech will make the torch in the hall gutter),[181] while ᚣ, '*yr*' (the 'bow', line 800) and ᚾ, '*ned*' ('need', line 800) could find comfort (less easily explained but perhaps referring to those having been wounded or slain in battle or having suffered poverty in life).[182]

In *Juliana*, the name *Cynewulf* is spelled in eight runes that are distributed over five lines of alliterative verse (lines 704-708).[183] Here the names of the runes do not seem to be in play. Rather, the letters appear to represent Cynewulf himself; they will go forth penitentially to the Last Judgement and await their fate before the angry king.[184] The runes are cunningly integrated into the fabric of the verse through alliteration and also through internal rhymes, for example, . ᚳ. ᚣ. ᚷ. ᚾ. (*c, y, and n*), the first three runes of Cynewulf's name in the *a*-verse, are echoed in "*cyning*", Cynewulf's feared judge, in the *b*-verse,

---

[178] Cynewulf, *Elene*, lines 1263-1264.

[179] Cf. M. HALSALL, "Runes and the mortal condition in Old English poetry", *The Journal of English and Germanic Philology* 88.4 (1989), pp. 477-486, at p. 485.

[180] *Anglo-Saxon Poetic Records: A Collective Edition*, ed. G.P. KRAPP and E.V.K. DOBBIE, 6 vols. (New York, 1931-1942), 3, p. 25, lines 797-807. For the interpretation cf. ORTON, *Writing in a Speaking World*, pp. 122-123.

[181] However, Orton proposes that the torch stands for Cynewulf (ORTON, *Writing in a Speaking World*, p. 123).

[182] On these two runes Orton comments, "it is not clear how they are to be understood" (ORTON, *Writing in a Speaking World*, p. 123).

[183] *Juliana*, ed. R. WOOLF, 2nd edn. (London, 1966), pp. 53-55.

[184] Cf. ORTON, *Writing in a Speaking World*, p. 124.

90   *Chapter 1*

and "*lifes to leane*" (the life for which they will receive judgement) is echoed by the trembling of .ᚱ. ᚹ. (*l, f,*) in the *b*-verse. The names of the runes are necessary for the lines to scan, but their *potestates* as graphs that spell words are in play as part of Cynewulf's art here too.[185]

Analysis of the two scribes' responses to the runes shows differences in their practice, suggesting that the associations of runes and their relation with Roman script differed in the two scribes' communities of practice. Each scribe uses a modified Latin alphabet, incorporating the runic letters wynn and thorn, alongside runic script, but they treat the two scripts differently. The Vercelli manuscript has been damaged by reagent on the page in question in the *Fates of the Apostles* (MS Vercelli, Biblioteca Capitolare, CXVII, f. 54r). However, despite the damage to the page it is possible to see that the runes are foregrounded graphically, so that they stand out from the Insular Minuscule of the rest of the text. They are formed with angular strokes, are separated from the text by points either side, and are carefully positioned with equal distance above and below the line. The letter wynn, shared by the Insular Minuscule and the runic script, appears slightly more prominent and angular and looks to have a slightly shorter descender when it is used as a stand-alone rune than when used as part of the modified Latin alphabet (compare "ᚹ *sceal*" with "*hpa*"). In *Elene*, the Vercelli scribe's lineation and corrections mean that the runes are all clustered in the first half of the line of text – where the eye will look to find its place – and again the runes are written as angular shapes between points, and are carefully positioned equally above and below the line (MS Vercelli, Biblioteca Capitolare, CXVII, f. 133r). The runic letter wynn is quite distinct from its counterparts in the Latin alphabet text. That the scribe was paying special attention to the formation and positioning of the runes is evident from his corrections. The wynn rune is written twice in line 1268; the scribe's first effort is positioned at a height more usual for the rest of the text, whilst his second attempt is more prominent and raised. The rune ᚱ was first written at

---

[185] For the point about scansion see ORTON, *Writing in a Speaking World*, p. 124. The poet's use of runes to record his signature may echo the specialised use of runes to commemorate the dead and the names of makers on monuments. Cf. Halsall's argument that the Cynewulf-poet is exploiting an association between runic symbols and grief because runes were used on funeral monuments (HALSALL, "Runes and the mortal condition", p. 484) and Orton's proposal that Cynewulf's signatures "suggest[] a conception of the composed text as a made thing [...] related to the materialization of language that writing involves" (ORTON, *Writing in a Speaking World*, p. 234).

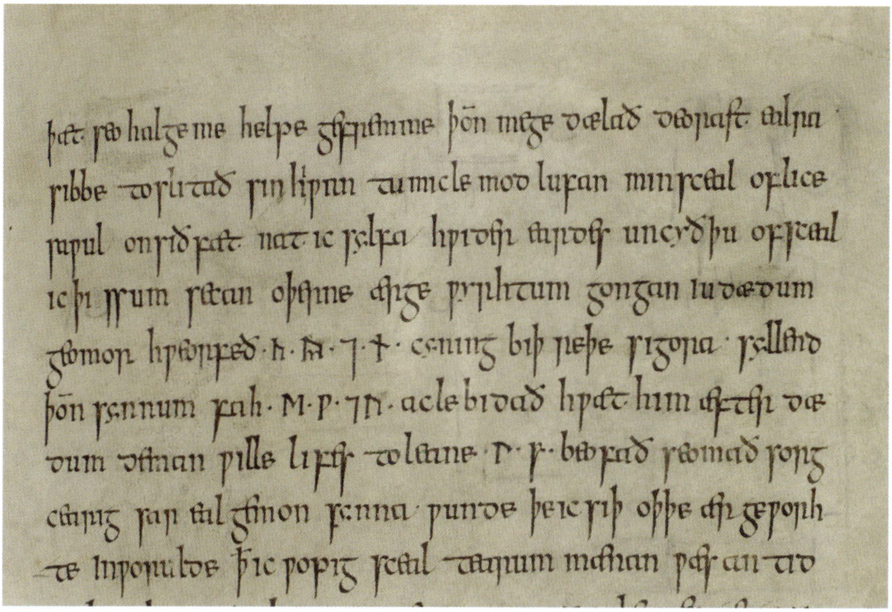

Graphs, Alphabets, and Scripts 91

Fig. 5.   Runes and Roman script in *Juliana*, in the Exeter Book, MS Exeter, Cathedral
Library, 3501, f. 76r (detail). Image reproduced with permission of the
University of Exeter Digital Humanities and the Dean and Chapter, Exeter
Cathedral.

the end of a line, then the correction is written more prominently at the beginning of the next line.

In the Exeter book texts of *Christ II* and *Juliana*, the practice is similar in
some respects to that in the Vercelli book. In Exeter, as in Vercelli, the runes
are distinguished from the other letters by points either side of each character.
In doing this, the scribe follows the practice that he uses to distinguish numerals and other single characters, for example "*XXX*" and "*æ*" ("law") in *Juliana*,
ff. 75v, 65v.[186] In other respects, though, the runes are not particularly distinct
in the Exeter scribe's hand. The vertical dimension falls within the *x*-height of
the Latin alphabet letters. Wynn in the *Juliana* signature is distinguished from
wynn in the rest of the text text only by the way it sits on the line when it is a

---

[186] For the scribe's punctuation see *The Exeter Book of Old English Poetry with Introductory
Chapters by R.W. Chambers, Max Förster, and Robin Flower*, ed. R.W. CHAMBERS, M. FÖRSTER,
and R. FLOWER (London, 1933), p. 62.

92   *Chapter 1*

rune, whereas it has a pronounced descender when it is used as part of the modified Latin alphabet (f. 76v, line 6; see Figure 5); compare "*hpæt*", in the same line and the majuscule wynn in "*HÞær*" (f. 25v).

The scribe's treatment of the runes in the Exeter Book Riddles is similarly indistinct.[187] Perhaps this lack of distinction between the scripts suggests that the scribe recognises that the runes are important but is unsure how to write them; he may be attempting to replicate the visual appearance of his exemplar closely rather than having knowledge of how to write runes. But the Exeter Book scribe's practice could also, or in addition, be accounted for as an attempt to minimise the visual difference between the runic and Roman scripts. By comparison with the Vercelli Book scribe, the scribe of the Exeter Book minimises the visual differences between the runic letter-forms and letter-forms in the modified Latin alphabet, changing the shapes and positioning of the graphs, especially those shared between the two scripts. Page has observed that "[w]hen the runic forms thorn and wynn were adopted into bookhand, their distinctive epigraphical forms were disguised [...] [t]hey were made to conform to the general appearance of written Roman characters".[188] But these examples show that practice varied. The Exeter Book scribe appears to follow this attempt to 'disguise' the runes, especially thorn and wynn, while the Vercelli scribe does not.

The scribes of the Exeter and Vercelli Books do not, of course, substitute one script for another. But script similarity and difference appear to be of consequence for them. Looked at through this lens, the preference of the Exeter Book scribe for minimising the difference between the runic script and the Roman one, and the preference of the Vercelli scribe for visually distancing the two scripts might be a choice that had acquired the power to mark identity. They treat the relation between runes and the modified Latin alphabet differently. The Vercelli scribe's practice emphasises a distinction between the two script traditions, while the Exeter Book scribe displays the overlap between them.[189] Possibly, the Exeter Book scribe and his community preferred not to

---

[187] In the Exeter Book, Riddles 19, 24, 64, and 75 use runes to spell out words. In other cases runes represent words logographically rather than graphically, standing for the entity that is the name of the rune. For further discussion of the Riddles see Chapter Three.

[188] PAGE, *An Introduction to English Runes*, p. 221.

[189] There are examples of the mixing of runic and Latin alphabets within single inscriptions, such as the Manchester gold ring inscription "Ædred owns me, Eanred engraved me" and the Llysfaen gold ring inscription "Alhstan" which is written in Roman letters save for a runic *n* at the end (ORTON, *Writing in a Speaking World*, pp. 65, 74, 86). Discussing the mixing of Roman

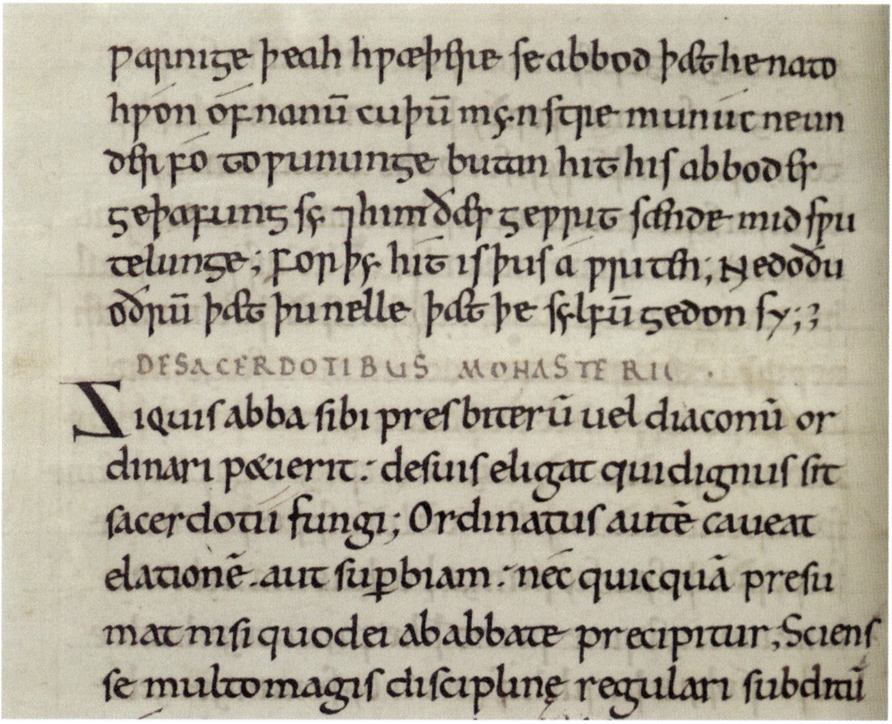

Graphs, Alphabets, and Scripts 93

Fig. 6. Script-language specialisation, MS Oxford, Corpus Christi College, 197, f. 90v. Photo: © Corpus Christi College, Oxford. By permission of the President and Fellows of Corpus Christi College, Oxford, MS 197, f. 90v.

consider runes as completely different from the modified Latin alphabet, whilst the Vercelli scribe and his audience maintained a visual and conceptual difference between the two scripts. Both practices can be understood within the pedagogical traditions of the early grammarians that taught that script choice mattered and could mark identity, and that scripts could be legitimised through comparison and historical discussion.

and runic letters on coins, Seiler notes that some letters, such as *R*, had the same shape in both alphabets, deducing that "runes were not considered completely different from the Roman alphabet" and attributing the mixture of letters to the inability of the writers to distinguish them clearly (SEILER, "The scripting of Old English", pp. 159-160). However, in light of the varying attitudes to the relations of the two scripts that we have discussed there may be more to this phenomenon than lack of ability on the part of the writers.

94 *Chapter 1*

The argument that the Vercelli scribe is concerned with maintaining a visual and conceptual distinction between the two scripts while the Exeter book scribe attempts to minimise the differences between runes and Roman script should not be surprising or seem farfetched if we consider the close attention paid by some scribes to the use of variant *figurae* to reinforce the differences between Latin and Old English. This occurs when, in some manuscripts from about 1000, the Insular script-style is used for Old English and the Caroline style is used for Latin. The letters that varied in shape according to language were *a*, *d*, *e*, *f*, *g*, *h*, *r*, and *s*, and sometimes *c*, *o*, *y*, ascenders, and abbreviation marks.[190] Ker infers that "scribes were trained to observe the conventional distinctions of letter-form with the utmost care", citing as an example the Rule of St. Benedict in MS Oxford, Corpus Christi College, 197, where he notes "not only two sets of letter-forms, but two distinct scripts".[191] F. 90v offers a good example (see Figure 6). Here the shapes of *a*, *d*, *f*, *g*, *r*, and *s* are clearly different, while the presence of eth, wynn, ash, and thorn in the Old English also contribute powerfully to the visual differences between the languages. Arguably, the decision of these scribes to exaggerate the difference between English and Latin through visual means might also be understood in relation to the variant understandings of the relations between the alphabets for Latin and English that we have traced back to the grammarians' teaching.[192]

---

[190] KER, *Catalogue of Manuscripts Containing Anglo-Saxon*, p. XXVI. Having "looked much like Latin, except for the tendency to import letter-forms designed to express specifically Germanic sounds", by 1000, Crick writes, "English vernacular writings were visually distinct from their Latin counterparts, written in a script effectively reserved for the vernacular" (CRICK, "English vernacular script", p. 176). Caroline Minuscule, "signalled the presence of Latin" (p. 178); script specialisation "created a visually distinct vernacular realm or rather cordoned off a separate Latin enclave" (p. 180). Dumville refers to this phenomenon of using distinct script-styles as "alphabetic apartheid" (D.N. DUMVILLE, *English Caroline Script and Monastic History: Studies in Benedictinism, AD 950-1030* (Woodbridge, 1993), p. 19), speculating that perhaps the use of two script-styles may reflect "a spirit of compromise" by the introducers of Caroline script, or it might mean that they viewed the old script-style as "an uncouth alphabet" only fit for "Englishmen's earthly vernacular grunts" (p. 19).

[191] KER, *Catalogue of Manuscripts Containing Anglo-Saxon*, p. XXVI.

[192] As Ker notes, the visual distinctions between the vernacular and Latin continued to be observed into the twelfth century. The archaistic script of the charter bounds in MS London, BL, Harley, 3763, discussed above, could also be considered to be part of this tradition. Another late example is the Eadwine Psalter (MS Cambridge, Trinity College, R.17.1), a trilingual Psalter where, Elaine Treharne notes, the English gloss is differentiated by its script "[v]isually [...] the script of the English gloss differentiates it from all surrounding texts and hands" (E. TREHARNE, *Living Through Conquest: The Politics of Early English, 1020-1220* (Oxford, 2012), p. 179). She observes that the Insular Minuscule script "reinforc[es] the impact of English from a visual, as well as linguistic, perspective with its multitude of ascenders and descenders" (p. 180).

Graphs, Alphabets, and Scripts 95

Fig. 7. Female name *Osgyth* in both runes and Roman script on Lindisfarne 24 grave marker. © Corpus of Anglo-Saxon Stone Sculpture, photographer T. Middlemass.

96   *Chapter 1*

Monument Inscriptions

Pre-Conquest stone sculpture offers many examples of the relational use of Roman and runic scripts.[193] The variations in practice in the corpus of inscriptions across place and time suggest that script choice and variation could be associated with local identity: what 'we' do helps us to understand who 'we' are. The apparent uniformity of practice in some communities and the apparent diversity of practice in others might suggest differences in the meaning of script choice that relate to identity.[194] The focus of interest here is those biscriptal monuments that bear English-language inscriptions in both runes and Roman script, for arguably they give us glimpses of the application of the pedagogy of *littera* to understanding the practices of making and reading inscriptions in English.

Several gravestones from the community at Lindisfarne provide evidence for a practice where *both* runes *and* Roman script are used to encode the same

---

[193] Okasha's corpus of monuments from England in the period from the seventh to eleventh centuries numbers 120 items in Roman script, or Roman script that includes some runes, and twenty-four solely in runic script. Of the eighty-four Roman-script items that are legible enough for their language to be identified, nineteen (twenty-three per cent) have inscriptions in Old English (or Latin and Old English). All of the twenty-four runic inscriptions are in Old English (E. OKASHA, "Vernacular or Latin? The languages of Insular inscriptions, AD 500-1100", in: *Epigrafik 1988: Fachtagung für mittelalterliche und neuzeitliche Epigrafik, Graz, Mai 1988*, ed. W. KOCH (Vienna, 1990), pp. 139-150, at p. 146). Choice of script partly correlates with language: Okasha notes that "stones with Latin texts in non-Roman script are very rare" (p. 145), while Orton proposes that there was a "general restriction of runes to the vernacular" (ORTON, *Writing in a Speaking World*, p. 232). Two exceptions are the Ruthwell Cross, which appears to have borne Latin inscriptions in both runic and Roman scripts, and the Bewcastle Cross, which likewise appears to bear Latin and English inscriptions in runes, although the readings are uncertain (see OKASHA, "Vernacular or Latin?", p. 145; PAGE, *An Introduction to English Runes*, pp. 144-45, and ID., "The Bewcastle Cross", *Nottingham Medieval Studies* 4 (1960), pp. 36-57).

[194] The *Corpus of Anglo-Saxon Stone Sculpture* is online at <http://www.ascorpus.ac. uk/index.php>. Monuments are referred to in the present chapter using the system in this resource. Items associated with York seem to show a preference for Roman script. York Minster 20, a fragment of a grave-marker of late seventh to early ninth century, bears an Old English personal name in Roman capitals. York Minster 22, a fragment of a grave-marker of late seventh to early ninth century, bears a fragment in Latin with a personal name (perhaps *Wulfhere*) in Roman capitals. York St. Mary Castlegate 07, a foundation stone of the tenth or eleventh centuries, is inscribed in Latin and Old English in Roman capitals. Hartlepool grave-markers appear to have been more diverse than those in York. Hartlepool 02, of the mid seventh- to mid eighth-century, bears the feminine personal name "*hilddi*[g]*yþ*" in runes. Hartlepool 03 is similar to Hartlepool 02, though the runic name is illegible. Hartlepool 04 and 05 bear Latin "*ora pro*" and two personal names in majuscules.

Graphs, Alphabets, and Scripts 97

name on the same stone.[195] Lindisfarne 24, a grave marker dated mid seventh-to mid-eighth century, bears the female name *Osgyth* in both runes and in majuscules in the quadrants of a cross that lies within a decorative border. In the upper two quadrants the name is written in runes, "ᚠᚻ" appearing in the left-hand quadrant and "ᚷᚣᚦ" on the right. In the quadrants below, the text reads "+ O S" on the left and "G Y Ð" on the right (see Figure 7).

It is possible that the inscribing of the runes was a separate process from the inscribing of the frame and the Roman script. The Roman letters in the lower quadrants are large, deeply incised, and generously shaped. They are well positioned relative to the framing of the cross, and the disposition of three characters on each side creates visual balance. The small cross that precedes the name is echoed at the end of the inscription by a cross that comprises the upper portion of the letter eth. By contrast, the runes above are smaller, unbalanced, and do not sit horizontally but rather the line of runes slopes slightly upwards as one reads across the word. Another example of this kind of stone where an English name appears in two scripts is Lindisfarne 29. Like Lindisfarne 24, this too is a grave-marker with a rounded head, a decorative border, and a cross in whose quadrants a name has been written twice, in runes in the upper quadrants and in Roman script in the lower quadrants. The name is only partly legible (the right-hand quadrants appear to read "ᛈᛁᛏᛁ" above and "*UI-NI*" below). Both the runic and the Roman texts are formed from deeply-inscribed, tall, closely-spaced vertical lines. Possibly it is a happy accident of the spelling of the name, but there is a distinct impression of an attempt to bring the visual appearance of the two scripts into harmony. In this way Lindisfarne 29 contrasts with Lindisfarne 24, though they are in other ways similar. Lindisfarne 26 is of a similar bi-scriptal design though it is too fragmentary for its text to be read. Lindisfarne 27 may also have been of this type though it has lost its bottom quadrants. Lindisfarne 31 looks similar to Lindisfarne 29, though its inscriptions are too worn to be read. Also from Northumbria, Falstone 02, a memorial stone of the mid-eighth to mid- ninth centuries, bears English inscriptions recording the name of the dedicatee *Hroethberhte* in both runes and majuscules.[196]

---

[195] For the Lindisfarne monuments see *The Corpus of Anglo-Saxon Stone Sculpture I: County Durham and Northumberland*, ed. R. Cramp (London, 1977), <http://www.ascorpus.ac.uk/catvol1.php>.

[196] *The Corpus of Anglo-Saxon Stone Sculpture I.*

98   *Chapter 1*

Lindisfarne 24 and 29 and probably 26, 27, and 31 follow a variant of a pattern found on other grave-markers where text appears in all four quadrants of a cross and where two quadrants are used for a name and two for other text. In one version of this pattern, different scripts are used for the text in the upper and lower quadrants. For example, Hartlepool 01 has Greek omega and alpha in the upper quadrants and the name "*hildiþryþ*" in runes in the lower two quadrants.[197] On Hartlepool 06, alpha and omega appear in the upper quadrants and the name "*berchtgyd*" appears below in majuscules.[198] Billingham 13 may have followed a similar pattern with the addition of a Latin inscription in a border; unfortunately the stone is fragmentary and the lower quadrants of the cross have been lost.[199] With Lindisfarne 24 and 29 and probably 26, 27, and 31, runes stand in place of the Greek script on Hartlepool 01, and 06, and possibly Billingham 13. These three characteristics: repetition of the name in two scripts, the departure from the more usual use of the quadrants, and the difference in the inscription of the two scripts, suggest that it was the scripts themselves that mattered to those who were commemorating the deceased. Even if it was the case that the monuments were intended both for audiences who read runes and for different audiences who read Roman script, the practice may have other or additional implications. Providing the name of the deceased in both scripts suggests some kind of alignment or parity between the futhorc and the Latin-based alphabet for the community for whom the monument was created, while the use of runes where symbolism-laden Greek alpha and omega were sometimes found may also suggest that runes are firmly considered to be a Christian graphic practice in the community for which these monuments were made.

Parallelism between alphabets is clearly reflected in the use of both Roman and Greek scripts on Hartlepool 01 and 06. Conceivably, the paralleling of runes and Roman script on Lindisfarne 24 and 29 and probably 26, 27, and 31, where the Greek-Roman equivalence is replaced by runic – Roman equivalence, could be seen as a legitimate application of the kinds of parallels among various scripts in 'our' grammars that parallel futharks (and other exotic alphabets) with Latin.[200] The inscribers who formed runes and Roman script with

[197] *The Corpus of Anglo-Saxon Stone Sculpture I.*

[198] *The Corpus of Anglo-Saxon Stone Sculpture I.*

[199] *The Corpus of Anglo-Saxon Stone Sculpture I.*

[200] Also reminiscent of the grammars that compare exotic alphabets is Hackness 01a-b from East Yorkshire, a late seventh- to early ninth-century cross-shaft that bears five areas of inscription in four writing systems. Three inscriptions are in Latin in script based on Roman capitals.

Graphs, Alphabets, and Scripts   99

similar strokes were perhaps heightening this sense of parallelism through paying very close attention to showing equivalences between the *figurae* that they carved. Those communities who eshewed runic script altogether perhaps saw their contrasting practice as a marker of Christian legitimacy, mindful that 'our' grammars did not admit of alphabets unrelated to Hebrew, Greek, and Latin.

Conclusion

In this chapter I have presented evidence that when scribes and their communities made choices between scripts, letters, and orthographies and arrived at an analysis of their alphabet they used graphic practice as a resource for identity-making. Letters and alphabets were given the potential to become identity markers by the ways that they were framed in the basic grammar writings that persisted from classical times. The grammarians provided narratives about graphic practice and invested it with identity-making potential. The pedagogical rhetoric of these works framed graphic practice as an activity that defines a community: the 'we' of these texts was available for inhabiting by members of any number of different communities. The theory of *littera* provided models for relating different scripts and for incorporating letters from one script into another. It provided a framework for analysing letters and creating narratives about relationships and difference. Similarity of letter shape could signal a relationship between letters and alphabets and the communities that used them. Usage of given letters could be justified on the authority of biblical precedent. The earliest grammarians did not, however, provide a clear framework for practice within medieval communities where English was read and written; they did not model the treatment of 'barbarous' letters in the writing of English. This left scribes and their communities with decisions to make, variants decided between, decisions to be made about what was one *littera* and what was two, and legitimising narratives about their choices to be developed. Various solutions emerged that, developed within the basic framework of Latin literacy training, could mark identity and distinguish communities. There was,

One inscription is in hahal-runes, a code for runes that uses numbers. There is also a runic inscription and an inscription in "cryptic characters" the languages of which are unknown. The Latin inscriptions may relate to an abbess *Oedilburga* (*The Corpus of Anglo-Saxon Stone Sculpture III: York and Eastern Yorkshire*, ed. J. Lang (London, 1991), <http://www.ascorpus. ac.uk/ catvol3. php>).

in fact, no fixed repertoire of graphs but a process of varied and changing analysis of what constituted a *littera* and what its *nomen* and *potestas* or *potestates* were. In this chapter we have observed this process across a range of sources from early monuments and codices to late medieval primers. We have also identified a tradition of *Anglice littere* texts from the twelfth to the late fourteenth centuries that continues the work of the grammarians and enables us to glimpse attempts to analyse 'English' letters and to incorporate them into the ancient grammatical frameworks. This tradition provides evidence of a framework of graphic identity-making that is operative every time a scribe of English chooses between graphic variants and thinks of his practice as the one that 'we' use.

Chapter 2: Graphic Models

Nescimus, domine, bene scribere [...] Da nobis exemplaria aut scribe, et humiliter cotidie uolumus scribere ut diligenter discere.

Sir, we don't know how to write well [...] Give us some exemplars, or write for us! We humbly want to write and learn diligently every day.

(Ælfric Bata, *Colloquies*)[1]

'*Mashq*', or the act of copying, took up the greatest part of classroom activities and served as one of the key factors in the organization of social, cultural, and emotional life in the literacy socialisation processes.

(Amir Sharifi, "Orthography and calligraphic ideology
in an Iranian-American heritage school")[2]

In the imagined pre-Conquest classroom of Ælfric Bata and his pupils, *c.* 1050, writing is learned from models and copy-texts – *exemplaria* – under the authoritative tutelage of a master.[3] Ælfric Bata's colloquies, written in Latin, are fictional dialogues designed to teach Latin vocabulary and grammar.

---

[1]   Ælfric Bata, *Colloquies*: *Anglo-Saxon Conversations: The* Colloquies *of Ælfric Bata*, ed. and trans. S. GWARA and D. PORTER (Woodbridge, 1997), No. 15, pp. 116-119, at p. 116.

[2]   A. SHARIFI, "Orthography and calligraphic ideology in an Iranian-American heritage school", in: *Orthography as Social Action: Scripts, Spelling, Identity, and Power*, ed. M. JAFFE, J. ANDROUTSOPOULOS, S. JOHNSON, and M. SEBBA (Berlin, 2012), pp. 225-254, at p. 229.

[3]   I use 'model' to cover both copy-texts and non-lexical material for writing practice such as individual letter-forms, alphabets, and pangrams. By 'copy-text', I mean any piece of text used as a model in the course of writing practice. A copy-text may be a formula that is subject to variation, for example, the opening salutation of a letter, or a model Latin translation of a text (in which case the pair of original and translation constitute the model), or it may be a more fixed text such as a proverb or prayer. A copy-text is not necessarily a written text; it may be held in the memory.

They include a great deal of reference to learning to write, indicating that pupils (probably the target audience was the monastic school) were expected to aspire to this skill and to be able to talk about it in Latin using topics and vocabulary provided by the master. Ælfric Bata's colloquies also build an understanding of the identity of the literate person and their relationships with others. Models for writing Latin also model identities. Recent work on literacy training helps us to understand how the process of modelling written language transmits not only competence in reading and writing but associates that knowledge and skill with community values and identity. Amir Sharifi, quoted in the epigraph to this chapter, offers the example of the Iranian-American calligraphy classroom, where the child learns the values of his or her Persian heritage through the discipline of copying calligraphic and orthographic models. The concept that Shafiri invokes of "literacy socialisation", a concept recently developed in sociolinguistics within the paradigm of language socialisation, helps us to understand how the development of graphic awareness and competence in a written language is a vehicle for socialisation into community identities. Writing models are models both of how 'we' write *and* who 'we' are. In Chapter One we saw that traditional grammatical teaching texts gave variation in graphic practice the potential to signify identity. The present chapter investigates the contribution of pedagogic processes to the formation of identity in the graphic medium. This chapter will identify evidence for the application of a pedagogy of imitation of graphic models and copy-texts to Anglophone literacy learning and their contribution to identity formation among readers and writers of medieval English.

Historians of literacy have traditionally viewed literacy training as a "decontextualised technology" that works to inculcate the knowledge and skills needed to read and write in a meaning-free and neutral way.[4] By contrast, drawing on Pierre Bourdieu's notion of habitus, the literacy socialisation tradition in sociolinguistics provides a framework in which to identify and interpret the ways in which the formation of graphic awareness imbues literacy practices with social and cultural values and meanings.[5] A focus on language acquisition has given way to a desire to "document how, in the course of acquiring language, children [become] particular types of speakers and members of commu-

---

[4] L. STERPONI, "Literacy socialisation", in: *The Handbook of Language Socialisation*, ed. A. DURANTI, E. OCHS, and B.B. SCHIEFFELIN (Oxford, 2012), pp. 227-246, at p. 227; L. AHEARN, *Living Language: An Introduction to Linguistic Anthropology* (Oxford, 2012), pp. 145-147.

[5] STERPONI, "Literacy socialisation", p. 227.

Graphic Models 103

nities".[6] Much of the work in this tradition focuses on modern and contemporary case studies and in some cases it is assumed that the paradigm is definitively post-medieval, for example by Sterponi:

> we can analyse the modes of production and reception of the written word that dominate educational institutions as products of a historically-evolved textual ideology, one that began to emerge at the inception of the modern age.[7]

The present chapter will aim to demonstrate that the literacy socialisation framework has value for illuminating pre-modern graphic culture. However, some adaptations of the paradigm are required for pre-modern applications of this approach. Literacy socialisation studies often focus on children and case studies often focus on practices in the classroom. Of course, even today the acquisition of literacy is not confined to children, and we know that in many medieval communities learning to read and write was not confined to the classroom or to children. For present purposes, we should also be alert to the possibility, even probability, that for any given medieval individual, the development of literacy in English could happen at a different time and in different circumstances from their acquisition of literacy in Latin even though, as the present study argues, it was always framed conceptually and in practice by Latin pedagogy.

This chapter will present substantial new evidence for the adaptation to medieval English of *littera* pedagogy and associated resources for literacy socialisation and in particular for the use of models and copy-texts among communities of Anglophone literate practice and for their importance in constructing social identities. It will provide evidence that the pedagogy of imitation was applied within those communities and that graphic models and copy-texts were associated with their values.

Imitation, Pedagogy, and Identity

In medieval literacy pedagogy, the imitation of models and replication of copy-texts was a key process in learning how to put the theory of *littera* into

---

[6] E. Ochs and B.B. Schieffelin, "The theory of language socialisation", in: *The Handbook of Language Socialisation*, pp. 1-22, at p. 2.

[7] Sterponi, "Literacy socialisation", p. 234.

104   *Chapter 2*

practice. Exercises involving elementary copying from and imitation of models
and copy-texts were designed to support early lessons in the doctrine of *littera*.
Elementary teaching focused on making the shapes of the letters of the alphabet correctly, on naming them, and on being able to produce their *potestates* by
making them, singly and in groups, sound as others pronounced them. A story
told by Bede in the *Historia Ecclesiastica* of the miraculous healing of a mute
boy may give us an insight into literacy training in seventh-century Britain.[8] It
describes the pedagogy of naming and sounding the letters, and then sounding
syllables. Having performed the sign of the cross over the mute boy's tongue,
Bishop John of Hexham instructs him to speak, first the word '*gae*' ('yes',
DOE, *gea*), and then the names of the letters of the alphabet in order. After that,
the boy is instructed to repeat syllables and then words and sentences.[9] Similar
elementary lessons involving imitation and repetition are still in evidence some
seven centuries later. The verse preface to John Trevisa's translation of *De
Proprietatibus rerum* by Bartholomaeus Anglicus describes the learning of
letter-names using an alphabet row as "*þe firste lessoun þat I took*":

> *Croys was maad al of reed*
> *In þe bigynnynge of my book*
> *That is clepid God me spede.*
> *In þe firste lessoun þat I took*
> *Thanne I lerned 'a' and 'be'*
> *And oþir lettres by here names.*

> A red cross was at the beginning of my book that is called 'God me speed'. In my
> first lesson I learned 'a' and 'be' and other letters by their names.[10]

Recognition of letters, naming and sounding them, was often supported by
exercises in copying. As far back as antiquity, teaching methods included guid-

---

[8]   A. KING, "Old English ABCs", in: *History of Englishes: New Methods and Interpretations
in Historical Linguistics*, ed. M. RISSANEN, O. IHALAINEN, T. NEVALAINEN, and I. TAAVITSAINEN
(Berlin, 1992: *Topics in English Linguistics* 10), pp. 130-143, at p. 131.

[9]   KING, "Old English ABCs", p. 272; I. DUMITRESCU, *The Experience of Education in
Anglo-Saxon England* (Cambridge, 2018), p. 19. Cf. Parkes: "[pupils] had to copy model letters
to register their *figurae*, and pronounce them according to their *potestas*" (M.B. PARKES, "*Rædan,
areccan, smeagan*: How the Anglo-Saxons read", *Anglo-Saxon England* 26 (1997), pp. 1-22, at
p. 6.

[10]   Bartholomaeus Anglicus, *On the Properties of Things: John Trevisa's Translation of
Bartholomaeus Anglicus De Proprietatibus rerum*, ed. M.C. SEYMOUR *et al.*, 3 vols. (Oxford,
1975-1988), 1, p. 40, lines 4-9.

Graphic Models   105

ing the pupil's hand, demonstrations, and the setting of copying exercises.[11] Copying from models would have taught how letter shapes were built from strokes, and in what order the strokes should be written (the dynamic aspect of writing that is termed 'ductus' in modern palaeography).[12] It would also have supported acquisition of skill in forming graphs of the desired size and in their placement in relation to one another on the page by training muscle memory. Repeated replication of copy-texts would have reinforced this learning. Wax was the usual surface for copying and practising graphs throughout the Middle Ages; learners traced letters and words in the wax with a stylus. One end was pointed, used for inscribing letters in the wax; the other end was blunt, used for erasing. The wax tablet continued to be the basic equipment for learning to write until the sixteenth century, though paper became an important support from the fifteenth century.[13] Examples of the wax tablet from medieval Britain

---

[11] From Seneca we learn that someone might guide the hand of the pupil, presumably teaching 'ductus' – the sequence in which letter-forms should be built up from their component strokes (P. FIORETTI, "Ink writing and '*A sgraffio*' writing in ancient Rome: From learning to practical use", in: *Teaching Writing, Learning to Write: Proceedings of the XVIth Colloquium of the Comité International de Paléographie Latine*, ed. P.R. ROBINSON (London, 2010), pp. 3-16, at p. 3). Pupils may also have traced shapes over models (under-writings) provided by teachers (S. BONNER, *Education in Ancient Rome: From the Elder Cato to the Younger Pliny* (London, 1977), pp. 166-167). A second-century tablet (MS London, BL, Addit. 34186, No. 1) where moral precepts in Greek, at least partly by Menander (you should only accept advice from someone wise; you should not believe all your friends), are modelled and have been copied twice below within writing lines of different sizes, is material evidence of a practice described by Plato in which a teacher models writing on a tablet and the pupil copies (FIORETTI, "Ink writing and '*A sgraffio*' writing", p. 9). In later centuries and at all stages of the learning process, learning by copying from models of writing is in evidence. David Ganz offers evidence of master-scribes and pupils in early medieval writing centres (D. GANZ, "Risk and fluidity in script: An Insular instance", in: *Teaching Writing, Learning to Write: Proceedings of the XVIth Colloquium of the Comité International de Paléographie Latine*, pp. 17-24, at pp. 17-19). Aliza Cohen-Mushlin has shown that scribes in the house of Augustinian Canons in Frankenthal in the twelfth century were allocated samples to copy (A. COHEN-MUSHLIN, "A school for scribes", in: *Teaching Writing, Learning to Write*, pp. 61-87). Scribes being trained in business environments also followed models. A sheet of paper that survives in the papers of the Francesco and Iacopo Del Bene Company of 1361-1366 bears the sentence "*Al nome sia di Christo Benedetto et della madre vergine Maria*" copied twenty-three times beneath a model (I. CECCHERINI, "Teaching, function, and social diffusion of writing in thirteenth- and fourteenth-century Florence', in: *Teaching Writing, Learning to Write*, pp. 177-192, at p. 192, plate 13.2).
[12] For 'ductus' and other terms for the dynamic process of writing see A. DEROLEZ, *The Palaeography of Gothic Manuscript Books from the Twelfth to the Early Sixteenth Century* (Cambridge, 2003), pp. 6-7.
[13] For tablets see R.H. ROUSE and M.A. ROUSE, "Wax tablets", *Language and Communication* 9 (1989), pp. 175-191, and M.P. BROWN, "The role of the wax tablet in medieval

106   *Chapter 2*

are scarce. A tablet of *c.* 650-*c.* 850 found at Blythburgh, Suffolk, bears traces of writing in runes where the wax would have been (London, British Museum, No. 1902,0315.1); it has been suggested that these could be writing practice: the sequence on the bottom line transliterates as "*m a m æ m æ m*" which obviously makes no sense. Although we have no clear survivals from medieval Britain, the plentiful evidence of other kinds for wax tablets for education across medieval Europe at all periods demonstrates that learning to write through practice of letter shapes and of spellings must have been part of the experience of many.[14] The possession of a wax tablet meant that the individual pupil was expected to practise writing for himself, and the ability to erase writing from the wax meant that various exercises could be attempted, and learning could be by practice and repetition of exercises under the supervision of a teacher of some kind.

Through putting into practice the theory of *littera* by imitating models and replicating copy-texts, learners would have been exposed to the particular implementation of the theory that was adopted in their community of practice. They also would have become aware of the boundaries between belonging and difference erected by their community's practice. Medieval educational literature provides evidence for this claim. In the pedagogic literature, the equipment and methods for practising writing are associated with a discourse about the moral and social significance of learning letters. The ancient pedagogical genre of the colloquium or dialogue provided a structure for the presentation of teaching material that placed literacy learning in social contexts and offered subject positions for the learner.[15] In Ælfric Bata's *Colloquy* 3, a studious pupil berates a lazy fellow student who does not want to write on a tablet, nor a sheet, nor a piece of parchment nor a quire: "*scribere in tabula, nec in scedula*

---

literacy: A reconsideration in light of a recent find from York", *British Library Journal* 29 (1994), pp. 1-16. For the adoption of paper in educational contexts see N. ORME, *English School Exercises, 1420-1530* (Toronto, 2013: *Pontifical Institute of Mediaeval Studies, Studies and Texts* 181), p. 9.

[14] For a comprehensive discussion of the making and use of wax tablets in Europe see E. LALOU, "Les tablettes de cire médiévales", *Bibliothèque de L'Ecole des Chartes* 162 (1989), pp. 123-140.

[15] For the genre and some classical and medieval examples see *A Fifteenth-Century School Book: from a Manuscript in the British Museum (MS Arundel 249)*, ed. W. NELSON (Oxford, 1956). Cannon sees question and answer structures as one of several techniques that characterise "grammar-school style" (C. CANNON, *From Literacy to Literature: England, 1300-1400* (Oxford, 2016), pp. 92-99).

Graphic Models   107

nec in ullo pergameno nec in ulla quaternione".[16] *Colloquy* 14 includes a class-room dialogue in which a master accepts a pupil's excuse for not getting any writing done because he lacks the basic tools for writing. The master equips the pupil with pens "*ut in ea cotidie possis discere ad scribendum*", so that he can learn to write every day on a tablet or sheet: "*Et hic sunt pennae dure et bone ad tale opus, et secundum tuum exemplar, quod scriptum est in tabula siue in scedula tua, omni die scribe*".[17] One of the aims of the dialogue, clearly, is to equip pupils to be able to talk in Latin about learning to write. The (implicitly cowardly and unconvincing) 'my pen has run out' excuse may have been a perennial topic set for writing practice. An exuberantly decorated fifteenth-century grammar book associated with the Cistercian abbey of Sawley includes a Latin translation of an English phrase on the pupil's lack of a pen: "*I haue no pen to wrytt my lattyng with. Deest mihi pena sermone^m scribendum latinu^m*" ("I have no pen to write my Latin with", MS London, BL, Harley 5751, f. 146r).[18] Such texts indicate that the teacher and the community expect diligence, hard work, and commitment from literacy pupils. Another topic in the textbooks was the cultural capital to be gained from learning to write. An early sixteenth-century school-book from Somerset includes the sentences "*Legere et scribere faciunt scolarem peritum*" and "*Scribe [...] si vis vrbanus haberi*" (Orme translates, "Reading and writing make a scholar skilful"; "Write if you wish to be held courteous").[19]

A late-medieval compilation of *vulgaria* (passages in English for translation into Latin) associated with Magdalen School, Oxford, surviving in MS London, BL, Arundel 249, ff. 9r-61r, clearly illustrates how literacy training is also socialisation into a literate identity, erecting boundaries between belonging and difference. The text provides samples of English prose with parallel Latin translation. A heading reads "*Donet principiu^m*" (f. 9r).[20] Many of the

---

[16] Ælfric Bata, *Colloquies*, p. 84.

[17] "Here are stiff pens, good for this kind of work. Write every day following your exemplar from a wax tablet or parchment scrap", Ælfric Bata, *Colloquies*, p. 112.

[18] I identify the provenance as Sawley on the basis of the signature of the scribe on f. 3r, where the name "*Rofhus Sallay*" (Sawley) occurs in the lower portion of the frame border on the opening page. The initials "*RS*" occur in the top bar of the border. The border is decorated with the *Arma Christi*. The scribe has also signed f. 232v with "*RS*". The manuscript does not appear in MLGB3.

[19] ORME, *English School Exercises*, pp. 371, 737 (lightly edited).

[20] The edition, *A Fifteenth-Century School Book: from a Manuscript in the British Museum*

108   *Chapter 2*

paragraphs are in the first person, expressing the thoughts and beliefs of a model school-boy. The subject is given "*a pennare and an ynke horne*" ("a pen-case and an ink-horn") by his "*unkle on my fathers syde*" ("uncle on my father's side"), while the "*unkle of my mothers syde gaue me a peny knyff*" ("uncle on my mother's side gave me a pen-knife"); if he had a "*payre of tabullys*" ("a set of tablets") as well, he reflects, he would lack nothing (f. 9v). Below, a translation is provided in Latin and difficult terms for the uncles of the mother's and father's side are glossed in English interlinearly as well as translated. This little fiction about investment in a young kinsman's education conveys the reminder that practising a fine hand is supported financially by the family and conveys the message that learning letters is associated with their values. Literacy training is a social responsibility and kin invest in the pupil's training. In a later model prose, the pupil records that he has sent a letter to his mother and father "*for such book^es^ as I haue nede of*" ("for such books as I have need of"); he knows it "*for a suerty*" ("for definite") that as soon as they receive his message they will "*ordeyn for me all thing^es^ after my desire*" ("provide me with all the things I want", 12r). The school community and wider networks also feature. The pupil measures his progress against that of his classmates: he has "*playde longe and for gete mych the litle children that were sett to schole with me be gone afore me fare ther fore I must se or take hede that I may ou^er^ take them*" ("played long and forgotten much; the little children that started school with me have far overtaken me, therefore I must look to catch up", f. 9v). One paragraph provides a dialogue between some pupils and a master: the master asks where the children have learned their grammar. Some have studied at Winchester and some in other places and one says, "*I am an Oxford man*". "*[W]oll youe we shall assay how we can talke in latyn*", "if you please we shall try talking in Latin", says the master; the pupil is being socialised into a community of those who have studied their grammar (f. 10r). The pupil is discriminating about the use of writing in social circumstances. He has written a letter to a friend, including things that will please him, but he has left certain topics out which are more suitable to be communicated orally when his friend is in town (f. 10r).

A dialogue in MS Cambridge, Trinity College, O.5.4, a fine, early fifteenth-century grammar book, teaches the meanings of word case using examples drawn from relationships in the school and community. The text proceeds

---

(MS Arundel 249), ed. W. Nelson (Oxford, 1956), only includes the Middle English material; for this reason I quote from the manuscript.

Graphic Models 109

through the material by means of question and answer. A question asks for an example of a case and the answer provides an example in English and then in Latin, for example, "*How by gynnestowe by a nominatyf case ¶ As the mayst^er syttyth in the scole*" ("how do you make a nominative case, as for example, 'the master sits in the school'", f. 4r).[21] An impersonal verb construction is illustrated by the phrase, "*As me syttyth in scole*" ("as in, 'one sits in school'", f. 4r). The ablative absolute is illustrated by "*As the mayst^er stondyng in the scole I am a gast*" ("as in, 'the master standing up in the school, I am frightened'": presumably the master stands when he prepares to beat a boy, f. 4r). "*As Wyllyam come hydere and haue a peny*" ("as in, 'William, come here and have a penny'", f. 4r) illustrates the vocative case with a more positive example. The agreement of a noun in the nominative case is double: in number and person, "*As my felowe redyth hys bokes*" ("as in, 'my class-mate reads his books'", f. 4r). Similarly, some of the example texts in later fifteenth-century pedagogical manuscript MS London, BL, Addit. 19046 are about scholarship and writing. For example, "*Incaustu^m et penna scolasticis su^nt oportuna*" ("ink and a pen are needful for school-boys", f. 50v) is chosen to illustrate the use of a plural adjective and to discuss why the adjective "*oportuna*" is grammatically neuter in this example (ff. 50v-51r). Texts in this tradition offer subject positions that the learner can inhabit and other roles – master, fellow – in which he can cast other members of his community and understand his relationships with them.

Traces of Imitation Pedagogy in School-Books

In many of the late medieval school-text manuscripts (which survive in large numbers), as we might expect, there are traces of the process of imitating models and using copy-texts as part of the pedagogy associated with *littera*. We can see particularly clearly in these sources the processes of learning to imitate *figurae*: to trace the *shapes* of letters and words and follow the order in which strokes should be made correctly ('ductus'). For example, much of MS London, BL, Addit. 19046 is in the messy and varied hand of one John Jones, and appears to be the record of, or output from, teaching exercises.[22] Informal

---

[21] For an edition see "A collection of proverbs in Rawlinson MS D. 328", ed. S.B. MEECH, in: *Modern Philology*, 38 (1940-1941), pp. 113-132; see also S.B. MEECH, "Early application of Latin grammar to English", *Proceedings of the Modern Language Association* 50.4 (1935), pp. 1012-1032; and CANNON, *From Literacy to Literature*, pp. 71-72.

[22] Typically, the exercises begin with a brief Latin phrase. This is followed with grammar-

110 *Chapter 2*

Latin-English vocabulary notes appear on a blank page and in margins, supplementing vocabulary lists (ff. 69r- 82v). There are plentiful traces of imitative *littera* pedagogy alongside this material. For example, an attempt has been made to produce an elaborate flourished *S* with tendrils, leaves, and flowers (f. 119v). Practice writing appears in gaps, imitating the last line of texts (ff. 16v, 83v). Prayers run across the top margins, usually "*I^{esus} m^{er}cy*"; sometimes with an additional "*ladi helpe*" (f. 50r). John Jones signs on f. 5v "*Quod Ihoanni Ionys Carlai*" with some macaronic verses: "*Qui sc^{ri}psit sc^{ri}pta sua dext[er]a sit b^{e}n^{e}dicta / Qui sc^{ri}psit scrape A wey 'no^n possu^m scrib^{er}e Al day' / Qui sc^{ri}psit certe Ioh^{ann}es vocatur A perte / Qui legit eme^{n}dat non rep^{re}hendat*" ("May he be blessed who wrote correctly, whoever wrote may he scrape away 'I cannot write all day'. He who wrote is called *John*; may he who reads emend not reprehend").[23] Although this text looks like a typical scribal colophon, in context it functions both as writing practice and as identity formation: as John imitates scribal colophons and names himself through them he also inhabits the identity of a writer, a writer who makes mistakes and has to emend them, who finds it tiring to write all day, who leaves further correction to readers, and who is called *John*. The pages of this book become a site where the imitative processes and structures of pedagogy are replicated in the graphic practice of the novice writer.

Rare material formerly bound up with teaching materials now in MS Oxford, Lincoln College, Lat. 129/130 also consists of pedagogic exercises written in unpractised hands. MS Lat. 129, dated 1427-1428, is a composite manuscript of teaching materials, some of them copied by Thomas Short of Bristol, though the material is thought also to relate to Oxford and a number of west-country classrooms; perhaps it was compiled later while some of the fragments were repurposed as binding material. The material collected extends from grammar texts to less formal pedagogic models and copy-texts such as a Middle English alphabet poem on plant names (*DIMEV* 2775).[24] The fragments

---

focused questions about the phrase in English, and answers in English. Then follows the instruction, "*Say thys in latyn*" ("express this in Latin"). The passage is then given in Latin. A two-line verse that is preceded by the phrase "*vnde versus*" ("whence the verse") sums up the teaching point. Informal English glosses are added (ff. 95v, 96r).

[23] For other examples of these colophons see L. THORNDIKE, "More copyists' final jingles", *Speculum* 31.2 (1956), pp. 321-328, at p. 321; D. WAKELIN, *Scribal Correction and Literary Craft* (Cambridge, 2014), p. 29; and see further below and Chapter Three.

[24] E.M. WILSON, "An unpublished alliterative poem on plant-names from Lincoln College, Oxford, MS Lat. 129 (E)", *Notes and Queries* n.s. 26.6 (1979), pp. 504-508; for the provenance of the manuscript see pp. 504-505.

Graphic Models 111

formerly bound with Lat. 129 are now remounted separately as MS Lat. 130. Some of the fragments contain the Middle English grammar teaching texts *Accedence* and *Regeminia*.[25] Fragment 2 and Fragment 3, folded sheets of paper, include repeated Latin copy-texts (sentences) and many attempts at the alphabet. Fragment 6 is similar. The writing is messy and uneven and there are many crossings out. Given that this material is associated with teaching materials, and given its scruffiness, it seems likely that this material was produced by a learner or learners.

Fragment 3 provides traces of the pedagogy of copying models and repeating copy-texts. On f.ii r the phrase "*Omnibus est notu^m quod multu^m diligo potu^m*" ("it is known to all that I greatly love a drink") has been written. This phrase is recorded as a scribal colophon but here its function is clearly as a copy-text for writing practice.[26] The colophon provides material to copy out and an occasion for practising letter-forms and their placement. The text has been copied out five times in the same hand, each time over one line, the lines being placed immediately under one another to aid visual imitation of the letter and word shapes and to facilitate comparison and assessment of the results. Below the five lines occurs the nonsense pangram "*Equore cum gelido Zepherus fert et ex[he]nnia kymbis*". Like the sentence that used to be used for typewriting practice, 'the quick brown fox jumps over the lazy dog', the "*Equore*" pangram is a copy-text that includes all of the letters of the alphabet, facilitating practice of each letter in the context of writing a text-like line. This exercise would be a useful exercise for writing Latin, English, French – or any other language in Roman script.[27] Several examples of this pangram survive.[28]

---

[25] See *The Teaching of Grammar in Late Medieval England: An Edition, with Commentary, of Oxford, Lincoln College, MS Lat. 130*, ed. C.R. BLAND (East Lansing, 1992).

[26] For the colophon see BENEDICTINS DU BOUVERET, *Colophons de manuscrits occidentaux des origines au XVIe siècle* (Fribourg, 1965-1982), 1, p. 193, No. 1555. Other examples of this text as writing practice occur in school-book MS Nottingham, UL, Mi LM 2, ff. 126v (two examples) and 142v (recorded in *The Wollaton Medieval Manuscripts: Texts, Owners, and Readers*, ed. R. HANNA and T. TURVILLE-PETRE (Woodbridge, 2010), pp. 14, 111). For examples in literary manuscripts see below.

[27] The extent to which written models of English were offered in classroom settings seems to have varied in different communities of practice. Wieland deduces that in the pre-Conquest classroom lines of Latin text would have been dictated to pupils for copying on their wax tablets. The master would then expound difficulties drawing on glosses (some of them in English) in his textbook (G. WIELAND, "The glossed manuscript: Classbook or library book?", *Anglo-Saxon England* 14 (1985), pp. 153-173, at p. 171). English glosses are often found in later teaching texts, for example, MS Oxford, Bod. Lib., Rawlinson D. 328 (*c.* 1445, associated with Exeter) includes interlinear English glosses to Latin degrees of comparison: "*Res bona*" is glossed "*a god*

112   *Chapter 2*

Below the pangram the same hand has written an alphabet with allographs for
a, r, s, and *x*. The letters *m* and *n* occur twice: perhaps the novice writer has
become confused when counting the minims or has lost his place. Below the
alphabet are multiple attempts at selected letters and letter clusters, including
b, d, h, p, and "*est*", and another attempt at the pangram text. Similar practice
graphs occur in the left margin beside and above the "*Omnibus est notum*"
lines, including double *l* and double *u*. Another copy-text for writing practice
here is a rhyming tag, "*Adam p^{ri}mus h^{om}o dampnauit secula pomo*" ("Adam the
first man damned the world with an apple"). This text is found elsewhere as a
writing exercise.[29] Also on the page is a garbled medical maxim: "*Qui bene*

---

thyng", "*res melior*" "*a beter thyng*" ("a good thing", "a better thing") and so on (f. 80v). By this
time, learning to write Latin frequently involved the use of English texts as grammatical models
for turning into Latin. The Middle English *Informacio*, a dialogue attributed to grammar master
John Leylond († 1428), gives one picture of what might have happened. The "master" asks
"*[w]hat schalt thow doo whan thow hast an Englysch to make yn Latyn?*" and the pupil replies
"*I schall reherse myne Englysche onys, ij or iij*" ("What will you do when you have a piece of
English to turn into Latin? I will repeat the English once, twice, or three times"; *An Edition of the
Middle English Grammatical Texts*, ed. D. THOMSON (New York, 1984), p. 111). This seems to
imply that the pupil is required to repeat ("*reherse*") the English text, rather than to write it
(perhaps he did not write down his Latin either). The grammar text *Formula*, a revision of the
Informacio possibly by one of Leylond's pupils, perhaps John Cobbow, suggests that the pupil
may be working entirely from dictation and memory: "*How schalt thou doo when thou hast a
Englys to make en Laten? I must reherse my Englys tyll I haue yt perfitely be hart*" ("What will
you do when you have a piece of English to turn into Latin? I must repeat the English until I
know it perfectly by heart"; *An Edition of the Middle English Grammatical Texts*, p. 214). Having
the English text "perfectly by heart" confirms that rehearsing a text was not expected to involve
writing it down and perhaps did not involve reading a written model. But different communities
of practice would have had different priorities: some masters may have provided written models
of English, others may have stuck to the traditional methods, and others still may have developed
models along with their pupils. The literacy socialisation paradigm leads us to expect such a
scenario.

      [28] This pangram is copied twice in MS London, BL, Addit. 12195, f. 59v, with some alpha-
bets: see below. Other examples include the school-book MS Nottingham, UL, Mi LM 2, f. 123
(*The Wollaton Medieval Manuscripts*, p. 109 and see the other examples provided there). See
further below.

      [29] This verse also occurs in MS Cambridge, Gonville and Caius College, 468/575, on a fly-
leaf. This manuscript, which contains logic and other material, is dated thirteenth century and
tentatively given a Franciscan provenance (M.R. JAMES, *A Descriptive Catalogue of the Manuscripts in the Library of Gonville and Caius College*, 2 vols. (Cambridge, 1914), 2, p. 543). The
line also occurs as part of a writing exercise in MS Cambridge, Gonville and Caius College,
791/827 (two paper folios): "*Addam primus homo damnauit secula pomo, ex quodam pomo fit
miser omnis homo*" (M.R. JAMES, *Supplement to a Descriptive Catalogue of the Manuscripts in
the Library of Gonville and Caius College* (Cambridge, 1914), p. 40).

Graphic Models 113

degerit ingerit egerit est homo s[cancelled?] *fanus Qui male degerit ingerit egerit est homo sanus*" ("he who digests, ingests, and excretes well is a diseased man; he who badly digests, ingests, and excretes is a healthy man"). The unwitting inversion of the teaching betrays the difficulties of a learner: the writer seems to have confused *s* and *f* and the rhyme words have been marked for reversal. Several attempts at the word "*versus*" ("verse") are entered below. The opening words of the maxim have been entered above it in the top margin in a thicker pen but possibly by the same writer. More writing practice at the bottom of the page consists of several attempts at Psalm 116:2, the fullest version reading: "*Quoniam confirmata est sup^{er} nos misericordia eius et veritas*"; the writer has turned the page upside down before writing these lines. Five attempts have been made, one of them is the first letter of the line only. Beneath these lines are some practice *h* letters. This page exemplifies some basic writing practice exercises: alphabets, practice graphs, pangrams, and copies of brief, memorable verse texts. The adjoining page is similar. Here occur four attempts at the phrase "*Multi clerici sedent in scola quos magister docebit*" ("many clerks sit in school, whom the master will teach") along with "*Saculus meus est plenus librorum vel libris*" ("my satchel is full of books or with books"), the first word of the '*Equore*' pangram (two other attempts at this occur on f. i r, one at the bottom, upside down), and the name *John* ("*Iohannis*", "*Ioha^{nn}em*").[30] While copying out the texts, the learner forms both his hand and his identity: he belongs among scribes who love a drink; he may be one of those with healthy or unhealthy habits; he may be one of the many who sit ready to be taught by the school-master; he has a bag full of books; he belongs among the fallen and the saved ('we' are fallen owing to Adam's sin, but he assured 'us' of mercy); and he may be named John.

Names and ownership inscriptions are frequently associated with such traces of pedagogic imitation and, I would argue, are an important kind of writing exercise. For example, in MS London, BL, Addit. 62080, the text of the *Medulla grammaticae*, a Latin-English vocabulary in alphabetical order, has attracted numerous signatures that date from the later fifteenth century and well beyond. Here, the signatures of one Edward Lyster are ownership inscriptions, but they are at the same time, arguably, writing practice, as is indicated

---

[30] Bland suggests that the material is for practising conjugating, parsing and so on but the repetitions and abortive attempts suggest that the process here is one of attention to *figurae*, i.e., physical writing exercise as well as grammatical analysis (BLAND, *The Teaching of Grammar in Late Medieval England*, p. 119).

114   *Chapter 2*

by their frequency and variation. "*Edwardus Lyster bouke*" ("Edward Lister's book", f. 1v), written in an angular display hand, sports fantasy animal heads and pennants on the ascenders. Another attempt at a display hand occurs on f. 145r, "*Iste lyber p[er]tinet ad edwardus lyster*" ("this book belongs to Edward Lister"). That this is practice writing is indicated by the placing of the phrase at right-angles to the text on a vertical line ruled with a sharp implement and the repetition of the phrase in the same orientation to the right. Below right occur three short ruled lines of practice minims. The same phrase occurs in the top right of the folio, this time with a fancy majuscule *I* in "*Iste*". "*Who so wylle opyne and louke / thys ys Edward Lystere booke*" ("to whomsoever will open and look, this is Edward Lister's book", bottom margin of f. 2r) is in a more informal cursive, as is "*edward lyst^{er}*" written along the gutter of a stub before f. 2r.

Many practice alphabets are found in the collection of school-texts, MS London, BL, Addit. 12195, the manuscript apparently partly copied by one John Leke that we encountered in Chapter One. As well as the treatise on versification mentioned in Chapter One, this composite volume includes vernacular culinary, medical, and practical recipes, along with grammatical treatises and a dialogue that debates whether a layman who knows the alphabet is "*litteratus*" (ff. 67r-70v) despite not identifying as a cleric.[31] The materials are in many hands. On spare pages and in gaps occur practice alphabets that are not in Leke's hand. For example, on f. 59v occur two attempts at writing the '*Equore*' pangram, one under the other, the longer of which reads "*Equore cu^m gelido Zephyarus fert est[?] kymbus*", together with various majuscules and minuscules. The same unpractised hand has also attempted to imitate a framed explicit at the end of the text that finishes on the page. In MS London, BL, Harley 1277, a book of grammar texts that we encountered in Chapter One, traces of imitation pedagogy occur together with traces of Latins. A Latin verse text about the parts of the body that opens, "*Os facies mentu^m dens*" has been glossed in Middle English ("mouth", "face", "chin", "tooth") and post-production texts related to English-Latin translation occur, "*On of my frendys wonet*

---

[31] "*[N]o^n su^m cleric^{us} s^{et} su^m aliq^{ua}lit^{er} litt^{er}atus cont^{ra} nullus laicus est litt^{er}atus s^{et} tu es laic^{us} ^{er}g^o non es litt^{er}at^{us} M^{agister} p^{ro}bo si sis litt^{er}at^{us} tu scires alphabetu^m tuu^m set tu nesc^{is} tuu^m alphabetu^m ^{er}g^o no^n es litt^{er}at^{us}*" ("I am not a cleric but I am somewhat lettered; *contra*, no layman is lettered but you are a layman therefore you are not lettered. Master: I prove if you know your alphabet you are lettered but you do not know your alphabet therefore you are not lettered", f. 67r).

Graphic Models

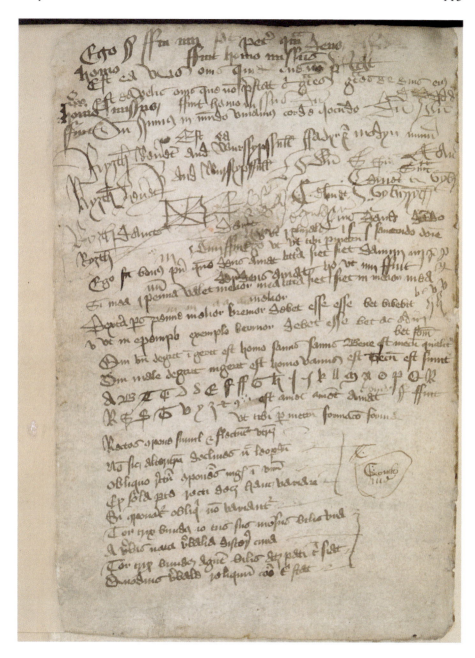

Fig. 8. Practice writing in a school-book, MS London, BL, Harley 1002, f. 187v. © The British Library Board, MS British Library, Harley 1002, f. 187v.

116   *Chapter 2*

be thys half a toun y^{at} ys be yis half lundene Vnus amicor^{um} meor^{um} [...] *hender cherche ys feryere fro god Eccl^{esi}e tanto p^{ro}pe* [...]" ("one of my friends lives by this side of town that is by this side of London [...] the closer to the church the further from God [...]", ff. 221r-222v). Practice graphs appear on a blank end leaf (f. 247v).

MS Cambridge, Trinity College B.14.39-40 (James numbers 323, 324) offers an example of a resource to teach French via English where traces of writing practice occur. We encountered the thirteenth-century portion of this volume in Chapter One. The fifteenth-century portion of the volume (B.14.40) provides the text of the French-English teaching text *Femina*. This section of the volume has attracted practice letter-forms that look to be in the hand of a learner. On f. 88v, a writer has attempted versions of *b* and *c* in various degrees of formality. A few folios later are some shaky attempts at the letters *d* and *a* and possibly *q* and *h*, along with some doodles (ff. 96v-97r). One wonders if this writing practice is by the "*Iohannes*" who has signed his name in rather uncertain Textura a few folios earlier (f. 95r), although judging from the quality of the script the writer here was more advanced. The graphs of the writing practice could be modelled on those in the text, but their forms might be reinforced by the alphabetised French-English dictionary. The alphabetical order here gives plenty of easily locatable model letters.

Material in MS London, BL, Harley 1002, a late fifteenth-century composite manuscript of grammar teaching texts in different hands that we encountered in Chapter One, displays traces of imitative writing practice similar to those found in MS Oxford, Lincoln College, Lat. 130, MSS London, BL, Addit. 62080, Addit. 12195, and Harley 1277, and MS Cambridge, Trinity College, B.14.39-40.[32] A Latin orthographic treatise on ff. 31r-81r that begins "*Orthog^{ra}phiam pu^{er}os p^{ro}pono docer^{e}*" ("I propose to teach orthography to boys") provides an account of each letter in alphabetical order. In a space between the chapters on *y* and *z* an informal hand has inserted some English-Latin translation exercises (f. 80v). Later in the volume on a formerly blank page an unformed hand (or hands, f. 187v, see Figure 8) has left particularly revealing traces of pedagogic imitation. The medical maxim we encountered in Lat. 130 occurs here too but in a slightly different form: "*Qui b^{e}n^{e} degrit* [*sic*] *i^{n}gerit est homo sanus sanus* [*sic*] / *Qui male degirit ingerit est homo vanus est* [*sic*]". Among other Latin verses on the page is one that begins, "*Si mea penna valeat melior mea litt[er]a*

---

[32] C.E. WRIGHT, "Late Middle English *parerga* in a school collection", *Review of English Studies* 2 (1951), pp. 114-120, at p. 115, summarises the contents of MS London, BL, Harley 1002.

Graphic Models 117

fiet fiet [*sic*] *in melio*[*r*] *mea*" ("if my pen had been better my writing would have been better"). Like "*Omnibus est notu^m quod multu^m diligo potu^m*" in MS Lincoln College Lat. 130, this verse is sometimes found as a scribal colophon but here it is clearly a text used for writing practice, judging from the repetitions and mistakes.[33] Text on the line below the verse reads, "*v* [*sic*] *vt in exemp*[*l*]*o exemplo beruior* [*sic, for breviore?*] *debet esse esse bet ac* [...]" ("as in the briefer example ought to be"). This line appears to imitate the one above: perhaps this is the "example" referenced? Towards the top of the page are at least two attempts at John 1:7, "*Homo missus fuit homo missus fuit*"; evidently the focus here is on the form of *figurae* rather than word order. Beneath is the opening salutation of a model letter to parents, in English, "*Ry3th reuer^en t and wurssypffull fadyr ^and mody*[*r*]" ("Right reverent and worshipful father and mother"); immediately below which occur three more attempts at "*Ry3th*" on different lines and one more "*and wurssypffull*"; again these subsequent iterations of the copy-text are clearly modelled on the word-shapes in the lines above. This material is surrounded by various repeated letter-forms and an alphabet of majuscules. At the foot of the page occur some lines of Latin verse on the grammatical inflections. Copying scribal colophons, aphorisms about healthy living, grammatical mnemonics, biblical tags, and respectful letters to his parents, the novice writer learns to imitate a literate in his community of practice while he learns to form graphs.

The relation of books such as those discussed above to actual classroom learning exercises in grammar-school communities of practice is not always simple.[34] David Thomson claims that most school-texts were produced by pupils, "most of the actual [grammar] texts we have in front of us were the productions of boys [...] and the transmission of the texts through their hands may account for much of the distortion that marks most of them".[35] We should be cautious, though, about assuming that pedagogic texts were always produced in formal classroom settings. Although unpractised hands are probably

---

[33] For example, the verse occurs in a fifteenth-century manuscript of science and medicine, MS Cambridge, Trinity College, O.1.57 (James 1081), f. 125r, in a showy scribal signature by one William.

[34] For the problem of distinguishing manuals from classroom books in the pre-Conquest period see WIELAND, "The glossed manuscript: classbook or library book?". Many examples of actual school-room practice may not survive because they were written on wax (ORME, *English School Exercises*, p. 9).

[35] D. THOMSON, *A Descriptive Catalogue of Middle English Grammatical Texts* (New York, 1979), p. 13.

118   *Chapter 2*

those of learners, they are not necessarily of learners in a formal education setting. Furthermore, some school-texts are in competent hands that may be those of masters, but they may be of uncertain relation with scholastic communities of practice. Orme regards some of the school-books in which Latins appear with English for example, MS Kew, TNA, C47/34/13, and MSS London, BL, Harley 1587, and Arundel 249, as fair copies; perhaps therefore these were not actually produced in an educational community of practice.[36] An example of a volume of school-texts that may also be resources owned by masters or others for whom pedagogic material is of value and where later traces of pedagogic imitation appear is MS London, BL, Addit. 60577, also known as the Winchester Anthology. This volume is in the "reasonably practised" hand of a Benedictine monk of St. Swithun's Priory, Winchester who was active *c.* 1487 and may, Wilson surmises from the manuscript's contents, have been a teacher at the almonry school, or responsible for teaching novices.[37] But another hand is that of Thomas Dackomb, who entered his material into the volume in 1549, well after his years of education (he was rector of St. Peter Colebrook, Winchester, in 1519).[38]

MS London, BL, Addit. 60577 contains basic primer texts and other teaching materials (*Pater noster*, *Ave Maria*, *Creed*, and texts on the Commandments, the works of bodily mercy, alphabet poems, and so on) from f. 120r.[39] This pedagogic section of the manuscript displays several examples of writing practice. Notably, the text that follows the alphabet on f. 120r is treated as a model and may have been intended as such. On f. 123r in the right-hand margin a writer has imitated the word (or plural ending) "*ys*" and then practised a *d* with looped ascender, as modelled in the text nearby ("*word*[ys]", "words"). Unusually, the text is written on alternate ruled lines, and a writer has taken advantage of the blank lines in a treatise on the *Pater noster* to imitate "*come thy*" (f. 142v). The same thing happens with "*alle dettes*" ("all debts") on f. 143r, while "*And*" is imitated in the margin on that page. On f. 126r a majuscule *I* is imitated on the spare line above. A particularly clear use of interlinear imitation occurs within the Form of Confession on f. 172r. F. 144r has attracted

---

[36] N. ORME, "School exercises from Canterbury, *c.* 1480", *Archaeologia Cantiana* 131 (2011), pp. 111-128, at p. 111; cf. ORME, *English School Exercises*, pp. 15-18.

[37] *The Winchester Anthology: A Facsimile of British Library Additional Manuscript 60577*, ed. E.M. WILSON and I. FENLON (Cambridge, 1981), pp 8-10, 13; see also ORME, "School exercises from Canterbury, *c.* 1480", pp. 146-154 and n. 57.

[38] *The Winchester Anthology*, p. 12.

[39] *The Winchester Anthology*, pp. 18-36.

Graphic Models 119

imitation of the word "*shal*" ("shall"), the letter *y*, and the syllable "*no*". Later in the volume, a formulary letter has attracted imitation of the large initial *I* (f. 157v). The imitating hands are obviously later – perhaps considerably later – than the main hand. Another example of writing practice occurs on f. 94v, where a very inexpert hand has written a twenty-two letter alphabet. Here is a mixture of majuscules and minuscules, a reversed *e*, and unidentifiable final letters. The writer has taken advantage of an almost blank ruled page, but has been unable to write uniformly between the lines. We have therefore several examples of post-production writing in this manuscript suggestive of the methods of learning to write prompted by the particular graphic environment of model alphabets, primers, and school-texts. Possibly the layout of the text on alternate lines with blank spaces in between was a feature of elementary learning resources.[40]

Many copy-texts imagine the learner as a young male who is part of a pedagogic community of practice: he is a school-boy with a master and fellow pupils. But the existence of fair copies of school-books or their possession by those who may no longer be pupils or teachers suggests that this pedagogy spread beyond the classroom and that its practice had significance for other communities as well as continuing to have significance for people whose school-days were well behind them. The next section will develop these points, demonstrating that we should not assume that the communities of practice in which the theory of *littera* was taught through models and the replication of copy-texts were always composed of formal pedagogic actors, institutions, and structures. The next section will also demonstrate that we may find traces of the pedagogy of imitation in sources well beyond those that are obviously pedagogic and it will argue that we have overlooked the functions of these traces – pen-trials, ownership inscriptions, colophons and so on – as writing practice imbricated in imitation pedagogy. These are particularly important points for investigating the application of the pedagogy of *littera* to Anglophone literate practice.

---

[40] Double line spacing runs from ff. 120r to 180r. Possibly the practice derives from the generous spacing of texts in some school-books, which leaves space for glossing. Wilson comments: "I have not seen this [double-spacing] before, and can offer no certain explanation" (*The Winchester Anthology*, p. 6).

120   *Chapter 2*

Copy-texts beyond the Classroom

Applications of *littera* imitation pedagogy in communities of Anglophone literate practice are found in a wide range of sources. Examples of the imitative writing practice we have observed in school-books – practice graphs, alphabets, and pangrams, and writing of names, proverbial texts, brief prayers, and book ownership inscriptions – are associated with a wide range of materials, including the micro-texts in copies of English literary prose and verse that have often been called 'pen-trials'. This evidence suggests that the communities of practice in which this pedagogic process was adapted and applied were very varied, extending well beyond the classroom and socially well beyond its demography.[41] Despite the stereotypes in the pedagogic literature, we shall see that masters might be mistresses, learners were not always young and male, and writing and reading practice were not always – were perhaps not often – carried out in grammar school. Applications of copying pedagogy supported identity formation in a wide variety of communities of Anglophone literate practice.

Practice Letters, Alphabets, and Pangrams

Countless manuscripts bear practice letters and alphabets that can be related to communities of Anglophone literate practice. Some use the text as a model, or replicate other copy-texts. These traces of imitative pedagogy are extremely challenging to study. First, they comprise a huge corpus of material. Second, their presence has not usually been systematically recorded by cataloguers and editors. Third, a consistent descriptive vocabulary is lacking; material relevant to this enquiry may also be described in catalogues and manuscript

---

[41] 'Pen-trial' (Latin *'probatio pennae'*) refers to test writing carried out to test the pen after the nib has been trimmed. Bischoff views pen-trials as evidence for elementary literacy teaching in the schoolroom (B. BISCHOFF, *Latin Palaeography: Antiquity and the Middle Ages*, trans. D. Ó CRÓINÍN and D. GANZ (Cambridge, 1990), p. 39) and he offers many early medieval examples of *"probationes pennae"* that, he argues, are an "image" (*"Abbild"*) of early learners' humble work in school (B. BISCHOFF, "Elementarunterricht und *probationes pennae* in der ersten Hälfte des Mittelalters", in: ID., *Mittelalterliche Studien: Ausgewählte Aufsätze zur Schriftkunde und Literaturgeschichte*, 1 (Stuttgart, 1966), pp. 74-87, at p. 77). The present chapter argues that in manuscripts associated with communities of Anglophone literate practice such micro-texts are not simply *reflections* of what happened in school, they *are* writing practice.

Graphic Models 121

descriptions as 'pen-trials', 'scribbles', even as 'graffiti'. Here a small sample must serve to illustrate this vast corpus of evidence.

Features of the modified alphabet in MS London, BL, Harley 208 that we encountered in Chapter One suggest that it may have been produced by a learner and there is evidence that the writer was using other texts in this book as a model. The alphabet is followed by the *Pater noster*, which, as we have seen, is a text often associated with the first steps of reading and writing. Peter Stokes classifies the alphabet on these pages as a "pen-trial".[42] However, as well as, or instead of, testing the pen such materials are arguably products of the testing of the writer within the model and imitation frameworks of literacy socialisation. Even if testing the *pen* was the immediate purpose of such texts, in writing out the alphabet and the *Pater noster*, writers of these micro-texts are repeating an early pedagogic exercise. If we reframe our understanding of pen-trials as 'writing practice', not just testing the pen, but testing the writer, this opens the way to consideration of the relations between post-production inscriptions, pedagogic and graphic contexts, and literacy socialisation.

The alphabet in MS Harley 208 is written in an uneven hand, not the hand of the main text, without ruling and with graphs of various sizes, and it is set out in a spare space on the page opening without regard for the layout of the main text. The letter *b* is erroneously reversed, appearing like a *d* (Figure 1). In modern educational psychology, *b-d* reversal and other letter misorientations are a recognised phenomenon among learners.[43] The entire alphabet-*Pater noster* sequence runs across the opening from verso to recto, where it trails off unfinished (Figure 2). Along the bottom margin appear scraps of writing that

---

[42] P.A. STOKES, *English Vernacular Minuscule from Æthelred to Cnut c. 990-c. 1035* (Cambridge, 2014), pp. 178, 180). Stokes refers here to MS London, BL, Harley 526 but it is clear from his discussion that this is a slip for MS Harley 208.

[43] R. TREIMAN, J. GORDON, R. BOADA, R.L. PETERSON, and B.F. PENNINGTON, "Statistical learning, letter reversals, and reading", *Scientific Studies of Reading* 18 (2014), pp. 383-394. Compare the engraving of the letter *b* upside down and reversed in a partial alphabet on a silver ring found at Flixborough and dated eighth or ninth centuries on the basis of script-style (M.P. BROWN and E. OKASHA, "The inscribed objects", in: *Life and Economy at Early Medieval Flixborough, c. AD 600-1000,* ed. D.H. EVANS and C. LOVELUCK (Oxford, 2009), ch. 3.3 (n.p.) and figure 3.5). A piece of lead inscribed with an alphabet in two lines was found in the remains of a Viking hall at Waltham, Essex. Okasha dates the find between the ninth and early eleventh centuries and interprets the alphabet as probably "practice letters" (E. OKASHA, "A supplement to *Hand-List of Anglo-Saxon Non-Runic Inscriptions*", *Anglo-Saxon England* 11 (1982), pp. 83-118, at p. 100; cf. E. OKASHA, "The Waltham alphabet: An Anglo-Saxon inscription", *Medieval Archaeology* 20 (1976), pp. 129-131 and Plate 11a). Perhaps supporting Okasha's suggestion are the strangely formed graphs *f* and *k*.

122   *Chapter 2*

could also be practice writing, one meaningless and one reading "*hwæt ic eall feala ealde sæge*" ("Lo, I [have heard] many old sagas", f. 88r). The same hand may be responsible for nonsense syllables at the top of f. 67r. The script and letter-forms of the alphabet differ from those of the main text.[44] However, I believe that a case could be made for the writer's attempting to imitate the shapes of some of the letters of the main text. On f. 88r, compare "*qui*" in the *Pater noster* and the main text, line 1; "*reg*" in the *Pater noster* and the main text, line 1, where the *g* of the text has been imitated even though the alphabet has Caroline *g*; and the use of the top stroke on *t* to form a ligature with adjacent letters ("*sanctificetur*" in the *Pater noster* and "*hortatur*" in line 10). Is the alphabet writer studying the Latin text's letter-forms, seeking to modify his Anglicised alphabet with the use of an older model?

A similar alphabet sequence and unfinished *Pater noster* are found in MS London, BL, Cotton Vespasian D.xxi, f. 40v, in a section of the manuscript that contains Felix's *Life of St. Guthlac*.[45] The main text is written by one hand in Insular Minuscule. This section was formerly part of MS Oxford, Bod. Lib., Laud Misc. 509, an Ælfric manuscript.[46] The main text is dated second half of the eleventh century, but the addition is dated twelfth century.[47] It is arguable that this alphabet too has been modified in relation to the graphic environment, though in a different way from MS Harley 208. If we align the letter-forms of the main hand with those of the alphabet we can see clearly both differences and close similarities. Some of the letter-forms of the alphabet are clearly different from those of the Insular Minuscule of the main text hand. In the alphabet, *d* has a straight vertical ascender while the ascender in the main hand curves to the left, and *g* in the alphabet has a closed bowl while in the main

---

[44] Stokes discusses the difficulties of interpreting the functions of "scribble[s]" and of identifying the characteristics to be expected from a learner: "If a given scribble is the result of a novice-scribe practising his new skills, or of a more experienced scribe trying out a new script, then we might expect mistakes rather than deviations [from a book-hand], and perhaps the introduction of features from other scripts" (STOKES, *English Vernacular Minuscule*, p. 180).

[45] *Digipal* notes "A very similar alphabet, also accompanied by the beginning of the *Pater noster*, was added s. XII (or s. XI?) on 40v of BL Cotton Vespasian D. xxi" (*DigiPal: Digital Resource and Database of Manuscripts, Palaeography, and Diplomatic* (2011-2014), <http://www.digipal.eu/>).

[46] N.R. KER, *Catalogue of Manuscripts containing Anglo-Saxon*, reissued with supplement (Oxford, 1990), item 344; N.R. KER, "Membra disiecta", *British Museum Quarterly* 12 (1938), pp. 130-135, at pp. 132-133.

[47] See the entry in O. DA ROLD, T. KATO, M. SWAN, and E. TREHARNE, *The Production and Use of English Manuscripts 1060 to 1220* (Stanford, 2018), <https://em1060.stanford.edu/>.

Graphic Models 123

hand it follows the Insular open form. In the alphabet, *f*, *r*, and sometimes *s* sit on the ruled line, while in the Old English text, they descend below it. The character set is different too. The alphabet includes ampersand, a form missing from the main hand, as well as the Tironian *et*. Thorn is not included in the alphabet. Perhaps this is simply a slip; alternatively, possibly the alphabet scribe is less familiar with the non-Roman letters, the alphabet scribe's character set does not include it, or thorn here is conceptually aligned with the abbreviation for *þæt*, *þ*. When it comes to the non-Roman letters there are close similarities between the hand of the text and the hand of the alphabet. The letters of the alphabet are well spaced and clearly legible, mirroring the clarity of the main hand. The alphabet graphs ash, wynn, eth, and the abbreviation *þæt* are particularly close in form to those in the main hand. These are all letter-forms which potentially could have been less familiar to a twelfth-century scribe. Writing the alphabet could have served the purpose of exploration, comparison, and practice.

Although the alphabet and the *Pater noster* in MS Cotton Vespasian D.xxi are both dated twelfth century, the scripts (and ink colour) are strikingly different from one another. The *Pater noster* below, written as a continuation of the alphabet (after the tittle) perhaps represents the more usual graphic experience of the alphabet scribe, or is perhaps written in his own, usual hand. Further evidence for the graphic culture in the alphabet scribe's community of practice is offered by Latin interlinear glosses to the Old English in MS Bod. Lib. Laud Misc. 509, formerly part of the same manuscript. The glossator annotates the Old English Heptateuch. Marsden suggests that as the glossator was working *c.* 1100, only "a generation or two" after the Old English text was copied but struggles to understand the Old English, he may have been a Norman.[48] Marsden shows that the glossator checks the Old English text against the Vulgate and sees him as privileging the Latin. An alternative interpretation is that the glossator is studying Old English traditions of writing. The twelfth-century users of MS Cotton Vespasian D.xxi and MS Laud Misc. 509 were perhaps studying Old English texts and making them more comprehensible with the addition of glosses in Latin, which was presumably a written language that was more readily accessible to them. The alphabet scribe's imitative copying exer-

---

[48] R. MARSDEN, "Latin in the ascendant: The interlinear gloss of Oxford, Bodleian Library, Laud Misc. 509", in: *Latin Learning and English Lore: Studies in Anglo-Saxon Literature for Michael Lapidge*, ed. K. O'BRIEN O'KEEFFE and A. ORCHARD, 2 vols. (Toronto, 2005), 2, pp. 132-152, at p. 148.

124   *Chapter 2*

cise is perhaps part of this project. Sara Harris describes a spectrum of knowledge of and attitudes towards Old English in the twelfth century.[49] We may surmise that this scribe's efforts to model a hand on Old English examples reflect a community of practice's high valuation of the English-language biblical text and that this learner's attentive graphic practice is a means of identifying with the beliefs of his community.

Both the alphabet in MS Cotton Vespasian D.xxi and that in MS Harley 208 belong with the tradition of learning letters through the imitation of an alphabet, and with the tradition of an alphabet that has been adapted to an environment in which English was copied. In MS Harley 208 we see the modelling of the alphabet in relation to the earlier Latin graphic model. In MS Cotton Vespasian D.xxi we glimpse the practice of this tradition of learning the English alphabet enacted as part of a process of close engagement with the model of earlier written English.

Countless examples of practice graphs and alphabets occur in manuscripts of Middle English texts. In the present study only a small fraction of this material – a selection of examples chosen to illustrate its basic characteristics – can be discussed. MS London, BL, Harley 63, a fifteenth-century *Brut* whose text goes up to Henry VI, includes *"and hys modir"* ("and his mother") modelled on the text in the upper margin of f. 12r (the learner writes the first *d* with a looped ascender but the second one with a simple ascender as in the text). In a blank space at the end of the text, practice minims and human faces are traced alongside a drawing of Christ displaying his wounds and a Middle English Holy Name prayer (f. 44v). In the lower margin of f. 9r occur three attempts to imitate the simplified secretary *w* of the scribe's hand (compare *"wroth"*, line 1), while imitations of the scribe's 'and' occur here and over the leaf (the learner produces a looped *d* in both cases).

An even less proficient learner has left his or her traces in MS London, BL, Harley 53, a late fifteenth-century paper manuscript of the *Brut*. In the right margin of f. 44r appear a large, poorly-formed *e* and two attempts at a plosive which may be *p* or *b*. In the lower margins of ff. 95v-96r occur what may be attempts to form curves and straight strokes; components of letter-forms rather than recognisable letters. On f. 151r, on freehand horizontal lines, a few faint minims have been traced. The person who drew the lines either did not know or did not care that ink would transfer onto a conjoint page if an opening was allowed to close before the ink was dry, for traces of the lines also appear on

---

[49]   S. HARRIS, *The Linguistic Past in Twelfth-Century Britain* (Cambridge, 2017), pp. 63-89.

Graphic Models 125

f. 150v. This learner's additions are so poorly formed that they do not reflect any recognisable script and hence are hard to date.

A rear flyleaf in *Brut* manuscript MS London, Society of Antiquaries, 93, bears an uneven alphabet of majuscules, two attempts at a row of the five vowels, and several attempts at a majuscule *R* (f. 97v).[50] A fancy but uneven partial alphabet that is preceded by a cross occurs upside down in the margin in MS Manchester, John Rylands Library, Eng. 75, a Wycliffite Bible (f. 23v) while various random majuscules occur in the margin at right-angles to the text in what is probably a significantly later hand (f. 34v) and, again at right-angles to the main text, numerous repeated letters of the alphabet (with a particular focus on minuscule *d*) in what may be the same hand occur on ff. 108v, 110v, and 126v. The tradition of using the margins of this volume for writing practice continued very late, to judge from, for example, the rather fine alphabet signed by James Forster (f. 188v; compare the wobblier "*Phillis Forster*" signature on f. 125r), and an alphabet of majuscules and minuscules on f. 150r.

MS Glasgow, UL, Hunter 232 (U.3.5) displays numerous practice letter-forms in the margins of a text of Lydgate's *Life of Our Lady*. On f. 58r there are practice attempts at the graph *a*, some of which echo the fine majuscule versions of *A* in the text, some yoghs, and the phrase 'in the name of' in various different scripts.[51] On f. 99v occur various attempts at *h*. Some of the practice letter-forms on f. 99v are incomplete, suggesting that the writer is trying to work out the sequence of strokes for making these graphs. Also on this page, the opening five lines of the text have been imitated in the lower margin, the attempted imitation even extending to the decorative initial that opens the stanza. Johanna Green has referred to the marginal material in this book as "pen-trials".[52] But it is perhaps better described as writing practice, especially as she also argues that "doodles" in the manuscript may be in the hands of children. Such so-called 'pen-trials' display the characteristics of writing practice based on models even when, as here, they occur in books whose vernacular texts are not pedagogic.

---

[50] I owe this reference to Ryan Perry.

[51] For a transcription of the marginalia in this manuscript see C.I. CAMPBELL, "A study of Glasgow, University Library MS Hunter 232: John Lydgate's 'Life of Our Lady'" (unpublished M. Phil. thesis, University of Glasgow, 2009), pp. 23-52. Campbell sees the activity in relation to the Reformation and the loss of interest in the text on behalf of the manuscript's sixteenth-century owners.

[52] J. GREEN, "The mystery of the medieval doodle" (BBC Radio 4, 2016: *Today Programme*), <https://www.bbc.co.uk/programmes/p04jq01b>.

126   *Chapter 2*

On an endleaf of the *Pore Caitif* manuscript MS Manchester, John Rylands Library, Eng. 87, dozens of attempts at the letter *y* appear in a row on a formerly blank page (f. 121r). The page is ruled but the practice row is orientated at right-angles to the lines. More attempts at *y* appear on the lines, along with many practice minims and attempts at *o* and *v*. Rows of the letter *y*, very badly formed, also occur in *Brut* manuscript MS Manchester, John Rylands Library, Eng. 102, in the lower margin of f. 75r. Other letters being practised here and on the facing page include *o*, *h*, and *p*. Rows of practice letters *s*, *p*, *d*, and *g* appear on a flyleaf in *Brut* manuscript MS Manchester, John Rylands Library, Eng. 105 (f. 2r). Uneven rows of cursive minims appear on the inner upper cover of *Canterbury Tales* manuscript, MS Manchester, John Rylands Library, Eng. 113. Several rows of the letter *s* appear on an endleaf of MS Manchester, John Rylands Library, Eng. 895 (f. 125v), a manuscript containing the *Process of The Passion* and the *Gospel of Nicodemus*. In the mid fifteenth-century Middle English and Latin literary miscellany MS Aberystwyth, National Library of Wales, Brogyntyn ii.1 (Porkington 10) several rows of Secretary *a* appear on the same page as various attempts at the letter *d* and at the name *William* in the same hand (f. 26v); some Welsh names appear here and on the previous page suggesting that multlingual communities of practice were associated with this volume. Also in this manuscript, attempts at the letters *b* and *r* are associated with wobbly and uneven linked cursive loops (f. 17r, lower margin), while attempts at *a*, a partial alphabet, *d-g*, more attempts at *d*, and some illegible letters (possibly *p*, *q*, and majuscule *I*) occur in the lower margin of f. 53r and some very poorly formed attempts at ampersand, *p*, and *v* on f. 55r. On f. 61r a full alphabet row appears in the lower margin (with some omissions and confusions).

In the Findern manuscript, MS Cambridge, UL, Ff.1.6, a practice alphabet fragment (*a-h*) occurs in a lower margin and in the opposite lower margin a complete alphabet is entered over two lines, the upper sequence ending at *m* and the lower sequence running from this *m* in reverse order to *z* (ff. 137v, 138r). Fragmentary alphabets appear in a similar position in a different, shakier hand on f. 119r; the letter *m* intrudes between *a* and *b* and between *b* and *c* in the first row. A scratchy and rudimentary fragment of a majuscule alphabet occurs on f. 13r. A fragment from the middle of the alphabet that includes several attempts at *r* and *s* appears in the upper margin of f. 22r. A full alphabet ending "*est amen*" occurs in a formerly blank space on f. 48v, together with a

Graphic Models 127

few very poorly formed majuscules. Contrastingly steady and proficient hands have written the names "*Elizabet Koton*" and "*Elisabet frauncys*" on f. 93v.

Primers encountered in Chapter One provide plentiful examples of writing practice in English where a book has served as prompt and sometimes as model. Spaces in the margin and a blank page at the end of the primer MS New York, Columbia University, Plimpton 258 have attracted some informal writing. Two starts at writing the Ten Commandments in English, a copy-text associated with elementary learning primers, occur on f. 8v. In both cases the hands look like those of learners. The nib of the top writer is broad and splayed and the spelling uncertain ("*frist*" for '*first*'). The lower writer reverses the page and starts again. He or she centres the writing on the line ruled for the script. Perhaps this use of lines related to a method of guiding the hand of the learner. The writing appears to be prompted by, though not to be modelled closely on, the pedagogic environment provided by the manuscript. MS Manchester, John Rylands Library, Eng. 85 has also acted as a stimulus for informal writing practice by later writers. A clear example occurs on the lower margin of a treatise on the *Pater noster* (f. 46v). Here there are numerous attempts at various forms of *a*, and some attempts at *p*, and perhaps *f*, *q*, and *e*. The forms are not modelled after the text; notably there is no example of single compartment *a* in the text but the writer has made many attempts at this form.

Along with alphabet rows and practice graphs, pangrams are frequently found in manuscripts of Middle English literature. For example, the school-text '*Equore*' pangram occurs twice in upper margins of thirteenth-century multilingual miscellany MS Oxford, Bod. Lib., Digby 86 (ff. 113v, 189v) and the first word only of the pangram occurs again, in the same hand, on f. 117v, along with the names "*Galfridus*" and "*Will*^{ielmus}*s*", the latter occurring twice (see further below). The pangram also occurs in MS London, BL, Harley 2248, f. 18v, another text of the *Brut*;[53] at the end of *Piers Plowman* in Oxford, Bod. Lib., Ashmole 1468, part 3, p. 378; and in another *Piers* manuscript, London, BL, Harley 6041, f. 96v.[54]

---

[53] See the entry in J.J. THOMPSON, S. KELLY, and R. PERRY, *Imagining History: Perspectives on Late Medieval Vernacular Historiography, Database of Manuscript Descriptions* (Belfast, 2013-2017), <https://web.archive.org/web/*/http://www.qub.ac.uk/imagining-history/resources/wiki/index.php/ Special:Allpages>.

[54] Warner notices that the *Piers* examples of the '*Equore*' text are pangrams but not that their context in both cases is writing practice (L. WARNER, *The Myth of* Piers Plowman: *Constructing a Medieval Literary Archive* (Cambridge, 2014), pp. 55-56).

128   *Chapter 2*

In MS Ashmole 1468, the '*Equore*' pangram occurs in the midst of several unconnected lines of Latin, some of them imitating the text (for example, "*Primus passus de vicione Passus secundus de dowel*"). There is no ruling and the lines are centred rather than being justified on the left margin, further signs of unpractised writing. The imitation of a rubric in *Piers Plowman* manuscript MS Ashmole 1468 is paralleled in other manuscripts. Perhaps rubrics lent themselves for use as copy-texts for imitation because they catch the eye and are often written in a script that is more calligraphic than the main text and hence were felt to provide a challenging and aspirational model. An example occurs in MS Manchester, John Rylands Library, Eng. 78, a Wycliffite Bible. Here, the rubric that announces the end of the gospel of John and the beginning of Romans is replicated in a later hand (and spelling) in the lower margin (f. 142r). In *Piers Plowman* manuscript Aberystwyth, National Library of Wales, 733B, a learner practises writing in the lower margin beside a catchword that is decoratively framed in a scroll. The catchword reads "*And al his*" ("and all his") and it may be that this model has attracted the attempts at the letter *a* and even perhaps the fragmentary phrase "*and her*" (p. 128).[55] Also in National Library of Wales 733B, an immature hand has imitated the last line on the page, "*lyf seiþ þ^{at} he lykþe / & haþ leyde his lyf*" ("Life says that he likes and has laid his life", p. 148). The learner struggles: *l* and *k* are very badly formed, appearing like *p* and *ff*, and the imitation stops at "*leyd*". Interestingly, the learner replicates the virgule and the ampersand. He or she appears to be copying *figurae* without understanding the meanings of the words. A few pages later, the same hand starts to copy the bottom line of text, "*þ^{at} my tale*" ("that my tale"). The first two words are imitated fairly legibly and accurately (the abbreviated "that" is imitated exactly), but "tale" is a disaster (p. 151). The use of the catchword and text on the lowest line of the writing frame as copy-texts

---

[55] A *possible* example of rubric imitation occurs in *Prick of Conscience* manuscript MS Manchester, John Rylands Library, Eng. 50. The rubric "*Of the peyn[es] of helle*" ("Concerning the pains of hell", p. 135) is imitated in the margin to the left of the main text. At first sight this text is a side-note designed to catch the eye that is looking for this part or topic or alternatively it might be guide text for the rubricator. However, evidence in favour of its being writing practice is the fact that it is written in a fainter medium than the text (plummet?), that it is in a careful, round hand that imitates the main text letter-forms and spellings exactly (save for the plural ending of "*peynes*", but this is probably missing as a result of later cropping), and as a note to aid finding a place in the text it is unnecessary, since the bold red rubric already fulfils this function. This hand imitates the rubric "*Of þe firste blis of heuene*" in the same faint medium and round script, the large letters necessitating a break in the last word over two lines ("Of the first bliss of heaven", p. 156).

Graphic Models 129

suggests an imitative pedagogic practice in which a learner writes the same text again and again on a succession of lines, facilitating comparison of attempts at the same text, a phenomenon we observed frequently in the school-books.

We will now turn to copy-texts that engage with various genres of micro-text to generate matter for writing practice. We saw that in school-books writing practice often masquerades under genre classifications such as ownership inscriptions, colophons, signatures, prayers, dictaminal formulas, and religious tags. In manuscripts of Middle English literary verse and prose also, texts for practice often belong to these genres. Clues for identifying micro-texts in these genres as writing practice involving replication of a copy-text include repetition, false starts, fragments, copying of a model in the book, execution in a hand and ink other than that of the main text, especially in immature and un-practised writing, and association with repeated letter-forms, alphabets, and pangrams.

Ownership Inscriptions

As we saw in relation to the school-books, names and ownership inscriptions may also function primarily as writing practice. Between rubrics in MS Manchester, John Rylands Library, Eng. 50 a different, Secretary, hand has written the names "*Jhon Campian*", "*Ales Camp\i/an*", "*schacspere*", and "*edwarde ketty*[?]*s*" (p. 184); nearby attempts at some Secretary *r* letter-forms, the rough correction in the second name, and the fact that all four different names are in the same hand, suggest that this is writing practice. Together with practice letter-forms, MS Glasgow, UL, Hunter 232 (U.3.5), displays signatures and other trial writing in various scripts. On f. 58r, one John has signed his name in various scripts, spellings, and orientations on the page; the repetition and variation suggest that recording a name is writing practice and this is further supported by the appearance on this page of the phrase 'in the name of' in various different scripts. In a similar way, the name *John* also occurs in various scripts along with the alphabets in *Brut* manuscript Society of Antiquaries 93 (f. 97v). The primer MS John Rylands Library, Eng. 85 also includes many signatures, some repeated (for example, "*Wyllyam Vicary*", f. 83r). Also in this manuscript, four ownership inscriptions appear on an endleaf, all in the same hand and all of them variants on the phrase "*Iste liber co^{n}stat Joh^{anni}*

Fig. 9. Practice writing in a *Canterbury Tales* manuscript, MS Manchester, John Rylands Library, Eng. 113, f. 195v (detail). Imaging: Copyright of the University of Manchester.

Ade[?]" ("this book belongs to John Ade[?]", f. 83v), while faint traces of another '*Iste liber*' inscription appear on the facing page (f. 84r). The repetition of the phrase suggests an imitative writing exercise with clear implications for identity: John models an identity as book owner as he learns to write. In MS Manchester, John Rylands Library, Eng. 87, the name "*Myles Gre*[...]*d*" appears three times in the lower margin of successive pages (ff. 100v, 101r, 102r). The repetition of the name and above all the immaturity of the hand (the surname is illegible) suggest that the writer is practising.[56] In MS John Rylands Library, Eng. 78, an ownership inscription in a late hand occurs in the lower margin of f. 172v, "*this is John dishe* [?] *is boke*", and a similar inscription appears on the lower margin on f. 72r. The poor formation of the hand and the repetition both suggest that this is writing practice. In *Piers Plowman* manuscript Harley 6041, the '*Equore*' pangram occurs with an ownership inscription and two attempts at "*Ego sum bonus puer que^m deus amat*" ("I am a good boy whom God loves"), both in a very immature hand, and several drawings of fish. In *Canterbury Tales* manuscript, MS Manchester, John Rylands Library, Eng. 113, Johannes Brode has written his name and "*Iohannes Brode constat iste liber*" (f. 1r). This looks like writing practice as well as announcing his name

---

[56] The catalogue reads "*Garard*".

Graphic Models 131

and ownership of a fine book: he writes two kinds of majuscule *B*, corrects *h* in "*Iohannes*" in the signature, and perhaps attempts cancellation of the inflexion on "*Iohannes*" in the ownership inscription. The signatures of one John Hull also appear in this manuscript (e.g., ff. 1r, 196r, 196v) and they appear to have been used as occasions for writing practice by another hand. A couplet addresses John Hull, "*yf ye wyll me be lyef / I haue gret honde yn the botom of my slyfe*" ("if you will me believe, I have a great hand in the bottom of my sleeve", f. 195v, see Figure 9). Another hand has copied the verses below with some emendation and error and similar lines also appear on f. 195r, with an apparent authorship claim on the facing page, "*By me you' frynde to ys pore John Hull*". Is the reference to his having *a great hand* concealed within his sleeve jocularly aggressive? Perhaps learning to *write* a hand is here associated with a community of practice of social equals and joshing male friends (who conceal in their sleeves hands that are ready to strike?).

The pedagogy of imitation that uses signatures and book ownership inscriptions as copy-texts may shed light on an extraordinary example of post-production writing in *Brut* manuscript, MS San Marino, Huntington Library, HM 136.[57] Many of the numerous sixteenth-century ownership inscriptions in this later fifteenth-century copy of the *Brut* relate to one of the owners of the book, one Dorothy Helbarton. Apparently written by a male ("*I ham he that wyll bere re corde*", "I am he that will bear record", f. 81r), most of them are in the idiom used by Edward Lyster in the school-book MS London, BL, Addit. 62080, discussed above. "*Who so wylle opyne and louke / thys ys Edward Lystere booke*" (bottom margin of f. 2r), for example, is echoed in several phrases that use the 'book / look' rhyme, such as, "*Thys ys Dorethe helbartun boke / And she wyll a pon ym loke*" ("This is Dorothy Helbarton's book / If she will upon it look", MS Huntington Library, HM 136, f. 50r), "*Thys ys my mystrys boke wo woll A pon ym loke*" ("This is my mistress's book / whoever will upon it look", f. 52r), and "*I tel the playne yt ys my* [an untranscribable squiggle follows] *mystrys boke / Who ys yovr mystrys toren over and loke*" ("I tell you plainly it is my [...] mistress's book / Who is your mistress? Turn over and look", f. 101r). Anthony Bale compares these inscriptions with bookplates and sees their writing as "an act of ownership" carried out on Dorothy's behalf by a scribe; "Dorothy and her scribe [...] assert ownership in the context of rival claimants".[58] But features of the material seem to me more consistent with

---

[57] I owe this reference to Ryan Perry.

[58] A. BALE, "Belligerent literacy, bookplates, and graffiti: Dorothy Helbarton's book", in:

132   *Chapter 2*

writing practice. For example, the hand is messy, inconsistent, and sometimes illegible (for instance, "*tell*" on 103r has been messily corrected and the writer has had two goes at the *h* in "*hel bartun*" on f. 110r, writing the second attempt partially on top of the first without erasing it). The writer intensifies the illegibility and messiness by writing over text written by the main scribe, showing an inability to size text to fit in the space available (for example, "*boke*" partially runs over "*Edwardus*" on f. 110r). The writer sometimes experiments with fancy majuscules (*M* in "*Mystrys*" on f. 104r is a displayed majuscule that is quite out of keeping with the rest of the inscription; on f. 108r the name "*Dorethe Helbartovn*" is written entirely in fancy majuscules; on f. 20r majuscules *DH* stand for the name; on f. 25r the ownership phrase is written as an acronym in majuscules *TYDHB* ("this is Dorothy Helbarton's book") while three versions of a monogram *KR* (the writer's own initials?) occur on f. 109r. The word divisions are variable, giving the impression that the writer is modelling the text on the basis of common spellings. For example, *Dorothy* is spelled as two words 'door' and 'thee / thy', "*Dore the*" (ff. 9r, 29r), "*dore the*" (ff. 33r, 104r), and "*Dore thy*" (f. 54r) as well as "*Dorethe*" (ff. 48r, 50r, 59r, 102r) and just "*Dore*" (endleaf, f. i r). Likewise *Helbarton* is sometimes "*helbar tun*" (f. 29r) or "*hel barton*" (f. 35r) as well as "*el bartvn*" (endleaf, f. i v) and "*helbartun*" (ff. 50r, 54r, endleaf, f. i r). Viewed in the light of such features, it is possible that all of these variations on the 'bookplate' formula are a kind of writing practice exercise; the ownership announcements and pious prayers for the owner (for example, "*Ihesu save her that do howe thys boke*" ("Jesus save her that owns this book", f. 63r); "*god save her that do owe thys boke*" ("God save her that owns this book", f. 72r)) providing copy-text for writing just as they did for the learners whose hands are found in the school-books. Unlike many of those learners, this writer does not model most of his output on the text of the book (with the exception of "*After kynge henry V regned henry his sone*" ("after King Henry V, his son Henry reigned", modelled on the penultimate line of f. 158r) but rather, on the book's earlier owners' signatures. One of the Dorothy ownership inscriptions sits on the same page as the earlier calligraphic ownership mark of John Leche, "*Liber Ioh^{ann}is Leche de wico Malb^ano in Com^{itatibus} Cest^{ria}*" ("the book of John Leche of Wich Malbank [Nantwich] in Cheshire", endleaf). Another version of John Leche's ownership inscriptions

---

Book Destruction from the Medieval to the Contemporary, ed. G. Partington and A. Smyth (Basingstoke, 2014), pp. 89-111, at pp. 92, 95.

Graphic Models 133

occurs on front flyleaf, f. i r.[59] The repetition with variation of the basic formulas, using them as copy-texts, echoes the traces of imitation pedagogy we have observed in the school-books.

Dorothy Helbarton's role and the wider learning scenario are unclear. As the writer's "mistress", was she in some way responsible for his education? Whether or not Dorothy had a role in the education of the learner writer, she certainly provided a role model. While the learner composes phrases and sentences about Dorothy, he also records that she is a book owner, that she was given the book by Mary her mother, and that she is worthy of prayers for her salvation. While the learner copies variations on the ownership formula, he also writes himself into a literate community of practice associated with this book: "*I tel the playne* [...] *toren over and loke*" ("*I* tell *you* plainly, turn over the leaf", f. 101r, my emphasis); "*Wyll yow say thys ys not mystrys Derethe boke then yow ly*" ("If *you* say this is not mistress Dorothy's book then *you* lie", f. 13r, my emphasis); "*I wyll tell yow playne yt ys her boke wetnes of me*" ("*I* will tell *you* plainly it is *her* book, take witness of *me*", my emphasis), "*truyst yt ys her boke And I wyll say so*" ("trust it is *her* book if *I* say so", f. 16r, my emphasis); "*I ham he that wyll bere re corde*" ("*I* am *he* that will bear record", f. 81r, my emphasis). In writing these texts to practise his hand, the writer inscribes an identity within this community: male, literate, familiar with the structure of books and how to discuss them, using the book under the tutelage of a book-owning mistress, and an *I* who shares the book with others who belong to this circle.

Signatures, Colophons, Formulas, and Tags

Alongside ownership inscriptions, scribal signatures sometimes can be identified as practice writing. Texts that announce responsibility for writing in

---

[59] Bale identifies this John Leche as John Leche III, a member of a Cheshire gentry family, b. *c.* 1480, dead by 1553, who was possibly an attorney. According to Bale, Leche also copied some of the material in MS HM 136 (ff. ii v, 83v-86r, 102v-130r). Bale identifies ownership and other signatures related to this Leche family in seven further manuscripts. He notes that the signatures in these books are similar but not identical, suggesting that they may be "by different members of the same family who taught each other to write" (A. BALE, "Late medieval book-owners named John Leche", *Bodleian Library Record* 25.1 (2012), pp. 105-112, quotation at p. 109). This example and explanation for it chime with the argument about copy-texts that I am developing in the present chapter.

134   *Chapter 2*

the manner of scribal signatures occur several times in MS Oxford, Bod. Lib., Digby 86. "*Will[ielmu]s de Vnd[er]hulle scripsit*" (f. 141v) and "*Galfridus Willielmus Robertus de penedok scripsit*" (f. 89v) are not in the hands of the main scribes, however; these formulas must be writing practice. More attempts at "*Will[ielmu]s*" occur on f. 87v. These names are not even necessarily those of the writers; Geoffrey, William, and Robert could not all have written the phrase on f. 89v, for it is in one hand. Copying these naming phrases is a different means of asserting identity made available by imitation pedagogy: by imitating a scribal signature, the learner also imitates the identity of a literate in his community of practice.

What looks like a scribe's signature but is more likely writing practice occurs in fifteenth-century medical / commonplace manuscript MS London, BL, Harley 1735, among the notes of one John Crophill (f. 42v, pencil foliation), on what may have been the blank last leaf of a bifolium devoted to a monthly health regimen. The blank page has been used for writing practice: a prayer in English signed with a rhyming colophon, "*God þ[at] is so foul of meght Saue har[e]* [sic] *solys bothe day [and] neght / Amen be skyel q[uod] Joh[n] Crophyl*" ("God that is so full of might, save our souls both day and night. Amen by skill [amen to that reasonable prayer] quod John Crophill").[60] The prayer and signature occur twice in two different hands, therefore at least one of these instances must be writing practice. A similar rhyming colophon and possible model for these signatures occurs with another item in the book, where it is associated with a poem of which Crophill claims authorship ("*my name Is crephill / I can þis coppe fyell*", f. 49r, my name is Crophill; I can this cup fill, *DIMEV* 1455): "*Be Resoun [and] skyell q[uod] Ioh[n] Crophill*".[61] Further evidence that one or both signature colophons on f. 42v are writing practice is the appearance on the same page (in yet another hand) of the nonsense couplet "*Altaris lassis priuat[ur] decipiendo / Istuc mandragora nescit balare negando*" and its English crib "*Allas Pryde ys mannes bane*", used in grammar pedagogy for practising syllables and their pronunciation.[62] Colophons also provide material for writing practice in *Piers* manuscript MS Oxford, Bod. Lib., Ashmole 1468, where the '*Equore*' pangram occurs with the text, "*Omnibus est notu[m] quod multu[m] diligo*

---

[60] *DIMEV* 1606.

[61] Playful scribal signatures such as this are discussed further in Chapter Three.

[62] For this crib see further in Chapter Three.

Graphic Models 135

potu^{nn}" (part 3, p. 378). The same copy-text also occurs at the end of *Piers Plowman* in MS Huntington Library, HM 137, f. 89v.[63]

Formulas from letter and charter writing are often used as copy-text material for writing practice. Elsewhere in Crophill's manuscript, a fragmentary opening salutation of a letter appears in a top margin ("*Ryght reu^{er}ent And w*", "right reverent and w[orshipful]", Harley 1735, f. 40r), recalling the examples of the same salutation tag found in school-book Harley 1002 and perhaps explaining the particular focus on the majuscule *R* shown in MS London, Society of Antiquaries, 93. The single word "*Right*" occurs on an endleaf in MS Manchester, John Rylands Library, Eng. 895 (f. 125v). In *Brut* manuscript MS Manchester, John Rylands Library, Eng. 105, the opening salutation "*To the right worshipfvll Maior* [mayor] *of this* [...]" appears amidst various ownership inscriptions (f. 2r). On a formerly blank end-leaf in *Canterbury Tales* manuscript, MS Manchester, John Rylands Library, Eng. 113 appears another epistolary formula, "*Ser I co^{m}mende me vnto you*" ("sir, I commend myself to you", f. 195v). A very immature hand has written "*ryght*" ("right") in a spare space on f. 51v in MS Cambridge, UL, Ff.1.6 (the Findern manuscript) and what is possibly the same hand has written "*ryght worshipfull*" ("right worshipful") on f. 79v.

Several attempts at the opening of a will and a charter occur in the upper margins of MS Digby 86, on ff. 39v-40r, in the upper margins.[64] "*Pateat vniu^{er}-sis per presentis*" ("let it be known to all by these presents", ff. 49v- 50r) also occurs in the upper margin, possibly in a different hand, while a similar phrase occurs in another upper margin, "*pateat vniu^{er}sis per pp^{re}sentis* [*sic*] *quod ego*" (f. 76r), again on f. 88r, and more fully on f. 98v, "*Pateat vniu^{er}sis per p^{re}sentis quod ego Rob^{ertus} filius Rob^{ert}i de Penedoch*" while a variation on the formula appears on the opposite page, "*Pateat vniu^{er}sis per p^{re}sentis quod ego Will^{ielmus}*" (f. 99r). What appears to be the same hand then turns to the opening formula of a charter, "*Sciant p^{re}sentes ^{et}futuri quod ego Will^{ielmu}s filius simonis de Vnd^{er}-*

---

[63] Again, Warner notices these examples but not that they are writing practice (WARNER, *The Myth of* Piers Plowman, pp. 55-56, 162 n. 13).

[64] At least one imitative drawing occurs in MS Digby 86: a manicule that points to the head of a woman drawn in red ink on the lower margin of f. 84r has been imitated crudely in brown ink in the lower margin of f. 84v. Noting that the scribe's "occasional drawings" are "frequently labelled with tags", Fein comments that it is "almost as if they are designed for pedagogy in reading Latin" (S.G. FEIN, "Introduction", in: *Interpreting MS Digby 86: A Tri-lingual Book from Thirteenth-Century Worcestershire*, ed. S.G. FEIN (Woodbridge, 2019), pp. 1-9, at p. 1). In my view, the imitations suggest the learning of practical graphic skills and not just reading.

136 *Chapter 2*

hulle" ("know all people present and those to come that I, William, son of Simon Underhill", f. 99v). The same hand writes a variation on this formula in a later upper margin; here, though, "*ego*" is "*Joh^{anne}s d^{omi}n^{u}s de Penedoch*", not William ("*Sciant p^{re}sentes ^{et} futuri quod ego Joh^{anne}s do^{mi}n^{u}s de Penedoch dedi et consessi*", f. 111v). Below this formula the same hand has made another attempt at "*Sciant*" and the *p* in "*p^{re}sentis*", and two attempts at "*quod*". We need not even assume that the writer was named William or John; by imitating these formulas he (or even she) also imitates the identity of members of a multilingual community of literate practice who use writing to strengthen kinship and social bonds.[65] Perhaps an exercise in dictaminal practice also lies behind the phrase "*E Edwardus [sic] dei gracia Rex anglie*" (191v, upper margin) with its two attempts at a fancy majuscule *E*.

In Wycliffite Bible manuscript, MS Manchester, John Rylands Library, Eng. 78, the opening formula of a charter appears in the lower margin upside down: "*Vnto all trw cristyan^{e} peple to whome thes p^{re}sente dede Indentyd*" ("unto all true Christian people to whome these present indented deeds", f. 57r), while a shorter and messier version of the same phrase, probably in the same hand, occurs in a similar position on f. 95v and a longer version occurs in the left margin at right-angles to the main text on f. 93v. What could be a fragment of a salutation formula occurs, perhaps in the same hand, upside down on f. 132v, "*my lorde byschep of baathe and welle[s]*" ("my lord bishop of Bath and Wells") and a similar salutation to the same bishop occurs on f. 133r and again on f. 156v, vertically in the left margin. More copy-text phrases drawn from dictaminal practice occur in the left margin of f. 160v (for example, "*trustyng that ye merye and in good hellth*", "trusting that you are happy and well") and on f. 171v "*moste welbelouyd*", "most well-beloved". From these examples we may deduce that dictaminal and diplomatic formulas provided copy-texts for writing practice. While the learner may not have been aspiring to be a professional scribe, this exercise in imitation also modelled literate identities of those who used writing for social and legal purposes within their communities of practice.

Prayer tags are another common subject for writing practice. The prayer *Jesus mercy* that appears in the top margins of school-text MS London, BL,

---

[65] By contrast, Hines and Julian-Jones describe this material as "pen-trials" and attribute them to the people named (J. HINES and M. JULIAN-JONES, "Below Malvern: MS Digby 86, the Grimhills and the Underhills and their regional and social context", in: *Interpreting MS Digby 86*, pp. 255-273, at p. 256).

Graphic Models 137

Addit. 19046, also appears in the primer MS Oxford, Bod. Lib., Rawl. C. 209 ("*Ihesu m^{er}cy*", "Jesus, mercy", f. 2r, top margin). On a flyleaf in the primer MS John Rylands Library, Eng. 85, f. iv v, the *Ave Maria* is copied in a messy cursive hand. This writer could be the same as the one who tries out the letter-forms. As on f. 46v, here are single compartment *a* and double *f*. The writer again uses a repertoire of spellings and letters different from those in the text. He or she prefers *th* to thorn, and adds final -*e* liberally ("*lorde*", "lord"; "*fruyte*", "fruit"). There is no attempt to imitate the neat Textura bookhand of the main text. It is possible that the presence of the basic primer text of the *Ave Maria* prompted the writer's own attempt at writing the prayer in English. Perhaps the writer has been prompted by the primer to rehearse a writing exercise as well as some letter-forms. The choice of copy-text for the practice writing perhaps demonstrates the close association of piety with graphic performance in the literacy socialisation of the writer. On a rear flyleaf in MS John Rylands Library, Eng. 85, "*Ih^{es}us mary a amen* [*sic*]" ("Jesus, Mary, amen") occurs twice with variations and several attempts at writing the letter *a* (f. 82v). An ornate 'amen' composed of fancy majuscules separated by red and brown minims so that it fills the line serves as the first line of the colophon to the *Prick of Conscience* in MS Manchester, John Rylands Library, Eng. 50. A wobbly hand has made two attempts to imitate the *A* and one to imitate the *M* (p. 204). In MS John Rylands Library, Eng. 78, "*the lord haue me*[*rc*]*ye*" appears on a top margin ("the Lord have mercy", f. 47v), the final word being rather bodged and unclear. More poorly formed attempts at a pious phrase, "[illegible] *the lord god god In the lord* [struck through] [illegible] *god god*", appear on f. 154r, while "*god knowythe all thyngis moste*" ("God knows all things in the highest degree") occurs in the top margin of f. 159r, possibly in the same hand.

Biblical tags also offer copy-texts for writing practice. In MS Digby 86, the biblical tag "*amen dico uobis sup^{er omni}a bona sua*" (Matt. 24:47) occurs in the upper margin of f. 180v, the usual place for writing exercises in this codex. An imprint of the line appears on the opposite page, suggesting that the writer closed the book in haste, being too inexperienced or hasty (or both) in writing in ink to avoid making blots. The same phrase occurs in the upper margin of f. 193v, in an even less assured hand. Below, the same hand has written, very uncertainly, the opening of Psalm 8, "*D^{omi}ne d^{omin}us n^{oste}r quam admirabile est Nomeⁿ tuv^m in universa t^{er}ra*": there is an otiose mark of abbreviation over "*est*", the opening majuscule of "*Nomen*" is poorly formed and drops below the

138   *Chapter 2*

line of the other letters, and the opening minims of "*universa*" are a zigzag. Another, truncated attempt at this phrase occurs on the opposite page (f. 194r) along with the name "*Robertus*". In *Piers Plowman* manuscript MS Ashmole 1468 this phrase also occurs in the context of writing practice: here three attempts at the word 'amen' are associated with the biblical line "*amen dico uobis*" (part 3, p. 378).

Discussion

In this section we have seen that Latin literacy training and socialisation processes were transferred and adapted for the acquisition of literacy in communities of Anglophone literate practice. The process of imitating graphic models which is so central to Latin literacy training and socialisation is replicated informally in these contexts. Learners make use of informal models and copy-texts to assist their recognition and production of letter and word shapes. Many of the exercises associated with imitation pedagogy – replication of letter-forms, alphabets, pangrams – would have been immediately or at least fairly easily adaptable to reading and writing English. Replication of Latin copy-texts would also have promoted literacy skills applicable to English, while in some cases the models and copy-texts themselves are written in English. Traces of this informal process are ubiquitous: writing practice is to be found in many genres of books valued by given communities and we have seen that imitation pedagogy frames much post-production writing in vernacular literary manuscripts. Writers adapt the exercises associated with school-books in a wide variety of contexts, often using vernacular books as *ad hoc* models and sources of copy-texts and opportunities for imitative writing practice. The traces of this activity have often gone unrecognised, concealed under classifications such as pen-trial, colophon, ownership inscription, signature, and biblical and prayer tags. When they imitated graphic models they also imitated literate identities, expressing belonging and difference within their diverse communities of Anglophone literate practice. Many of the learners' hands found in vernacular literary manuscripts are too unformed for dating with any kind of precision. All that can be said is that they obviously post-date the production of the manuscripts in which they appear. Nonetheless, some of this material is datable and it is clear from the varieties of script used by learners

Graphic Models 139

that vernacular literary manuscripts continued to be used as sites for imitation exercises for a long time.

Pattern Books

We now turn to other evidence for imitative pedagogy among communities of Anglophone literate practice: model or pattern books. While vernacular manuscript books were used as informal, *ad hoc* models and opportunities for writing practice, pattern books are formal models used by those with more ambitious calligraphic aspirations. The late medieval pattern book typically provided alphabets in majuscule and minuscule in various scripts, and examples of graphs in use in words and longer texts. Continental examples of pattern books are known, some of them supporting writing in vernaculars. Several examples of English provenance have been recognised as pattern books, though they have not previously been discussed as a group. This section will assemble seven extant examples, demonstrate the evidence for the use of pattern books as models for writing English as well as Latin, and investigate their use in particular communities of Anglophone literate practice.

According to Steinberg, increasing demand in the later medieval period from those involved in business for tuition in writing led to the emergence of itinerant writing-masters who taught both document hands and book-hands.[66] Steinberg assembled evidence from France, Italy, and the German-speaking lands – handbooks on writing, advertisements, and model books with specimen scripts – showing that the itinerant writing-master who could teach calligraphic writing in Latin and the vernacular must have been a common feature of fifteenth- and sixteenth-century society. Steinberg's evidence includes a sheet that displays varieties of scripts from early fifteenth-century Saxony.[67] Steinberg showed that this sheet was an advertisement of a writing-master, Johan vom Hagen.[68] Even more clearly intended as a model is the pattern book of

---

[66] S.H. STEINBERG, "Medieval writing-masters", *The Library* 22 (1941), pp. 1-24.

[67] MS Berlin, Staatsbibliothek Preussischer Kulturbesitz, lat. fol. 384, verso, reproduced in A. DEROLEZ, *The Palaeography of Gothic Manuscript Books*, plate 17.

[68] For a recent find (of fifteenth-century German provenance), see P. KIDD, "An unpublished medieval scribe's advertisement sheet" (10 January 2015), <https://mssprovenance.blogspot.co.uk/2015/01/an-unpublished-medieval-scribes.html>. M. SMITH, "Writing models and the formation of national scripts", unpublished First Lyell Lecture in the 2020 Series, University of Oxford, Bod. Lib., <http://podcasts.ox.ac.uk/writing-models-and-formation-national-scripts>,

140   *Chapter 2*

Gregorius Bock, of *c.* 1510-1517. On the first page after the introductory page, the letters *a-z* are broken down into their component strokes and the correct sequence for making them is indicated.[69] The fifteenth-century *Liber de arte scripturali* by Robert of Nantes is also clearly a training model. Each letter of the alphabet in turn is modelled with a fancy flourished capital, followed by text (largely liturgical in content) in named minuscule scripts such as "*Lettre Curialle*", and "*Lettre bastarde*".[70] Some of the initials are decorated with finely modelled grotesque human heads. Each letter is devoted several pages until the alphabet ends (f. 50r). Then follow recommendations of Robert and his curriculum in the arts of writing in brief Latin and French prose texts (ff. 50v-51r). Steinberg declared that there must have been writing-masters in England but he had not found any of the usual evidence for them and no English example of a pattern book appears in his list of sources.[71]

Our first two examples of pattern books of English provenance demonstrate their use in England though not their applications in communities of Anglophone literate practice. Surviving in fragments, MS Oxford, Bod. Lib., e. mus. 198 appears to be an early fourteenth-century model for Latin liturgical scripts from Oxford that was probably a scribe's advertisement or specimens of a specialised writing-master.[72] MS Cambridge, Magdalene College, Pepys 2981, a fragment of five heavily-cropped leaves that now measure 13.5 cm high x 10.5 cm wide, contains the criss-cross row preceded by a showy *IHC* monogram whose letters are pierced by a spear, a vinegar sponge on a pole, and three nails (f. 1r).[73] On other pages in the fragment occur showy Textura minuscules (f. 1v) and majuscules (f. 2r). Four pages display an alphabet of penwork initials arranged on bar borders (ff. 2v-4r). Wolpe suggests that the fragment is "probably of English provenance" and dates it *c.* 1400; comparing the alphabets with those in primers, he proposes that the fragment is "either the remainder of, or a scribe's copy-book for, such a primer".[74] But the material

surveys much of the known material.

[69] MS New Haven, Yale University, Beinecke Library, 439, ff. 1v-2r.

[70] MS Paris, BnF, lat. 8685, for example, ff. 8r, 9r, 10r.

[71] STEINBERG, "Medieval writing-masters", pp. 2-3; S.H. STEINBERG, "A hand-list of specimens of medieval writing-masters", *The Library* 23 (1942), pp. 191-194.

[72] F. 8v. S.J.P. VAN DIJK, "An advertisement sheet of an early fourteenth-century writing master at Oxford", *Scriptorium* 1 (1956), pp. 47-64.

[73] For reproductions see B. WOLPE, "Florilegium alphabeticum", in: *Calligraphy and Palaeography: Essays Presented to Alfred Fairbank on his 70th Birthday*, ed. O.S. OSLEY (London, 1965), pp. 69-75, and plates 22-25.

[74] WOLPE, "Florilegium alphabeticum", p. 72.

Graphic Models   141

makes better sense as training resources for a scribe. Whereas alphabets in primers generally are restricted to a single criss-cross row, this booklet has four alphabets in different script- styles and the practice word "*honorificabilitudini-tatibus*".[75] Four of the pages bear an alphabet of pen-work initials with letter labels, though these are not accurately positioned, for example, the initial *K* occurs on a different page from the label *K* (ff. 3r, 4v). The page with the labels criss-cross to *D* contains the initials *A* to *E* but no cross. Possibly the labels were written first with gaps between for the insertion of the pen-work initials by a learner. Having supplied *A* in the space for the criss-cross, the scribe therefore positioned every initial thereafter on this page one place too early, meaning that *E* was displayed where *D* should have been, and so on. This evidence suggests that the leaves are from a working 'exercise' book. Possibly the labels were written first as an exercise and the scribe struggled to fit the required pen-work initials in the spaces provided. In addition, outlines for painted initials *A*, *B*, and *C* with sprigs and cusped grounds occur (f. 4v). A start has been made on filling the initials: parts of daisies on the *C* and the acorns on the *B* have been coloured. Furthermore, there is evidence that this was material used as a model: practice *A*, *B*, and *D* occur on a page with model capitals. The outline for the painted initial *C* has been copied again rather roughly in ink (f. 5r), Unfortunately that last page is pasted down (the item survives in a calligraphy scrap book) but further practice graphs and words show through the vellum (f. 5v). The alphabet lacks thorn and yogh, and *z* has no 3-shaped allograph. We have seen that this alphabet occurs widely in English-language reading and writing environments so the possibility that the scribe was learning to write English as well as Latin cannot be ruled out, but there is no positive evidence for this.

A model book that is definitely associated with a community of Anglophone literate practice occurs in MS Oxford, Bod. Lib., Ashmole 789. What I am identifying as a pattern book in this manuscript is in a quire that is now bound into the front of the codex (ff. 1r-5v).[76] MS Ashmole 789 is a composite

---

[75] Perhaps chosen because '*honorificabilitudinitatibus*' was thought to be the longest Latin word (*DMLBS, honorificabilitudinitas*).

[76] This quire in MS Ashmole 789 has not previously been identified explicitly as a pattern book used in a community of Anglophone literate practice. Eldredge describes the two Middle English *epistles* in the codex as "perhaps models", implying that it is a formulary, but making no comment on its calligraphic purpose (see the entry in L.M. ELDREDGE, *Index of Middle English Prose, Handlist IX: Manuscripts in the Ashmole Collection, Bodleian Library, Oxford* (Cambridge, 2007). The Bodleian Library online collection catalogue describes f. 4v as a "notarial ex-

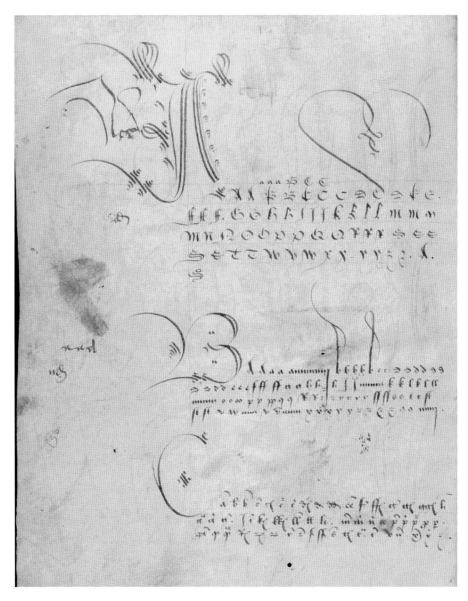

Fig. 10. Page from a model writing book, MS Oxford, Bod. Lib., Ashmole 789, f. 4v. Photo: © Bodleian Libraries, University of Oxford. Creative Commons licence CC-BY-NC 4.0.

Graphic Models 143

manuscript of materials known, from a note on the first leaf, to have been collected by a bishop of Hereford in the sixteenth century. The note expresses a wish that the volume remain in the Registry at Hereford. This note relates to Charles Booth, Bishop of Hereford from 1516. The main item in this manuscript is a formulary associated with Bishop Thomas Bekynton († 1465), secretary to Humphrey Duke of Gloucester, that includes correspondence related to Reginald Pecock.[77] The quire is not itself part of the formulary, though: it is clearly distinct, codicologically, from the rest of the volume. It is the only part of the volume that is on parchment apart from ff. 360-end and a stray leaf earlier. Also, its dimensions are smaller than those of the rest of the manuscript. The note about Hereford is written on the first leaf (recto) of this quire. The final leaf carries a poem in a different hand and the verso is blank. Possibly originally this was a quire of two bifolia protected by a blank outer bifolium.

The MS Ashmole 789 pattern book includes specimen letters in *lettre bâtarde* script, for example alphabetised names from *A* to *Z* (ff. 3v-4r). On f. 2v is a sentence in which each word begins with a different letter of the alphabet, in alphabetical order. This is presumably an expanded pangram, a text designed to provide opportunities for practising the formation of each letter in initial position in a given script. On f. 4v are found various alphabets (see Figure 10). These alphabets include majuscules and minuscules, forms for abbreviations, double letters, alternative forms of *r*, *s*, and so on. Some of the graphs are repeated but they are not allographs. This suggests that these alphabets may be practice work.

Writing in the margins on this and several other pages shows other attempts to imitate the models, for example, letters have been written above the alphabet lines on f. 4v (these may be alternative forms added later). The alphabets include no separately-distinguished non-Roman letters. However, the entire book was obviously intended for the use of writers of Latin *and* English since the specimen texts include material in both languages, for example brief formal epistles addressed to illustrious recipients (ff. 1v-2r). Evidence that at least one user was a writer of English is provided by the practice word "*and*" in the margin beside the practice alphabets, and above them the word "*Trust-*

---

ercise" and the online catalogue refers to the material as "writing exercises"; cf. "*Exercitia Notarialia*", in the Ashmole Catalogue. Smith discusses the manuscript in relation to continental examples in his first Lyell Lecture (SMITH, "Writing models and the formation of national scripts").

[77] W. SCASE, *Reginald Pecock* (Aldershot, 1996: *Authors of the Middle Ages* 8), pp. 112, n. 239, 132-140.

144   *Chapter 2*

[...]" has been partially erased (f. 4v). The main hand has been identified as "perhaps" that of Ricardus Franciscus, exponent of fine *lettre bâtarde* script at this date.[78] However, we have no evidence that Ricardus – whom we encountered in Chapter One – worked as a writing-master. The quire does however provide evidence that by the mid or later fifteenth century alphabetic specimen books had appeared in England and that the form had been adapted to support fine calligraphic writing in English. It is established by the note on the first page that by the early sixteenth century this example had found its way to the Registry of the Bishop of Hereford and that it was there collected up with model letters of correspondence, but indications of its earlier provenance, of the community or communities of practice in which it attracted imitative writing, are unfortunately lacking.

Fuller evidence for pattern books and their use in an identifiable community of Anglophone literate practice occurs in MS Oxford, Bod. Lib., Lat. Misc. c. 66, also known both as the Commonplace Book of Humphrey Newton (1466-1536) and as the Capesthorne manuscript. Newton was a member of a prominent Cheshire gentry family.[79] MS Lat. Misc. c. 66 is a composite manuscript that contains items of various sizes, shapes, and genres including genealogical, legal, medical, religious, and literary material, some of it signed by Newton himself as scribe. Some of the material is on single sheets or individual quires and it may not have originally been bound up together: MS Lat. Misc. c. 66 is perhaps better thought of as a collection rather than a codex.

Among the resources in Humphrey Newton's collection are several alphabetic pattern books. The presence of these materials has been noted before but

---

[78] O. PÄCHT and J.G. ALEXANDER, *Illuminated Manuscripts in the Bodleian Library, Oxford*, 4 vols. (Oxford, 1966-1974), 1, p. 57; cf. M. DRIVER, "'*Me fault faire*': French makers of manuscripts for English patrons", in: *Language and Culture in Medieval Britain: The French of England c. 1100-c. 1500*, ed. J. WOGAN-BROWNE with C. COLLETTE, M. KOWALESKI, L.R. MOONEY, A. PUTTER, and D. TROTTER (York, 2009), pp. 420-443.

[79] For Humphrey and his family see D. YOUNGS, *Humphrey Newton (1466-1536): An Early Tudor Gentleman* (Woodbridge, 2008). The manuscript has been viewed as typifying the cultural interests of an unsophisticated late medieval provincial gentleman. Rossell Hope Robbins, editor of the Middle English lyrics in the manuscript, argues that the volume is important as a source of evidence for Cheshire dialect and is in many ways typical of the interests of a late medieval provincial gentleman something of whose life is known (R.H. ROBBINS, "The poems of Humfrey Newton, Esquire, 1466-1536", *Proceedings of the Modern Language Association* 65.2 (1950), pp. 249-281, at p. 249). In his detailed examination of the codicology and contents of the manuscript, Ralph Hanna concludes that "the impulse for producing this book should be placed somewhere between the pedestrian and the perverse" (R. HANNA, "Humphrey Newton and Bodleian Library MS Lat. Misc. c. 66", *Medium Aevum* 69.2 (2000), pp. 279-291, at p. 289).

Graphic Models

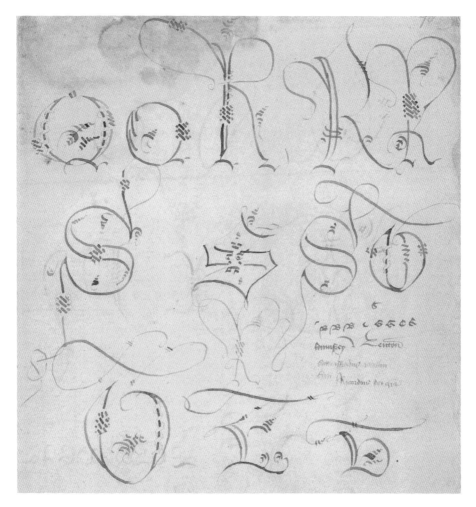

Fig. 11. Practice writing based on models in Humphrey Newton's manuscript, MS Oxford, Bod. Lib., Lat. Misc. c. 66, f. 98r. Photo: © Bodleian Libraries, University of Oxford. Creative Commons licence CC-BY-NC 4.0.

their significance and the relationships of the various sets of models have not been discussed.[80] One item is a fine pattern book containing model letters of

---

[80] ROBBINS, "The poems of Humfrey Newton", p. 257; HANNA, "Humphrey Newton", p. 284.

146   *Chapter 2*

the alphabet.[81] It also includes model documents with fine flourished lettering. Now ff. 112-121, this pattern book is the only component on vellum in the collection and this property, together with the expertise of the hand, suggests that it was a distinct item used as a resource by Newton but not created by him.[82] Evidence for Newton's response to this resource comes from his entry for it in his table of contents for part of the manuscript, "*De exemplis scribendi p*^{ro} *sc*^{ri}*ptore*" (f. 92r).[83] But Humphrey did not just note the presence of the pattern book ("*de exemplis scribendi*"); he engaged with it, making further pattern-book sets on paper which appear to have used the vellum item as a model.[84] F. 114v of the vellum pattern book, for example, is replicated by Humphrey on f. 98r, a page on which his signature appears twice (see Figure 11). There are many other alphabets and practice letters. A tiny alphabet appears in the left margin of f. 93r, along with draft poetry by Humphrey. A fragmentary alphabet (*a* to *h*) where each letter has been written at least twice appears on f. 100r, where an alphabet row of practice fancy majuscules also appears. Among the practice letters in the manuscript, *h* is particularly common; no doubt Humphrey's name is the cause of this (for example, ff. 95v, 100r); "*Humphrey*" and "*Humphrey Newton*" appear many times in various scripts and spellings and in both Latinised and Anglicised forms (for example, ff. 92r, 98r, 99r, 122r). Various forms of *g* are explored in repetitions of the word "*gracia*" on f. 92r, while many forms of complex *w* appear on f. 117r, along with many alphabets and syllables, "*ba be bo*", for example.

Many pages in the collection bear writing practice in the form of repeated copy-texts. For example, the opening words of a salutation for a letter, "*Right*

---

[81]   The presence of a *figura* that resembles thorn as an allograph of *y* and of two shapes for *z* suggests that thorn has merged conceptually with *y* and yogh has fallen together with zed (f. 114v).

[82]   The Digital Bodleian catalogue describes this quire as "[i]nserted parchment booklet (ff. 112r-121v) of calligraphic samples (fancy alphabets, specimens of documentary hands, etc.) by a late 15th-century English professional writing-master" (BODLEIAN LIBRARY, *Digital Bodleian* (2020), <https://digital.bodleian.ox.ac.uk/>).

[83]   The table of contents is written in a careful and showy Secretary hand which is very probably Humphrey's; if it is not, he certainly used the page, as is evidenced by his signatures and other copy-texts written in his hand in the margins. I am grateful to Bodleian Library Special Collections staff for providing mediated copying of this page.

[84]   The Bodleian online catalogue notes "ornamental letters and beginnings of petitions, copied by H. Newton from the models written on parchment" (BODLEIAN LIBRARY, *Medieval Manuscripts in Oxford Libraries* (2017-), <https://medieval.bodleian.ox.ac.uk/>), but Robbins, Hanna, and Youngs do not discuss these relationships. The manuscript has been rebound in separate fascicules making it difficult to ascertain the original codicological relationships of the parts.

Graphic Models 147

worshipfull", occur several times with alphabets on f. 100r, sometimes just in the form of "*Right*" or even just *R*. Numerous attempts at an elaborate majuscule *R* appear on f. 92r, apparently modelled after two of the three models in the pattern book (f. 98r, see Figure 11). The opening formula of a charter appears at least eight times in Latin on f. 92r, "*Nou^{er}unt vniu^{er}si per p^{re}sentes*", and three times in English, "*be it knowen to alle*"; the same English phrase is copied twice on f. 99r and the Latin on f. 100r. The opening of an indenture document appears twice on f. 94v, the longest version reading, "*This indenture made the fou*[...]". Also on this page appear two attempts at another opening formula of a charter, "*Pateat pateat* [sic] *uniu^{er}si* [sic] *p^{er} present^{is}*". A political maxim, "*decet regem reg^{er}e legem*" ("it is fitting that the king administers the law") appears on ff. 92r (twice) and 100r. Other tags include "*Iudica nemo*" (?; "judge [yourself], no-one [will judge you]") and "*herkens now alle that*" ("listen now all that", f. 92r, twice).[85] Humphrey signs some of the material he has copied with conventional scribal colophons, for example, "*Qui sc^{ri}pcit carmen Humffridus est sibi nomen*" ("he that wrote this verse, Humphrey is his name", f. 98v), "*Explicit liber quod Humfrey*" ("here ends the book quod Humphrey", ff. 106r, 122v), "*Explicit* Fabula de Philomena *Humfrey Newton*" ("here ends *The Story of Philomena* [copied by] Humphrey Newton", f. 11r), and "*nomen scripto^{ris}* [sic] *H*" ("the name of the scribe is H", f. 112r). This last example of a scribal colophon is clearly a copy-text since it is not appended to any work copied by Humphrey. Earlier, we identified as writing practice micro-texts of all of these kinds in school-texts and in the margins and on the flyleaves of manuscripts associated with communities of Anglophone literate practice. Humphrey supplements these imitative copying exercises with his engagement with a pattern book.

Many features of Humphrey's work could be considered experimentation with graphic resources: with line and form.[86] Drifts of pen-work foliage and

---

[85] For the last tag, compare "*Now herken, all that be here*", in the early sixteenth-century morality play *Everyman*, in Everyman's address to Knowledge, Good Deeds, Beauty, Strength, Discretion, and the Five Wits, as he prepares to outline his testament (*Everyman and Medieval Miracle Plays*, ed. A.C. CAWLEY (London, 1974), p. 227, line 696). Some of the early prints of the play include a woodcut of Everyman and Death where the latter is represented as a skeleton (e.g., frontispiece, STC (2nd edn.) 10606), however Newton's line drawing of a skeleton on this page does not resemble the woodcut in any specifics.

[86] This broader graphic aspect of the manuscript has not been much discussed. Deborah Youngs offers the opinion that Humphrey's scribal aspirations ran ahead of his achievements: he "was prone to doodling", was "attracted to the use of colour", and "recorded and practised the skills" needed to create a more polished manuscript than that he actually achieved (YOUNGS, *Humphrey Newton*, p. 189).

Fig. 12. Practice writing and drawing in Humphrey Newton's manuscript, MS Oxford, Bod. Lib., Lat. Misc. c. 66, f. 95v. Photo: © Bodleian Libraries, University of Oxford. Creative Commons licence CC-BY-NC 4.0.

Graphic Models 149

entwined letters occur on f. 122r. A page of prayers is illustrated with a lurid image that depicts Christ's wounded heart (f. 129v). A pastiche of a *Gawain*-like poem (*DIMEV* 4262) begins with an outsized historiated initial *O* that features, incongruously, Veronica displaying her veil (f. 106v). A striking example of experimentation with lines and letters is a quatrain about a bird of paradise (*DIMEV* 3584) that is enclosed in a kind of speech bubble beside a sketch of the bird that is labelled "*papeiaye*" ("parrot", f. 95v, see Figure 12). The strokes used to depict the bird and the leaves and branches of the tree in which it sits echo those used to make the letters in the speech bubble. The descender on *q* in "*qwene*", for example, is similar to the stroke used to describe the left edges of the leaves, while three of the leaves on the lower right of the trunk are described with an enlarged *m* such as that in "*am*". The curving mark that demarcates the left of the upper trunk is like that of the *I* in the last line of the stanza. And the effect works reciprocally, so the writing of the poem suggests yet more leaves, and the leaves suggest writing. The scribe is deploying the conventional marks of graphs in a creative, ludic fashion. Further down on the same page, Humphrey tries out the strokes in series for depicting facial features and hair braiding (Figure 12). Humphrey here engages with a kind of 'ductus' of the human face. It appears that a face in three-quarter profile that looks towards the left may begin with a descender that curves to the left and then the right to describe the eyebrow and nose, then a bowl is added to describe the eye, and then a descending stroke that finishes with an abrupt upwards curve is added to describe the furthest edge of the face, chin and neck. On the same page, where Humphrey experiments with the trace of *h*, he deploys a similar stroke to that used for the far edge of the face. On f. 92r he draws a full-length figure of an astronomer who holds a book in a bag in his right hand and a portable astrolabe in his left. The draping of the hem of the astronomer's garment is suggested with curves and straight lines similar to those used for the extravagant majuscule *R* forms on the same page, while more attempts at drapery also appear. Opposite the astronomer a skeleton grins, the bones of his limbs and digits recalling the spilt first strokes of the *R* majuscules, and his vertcbrae resembling the cadels on the extravagant ascenders that rise from a Middle English model petition (f. 107a).[87]

---

[87] For reflections on the tension between the line as component of a letter and the line as figural, see J.-F. LYOTARD, *Discourse, Figure*, ed. and trans. J. MOWITT and A. HUDEK (Minneapolis, 2010): "It [the "plastic object", i.e. a graphic trace] can be either letter or line. The letter is the support of a conventional, immaterial signification, identical in every respect to the presence of the line and the letter phoneme. Moreover, the support disappears behind what it

150   *Chapter 2*

Humphrey Newton's pattern book is very reminiscent of the one in MS Oxford, Bod. Lib., Ashmole 789, but in this case we have more evidence for the community of practice in which it was used. The materials in the manuscript appear to be in many hands and, while it seems that Humphrey was capable of writing several scripts with different letter-forms and grades of formality, some apparently responding to his models, and while the material in professional hands, such as the pattern book, was almost certainly sourced from outside the household, some of the hands most probably are those of other members of his household and wider community of literate practice. On f. 8v, for example, a later hand has added some memoranda in an empty space above where Humphrey has drawn a diagram with notes concerning how a harp should be strung. Recipes on ff. 89r to 90v are in Humphrey's and a later hand. The hand of the French material on f. 101v may not be Humphrey's. The presence of several hands suggests that others identified with his graphic enterprises, continuing to use the resources he had compiled and to add to them. Other materials in Humphrey's manuscript give us an insight into the community of Anglophone literate practice to which Humphrey belonged and suggest how their creation was related to and resourced social links and relationships. The manuscript includes draft love poems, some marked "*mittit^{ur}*" ("it is sent", for example, f. 92v), that is, presumably, actually sent to someone in fair copies, acrostics on family names, and engagement with the arts and language of heraldry with relevance to the Newton family.[88] For Humphrey and his community of Anglophone literate practice, writing is a mode of social exchange with household and family, bearing local, identity-forming and boundary-erecting meanings.

upholds, since the letter occasions only instantaneous recognition, in the service of signification" (pp. 205-206). While Lyotard approaches the subject from the perspective of postmodern cultural theory, a fuzziness between letters and drawing is also associated with literacy studies by Garipzanov who notes "a new academic awareness of a thin and somewhat blurry line between script / text and visual image", which he traces to early twentieth-century work in visual literacy (I. GARIPZANOV, "Introduction", in: *Graphic Signs of Identity, Faith, and Power in Late Antiquity and the Early Middle Ages*, ed. I. GARIPZANOV, C. GOODSON, and H. MAGUIRE (Turnhout, 2017), pp. 1-22, at p. 6). Published in the same year as Lyotard's study was Nicolete Gray's *Lettering as Drawing*, an exploration of script in the terms of drawing analysis such as line weight, direction, speed of execution, and shape (N. GRAY, *Lettering as Drawing* (London, 1971))

[88] On Humphrey's interest in heraldry see further W. SCASE, "Parrot poet: Humphrey Newton and Bodleian Library, MS Lat. Misc. c. 66", in: *Medieval Literary Voices: Embodiment, Materiality and Performance, Essays in Honour of David A. Lawton*, ed. S. RÍKHARÐSDÓTTIR and L. D'ARCENS (Manchester, forthcoming), pp. 172-190. For his acrostics see Chapter Three and for his *ABC of Aristotle* see Chapter Four.

Graphic Models 151

Humphrey Newton's interest in letters *and* drawings aligns his work with three very fine late medieval figurative pattern books of English provenance and it seems likely that he numbered material such as these among his resources, albeit most probably humbler specimens. MS Cambridge, Magdalene College, Pepys 1916 is a pattern-book of drawings, many of them coloured, with some calligraphic lettering (an *IHC* monogram and a crowned *M* accompany a drawing of the Virgin and Child and some architectural designs (f. 22r); another Virgin with Child is labelled "*santa maria*" in a careful display hand (f. 6r). The provenance of the volume is unknown, but some of the creatures are labelled in English in a hand of the fourteenth or fifteenth century (for example, "*a hors*", "*talbott*", "*con^{n}e*", "*a catte*" ("a horse", "dog", "coney", "cat", f. 9v); "*Iay*" ("jay", f. 10r), "*boterfly*", "*partriche*", and "*woodecoke*" ("butterfly", "partridge", "woodcock", f. 10v); and "*malard*" ("mallard", f. 11r)), suggesting that use of the volume and at least some stages of production occurred in later medieval England. Newton's female faces look like crude attempts to produce something like the profile face of the Virgin in the same volume (f. 21r) or the faintly-traced male faces on f. 20v, or the naked female figure on f. 16v whose face is in profile and whose unbraided hair tumbles behind her shoulders (a faintly-traced item that may be a spindle in the woman's left hand may suggest a user's identification of her as Eve). Newton's bird of paradise drawing and its label "*papeiaye*" recall the numerous bird drawings and labels in Pepys 1916.

Focusing on "sketchbooks", Scheller argues that drawings were made by artists by copying from earlier works to compile a repertoire of resources for future use; "incorporated in a compositional structure", books of drawings served as "reservoirs of ideas for all branches of art".[89] The drawings in Pepys 1916 are in a range of styles and degrees of proficiency, suggesting that it may be a compilation of material gathered from various sources. Less proficient practice drawings in Pepys 1916 respond to its more proficient content (for example, the profile face of a centaur is repeated in smaller and cruder form on f. 2r; the "*Talbotte*" on f. 22v is less easily identifiable than the "*talbott*" who follows a scent on f. 9v). They and Newton's drawings suggest this kind of usage pattern of collecting models and imitating them attentively and creatively. Creativity is reflected not only in the variations in the copies but their placing on the page. For example, f. 19v is a riotous page of animals and human figures wittily positioned in relation to one another: a fox catches a hen,

---

[89] R.W. SCHELLER, *A Survey of Medieval Model Books* (Haarlem, 1963), p. 3.

152 *Chapter 2*

a lion pounces on a small quadruped beside a squirrel that eats a nut; a horse bucks over a dog, nearly unseating its naked rider, and a dog licks its back paw.

In some ways also comparable with Humphrey Newton's imitative experiments are the decorated alphabets and associated materials in MS London, BL, Sloane 1448A, an English pattern book of the second or third quarter of the fifteenth century.[90] Both Newton's and this book demonstrate that alphabetical models, decorative models, and figurative models were collected together, providing further evidence that some individuals compiled all of these kinds of resource for use in their own graphic work.[91] The surviving leaves of Sloane 1448A bear a variety of experiments with initial letters. Various kinds of initials appear here, some free-standing and some integrated into borders. Some initials are unfinished. None has received paint, though some have been inked over (e.g., f. 27v) and one feature, a rose in the middle of an initial *L*, appears to have been pricked for use as a model (f. 11r). Backhouse suggests that "the Sloane sketches appear to represent a stage in a particular individual's creative process".[92] Notably, one of the alphabets, in which letters are formed from human and animal figures in various poses (ff. 25r-26v), appears to be earlier than the mid-fifteenth century date for most of the material and it may be model material collected by the user.[93] The letters evidence an overlap between the formation of letters and drawing. All depict fantastical scenes, for example *L* is formed from a standing female figure and a seated figure whom she holds on a lead that is attached to a collar around its neck. Perhaps this figure is meant to represent a pet monkey (f. 25v). Somewhat comparable is a pattern book of *c.* 1400 that is associated with MS Bergamo, Biblioteca Civica, cod. Δ VII.14. Sewn into the volume appears an "anthropomorphic alphabet" of Textura letters whose strokes are formed from intertwined images of animals and humans.[94]

The figures in Sloane 1448A display features that suggest experimental engagement on behalf of their copyist or copyists. For example, from the head of the 'monkey' protrudes a branching structure that is crudely drawn in darker

[90] Images, date, and provenance from the British Library Illuminated Manuscripts online catalogue.

[91] Five of the items in Scheller's catalogue of medieval model books include alphabets (SCHELLER, *A Survey of Medieval Model Books*, p. 154, n. 21).

[92] J. BACKHOUSE, "An illuminator's sketchbook", *The British Library Journal* 1.1 (1975), pp. 3-14, at p. 12.

[93] BACKHOUSE, "An illuminator's sketchbook", p. 12.

[94] See SCHELLER, *A Survey of Medieval Model Books*, p. 149 and fig. 109.

Graphic Models 153

ink, while the letters are crowded on the page, overlapping one another in places. A similar structure appears in the margin of f. 29v, and a similar but much more complex branching structure appears in the space surrounded by a model *D* initial and full border (f. 18v). Elaborate intersecting loops appear in the middle of an *A* model border (f. 3v), the originally blank centre of the *A* having been filled with hatching in a darker ink. Similar exuberant looping decorates the signature of Robert Johnson (27v), while elsewhere it becomes a top horizontal for an initial *T* where it doubles as an extravagant graphic headdress for the fantastical profile head that inhabits the initial (f. 26v). Indeed, amusing pictures and scraps of writing intrude frequently. A model for *T* with a full border has been ruled and inscribed and signed by one Young (f. 29v). A blank leaf bears an image of two figures in dress that is perhaps of the sixteenth century. One figure, drawn in red ink, bears a square object inscribed with the letter *s* and is labelled "*superbia*"; a gallant, labelled "*amator illius*" holds (?) her hand ("her lover", f. 13v). Another gallant figure, oriented upside down on a page with a model *D*, labelled "*iuuentus*" and "*youthe*" ("youth"), appears to incorporate earlier foliate underdrawing, while a riderless saddled horse stands on the inverted base of the initial *D*, his tail extending from the foliage of the serif (f. 17r). Above the horse appear two lines of verse about a schoolboy's motivation to study, "*currere cogit equu^m sub milite calcar acutu^m, Sic pueru^m studio virga vacare suo*", apparently a copy-text extract from a collection of proverbs and sayings ("the sharp spur drives the horse beneath the knight to run; just so the rod drives the boy to attend to study").[95] The hand that wrote these verses may also be the one that inscribed "*A Gen^er all confessyou^n of synnes*" ("a general confession of sins") on the verso of the leaf (which is otherwise blank). A page bearing a model initial *G* has attracted much practice writing (f. 8r) and the model *H* on the verso (f. 8v), inverted, provides a standing place for a fallow deer doe who rests her front hooves on the foliate limb of the letter. The doe, labelled "*dama*", is hotly pursued across the page by a hunting dog that wears a collar and runs with his snout protruding, his ears swept back, and his tail extending horizontally behind him. When one turns the page (still with the book inverted), a similar hound appears but this time it appears to be at rest, with its ears drooping and its tail curved. All of these examples are probably based on other models (compare the model of the fallow deer in MS Vienna, Nationalbibliotek, Cod. 507, an early thirteenth-century

---

[95] Cf. MS London, BL, Lansdowne 762, f. 99r, associated with *DIMEV* 2635.

154   *Chapter 2*

pattern book from Graz).[96] Also similar are the fallow deer and seated grey-
hound in MS Bergamo, Biblioteca Civica, cod. Δ VII.14, but in Sloane 1448A
they seem to be graphic responses to the experimental crafting of the initials.[97]

The Macclesfield Alphabet book, MS London, BL, Addit. 88887, is perhaps
the finest of these three late medieval English figurative resource books. This
volume dates from the second half of the fifteenth century (after 1464) with
some sixteenth-century additions, and is of English provenance.[98] The plainer
Textura alphabets on the opening leaves (ff. 1r-2v), appear to have been copied
by one "*Baldry*" who has signed the first alphabet "q^{uod} *Fryer* [friar, or Roger?
erased, reading uncertain] *Baldry*" (f. 1r). The initials *RB* formed from fantastical letters occur in a shield (f. 9v). It has been suggested that the owner could
have been Roger Baldry, prior of the Cluniac priory of St. Mary, Thetford,
1503-1518.[99] The resources collected here resemble the materials in the Sloane
manuscript. The volume includes various arrangements for initials with borders
(f. 27v), anthropomorphic initials (f. 8v), and initials with pen-work that incorporates fantastical heads (f. 3v). The accumulation of fifteenth- and sixteenth-
century materials testifies to an ongoing process of assembly; some pages have
still not been completed (for example, f. 26v). It is also a resource that is exper-
imented with. For example, some of the techniques have been exploited in the
monogrammed shield (f. 9v). De Hamel and Lovett note parallels with liturgical manuscripts, arguing that the Macclesfield book may not, however, have
been intended as a model for practising illuminators but may be a book of "of
pictorial information for wealthy patrons".[100] Perhaps, in assembling and engaging with pattern-book resources, Humphrey Newton was aping social superiors like the patrons of the Macclesfield book, seeking to display similar tastes
and aspirations and to model them for his own community.

The pattern books discussed in this section give us an insight into the kinds
of formal models for writing and graphic production more broadly to which
some evidently more privileged and aspirational later medieval writers had
access. Users of pattern books practised the close imitation of exemplars that
we observed in the humbler pedagogic and non-pedagogic environments discussed in the previous sections. But by means of engagement with these formal

---

[96] Reproduced in SCHELLER, *A Survey of Medieval Model Books*, fig. 40.

[97] Reproduced in SCHELLER, *A Survey of Medieval Model Books*, figs. 98, 105.

[98] C. DE HAMEL and P. LOVETT, "Introduction", in: *The Macclesfield Alphabet Book: A Facsimile*, introduced by C. DE HAMEL and P. LOVETT (London, 2010), pp. 7-21, at pp. 8, 13.

[99] DE HAMEL and LOVETT, "Introduction", pp. 15-16.

[100] DE HAMEL and LOVETT, "Introduction", pp. 18-19.

and more advanced materials, they extended their education in the understanding of the *figura*, practised their reproduction in various scripts, and discovered how the marks that comprise a graph related to those marks from which decorative and figurative devices were built. The collection of resources for study and imitation characterises the aspirational scribe and perhaps in itself signals belonging to a cadre of elite literates. From the inclusion of English-language material both as models and as learners' practice output, we can see that readers and writers of English engaged with such materials and made them part of their own process of learning and identity formation. Through collection of, skilful imitation of, and experimentation with formal writing models, writers of English could index belonging to literate elites.

Conclusion

The present chapter has shown that medieval *littera* pedagogy rested on the imitation of models and replication of copy-texts. Writing models and copy-texts were associated with individual and community identities and values, and learning to replicate a graphic model contributed to the identity-formation of the individual. We have seen that the literacy training methods and resources used for Latin were appropriated in communities of practice where English was read and written and at the same time their potency for indexing identity was deployed in these communities. The medieval framework of Latin literacy training was adaptable to local literacy conditions and to local values and identities as the basic processes of literacy socialisation in Latin were replicated in English literacy acquisition. Models encountered by readers and writers of English ranged from *ad hoc* copy-texts to formal calligraphic pattern books. This chapter brings together for analysis examples of both categories of material for the first time. Traces of this pedagogic process are often categorised as pen-trials, colophons, ownership inscriptions, and so on, but, this chapter has argued, it is often more appropriate to think of them as writing practice that contributes to the educational and social formation of the writer and draws boundaries between belonging and difference.

Chapter 3: Graphic Play

Hire nome is in Anote of the nyhtegale,
In annote is hire nome. Nempneþ hit non!
Whose ryht redeth, roune to Johon.

Her name is in Anote of the nightingale / In a note is her name. / Let no-one say it aloud! / Whoever can interpret it rightly, whisper to John.

("*Annot and John*", MS London, BL, Harley 2253, f. 63r-v)[1]

Language play [...] contributes greatly to [...] *metalinguistic awareness*

(David Crystal, *Language Play*)[2]

Reduced transparency of messages heightens metalinguistic awareness, and leads us to treat words, letters, and other typographic symbols as objects, and to play with them.

(Brenda Danet, *Cyberpl@y*)[3]

"*A*nnot and John*", one of the celebrated love lyrics in MS London, BL, Harley 2253, offers a rich experience to the graphically-aware reader. Courteously concealing the identity of the lady whom he

---

[1] My transcription and translation. For my translations of "*Nempneþ*" and "*redeth*" see *MED*, nemnen, v., 1b and *MED*, reden, v. 1, 6a. For some different transcriptions and translations see *The Complete Harley 2253 Manuscript: Volume 2*, ed. S.G. FEIN with D. RAYBIN and J. ZIOLKOWSKI (Kalamazoo, MI, 2014: *TEAMS Middle English Texts Series*), No. 28; and *Wessex Parallel WebTexts*, ed. B. MILLETT (Southampton, 2003), <https://ota.bodleian.ox.ac.uk/repository/xmlui/bitstream/handle/20.500.12024/2463/AW-front-pref.html>.

[2] D. CRYSTAL, *Language Play* (Harmondsworth, 1998), p. 180.

[3] B. DANET, *Cyberpl@y: Communicating Online* (Oxford, 2001), p. 6.

158   *Chapter 3*

praises, in the lines quoted in the epigraph to this chapter the poet says that her name is found in a note in the nightingale's song. Solvers of modern cryptic crosswords will readily recognise the classic misdirection here. Read literally, the lines appear to state that the lady's name is a musical sound in the bird's song. But, as in many a modern cryptic crossword clue, "*in*" has another meaning, directing attention to the graphic level of the text: the name is embedded graphically in "*A note*" and "*an note*". The name is available to anyone who *sees the letters*, either in a manuscript or perhaps in his or her mind's eye. The Harley 2253 scribe too stresses the meaning-bearing property of the graphic material. Taking advantage of the flexible word division at this period, he inserts no space between the indefinite articles and "note" (f. 63r). He also hints that "*Anote*" / "*annote*" is a name by making the initial letter of the name "*Anote*" a *littera notabilior*, a more *noticeable* letter in the nomenclature of modern palaeography, just as he has for the name "*Iohan*". The poet and the scribe both draw attention to the graphic material of the poem, inviting the reader to inspect and play with its graphic components.

Graphic play might appear to be precluded by the medieval literacy pedagogy that we have traced in Chapters One and Two. We have seen that who 'we' are is bound up in how 'we' write and this and the strong evidence for the use of models to transmit practice and its social meanings would seem, on the face of it, to preclude playing around with letters. The presumption in favour of constraint is reinforced by the history of medieval graphic communication, where graphic playfulness in medieval manuscripts is held to be tightly constrained by the demands of legibility. Malcolm Parkes defines the "grammar of legibility" as:

> a complex of graphic conventions by which the written manifestation of language operates to facilitate access to the information it conveys [...] at all levels: the letter, the word, the sentence, the paragraph, and the page.[4]

His account of the ways that the *ordinatio* of the scholastic text was developed to aid rapid access to its content proposes that the unimpeded access of the reader to the semantic content of the written text is the goal of scribal practice from at least the twelfth century.

---

[4]   M.B. PARKES, "Introduction", in: ID., *Scribes, Scripts, and Readers: Studies in the Communication, Presentation, and Dissemination of Medieval Texts* (London, 1991), pp. XV-XXII, at p. XV; cf. M.B. PARKES, "The contribution of Insular scribes of the seventh and eighth centuries to the 'grammar of legibility'", repr. in: ID., *Scribes, Scripts, and Readers*, pp. 1-18, at p. 2.

Graphic Play 159

But at the same time, it is well known that graphic play was a core component of medieval literacy pedagogy. Riddling and cryptographic texts are recognised to have had a pedagogic function as far back as antiquity and examples of their use in the medieval classroom are well known.[5] These genres trained essential literate skills by promoting close, creative, and agile attention to the *figurae*, *potestates*, and *nomina* of *litterae*. This chapter will propose that pedagogic genres and practices that harnessed play for literacy education became mediators of belonging and difference. It will argue that reading and writing in the medieval English language created graphic challenges similar to those for which training was offered in the course of *littera* pedagogy and literacy training processes and provided new applications for these skills. Written English must have been less immediately legible than written Latin because the language was written and read phonetically. Two stages must have been involved in decoding English writing since graphs signified sounds which in turn signified things. In addition, if the orthography of an English-language text was unfamiliar to the reader, or a text was written in a mixture of orthographic systems, ease of legibility must have been further reduced and lack of legibility increased. The problems associated with reading and writing English offered distinctive scope for display of the graphic skills developed by pedagogic play and therefore opened up new modes of literate belonging.

To assist in analysis of this medieval tradition, the present chapter will invoke ideas about graphic play, pedagogy, and identity that have been developed in recent sociolinguistics and in particular in work on electronic text and digital media. Sociolinguists see language play as conferring a kind of metalinguistic awareness that is an important component of language development among learners. Crystal, who defines play as "bending and breaking the rules of the language" for the enjoyment of the self or others, suggests that language play involves "operating within two linguistic worlds at once, the normal and the abnormal" and as he writes in the passage quoted in the epigraph to this chapter, proposes that this experience reinforces metalinguistic skills.[6] He draws attention to the relationships between graphic play and metalinguistic skills. Language play contributes to understanding about language. Both using metalanguage – talking about language – and linguistic play require "a stepping

---

[5] For an excellent survey of how riddles were used in early medieval education, see W. RUDOLF, "Riddling and reading: Iconicity and logogriphs in Exeter Book riddles 23 and 45", *Anglia* 130.4 (2012), pp. 499-525.

[6] CRYSTAL, *Language Play*, pp. 11, 181.

160 *Chapter 3*

back" into a more abstract realm in which it is possible to understand "how letters, punctuation marks, and other features of graphic expression relate to speech sounds".[7] Making a case for the inclusion of opportunities to play with language in the modern primary school curriculum, Crystal draws on education research that sees "play as practice" and concludes that "language play is a continuing feature of [child] development".[8]

In recent work on texts in digital media, graphic play – play with digital words and graphs – and its association with learning and identity have attracted considerable interest. Sociolinguists and literacy theorists have, especially since the advent of digital electronic media, become interested in the ways in which graphic phenomena in the digital environment become objects of attention, interactivity, and play for readers and authors. With digital media, Lanham argues, play happens because the reader's conditioning to look "through" the text instead of "at" it is disrupted.[9] Lanham imagines "playfully blasphemous rearrangement" of *Paradise Lost* and other texts in the undergraduate curriculum: presented with a digital copy of *Paradise Lost*, "wouldn't you begin to play games with it?" Lanham's speculations on looking 'at' versus looking 'through' a text emerge from his reflections on the power that digital media give authors and readers to attend to and play with the graphic properties of the text. In Lanham's view and that of other scholars, a perceived reduction in the transparency of text, which is seen as a phenomenon of the digital age, is a kind of return to practices in earlier literacies. The materiality of the visual is always there, but in certain periods, stages of literacy education, and media it is less obvious. Literacy and discourse theorists have demonstrated that the ability to ignore or see through the surface of the text – in other words, to access meaning without having to think about the code – is acquired in the process of literacy acquisition by the learner.[10] Awareness of the graphic medium is an essential stage in literacy acquisition.

Graphic play and the disruption of transparency are viewed as tools for the exercise of agency and alternative identity-making in digital environments. Danet builds on Lanham in her investigation *Cyberpl@y*, suggesting, in the passage quoted in the epigraph to this chapter, that graphic play is spurred by

---

[7] CRYSTAL, *Language Play*, p. 181.

[8] CRYSTAL, *Language Play*, pp. 179, 178.

[9] R. LANHAM, *The Electronic Word: Democracy, Technology, and the Arts* (Chicago, 1993), p. 5.

[10] J. BLOMMAERT, *Discourse: A Critical Introduction* (Cambridge, 2005), p. 116.

Graphic Play 161

the "reduced transparency" of digital text.[11] Deumert analyses 'Bbz', a language used on South African *Twitter*, in relation to the typographic and orthographic art of the Futurists where "artists played around with the spelling of words, the typeface of letters and the arrangement of letters on the page". She traces the Futurists' legacy in global branding and advertising (she gives the example of the chain-store name *Toys Я Us*, in which the verb was represented by a playfully reversed capital *R*). In digital writing, graphic play is recontextualised once again. In 'leet', non-alphabetic keyboard characters are used for letters of the alphabet (for example, the figure 4 is used for *A*) to express subversion of the "capitalist-consumerist logic of the internet"; the term 'leet' is an ironic subversion of 'elite'. 'Bbz' language in South African digital writing uses similar graphic play but its meanings are different, "Bbz language [...] might look like SMS / MXit / Twitter language, but it means different things: it is a way of writing that is, indexically, positioned as intimate, personal and sociable; at the same time, it challenges the hegemonic and monolithic norms of English iconically".[12] 'Bbz', Deumert argues, harnesses graphic play for post-colonial purposes. Wilkie, by contrast, takes a less sanguine view than Lanham (and Deumert and Danet) of the power of play with the cybertext to liberate, empower, and democratise.[13]

"*Annot and John*" offers a test case for the application of this approach to a medieval text. The poet codes his poem as virtuosic linguistic creativity by deploying a huge repertoire of richly alliterative similes for the lady – she is like precious stones, birds, flowers, spices, and romance heroines. While he offers many similes for the lady, he craftily conceals her name in the fabric of his text. The scribe too engages in graphic play. By exploiting flexibility over word division and spacing in Middle English, and by deploying *litterae notabiliores*, the Harley 2253 scribe is, to adapt Deumert's phrase, 'playing with the arrangement of letters on the page'. The reader also is invited to oscillate in his or her attention, to look both at and through the text. Before the reader can look through the text, he or she must look at the orthography, especially at the unfamiliar words, to decode them (for example, "*Wyrhale*" ("Wirral") might cause difficulties). The poet and scribe invite him or her to enjoy the challenge of looking at and through, inviting oscillation between reading

[11] DANET, *Cyberpl@y*, p. 6.

[12] A. DEUMERT, "Mimesis and mimicry in language – Creativity and aesthetics as the performance of (dis-)semblances", *Language Sciences* 65 (2018), pp. 9-17, at p. 13.

[13] R. WILKIE, *The Digital Condition: Class and Culture in the Information Network* (New York, 2011), pp. 122-166.

162   *Chapter 3*

for semantic content and looking at the letters on the page (or in the mind's eye) to solve the riddle of the lady's name. The poet's injunction that the name should not be *spoken aloud* ("*Nempneþ it non!*") and his command that anyone who finds the solution should only whisper it to the poet ("*roune*") mean that those who can puzzle out the solution for themselves by playing with the letters are distinguished from those who cannot: finding the solution means belonging to a literate elite.

The first section below surveys traditions of letter-play and puzzling in the pedagogy of Latin literacy training and its use as a resource for indexing identity. Graphic playfulness in pedagogic texts and traditions is identified in both composition and copying of texts. The second and third sections examine the transfer of these pedagogic traditions to English, examining selected genres in Middle and then Old English that require scribe and reader apply *littera* teaching to English and to pay careful attention to the arrangement and display of letters. We shall see that the teaching on the alphabet discussed in Chapter One and the models and copy-texts discussed in Chapter Two become occasions for playful learning and challenging puzzles and resources for forming identity.

Pedagogy and Graphic Puzzles

"*Annot and John*" tests skill with the building of letter sounds into syllables and the use of syllables to form words. In this way, "*Annot and John*" is typical of puzzle texts that give scribes and readers opportunities to test their knowledge of the theory of *littera* and to demonstrate skills in its application. Puzzle texts train skills in decoding and in understanding how the *littera* relates to the *potestas* and the *figura*. They also reinforce knowledge of the alphabet.

In early grammatical writings these modes of writing are associated with pedagogy and the socialisation of the pupil into a 'we' who are familiar with and can deploy elite and special literacies. In his preface to his riddle collection, Aldhelm († 709-710), first abbot of Malmesbury, describes riddles as a rudimentary pedagogic exercise, and evidence that riddle collections were used for pedagogic purposes is provided by the numerous glosses in the manuscripts.[14] In his chapter "*De notis litterarum*" ("concerning codes of letters"),

---

[14] F.H. WHITMAN, "Medieval riddling: Factors underlying its development", *Neuphilologische Mitteilungen* 71.2 (1970), pp. 177-185, at p. 181; F.H. WHITMAN, "Ænigmata Tatwini", *Neuphilologische Mitteilungen* 88.1 (1987), pp. 8-17, at pp. 10-11.

Graphic Play 163

in his classroom classic *Etymologiae*, Isidore records the tradition of writing in code so that secrets could remain hidden. He gives the examples of Brutus, who wrote his plans in code so that everyone else remained ignorant of his intentions. He also describes how Caesar Augustus instructed his son in the use of a cipher so that the two of them could write in a way that would be secret from others:

> *habeamus inter nos notas si vis tales ut, cum aliquid notis scribendum erit, pro unaquaque littera scribamus sequentem hoc modo, pro* a b *pro* b c *et deinceps eadem ratione ceteras.*

> let *us* have *between us* notations, if you wish, so that when something is to be written in cipher, for each letter *we* will use the following one in this way: for *a*, *b*; for *b*, *c*; and so on.[15]

Isidore also records another mode of encryption in which words are written backwards. Bede records a method of encrypting Latin in Greek letters. The numerical equivalent of the Greek letter would signify the place in the alphabet of each letter of the coded Latin word.[16] These grammarians therefore treat cryptographic skills as granting entry to a literate elite. Pedagogy transmits that skill and that identity. The seventh-century grammarian Virgilius Maro Grammaticus, thought to have been Irish, recommends that scrambling of words ("*scinderatio fonorum*") has a pedagogic function. "*Scinderatio fonorum*" refers, among other things, to "changing the order of syllables or letters in a word, transforming the word by adding or omitting some of its letters or syllables, as well as changing some letters or syllables" and its primary purpose is to sharpen the "ingenuity of *our students*" in finding what is hidden ("*sagacitatem discentium nostrorum*").[17] Evidence for the proposition that cryptography was – and had long been – an outlet for scribal play is offered by

---

[15] Isidore of Seville, *Etymologiae: Isidori Hispalensis Episcopi,* Etymologiarum *sive* Originum, ed. W.M. LINDSAY, 2 vols. (Oxford, 1911), 1, Book 1, ch. 25, section 2; my emphasis in the translation.

[16] Bede, *De Temporum ratione*, Book 1, ch. 1, in: PL 90, col. 298; cf. S.J. HARRIS, "Anglo-Saxon ciphers", in: *Material History of Medieval and Early Modern Ciphers: Cryptography and the History of Literacy*, ed. K. ELLISON and S. KIM (New York, 2018), n.p. (e-book).

[17] L. DOLEŽALOVÁ, "On mistake and meaning: *Scinderationes fonorum* in medieval *artes memoriae*, mnemonic verses, and manuscripts", *Language & History* 52.1 (2009), pp. 26-40, at p. 27, my italics. Cf. B.A. SALTZMAN, "*Vt hkskdkxt*: Early medieval cryptography, textual errors, and scribal agency", *Speculum* 93.4 (2018), pp. 975-1009, at p. 984.

164   *Chapter 3*

Saltzmann's recent work on scribal "errors" in cryptographic texts. Apparent deviations from cryptographic systems in the transmission of early medieval encrypted texts have been treated by editors as errors. However, Saltzman proposes that scribes of early medieval texts who deviate from or even make errors in cryptographic texts may be "creative" and engaged in "scribal play".[18] Scribes may be attempting to ring the changes on systems of encryption or to make cracking the code harder for the reader, Saltzmann suggests.[19] If Salzmann is correct, this addition of difficulty could be a way of displaying and inviting membership of an elite group of literates that builds on elementary *littera* pedagogy.

The basic teaching on *littera*, especially on the alphabet and letters, is the subject of many of the Anglo-Latin riddles or *enigmata*, a genre characteristically used in pre-Conquest pedagogy,[20] such as the series by Aldhelm, Tatwine (*c.* 670-734; Archbishop of Canterbury), and Tatwine's follower Eusebius. Tatwine's fourth riddle, *De litteris*, reflects on the way that letters combine to make words: if a letter is taken away, a word does not dawn ("*Littera tollatur, non fulget nominis ortus*").[21] This also provokes reflection on cryptography, where letters are deliberately taken away so that the reader has to work hard to make the encrypted words come to light. Tatwine's tenth riddle, whose solution is 'lectern', engages with the relation between words and writing. A "*vox*" comes forth from the "*caua guttera*" ("wide throat") of this mystery object, even though it cannot speak.[22] Eusebius, who added to Tatwine's riddle sequence, plays with the mysteries of *littera* in his riddle whose solution this is. We are numberless; we make sound all at the same time although no sound reaches the ear; black, we play on white ("*nos tetrae, ludimus albis*").[23] In a number of elegant paradoxes this riddle alludes to the *potestates* and *figurae* of letters, and the theory of *vox*. Black but playing on white, letters are *figurae* on

---

[18] SALTZMAN, "*Vt hkskdkxt*: Early medieval cryptography", p. 994.

[19] SALTZMAN, "*Vt hkskdkxt*: Early medieval cryptography", p. 998.

[20] P. LENDINARA, "The world of Anglo-Saxon learning", in: *The Cambridge Companion to Old English Literature*, ed. M. GODDEN and M. LAPIDGE, 2nd edn. (Cambridge, 2013), pp. 295-312, at p. 308; M. SALVADOR-BELLO, *Isidorean Perceptions of Order: The Exeter Book Riddles and Medieval Latin Enigmata* (Morgantown, WV, 2015), p. 25.

[21] Tatwine, *Aenigmata*, ed. F. GLORIE, in: *Tatvini Opera Omnia Variae collectiones aenigmatum Merovingicae aetatis*, ed. M. DE MARCO *et al.* (Turnhout, 1968: *Corpus Christianorum, series Latina* 133), pp. 165-208, at p. 171.

[22] Tatwine, *Aenigmata*, p. 177.

[23] Riddle 7: Eusebius, *Aenigmata*, ed. F. GLORIE, in: *Tatvini Opera Omnia*, pp. 209-271, at p. 217.

Graphic Play 165

parchment but also riddling: obscure and playing. A similar conceit is at play in his riddle 32, where parchment is accustomed to produce words without a voice ("*Distincta sine nunc uoce edere verba solemus*").[24] Eusebius's riddle 35, whose solution is 'quill', returns to the *figurae* with another black-white paradox; the quill is a white thing that leaves black traces: "*Candida conspicior, uestigia tetra relinquens*".[25] Several of Eusebius's riddles engage with theories of the alphabet. His ninth riddle, on the letter *a*, alludes through a paradox to the learning of the alphabet: "Adam, the first to be called, began with me". Riddle 14 by Eusebius alludes to the unusual properties of the letter *x*, first adopted into the alphabet by Augustus, while his riddle 19 refers to the grammatical analysis of the letter *u*, at once categorised as a vowel, a consonant, and a semi-vowel.[26] Eusebius's riddle 39 plays with the *figura* of the letter *i*, the most slender but, like a sceptre, most powerful of the letters.[27] Aldhelm also plays with the basic pedagogical doctrine of the alphabet. His riddle 30 is voiced by seventeen voiceless sisters who declare six others not numbered among them, an allusion to the teaching on the Latin alphabet and additions to it. The seventeen voiceless "sisters" are the letters *abcdefgilmnoprstv*, thought to be genuine Latin letters, and the six other "bastards" are *hkqxyz*.[28] Aldhelm's riddle 32 refers to the tracings of *figurae* on wax with a stylus as being like the furrows traced by a plough.[29] All of these examples test the student's knowledge of *littera* by cloaking the basic teachings about the alphabet and letters in riddling metaphors and paradoxes. They do not use the language of *littera* but use word play to make the student use it himself when he finds the solutions.

Acrostics, which test the combination of letters to form syllable sounds and words, are also found in pedagogic riddles. Such texts belong with an ancient tradition of alphabetical acrostics that has biblical and classical precedents.[30] Tatwine embeds an acrostic in his riddles using the first and last letters in each

---

[24] Eusebius, *Aenigmata*, p. 242.

[25] Eusebius, *Aenigmata*, p. 245.

[26] Eusebius, *Aenigmata*, pp. 224, 229.

[27] Eusebius, *Aenigmata*, p. 249.

[28] Aldhelm, *Aenigmata*, ed. F. GLORIE, in: *Tatvini Opera Omnia*, pp. 382-540, at p. 419; cf. R.J. DEWA, "The runic riddles of the Exeter Book: Language games and Anglo-Saxon scholarship", *Nottingham Medieval Studies* 39 (1995), pp. 26-36, at p. 26, and D. BITTERLI, *Say What I Am Called: The Old English Riddles of the Exeter Book and the Anglo-Latin Riddle Tradition* (Toronto, 2009), pp. 114-115.

[29] Aldhelm, *Aenigmata*, p. 417.

[30] For the tradition see G.R. CRAMPTON, "Chaucer's singular prayer", *Medium Ævum* 59 (1990), pp. 191-213, at p. 193.

166 *Chapter 3*

line, as he explains at the end of the sequence, while Aldhelm embeds an acrostic in his prologue.[31] Lendinara speculates that the interest in acrostics, found in Aldhelm, Tatwine, and Boniface, and in cryptography (also Boniface) reflect concern with the alphabet.[32]

Graphic puzzles continued to be used for pedagogic purposes into the later medieval period. MS Manchester, John Rylands Library, Lat. 394, a fifteenth-century collection of Latin riddles and English proverbs with translations, offers an excellent example of their variety and basic pedagogic purposes. The riddles and puzzles in the manuscript (ff. 27r-28r) play with the arrangement of letters in various cryptographic ways.[33] For example, the Latin "*Margareta amor mei cordis salue*" ("Margaret, love of my heart, save [me]") is written backwards: "*Ateragram roma*" and so on. Until the puzzler realises that the line is written backwards, he may be misled in his interpretation of the letters; for example, "*mei*" looks like "*rem*" ("thing", f. 28r). This puzzle, which is a kind of cryptograph of the sort described by Isidore, tests flexibility in the recognition of *figurae* and the ability to try out different ways of making the letters form meaningful syllables and words. Another puzzle conceals the solution "*amo te*" ("I love you", f. 27r), testing knowledge of *figurae* to solve the problem. The first line must be solved by matching the words to letter-shapes: "*Prima triangula sit tripodem postpone rotundum*" is glossed *A* (triangle) *M* (tripod) *O* (round), while the second line, "*Et conuerte scies quid sit tibi* [*erased*] *m^{ihi} morbus et vnde*" conceals '*te*' ("*Et*" in reverse).[34] Another puzzle requires the solver to replace *d* with *f* (f. 27r) and another requires subtraction of the first and last letters from "*navem*" ("ship") to yield "*ave*" ("hail!", f. 27v).

While these puzzles in MS John Rylands Library, Lat. 394 train close attention to *figurae*, concealing of words and grappling with their arrangement is also used in this manuscript to train the conversion of *figurae* into *potestates* and to turn groups of *potestates* into syllables. An example is the nonsense couplet "*Altaris lassus priuatur decipiendo / Istuc mandragora nescit balare negando*" (f. 27r). Above the syllables are written the words of the saying,

---

[31] Tatwine, *Aenigmata*, p. 208; WHITMAN, "Ænigmata Tatwini", pp. 14-15.

[32] LENDINARA, "The world of Anglo-Saxon learning", pp. 308-309.

[33] Pantin finds ten different kinds of puzzle, but he does not give solutions (W.A. PANTIN, "A medieval English collection of proverbs and riddles from the Rylands Latin MS 394", *Bulletin of the John Rylands Library* 14 (1930), pp. 81-114, at pp. 89-90).

[34] Pantin records another text in MS London, BL, Harley 3362, f. 33r (PANTIN, "A medieval English collection of proverbs and riddles", p. 110).

Graphic Play 167

"*Allas p^{ri}de ys ma[nys] bane*" ("alas pride is the bane of man", with the errone-
ous omission of the end of '*mannys*'). Each syllable of the Middle English
saying is the first syllable of each word of the Latin couplet. This text has been
described as a bilingual "riddle" whose solution is the English saying.[35] It
could perhaps provide support with reading Latin – as a 'gamified' form of
learning to sound out syllables. Pupils who solved the riddle would be
rewarded by making sense – but sense would be made when the pupil heard the
familiar English saying as he sounded out the syllables, not when he construed
the meaning of the Latin. This is perhaps why a nonsense couplet is used: the
master aims for the pupil to sound Latin correctly aloud, not to construe it. The
exercise relies on the mapping of syllable sounds onto groups of two *figurae*.
In the John Rylands Library manuscript this puzzle is made more difficult
because of an imperfect correlation between the spelling systems ("*is*" = "*ys*",
"*lass*" = "*las*"), which adds to the challenge of solving the riddle. This text also
occurs in MS London, BL, Harley 1735, John Crophill's notebook (f. 42v, pencil foliation), on what may have been the blank last leaf of a bifolium devoted
to a monthly health regimen, a page used for writing practice, as mentioned in
Chapter Two.

The proverbs in MS John Rylands Library, Lat. 394 (ff. 2r-26v) are organised alphabetically. Grammatical and linguistic material was often organised
alphabetically, for example, in alphabetical glossaries.[36] Alphabetical order
was practical but also offered opportunities to display linguistic virtuosity. In
fourteenth-century Oxford, Adam of Nutzard wrote treatises on transitive and
intransitive verbs in the form of alphabetical verse lists of verbs. For example,
the *B* lines include the intransitive verbs, "*Bello, belligero, bombizo, bauloque,
balo, / Et barbarizo, boo, bito, buccino, burso*" ("I fight, wage war, and buzz,
and sway and bleat; I barbarise and roar, I go, I trumpet, pack").[37] These traditions from Latin pedagogy inform cognate texts in Old and Middle English and
many of our examples are found in medieval school-books from England and
in Anglophone reading and writing environments as well as in those of Latin.
We shall see below that the skills taught proved especially valuable for authors,
scribes, and readers confronted by the challenges of graphic diversity in Old
and Middle English.

---

[35] N. ORME, "Games and education in medieval England", in: *Games and Gaming in Medieval Literature*, ed. S. PATTERSON (New York, 2015), pp. 45-60, at p. 52.

[36] LENDINARA, "The world of Anglo-Saxon learning", pp. 304-305.

[37] Edited and translated in G. RIGG, *A History of Anglo-Latin Literature 1066-1422* (Cambridge, 1992), p. 229.

168   *Chapter 3*

Alphabet Games, Acrostics, and Riddles

The theory and practice of *littera* inform many graphic puzzles. In the Anglophone graphic environment new layers of challenge are introduced for authors, scribes, and readers, and therefore opportunities arise to perform belonging to new, select literate identities through displaying skill in solving the challenges. This section will examine graphic puzzling and its identity-forming potential in relation to *ABC* poems, acrostics, and riddles written in English. The first part of this section will focus on the *ABC of Aristotle*, arguing that it illustrates modes of playful pedagogy also found in relation to Chaucer's *ABC Hymn to the Virgin*, several literary game texts, and earlier *ABC* poems. The final parts will consider the pedagogy of graphic play in relation to two genres of puzzle poem: later Middle English acrostics and Old English riddles.

Alphabet Poems and Pedagogic Play

Many puzzle texts are organised around the alphabet. Like model alphabets and alphabet copying exercises, these puzzle texts belong with a long tradition of literacy pedagogy designed to teach about the alphabet and its letters. But once the tradition is transferred to the vernacular, the graphic challenge of the texts is increased by the difficulty about the composition and order of the alphabet that we encountered in Chapter One. One of the most ubiquitous alphabet texts, and one of the most interesting as evidence for graphic puzzling, is the *ABC of Aristotle*.[38] The poem urges moderation in all things and avoidance

---

[38] *DIMEV* 6054, surviving in eleven manuscripts; another version, *DIMEV* 6654, has a prologue and survives in five manuscripts. For a recent edition and discussion of themes, possible authorship, and manuscripts, see M.D. RUST, "The 'ABC of Aristotle'", in: *Medieval Literature for Children*, ed. D.T. KLINE (London, 2003), pp. 63-78; edition based on MS London, Lambeth Palace Library, 853. For an older edition with some variants see *ABC of Aristotle*, "Das stabreimende *ABC des Aristoteles*", ed. M. FÖRSTER, in: *Archiv für das Studium der neueren Sprachen und Literaturen* 105 (1900), pp. 296-310. The manuscripts are as follows. *DIMEV* 6054: MS Cambridge, Trinity College, O.2.53, f. 69v; MS Dublin, Trinity College, 509, p. 104; MSS London, BL, Addit. 36983, f. 263r-v; Addit. 37049, f. 86v; Addit. 60577, f. 56v; Harley 541, f. 228r; Harley 1706, f. 94r; and Harley 5086, f. 90v; MS New Haven, Yale University, Beinecke Library, Takamiya 61, f. 56v; MSS Oxford, Bod. Lib., Lat. Misc. c. 66, f. 26br and Rawl. B. 196, f. 110v. *DIMEV* 6654: MS Cambridge, UL, Ff.5.48, ff. 8v-9r; MSS London, BL, Harley 541, f. 213r-v and MS Harley 1304, f. 103r-v; MS London, Lambeth Palace Library, 853, pp. 30-32. I have used the text of MS Lambeth 853 in Rust's edition and for the variants in MS Cambridge, UL, Ff.5.48 I have consulted Rust's and Förster's editions. I have not had access to the MS Oxford, Bod. Lib.,

Graphic Play 169

of a catalogue of vices that is organised alphabetically: each line lists a number of vices that begin with a different letter of the alphabet. Examination of the texts reveals that these vary considerably. I argue below that engagement with the alphabetical structure is an example of pedagogic play that involves both readers and scribes. I shall argue that the differences among the texts are not just textual variants caused by transmission as they have been treated by editors and critics;[39] they are creative interventions that address the challenges of finding several words that begin with a given letter and of variation in the composition and order of the alphabet. I shall also present evidence that the poem could have been a text for playing a social pedagogic game somewhat like the Middle English dice and fortune poems.

Through including several lines about play and pedagogy, the poem invokes consideration of the extent to which scribes and readers are licensed by the doctrine of the golden mean to play with the text. MS London, BL, Addit. 36983 advises *"ne boorde thou nat to large"* – "do not joke *too* much"; a balance is required between being *"to dulle"* and *"to medleus, to mury"* ("too dull", "too meddlesome, too merry", f. 263r-v). Harley 541 advises that the addressee should *"jape not to moche"* ("jape not too much", f. 228r) and that he should not be *"to medelous to mery but as gode man*er*e askith"* ("too meddlesome, too merry, but as good manners require"). He should not be *"to quesytise of questions"* (perhaps he should not ask what the playful, invented word *"quesytise"* means?). While Harley 541 advises that the addressee should not do too much japing, BL, Addit. 37049 advises that he should *"Iape not to large"* ("do not jape too unrestrainedly", f. 86v), MS Oxford, Bod. Lib., Rawl. B. 196 enjoins him not to do it too frequently, *"Iape nat to oftyu*m*"* ("jape not too often", f. 110v), and MS Oxford, Bod. Lib., Lat. Misc. c. 66 adds that he should not be *"To joconde to Ioly"* ("too jocund, too jolly", f. 26ar). In MS Dublin, Trinity College, 509 the line reads *"To Iettyng to Iangelyng and Iape þu not to ofte"* ("too jetting, too jangling, and jape not too often", p. 104). MS

Douce 384 fragment (on which see below, note 42). The copy in MS Addit. 60577 was identified in E.M. WILSON, "A newly identified copy of the *ABC of Aristotle* in the 'Winchester Anthology'", *Notes and Queries* n.s. 47.3 (2000), p. 296.

[39] For example, Rust treats the different readings as textual variants derived from scribal transmission rather than as active engagement by scribes with the challenge posed by the poem and the Middle English alphabet (RUST, "The 'ABC of Aristotle'", pp. 72-78), and Cornelius argues that the Winchester Anthology text is a "rewritten poem" on the basis of his "standard analysis of (written) textual transmission" (I. CORNELIUS, "The text of the *ABC of Aristotle* in the 'Winchester Anthology'", *Anglia* 139.2 (2021), pp. 400-418, at pp. 415, 411).

170   *Chapter 3*

London, Lambeth Palace Library, 853 has a similar reading, "*to iettynge ne to iangelinge ne iape not ofte*" (p. 31), as does MS Bod. Lib., Rawl. B. 196 (f. 110v). MS London, BL, Harley 1706 counsels not against too much japing but against too much joy, "*Ne Ioye thow nat ofte*" (f. 94r). Many of the texts explicitly evoke a pedagogic scenario in which the reader is positioned as a learner who is studying under the tutelage of a master. The version in Addit. 36983 instructs that it is important "*to queme well þⁱ maystᵉʳ*" (f. 263v); the learner must adjust his behaviour in relation to his master's standards. MS London, BL, Addit. 37049 enjoins, "*kepe wele þⁱ maystᵉʳ*" (in the *Q* line, f. 86v, perhaps meaning honour or serve, *MED, kepen*, v. 14a). MS London, BL, Addit. 60577 specifies that the addressee should not be *too* playful with his master, "*to Iangelynge to Iapeynge neuᵉʳ wⁱᵗʰ thy maystᵉʳ*" (f. 56v). Harley 5086 (like other versions) enjoins the learner to please his master even though he should not flatter other social superiors, "*To Preysyng to Preve with Prynces and Dukes / To Queynt to Querelous and Queme well thy maistre*" (f. 90v).

The variants found in the lines about play are evidence for playfulness and creativity with the alphabet. They are traces of the ways the poem has tested the resourcefulness of the scribe to find appropriate words for each letter of the alphabet and tested the taste of the reader who is given opportunities to recognise scribal achievement as part of learning how to be an ideal pupil. Finding enough appropriate words requires creative solutions to problems of the alphabet in Middle English, and the *ABC of Aristotle* scribes present various solutions to the problem of the different Middle English alphabets. The letters of the alphabet row in the various texts of the poem vary. Few texts go beyond *v* or *w*. However, in MS London, BL, Addit. 60577 (the Winchester Anthology, encountered in Chapter Two), the alphabet is *A[...]TVX* (f. 56v). A use for *x* is created using the chi-rho-sigma abbreviation for '*Christus*':

>   X *to Cryste pray we where soo wee bee*
>
>   *xpc*
>   *. That we may lerne thys A . B . C .*

>   *X* To Christ we pray wherever we be / That we may learn this *ABC*; *Christus*

This is a clever and resourceful way of including *x*. Like lines *A* to *V*, the first line begins with "*to*", for example, "A *to amerous to aventurous avyse or ye answere*", but where they begin with the adverb "*to*" ("too"), the *X* lines use

Graphic Play   171

"*to*" as a preposition.[40] MS London, BL, Harley 1706 is also resourceful, including the whole alphabet to *XYZ*, abbreviations, tittle, and "*amen*" to feature the final portion of the alphabet in the final lines of the poem:

> W *To Wylde ne to wrathfull ne to wyse deme the*
> *ffor a mesurable meane ys best for vs all*
> XYZ xy *wy*[*t*]*h esed* ^*and*^ p^*er*^ *se*
> *Tytell Tytell Tytell*
> *Amen*

> *W* Too wild nor too wrathful nor judge yourself too wise / for a happy medium is best for us all / *XYZ xy* with zed, 'and' by itself / tittle [the symbol for '*est*'], tittle, tittle, Amen

> (MS London, BL, Harley 1706, f. 94r)[41]

The fact that some *figurae* have more than one *potestas*, and that different *figurae* may be used to represent the same *potestas* is an additional part of the graphic challenge posed by the poem, and the scribes vary in their linking of *potestates* and *figurae*. For example, the letters *v* and *w* may be treated as one letter with two *potestates*, both of which are represented by *v*. This happens in MS Bod. Lib., Lat. Misc. c. 66, where the poem runs from *A* to *V* and the scribe (Humphrey Newton, encountered in Chapter Two) uses only the *figura v*, "V *to vastyng* [wasting] *to vengable and vade* [wade] *not to depe*" (f. 26rb) even though the line mixes *potestates*, both /w/ and /v/. In some texts the *V* line includes single (*v* / *u*) and digraph (*w*) forms. In MS London, BL, Addit. 37049, f. 86v, the alphabet runs *A* to *V*. The letter *v* is given two lines which subsume *w* and *v*, "V *To venomos to vengeabyll Ne wast not þi tyme* / *To wylde ne to wrathfull Ne wade not to depe*" ("*V* too venomous, too vengeful, nor waste not your time, too wild, nor too wrathful, nor get too deeply involved [in love]"). The *ABC of Aristotle* occurs twice (in different hands and codicologically distinct sections) in MS London, BL, Harley 541, ff. 213r-v and 228r. The alphabet row at f. 213v is *A* [...]*TVW*, while that at f. 228r runs *A*[...]*TV*. The *A*[...]*TV* version later in MS Harley 541 simply ends the alphabetical sequence with the mixed line, "*to venemo*^*us*^ *to vengeable* ^*and*^ *wast not moch*" (f. 228r). The *A*[...]*TV*

---

[40] Cornelius describes this redaction as "artful" (CORNELIUS, "The text of the *ABC of Aristotle*", p. 415).

[41] A later hand has inserted "*than est a*" before "*Amen*"; see further below.

172   *Chapter 3*

version of the text in MS Bod. Lib., Rawl. B. 196 has a similar final line (f. 110v). Sometimes *w* words are included in the *V* line even where there is also a *W* line. The version in MS Harley 541 that includes *v* and *w* in the alphabet has a line that mixes initial *v* and initial *w*, "*To venemous to vengeable ^{and} wast not to myc[h]*" (f. 213v), followed by a line that alliterates exclusively on *w*, "*To wyld to wr\o\thfull ^{and} wade not to depe*". MS London, BL, Addit. 36983 has similar *v* and *w* lines (f. 363v). Likewise in Cambridge, Trinity College, O.2.53 there are *v* and *w* lines where a *w* word is included under *v*, "*To venomous to vengeable and wast not moche / To wylde to wrathfull and wade not to depe*" (f. 69v). Other manuscripts of the *ABC of Aristotle* display further solutions. MS Dublin, Trinity College, 509 has a line for each of the letters *v* and *w*, but the digraph occurs in both lines and at the end of each line the graph *v* is written (p. 104). This is echoed in Beinecke, Takamiya 61 (f. 56v). MS London, Lambeth Palace Library, 853 moves '*waste*' to the *W* line and adds some more *v* words to replace it, "*V to venemose. ne to veniable. ^{and} voide al vilonye. W to wielde ne to wraþful neiþer waaste ne waade not to depe*" (p. 31). We might see such variation in the understanding of the alphabet row and links between *potestates* and *figurae* as displays of ingenuity caused by the need to adjust the alphabet for English-language contexts and invitations to the reader to learn from these playful examples. The *ABC of Aristotle* provides a copy-text and a reading-text that provides playful pedagogic opportunities for writers and readers to test their understanding of the doctrine of *littera* and to exercise skill in applying it to Middle English.

Similar opportunities for graphic ingenuity are presented by other lines. The choice of words used to exemplify *g* and *i* was a particularly challenging opportunity for the display and appreciation of graphic dexterity. Scribes had the opportunity to devise the most interesting *I* line, and to display their ability to find appropriate terms from the limited lexicon of borrowed French words beginning with /dʒ/. Harley 541, f. 213v reads "*To Iettyng to Ianglyng and Iape not to oft*", and MS London, BL, Harley 5086 (f. 90v) and Beinecke, Takamiya 61 (f. 56v) have similar readings. The *ABC of Aristotle* in MS London, BL, Addit. 36983 reads "*To Iettyng to Ianggelyng beware of knaves tacches*" ("too jetting, too jangling, beware of wastrels' habits", f. 263v), while MS London, BL, Addit. 60577 (the Winchester Anthology) reads "*To Iangelynge to Iapeynge neu^{er} w^{ith} thy mayst^{er}*" ("too jangling, too japing, never with your master", f. 56v), both of these manuscripts failing to find more than two words for the *I* line. In MS Bod. Lib., Lat. Misc. c. 66, the *I* line reads, "*To Ioconde to ioly*

Graphic Play 173

ne iape not to I [struck through] *ofte*" (f. 26br); perhaps the scribe failed to find a fourth appropriate alliterating term. Likewise, in MS Cambridge, Trinity College, O.2.53, the *I* line reads, "*To Iettyng to Iangellyng and Iape þ^u not to I* [struck through] *ofte*" (f. 69v). The odd *I* line admonition against being joyful too frequently in Harley 1706, "*To Iocunde ne to Iangelyng ne Ioye thow nat ofte*" (f. 94r, pencil foliation), is perhaps a sign of a scribe who struggled to meet the challenge of the line.

As well as rising to the challenge of creating the best *I* line, scribes of the *ABC of Aristotle* had to consider its relationship with the *G* line. Since *g* could represent /g/ or /dʒ/, in one of its *potestates g* overlapped with *i*. Scribes had to decide whether the *figura-potestas* relationship should be consistent, or whether the aim was simply for the key *figurae* in a given line to be the same. Another decision was whether a given *potestas* could be represented by different *figurae* in different lines. In many texts the *figurae* match in a given line but their *potestates* do not. The *G* line in the second version of the *ABC* in Harley 541 reads, "*to glad to gloryous ^{and} gelosy þu hate*" ("too glad, too self-glorying, and hate jealousy", f. 228r). Harley 5086, f. 90v is similar, as are MS Dublin, Trinity College, 509, p. 104, and MS Oxford, Bod. Lib., Rawl. B. 196, f. 110v. In MS Cambridge, Trinity College, O.2.53, the *G* line likewise mixes *potestates*, "*To glad ne to glorius and gelosye þ^u hate*" (f. 69v) and Lambeth 853 has a similar line, "*to glad. ne to gloriose. ^{and} gelosie þou hate*" (p. 31), as does Beinecke, Takamiya 61 (f. 56v). Similarly, in the *ABC of Aristotle* in BL, Harley 1304, the *G* line reads "*Be not to Glosynge ne to gelous gay and gap*[?MS corrected]*e not to wide*" ("Be not too flattering nor too jealous, gay, and do not open your mouth too wide", f. 103v), while in MS London, BL, Addit. 36983, f. 263r, it reads "*To glade ner to glorious and gelowʒy thou hate*".[42] By contrast, other texts limit the *G* line to a single *potestas*, /g/. For example, in the Winchester Anthology both *potestates* and *figurae* match in the *G* line: "*To gry^mme to grounfulle goode gouernauⁿce suffyce*" ("too harsh nor too scolding, good governance is enough", f. 56v). Likewise in Harley 1706 the *figura g* represents a single *potestas*, "*To gladde ne gloryous Ne to galaunt neuer*" ("to glad nor too self-glorying nor too much like a dandy", f. 94r). In Humphrey Newton's manuscript the *G* line has a single *potestas* but unusually it is /dʒ/; Humphrey respells with initial *g* many words often found elsewhere

---

[42] The text in MS Harley 1304 runs to the *K* line; the leaf on which it would have finished was removed by Peter Le Neve in 1695 and its text appended by him under the *K* line. The extracted leaf is now MS Oxford, Bod. Lib., Douce 384, f. 3.

174   *Chapter 3*

in the *I* line, "*To Gettyng to gangelyng* ^{and} *gelosy þu hate*" (MS Bod. Lib., Lat. Misc. c. 66, f. 26br). In MS London, BL, Addit. 37049, f. 86v, we can see the process of addressing the challenge of the *I* and *G* lines at work. The scribe mixes /g/ and /dʒ/ in the *G* line, "*To* [erasure] *glad ne to glorius and gelyosnes þu hate*", but in the *I* line, he first wrote "*gettyng*" ("jetting") then corrected the spelling to "*Iettyng*" ("jetting"). The correction suggests that the scribe was thinking about the relation between *figurae* and *potestates* and that he decided that the *figurae* must match in a given line, but not necessarily the *potestates*.

The manuscripts provide evidence that as well as focusing on the graphic challenges of the *ABC of Aristotle*, scribes had to consider a visual presentation that was appropriate to an alphabet structure. They faced the problem that the initial letters of the lines do not form an alphabet acrostic, since in some versions the lines begin with '*To*' and in others with '*Be*'. Some scribes solved these challenges by highlighting the alphabet structure using layout, rubrication, or the provision of alphabet rows. Some scribes of the '*To*' version solved the problem by placing the first word of each line at a distance from the following alphabet word. In Beinecke, Takamiya 61, for example, this occurs and the alphabetical arrangement is enhanced with the use of a majuscule at the beginning of each first alphabet word and the tipping in red of both "*To*" and the following word (f. 56v), while the letters of the alphabet are also arranged at the extreme right of each line, again in majuscules tipped with red. Others solved the problem by inserting an alphabet row in a column to the left of the poem. In MS London, BL, Addit. 60577, the alphabet row is inserted in majuscules in a specially ruled column (f. 56v). The layout of both texts in Harley 541 is similar, with the letters of the alphabet clearly set out in a column on the left (ff. 213v, 228r). Likewise, in MS Bod. Lib., Rawl. B. 196, f. 110v, "*To*" is preceded by the requisite letter of the alphabet in majuscule form. Similarly, in MS London, BL, Addit. 37049, f. 86v, letters of the alphabet precede "*To*", the first word of each line. In this manuscript, each of the verse lines is written over two lines because the page is laid out in two columns with short lines; the scribe brackets the two halves of the line to make clear which letter they exemplify. The scribe of Harley 5086 does not provide a vertical alphabet row, but he foregrounds the alphabet by rendering the alliterated letters in showy majuscules (f. 90v). Not all scribes reflected the alphabetical structure of the poem in the layout and visual presentation however. In MS London, Lambeth Palace Library, 853 the poem is set out like prose, the letters of the alphabet at the

Graphic Play 175

start of each line of verse occurring at various points in the line in this layout.[43] In Harley 1304, where each line of the *ABC* text begins "*Be not*", no attempt has been made to highlight the alphabet (f. 103v). In MS Cambridge, Trinity College, O.2.53, f. 69v, whose lines begin with "*To*", the poem is rather plainly set out with no attempt to draw attention to the alphabet. MS London, BL, Addit. 36983 is similar (f. 263r-v), as is MS Dublin, Trinity College, 509 (p. 104). Scribes vary, therefore, in the degree to which they help the reader. Some display resourcefulness in solving the graphic challenges of the poem while some choose a form of presentation that makes the reader discover the alphabetic structure of the poem for themselves.[44]

While layout and visual presentation contribute to highlighting – or hiding – the alphabetic structure of the *ABC of Aristotle*, paratextual devices are also important to its pedagogic framing. Paratextual framing of various kinds emphasises its pedagogic functions. In MS London, BL, Addit. 37049, the poem is headed by a title rubric, "*Þis is þe* A . B . C . of Arystotyll *of gode doct^{r}ine*" ("this is the *ABC of Aristotle* of good instruction", f. 86v).[45] Describing the poem as an *ABC*, endorsing its teaching, and attributing it to Aristotle, the rubric frames the text as pedagogic. The version of Harley 541 at f. 213r is preceded by a prologue that recommends "[*w*]*hoso wyll be wyse and worshyp to wynne leern he on lettur and loke vpon an other of the* .A.B.C. *of Arystotle*" ("whoever wishes to be wise and respected, let him acquire literacy and study another version of the *ABC of Aristotle*"). The author of the header indicates his own success in this regard and models it to his readers by imitating the structure of the alliterating lines of the poem. But whereas the poem alliterates extremes to be avoided, the header alliterates virtues. The header-author is explicit about the identity on offer to those who, like himself, possess skill and knowledge "*on lettur*" and study this poem: it will bring wisdom and respect. A similar imitative alliterative phrase which urges learning and models it with graphic accomplishment forms an explicit to the poem in MS London, BL, Harley 5086, "*Yitte Lerne or be Lewde*" ("again, learn or be ignorant"). The previous item in MS Harley 5086, *DIMEV* 2643, has the explicit "*Lerne or be Lewde*" (f. 90r), and the scribe notices the connection. The scribe in Harley 1706 inserts the opening

---

[43] Rust's transcription reproduces this layout (RUST, "The 'ABC of Aristotle'", pp. 72-73).

[44] Humphrey Newton, scribe of the poem in MS Oxford, Bod. Lib., Lat. Misc. c. 66 (f. 26r-v), makes a pertinent remark about its visual display potential for audiences; see further in Chapter Four.

[45] For this manuscript, thought to be Carthusian, see further in Chapter Five, pp. 327-328.

Fig. 13. Master-scribe and the *ABC of Aristotle*, MS London, BL, Addit. 37049, f. 86v (detail). © The British Library Board, MS British Library, Addit. 37049, f. 86v.

Graphic Play 177

rubric "*Here begynneth Arystotoles* A B C *made by mayster Benett*" ("here begins the ABC *of Aristotle* made by Master Benett", f. 94r). Possibly "*made be mayster Benett*" here credits the author of the version in this manuscript.[46] Whether or not Benett was the version-scribe's name, crediting the poem to a "master" offers the text as pedagogic and positions its readers as pupils. The provision of a criss-cross at the beginning of the poem also serves its pedagogic framing. Recalling the layout of the primer alphabets discussed in Chapter One, the criss-cross helps to associate the text with elementary *littera* teaching. Examples occur in Harley 541 (f. 228r); Harley 1706 (f. 94r); and MS London, BL, Addit. 60577, f. 56v, where a cross precedes an opening couplet "*C[r]ystys crosse be oure spede w^{ith} grace m^{er}cye in all oure nede*" ("may Christ's cross be our helper with grace and mercy whenever we have need", f. 56v).

In MS London, BL, Addit. 37049, images contribute to the paratextual pedagogic framing of the poem. Complementing the presentation of the text as being "of gode doctrine", the *ABC* is provided with an illustration of a figure who is depicted as a scribe seated at work copying a text. Although at first sight one might interpret this figure as the 'author' Aristotle, in the context of the illustration of these pages it is more likely that he would have been seen as a teacher. The figure is wearing a long blue robe and an academic's or teacher's skull-cap (see Figure 13). A figure in similar skull cap and attire appears at the beginning of moral couplets on the previous page (f. 85v). This figure, who is standing, is plainly a teacher. He gestures to the verse from the left of the text while on the right a figure looks at the verses with his right hand on his heart. Wearing a shorter gown and sporting long hair and no headwear, this second figure is a youth, and plainly a pupil. A similar pair appear with the moral couplet text *DIMEV* 917 (f. 85r). Here the teacher figure carries a scroll (?) and the learner a book.

Inclusion in a compilation can also provide pedagogic framing for the text. In Harley 1304, the *ABC* is found in a compilation with other elementary pedagogic material in spare leaves at the end of Lydgate's *Life of Our Lady*. A dialogue between master and pupil, "*Questiones bytwene the maist^{er} of Oxenford and his clerke*" ("questions discussed between the Oxford master and his student", ff. 100r-102v) rehearses basic religious teaching in the form of a riddle-like question posed by the pupil and an answer supplied by the master, for example:

---

[46] By contrast, Rust suggests that Benett may refer to authors Benedict Burgh or Benedict Anglus (RUST, "The 'ABC of Aristotle'", p. 64).

178   *Chapter 3*

C[*lerke*]	*What was he þ^{at} neu^{er} was bore ^{and} was buried in his mod^{ur}*
	wombe and sithe was C^{ri}stened and saued
M[*aister*]	*That was owre fad^{ur} Adam*

Student:	Who was never borne in a mother's womb and was buried
	and afterwards was cristened and saved?
Master:	That was our father, Adam.

(MS London, BL, Harley 1304, f. 100v)

A version of the prologue found in Harley 541 at f. 213r is also worked into this compilation. Learning of letters, says the Harley 1304 compilation, is good for thousands of knights and clerks and can amend common men:

And it is cownsell to clerkis ^{and} knyght^{is} a thousand
Yutt it myte a men man amend ful ofte
The lernynge of ou^{re} lett^{er} and his lif safe

And it is guidance for thousands of clerks and knights and still the study of our letters may often reform an ordinary man and save his life.

(MS London, BL, Harley 1304, f. 103r)

A poem structured on the alphabet follows, advising avoidance of sin and following of virtue in alliterative lines that recall those of the *ABC of Aristotle* (f. 103r-v), and then another stanza enjoins the virtues of measure in all things (f. 103v). The *ABC of Aristotle* completes the compilation.

I have been arguing that the *ABC of Aristotle* functions as a copy-text used for writing practice of the kind – albeit more challenging – that we encountered in Chapter Two. This argument about the function of the text is reinforced by its codicological and palaeographical relationships to some of the manuscripts in which it survives. In some manuscripts the *ABC* looks like a copy-text that sometimes travelled independently of larger copying campaigns, just as the simpler writing practice copy-texts discussed in Chapter Two did. It may be on a support that was not originally part of a codex, or may be written in a different hand from the main texts in spare space in a codex. For example, in Humphrey Newton's manuscript (MS Oxford, Bod. Lib., Lat. Misc. c. 66) it appears on a separate, narrow leaf which was formerly folded into four; it was not originally part of a codex at all. In several manuscripts it is given a page to

Graphic Play 179

itself. In MS London, BL, Addit. 60577 the poem is given a page to itself (f. 56v), ends with many lines to spare on the page, and faces a blank ruled page. In Harley 1706 is it is given a page to itself (f. 94r), follows a blank facing verso page, is written in a large Secretary display hand, and is laid out in double columns with each line of verse set out over two lines. This hand and format in Harley 1706 are quite different from those of the surrounding materials. In MS Oxford, Bod. Lib., Rawl. B. 196, the *ABC* has been entered with a few other short texts on blank pages at the end of a text of the Middle English prose *Brut* (f. 110v). In Harley 541 the version of the poem at f. 228r occurs in a small booklet made of what was originally largely blank paper that was later used by many hands for household purposes of various kinds.[47] The prologue in Lambeth 853 instructs *"Reede ofte on þis rolle"* ("read this roll often", p. 30), while the versions in Harley 541 (f. 213r) and in MS Cambridge, UL, Ff.5.48, ff. 8v-9r, respectively enjoin the reader to read this *"ragment"* and *"ragmon"* suggesting that it was imagined not just as a separate roll or document but as a kind of literary game (a 'ragman roll') that involved random selection of separate text pieces. A crucial piece of evidence for use in this way is the survival of a version of the *B* line in a graffito at Great Bardfield Church (*DIMEV* 770).[48]

Framed as a pedagogic text, the *ABC of Aristotle* is not surprisingly associated with informal literacy training in a variety of communities of Anglophone literate practice. There are traces of evidence beyond the text itself for the displays of graphic ingenuity invited by the *ABC of Aristotle* among its scribes and readers and the identities offered by these activities in the communities of practice where this text was used. In Harley 1706 another hand has completed the alphabet of the *ABC of Aristotle*, inserting *"than 'Est' a"* (then [the symbol for] 'est' a) between *"Tytell Tytell Tytell"* and *"Amen"* (f. 94r). In Harley 1304, the explicit of the *Questiones* in the compilation associated with the *ABC* is

---

[47] For the booklet, much of which was originally blank and whose pages were used for household composition such as the compilation of a chronicle see A. SUTTON and L. VISSER-FUCHS, "'The making of a minor London chronicle in the household of Sir Thomas Frowyk (died 1485)", *The Ricardian* 10 (1994), pp. 86-103.

[48] For the Great Bardfield graffito see Chapter Four. By contrast, Rust – who does not mention the graffito or survival with other game texts – sees play and pedagogy as opposed, "[i]f the *ABC of Aristotle* was used for the game of Rageman, its apparent didacticism would have been turned to quite a different use" (RUST, "The 'ABC of Aristotle'", p. 76, note to line 10 of her edition, comment on the word '*Rageman*'). In the next part of this section, 'Alphabet Poems and Literary Games', we shall see that the poem survives in the company of other such literary game texts.

180 *Chapter 3*

imitated twice in spare space beneath, and the copy-text *"amen dico vobis"*, which we encountered in Chapter Two, is also found here with an English translation in a wobbly hand (f. 102v). A pedagogic context for the poem in MS Cambridge, Trinity College, O.2.53 is suggested by the appearance of Latins with English translations and glosses, possibly in the same hand as the poem (f. 72r) and, in a different hand, a copy-text practice letter from a school-boy to his parents (f. 45v).[49] The *ABC of Aristotle* in this manuscript has no rubric, but somewhat in the style of Latins the scribe follows the last line, *"For a mesurable mene is best for vs all to kepe"* ("it is best for us all to observe a happy medium") with a similar Latin maxim about moderation, *"Tene* [above illegible crossed-out text] *mediu^m si non vis p^er̄dere modu^m̄"* ("keep a moderate course if you do not wish to lose the way of virtue", f. 69v).[50] Use of Beinecke, Takamiya 61 for writing practice is suggested by many appearances of the copy-text *"Ego sum bonus puer que^m deus amat"* (f. 3r, f. 68v, and f. 69r);[51] part of the copy-text prayer-tag, *"[Iesu] m^er̄cy lady helpe"* (f. 22v, top margin); many attempts at the letters *d, x,* and *z,* and other practice writing that imitates a set of accounts, on f. 68v; various attempts at the end of the alphabet row *"Est amen"* on f. 69r; a partial alphabet row, *d* to *v,* with repeated attempts at some of the letters (f. 81r); a full alphabet row along with some cursive loops and minims, faces in three-quarter profile, and several attempts at the name *Richard* (f. 81v); strokes for fancy majuscules (f. 82r); and *"deus est animus nobis vt carmina dicu^nt"* ("God is our inward understanding as verses say") twice as a copy-text on f. 82v.[52] In MS London, BL, Addit. 37049, the copy of the *ABC* is very messy; the scribe has crossed out errors as he copies and has inserted corrections between the lines. One wonders if the whole book was some kind

---

[49] That the letter is practice writing is suggested by its repetitiousness (*"praying you to sende me your dayly blessyng Father the cause of my wrytyng vnto you at this tyme Is praying you to sende me your dayly blessyng"*, "praying you to send me your daily blessing; Father, the reason that I am writing to you at this time is praying you to send me your daily blessing"). It is followed by another repeated copy-text, *"My loue she morns For me for me my loue she morns for me"* ("my love she mourns for me for me my love she mourns for me").

[50] The maxim is from Bernard of Clairvaux, *De Consideratione*, Book 2, ch. 10, para. 19, ed. in: PL 182, col. 753D.

[51] We encountered this copy-text in Chapter Two in the informal pedagogic environment of MS London, BL, Harley 6041.

[52] The opening lines of Benedict Burgh's *Cato major* translate this tag; the full Latin couplet appears in two of the manuscripts, MS Cambridge, UL, Ee.4.31, f. 7v, and MS Oxford, Bod. Lib., Rawl. C. 48, f. 84r; see *DIMEV* 1418. MS Beinecke, Takamiya 61 is fifteenth-century composite manuscript on paper that contains medical and scientific texts along with much informal post-production material in English and Latin in many hands.

Graphic Play 181

of apprentice piece. After the last line of the text, "*For a mesurabyl mene is best for vs all*" ("for a happy medium is best for all of us"), the scribe has filled a gap at the base of the column with a brief moral advice text about not being a lender to a friend (f. 86v), the kind of material often used as copy-text for writing practice. In addition, a few traces of rudimentary practice writing appear in the lower margin of f. 15r and on the right margin of f. 16r (*R* both times?). The pages of the volume are full, with space not used for text taken up with much illustration, so there may not have been much practice writing in the margins of this manuscript. However, many edges of pages are worn so some traces of practice may have been lost. In MS London, BL, Addit. 60577, beneath the *ABC of Aristotle*, a wobbly hand has copied again the last line of the poem (f. 56v). As we saw in Chapter Two, this manuscript is associated with a Benedictine monk of St. Swithun's Priory, Winchester who was active *c.* 1487 and may have been a school teacher. In 1549, Thomas Dackomb – a petty canon of Winchester Cathedral – added another alphabet poem to MS London, BL, Addit. 60577 (ff. 59r-60v). Here the letters of the alphabet start each stanza in order, and the pattern is emphasised through the placing of each letter at the midpoint of a blank line before each new stanza. As with the *ABC of Aristotle* in this manuscript, this scribe's attention to layout and letter-placing promotes visual recognition of the *figurae* and their place in the alphabet. With the first version of the poem in Harley 541, practice letters in the margin below the explicit of the first text confirm the educational associations of the material (f. 213v). The second version of the poem in Harley 541 is on a leaf on whose verso occur the name of Sir Thomas Frowyk, London merchant, probably not in his hand, and the symbol he put on the beaks of his swans (f. 228).[53] In Harley 1304, practice letters occur on the end leaves, on ff. 1av (with a drawing of an axe and some names and brief copy-texts), and 104r-v, while practice writing in a late hand is modelled on the first lines of text (Lydgate's *Life of Our Lady*) on ff. 10v and 11r, where it is accompanied by the name "*Elizabeth*" and in the lower margin the penultimate line of text on the page is copied. Another late, immature hand copies the penultimate line on f. 20r in the lower margin, also writing there "*amen in mysery*"(?) between two roughly ruled lines. Drawings of a pair of yoked oxen, viewed from above, appear on a formerly blank page (f. 99v). On a blank verso of Harley 1706 opposite the *ABC* a reader has

---

[53] On the symbol and the hand see SUTTON and VISSER-FUCHS, "'The making of a minor London chronicle" and M.D. RUST, *Imaginary Worlds in Medieval Books: Exploring the Manuscript Matrix* (Basingstoke, 2007), pp. 73-79.

182   *Chapter 3*

signed *"Elysabeth Oxnford"* and has entered a few practice letters (Elisabeth's signature also occurs on f. 95r, a table of contents of ff. 3r-94r that could also be in the hand of the *ABC* scribe, and elsewhere).[54]

We have seen that making a copy of, and reading, the *ABC of Aristotle* posed graphic puzzles and challenges. The textual variation that I have described above is, arguably, not simply the product of scribal transmission of an authorial text. Surviving in many variant copies, the *ABC* is in some ways comparable with the copy-texts discussed in Chapter Two such as colophons and ownership inscriptions that also gave matter for practice reading and writing in communities of Anglophone literate practice. And like those more elementary copy-texts, the *ABC* is found not as part of sustained copying campaigns but in other hands on end leaves or on single sheets, anywhere that there was opportunity for testing and playful display of skill. Whether it was copied from memory, as many of those copy-texts perhaps were, or adapted from an exemplar, the text served as a challenging copy-text, engaging readers and writers in testing and displaying their knowledge of the doctrine of *littera* and their ingenuity in applying it to the alphabet and graphic practice in Middle English. Variation in the text provides traces of the creative and playful responses of writers and readers to those challenges. But while it is a version of this material, the *ABC* is much more challenging, a graphic puzzle that engaged the skills of practised writers rather than those still at the stage of trying out wobbly hands in the margins of books.

Alphabet Poems and Literary Games

We saw above that the *ABC of Aristotle* is sometimes referred to in its prologues as a 'ragman' or a 'roll'. A 'ragman roll' was a record of witness testimony in shire courts[55] but it became associated with literary games in which a series of brief texts concerning courtly behaviour and character were randomly allocated to players. *Ragmanys Rolle* (*DIMEV* 3618) was a game of fortunes based on the rather more scurrilous *Ragemon le Bon*.[56] It is clear from the com-

---

[54] She is identified in the British Library Catalogue as Elisabeth Beaumont († 1537),who married John de Vere, Earl of Oxford, *c*. 1508; she owned the book before this marriage.

[55] W. SCASE, *Literature and Complaint in England, 1272-1553* (Oxford, 2007), p. 133.

[56] S. PATTERSON, "Sexy, naughty, and lucky in love: Playing *Ragemon le Bon* in English gentry households", in: *Games and Gaming in Medieval Literature*, ed. S. PATTERSON (New York, 2015), chapter 4, n.p. (e-book).

Graphic Play 183

plete text that the stanzas were supposed to be copied separately and to be allocated to players of the game by drawing lots, so some improvising on behalf of the reader would have been required, perhaps recopying the stanzas, or dipping into the text with eyes shut. The *ABC of Aristotle* could easily have been used as a game text along these lines. It would have been a simple matter to find a process for random distribution of lines. For example, a player could dip into the alphabet with his or her eyes closed. As mentioned above, the *ABC of Aristotle* is known to survive in a single-line form – in a graffito at Great Bardford. This survival could be the *result* of selection of a line.

Reinforcing the association of the *ABC of Aristotle* with literary game-playing, the poem is on occasion found in the manuscript environment of such graphic games. A trace of this kind of use of the text may lie behind the appearance of a single stanza from *Ragmanys Rolle* in *ABC of Aristotle* manuscript MS London, BL, Addit. 36983, f. 263v (*DIMEV* 6543). The sole stanza from *Ragmanys Rolle* (stanza 11) is in praise of the Virgin Mary, reflecting on how members of different estates strive to emulate her.

Another alphabet poem that appears in Addit. 36983 is Chaucer's *ABC Hymn to the Virgin* (ff. 175r-178v, *DIMEV* 414). Based on an alphabet poem in Guillaume de Deguileville's *Pèlerinage de la Vie Humaine*, Chaucer's *ABC*, one of the best known and most copied alphabet poems of the late medieval period, comprises twenty-three stanzas of eight rhyming lines. The first word of each stanza begins with one of the letters of the alphabet and they are arranged in order, from *a*, "*Almighty and al merciable queene*" ("almighty and all-merciful queen", line 1) to *z*, "*Zacharie yow clepeth the open welle*" ("Zechariah calls you the open well", line 177). Each stanza is an elegant and courtly prayer to the Virgin Mary, and each forms a complete sense unit so it may be read or written independently.[57]

Evidence that selected stanzas of Chaucer's *ABC* were used for playful (but pious) writing practice is provided by a manuscript that includes an incomplete text of the poem. In MS Durham, UL, Cosin V.i.9, the first two stanzas of Chaucer's *ABC* have been entered in a blank space at end of a late fourteenth-century copy of Henry de Gauchy, *Gouvernement des princes* (f. 203r). The *ABC* stanzas are in a completely different hand from the main text. The writing gives the impression that its scribe was unpractised: the text is not well fitted into the ruled frame and the rhymes are bracketed inaccurately. The scribe treats the

---

[57] Geoffrey Chaucer, *ABC Hymn to the Virgin*, in: *The Riverside Chaucer*, ed. L.D. BENSON, 3rd edn. (Oxford, 1988), pp. 637-640 (text) and pp. 1076-1077 and 1185 (notes).

184   *Chapter 3*

two stanzas as a complete work, finishing with a colophon of one rhyming couplet "*Thenkyth on hym that this wrote / Qwanne ye seen hym not*" ("think about the person that copied this when he is absent from you").[58] Had the two stanzas been penned as a gift for the recipient who is addressed in the colophon? Had they been selected because particularly liked by or appropriate for the addressee?[59]

Scribal treatment of Chaucer's *ABC*, accompanying game texts, and traces of practice writing all provide evidence of playful pedagogic engagement with the text. As mentioned above, in MS London, BL, Addit. 36983 Chaucer's *ABC* occurs along with the *ABC of Aristotle* and the stanza from *Ragmanys Rolle*. Unusually among the scribes of the poem, the scribe of Addit. 36983 calls attention to the graphic subject of the poem by inserting the rubric "*Incipit carmen Secundu^m ordinem litteraru^m alphabetu^{m}*" ("here begins a poem organised in alphabetical order").[60] He also enhances the alphabet structure visually. This scribe characteristically adorns his letters with ludic initials in red ink and exaggerated flourished ascenders and descenders in upper and lower margins and sometimes in left and right margins (for example, f. 242r).[61] His copy of the *ABC of Aristotle* begins each line with the word "*To*" written with an extravagantly formed *T* (f. 263r-v). When copying Chaucer's *ABC* this scribe gives full rein to his ludic and showy hand. The alphabetical initials are generously embellished with a variety of graphic motifs including cadels, illusionistic ribbons, creatures, and faces. The scribe's showy initials have been treated as

---

[58] This couplet is not recorded in *DIMEV*. The text of the colophon, read under ultra-violet light, is quoted from the online library catalogue; the manuscript was stolen in 1998 and the text is only partially visible on the digitised microfilm.

[59] Incomplete texts of Chaucer's *ABC* also occur in MS London, BL, Harley 7578, f. 20v (lines 1-48), and MS Cambridge, Magdalene College, Pepys, 2006, pp. 386-388 (lines 1-59). The Harley text may once have continued in a further booklet. The Pepys text ends with a stanza fragment that has been completed with a spurious line (see *DIMEV*).

[60] This rubric is also found in MS Cambridge, UL, Ff.5.30 and MS London, Lambeth Palace Library, Sion College, Arc. L. 10.2/E44 (Geoffrey Chaucer, *ABC Hymn to the Virgin*, p. 1185).

[61] Thompson *et al.* find three hands in the volume, attributing to the scribe of the *ABC* (scribe B), ff. 3r-178v, 230r-263v, 305v (J.J. THOMPSON, I. JOHNSON, S. KELLY, R. PERRY, and A. WESTPHALL, *Geographies of Orthodoxy: Mapping English Pseudo-Bonaventuran Lives of Christ, 1350-1550* (Belfast and St. Andrews, n.d.), <https://geographies-of-orthodoxy.qub.ac.uk/ discuss/>. Though scribe C's stint is distinct (and dated by him 1442), it is less easy to be sure that scribes A and B are not the same hand, since the exuberance and extravagance of the scribe of the *ABC*s are shared with the hand designated A, ff. 1r-2v, 216r-229v, 264r-305r.

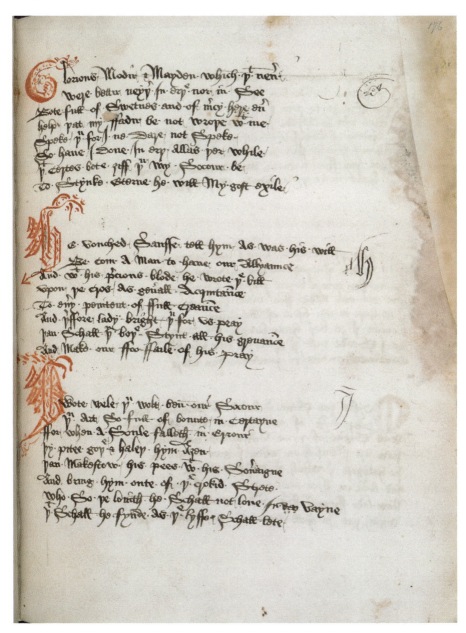

Fig. 14. Chaucer's *ABC* with embellished initials and imitation, MS London, BL, Addit. 36983, f. 176r. © The British Library Board, MS British Library, Addit. 36983, f. 176r.

186   *Chapter 3*

models for practice writing carried out by later users of the book. For example, his red pen-work *G*, *H*, and *I* on f. 176r have been imitated to the right of the relevant stanzas (see Figure 14). Practice letters *A* and *P* decorated with lacy pen-work that imitates that of the scribe occur on f. 177r. The copy-text "*Ihesu mercy lady helpe*" is repeated twice on ff. 255r and 261v. These features suggest that some users of the volume demonstrated appreciation of and aspired to emulate the scribe's graphic exuberance and aspiration.

The scribe of Addit. 36983 follows a tradition in which the alphabetical structure of Chaucer's *ABC* is foregrounded visually by a layout in stanzas with decorated initial letters.[62] In MS Glasgow, UL, Hunter 239 (U.3.12), an early fifteenth-century copy of the *ABC*, the alphabet is made prominent by virtue of fine blue initials decorated with red pen-work. The text is embedded in a Middle English translation of Guillaume de Deguileville's *Le Pèlerinage de la Vie Humaine*, where Chaucer's translation forms the text of a "*skripture*" ("piece of writing") that is handed down to the pilgrim out of a cloud by Grace Dieu (ff. 80v-83v). The text's focus on writing is enhanced by the scribe's switch from a prose to a verse layout with regular decorated initials that foreground the alphabetical sequence. This scribe's interest in graphic arts is betrayed by his fine, exuberant ascenders (e.g., ff. 3v-4r). In MS London, BL, Harley 2251, attributed to the Hammond scribe and dated after 1465 (*Late Medieval English Scribes*), the first line of each stanza is marked with a rubricated paraph (the scribe's usual method for laying out stanzaic verse in the manuscript); in addition, after *A*, which receives a three-line pen-work initial, the letters of the alphabet are given prominence by being written beside the appropriate stanza in the margin in majuscules in the same ink and (usually) letter-forms as in the text. In MS London, BL, Harley 7578, f. 20v, the scribe has left spaces to demarcate the stanzas and has written guide letters for a decorator to fill with large initials, though the gaps remain unfilled. An exception is MS Oxford, Bod. Lib., Laud Misc. 740, ff. 103v-106v, where the scribe has marked the rhymes with brackets but the stanzas and the alphabetical arrangement completely disappear. This must be purposeful as the scribe is calligraphically exuberant, as shown by his elaborate, ludic ascenders for example, on ff. 47v-48r and f. 18r in the *Pilgrimage of the Life of Manhood* (see Figure 15). Perhaps the scribe is trying to make the *ABC* conform with the *mise en page* of the prose that occu-

---

[62] For brief descriptions of the treatment of the initials in the manuscripts see G.B. PACE, "The adorned initials of Chaucer's *ABC*", *Manuscripta* 23.2 (1979), pp. 88-98.

Graphic Play

Fig. 15. Exuberant ascenders in the *Pilgrimage of the Life of Manhood*, MS Oxford, Bod. Lib., Laud Misc. 740, f. 18r (detail). Photo: © Bodleian Libraries, University of Oxford. Creative Commons licence CC-BY-NC 4.0.

pies the rest of the volume. But his treatment of the text would also have given readers the opportunity to test and display their graphic knowledge by discerning the alphabetical structure for themselves.

Chaucer's *ABC* is associated with game poems in other manuscripts. In MS Oxford, Bod. Lib., Bodley 638, ff. 204r-207v, a late fifteenth-century anthology of poetry, Chaucer's *ABC* directly follows the game poem the "*Chaunce of the Dyse*" (*DIMEV* 1318, ff. 195-203v) while *Ragmanys Rolle* follows later in the volume (ff. 214v-218v). Players of the "*Chaunce of the Dyse*" would throw dice and seek out the appropriate stanza, submitting themselves to the power of Fortune who "*hath of all thinge gou^{er}naunce*" ("rules over all things", f. 195r) and to the risk of insult. A throw of two sixes and a one meant that one was a glutton, "*all the strete may here youre body clokke*" ("everyone in the vicinity can hear your body make animal sounds", f. 196r); three threes, a loyal unfortunate, "*Whi nas fortune take hede of youre sadnesse*" ("why has Fortune not taken heed of your steadfastness", f. 202r); two threes and a one meant that one was a resilient wise person that "*no rech what auenture god sende*" ("does not mind what befalls him", f. 202v). The poem permits its readers to play with the selection, order, and application of the stanzas. The scribe of MS Bodley 638 displays creativity and playfulness in the layouts of the *ABC* and the dice poems and invites similar freedom from the reader. Three stanzas are allocated to a page, the alphabetical arrangement being highlighted with both a rubricated initial at the opening of each stanza and a pen-work initial in the left margin. The "*Chaunce of the Dyse*" also has three stanzas to a page divided by red lines and a rubricated running header, and the letters of the alphabet in the *ABC* mirror depictions of throws of three dice in the margin. A fancy calligraphic explicit fills the stanza space at the end of both poems (ff. 203v, 207v). *Rag-*

188   *Chapter 3*

manys Rolle in this volume (ff. 214v-218v) has a similar layout. Perhaps the parallels between the layout of the *ABC* and those of the dice poem and *Ragmanys Rolle* would have suggested that the reader is likewise free to play with the selection, order, and application of the stanzas of the *ABC*, to play around with their alphabetical order or to choose a favourite stanza.

Chaucer's *ABC* occurs together with *Ragmanys Rolle* in the only other surviving full manuscript of the latter poem in English: MS Oxford, Bod. Lib., Fairfax 16, another later fifteenth-century anthology of poetry, where the *Rolle* occurs on ff. 47r-50r and the *ABC* on ff. 188v-191r.[63] This second example of Chaucer's *ABC Hymn to the Virgin* and the *Ragmanys Rolle* together in a manuscript strengthens the argument that the *ABC Hymn* is associated with graphic play and games. Another gaming text in MS Fairfax 16 is "*Chaunce of the Dyse*" (*DIMEV* 1318) which, we saw above, occurs together with *Ragmanys Rolle* and Chaucer's *ABC* in MS Bodley 638. However, the Fairfax scribe engages less with the graphic potential of the texts than the scribe of MS Bodley 638, preferring to maintain the consistent page layout of the volume. In imposing a rigid layout regime he introduces textual opacity.[64] In both texts the stanzas run over from page to page, and in the *ABC* the top line receives an embellished initial even when the letter is not one of the alphabetical sequence (for example, "*Han take on me a grevouse accion*" ("have subjected me to a grievous lawsuit") receives an enlarged and rubricated initial in the *C* stanza (f. 89r), and likewise "*There as that mercy euer shal soiourne*" in the *V* stanza ("where mercy will forever remain", f. 191r). This example particularly disrupts the appearance of the vertical alphabetical sequence as the embellished *T* mirrors visually that of the previous *T* stanza. The similar treatment of *Ragmanys Rolle* means that anyone trying to use the text to play the game could be misled as to

---

[63] A French version, *Ragemon le Bon*, occurs in MS Oxford, Bod. Lib., Digby 86, ff. 162r-163v. For the continental history of the genre and its appropriations in English gentry households see PATTERSON, "Sexy, naughty, and lucky in love: Playing *Ragemon le Bon*".

[64] My term 'opacity' is indebted to Jean-François Lyotard via Ganz's comment on ornamentation in early medieval display scripts, "[it] can augment its effects or confuse the reader grappling with an unfamiliar visual grammar. Script is not concerned with representation but with differentiating letters as they compose words. But the line of writing embodies meaning [...] as Jean-François Lyotard recognised: 'The trace must leave behind communicable transparency; the mind used to language can only perceive as opacity the way in which meaning invests the line'" (D. GANZ, "Early medieval display scripts and the problems of how we see them", in: *Graphic Signs of Identity, Faith, and Power in Late Antiquity and the Early Middle Ages*, ed. I. GARIPZANOV, C. GOODSON, and H. MAGUIRE (Turnhout, 2017), pp. 125-143, at p. 126, quoting J.-F. LYOTARD, *Discourse, Figure*, ed. and trans. J. MOWITT and A. HUDEK (Minneapolis, 2010), p. 212).

Graphic Play 189

stanza divisions. For example, the stanza that begins "*To chirche as swyftly as a snayl ye hey*" ("you go to church as swiftly as a snail") is spilt with three lines at the bottom of f. 47v and five at the top of f. 48r. Occurring at the top of the page and bearing a rubricated initial, the five lines that begin "*Ful spedful ye rennyn and ful yerne*" ("you run eagerly and very fast") might be mistaken for a stanza. The player winning this truncated stanza would receive a more positive character assessment than one who received the full stanza where the object of his eager running is specified:

> *To chirche as swyftly as a snayl ye hey*
> *But to the temple of bachus the tauerne*
> *To moystyn ther your appetitys drey*
> *Ful spedful ye rennyn and ful yerne*

> You go to church as swiftly as a snail, but to the temple of Bacchus to relieve your thirst you run eagerly and very fast

> (MS Oxford, Bod. Lib., Fairfax 16, ff. 47v-48r)

The Fairfax scribe's intolerance of graphic play, paradoxically, generates textual opacity and creates challenges for readers.

Surviving together with gaming texts such as *Ragmanys Rolle* and the "*Chaunce of the Dyse*", Chaucer's *ABC Hymn to the Virgin* and the *ABC of Aristotle* belong to a social environment – whether actual, or imagined. Through picking or winning a stanza, players of these games are attributed with attributes of courtly or uncourtly character. Graphic skill and being able to admire graphic virtuosity are associated with social transactions in which identity is negotiated. The lavish care and expense devoted to decorating the initials of Chaucer's *ABC* suggest that the text provided opportunities for readers as well as scribes to demonstrate graphic learning and skill. The attention to decoration suggests valuation of the alphabet and flatters the reader and patron by implying that they will recognise the *ABC* and prize it. It suggests that they are informed and skilled readers of the poem and not just listeners. It provides opportunities for identifying with the 'we' who value and understand letters and draws a boundary between this 'we' and 'others' who would not be able to recognise the alphabet acrostic.

190   *Chapter 3*

Early Middle English Alphabet Play

The *ABC of Aristotle* and Chaucer's *ABC* have precedents in earlier Middle English alphabet poems. These texts too show creative engagement with the challenges of displaying the alphabet: their poets, scribes, and decorators too exhibit resourcefulness and display graphic virtuosity when they tackle graphic problems. The *Alphabetical Praise of Women* (*DIMEV* 901) in the Auchinleck manuscript (MS Edinburgh, National Library of Scotland, Advocates' 19.2.1, ff. 324r-325v) is composed of eleven-line rhyming stanzas each of which begins with a new letter of the alphabet. The stanzas praise women and the poem seems to counter what Mary Dove calls a tradition of "misogynistic alphabet poems".[65] The *Alphabetical Praise of Women* poet's playfulness and graphic virtuosity are demonstrated by comparison of the poem with a possible Insular French source, the *ABC à Femmes* in MS London, BL, Harley 2253, ff. 49r-50v. The alphabet in the French poem ends *TVXYZ*. In the Middle English version in Auchinleck the alphabet is different, ending *TVXÞ/YZÞ/Y*. The poet of the Middle English version has replaced the *Y* stanza of the Harley poem (that begins "*Ysope fenoil columbyn*"; "hissop, fennel, columbine", f. 50r) with a *Þ* stanza that begins "*Þei a schrewe on woman lyȝe*" (f. 325r, "even if a wicked man should malign a woman"). He has added another, new *Y* stanza at the end of the sequence, after the *Z* ("*Zabulon*") stanza (the French letter sequence ends with "*Zabulon*", f. 50v): "*Yv were as douhti a swai[n]*" ("formerly [*MED*, *yu*, adv.] were as strong a knight's lad" (in the following lines the poet gives the examples of bygone doughty lads: Samson, Gawain etc.), f. 325r).[66] Pickering believes that the *Y* stanza after *Z* is a mistake on the part of the poet.[67] But it seems to me more likely that in the poet's alphabet thorn has been assimilated conceptually with *y* as a *figura*, though it has two *potestates*, and

---

[65] M. DOVE, "Evading textual intimacy: The French secular verse", in: *Studies in the Harley Manuscript: The Scribes, Contents, and Social Contexts of British Library MS Harley 2253*, ed. S.G. FEIN (Kalamazoo, MI, 2000), pp. 329-349, at p. 334.

[66] Burnley and Wiggins read "*Þei y were*" ("though I were"), emending silently (*The Auchinleck Manuscript*, ed. D. BURNLEY and A. WIGGINS (Edinburgh, 2003), <http://auchinleck. nls.uk/>. But a word with initial /j/ is needed here and there is no sign of missing '*ei*' in the manuscript. However, what may be a faint cross appears beside the line, possibly marking an error.

[67] O. PICKERING, "Stanzaic verse in the Auchinleck manuscript: *The Alphabetical Praise of Women*", in: *Studies in Late Medieval and Early Renaissance Texts in Honour of John Scattergood*, ed. A.M. D'ARCY and A.J. FLETCHER (Dublin, 2005), pp. 287-304, at p. 296. Pickering reads "*Y y were*".

Graphic Play 191

hence, perhaps, it has two positions in the alphabet: it can replace the "*Ysope*" stanza since thorn is equivalent to *y* figurally, while the *figura* requires two positions in the alphabet as it has another sound, /j/, also.[68] In fact, "*Yv were as douhti a swai[n]*" is superior to "*Ysope fenoil columbyn*" as a *Y* line, since "*Ysope*" begins with /i/ not /j/; the poet who writes Insular French has included two stanzas beginning with /i/, the other *I* stanza beginning "*Il ny out unqe homme nee*" ("there has never been any man born", Harley 2253, f. 49v). In addition to displaying this impressive graphic resourcefulness, the Middle English poem even incorporates the closing words of the alphabet prayer '*est*' and '*amen*' as opening words of two stanzas after the "*Yv*" stanza (loss of the opening of the poem means we cannot know if it also began with a cross). Here "*Est*" (Latin "is") becomes the first word in an English line that begins "*Est and west*" ("east and west", f. 325r). The pleasure of this play resides at the graphic level: only someone who was *looking at* the vertically embedded alphabetical sequence would detect the visual pun on Latin '*est*' ('is') and English '*est*' ('east'). The poet's incorporation of "*est*" into the poem is not paralleled in the source. While addressing the challenges of creating an alphabet poem in English, the poet demonstrates his graphic virtuosity by improving on the French model.[69] Readers might well have been expected to know both and to admire his skill. And any reader who knew either the Middle English poem or the French version could have been mischievously misdirected by an echo when trying to solve the "*Annot and John*" puzzle in Harley 2253 with which this chapter began, for the "*Note of þe niȝtingale*" is the first line of the *N* stanza (f. 324v, "*Note de la russinole*" in the French of Harley 2253), the phrase attracting attention to the *N* graph and directing attention away from the '*Annot*' reading.

The scribes engage with the poems' graphic structure with various degrees of proficiency. The *ABC à Femmes* stanzas are laid out in four lines with offset shorter lines. The scribe has left spaces and guide letters for the letters of the alphabet which are displayed boldly in two-line red initials. However, the start of a stanza that begins "*Amen*" is only highlighted with a paraph (f. 50v). The

---

[68] Compare the treatment of thorn / *y* and yogh / zed in some *Polychronicon* indexes, discussed in Chapter Five.

[69] This improvement adds evidence in support of the French text's being the source for the English rather than the other way round, as argued by Dove (DOVE, "Evading textual intimacy: The French secular verse", pp. 331-332). Cf. Pickering's argument that the English is based on the French on the grounds of the poet's replacement of the *Y* stanza with a thorn stanza (PICKERING, "Stanzaic verse in the Auchinleck manuscript", p. 297).

192   *Chapter 3*

scribe's layout of the stanzas of the Middle English *Alphabetical Praise of Women* likewise emphasises their alphabetical arrangement. The initial letter of each line is offset in the left margin and the alphabetical sequence is displayed as large initials of two or more lines with blue letters and delicate red pen-work, giving the letters of the alphabet the appearance of being linked as in a necklace or daisy-chain. The scribe has allowed space for the large initials by indenting the first letters of the opening two lines of each stanza. However he has overlooked *G* and *V* (ff. 324r, 325r). Someone (perhaps the decorator) has tried to make good the omission by marking the new stanzas with red paraphs but the visual disruption to the alphabetical sequence goes unremedied. The decorator displays the witty incorporation of "*Est*" and "*Amen*" into the sequence by including large initials for these words. The decorator's thorn (f. 325r) has the same *figura* as his *Y*; perhaps like the poet he sees *Y* and *Þ* as a single *figura* with two *potestates*. The deficiencies and attempts at remedy would have given alert readers opportunities to test their own understanding of the poems' alphabetical structure.

Acrostics

Many of the *ABC* poems that we have been discussing are acrostics of a sort. Those familiar with the *figurae* and order of the letters of the alphabet and aware of the applications of this learning to English are invited to display and take pleasure from their learning by poems in this tradition. Poems that conceal personal names in acrostics also align graphic skill and understanding with social belonging. They require writers and readers to play with their knowledge of how *figurae* and *potestates* relate, and how to assemble syllables and words. Some acrostics play with religious keywords and brief texts that would be widely known, such as '*mors solvit omnia*' ('death dissolves all things'), but many embed personal names whose significance would be known to only a few. The particular pleasures taken in the form in such cases must have been confined to small circles, perhaps going some way to explaining why the texts were not, apparently, widely circulated. It is noticeable that most of the twenty-six non-alphabetic Middle English acrostics – acrostics that conceal words rather than the alphabet – recorded in *DIMEV* survive in only one manuscript. In some cases the author and the scribe are probably one and the same. Often, a significant name is distributed as the first letter of each line of a poem. An

Graphic Play 193

acrostic poem by Charles D'Orléans, "*Alas mercy where shall mine heart you find*" (*DIMEV* 289), reveals the full name *Anne Molins* if the first letter of each line is read vertically. The inclusion of a name in an acrostic enables the author to display his compositional skill, since it determines the number of lines in a poem and limits the choice of opening words in each line. Here, Charles D'Orléans has chosen the *chanson* form, a ten-line form where the first two lines are repeated twice more as a refrain, making fourteen lines in all. As well as concealing the lady's name in the opening letters of each of the ten lines, Charles conceals the lady's initials in the first two words of the refrain, "*Alas mercy*". Acrostics also require graphic creativity on the part of the scribe. In Paris, BNF, fr. 25458, p. 311, a manuscript in several hands that is said to have belonged to Charles, the acrostic is foregrounded visually by the space left between the fourth and fifth lines, where the division between the lady's first and second names falls.[70] The repetitions of the refrain include only the key opening words that conceal the lady's initials. Despite this graphic resourcefulness, the scribe has not solved the problem of having to leave space for a two-line initial *A*, meaning that the first *n* in '*Anne*' is displaced from the vertical column.

An acrostic about St. Katherine (*DIMEV* 961) with a similar layout has been added in a blank space at the end of a prayer to the saint in MS Cambridge, Trinity College, B.11.18 (James No. 257), f. 9v, a Book of Hours thought to date to the mid fifteenth century. The addition is in a later, informal hand. The scribe foregrounds the acrostic by placing the letters *KATIRIN* in large capitals in the margin, leaving a wide gap before the rest of the poem which is enclosed in the ruled writing space. Not all scribes are alert to the art of the acrostic: scribal error demonstrates that they sometimes were unaware that an acrostic was present. This is the case with *DIMEV* 3454, a fifteenth-century lyric in which death addresses a beautiful person – according to the French rubric, death is a mirror for young ladies at their toilet.[71] The first letters of the fourteen lines of the poem spell out the warning in Latin: "*MORS SOLVIT OMNIA*". The scribe of the only manuscript copy, MS London, BL, Harley 116, f. 128r-v, has corrupted the acrostic by spelling '*Vche*' (needed for the letter *v* in '*solvit*') as "*Yche*" and miscopying '*Ne*' (needed for the *n* in '*omnia*') as "*Be*". No effort

---

[70] The acrostic poem is not attributed to the scribal hand of Charles himself; Champion attributes it to "*un scribe anglais*" ("an English scribe"; P. CHAMPION, *Le manuscrit autographe des poésies de Charles D'Orléans* (Paris, 1907), p. 47); for material in this manuscript in Charles's hand see pp. 1-11.

[71] J.L. CUTLER, "A Middle English acrostic", *Modern Language Notes* 70.2 (1995), pp. 87-89, at p. 88.

194   *Chapter 3*

is made to foreground the initial letters of each line; they are tipped with red ink just like the first letters of each line in other poems in this scribe's hand (for example, *DIMEV* 1563, ff. 127r-128r).

Six acrostics occur in Humphrey Newton's manuscript, MS Oxford, Bod. Lib., Lat. Misc. c. 66: an acrostic on *Brian, DIMEV* 785 (f. 93v); two on *Elin, DIMEV* 1219 (f. 93v), and *DIMEV* 1220 (f. 94v); two on *Humphrey, DIMEV* 1938 (ff. 92v and 95r), and one on *Margere, DIMEV* 3561 (f. 93v; *DIMEV* reads *Margaret* but the first words of the final line are corrected and illegible). F. 93v, where four of the acrostics occur, is headed "*Litt^{er}a amandi ^{et} nomeⁿ de illa ^{est} expressum hic*" ("the letter [or epistle] of the beloved and her name are expressed here"). Humphrey's graphic experimentation and engagement here clearly index belonging in a social circle.[72] The general disorganisation of the texts, which are crammed on the page and written in different inks and sizes of script, and the inclusion of two versions of the *Elin* acrostic, suggest personal drafting and collection of material for playful experimentation. The recurrent annotation "*mittit^{ur}*" ("it is sent"), as mentioned in Chapter Two, may record the sending of a fair copy to someone; most probably the person named in the case of the acrostics (ff. 93v, 94r, 94v). Playful graphic skill and accomplishment here are clearly seen as modes of social belonging.

Littera *and Early English Riddles*

The present section on pedagogic play in medieval poems in English will finish with some brief reflections on the ways in which the pedagogy of graphic play informs riddles and related riddling texts in Old English. We saw in Chapter One that the Old English Cynewulf acrostics, themselves graphic puzzles and challenging cryptic signatures, repay consideration in the framework of teaching about graphs and alphabets. The present discussion will focus on applications of *littera* teaching facilitated by riddles and related texts and how they could have provided vehicles for identity formation. Whether or not these texts were actually used in the classroom, like the Latin examples discussed in section one of this chapter, is undecided.[73] Rudolf has argued con-

---

[72] Perhaps those who gathered in "*þe halle*" ("the hall", f. 26br) for which the *ABC of Aristotle* is proposed as a decoration; see Chapter Four.

[73] There is of course a huge literature on the riddles, and their general links with the Anglo-Latin traditions of pedagogic riddling are well known; see A. ORCHARD, "Enigma variations: The Anglo-Saxon riddle-tradition", in: *Latin Learning and English Lore: Studies in Anglo-Saxon Lit-*

Graphic Play   195

vincingly that "Anglo-Saxon readers *could* use the vernacular riddles to practise the medieval reading modes of *lectio* [the elementary stages of *littera*], *enarratio*, and *iudicium*".[74] This section builds on that insight, arguing that whatever their role in formal education, the riddles offer early examples of the application of pedagogic play to the special challenges of reading and writing English.

The earliest example of an alphabet puzzle in English – and the single Old English specimen – is the *Rune Poem*. Actually, it is more complicated and a more challenging exercise than many later alphabet poems, since it engages knowledge of both the modified Latin alphabet and the rune row or futhorc. It is comprised of a series of sections, each one offering a riddling definition of the name of the rune. The rune ᚻ that is called '*hægl*' ('hail'), for example, is described in the poem as the whitest of grains, a substance that comes down from the skies before turning to water. The manuscript, MS London, BL, Cotton Otho B.x ff. 165r-165v, was lost in the Cotton collection fire of 1731, so we have to rely on early modern transcriptions and editions to try to deduce what the original looked like.[75] The edition of George Hickes is the base text used by editors. Hickes prints the rune in the left margin together with its name, printing the riddling verse that identifies the rune name when solved to the right.[76]

---

erature for Michael Lapidge, ed. K. O'BRIEN O'KEEFFE and A. ORCHARD, 2 vols. (Toronto, 2005), 1, pp. 284-304. For details of riddles in the Exeter book that are based on Aldhelm's Latin riddles, see H. SOPER, "Reading the Exeter Book riddles as life writing", *Review of English Studies* 68 (2017), pp. 841-865, at p. 842, n. 4. For the relationships of the thematic organisation of the Exeter Book riddles with those of Latin collections and their grounding in Isidore's *Etymologiae* see SALVADOR-BELLO, *Isidorean Perceptions of Order*. Lendinara's picture of pre-Conquest Insular education as Latinate implies that English only had a role as a medium for glosses to assist teachers (LENDINARA, "The world of Anglo-Saxon learning"). If so, the Old English riddles may have found only informal pedagogic uses in communities of Anglophone literate practice. However, Salvador-Bello sees the Exeter riddle collection as "originat[ing] in a monastic center, in which they were probably used for teaching purposes" (p. 450), still, riddling should not be considered "only as an exclusively educational phenomenon" (p. 451). Cf. Drout who argues that the 'wisdom' poems in the Exeter Book are "instructional" and that they and the manuscript are associated with the Benedictine Reform (M.D.C. DROUT, "Instructional effects of the Exeter Book 'Wisdom Poems'", in: *Form and Content of Instruction in Anglo-Saxon England in the Light of Contemporary Manuscript Evidence*, ed. P. LENDINARA, L. LAZZARI, and M.A. D'ARONCO (Turnhout, 2007: *Fédération Internationale des Instituts d'Etudes Médiévales, Textes et Etudes du Moyen Age* 39), pp. 447-466, at p. 466).

[74] W. RUDOLF, "Riddling and reading: Iconicity and logographs in Exeter Book Riddles 23 and 45", *Anglia* 130.4 (2012), pp. 499-525, at p. 523, my italics.

[75] See *The Old English Rune Poem: A Critical Edition*, ed. M. HALSALL (Toronto, 1981).

[76] *The Old English Rune Poem*, in: *Linguarum vett. septentrionalium thesaurus*

196   *Chapter 3*

Symons argues that editors like Hickes err when they insert the rune name after the rune because solving the riddle *supplies* the rune name.[77] If we accept this plausible suggestion it follows that the point of the riddles is to offer the reader opportunities to give the correct *nomen* for each runic *figura*. This process would also have invited the reader to give each rune its correct *potestas*, since the names of runes are acrophonic, "beginning with the phoneme expressed by the rune".[78] The runes may have been placed in the left margin, as they are by Hickes, Symons suggests, so that they formed "a visually distinct runic acrostic".[79] If this is correct, the poem would in addition have invited flexibility and directional versatility in the reading process, requiring a mixture of horizontal and vertical reading, the latter reading revealing the entire futhorc in order and the place of each rune in the row. The *Rune Poem* engages with *littera* pedagogy, but transfers it to the more challenging environment of bi-scriptal vernacular literacy, requiring the reader to work in two overlapping scripts and to distinguish between the shapes of the graphs they share, such as thorn, which is present both as a component of the futhorc and in the modified Latin alphabet here.

Like Aldhelm's riddle 30, some of the Old English riddles in the Exeter book (described as a "perceptual game" and as a "literary game", by Williamson)[80] likewise encourage reflection on and engagement with the names, shapes, and *potestates* of letters. If there is no firm evidence that the Exeter Book itself was used for pedagogic purposes, its riddle texts undoubtedly reflect that tradition. Many of the English riddles involve playing around with letters. Riddle 36[81] encrypts the Latin words '*mulier*' and '*equus*' by substituting the vowels with the next letter in the alphabet, so for example *u* in '*mulier*' and '*equus*' is spelt with *x* (f. 109v). Riddle 23 begins with the solution, '*boga*' ('bow', n.) but the word is encrypted by means of word reversal. The line in-

---

grammatico-criticus et archaeologicus, ed. G. HICKES, 2 vols. (Oxford, 1705), 1, p. 135.

[77] V. SYMONS, *Runes and Roman Letters in Anglo-Saxon Manuscripts* (Berlin, 2016), pp. 184-188.

[78] R. DEROLEZ, "Runic literacy among the Anglo-Saxons", in: *Britain 400-600: Language and History*, ed. A. BAMMESBERGER and A. WOLLMANN (Heidelberg, 1990), pp. 397-436, at p. 405.

[79] SYMONS, *Runes and Roman Letters,* p. 186.

[80] *The Old English Riddles of the Exeter Book*, ed. C. WILLIAMSON (Chapel Hill, 1977), pp. 24-25, 28.

[81] I follow the numbering in *The Exeter Book of Old English Poetry with Introductory Chapters by R.W. Chambers, Max Förster, and Robin Flower*, ed. R.W. CHAMBERS, M. FÖRSTER, and R. FLOWER (London, 1933).

Graphic Play 197

cludes a clue as to how to solve the riddle: "*ago[b] is min noma eft onhwyrfed*" ("'*agob*' is my name when it is reversed"). In fact, the manuscript reads "*agof*", and Saltzmann suggests that this spelling might not be an error: it might have been intended to make the riddle harder to solve.[82] Orchard suggests that the opening line was a solution in an exemplar that has been mistakenly incorporated in the text.[83] Rudolf suggests that the *f* might challenge the reader to recall the use of *b* for the voiced fricative in earlier Old English texts, such as '*heben*' ('heaven').[84] Whatever the case, solving the puzzle would have involved substitution of graphs with different *potestates* to replace the misleading *f* and application of knowledge about the assembly of letters into syllables and words.

Six of the Exeter Book riddles employ runes to test the reader's understanding and skill with *litterae*. Four include runes that require their *figurae* to be read as futhorc letters with *potestates* that spell words (Riddles 19, 24, 64, 75) and two, Riddles 42 and 58, name runes to designate *figurae* that spell the solution.[85] Dewa observes that decoding the runes "requires a variety of problem-solving approaches from the reader".[86] For our present purposes it is important to note that the use of runes engages poet, scribe, and reader in testing and developing their elementary graphic knowledge and skills through play. Riddle 19 uses reversed spellings like Riddle 23, but using runes. Reversal is combined with an acrostic: the word 'ᚻᚾᚪᚳ' ('*snac*', 'a fast warship') is revealed by reading the final runes of each runic word, confirming the solution 'ship'.[87] Riddle 24 deflects attention from the solution by describing the impossibly varied *sounds* made by the speaker of the riddle: "*hwilum beorce swa hund, hwilum blæte swa gat / hwilum græde swa gos*" and so on ("sometimes I bark like a dog, sometimes I bleat like a goat, sometimes I honk like a goose").[88] The final lines draw attention to the graphic material as the source of the solution: the six runic letters "*mec nemnað*" ("name me", line 7); "*Nu ic haten eom / swa þa siex stafas sweotule becnaþ*" ("now I am named as those

---

[82] Saltzman, "*Vt hkskdkxt*: Early medieval cryptography", p. 998.

[83] Orchard, "Enigma variations: The Anglo-Saxon riddle-tradition", p. 290.

[84] Rudolf, "Riddling and reading", p. 505.

[85] Bitterli, *Say What I Am Called*, pp. 85-86, categorises the runic riddles but not in relation to the theory of *littera*.

[86] R.J. Dewa, "The runic riddles of the Exeter Book: Language games and Anglo-Saxon scholarship", *Nottingham Medieval Studies* 39 (1995), pp. 26-36, at p. 36.

[87] M. Griffith, "Riddle 19 of the Exeter Book: '*Snac*', an Old English acronym", *Notes and Queries* n.s. 39.1 (1992), pp. 15-16, at p. 15; Bitterli, *Say What I Am Called*, pp. 87-89.

[88] *Anglo-Saxon Poetic Records*, 3, pp. 192-193, lines 2-3.

198   *Chapter 3*

six characters show clearly", lines 9-10). The six runes ᚷᚠᚱᚠᚻᛁ encode an
anagram of '*higoræ*', interpreted as 'jay', a supreme avian mimic.[89] The emphasis on sound in this puzzle perhaps directs the reader to think about the
potestates of the runes and to convert them into syllables and a word. Riddle 58
does not include rune graphs but it does describe and name them as a clue to its
solution: "*Þry sind in naman / ryhte runstafas, þara is rad fruma*" ("there are
three upright runes in my name, of which [the rune called] '*rad*' is the first").[90]
Describing the runes as "*rihte*" ("upright"), the poet invites the reader to imagine the visual appearance of runes and their graphic composition. The solution
'*rod*' (apparently the word for a well-sweep, a device for drawing water from
a well) written in runes, would contain three graphs that each include a straight
vertical initial stroke.[91] The riddle provides a metaphorical description of the
structure of the well-sweep, with its pole topped by a fulcrum and another pole
positioned as a lever in the fulcrum to raise and lower a bucket. Arguably,
possibly by imagining this structure the reader could also bring to mind the
figurae of some runes. Viewed from the side, with the lever angled to raise the
bucket, the well-sweep components would perhaps form the shape of the *n*-
rune: ᚾ. Viewed with the well behind the well-sweep, where both sides of the
fulcrum could be seen, the same configuration would perhaps form the image
of the *x*-rune: ᛉ, the left and right strokes at the top of the graph being formed
by the fulcrum. If this sounds far-fetched, there is other evidence that runes
could signify through their shape, as well as through their names and sounds:
on the Bewcastle Cross (Bewcastle 01), the first rune of the word '*Jesus*' is the
g-rune ᚷ that, shaped like a cross, perhaps echoes the use of the Greek letter
chi, the first letter of *Christus*, as a representation of Christ's body.[92] Were we
to know more about the precise well-sweep construction usual in pre-Conquest
England we might hazard further rune shape interpretations for Riddle 58. The
runic riddles, then, like the *Rune Poem* and like Cynewulf's acrostic signatures,
discussed in Chapter One, transfer exercises related to Latin literacy training

---

[89] *The Exeter Book of Old English Poetry*, p. 64; DEWA, "The runic riddles of the Exeter
Book", p. 29; BITTERLI, *Say What I Am Called*, p. 92.

[90] *Anglo-Saxon Poetic Records*, 3, pp. 208-209, lines 14-15; last line as emended by
BITTERLI, *Say What I Am Called*, p. 99.

[91] BITTERLI, *Say What I Am Called*, p. 105.

[92] B.C. TILGHMAN, "The shape of the word: Extralinguistic meaning in Insular display
lettering", *Word & Image*, 27.3 (2011), pp. 292-308, at p. 296. As we saw in Chapter One, Isidore
notes the symbolism of *X*: cf. "*figura crucem significat*" ("the letter signifies the cross";
Etymologiae, Book 1, ch. 3, section 11).

Graphic Play 199

to a bi-scriptal vernacular environment, increasing the difficulty of the puzzles with which the reader is confronted. These bi-scriptal poems make available to those who can solve them belonging to an elite and, one imagines, particularly highly select, literate identity.

The scribe of the Exeter book engages in the graphic play of the riddle texts.[93] As with his copies of Cynewulf's *Juliana* and *Christ II*, discussed in Chapter One, he distinguishes the runes from the Roman script by using angular strokes and delineating each rune with a point either side.[94] He draws attention to the first letter of reversed '*boga*' with a decorative majuscule in the margin (this graph also marks the beginning of the riddle, f. 106v). The runes in Riddle 19 are formed with extremely straight strokes and there may be evidence of erasure beneath the first runic word (f. 105r). The runes in Riddle 24 are similarly formed (f. 106v). The ratio of runes to Roman characters in Riddle 64 means that the runes, separated by points, are prominent on the page (f. 125r). Here the opacity of the graphs is increased by the scribe's treatment of thorn and wynn, which are hardly distinguishable in the runic and Roman scripts. This would have added to the challenge with which the reader is confronted. Opacity is also compounded by the scribe's treatment of Tironian *et*. Whereas usually the scribe encloses both the symbol for '*et*' and a rune within one pair of points (for example, in the *Christ II* Cynwulf signature, f. 19v, line 9), here Tironian *et* is also given separating points giving it, too, the appearance of a rune. Opacity is increased as the codes to which the graphs belong are not instantly apparent. The way in which the runes communicate in this highly cryptic riddle is also called into play. Since Tironian *et* is a logograph, a symbol that represents a word, the similar treatment of the runes suggests that they too should be read for their *nomina*, logographically, as symbols for the entities they name, rather than for their *potestates*. However, the placing of 'and' between two runes may signal that the two runes thus linked should be read as the first two graphs of a concealed word.[95] This use of runes would challenge the reader to try out various modes of decoding and arriving at the solution would require him or her to draw on knowledge of *potestates* and how they combine to form syllables and in turn how syllables form words. An unde-

---

[93] Cf. Rudolf's point that the material instantiation of the riddles and especially the "singularities of medieval handwriting" are essential to appreciating their "full literary and cultural potential" (RUDOLF, "Riddling and reading", p. 523).

[94] Bitterli finds a possible exception to this practice in Riddle 64, where one point appears to be missing (BITTERLI, *Say What I Am Called*, p. 90).

[95] S.J. HARRIS, "Anglo-Saxon ciphers", paragraph 13.10.

200   *Chapter 3*

coded runic inscription by a later reader in drypoint in the top margin of this page adds to the mystery. The runes in Riddle 75 stand out by being at the end of a line and being formed of unusually thick, heavy lines (f. 127r). The four runes are separated by points at either end rather than individually. It has been suggested that the scribe has erroneously copied a note in the margin of the exemplar into the text.[96] Like the inconsistency in rune formation elsewhere in the hand of this scribe (discussed in Chapter One), such an error would suggest that the scribe is paying very close attention to replicating the graphic substance of his exemplar, perhaps without decoding it. His error may have added to the opacity and graphic challenge of his output and, ironically, increased the opportunities it presented for belonging to an elite literate identity of those who could overcome the difficulties.

Exploring cryptography as a theme in pre-Conquest literature, Christie argues that it thematises the world view in which the universe is "an opaque testament to God's invisible architecture".[97] This "conception of the natural world as a cipher" provides, for Christie, context and authority for the "ludic textuality of Anglo-Saxon manuscripts", leading to "literary toying" with letters seen as "discrete, material objects" and "material conduits of meaning".[98] The Blickling Homily for Easter, for example, describes the Last Judgement as a time when the transcendent will be revealed and "all men shall see".[99] However, with the Old English riddles, as we have seen, an alternative view is possible in which human engagement with graphic play offers a different kind of belonging. Readers of the English riddles are offered opportunities to identify, not with all men, but with an elite group who arrive at solutions through their graphic puzzle-solving powers.

[96] V. SYMONS, "Commentary for Riddles 75 and 76", in: *The Riddle Ages: An Anglo-Saxon Riddle Blog*, ed. M. CAVELL, V. SYMONS, and M. AMMON, Blog Post 26 March 2018, <https://theriddleages.wordpress.com/>.

[97] E.J. CHRISTIE, "The cryptographic imagination: Revealing and concealing in Anglo-Saxon literature", in: *Material History of Medieval and Early Modern Ciphers: Cryptography and the History of Literacy*, ed. K. ELLISON and S. KIM (New York, 2018: *Material Readings in Early Modern Culture*), n.p. (e-book), para. 14.5.

[98] CHRISTIE, "The cryptographic imagination", paras. 14.5-6.

[99] CHRISTIE, "The cryptographic imagination", para. 14.15.

Graphic Play 201

Discussion

In this section we have seen that the basic elements of the teaching of *littera* through graphic puzzles and play were transferred to English-language writing environments in the periods studied by this book. With this transfer, new layers of challenge were added to traditional puzzle activities as scribes, authors, and readers had to grapple with the variability and uncertainties associated with graphs and alphabets in the vernacular. If one were to compare graphic puzzling with modern computer gaming, one could say that Latin pedagogic puzzles are like the entry level of a game while vernacular graphic puzzles constitute a higher game level. English-language riddles, alphabet poems, and acrostics also demanded a higher level of skill and knowledge of the arts of *littera* than did the imitation of models and copy-texts in Anglophone literate environments that we explored in Chapter Two. Traces of individuals' engagement with these challenges appear in scribes', readers', and players' responses to the material. In some cases scribes' struggles may have added extra levels of pleasurable challenge for other readers. In other cases, such as some of the examples of the *ABC of Aristotle*, we can see displays of graphic ingenuity and resourcefulness in the variant texts. One possible reader response was evidently the display of valuation of the alphabet through commissioning a manuscript copy of an alphabet poem. Another was engaging with the opportunity to recognise and appreciate the structure of a lavishly decorated alphabet poem such as Chaucer's *ABC*. These puzzles and displays offered opportunities to belong to new, select literate identities. The close association between the *ABC* poems and literary games provides further evidence that engaging with and appreciating graphic challenges contributed to social identity and belonging. In the case of the acrostics of personal names, a further boundary was drawn between those who could spot the acrostic and those who could both spot it and identify the person to whom it referred.

Signature Playfulness

We will now turn from puzzle and game poems to another genre where the resources of pedagogic play are mobilised: scribal signatures and colophons.[100]

---

[100] Scribal colophons are a neglected subject. Reynhout writes "[p]eu de phénomènes *codicologiques semblent si connus et ont été en réalité si peu étudiés pour eux-mêmes que les*

202   *Chapter 3*

In Chapter Two we encountered the colophon and the signature as models and copy-texts for writing practice. This final section of the present chapter will argue that as well as providing opportunities for elementary writing and reading practice, the scribal colophon is often associated with more challenging graphic play. Signature colophons use cryptography and other playful conventions as resources for signalling belonging to groups distinguished by their special accomplishment in the arts and skills associated with *littera*. Many scribes harness these resources to indicate social belonging and the tradition is widely found among medieval scribes of Latin texts. This section will examine the deployment of the tradition among later medieval scribes of English-language texts. It will argue that these scribes deploy graphic puzzles, codes, and play to express new identities and forms of belonging for those who were skilled in the specialist arts of copying English as well as Latin.[101] But before turning to the opportunities offered by colophons for graphic play, a brief survey of some of the more common signing formulas is necessary.

A restricted number of conventional themes typifies all scribal signature colophons, including those in manuscripts that contain English language texts. Furthermore, there are distributional patterns to be found. Reynhout presents quantitative data showing the chronological and geographical distributions of

---

colophons de manuscrits médiévaux" ("few features of the codex seem to be as well known and have been in reality so little studied in their own right as colophons in medieval manuscripts"; L. REYNHOUT, *Formules latines de colophons*, 2 vols. (Turnhout, 2006), 1, p. 17). The main analyses of colophons seem to have been undertaken to derive provenance information and in some cases insights into the motivations of scribes, their working conditions, social status, and so on (for example, the catalogue of colophons in the Brussels Bibliothèque Royale, T. GLORIEUX-DE GAND with A. KELDERS, *Formules de copiste: Les Colophons des manuscrits datés* (Brussels, 1991). The massive reference work BENEDICTINS DU BOUVERET, *Colophons de manuscrits occidentaux des origines au XVIᵉ siècle* (Fribourg, 1965-1982) lists colophons in name order so that information about scribes can be retrieved and collated.

   [101] Graphic playfulness in scribal colophons has not previously been studied, to my knowledge, and my claim that it is a resource for identity-formation extends our understanding of the functions of colophons. Studying pre-Conquest Insular scribal colophons, Gameson stresses that they are transactional and conventional: "By and large, early medieval colophons were written less to tell the reader something about the scribe than as an expression of scribal activity itself and in order to get the reader to do something for the transcriber" (R. GAMESON, *The Scribe Speaks? Colophons in Early English Manuscripts* (Cambridge, 2002: H.M. Chadwick Memorial Lectures 12), p. 32). I explore some of the paratextual and codexical functions of scribal colophons in manuscripts of medieval English in W. SCASE, "Threshold-switching: Paratextual functions of scribal colophons in Old and Middle English manuscripts", in: *The Dynamics of Text and Framing Phenomena in the History of English*, ed. B. BOS and M. PEIKOLA (Amsterdam, 2020), pp. 91-113.

Graphic Play 203

formulas.[102] His data shows that there were fashions and that in particular regions and periods particular formulas had prominence. The variation in colophons over time and location recorded by Reynhout suggests that as well as performing identity work through recording the name of the scribe, the colophon offered a choice of format in which to be named and that this selection could itself potentially perform identity-work.

Some colophons provide the opportunity for a scribe literally to inscribe his identity through inserting his name in a ready-made textual formula – a 'lacuna formula'[103] – that identifies him as a scribe via words and phrases such as '*qui scripsit*' ('he who wrote') or '*scriptor*' ('scribe').[104] In sociolinguistic approaches to identity, this constitutes a mode of "direct indexicality", a process of indexing identity as a scribe via "overt mention of identity categories and labels".[105] An extremely common type is one that I shall call the '*nomen scriptoris* [name of the scribe] formula', where a line that ends on a rhyme with '*scriptoris*' provides a gap where a scribe may insert his own name. A well-known and extremely common version of this formula is '*nomen scriptoris* [...] plenus amoris*' ('the name of the scribe [...] full of love'). Reynhout finds dozens of examples of this formula across the thirteenth to the sixteenth centuries, predominantly in England and France.[106] Formerly held to be a family name for scribes, a translation of the surname 'Fullalove', '*plenus amoris*' is now widely

---

[102] REYNHOUT, *Formules latines de colophons*.

[103] Cf. REYNHOUT, *Formules latines de colophons*, 1, p. 187.

[104] These formulas are a subset of frequently-used colophon formulas where the scribe is mentioned but not named. For example, the *Prick of Conscience* in MS Manchester, John Rylands Library, Eng. 51 ends "*Qui sc^ripcit carmen sit benedictus Amen*" ("may he who copied the verse be blessed", f. 116v) as does the text of *Femina* in MS Cambridge, Trinity College, B.14.39 (p. 118). MS Aberystwyth, National Library of Wales, Peniarth 356B, a text of the Middle English *Accedence*, ends with another common colophon, "*explicit expliciunt, ludere scriptor eat*" ("it is ended, they are finished, let the scribe go out to play"; *An Edition of the Middle English Grammatical Texts*, ed. D. THOMSON (New York, 1984), p. 80). MS Oxford, Bod. Lib. Fairfax 16, f. 201r bears the colophon "*Qui legit emendat scriptorem non reprehendat*" ("Let him who reads make corrections; let him not blame the scribe"; quoted and translated by J. SCATTERGOOD, "The copying of medieval and renaissance manuscripts", in: J. SCATTERGOOD, *Manuscripts and Ghosts: Essays on the Transmission of Medieval and Early Renaissance Literature* (Dublin, 2006), pp. 21-82, at p. 51).

[105] K. BUCHOLTZ and K. HALL, "Locating identity in language", in: *Language and Identities*, ed. C. LLAMAS and D. WATT (Edinburgh, 2010), pp. 18-28, at p. 21; cf. K. BUCHOLTZ and K. HALL, "Identity and interaction: A sociocultural linguistic approach", *Discourse Studies* 7.4 (2005), pp. 585-614, at p. 594.

[106] REYNHOUT, *Formules latines de colophons*, 1, pp. 186-94.

204 *Chapter 3*

recognised to be part of a scribal signing-off formula.[107] Friedman – who keeps an open mind as to whether '*plenus amoris*' is a surname – lists "around forty" examples from English manuscripts.[108] The copy of the *Prick of Conscience* in MS Oxford, University College, 142 ends with the formula after the explicit, "*Nomen scriptoris thomas plenus amoris*" (f. 125v).[109] In MS Cambridge, St. John's College, 137 (E.34), f. 118r, the *nomen scriptoris* formula follows a macaronic explicit and colophon:

> *Explicit tractatus* Stimulus consciencie *nominatus*
> *Here endiþ þe tret[...] þat* prik of conscience *clepid ys*
> *Floure of maydens alle*
> *Tu gloria virginitatis*
> *Whan we to þe calle*
> *Rege nos sociando beatis*
> *He þat wrote þis tretis*
> *God graunte hym hevene blis*
> *Nomen scriptoris est Ricardus plenus amoris.*

> Here ends the tract called *Prick of Conscience*. Flower of all maidens, glorious virgin, when we call to you, rule by uniting us with the blessed. May God grant heavenly bliss to the one who wrote this treatise. The name of the scribe is Richard full of love.[110]

A similar formula is a lacuna version of '*Qui scripsit carmen benedictus amen*' ('let him who wrote the song be blessed, amen'). The lacuna version rhymes '*dictus*' and '*benedictus*', providing a space for the scribe's name at the beginning of the line. For example Robert Thornton, the fifteenth-century amateur copyist, signs "*R Thornton dictus q^{ui} scripsit sit benedict^{us}*" in three places in the two manuscripts that he produced ("may the said R. Thornton who wrote [this] be blessed", MS Lincoln, Cathedral Library, 91, ff. 98v, 213r and MS

---

[107] T. HEFFERNAN, "The use of the phrase '*plenus amoris*' in scribal colophons", *Notes and Queries* n.s. 28.6 (1981), pp. 493-494; REYNHOUT, *Formules latines de colophons*, 1, p. 186. Scattergood suggests that '*plenus amoris*', "simply represents a conventional gesture of goodwill" (SCATTERGOOD, "The copying of medieval and renaissance manuscripts", p. 60).

[108] J.B. FRIEDMAN, *Northern English Books, Owners, and Makers in the Late Middle Ages* (Syracuse, NY, 1995), pp. 67-72.

[109] R.E. LEWIS and A. MCINTOSH, *A Descriptive Guide to the Manuscripts of the* Prick of Conscience (Oxford, 1982), p. 122.

[110] LEWIS and MCINTOSH, *A Descriptive Guide to the Manuscripts of the* Prick of Conscience, p. 41.

Graphic Play 205

London, BL, Addit. 31042, f. 66r).[111] Such formulas, where there was a space for a name, any name, to be inserted illustrate particularly well how the colophon presented an opportunity for a scribe literally to inscribe himself through his own graphic practice into a ready-made identity. The availability of variants of this formula indicates that the scribe had a choice of what kind of scribal identity he wished to express: playful or pious. His choices were of course framed by the literary and cultural stereotypes of the medieval scribe which pivoted around the two poles of the careless introducer of error and the pious labourer.[112]

Another way of signing was to add a name to an attribution formula. Scribes had available to them a number of conventional expressions to precede their name. William Cotson, canon of Dunstable, uses the formula '*per manus*' at the end of his copy of Chaucer's *Second Nun's Tale* in MS Manchester, Chetham's Library, 6709 (Mun.A.4.104): "*Explicit vita S^{an}cte virg^{in}is ^{et} / Martiris Cecilie scripta p^{er} Man^{us} / Do^{mi}n^i Will^{elm}i Cotson* ["*Cots*" struck through] *Canonici*" ("here ends the life of the martyr Cecilia by the hand of Master William Cotson, canon", f. 173r). A briefer version of this formula is simply '*per*', as for example in a late fourteenth-century *Prick of Conscience* manuscript, "*Per fratrem Johannem de Bageby commonachum Monasterii beate Marie de fontibus*" ("by Brother John of Bagby, monk of Fountains Abbey"; MS London, BL, Addit. 24203, f. 150v).[113] Another variant is '*secundum*', or '*secundum manum*', as for example in MS London, BL, Addit. 32578, signed by one John Farnley at the end of *Prick of Conscience*, "*secundum manum Johannes ffarnelay capelani*" ("according to John Farnley, chaplain", f. 103).[114] Yet another version is '*script[us] per*' as in MS Oxford, Bod. Lib., Rawl. Poet. 149 ("copied by", f. 136v).[115]

---

[111] Quoted from S.G. FEIN, "The contents of Robert Thornton's manuscripts", in: *Robert Thornton and his Books*, ed. S.G. FEIN and M. JOHNSTON (Woodbridge, 2014), pp. 13-65, at p. 20.

[112] Of course, these stereotypes were well established centuries before the castigation of Adam Scriveyn in the poem attributed to Chaucer and Johannes Trithemius's praise of the labour of scribes. Ælfric (*c.* 950-*c.* 1010) exhorted scribes of his *Sermones catholici* that they would be held to account for their errors on the day of judgement, while Alcuin (*c.* 735-804) stated that copying books was better for the soul than planting vines (GAMESON, *The Scribe Speaks? Colophons in Early English Manuscripts*, pp. 20, 31).

[113] LEWIS and MCINTOSH, *A Descriptive Guide to the Manuscripts of the* Prick of Conscience, p. 74.

[114] LEWIS and MCINTOSH, *A Descriptive Guide to the Manuscripts of the* Prick of Conscience, pp. 76-77.

[115] See the entry in D.D. MOSSER, *A Digital Catalogue of the pre-1500 Manuscripts and*

206   *Chapter 3*

The attribution formulas were associated with playful and coded signatures: the scribe could *perform* his identity as a skilled literate by engaging in graphic play as part of his signature. Cryptography is an important form of graphic play in scribal signatures. Involving such devices as adding at least one extra stage to the process of encoding and decoding text, cryptography was, as we saw in section one, one of the identity-marking resources with roots in basic Latin literacy training.[116] Substitution of graphs is a common system of encipherment that is used by scribes.[117] In one system all letters are substituted by the letter next in order in the alphabet. In another system, only vowels are substituted. A means of encryption in which vowels only are shifted forward one alphabetical place is found at the end of a copy of Chaucer's *Clerk's Tale* in MS Naples, Biblioteca Nazionale, XIII.B.29, p. 146: "*Hic pennam fixi penitet mi si male scripci q[ᵘᵒ]d mprf*" ("here I set my pen to rest; I am sorry if I have copied badly, quod Mprf [More]", p. 113).[118] It is also used by the scribe Rose who signs a *Temporale* from the *South English Legendary* in MS Cambridge, St. John's College, 28 (B.6): in one place he signs "*Rpsf*" using this cipher system (f. 21v).[119] In other cryptographic systems, letter and word order are played with. In one system, encountered above in the Exeter Book Riddles, the order of letters in a word is reversed. This system is used by William Stevens whose *Canterbury Tales* in MS Rawl. Poet. 149 has the colophon: "*Expliciunt fabula script[a?] per snnevets mlliW*" ("here end the tales copied by Snnevets Mlliw", 136v).[120] Some scribes use visual codes or rebuses. Rebus signatures were used by notaries and the addition of such cryptographic elements may have been an authenticating device.[121] Scribes of English literature adopt the tradition. For example, Leweston, a scribe of some Chaucerian verse in the Findern manuscript, signs with a line drawing of some fish and a barrel, said to

Incunables of the Canterbury Tales, 2nd, online edn. (2010), <http://mossercatalogue.net/index. html>.

[116] For a survey of various medieval cryptographic systems see B. BISCHOFF, "Übersicht über die nichtdiplomatischen Geheimschriften des Mittelalters", *Mitteilungen des Instituts für Österreichische Geschichtsforschung* 62 (1954), pp. 1-27.

[117] For this method see SALTZMAN, "*Vt hkskdkxt*: Early medieval cryptography", pp. 983-984.

[118] See the entry in MOSSER, *A Digital Catalogue*.

[119] M.R. JAMES, *A Descriptive Catalogue of the Manuscripts in the Library of St. John's College Cambridge* (Cambridge, 1913), p. 36.

[120] See the entry in MOSSER, *A Digital Catalogue*.

[121] Fraenkel suggests that the addition of cryptographic elements to a notarial signature was a way of distinguishing and authenticating the text copied (B. FRAENKEL, "Rebus-signatures", in: *Sign and Design: Script as Image in Cross-Cultural Perspective (300-1600 CE)*, ed. B.M. BEDOS-REZAK and J. HAMBURGER (Washington, 2016), pp. 71-84, at pp. 79-80).

Graphic Play 207

be a pun on '*luce*' ('pike') and '*tun*' ('barrel'; MS CUL, Ff.1.6, f. 120r). Robert Thornton signs his copy of the prose *Life of Alexander* with an image of a thorn tree above a barrel that fills a pen-work initial *A* (MS Lincoln Cathedral 91, f. 23v).[122] Rate, scribe of MS Bod. Lib., Ashmole 61, signs with his name, an image of a fish, and geometric devices which may be protection marks or apotropaic symbols (ff. 16v-17r).[123]

Another form of cipher is alpha-numeric, for example, when each letter of the alphabet is substituted by a number. The scribe John Cok signs Cambridge, Gonville and Caius 669*/646, "*Amen quod Iohn cok*" (p. 210) but also "*Quod .IX. and. III.*" (p. 209 at the end of item 3). John Cok's interest in cryptography is also attested by a key to a cipher of numbers, letters, and a symbol signed by him on a flyleaf of MS Cambridge, Trinity College, B.11.14 (first flyleaf, verso). Grounded in the elementary pedagogy of graphic play, and commonly used in signatures of scribes of Latin texts, these various kinds of cryptic signature would indicate highly developed skills in organising letters on the page and invite recognition from and decoding by others with the same skills. Copyists of English-language texts like John Cok, More, Rose, and William Stevens adapted these traditions to a new purpose when they turned their English names into cipher to sign their work.

Many of the examples above use the attribution formula '*quod*'. '*Quod*' is one of the most common, and typical, late-medieval signing formulas, typically represented in the abbreviated forms '*qd*' or just '*q.*' with a mark of suspension (see for example the signature of John Benet, Figure 16). Reynhout finds that '*quod*' is an exclusively English formula and that it was used predominantly in the fifteenth century; he records around 225 examples, and he speculates that it might mark belonging ("*appartenance*").[124] Finding many examples in manuscripts associated with Oxford and Cambridge (about ten percent of the total examples), he suggests that the formula '*quod*' indicates belonging to one of those universities.[125] If Reynhout is right, then this would indeed be another

---

[122] It is not clear whether Thornton was responsible for the initial. An instruction (a faint sketch of a thorn and some illegible guidance) appears beside the initial which suggests that Thornton may not have been the pen-work artist; Thompson, however, states that the artist was "probably Thornton himself" (J.J. THOMPSON, *Robert Thornton and the London Thornton Manuscript* (Cambridge, 1987), p. 59).

[123] The compass-drawn symbols found with Rate's signature are commonly seen on the fabric of churches and other buildings; see further in Chapter Four.

[124] REYNHOUT, *Formules latines de colophons*, 1, p. 196; 2, pp. 66-67; 1, p. 196.

[125] REYNHOUT, *Formules latines de colophons*, 1, p. 198.

208   *Chapter 3*

example of how a scribal colophon can mark identity. I would argue that, in addition, '*quod*' was played with among particular communities of scribes who copied English to mark group belonging.

'*Quod*' was not only mobilised by university scribes. To the examples above many further instances of use among scribes of English-language texts may be added. John Bagby, scribe of the *Prick of Conscience* in MS London, BL, Addit. 24203 signs "*Amen quod Bagby*" while also using the attribution formula "*per fratrem Johannem de Bageby*" (f. 150v).[126] In MS London, BL, Addit. 32578, John Farnley signs "*amen quod ffarnelay*" at end of *Apostles' Creed* (*DIMEV* 1200), alongside his "*secundum manum*" formula at the end of the *Prick of Conscience* (ff. 105v, 103r).[127] In MS Chicago, Newberry Library, 32.9, the *Lapidarye of Philippe of France* is signed "*quod Hull*" (f. 113v).[128] While Nicholas signs his contribution in the Findern manuscript using the '*nomen scriptoris*' formula, "*Explicit Pyramus et tesbe / Nomen scriptoris nicholaus plenus amoris*" ("here ends *Pyramus and Thisbe*; the name of the scribe is Nicholas full of love"; MS Cambridge, UL, Ff.1.6, f. 67v), and there are the ciphers and witty jingles in the hands of other scribes in the manuscript that we have already noticed, other scribes of Findern choose the '*quod*' signing formula, for example W. Calverley (f. 35v) and Leweston (ff. 47v, 48r). Other scribes of English texts who sign '*quod*' include John Cok (MS Cambridge, Gonville and Caius College, 669*/646, pp. 209, 210), M.J. Combe (MS Oxford, Bod. Lib., Ashmole 50, f. 9r),[129] William Cotson (MS Manchester, Chetham's Library, 6709 (Mun. A.4.104), ff. 274v, 284r), "*Duxwurth*" (MS BNF, fonds anglais 39, f. 83v), Richard Heege (MS Edinburgh, National Library of Scotland, Advocates' Library, 19.3.1, f. 29v),[130] Herrysoun (MS Cambridge, Gonville and Caius College, 249/277, f. 227v),[131] Leghrewell (MS Oxford, Bod.

---

[126] LEWIS and MCINTOSH, *A Descriptive Guide to the Manuscripts of the* Prick of Conscience, p. 74.

[127] LEWIS and MCINTOSH, *A Descriptive Guide to the Manuscripts of the* Prick of Conscience, pp. 76-77.

[128] LEWIS and MCINTOSH, *A Descriptive Guide to the Manuscripts of the* Prick of Conscience, p. 49.

[129] See the entry in *DIMEV*.

[130] J. BOFFEY and J.J. THOMPSON, "Anthologies and miscellanies: Production and choice of texts", in: *Book Production and Publishing in Britain 1375-1475*, ed. J. GRIFFITHS and D. PEARSALL (Cambridge, 1989), pp. 279-315, at p. 296 and plate 25.

[131] M.R. JAMES, *A Descriptive Catalogue of the Manuscripts in the Library of Gonville and Caius College*, 2 vols. (Cambridge, 1914), 1, p. 304.

Graphic Play 209

Lib., Laud Misc. 598, f. 49r),[132] More (MS Naples, Biblioteca Nazionale, XIII.B.29, p. 113),[133] Rate (MS Oxford, Bod. Lib., Ashmole 61, ff. 16v-17r), Rose (MS London, Dulwich College, 24, f. 16v),[134] Rose (MS Cambridge, St. John's College, 28 (B.6), f. 79),[135] John Benet (MS Dublin, Trinity College, 516, for example, f. 118r, as already mentioned; see also ff. 121r, and 195v),[136] and Robertus Lefydys (MS Cambridge, St. John's College, 137 (E.34), f. 113v).[137] Some scribes follow '*quod*' with just initials, such as "*A*" in MS Cambridge, St. John's College, 29 (B.7), f. 119v,[138] and "*R T*" in MS London, BL, Arundel 140 (f. 146v).[139]

Arguably, while '*quod*' may have signified belonging among university scribes, it may also have become a signifier of belonging to the subset of scribes to which these scribes belonged: scribes with the skills to copy English. For scribes competent in both English and Latin, I would argue, '*quod*' offered the opportunity for a fitting form of linguistic play: it is linguistically ambiguous, analysable as both English and Latin. Reynhout proposes that '*quod*' is the Latin relative pronoun: "*la signification latente de cette formule pourrait être:* '[*Livre / ouvrage*] *que* [*fit / ecrivit*] *nom de copiste*'" ("the hidden meaning of this formula could be 'the [book / work] which [composed / copied] name of the copyist'"), citing expanded examples in support, for example "[*explicit*] *computus manualis* [...] *quod Bernys scripsit*" ("[here ends] the computus manual that Bernys wrote").[140] However the word has an alternative analysis as the Middle English word meaning 'said'. *OED* analyses '*quod*' in attribution formulas as the past tense of Middle English '*quethen*', 'to say' (*quoth*, v. 1c). *MED* does not corroborate the *OED*'s analysis, but support for the '*said*' analysis comes from a manuscript of *c.* 1275-1300 where a Middle English lyric is signed "*dixit Robertus seynte Mary clericus*" ("said Robert clerk of St.

---

[132] See the entry in *DIMEV*.

[133] See the entry in MOSSER, *A Digital Catalogue*.

[134] See *DIMEV*.

[135] See JAMES, *A Descriptive Catalogue of the Manuscripts in the Library of St. John's College Cambridge*, p. 36.

[136] On Benet, see further below.

[137] Lewis and MCINTOSH, *A Descriptive Guide to the Manuscripts of the* Prick of Conscience, p. 42.

[138] JAMES, *A Descriptive Catalogue of the Manuscripts in the Library of St. John's College Cambridge*, p. 39.

[139] Lewis and MCINTOSH, *A Descriptive Guide to the Manuscripts of the* Prick of Conscience, p. 57.

[140] REYNHOUT, *Formules latines de colophons*, 1, pp. 194, 195.

210   *Chapter 3*

Mary's"; MS Worcester Cathedral, Dean and Chapter Library Q. 50, f. 46r).[141] This suggests that '*quod*' may be a translation of a signing formula that used the Latin verb '*dicere*'. Indeed, two signing formulas could be viewed as having coalesced in '*quod*': one involving the Latin relative pronoun and one the verb translating '*dixit*'. The formula is, according to Reynhout, "*un anglicisme sur* [...] *latine '*quod*'*" ("an Anglicisation of Latin '*quod*'") and suggests that perhaps copyists themselves were unsure about which language the word was.[142] I would argue rather that scribes *played* with the ambiguity of the term. The spelling of the formula enables the play, which, Reynhout states, is nearly always spelt with a dental ('*quod*') rather than a fricative ('*quoth*').[143] The combination of Latin and English often found in the colophons also enables the ambiguity. As the examples above show, the names of the scribes who copy English-language texts are often Anglicised in their signatures, even though other parts of their signature colophon may be in Latin.[144] This ambiguity over language, I suggest, meant that '*quod*' was an ideal signature formula for scribes capable of copying English as well as Latin. A word whose linguistic status was unclear, a word that could be abbreviated and analysed as the Latin relative pronoun or conjunction as well as the vernacular '*quod*' / '*quoth*', it perhaps indexed that subset of scribes who had dual copying competence, an identity confirmed by almost all of the corpus of English-language manuscripts of the fifteenth century. Arguably, among certain scribes, a play on '*quod*' became a symbol of special linguistic versatility and accomplishment in the

---

[141] M. LAING, *Catalogue of Sources for a Linguistic Atlas of Early Medieval English* (Cambridge, 1993), p. 156. Reynhout cites some examples that give support for this interpretation. MS Durham, UL, C. IV. 23, dated *c.* 1200, bears the phrase "*quoth Fishburn*" after "*quod William Law*" (REYNHOUT, *Formules latines de colophons*, 1, p. 195; cf. BENEDICTINS DU BOUVERET, *Colophons de manuscrits occidentaux*, No. 5949). MS London, BL, Royal 15 C.xii, f. 147, also of the fourteenth century, bears the inscription "*quod Ellerker i. e. quoth Ellerker*" ("'*quod Ellerker*', that is, '*quoth Ellerker*'"; REYNHOUT, *Formules latines de colophons*, 1, p. 195; cf. BENEDICTINS DU BOUVERET, *Colophons de manuscrits occidentaux*, No. 3753).

[142] REYNHOUT, *Formules latines de colophons*, 1, p. 196.

[143] REYNHOUT, *Formules latines de colophons*, 1, p. 196.

[144] Among the rare examples that are only in English are a colophon to *Sawles Warde*, "*Par seinte charite biddeð a pater noster for Iohan þat þeos boc prat*" ("by saint Charity pray a *Pater noster* for John who copied this book"; MS London, BL, Royal 17 A.xxvii, f. 10v) and the note in MS London, Lambeth Palace Library, 223, a copy of the *South English Legendary* of *c.* 1400, "*her endeþ legenda aurea writen by R.P. of þis toun To a gode mon of þe same is cleped Thomas of Wottoun*" ("here ends the *Legenda Aurea* written by R.P. of this town for a good man of the same town called Thomas of Wottoun"; see M. GÖRLACH, *The Textual Tradition of the* South English Legendary (Leeds, 1974: *Leeds Texts and Monographs* 6), p. 83).

Graphic Play 211

arts of the scribe, that is, of membership of a community of scribes whose practice included special competence in English copying. The rest of this section endeavours to reconstruct some of these communities of Anglophone scribal practice to which playful signatures might have signified belonging.

Among scribes with competence in copying English-language texts one category that seems to have adopted showy and cryptic signatures are those who copy for their own amusement and that of their households. Indeed, Horobin suggests that the presence of a scribal signature in a manuscript is evidence that it was made for the scribe's personal use: "Because professional scribes carrying out a commission for a patron generally remained anonymous, the addition of a scribal signature suggests that a manuscript was being copied for the scribe's own use".[145] There is evidence that the work of such scribes was facilitated by network membership, and I argue below that networks of scribes who copied English-language texts for themselves and their households may have constituted communities of practice who adopted '*quod*' and other cryptic modes of signing their work as a badge of belonging.[146]

A community of scribal practice associated with late medieval manuscripts containing English is suggested by the Findern manuscript, MS Cambridge, UL, Ff.1.6, whose texts are in the hands of dozens of scribes who were interacting on the page and presumably sometimes in person. We have already met Calverley, Leweston, and Nicholas from this community. In total, six scribes sign

---

[145] S. HOROBIN, "Manuscripts and readers of *Piers Plowman*", in: *The Cambridge Companion to* Piers Plowman, ed. A. COLE and A. GALLOWAY (Cambridge, 2014), pp. 179-197, at p. 182.

[146] The phenomenon of the network of amateur scribes has been neglected in studies of such manuscripts; the emphasis has usually been on the scribe himself or herself and the principles behind the compilation and structuring of the individual manuscripts rather than on the scribal social networks that must have enabled their production (e.g., A. BAHR, "Miscellaneity and variance in the medieval book", in: *The Medieval Manuscript Book: Cultural Approaches*, ed. M. JOHNSTON and M. VAN DUSSEN (Cambridge, 2015), pp. 181-198). Work on access to networks that provisioned exemplars and supported readers (e.g., BOFFEY and THOMPSON, "Anthologies and miscellanies"; M. CONNOLLY, "Compiling the book", in: *Book Production and Publishing in England 1350-1500*, ed. A. GILLESPIE and D. WAKELIN (Cambridge, 2011), pp. 129-149; R. PERRY, "The Clopton manuscript and the Beauchamp affinity", in: *Essays in Manuscript Geography: Vernacular Manuscripts of the English West Midlands from the Conquest to the Sixteenth Century*, ed. W. SCASE (Turnhout, 2007), pp. 131-160; and D. YOUNGS, "Entertainment networks, reading communities, and the early Tudor Anthology: Oxford, Bod. Lib., MS Rawlinson C. 813", in: *Insular Books: Vernacular Manuscript Miscellanies in Late Medieval Britain*, ed. M. CONNOLLY and R. RADULESCU (Oxford, 2015), pp. 231-246) could be developed to encompass the possibility of scribe-to-scribe contact and exchange within these structures, whether textually mediated or face-to-face.

212   *Chapter 3*

their names in Findern, if one accepts Harris's analysis.[147] If the Findern manuscript is the product of a community of Anglophone scribal practice (albeit extended over time), perhaps this is a community whose members advertise their membership not only through contributing texts but also through witty and playful deployment of a wide repertoire of scribal signing formulas and colophons as well as through a variety of means of encoding their names, examples of which we have seen above.

In a smaller-scale example, father and son Geoffrey and Thomas Spirleng sign the *Canterbury Tales* they copied in MS Glasgow, UL, Hunter 197. A colophon records that they finished the text in 1456, when Geoffrey was aged fifty and Thomas was sixteen (f. 115v), providing evidence for copying by scribes in a familial structure. More of Geoffrey's relationships are indicated by the statement in the colophon that he is "court holder" in the city of Norwich (f. 102v). Perhaps it was to members of this community that his colophon spoke, who perhaps would have been used to the kind of precise dating included in the colophon. Knowledge of the circumstances of the book's production and responsibility for it is also suggested by a note immediately below the colophon that explains why the colophon has been cancelled and rewritten on f. 115v:

> *This writyng is drawen for the book of Cant^{er}bury is nat yet ended and therefor these woord^{es} arn writen in the XIJ leef folwyng by cause that IJ tales arn yet folwyng immediatly.*

> This copy of the *Canterbury Tales* is not finished and therefore these words are written on the twelfth leaf after because two tales follow immediately (f. 102v).

The rewriting of the colophon after the tales of the Clerk and the Canon's Yeoman may be the work of another member of this circle who was familiar with the circumstances, since the aspect of the second copy has a slight forward slant like that of another explanatory rubric about the place of the two missing tales added on f. 102v.

The acquisition of exemplars from many sources also provides evidence for the existence of informal communities of scribal practice among whom playful signatures may have signified belonging. John Benet († by 1474), vicar of Harlington, Bedfordshire, 1443-1471 and scribe of MS Dublin, Trinity Col-

---

[147] K. HARRIS, "The origins and bibliographical make-up of Cambridge University Library MS Ff.1.6", *Transactions of the Cambridge Bibliographical Society* 8.3 (1983), pp. 299-333, at pp. 302-303.

Graphic Play 213

lege, 516, compiled and partly copied *c*. 1460-1470, offers a portal onto one such set of scribes. As noted above, he frequently signs "*q^{uo}d Benet*" in this anthology of prophecies, satires, and chronicle material. On the basis of an anathema against purloining of his volume (f. 2v) and annotations in it by many hands, it has been suggested that Benet was "a member of a book-lending circle", while the patron of his final benefice, John Broughton, was himself a book collector.[148] Benet may have gained access to his materials via contacts in London.[149] He specialised in copying history and prophecy and marking it up for the use of others and it seems likely that lending was mutual and that others were copying Benet's materials.[150] Like many other compilers of history and prophecy, he seems to have belonged to circles that exchanged curious prophetic material and demonstrated their skill in interpreting arcane codes such as that of "*Ever is Six the best Chance of the Dice*" (*DIMEV* 1215), a text included in Benet's manuscript (see Figure 16).[151]

There are similar traces of many other such communities of Anglophone scribal practice. Humphrey Newton's manuscript, MS Oxford, Bod. Lib., Lat. Misc. c. 66, with its copious number of signatures of both himself and others testifies to his interaction with other scribes, as does his collection of extracts

---

[148] John Benet, "John Benet's chronicle for the years 1400-1462", ed. G.L. HARRISS and M.A. HARRISS, in: *Camden Society*, 4th series, 9 (1972), pp. 151-233, at pp. 172-173. Benet's hand is established by the ownership note and anathema on f. 2v.

[149] John Benet, "John Benet's chronicle for the years 1400-1462", pp. 153, 158; SCATTERGOOD, "The copying of medieval and renaissance manuscripts", p. 48.

[150] W. SCASE, "John Benet, scribe and compiler, and Dublin, Trinity College, MS 516", in: *Scribal Cultures in Late Medieval England: Festschrift for Linne Mooney*, ed. M. CONNOLLY, H. JAMES-MADDOCKS, and D. PEARSALL (Woodbridge, 2022), pp. 241-258.

[151] *Historical Poems of the XIVth and XVth Centuries*, ed. R.H. ROBBINS (New York, 1959), p. 120, No. 46. *DIMEV* 1215 is another textual game that provides multiple opportunities for expressing belonging through graphic play. Like the poem with a similar title in MS Oxford, Bod. Lib., Bodley 638, ff. 195-203v (*DIMEV* 1318), this poem uses dice but unlike *DIMEV* 1318 its subject is political rather than personal. The poem uses die throws in place of key words in political statements, for example, "*Whan that* [one] *beryth vp the* [six] *ynglond schal be as paradice*" ("when [one] bears up [six] England shall be like Paradise"), and "*Then* [...] [three] *set A-side and* [two] *clene schent*" ("then [...] [three] set aside and [two] clean destroyed"). Some of the throws appear more than once and the challenge is to decode the throws in ways that make sense in each of the instances in which they appear. Doubtless actually playing the game in that way would elicit much cynical laughter. The player must decode the throws of the die for himself or herself, or even devise a code. Perhaps, by including his own glosses, John Benet was displaying his own clever solution to the puzzle. For the poem as "a kind of puzzle, based on the use of dice-casting for the telling of fortunes, a kind of social 'game' in the Middle Ages" see L.A. COOTE, *Prophecy and Public Affairs in Later Medieval England* (Woodbridge, 2000), p. 36.

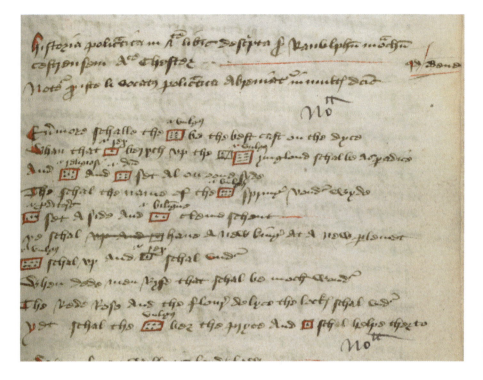

Fig. 16. John Benet's '*quod*' signature (above, right); below, encrypted prophecy game with dice and glosses, MS Dublin, Trinity College, 516, f. 118r (detail). The Board of Trinity College Dublin. Image may not be further reproduced from software. For reproduction application must be made to the Head of Digital Resources and Imaging Services, by post to Trinity College Dublin, College Street, Dublin 2, Ireland; or by email at digitalresurces@tcd.ie.

from literary texts. The prolific amateur scribe John Shirley composed prefaces and bookplates that tell us that he expected to lend his copies to others, and textually, Shirley's products link with other manuscripts, also suggesting some kind of circulation.[152] The audience for Shirley's work is usually spoken of as readers, but we may assume that some of his readers were copyists too: this is implied by his request to readers that they correct any errors in his "*meter or ortografyure*" ("metre or spelling"; MS London, BL, Addit. 29729, preface,

---

[152] BOFFEY and THOMPSON, "Anthologies and miscellanies", p. 187. For Shirley see M. CONNOLLY, *John Shirley: Book Production and the Noble Household in Fifteenth-Century England* (Aldershot, 1998).

Graphic Play 215

lines 66-77).[153] Robert Thornton appears to have drawn his material from, in Fredell's words, "locally circulating pamphlets", suggesting local production too, by others whom Thornton must have known, or known of, and who must have known, or known of, Thornton (Brewer infers "there must have been a number of manuscripts circulating around the country, large and small, perhaps often unbound gatherings, from which interested gentry, and probably clergy, read [...] and from which, when a piece was particularly valued, copies were made".[154] One of these persons who read and copied may have been the second hand that corroborates Thornton's showy scribal signature at the end of the alliterative *Morte Arthure*, "*Here endes* Morte Arthure *writen by Robert of Thornton*" ("here ends *Morte Arthure* copied by Robert of Thornton", MS Lincoln, Cathedral Library, 91, f. 98v); perhaps this suggests that the scribe who wrote the explicit had personal knowledge of Thornton. In the last quarter of the fifteenth century, Robert Reynes, a Norfolk man of some local prominence, compiled MS Oxford, Bod. Lib., Tanner 407, a miscellany that includes material related to his local gild of St. Anne and extracts from dramas and pageants,[155] all of which were likely circulated locally or at least reflect local collaborative cultural activities. Richard Heege collaborated with a scribe called John Hawghton and another hand.[156] The early sixteenth-century Welles anthology, MS Oxford, Bod. Lib., Rawl. C. 813, produced and owned by esquire Humfrey Welles of Staffordshire, is thought to have been "developed in a household context and shared among interested parties".[157]

The few amateur scribes known to us from their signatures, such as Robert Thornton, John Shirley, Richard Heege, John Benet, Humphrey Newton, and Humfrey Welles, must have been a small proportion of the actual number of such scribes (given the loss of such materials over the centuries), and each of these must have learned their practice and obtained their models as part of some kind of network of similar individuals who were doing likewise. We should remain open to the possibility that perhaps many or most of the scribes mentioned in this section, including some copyists of the longer religious

---

[153] CONNOLLY, *John Shirley*, p. 210.

[154] J. FREDELL, "The Thornton manuscripts and book production in York", in: *Robert Thornton and his Books*, ed. S.G. FEIN and M. JOHNSTON (Woodbridge, 2014), pp. 109-130, at p. 125; *The Thornton Manuscript (Lincoln Cathedral MS 91)*, ed. D.S. BREWER and A.E.B. OWEN (London, 1977), p. X.

[155] BOFFEY and THOMPSON, "Anthologies and miscellanies", p. 293.

[156] BOFFEY and THOMPSON, "Anthologies and miscellanies", p. 295.

[157] YOUNGS, "Entertainment networks, reading communities", p. 234.

216   *Chapter 3*

works and members of the clergy or religious orders, such as John Farnley who copied the *Prick of Conscience*, operated within the informal scribal network model. The various playful means of signing discussed above made available to the scribes of these networks resources for them to index their membership of a group of specialised scribes.

Conclusion

In this chapter we have seen that graphic puzzle texts and games belong with a long tradition of pedagogic play that taught *littera* and shaped identities. Graphic puzzles, codes, and games provided opportunities for identity formation, creating boundaries between those who could solve the puzzles and play the games and those who could not. These pedagogic traditions were transferred to the vernacular and framed graphic culture in the English language and understanding of the particular challenges it posed. When these traditions of graphic challenge and skill were transferred into English, special demands were made and special opportunities for the display of graphic skill were presented to authors, scribes, and readers. Earlier scribes and readers engaged with the challenges of runic as well as Roman script. Variation in Middle English offered particular challenges to solve. Spelling and decoding English exercised the skills learned through graphic play. As new opportunities emerged to display in-group membership, new identities became available. The display of graphic virtuosity and accomplishment in English and appreciation and understanding of this display fostered feelings of belonging to new, specialised, literate elites.

Chapter 4: Graphic Display

ᛁᛚ ᚱᛁᛁᚴᛏᚪ ᚷᚪᚾᛁᚷᛚ ᚻᛏᛈᚾᛏᚠᛋ ᚻᛚᚠᛈᚠᚱᛗ ᚻᚠᚦᛗᚠ ᛁᚴ ᛏᛁ ᛗᚠᚱᛋᛏᚠ

[I]c riicnæ kyningc, heafunæs hlaford, hælda ic ne dorste [...]

I [held aloft] the powerful king, heaven's lord, I dared not bend
(Inscription, Ruthwell Cross, east side)[1]

To the extent that linguistic tokens are artefacts of a central government, they may reflect the overt language policies of a given state. In this sense they are markers of status and power [...] Other linguistic artefacts within a given linguistic landscape, for example signs and advertisements of local businesses, notices posted by individuals and other locally produced tokens, are a manifestation of the covert language policy of a community, and may display the grass roots cultural identity and aspirations of its members.
(Thom Huebner, "Bankok's Linguistic Landscapes")[2]

Perhaps one of the best-known, earliest, and most exotic examples of medieval English that was displayed in a particular space accessible to view by a variety of individuals – what this chapter will call a 'graphic landscape' – is the runic inscription on the Ruthwell Cross, quoted in the epigraph. By means of the text that is inscribed on the borders of its decorated faces, the cross addresses its viewers, announcing that it was the instrument of Christ's

---

[1] I am grateful to Jeremy Smith for this transcription and transliteration of the runes; the translation is my own. Cf. Page's translation (R.I. PAGE, *An Introduction to English Runes*, 2nd edn. (Woodbridge, 1999), pp. 147-148), quoted below.

[2] T. HUEBNER, "Bankok's linguistic landscapes: Environmental print, codemixing, and language change", in: *Linguistic Landscape: A New Approach to Multilingualism*, ed. D. GORTER (Clevedon, 2006), pp. 31-51, at p. 32.

218   *Chapter 4*

crucifixion (see Figure 17). The massive Ruthwell Cross, perhaps a monument
or a preaching cross (or both), towers over five metres high. It may have stood
outside in an actual landscape from the time it was erected (evidence points to
somewhere near Dumfries, now in south-west Scotland, sometime in the eighth
century), until it was demolished by iconoclasts in the seventeenth century and
restored and moved to its current location inside Ruthwell Church, near Dumfries, in the nineteenth century. Famously, some of the inscriptions it bears are
related to (perhaps extracts from) the Old English poem *The Dream of the
Rood*.[3] Together with this material, the cross bears other inscriptions in Latin,
written in both runic and Roman script. The Ruthwell Cross poses numerous
complex questions of production, dating, and use which continue to be de-
bated. As an inscription-bearing object which must have been prominently
visible to the communities it was produced for, it also provides a case-study
appropriate for the present chapter. This chapter proposes that the theories and
practices associated with *littera* pedagogy examined in the previous chapters
inform English-language writing and inscription that was displayed to view.
When displayed, whether on objects, on walls, or on monuments such as the
Ruthwell Cross – to which we will return at the end of this chapter – the capacity of literacy pedagogy to draw boundaries between belonging and difference
was extended and amplified. Objects presented to view in display spaces could
extend and enrich the opportunities for applications of *littera* pedagogy in
communities of Anglophone literate practice. In such locations, the capacity of
literacy pedagogy to prompt recognition of belonging and difference was increased: display in spaces used by a variety of communities intensified awareness that graphic experience was not a collective experience. Differences in
literate taste, understanding, and accomplishment could be foregrounded by
display of alphabets, models and copy-texts, and texts that challenged graphic
skills and encouraged graphic play through riddling and puzzles.

The approach to the meanings and functions of the display of English
adopted in this chapter is informed to some extent by new work in epigraphy.
In his study of inscriptions in thirteenth- and fourteenth-century France, Debiais has urged that the study of inscriptions should incorporate all text that is
presented to public view, not just professionally engraved inscriptions on stone
monuments and metal plates. Inscriptions form a part of the "everyday graphic

---

[3]   R.I. PAGE, *An Introduction to English Runes*, pp. 145-148.

Graphic Display 219

Fig. 17. Poem related to the *Dream of the Rood*, inscribed in runes around decorative panel, Ruthwell Cross, east side (detail). © Corpus of Anglo-Saxon Stone Sculpture, photographer T. Middlemass.

220   *Chapter 4*

landscape" (*"le paysage graphique quotidien"*).[4] He urges, furthermore, that inscription material benefits from being approached as a form of communication that is defined by its publicness; it has *"une véritable vocation publique"* and what he calls epigraphic documents are writing that is exposed (*"l'écriture exposée par excellence"*).[5] This public dimension (*"la dimension publicitaire"*) is not just an inescapable fact but one of the parameters of the semiotic system that an inscription constitutes.[6] Each element of an inscription – its semantic content, writing, physical form, and so on – constitutes a sign.[7] A similarly broad understanding of the scope of inscriptions and a sense of them as communications frames Eastmond's collection of essays on the non-verbal codes of ancient and medieval inscriptions.[8] Similarly, Garipzanov sees the display of graphic signs across a range of media from monuments to coins as a medium for communication and for transmitting messages about religious identity.[9]

In order to investigate the public display of English writing, this chapter brings together Debiais's communication framework for epigraphy with approaches to language display developed to understand multilingualism in modern societies. 'Landscape' has emerged as an important concept in these traditions, providing a transformative way of thinking about the social meanings and identity-forming functions of language visibility in the form of what is sometimes called Linguistic Landscape research. This chapter proposes that the linguistic landscape paradigm can add a new dimension to our interpretation of displayed text, complementing the exciting new semiotic approaches offered in epigraphy by Debiais and others. Following Debiais, it focuses on the 'graphic landscape' rather than the 'linguistic landscape', for work in the latter tradition

---

[4]   V. DEBIAIS, *Messages de pierre: La lecture des inscriptions dans la communication médiévale (XIIIᵉ-XIVᵉ siècle)* (Turnhout, 2009), Abstract.

[5]   DEBIAIS, *Messages de pierre*, p. 49.

[6]   DEBIAIS, *Messages de pierre*, p. 59.

[7]   DEBIAIS, *Messages de pierre*, p. 60.

[8]   *Viewing Inscriptions in the Late Antique and Medieval Worlds*, ed. A.D. EASTMOND (Cambridge, 2015).

[9]   I. GARIPZANOV, "Introduction", in: *Graphic Signs of Identity, Faith, and Power in Late Antiquity and the Early Middle Ages*, ed. I. GARIPZANOV, C. GOODSON, and H. MAGUIRE (Turnhout, 2017), pp. 1-22. By contrast, Favreau focuses on durability as an essential feature of displays: *"L'inscription a pour fonction une information à la connaissance du public le plus large et pour la plus longue durée, d'assurer une communication en vue d'une publicité universelle et durable"* ("the inscription's function is the widest and most long-lasting public information, to guarantee universal and enduring communication", R. FAVREAU, *Epigraphe Médiévale* (Turnhout, 1997: *L'atelier du médiéviste* 5), p. 31).

Graphic Display 221

is primarily concerned with public writing as a proxy for the spoken languages of a given community rather than with graphic culture.

Linguistic landscape studies characteristically inventory visible language in a delimited area at a delimited time, the typical subject of study being urban, public areas. The linguistic landscape is typically defined as the publicly visible writing seen by anyone in a given area at a given time.[10] Beginning in the 1990s with seminal work by Calvet and Landry and Bourhis, linguistic landscape studies proposes that publicly visible written language can inform the viewer, but it also creates a space in which identity is negotiated symbolically.[11] A key method in linguistic landscape research is to analyse the data according to the salience of the languages. Landry and Bourhis, introducing the term within the field of language planning, define the concept thus: "[l]inguistic landscape refers to the visibility and salience of languages on public and commercial signs in a given territory or region [..] as a marker of the relative power and status of the linguistic communities inhabiting the territory".[12] The relations between communities may be symbolised by the languages visible in public spaces, and the symbolic resources of visible language are deployed by both authorities and private individuals.[13] In the study by Huebner quoted in the epigraph to this chapter, Bangkok exemplifies the ways in which a linguistic landscape provides numerous kinds of actors with identity-shaping resources. In another example, in their study of languages on signs in two streets

---

[10] For example, Gorter reflects that he and his research partner recorded "all texts to be seen" in major streets in selected towns in the Basque country and Friesland and he notes that typically, researchers conducting such research record their material by taking photographs (D. GORTER, "Introduction: The study of the linguistic landscape as a new approach to multilingualism", in: *Linguistic Landscape: A New Approach to Multilingualism*, ed. D. GORTER (Clevedon, 2006), pp. 1-6, at p. 3; Cf. F.M. HULT, "Language ecology and linguistic landscape analysis", in: *Linguistic Landscape: Expanding the Scenery*, ed. E. SHOHAMY and D. GORTER (London, 2009), pp. 88-104, at p. 90).

[11] J.-L. CALVET, *Les voix de la ville: Introduction à la sociolinguistique urbaine* (Paris, 1994); R. LANDRY and R.Y. BOURHIS, "Linguistic landscape and ethnolinguistic vitality: An empirical study", *Journal of Language and Social Psychology*, 16.1 (1997), pp. 23-49.

[12] LANDRY and BOURHIS, "Linguistic landscape and ethnolinguistic vitality", p. 23.

[13] Shohamy *et al.* claim "the design of [linguistic landscape] items may also eventually assert – among other interests – their actors' particularist identities [...] [t]his collective-identity principle, which is bound to regional, ethnic, or religious particularisms, should express [...] a difference from the all-societal identity" (E. SHOHAMY, E. BEN-RAFAEL, and M. BARNI, "Introduction: An approach to an 'ordered disorder'", in: *Linguistic Landscape in the City*, ed. E. SHOHAMY, E. BEN-RAFAEL, and M. BARNI (Bristol, 2010), at p. XVIII). Thus, items in the linguistic landscape "may convey meanings in terms of identity markering, testifying to the special ties binding *a priori* actors and given categories of clients" (p. XIX).

222   *Chapter 4*

in Basque and Frisian-speaking communities, Cenoz and Gorter conclude that
the linguistic landscape communicates symbolically in places where language
is a dimension of ethnic identity.[14]

Focusing on speakers of minority languages in multilingual societies (the
languages of displayed writings being used as a proxy for the languages spoken
in a given society), the linguistic landscape framework does not precisely map
onto the approach of the present study, where the focus is on graphic culture
and on its contribution to the formation of identity among communities of
literate practice. However, the concept of the community of practice has started
to be invoked in some linguistic landscape work to promote more subtle and
granular understandings of how people engage with multilingual landscapes.[15]
Other recent work sees *written* material in the linguistic landscape as a field
with its own "dynamics".[16] And while the focus of the overwhelming majority
of linguistic landscape research is language in contemporary, urbanised societ-

---

[14] J. CENOZ and D. GORTER, "Linguistic landscape and minority languages", in: *Linguistic
Landscape: A New Approach to Multilingualism*, pp. 67-80, at p. 78.

[15] L. VAN MENSEN, H.F. MARTEN, and D. GORTER, "Minority languages through the lens
of the linguistic landscape", in: *Minority Languages in the Linguistic Landscape*, ed. L. VAN
MENSEN, H.F. MARTEN, and D. GORTER (Basingstoke, 2012), pp. 319-323, at p. 322. In Florian
Coulmas's definition, "[l]inguistic landscape is a viewpoint from which to study language in
urbanized society, the object of investigation being the multidimensional distribution of languages
and varieties in the city, as opposed to the regional distribution of varieties of language investigated in traditional dialectology" (F. COULMAS, *Writing and Society* (Cambridge, 2013), p. 38;
cf. F. COULMAS, "Linguistic landscaping and the seed of the public sphere", in: *Linguistic
Landscape: Expanding the Scenery*, pp. 13-24, at p. 14). Despite its use of the term "*environnement graphique*", Calvet's work is typical of earlier studies that treat written materials as
representative of the *spoken* language realities of plurilingual communities: "*en Europe les lan-
gages de migrants, turc à Munich et Berlin, arabe ou chinois à Paris, grec ou chinois à Londres,
coexistent avec des langues officielles et manifestent parfois leur présence jusque dans l'environnement graphique*" ("in Europe languages of migrants [...] co-exist with official language,
sometimes even showing their presence in the graphic environment", CALVET, *Les voix de la ville*,
p. 11).

[16] SHOHAMY, BEN-RAFAEL, and BARNI, "Introduction: An approach to an 'ordered disorder'", p. XII. In a related shift, the display context is seen as a contributor to the meaning of text.
Spitzmüller draws attention to the preference for the term 'linguistic landscaping' in some work.
The gerund signals that the linguistic landscape is shaped, "a space of power controlled by, as
well as controlling, people" (J. SPITZMÜLLER, "Graphic variation and graphic ideologies: A metapragmatic approach", *Social Semiotics* 25.2 (2015), pp. 126-141, at p. 127). For Spitzmüller,
analysis needs to take into account not only the emplaced typographic text, but also the meanings
of the location: "a look not only at the *discourse in place*, but also at the *discourse that frames
place* – will broaden our picture of emplaced communication" (p. 138, italics in original).

Graphic Display 223

ies, the potential for applications to written language of the past has been acknowledged.[17]

The following sections will examine displayed medieval English text in relation to *littera* pedagogy using materials from different periods and kinds of graphic landscape. First, we will consider the medieval parish church, using in particular graffiti surveys supplemented with some antiquarian records of later medieval inscriptions in churches, and focusing on the parish churches at Great Bardfield, Essex, and at Ashwell, Hertfordshire. Second, we shall consider graphic display in spaces in later medieval gentry, religious, and civic households and halls, focusing on records of such practices but also the recently reconstructed graphic landscape of the painted chapel of the guild of the Holy Cross at Stratford-upon-Avon. Finally, we shall consider pre-Conquest monumental landscapes, focusing on the Ruthwell Cross. These case studies will argue that graphic display reproduced, extended, and amplified the application of literacy pedagogy that we have identified and examined in previous chapters, providing additional opportunities for identity formation in relation to communities of Anglophone literate practice.

The Medieval Parish Church

Medieval parish churches were public spaces where much writing was displayed to view. Texts were found on windows and on walls, fittings, and monuments. As places of multilingual display used by a variety of speech and literacy communities they were perhaps the closest approximation in the medieval period to the linguistic landscapes defined by Calvet and Landry and Bourhis. The medieval parish church, this section will argue, provided a space where literacy pedagogy was implemented and amplified in particular ways in relation to the inscription of English, offering opportunities for identity forma-

---

[17] For linguistic landscape approaches to older writing, see L. ARONIN and M. Ó LAOIRE, "The material culture of multilingualism: Moving beyond the linguistic landscape", *International Journal of Multilingualism* 10.3 (2013), pp. 225-235, at p. 228; Coulmas writes that "[much] separates giant TV screens and running message displays [...] from stone stelae and rock inscriptions, but an essential function has stayed the same" (COULMAS, "Linguistic landscaping", p. 23); and see also A. PAVLENKO, "Linguistic landscape of Kyiv, Ukraine: A diachronic study", in: *Linguistic Landscape in the City*, ed. E. SHOHAMY, E. BEN-RAFAEL, and M. BARNI (Bristol, 2010), pp. 133-150.

224   *Chapter 4*

tion and constructing boundaries between belonging and difference among the various communities that used the space.

Comprehensive surveys of the linguistic landscapes of medieval parish churches in Britain are lacking.[18] The problem is compounded by the extensive loss of material; in particular, much of the writing displayed in the medieval parish church did not survive the Reformation. To reconstruct the graphic landscapes of the parish churches of Anglophone medieval societies we have to rely a great deal on antiquarian records such as those of the seventeenth-century antiquarian John Weever which are in some ways the closest we can come to the surveys made by linguistic landscape researchers. Weever recorded that inscriptions were regularly found beside or beneath images of the Trinity, pictures of Christ and Christ crucified, portraits of the evangelists, and near to altars, relics, and near and upon bells, while organs, pulpits, portals, crosses, candlesticks, roods, and crucifixes were also inscribed.[19] Resources for the linguistic landscape of the medieval parish church such as the antiquarians' records, however, may now be significantly supplemented by recent surveys of a much neglected source: graffiti. Overlooked by generations of antiquarians and epigraphy specialists, historic graffiti in parish churches are now the subject of intensive county-based surveys that use methods similar to those of linguistic landscape work, including surveys of sites and the recording of data in photographs. Often the photography is an essential component of discovery, not just recording of graffiti; high resolution photography of graffiti lit by raking light makes visible material that could not be seen clearly with the naked eye.[20] Comprehensive surveying has been associated with a thorough re-

---

[18]   There is currently no comprehensive corpus of Middle English inscriptions. Some of the verse material is catalogued in *DIMEV* under the heading of 'inscription', some under 'epitaph'. Edwards confines his discussion of Middle English inscriptions to literary examples rather than briefer formulae or place- and personal names (A.S.G. EDWARDS, "Middle English inscriptional verse texts", in: *Texts and their Contexts: Papers from the Early Book Society*, ed. J. SCATTERGOOD and J. BOFFEY (Dublin, 1997), pp. 26-43).

[19]   *Ancient Funerall Monuments of Great Britaine, Ireland, and the Islands adjacent*, ed. J. WEEVER, 2nd edn. (London, 1631) [*STC* 25223], p. 123. Some of the antiquarians' records were even of material that was no longer visible in their own time but were based on secondary sources, what Schwyzer has recently called "memorials to memorials": early modern writings about church walls that recorded the presence of earlier epitaphs (P. SCHWYZER, "'A tomb once stood in this room': Memorials to memorials in early modern England", *Journal of Medieval and Early Modern Studies* 48.2 (2018), pp. 365-385.

[20]   For links to the county surveys see the webpage at <http://www.medieval-graffiti.co.uk/page106. html>. As yet the surveys are in their infancy, with many sites not yet covered. Partial surveys have been made for counties in East Anglia, the south-west and south-east of England,

Graphic Display 225

theorisation of graffiti: it is now recognised that our modern associations of graffiti with unsanctioned, subversive, and illicit writing should not be applied unquestioningly to the past.[21] In the present chapter section it will be suggested that graffiti expand our knowledge of Anglophone literate practice and the kinds of identity that it made available to the communities who used medieval churches. Graffiti share many characteristics of the more formal inscriptions

and the Midlands, following a model established for the county of Norfolk. Survey photographs organised by UK county are also hosted by the Raking Light hub: <https://rakinglight.co.uk/>. These survey projects are adding immensely to the corpora of data assembled by early pioneers in the subject, especially Coulton, who surveyed around a hundred churches in Cambridgeshire, Hertfordshire, Essex, Suffolk, and Norfolk (G.G. COULTON, "Medieval graffiti, especially in the eastern counties", in: *Medieval Studies*, 2nd ser. 12 (London, 1915), pp. 53-62 and plates 1-16), and Pritchard who also concentrated on sites accessible from Cambridge (V. PRITCHARD, *English Medieval Graffiti* (Cambridge, 1967)). Champion has recently published an overview that includes some of the new finds and provides a framework for the continuing research (M.J. CHAMPION, *Medieval Graffiti: The Lost Voices of England's Churches* (London, 2015)). See also *Peregrinations: Journal of Medieval Art and Architecture* (Special issue: *New Research on Medieval and Later Graffiti*) 6.1 (2017). For study of continental graffiti see DEBIAIS, *Messages de pierre*, pp. 41-42.

[21] The modern category of the graffito is often associated with dissent, iconoclasm, and destructive aims. Waksman and Shohamy give examples of graffiti from the city of Tel Aviv-Jaffa "depicting words and ideas that contest the deletion of its past" (S. WAKSMAN and E. SHOHAMY, "Decorating the city of Tel Aviv-Jaffa for its centennial: Complementary narratives via linguistic landscape", in: *Linguistic Landscape in the City*, pp. 57-73, at p. 70), such a graffito that read "[h]ere once existed a Palestinian village that has been destroyed" (p. 71). Landry and Bourhis describe later twentieth-century graffiti campaigns that targeted public signs in support of minority languages, for example in the Basque-speaking areas of France and Spain, in Catalonia, in Quebec, and in Wales (LANDRY and BOURHIS, "Linguistic landscape and ethnolinguistic vitality", pp. 28-29). Using examples of graffiti on wall-paintings in fifteenth-century Italian churches, Plesch argues that graffiti may represent acts of cultural appropriation, perhaps somewhat aligning with the understanding of twentieth-century graffiti campaigns (V. PLESCH, "Memory on the wall: Graffiti on religious wall paintings", *Journal of Medieval and Early Modern Studies* 31.1 (2002), pp. 167-197). But this understanding of graffiti is not historically universal. Fleming points out that early modern ideas about graffiti may have been different from our own (J. FLEMING, *Graffiti and the Writing Arts of Early Modern England* (London, 2001), pp. 30, 41) and as Oliver and Neal point out, "recent research [...] emphasises the social efficacy of participating in the creation of wild signs [graffiti] [...] writing (or carving or painting), with and in the world of objects, is in itself creative of material meanings that are socially consequential" (J. OLIVER and T. NEAL, "Wild signs: An introduction", in: *Wild Signs: Graffiti in Archaeology and History*, ed. J. OLIVER and T. NEAL (Oxford, 2010: *Studies in Contemporary and Historical Archaeology* 6), pp. 1-4, at p. 2). Owen makes the case that "it is simplistic to assume that the expression of individuality in a public space has always been frowned upon or discouraged" (K. OWEN, "Traces of presence and pleading: Approaches to the study of graffiti at Tewkesbury Abbey", in: *Wild Signs: Graffiti in Archaeology and History*, pp. 35-46, at p. 35).

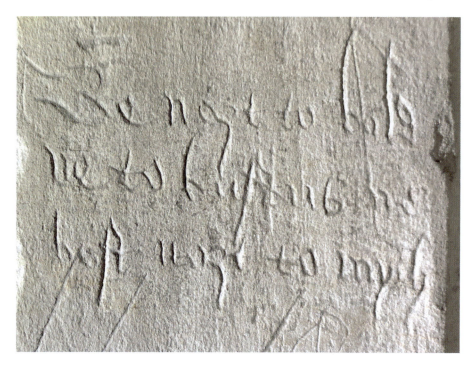

Fig. 18. *B* line from the *ABC of Aristotle*, graffito on pillar in north arcade, Great Bardfield Church, Essex. Photo: Anthea Hawdon of Raking Light (<www.rakinglight.co.uk>).

found in churches, but at the same time may relate to them in ways analogous to the ways in which the writing practice copy-texts in manuscripts relate to the codices in which they appear. The parish churches of St. Mary at Great Bardfield, Essex and Ashwell, Hertfordshire will serve as two case-study graffiti landscapes in this section. The section will also offer further examples from other churches of features identified in the case studies.

The church of St. Mary the Virgin, Great Bardfield, Essex offers a case study of graffiti as a medium for the extension and amplification of the applications of *littera* pedagogy to Anglophone literate practice, and its identity-forming potential in the linguistic landscape of the parish church. Dating from the twelfth century, the church walls are dressed with limestone and clunch, a soft material of the density of chalk. Perhaps their softness explains why the walls

Graphic Display 227

have attracted a mass of medieval graffiti.[22] I have studied the material at Great Bardfield using a corpus of high-resolution photographs taken under raking light.[23] The use of raking light and high-resolution photography for this corpus of photographs means that details are made clearer than would be seen by the naked eye in normal light. One graffito at Great Bardfield Church is particularly suggestive of how graffiti are framed by the understanding of graphic culture transmitted through *littera* pedagogy. At Great Bardfield, on a pillar, in a large, clear, and confident script, occurs the graffito, "*Be noʒt to bold ne to bustus ne bost noʒt to mych*" ("be not too bold nor too crude nor boast too much"; see Figure 18).[24] The graffito text, written over three lines that extend the full width of a face of a pillar in the north arcade, is similar to some of the lines in the *ABC of Aristotle*, the sequence of moralising exhortations in alphabetical order that, as was argued in Chapter Three, was used as an opportunity for the playful display of graphic skill. The graffito at Great Bardfield is a version of the *B* line comparable, for example, with the text of the *ABC* in MS Dublin, Trinity College, 509, p. 104: "*To bolde ne to besy ne borde þu not to large*" ("too bold nor too busy nor jest too unrestrainedly"). But the Great Bardfield graffito completes the line with a different *B* phrase: "*ne bost noʒt to mych*". The completing phrase is not found in the *B* lines of other surviving texts, instead, the phrase imitates a syntactical formula used in other lines, for example "*ne Rage nat to muche*" ("do not be too lusty") and "*Waste nat to muche*" ("do not squander too much") in MS London, BL, Harley 5086, f. 90v, or "*not to hevy in thy herte*" ("do not be too heavy of heart"; MS Oxford, Bod. Lib., Rawl. B. 196, f. 110v). Like some of these phrases, the instruction not to "*bost*" too much invites the reader to decide just how much is too much, and perhaps to question the morality of measure promoted by the poem. This selection and adaptation of material for display from longer texts is a small-scale example of the ingenious editing and rewriting of the text in the manuscripts, that, as we saw in Chapter Three, provided opportunities for the display of graphic virtuosity and for engagement in play. The graffito from the *ABC of*

---

[22] For the church see ROYAL COMMISSION ON HISTORICAL MONUMENTS OF ENGLAND, "Great Bardfield", in: *An Inventory of the Historical Monuments in Essex, Volume 1, North West* (London, 1916), pp. 105-113.

[23] I have used the digital images made with raking light published at <https://rakinglight.co.uk/uk/st-mary-the-virgin-great-bardfield-essex/>.

[24] Coulton misreads "*Be noght* [*sic*] *to bold / Be to bussi*[*ness*] ... *Bost noght* [*sic*] *to mych* [...]", describing the text as "very imperfect" (COULTON, "Medieval graffiti", p. 57); *DIMEV* 770 misreads "*Be noʒt to bold be to bustusne*[*s*] *bost noʒt to mych*".

Fig. 19. Graffito, "*Well fare my lady Cateryne*", encrypted with a die and musical notation, Lidgate Church, Suffolk. Photo: M.J. Champion.

Aristotle at Great Bardfield was perhaps an amalgam of favourite lines that took on particular meaning in its display place. Was the priest or a fellow parishioner perceived by the person who inscribed it as too bold or too boastful, too prone to arrogance? Did this inscription invite feelings of recognition and belonging from an audience, members of a community of Anglophone literate practice who used the space, who recognised its witty application? Had a *game* of the *ABC of Aristotle* been played, in which the *B* line was allocated to someone? Would such a community reflect on the extent of permissible boldness when they viewed the bold, confident script?

More evidence for engagement with graphic play on the part of the communities who used Great Bardfield Church appears on another column, where a fragment of a dice text is visible. Written across two lines, the text begins with an image of the throw of one, followed by "*þ^{at} fals* [...]" ("that false [...]"), the *f* being topped with an exuberant flourish. In the line below there is an image of a throw of three and before it the word "*huld*" ("loyal"?) and the number "*ix*". This appears to be a (previously unnoticed) fragment of a Middle English fortune-telling game-text in which the throws of the dice reveal charac-

Graphic Display 229

ter, a genre encountered in Chapter Three. Like the *ABC of Aristotle* line, it offered opportunities for graphic play and the creation of a sense of belonging and difference. At the same time as enabling them to distinguish between loyal and false persons, being able to play the game in itself gave the opportunity to experience belonging. The community of Anglophone literate practice that experienced belonging through the display of a dice text in a graffito was not alone. Another example of a dice text displayed in a graffito is "*Well fare my lady Cateryne*" ("fare well my lady Catherine") at Lidgate Church, Suffolk, which combines text with the die and with musical notation in a puzzling rebus that conceals the lady's name (see Figure 19). The musical notes are 'fa re mi la', representing the syllables in "*fare my la[dy]*"; the die shows the number 4, '*quater*' in French, representing the first two syllables in "*cateryne*". This witty puzzle recalls those of the school-books that we encountered in Chapters Two and Three, in particular the "*Allas p^{ri}de ys manys bane*" phrase that is encoded in nonsense Latin lines. Whereas the dice poems "*Ever is Six the best Chance of the Dice*" (*DIMEV* 1215) and "*Chaunce of the Dyse*" (*DIMEV* 1318), challenge the reader to puzzle with die images *and* text,[25] "*Well fare my lady cateryne*" deploys two kinds of musical notation alongside text and die diagram, setting the bar for the puzzle-solver even higher and recalling the cryptic scribal signatures, acrostics, and other puzzles that became resources for expressing in-group, literate identities.

As well as texts associated with graphic play, simpler writing practice copy-texts such as names and practice letters occur among the graffiti at Great Bardfield. Three names appear in a bold and confident script similar to that of the *ABC* text on another column, including "*Robert^{us} thetford*" and "*Ricardus spe*[...]". The name "*Alys*" appears on another column. The name "*Alkeryche*" appears in a large, bold, and stylish script with long, looped ascenders and quadrata feet just below a joint in a column. Another column bears the names "*Ioh^{ann}es* [...]" and "*Willielmus*" in a sloping, poorly formed script just above a join in the masonry. Lone practice letter-forms are hard to distinguish from fragmentary traces, but a lone majuscule *S* occurs above an otherwise illegible word that begins with a majuscule of the same shape.[26] Perhaps, as well as offering opportunities to express identity through displaying names, recognis-

---

[25] See Chapter Three, note 151.

[26] Other examples of names in medieval church graffiti: the name of the priest Bagot appears on the frame of the priest's door at Worlington, Suffolk (cf. PRITCHARD, *English Medieval Graffiti*, p. 164). The names "*William*", "*Johannes Lofte*", and "*Thom*" are among those at Coton, Cambridgeshire (COULTON, "Medieval graffiti", p. 55).

230 *Chapter 4*

ing the names also gave opportunities to experience belonging and difference. A graffito stanza on a pillar at St. John's Church, Duxford, Cambridgeshire (*DIMEV* 6757), makes use of initials instead of a name or names:

> *With wiel my herte is wa*
> *& closyd ys w^{ith} care*
> *L & S sekurly*
> *[Ca]use me to syth ful far*
> *I & [...]*
> *[...] for to smarte*
> *V & [...] Y withall*
> *[...] joy come to thin hert.*

With wei-la-wei! My heart is woeful and gripped with care. L and S truly cause me to sigh a great deal. I and [...] to smart with pain V and [...] along with Y [...] may joy come to your heart.[27]

Those who could decode the references belonged; those who could not – either because they could not read English at all, or because they did not know whose initials these were – were excluded.

The church of St. Mary, Ashwell, Hertfordshire, gives a second suggestive illustration of graffiti in the medieval church and its graffiti's relations with graphic culture developed in relation to literacy training. Built of flint rubble and faced with soft clunch, the church building dates from the mid fourteenth century with some fifteenth-century additions.[28] Containing much graffiti from medieval (and later) periods, Ashwell is entirely typical of the linguistic landscapes that modern graffiti surveys are beginning to discover. It is an exceptional site only in that some of its graffiti are well-known. Thirty graffiti texts and eight drawings are listed in David Sherlock's guide, which builds on the transcriptions of Coulton and others; yet others have been recorded by Lucy Parry.[29] In the description which follows, I offer transcriptions of material

---

[27] R.M. WILSON, "More lost literature in Old and Middle English", *Leeds Studies in English* 5 (1936), pp. 1-49, at p. 38, lightly edited.

[28] For St. Mary's, Ashwell see W. PAGE, "Parishes: Ashwell", in: *A History of the County of Hertford: Volume 3*, ed. W. PAGE (London, 1912: *Victoria History of the Counties of England*), pp. 199-209.

[29] D. SHERLOCK, *Medieval Drawings and Writings in Ashwell Church, Hertfordshire* (1978). L. PARRY, "Contributions [to Historic England List No 1102715] Church of St. Mary Ashwell", (n.d.), <https://historicengland.org.uk/listing/the-list/list-entry/1102715#contributions-banner>.

Graphic Display 231

previously undocumented and revise some of the existing transcriptions. My readings are based on my own photographs taken on a site visit and on images provided in the online church guide.[30]

As at Great Bardfield, the communities of literate practice who used the church as a graphic display space included those who wrote and read English. On the second pier from the chancel in the north aisle an inscription in English appears above a drawing of a church with a tower topped with a spire. Some of the material could read "*hery I þat*" ("?harrow I that"). Sherlock recorded this as two lines of writing in English but he did not transcribe the text, presumably using orthography to identify the language.[31] More attention to orthography and fragmentary material might reveal further inscriptions in English.[32] For example, a single word-fragment "*hys*" ("?his"; there is a macron over the *y*) appears on the second pier from the chancel in the north aisle, above a drawing of a church and above, "*Wa[?]l*" ("?wall"). A text fragment "*a synne*" or "*a synner*" ("a sin", "sinner") appears in the south aisle, on the fourth pier from the chancel. The preceding word appears to be "*artocop^{us}*" ("baker"). Perhaps the two fragments are unconnected, or perhaps they play with the form of a gloss: "a baker [in this parish, or perhaps bakers generally]: a sinner".[33] If it is a parodic gloss, the text engages with *littera* pedagogy, and shares an idiom with the displayed tombstone verses that translate Latin tags or provide both the English and the Latin. For example, the tombstone verses "*Lo all that ever I spent some time had I*" (*DIMEV* 3141) translate a Latin mortality quatrain "*Ecce quod expendi habui*". The earliest known example (1410) occurred beneath the effigy of a priest in St. Peter's Church, St. Albans.[34] A six-line English stanza at the tomb of William Read († 1477), St. Olave's, Hart Street, London, "*Who that passeth by this way*" (*DIMEV* 6574.5) is finished by the Latin couplet "*Qui*

---

[30] *St. Mary's Ashwell: History*, <http://www.stmarysashwell.org.uk/church/history.htm>.

[31] SHERLOCK, *Medieval Drawings and Writings in Ashwell Church*, p. 3.

[32] It seems likely that graffiti inscriptions in English have been overlooked generally given the difficulty of decoding most graffiti texts and the perhaps inexplicit, default assumption that medieval material is likely to be Latin. For the period from the twelfth to the sixteenth centuries, Pritchard states "[t]he inscriptions are written mostly in medieval Latin, a number in Middle English, and a few in Norman French" (PRITCHARD, *English Medieval Graffiti*, p. XII).

[33] Sherlock reads "*Archi[di]aconus Asemnes*" interpreting the text as a name, "[o]r possibly: 'The Archdeacon is an ass'" (SHERLOCK, *Medieval Drawings and Writings in Ashwell Church*, pp. 8-9).

[34] *Antiente Epitaphes (from A.D. 1250 to A.D. 1800) collected [and] sett forth in chronologicall order*, ed. T.A. RAVENSHAW (London, 1878), p. 5.

232   *Chapter 4*

pro aliis orat Pro se laborat" ("whoever prays for others helps himself").[35] The speaker in the late fifteenth-century seven-line tombstone stanza "*Farewell my friends the tide abideth no man*" requests that a "*requiem eternam*" be sung (*DIMEV* 1265).[36] Another possible instance of play with *littera* pedagogy at Ashwell is a fragmentary majuscule alphabet "*BCDEF*" that appears below a finely etched drawing of a church on the fourth pier from the chancel in the north aisle, just beneath a pattern of zigzag lines between two horizontals.

Like those at Great Bardfield, the graffiti texts in Ashwell Church include well-known pithy proverbs and sayings in verse common in *littera* pedagogy that I have included in the category of 'copy-texts'.[37] For example, in the south aisle, on the fourth pier from the chancel, appears the rhyming phrase "*ebrietas frang^{it} q^{ui}cq^{ui}d sapientia tangit*" ("drunkenness breaks whatever wisdom touches").[38] "*Ebrietas frangit quicquid sapientia tangit*" was evidently a proverb with some dissemination.[39] Coulton notes that it is found in a German manuscript.[40] But it is also found closer to home in John of Grimestone's preaching book, MS Edinburgh, National Library of Scotland, Advocates' 18.7.21, with the heading "*De Ebrietate*" and an English translation "*Drunkenchipe brekt Al þat wisdom spekt*".[41] On the pier nearest to the chancel in the south aisle occurs a fragmentary phrase reminiscent of the biblical injunction that pride goes before and other things follow – the other sins, or ruin or affliction, in commentaries – "*[s]up^{er}bia p^{re} seq^{uu}nt[ur]*".[42] A wall protruding into the nave from the south wall of the tower has "*finis virtutu^m est gl^{ori}a ^{et} no^n sc^{ienc}ia s^{i}n^e* [...]*" ("glory, not knowledge, is the end of virtues"), a phrase that circu-

---

[35]   *Antiente Epitaphes*, p. 11.

[36]   *Antiente Epitaphes*, p. 14; D. GRAY, "A Middle English epitaph", *Notes and Queries* n.s. 8.4 (1961), pp. 132-135.

[37]   Coulton describes this category of material as "moral saws" and notices that "[s]aws of this kind are of course commonly met with scribbled on the blank leaves and margins of medieval books" (COULTON, "Medieval graffiti", p. 56). Sherlock follows, describing these materials as "popular saws, or sayings" (SHERLOCK, *Medieval Drawings and Writings in Ashwell Church*, p. 2).

[38]   Cf. SHERLOCK, *Medieval Drawings and Writings in Ashwell Church*, p. 9.

[39]   Cf. *Novus Thesaurus Adagiorum Latinorum: Lateinischer Sprichwörterschatz*, ed. W. BINDER (Stuttgart, 1861), No. 923, p. 101.

[40]   COULTON, "Medieval graffiti", pp. 56-57.

[41]   Transcription from *DIMEV* 1156.

[42]   Cf. SHERLOCK, *Medieval Drawings and Writings in Ashwell Church*, p. 10. Cf. Prov. 16:18, "*contritionem praecedit superbia et ante ruinam exaltatur spiritus*". The final phrase of the graffito text has previously been read as "*fallum*"; for example, Coulton transcribes "*superbia precedit fallum*", calling this "a magnificent specimen of dog-Latin" (COULTON, "Medieval graffiti", p. 58). I cannot see how the marks can be construed in this way.

Graphic Display 233

lated in a popular theological compendium.[43] Also in this location occurs the rhyming phrase "*Quot g'auitas* [?] *sentis tot deles c^{ri}m^{in}a m^{en}t^{is}*" ("you delete as much sin as you suffer pain").[44] Fragmentary phrases "*per[f]ectus si uis*" ("?if you wish to be perfect"), "*temet*" ("yourself") and "*i^n celo pace^m*" ("in peace in heaven") occur on the pier nearest to the chancel in the south aisle. Perhaps the fragments echo Matt. 19:21, "*si vis perfectus esse vade vende quae habes et da pauperibus et habebis thesaurum in caelo et veni sequere me*", though they may not originally have been part of a single phrase.[45] The Christograms "*ihc*" on the fourth pier from the chancel in the south aisle, and another "*ihc*" on another face of the same pier recall the use of brief prayers and prayer fragments as copy-texts for writing practice in manuscripts and in graffiti at other churches.

The use of pithy and prayerful copy-texts for graffiti inscriptions at Great Bardfield and at Ashwell occurs widely in graffiti elsewhere. For example, a graffito quatrain in Barrington Church, Cambridgeshire, advises that folly should be given up because "*It ys almost XII of the clok*" ("it is almost twelve o'clock", *DIMEV* 3144).[46] A five-line abuses of the age text, "*a yong rewler wytles*" ("a senseless young reveller"), is found in a graffito at Ridgewell Church (*DIMEV* 2994).[47] This form of graffiti engages with the idioms of displayed texts in other material media. Many very brief Middle English moral and religious texts occur as part of epitaphs.[48] Many of these verses were gen-

---

[43] This text occurs in the *Compendium theologicae veritatis*, a popular theological compilation attributed to Albertus Magnus (see Albertus Magnus, *Compendium totius theologicae veritatis, septem libris digestum*, ed. J. DE COMBIS (Lyon, 1602), p. 400). Coulton misreads, "*Finis virtutis Dei gloria & non sancta sum omnibus*" (COULTON, "Medieval graffiti", p. 57). Sherlock follows, reading, "*Finis virtutis [pro] Dei gloria & non factum suum virtutibus / & non sancta omnibus*" (SHERLOCK, *Medieval Drawings and Writings in Ashwell Church*, p. 7).

[44] Coulton reads "*Quot gratias sentis tot deles crimina mentis*", translating, "as many thanks [or favours] you feel, so many faults of the soul do you wipe out" (COULTON, "Medieval graffiti", p. 57). Sherlock follows (SHERLOCK, *Medieval Drawings and Writings in Ashwell Church*, p. 7). However, the line requires a word that refers to something that one can physically sense to counterbalance sin.

[45] Sherlock, following Coulton, reads "*Patere si vis temet / in c[o]elo patere*", translating "suffer if you wish yourself to be seen in heaven" (SHERLOCK, *Medieval Drawings and Writings in Ashwell Church*, p. 10).

[46] COULTON, "Medieval graffiti", p. 57.

[47] For an image see PRITCHARD, *English Medieval Graffiti*, p. 76, fig. 103.

[48] Edwards describes the epitaph as the "most popular kind of inscriptional verse" (EDWARDS, "Middle English inscriptional verse texts", p. 35). David Griffith states that there are over 300 epitaphs in Middle English verse (D. GRIFFITH, "English commemorative inscriptions: Some literary dimensions", in: *Memory and Commemoration in Medieval England*, ed. C.M. BARRON

234   *Chapter 4*

eral reminders of mortality and therefore not specific to individuals and conse-
quently they were amenable to widespread imitation, giving opportunities for
ingenious and playful adaptation such as "*Farewell my friends*" (*DIMEV* 1265),
mentioned above. Floor and wall tiles, too, provided the opportunity for display
of short, pithy texts, for example, "*Thenke man thi life mai not ever endure*"
("think, man, your life cannot last forever") is found on a tile now in a pillar in
Malvern Priory (*DIMEV* 5635).[49] As with the traces of writing practice found in
manuscripts, brief prayer tags are common among texts displayed in churches.
For example, the couplet "*Mary for thine joys five / Teach me the way to right
live*" occurs in a wall-painting at Broughton Church, Banbury (*DIMEV* 3414).[50]
"*Cryst mote us spede And helpe alle at nede*" ("Christ support us and help all
who are in need") is found inscribed on the font in Holy Trinity Church,
Middleton, Suffolk.[51] In imitation of this mode, some graffiti texts in English
are brief prayers, for example, "*our ladi help*" ("Our Lady, help us") at Anstey,
Hertfordshire[52] and "*God help þe*" ("may God help you") twice at Steeple
Bumpstead, Essex.[53] Inscribed graffiti texts on wood (at one time part of seats)
at Warkworth Church, Banbury, include part of the *Creed* in Latin, and also
"*byttur passyon schylde vs frome*" ("shield us from hard suffering"), a fragment of the Middle English prayer "*Jesu for thy holy name*" (*DIMEV* 2840).[54]
The continuity between writing practice in manuscripts and graffiti on church
walls is powerfully exemplified by this example. *DIMEV* records twenty-two
manuscript witnesses to this brief prayer, many of them sole verse additions to
their codices, suggesting that they may often have functioned as copy-texts. In
the eighteenth century at Warkworth Church, a graffito was recorded as reading "*Ihs mercy Ihs*".[55]

On the north wall of the tower at Ashwell occur historical records of the
plague in 1350 and a record of a strong wind on St. Maur's day in 1361.[56]

---

and C. BURGESS (Donington, 2010: *Harlaxton Medieval Studies* 20), pp. 251-270, at p. 254.

[49] EDWARDS, "Middle English inscriptional verse texts", p. 35; another example survives
in Salisbury Museum.

[50] EDWARDS, "Middle English inscriptional verse texts", p. 30.

[51] EDWARDS, "Middle English inscriptional verse texts", p. 35.

[52] PRITCHARD, *English Medieval Graffiti*, p. 94.

[53] PRITCHARD, *English Medieval Graffiti*, p. 81 and fig. 108; Pritchard misreads "*me*".

[54] D. GRAY, "A Middle English verse at Warkworth", *Notes and Queries* n.s. 14.4 (1967),
pp. 131-132.

[55] D. GRAY, "A Middle English verse at Warkworth", p. 131.

[56] For comparable early modern inscriptions in Italian churches see PLESCH, "Memory on
the wall", pp. 177-178.

Graphic Display 235

These texts too engage with the pedagogy of *littera*. The historical events are recorded in a riddling way, in that the viewer is required to decode the date of the pestilence, "*M C t^er X penta*" (1350) and "*primula pestis i^n M t^er CCC fuit L minus uno*" (1349; "the first plague was one thousand three hundred fifty less by one").[57] The record of the wind, "[... *h*]*oc anno maurus in orbe tonat M CCC LXI*", coincides with a cryptic Latin verse on the topic "*Ecce flat hoc anno Maurus, in orbe tonans*" ("in this year Maurus thunders in the world").[58] This verse occurs in MS London, Lambeth Palace Library, 419 (f. 1a), a fourteenth-century manuscript of chronicles from St. Augustine's Canterbury.[59] The same verse is quoted in the chronicle of Adam Murimuth.[60] On the same pillar as the saying about drunkenness, in the south arcade on the fourth pier from the chancel, Sherlock recorded a graffito scribal signature, another genre that we have associated with graphic play: "*h*[*om*]*o que scriptus predictus* [...] *est*" as one alternative reading of a graffito text, but the grammar calls this transcription into question.[61]

Some of the graffiti at Great Bardfield and Ashwell may engage with the practices of writing taught at the elementary stages of *littera* learning through script choice and execution. Inscribing text on paint, plaster, and stone was a kind of deformational writing in which strokes were made by removing some element of the writing surface rather than by applying ink or pigment to it. Common to many of the inscriptions in both graphic landscapes is a script characterised by simplified letter-forms, lack of serifs, and a pronounced use of straight vertical and horizontal strokes. While they are related to forms used in cursive writing in ink on parchment, the graffiti letters are either very simply linked or not linked at all. For example, in the extract from the *ABC of Aristotle* at Great Bardfield, the letters in "*Be*", "*bold*", and "*ne*" are widely spaced from

[57] Cf. SHERLOCK, *Medieval Drawings and Writings in Ashwell Church*, p. 5.

[58] Cf. SHERLOCK, *Medieval Drawings and Writings in Ashwell Church*, p. 5.

[59] Quotation from the catalogue entry of Lambeth Palace Library, Database of Manuscripts and Archives, <https://archives.lambethpalacelibrary.org.uk/>.

[60] Adam Murimuth, *Adami Murimuthensis, Chronica sui temporis*, ed. T. HOG (London, 1846), p. 196. See P.J. BROWN, "'*Ventus vehemens et terribilis per totam Angliam*': Responses and reactions to a short-term crisis in the British Isles", in: *Waiting for the End of the World? New Perspectives on Natural Disasters in Medieval Europe*, ed. C.M. GERRARD, P. FORLIN, and P.J. BROWN (Abingdon, 2021), pp. 24-42, at p. 41 and n. 107.

[61] SHERLOCK, *Medieval Drawings and Writings in Ashwell Church*, p. 8. Though this reading is doubtful, graffiti signatures *are* found: the signature "*quod Cotton*" at Landwade, Cambridgeshire, in a private chapel that belonged to the Cotton family, accompanies the Middle English verse lines "*fare wel alle clene Felawis*" and "*fare well alle ladys*" ("fare well all decent fellows; fare well all ladies"; PRITCHARD, *English Medieval Graffiti*, p. 55, fig. 73).

each other. The approach stroke on *b* and the *l* in "*bold*", and the approach stroke on *b* in "*bost*", are long and only slightly or not at all curved and the ascenders are very high. The ascenders of *b* in "*bold*" and *h* in "*mych*" finish in a straight stroke that is angled down and to the right, giving the appearance of a simple serif. A simplified *st* ligature is used in "*bost*" and "*bustus*", the *s* being formed of a long, slightly angled vertical whose top is linked with the top of *t* with a slightly curved stroke. The descenders on *ʒ* in "*noʒt*", and on *y* and *h* in "*mych*" have a similar exaggerated length and slightly curved form. The *s* at the end of "*bustus*" is formed of a very simple shape that resembles the number six and is formed of two curving strokes that join at the bottom of the letter. Some of the script at Great Bardfield is more ambitious. The name "*Alkeryche*" is inscribed in a fine, large Textura script with elaborate ascenders and descenders and a fancy majuscule at the beginning. Below are traces of informal, smaller, cursive text: possibly "*obit*" ("died") and below, possibly, "*christ^us*". The initial majuscule *I* of another fine Textura inscription has been decorated with a trailing serif that ends with an outline trefoil, while the following majuscule *F* is a *ff* ligature graced by exaggerated descenders and a linking, curving upper serif.[62] The letters "*ull*" at the end of another inscription are formed from exaggerated verticals, the minims unlinked and with minimal feet and the *l* letter-forms being topped with slightly curved serifs and joined with a horizontal bar.

At Ashwell, the letters of the words in the plague and wind inscriptions in the tower are similarly broadly spaced. Even the *st* ligature does not appear here. The letter *l* in "*uiolenta*" is a simple vertical stroke. A similar 6-shaped *s* occurs at the end of "*gʹauitas* [?]" and "*sentis*" on the tower wall at Ashwell. The letter *s* at the end of "*pestis*" is formed from a curve that sits 'on the line' and the upper part of the letter is formed with two straight strokes joined at right-angles. (The formation of this letter is clarified by the *s* at the end of "*unus*", where only the curve part has been completed.) Notable in this inscription are the simplified forms used for *e* and *a*. The letter *e* is formed from a curve and a straight stroke angled upwards to the right that extends above the upper end of the curve. For the letter *a*, a simplified form is fashioned from two verticals linked at the top and in the middle with horizontals. The minims of the letters *u*, *n*, and *m* are not linked. Most of the other hands at Ashwell exhibit similar forms. The "*ihc*" inscriptions on the fourth pier from the chancel

---

[62] This inscription is perhaps a name: "*I Freans*[...]*ag^er*[...]".

Graphic Display 237

in the south aisle are exceptions: they display two attempts at Textura Quadrata that trace outlines of letters with squared-off serifs.

It seems obvious that the simplification of letter-forms of the graffiti inscriptions must be a response to the difficulties of writing on hard surfaces such as painted or plastered masonry, even if it was made of soft material such as clunch. The strategies used may relate to early writing pedagogy for which, as discussed in Chapter Two, wax tablets were often used for practice writing. Of course, the surface of wax would have differed from that of plastered or painted masonry and the tablets would have been laid flat or at an angle and perhaps used in a seated position whereas graffiti are applied to vertical surfaces and must have been done standing up, with additional strain on the arms and hands.[63] Nonetheless, elementary writing practice and graffiti were both kinds of deformational writing and learning to write on wax may have supported practice of the graffiti, especially since wax tablets were used for informal writing even once skill in writing had been acquired. A comparison of the forms and aspect of the graffiti at Ashwell and Great Bardfield with a sample of writing on wax supports this possibility. Such artefacts are extremely rare, but fortunately a set of tiny wax tablets dated to *c.* 1350 and still bearing writing was found in a York archaeological dig in 1989-1990. The tablets measure 50×30 mm, are made of wood, and were stored in a decorated leather pouch.[64] The tablets bear a Middle English text (tablets 2r-5r) which has been thought to be part of a love poem.[65] Also on the tablets are part of a Latin legal text and some accounts. The early graffiti at Ashwell and Great Bardfield share some features with this everyday, deformational writing on wax. For example, the

---

[63] The inscriptions that record the plague and the wind are raised high on the north wall of the tower at Ashwell, well above the reach of a standing person, though still easily legible owing to the large size, regularity, and deeply engraved script of the letters. But much of the material in the church – at least the material currently visible (some of the walls are whitewashed and may conceal further graffiti) – is positioned roughly between a standing adult's waist and head height.

[64] The measurement is from D. Tweddle, "Medieval love poem written in wax", *Minerva: The International Review of Ancient Art and Archaeology* 3.2 (1992), pp. 10-12, p. 11. The tablets were found in the backyard of 12-18 Swinegate, an area associated with metalworking and nail making (see J.M. McComish, *Archaeological Investigations at 12-18 Swinegate, 14 Little Stonegate, and 18 Back Swinegate* (York, 2015: *York Archaeological Trust Web-Based Report* 2015/ 4); and J.M. McComish, *The Wooden Writing Tablets from Excavations at 12-18 Swinegate: An Insight Report* (York, 2015)). Lalou terms tiny tablets of this kind "*carnets*" (E. Lalou, "Les tablettes de cire médiévales", *Bibliothèque de L'Ecole des Chartes* 162 (1989), pp. 123-140, at p. 138).

[65] M.P. Brown, "The role of the wax tablet in medieval literacy: A reconsideration in light of a recent find from York", *British Library Journal* 29 (1994), pp. 1-16, at pp. 12-13.

238   *Chapter 4*

majuscule *a* in *"Also"* on the tablets has a simple form and structure that recall the forms of *a* in the wind and plague inscriptions at Ashwell.[66] But the writing on the wax is more fluent and rounded than the graffiti.[67] It appears that the application of graffiti was not within the scope of just anyone who had been trained to write on a wax tablet at school; some further adaptation would have been needed. The transfer of the script used by the literacy learner to graphic production on the fabric of the church may reflect not just the replication and amplification of graphic culture in this environment but also the use of such spaces for literacy training.[68] In addition, while some graffiti appear to have been made with hefty metal tools, much of it must have been traced with something thinner and lighter, raising the question of whether styli normally used with wax tablets could have sometimes been used for this purpose.[69]

[66] See the images of the tablets in McCOMISH, *The Wooden Writing Tablets from Excavations at 12-18 Swinegate*, p. 3, upper image, line 4.

[67] For an example of very fluent, even, and rapid writing on wax tablets see the accounts of Jean Sarrazin, 1256-1257, MS Paris, Archives Nationales, Musée des documents français, Ancien fonds, AE/II/258, Cote d'origine: J//1168.

[68] Graffiti in the north chapel at St. John's Church, Duxford, Cambridgeshire is said to date from 1657 to 1847, the period when the space was used as the village school (B. COLBOURN and M. YNYS-MON, *Cambridgeshire Churches*, <druidic.org/camchurch/>). Schofield infers from the lack of archaeological or documentary evidence for special buildings for the parish schools in late medieval London that "[p]resumably much of the business of the school took place within the church itself" (J. SCHOFIELD, "Saxon and medieval parish churches in the city of London: A review", *Transactions of the London and Middlesex Archaeological Society* 45 (1994), pp. 23-146, at p. 74). School-children were trained to perform Our Lady Mass, celebrated in St. Dunstan in the East, London, from the late fourteenth century (J. LEDFORS, "St Dunstan in the East: An architectural history of a late medieval London parish church", *London and Middlesex Archaeological Society Transactions* 66 (2015), pp. 47-77, pp. 64, 67) which establishes the presence of pupils in the church building. Cf. Orme's description of "small, private, and temporary [school] operations in villages and parish churches" (N. ORME, *Medieval Schools: From Roman Britain to Renaissance England* (New Haven, 2006), p. 189).

[69] It is worth considering in particular whether a metal or metal-tipped stylus, a common writing implement for use with a wax tablet, would have been all that was needed to make some of the graffiti traces seen today, although most of the survivals do not seem strong enough to have been used in this way. For examples of later medieval styli that still retain their inset metal tips see the Museum of London, objects ID A7749, ID A1319, ID 10964, ID 17097, ID 1340, ID 1328, and ID 87128/24 (tipped with copper). Object ID 17156 is, like these other styli, made of bone but instead of having a metal tip or space for one the bone shaft itself has been sharpened. Object ID 87.128/19 is made of copper alloy, with a hexagonal section and a sharp point. Unfortunately these items do not have formal archaeological contexts (Meriel Jeater, Museum of London, personal communication). The collection of styli of the Museum of Writing of the School of Advanced Studies, University of London, includes medieval styli made of bronze (accession number 2011.4203), iron (accession number 2011.4202), and gilt bronze (accession

Graphic Display 239

The marks of the communities of Anglophone literate practice at Great Bardfield and Ashwell contrast with the traces of other graphic languages left by communities who identified themselves differently in the graphic landscape of the church using other modes of making meaning with line.[70] At Great Bardfield a series of embedded ellipses occurs on a pillar amidst a mass of textual graffiti. A simpler ellipse occurs at St. Mary the Virgin, Stone, near Dartford, Kent, on the south rectangular pillar, east end, where it has been interpreted as an apotropaic symbol rather than a mason's mark because the latter are not usually curved.[71] Masons' marks at Great Bardfield include a symbol comprised of two straight crossed lines with angled lower ends and a triangular device with a spiral and two small circles. Dense cross-hatched lines that describe shapes may be decoration or possibly the beginning of some kind of figurative drawing (perhaps a windmill: compare the post-mill graffito drawing at Dalham, Suffolk).[72] A crude freehand shield with a central cross that sits among illegible text may be a heraldic symbol. Below the "*Alkeryche*" inscription at Great Bardfield is an outline flower drawing and below that to the right an unusually complex apotropaic symbol formed of interlocking *V* and *W* shapes, thought to be "ritual protection marks".[73] Also at Great Bardfield, a

number 2011.4205). Alan Cole, collector and curator of the collection, writes "I do not feel that even metal styli could have stood up to rock as the writing end is quite thin and [...] iron ones were not that common" (personal communication).

[70] Perhaps only 5-10% of medieval graffiti is textual according to Matthew Champion (M.J. CHAMPION, "Writing on the wall: Workshop on historic graffiti", unpublished paper (University of Birmingham, 18 July 2019)). Of approximately fifty-nine inscriptions in All Saints Church, Leighton Buzzard, just under twelve percent are textual (B. WILLIAMS, "Monsters, masons, and markers: An overview of the graffiti at All Saints Church, Leighton Buzzard", *Peregrinations: Journal of Medieval Art and Architecture* (Special issue: *New Research on Medieval and Later Graffiti*) 6.1 (2017), pp. 38-64). Earlier surveyors of graffiti such as Coulton, Pritchard, and Sherlock tended to focus on the textual material, perhaps giving an undue impression of the prominence of this category. Even the county graffiti surveys recorded in the later digital scans, however, do not give a fully rounded picture of the material.

[71] <https://rakinglight.co.uk/uk/st-mary-the-virgin-stone-near-dartford-kent/>, AP13.

[72] Unless otherwise noted, all references to graffiti in Suffolk churches are based on the photographs published by the *Suffolk Medieval Graffiti Survey* (2014-), <http://www.medieval-graffiti-suffolk.co.uk/>.

[73] *Norfolk Medieval Graffiti Survey*, images at <http://www.medieval-graffiti.co.uk/page15.html>. Unless otherwise indicated all references to Norfolk graffiti are to this survey. Cf. M.J. CHAMPION, *Medieval Graffiti*, para. 12.8. Other examples are widespread, for instance these symbols occur at St. Mary's Church, Sedgeford, Norfolk and at St. George's, Crowhurst, Surrey (*Surrey Medieval Graffiti Survey* (2011-2019), <https://web.archive.org/web/20200815113317/http://www.medievalgraffitisurrey.org/the-project.html>, last accessed 2019). These marks were sometimes used by masons: see further below.

240 *Chapter 4*

crude shield, possibly bearing some kind of heraldic charge, sits amidst a mass of text, some of it apparently inscribed around the shield.[74] At Ashwell informal, freehand pentangles occur between deeply-etched lines on the fourth pier from the chancel in the south aisle, and a geometric 'frieze' occurs below an image of a church on the fourth pier from the chancel in the north aisle.[75] Drawings at Ashwell range from the figurative[76] – architectural images of medieval St. Paul's and other churches and faces – to ritual marks, geometric designs,[77] and outlines of shoes, perhaps associated with pilgrimages.[78] A male face in three-quarter profile with joined brows is found on the second pier from the chancel in the north aisle along with, on the same pier, an outline drawing of a church with a spire topped with a large cross, and much textual graffiti. A very fine graffito drawing of a church with carefully outlined windows and a castellated tower is found on the fourth pier from the chancel in the north aisle. On the fourth pier from the chancel in the south aisle occur concentric circles

[74] Graffiti heraldic badges and shields are common; examples elsewhere include the fine shield at Borough Green, Cambridgeshire, the superimposed shields at Coveney, Cambridgeshire (PRITCHARD, *English Medieval Graffiti*, pp. 25-26, 30-31), the shields at Worlington, Suffolk, and the scallop shell badge of Compostela pilgrims at Anstey, Hertfordshire (PRITCHARD, *English Medieval Graffiti*, pp. 94-95).

[75] Freehand figures occur at Cowlinge, Suffolk, including several complex interlaced knots, a kind of plait, and a decorative frieze.

[76] Examples of figurative graffiti elsewhere include an owl with a woman's head-dress at Stetchworth, Cambridgeshire (PRITCHARD, *English Medieval Graffiti*, pp. 59-60), a horned head at Sible Hedingham, Essex (p. 78), a windmill at Dalham, Suffolk (pp. 136-138), a ship, dagger, sword, a male head and torso, and a fashionably-dressed male at Kedington, Suffolk, a fanciful flower at Belchamp Walter, Essex (pp. 68-69), and three horned devils' heads, a fashionably dressed male with arms akimbo, a ship, and a bird with a long beak at Lindsey, Suffolk. At Stoke-by-Clare, Suffolk, occur a head with an extravagant hat, and another in three-quarter profile. At Troston, Suffolk, occur the sole of a foot (from which a devilish head appears to protrude), a ship with sails furled, the outline of a left hand, and a fish. At Worlington, Suffolk, a hand makes a symbol of blessing (the third and fourth fingers are bent) and a female face frowns.

[77] Geometric graffiti are common. Some graffiti appear to have been drawn with a hinged implement with two sharp metal points such as scissors or shears or, perhaps more rarely, with a stonemason's dividers (M.J. CHAMPION, *Medieval Graffiti*, para. 13.16). At Cowlinge, Suffolk occurs a circle that contains a pattern of six petals formed of curves that link the perimeter to the centre and a similar design where curves link the tips of the petals. Another circle includes three smaller circles linked by groups of tiny circles that give a floral impression. At Worlington, Suffolk, seven concentric rings surround a central point (perhaps this is a cosmographical diagram); nine rings occur on a second example of this diagram here.

[78] For this interpretation of graffiti shoe outlines see PARRY, "Contributions [to Historic England List No 1102715] Church of St. Mary Ashwell".

Graphic Display 241

on one face and on another rows of pentangles and other symbols inscribed between deeply etched lines.[79]

If the multilingual linguistic landscapes of modern urban environments shape identities and express relations among different speech communities, the graffiti landscapes of these parish churches carry out a similar function by displaying various graphic languages. Graffiti such as the *ABC of Aristotle* line, the dice text, the anglicised names, and the prayers draw boundaries between communities of Anglophone literate practice and communities of practice who use other graphic languages to express identity: the languages of masons' marks, heraldry, and evil-repelling symbols. In the parish church, English writing as a resource for identity construction is part of a public graphic landscape where other resources and modes of communication offer alternative graphic modes of identity formation to the communities that gathered in those spaces. Heraldic symbols, names, and masons' marks are obvious identity symbols. Graffiti have been seen as a "practice of scratching personal marks [... to] give permanence to [...] identity within a holy space".[80] Crosses, pentangles, and cosmographical diagrams readily lend themselves to explication in terms of belonging and one's place in the world. Drawing around one's hand recorded one's contact with the space and one's conversion of a graphic act into a memorial of the self (the outline representing both the hand that provides the model and the hand that produces it). The outline of a foot, perhaps achieved by drawing round the shoe one was wearing, may be associated with pilgrimage, as may, perhaps, the ships. The fashionably-dressed figures may represent the other, to be feared and shunned. The graphic resources for making English visible in these spaces resonated with and against these graphic alternatives for the expression of identity.

Some members of communities of Anglophone literate practice may, of course, have been competent in two or more of these graphic languages. The fifteenth-century scribe of MS Oxford, Bod. Lib., Ashmole 61 who signs himself *"Rate"* is competent in both Anglophone literate practice and the graphic language of graffiti symbols. He accompanies his signatures to *Isumbras* and the *Lay of Commandments* with a hexfoil image (f. 17r), linking the tips of the petals with concave curves, giving a kind of spider's-web effect and surrounding the whole figure with two circles; precisely similar figures occur at St.

---

[79] At Kedington, Suffolk, a pentangle (thought to be an apotropaic or protective symbol; see M.J. CHAMPION, *Medieval Graffiti*, para. 12.8) has been drawn freehand.

[80] OWEN, "Traces of presence and pleading", p. 41.

242   *Chapter 4*

Mary's, Wiveton, Norfolk and at St. Mary's, Troston, Suffolk. Rate's figure is enclosed in circles. Similarly, the graffiti hexfoil at St. Margaret's, Cowlinge, Suffolk, is enclosed in one circle and in the church of St. Peter, Belaugh, Norfolk, the spider's web feature is enclosed in five circles. At St. Catherine, Ludham, Norfolk, a graffiti-artist has attempted to build further hexfoils onto the spider's web curves. A similar figure occurs at St. Mary's, Sedgeford, Norfolk. Rate also associates his signature with two images of a fish (MS Ashmole 61, ff. 16v, 17r) drawn in profile with sharp teeth exposed and two fins above and below. This figure may be a heraldic device: depicted in side profile, with an open mouth and two fins on both the upper and lower body, it resembles, apart from a difference in the tail, the "*roches*" ("roach") that appear on the arms of Peter des Roches († 1238), as recorded in the *Boke of St. Albans*.[81] The fish at Troston, Suffolk, is equally fanciful, bearing a large dorsal fin that is fashioned from the repeated letter *M*. Perhaps it too is a heraldic device.

Other examples of Middle English manuscripts that contain graffiti figures include Humphrey Newton's manuscript, discussed in Chapters Two and Three, where the *VV* sign appears (MS Oxford, Bod. Lib., Lat. Misc. c. 66, f. 121v, upside down, beside a *B*). A fine ship drawing that recalls those of the graffiti occurs in MS Manchester, John Rylands Library, Eng. 895, f. 66v, beside a copy of the *Gospel of Nicodemus*, which, with its furled sails, is remarkably like the graffiti ships at St. Nicholas, Blakeney, Norfolk. There is another example of a ship in Lydgate manuscript, MS Glasgow, UL, Hunter 232 (U.3.5), f. 56r, along with the practice letters there that we encountered in Chapter Two.[82] Complex patterns of intertwining lines also in the margins of this manuscript resemble in some ways the endless knot found in graffiti, for example, at All Saints, Litcham, Norfolk. A similar figure appears in MS Cambridge, Trinity College, O.2.53, on f. 59r.

We cannot assume, however, that the scribes who used graffiti symbols shared the interpretation of those symbols with those who used them in the graphic landscape of the parish church. It is possible that similar inscriptions could take on different meanings in different communities of graphic practice. Some evidence for this is provided by the use of the various versions of the *VV* symbol on masonry. Sometimes these symbols are made professionally with

---

[81] Juliana Berner, The Boke of Saint Albans: *Containing Treatises on Hawking, Hunting, and Cote Armour by Dame Juliana Berner, printed at Saint Albans by the School-Master Printer in 1486, Reproduced in Facsimile*, ed. W. BLADES (London, 1901), sig. f. v[i].

[82] I owe this reference to Ryan Perry.

Graphic Display 243

the use of a chisel and in these cases they are masons' marks.[83] They may have still been understood to have apotropaic properties in these contexts, but by being appropriated to sign work, they take on new meanings within the masons' communities of graphic practice.[84] When the scribe Rate associated his signature with the graffiti symbols of the fish and the hexfoil, or the reader of Humphrey Newton's manuscript entered a *VV* symbol in it, they may have appropriated and repurposed these symbols to draw different boundaries between belonging and difference.

When considering the parish churches at Great Bardfield and at Ashwell as graphic landscapes where the display of various graphic languages expresses different social identities, we of course need to acknowledge that the graffiti recovered by the modern photographs was not necessarily all visible at the same time. Some columns at Great Bardfield and Ashfield display a mass of text. Probably these are places where inscription frequently occurred and was painted over, leaving the traces of numerous palimpsests in the masonry. But this does not mean that the approach is invalid. Linguistic landscape scholars acknowledge similar issues with their cityscapes. The linguistic landscape, Gorter notes, always has a historical dimension: all texts will have temporality and all landscapes historical layering and depth: "Although the landscape may change from day to day, some posters will be removed or added, but other signs may be fixed for many years".[85] Shep, exploring printing in Wellington, New Zealand, writes of the "contemporary semioscape" as a place of palimpsests, of layered "ghost signs" in an "architextural landscape".[86] Likewise, the palimpsest columns at Great Bardfield and at Ashwell speak eloquently of communities who shared graphic practices, an understanding of certain spaces as appropriate for graphic display, and used this shared understanding to create boundaries between belonging and difference.

---

[83] For the distinguishing features of masons' marks (repetition, regularity, professional execution) and for the use of these *VV* symbols as masons' marks see J.S. ALEXANDER, "Masons' marks and the working practices of medieval stone masons", in: *Who Built Beverley Minster?*, ed. P.S. BARNWELL and A. PACEY (Reading, 2008), pp. 21-40.

[84] Owen suggests that masons' marks may have had the purpose of leaving "some trace of [individuals'] identity within the church" (OWEN, "Traces of presence and pleading", p. 41).

[85] GORTER, "Introduction: The study of the linguistic landscape", p. 3.

[86] 'Architectural' / 'textual': S.J. SHEP, "Urban palimpsests and contending signs", *Social Semiotics* 25:2 (2015), pp. 209-216, at p. 210.

244   *Chapter 4*

Domestic and Civic Spaces

In this section we turn from the graffiti landscape of the parish church to graphic display in domestic settings: in halls and other rooms used for a household or other community and its guests. Writing on walls, windows, fireplaces and the like may have been the norm in late medieval England, if it is safe to extrapolate back from the ample early modern evidence discussed by Fleming.[87] There is much potential for study of the graffiti landscape in such environments, but surveys of graffiti in domestic interiors are not as far advanced as those of parish churches.[88] Instead, this section will draw on evidence for other aspects of the graphic landscapes of halls and other domestic rooms. We will begin with inscribed objects, such as the famous Studley bowl and other later medieval vessels, examining how their inscriptions engage with *littera* pedagogy and have the potential to speak to identity among the communities of literate practice that viewed them. We shall then turn to text displayed on walls and other architectural features in the domestic environment. First, we shall focus on the schemes of inscription at the houses of the Percy family at Leconfield and Wressle in East Yorkshire and other similar graphic landscapes. Our evidence for these schemes is for the most part largely literary and documentary. It will be argued that such manuscript records are valuable not just as traces of schemes but also as traces of the impacts of these schemes and their contribution to the formation of identity among communities of Anglophone literate practice. Our final example is the scheme of inscription at the chapel of the guild of the Holy Cross at Stratford-upon-Avon. Here restoration of the wall inscriptions combined with digital reconstruction of the original based on literary and documentary sources provide rich evidence for a civic graphic landscape. This section will argue that, as in the parish church, the display of English inscriptions in these locations was informed by basic understandings of reading and writing transmitted by formal and informal *littera* pedagogy. Resources drawn on for these purposes included familiar copy-texts such as

[87] FLEMING, *Graffiti and the Writing Arts*.

[88] We shall know more about this dimension of graphic display in domestic and civic spaces as our corpus of historic graffiti grows. The survey of graffiti in such buildings lags behind that in churches, but some properties have recently been surveyed, for example, under the auspices of the National Trust at Knole, Sevenoaks (N. COHEN, "Scratches and story-telling: Graffiti recording and interpretation at National Trust sites", unpublished paper (University of Southampton, 5 October 2019: *Making Your Mark: The First National Symposium for the Study of Historic Graffiti*)).

Graphic Display 245

Fig. 20. Alphabets on the Studley Bowl, London, Victoria and Albert Museum, M.1:1, 2-1914. Photo: © Victoria and Albert Museum, London.

proverbs and pithy moral texts and model alphabets. Display of pedagogic copy-texts and viewing of them in these environments provided opportunities for the experience of belonging to exceptional and prestigious social groups and alignment with their concerns for lordship, governance, and social order. It could also signify and construct belonging to groups of worthy citizens concerned with civic power, values, and harmony.

Medieval *littera* pedagogy provides a framework for interpreting many examples of inscribed objects. While inscriptions on rings and brooches cannot, perhaps, safely be regarded as for public display, since their legends are necessarily small in size and possibly not visible to others when in use on a finger or clothing, items used at the dining table or in other social and household settings could offer public display opportunities. A fine example of an inscribed object that displays engagement with *littera* pedagogy is the Studley bowl, a lidded silver bowl made in England *c.* 1400 (Victoria and Albert Museum M.1:1, 2-1914) that is decorated with alphabets (see Figure 20). The alphabets on the Studley bowl correspond closely with those of some of the primers discussed in Chapter One, where thorn and yogh have been assimilated

246   *Chapter 4*

with the Latin character set.[89] The object, even if too fine for actual *use* with learners, possibly *represents* the educational process.[90] The handle of the lid bears the letter *a*, perhaps suggesting that to begin the alphabet is to begin to receive nourishment. It also associates learning the alphabet with the active work of the learner's hand. This association is continued by the decorative scheme. The alphabet on the Studley Bowl is inscribed twice, identically, once on the bowl and once on the lid. A learner could be challenged to line up the letters by rotating the lid with the handle and to match the letter-forms and abbreviations.[91] The learning experience offered by the Studley bowl involves both the eye of the reader and the hand of the writer whom the learner would become. The bowl also implies learning in a community, since presumably it would be brought out for use at meals. And it associates the alphabet with the values of the community. The cross at the beginning might have prompted a prayer, and certainly indicated an association between the alphabet and Christian religion, as the bowl alphabets share the layout of the alphabet as a criss-cross row in primers which begin with a prompt to say the prayer "*Christ's Cross Me Speed*", implying that the user would have read the alphabet aloud as part of the prayer. This activity might have involved pronouncing the sounds of the letters aloud, so that the pupil knew the *potestas* of each letter. If, as suggested above, the quality and beauty of the object suggest that it was probably not intended for practical use, they also imply that the community that owns it values literacy and the recognition and use of letters. Even if they did not offer active participatory and learning activities, like the fine copies of Chaucer's *ABC* discussed in Chapter Three, objects such as the Studley bowl

---

[89] A description, partial transcription, and a useful photograph of the lid seen from above so the whole alphabet is visible are included in ANON., [Untitled Proceedings of 3 February 1910], *Proceedings of the Society of Antiquaries*, 2nd series, 23 (1910), pp. 46-49. I am grateful to Christopher Edgcumbe of the Victoria and Albert Museum for this reference. Orme transcribes "+abcdefghiklmnopqrstuxyz& *est :* [*con*]" (N. ORME, *Medieval Children* (New Haven, 2001), p. 271; the picture of the bowl on this page is mistakenly reversed so the letters are all mirror-images). For the view that this is an alphabet without thorn and yogh (rather than with assimilated thorn and yogh), see also J.G. ALEXANDER and P. BINSKI, *Age of Chivalry: Art in Plantagenet England 1200-1400* (London, 1987), p. 526, item 728 (citing A.I. Doyle's opinion); and R. MARKS and P. WILLIAMSON (ed.), *Gothic: Art for England 1400-1547* (London, 2003), p. 315, item 183.

[90] Clanchy, however, states that the Studley alphabets are "intended for a child" (M.T. CLANCHY, *Looking back from the Invention of Printing: Mothers and the Teaching of Reading in the Middle Ages* (Turnhout, 2018: *Utrecht Studies in Medieval Literacy* 40), p. 143).

[91] I am grateful to Christopher Edgcumbe of the metalwork department at the Victoria and Albert Museum for supplying me with a photograph of the bowl with the letters aligned.

Graphic Display 247

would also have provided opportunities for literate users and viewers to experience feelings of belonging to an elite community of literate practice through recognition of shared knowledge of and taste for letters. For such viewers, they drew a boundary between those who identified with such a community and those who could not.

The Studley bowl may belong with a tradition of literacy pedagogy in which valuable vessels express a community's high valuation of the learning of letters.[92] The association may derive from the iconography of the bowl, thought to have been an attribute of the personification of the liberal art *Grammatica*.[93] An item described as "*unum collok pece argenti cum scriptura A.B.C. in cooperculo*" ("one silver bowl with the *ABC* engraved on its lid") in a York will of 1431 sounds very similar.[94] The Royal Gold Cup, British Museum 1892,0501.1, a lidded bowl of similar date thought to be of French provenance, bears on the inside of the cup part an image of the young St. Agnes learning to read from a primer. An image on the underside of the lid (that is, directly above the St. Agnes image when the lid is in position) depicts Christ in an attitude of blessing and carrying a chalice and host.[95]

---

[92] From later medieval England there survives evidence for alphabets on objects of fine quality that would have drawn attention to the beauty of the letters that decorated them and implied their value. We know that alphabets were sometimes written on walls (ORME, *English Schools in the Middle Ages*, p. 62) and on "alphabet tables" (ORME, *Medieval Children*, p. 254). Alphabets also occurred on wooden and plaster tablets, leather belts, embroidered fabric, and even cakes and confectionery. Items of this kind that display the Roman alphabet are found across medieval Europe; for an immense range of evidence, especially of continental provenance, see D. ALEXANDRE-BIDON, "La lettre volée: Apprendre à lire à l'enfant au Moyen Age", *Annales. Economies, Sociétés, Civilisations* 44.4 (1989), pp. 953-992. See also B.L. ULLMAN, "*Abecedaria* and their purpose", *Transactions of the Cambridge Bibliographical Society* 3 (1961), pp. 181-186.

[93] L. CLEAVER, "Grammar and her children: Learning to read in the art of the twelfth century", *Marginalia* 19 (2015), n.p., <https://merg.soc.srcf.net/journal/09education/cleaver.php>.

[94] ANON., [Untitled Proceedings of 3 February 1910], p. 49. The testator was John Morton, Esquire of York, and the beneficiary his cousin Robert Gaytenby. Morton was a wealthy bibliophile; see J.B. FRIEDMAN, *Northern English Books, Owners, and Makers in the Late Middle Ages* (Syracuse, NY, 1995), p. 27.

[95] Some examples of alphabets on objects are very early, such as the silver ring found at Flixborough that bears a partial alphabet and the alphabet on a piece of lead from Waltham, Essex, mentioned in Chapter Two. A piece of sandstone found at Barton St. David, Somerset, is inscribed with the letters "*ABCDE*" (Barton St. David Sandstone; E. OKASHA, "A second supplement to *Hand-List of Anglo-Saxon Non-Runic Inscriptions*", *Anglo-Saxon England* 21 (1992), pp. 37-85, plate 1b); this object has been dated third quarter of the tenth century or eleventh century on stylistic grounds; its purpose is unclear: it could have been a "trial piece" (p. 41). On

Fig. 21. Drinking bowl with moralising inscription, New York, Metropolitan Museum of Art, Cloister Collection, 55.25. Photo: © New York, Metropolitan Museum of Art. Creative Commons Zero (CC0).

Domestic objects also provided spaces for the display of pedagogic copytexts in aristocratic and gentry households, in particular the short, pithy moral texts and precepts associated with *littera* pedagogy that we have observed in school-books, in manuscript margins, and in parish churches.[96] As in these cases, the display of such inscriptions on objects was an opportunity to show the selection and arrangement of the material while it also allowed for special

---

other faces some uninterpreted inscriptions, probably carved by another hand, include the letters thorn and wynn (pp. 41-42 and Plate 1b). These inscriptions are thought to post-date the alphabet. Cf. *The Corpus of Anglo-Saxon Stone Sculpture VII: South-West England*, ed. R. CRAMP (London, 2006), p. 138.

[96] Cf. Safran's comment about inscriptions at Salento, "The producers of formal or casual inscriptions intended them to be seen, to be viewed repeatedly and in perpetuity, although only hortatory texts express this objective explicitly" (L. SAFRAN, "Public textual cultures: A case study in southern Italy", in: *Textual Cultures of Medieval Italy*, ed. W. ROBINS (Toronto, 2011), pp. 115-144, at p. 118). Edwards notes that the moralising in displayed Middle English verses in domestic settings exhibits "an almost compulsive tendency to harangue the reader in contexts that might otherwise have been pleasant and private" (EDWARDS, "Middle English inscriptional verse texts", p. 29).

Graphic Display 249

ways of speaking to the community of Anglophone literate practice that would view or use it. A fifteenth-century lidded bowl (New York, Metropolitan Museum of Art, Cloister Collection, 55.25), bears the legend "*Resun bad [that] I Shulde writ th[i]nk micul + spek lite*" ("reason required me to write and think much and speak little", *DIMEV* 4448A; see Figure 21). A late fourteenth-century metal jug bears the inscription, "*He that wyl not spare whan he may / He schal not spend whan he wold*" ("he that will not save when it is possible shall not spend when he wishes to"; *DIMEV* 1911).[97] This proverb is accompanied on the jug by another on giving the benefit of the doubt: "*Deme the best in every dowt / Til the trowthe be tryid owte*" ("give the benefit of the doubt until the truth is known"). This couplet may have been selected from longer texts such as those witnessed in several manuscripts (*DIMEV* 1112). Another jug of similar date (London, Victoria and Albert Museum, 217-1879) bears the couplets, "*Stond uttir from the fyre / And lat on iust come nere*" ("stand further from the fire and let a just person come near") and "*Goddis grace / Be in this place*" ("God's grace be in this place").[98] Referring to the domestic space, to the fireplace and "this place", both couplets mandate generosity and pray for household harmony. Commissioning and using such objects gave opportunities for the wealthy to demonstrate their ability to select and manipulate appropriate pedagogic copy-texts – or at least to display their understanding and valuation of this graphic skill. Displaying inscriptions on household objects also suggested that the texts were models of conduct as well as literate skill for the social groups that viewed and used them. Viewers and users who recognised the texts and were capable of puzzling out their orthography were invited to consider themselves members of an elite social group. These displayed copy-texts offered literate viewers opportunities to experience belonging and a boundary between themselves and other viewers who could not read the texts or identify with the literacy training they represented.

Capable of being written as brief, discrete texts of a few short lines, pedagogic copy-text proverbs and precepts were also appropriate for display on the interior fabric of domestic and civic buildings. Again, the display of pedagogic material provided opportunities for those with power in households to demonstrate their graphic ingenuity and literate abilities and to model those skills and urge moral conduct at the same time. Selection and adaptation of material was required by the particular spaces of given buildings. A text that could be dis-

---

[97] Cf. *DIMEV* 5017; London, British Museum, item BM MLA 96, 7-27.
[98] *DIMEV* 5028, lightly edited.

250   *Chapter 4*

played in several short lines of text would be suitable for a small space of restricted size – in a border, on woodwork, above or below windows, on a tile, and so on. For settings where a more extensive programme of display was desired, short, pithy texts were also suitable. Copy-text proverbs and precepts could be gathered in sequence, meaning that they could be displayed in series in repeated architectural frames such as windows or decorative wall borders. For spaces where only one inscription was possible, a single precept could be selected and extracted from a longer sequence. Texts chosen for display may have been selected from pedagogic material that circulated in manuscripts as copy-texts, and the display of that material may have stimulated further circulation of the texts as copy-texts used for writing practice.

Percy Family Houses at Leconfield and Wressle

The houses of the Percy family at Leconfield and Wressle in East Yorkshire bore extensive schemes of displayed copy-text. We know of the Percy schemes and their texts from a fine manuscript copy in MS London, BL, Royal 18. D.ii; the portion of the manuscript that includes these texts dates between *c.* 1516 and 1527. The texts are a sequence of mono-rhymed quatrains that enjoin dreading God and fleeing vice and sin (*DIMEV* 1150); a selection of stanzas from Benedict Burgh's *Cato major* (*DIMEV* 1418), a pedagogic sequence of rhyme royal stanzas of advice on measure, temperance, and caution in conduct that translates the *Disticha Catonis*; and *DIMEV* 4423, a sequence of quatrains that exhort lords to dispense justice wisely. The *Cato major* stanzas at Wressle appear to have been selected and reordered when compared with the other manuscript copies of this text. Perhaps this reduction and re-ordering were responses to the exigencies of display in the chosen location and selection driven by the perceived appropriateness of the material to the household. Cameron Louis observes that Middle English proverb collections often provide some kind of frame that gives the proverbs authority, such as a parental speaker addressing a child (such as *How the Wyse Man Tawght his Son, DIMEV* 3241) or attribution to an author (for example, Cato, Aristotle, King Alfred).[99] We might add that these frames are pedagogic, authorities such as these often being attributed with authorship of copy-texts, as we have seen. In display situations

---

[99] C. LOUIS, "Authority in Middle English proverb literature", *Florilegium* 15 (1998), pp. 85-123.

Graphic Display 251

such structuring devices are not often found, and indeed would not normally have been practical in the restricted and discrete spaces provided by architectural settings. But perhaps public display was a substitute for pedagogic framing, the texts gaining authority by virtue of the act of display and the status of the household in which they were displayed.

There is evidence that the *Cato major* provided copy-text material elsewhere for selection and rearrangement and hence for the demonstration of graphic ingenuity. Another rearranged, selected sequence occurs in the Findern manuscript (MS Cambridge, UL, Ff.1.6, ff. 155r-159v). A single stanza of the *Cato major* that enjoins learning because it will help in times of bad fortune appears as an addition in a fifteenth-century manuscript containing materials on letter-writing, MS London, BL, Royal 17 B.xlvii (f. 3v) and in MS Cambridge, Trinity College, O.2.53 (James 1157, f. 60r), a fifteenth-century notebook in many hands that also includes the *ABC of Aristotle* and much evidence of writing practice.[100] The selection and arrangement of the stanzas for display offered opportunities for the demonstration of graphic ingenuity on the part of those who executed the schemes and provided opportunities for members of the Percy household to identify with a community of Anglophone literate practice endorsed by the lord. Rubrics that accompany the Percy texts in MS London, BL, Royal 18 D.ii record where in the building the texts were displayed and indicate the meanings of this practice and its identity-forming potential. "*The prouerbes in the roufe of my lordis library at lekyngfelde*" ("the proverbs in the ceiling of my lord's library at Leconfield"; f. 204v, *DIMEV* 1150); "*The prouerbes in the sydis of the Innere chambre \of\ the house in the garding at Wresill*" ("the proverbs on the walls of the inner chamber of the building in the garden at Wressle"; f. 207r, *DIMEV* 1418); and "*The counsell of Aristotill whiche he gayfe to Alexander kynge of massydony whiche ar writyn in the syde of the vtter chambre aboue of the house in the gardynge at wresyll*" ("the counsel of Aristotle which he gave to Alexander, king of Macedonia, which are written on the wall of the outer chamber at the top of the house in the garden

---

[100] "*Enforce thi wittes somwhat for to lere*" ("put your mind to learning something"), stanza 138, lines 969-975, Benedict Burgh, *Cato major*, "*Die Burghsche Cato-Paraphrase*", ed. M. FÖRSTER, in: *Archiv für das Studium der neueren Sprachen und Literaturen* 115 (1905), pp. 298-323 and 116 (1906), pp. 25-40, 304-323, 325-334, vol. 116, at p. 28. For the manuscript contexts of the *Cato major* see F.J. DALLACHY, "A study of the manuscript contexts of Benedict Burgh's Middle English *Distichs of Cato*" (unpublished PhD thesis, University of Glasgow, 2013), especially pp. 206-209. A different excerpted stanza was copied into MS London, BL Addit. 29729 by John Stow (f. 288v).

252   *Chapter 4*

at Wressle"; f. 209r, *DIMEV* 4423) suggest alignment of the texts with *littera* pedagogy: some of the inscriptions are seen as proverbs while *DIMEV* 4423 is attributed to Aristotle, recalling the attribution of the *ABC of Aristotle*. The rubrics also clearly express a sense that the display of the texts on the fabric of the buildings and their location within the buildings are important frames for reading the text. They are written from the viewpoint of someone who is implied to be part of the household: one of the texts appears in "*my* lord's library", while the records of the locations of the displayed texts imply someone familiar with the layout of the houses. The implied audience are equally insiders, for example the reference to "*the* house in the garden" not '*a* house in the garden' suggests that the reader will already know that there is a house in the garden. The language of display in the rubrics suggests that the texts are for a community of Anglophone literate practice that is associated with the Percy household and that the readers of the manuscript share – or aspire to share in – its values and literary tastes.[101] Here, for the communities of Anglophone literate practice associated with MS Royal 18 D.ii, English texts are mobilised in a graphic landscape as a resource capable of signifying belonging – and not belonging – to a literate, aristocratic household.

Humphrey Newton's Household

A comment associated with Humphrey Newton's copy of the *ABC of Aristotle* in MS Oxford, Bod. Lib., Lat. Misc. c. 66 also gives insight into the use of pedagogic copy-texts for display in a graphic landscape. The comment, "*These byn gode p^{ro}uerbus to set in þe bordor^e of þe halle*" ("these are good proverbs to display in the border in the hall", f. 26br) which runs vertically down the margin beside the text, suggests that Humphrey imagines the text as something to be publicly displayed, perhaps in a border around a window or even around the wall (*MED*, *bordure* n. 1c) given the length of the full text. In the previous section we saw that a modified extract from the *ABC of Aristotle* is displayed in a medieval graffito at Great Bardfield Church; Humphrey's note adds to the

---

[101] Blatt focuses on a different aspect of the text, arguing that it provides an insight into "participatory" reading associated with architecture and embodiment (H. BLATT, *Participatory Reading in Late Medieval England* (Manchester, 2018), pp. 128-142). Noting the oddity that the manuscript would be hardly necessary for someone with access to these houses, she suggests that the material for one of the houses would be relevant for persons who were at the other, or absent from both (p. 141).

Graphic Display 253

evidence that use of the ABC as a copy-text was amplified and endorsed in display locations. Perhaps the setting envisaged by Humphrey for the whole sequence was something like that for the Percy household proverbs or the extant moralising verse text that runs along the top of the walls of the Painted Room in Oxford, at the site of the former Crown Tavern (now 3, Cornmarket). Here a six-line stanza of rhyming couplets runs along the wall (*DIMEV* 560).[102] It may be significant that Humphrey has had two attempts at starting this text. He first began with a layout of one verse line per letter of the alphabet until he reached *C*, then cancelled this beginning and adopted a format where each verse line is written across two writing lines in the manuscript. In the second attempt, the letters of the alphabet are clearly displayed to the left, the run-on lines are attached by brackets, and the two lines of writing for each letter are separated from those for other letters by horizontal lines. Perhaps the second layout would have tested out the text's potential to be displayed in the architectural spaces of the border of the hall that the scribe has in mind. This layout, and the note that this material would be "good proverbs" for display, suggest that the scribe is aware of the practical and symbolic conventions of display of Middle English texts – significantly he uses the same genre language as the rubrics for the Percy texts – while his experiments with layout of the text in manuscript also give him an opportunity to exercise his own graphic ingenuity and to speculate on displaying it for the benefit of other members of his community of Anglophone literate practice.

Grafton Manor, Bromsgrove; Oxford Painted Room; Duke of Norfolk's House

There is other evidence that copy-texts associated with *littera* pedagogy were ingeniously selected and adapted for display with the constraints and affordances of the display location in mind and consideration given to the communities who used it. Another instance of selection of appropriate material for a specific location and household occurs in a frieze above the upper parlour window at Grafton Manor, near Bromsgrove. The text inscribed here attributes to Solomon the observation that social deference and distinction are necessary to harmony in the household:

---

[102] C. HOLE, *English Custom and Usage*, 3rd edn. (London, 1950), p. 106 and plate 42. See further below.

254   Chapter 4

> *Plenti and grase*
> *bi in this plase*
> *whyle everi man is plesed in his degre*
> *there is both pease and uniti*
> *Salaman saith there is none acorde*
> *when everi man would be a lorde*

Plenty and grace be in this place. While everyone is content with his status there is both peace and unity. Solomon says there is no peace when everyone wants to be a lord.[103]

This text probably dates from the restoration of the building in 1567 but the last two lines are found in a longer sequence of proverbs found in the fifteenth century. This is not the only instance of its use for display: above we met one of these copy-texts displayed on a jug: "*Goddis grace / Be in this place*".[104] The final four lines at Grafton Manor are the first two couplets of *DIMEV* 4954, a thirty-line set of proverbs in couplets that appears in MS Cambridge, Trinity College, O.9.38, a mid fifteenth-century commonplace book associated with Glastonbury Abbey, though here they are in reverse order: "*Salamon seyth ther is none accorde / There euery man wuld be a lord / Wher euery man is plesyd with his degre / Ther is both pece and vnyte*" (f. 70r).[105] The set in MS Cambridge, Trinity College, O.9.38 itself could be a personal selection and arrangement for writing practice: it has been entered in a different hand from those around it on a page from which the top has been removed, apparently before the text was written. Other copy-texts occur in various hands on f. 89v. Perhaps the two couplets at Grafton have been selected and arranged to associate the pithy prayer for blessing on the household with two proverbs about human responsibility for bringing about social harmony: copy-texts with very appropriate sentiments to display in a household. The couplets in the Oxford Painted Room mentioned above (*DIMEV* 560) may also have been selected and adapted to fit their spaces from longer texts, since one of the couplets, "*In the mornynge earlye / Serve god Deuoutlye*" ("early in the morning, serve God devoutly") is the opening of a poem of, variously, eleven or sixteen monorhyming lines (for example, in Richard Hill's commonplace book of 1501-1533, MS

---

[103] N. PEVSNER, *Worcestershire* (London, 1968: *The Buildings of England*), p. 157. This text is not recorded in *DIMEV*, perhaps because of its late date.

[104] *DIMEV* 5028, lightly edited; London, Victoria and Albert Museum, 217-1879.

[105] James number 1450.

Graphic Display 255

Oxford, Balliol College, 354, p. 340, where it is associated with other proverb copy-texts). Likewise, precepts and proverbs preserved in glass of the sixteenth-century or earlier and thought to have originated in the house of the Duke of Norfolk seem to have been selected from longer texts for display in the top, central lights of windows. Two of these texts counsel wise use of wealth: "*Goodis gotten in haste / Wyll shortly waste*" ("goods acquired in haste will not last") and "*Some man is a giver / And is the rycher*" ("he who gives away his wealth is richer").[106] Again this is a copy-text with some currency in the graphic landscape; above we encountered a similar precept on a late fourteenth-century jug, "*He that wyl not spare whan he may / He schal not spend whan he wold*".[107] The final surviving couplet in the glass counsels caution before speaking: "*For Impatiency / Uttreth moch folye*" ("impatience results in foolish speech").[108] A proverb similar to the first couplet (*DIMEV* 1651) is attributed to Solomon in Chaucer's *Tale of Melibee*, "*[Solomon] seith also that 'the richesse that hastily cometh to a man soone and lightly gooth and passeth from a man'*" ("Solomon says also, 'easy come, easy go'"; line 1579),[109] suggesting that this displayed text too engages with the copy-text traditions of *littera* pedagogy.

Launceston Priory Hall

Financial advice similar to that in the windows of the Duke of Norfolk is recorded as having been displayed in the dining hall of Launceston Priory, Cornwall, a house of Augustinian canons. The record survives in MS Oxford, Bod. Lib., Bodley 315 (f. 268r).[110] The scribe records not just the institution where the verses were found but the room and where in the room the verses were displayed. As with many of the displayed texts discussed above, some of the Launceston texts occur elsewhere, but it seems that in the hall they were

---

[106] E.A. KENT, "Some heraldic glass in Norwich", *Journal of the British Society of Master Glass-Painters* 4.3 (1932), pp. 137-141, at p. 138.

[107] *DIMEV* 1911; cf. 5017; London, British Museum item BM MLA 96, 7-27.

[108] KENT, "Some heraldic glass in Norwich", p. 138; cf. *DIMEV* 1651, 1363, 4963.

[109] Geoffrey Chaucer, *Canterbury Tales*, in: *The Riverside Chaucer*, ed. L.D. BENSON, 3rd edn. (Oxford, 1988), pp. 217-239.

[110] I am most grateful to Oliver House of Special Collections at the Bod. Lib. for providing me with images of relevant folios. See R.H. ROBBINS, "Wall verses at Launceston Priory", *Archiv für das Studium der neueren Sprachen und Literaturen* 200 (1964), pp. 338-343. Cf. *DIMEV* 2711, 6568, 1879, 6644, 6621.5.

256   *Chapter 4*

carefully disposed to give them social meaning when displayed *in situ. "Who so loueth wel to fare / Euer spende and neuer spare / Bot he haue the more good / His heer wol growe thurgh his hode"* ("he who loves to have the best, always to spend and never to save, unless he has more wealth his hair will grow through his hood") was displayed *"Supra tabulam valettor^{um}"* ("over the servants' table"; f. 268r).[111] Clearly, the writer seems to have thought that the position of the stanza in the hall was significant. Perhaps putting aside some savings was considered apt advice for younger male servants. Alternatively, the advice may be *about* the servants, but aimed at their masters, "his hair may grow through his hood" perhaps meaning that his expenses will outstrip his means. A similar quatrain is found in a playful scribal colophon signed by the scribe More at the end of *Libeaus Desconus* in MS Naples, Biblioteca Nazionale di Napoli, XIII.B.29: *"Qui scripcit carmen sit b[e]n[e]d[i]c[t]is Amen / Hic explicit libeus Disconyus / He that louyth well to fare / eur to Spend and neuer spare / But he have the more good / His here wol grow throw his hood q^{uo}d more"* (p. 113).[112] Looking at the stanza displayed above the servants would be an apt reminder of the counsel as well as reinforcement of the identities of masters and servants. Above the table for clerks (*"Supra tabulam cl^{er}icor^{um}"*), a six-line stanza advised that a guest should take as he finds, and if he does not, what he brings should be taken (*"Who so comyth to any hows / Ne be he nought dangerous / Tak that he fyndith / And but a wol do so / Resou^n wolde accorde þ^{er} to / To take that he bryngith"*, f. 268r).[113] A version of these verses is also found in the Glastonbury commonplace book where it is found among various copy-texts in a space at the end of a longer text (MS Cambridge, Trinity College, O.9.38, f. 47r). Above the table for workmen and lads (*"Sup^{ra} tab^ulam garcio^{num} et op^{er}arior^{um}"*), a quatrain advised that one should not be covetous in another man's house, *"For þ^{at} is þe condiciou^n of a knaue"* (f. 268r).[114] Those seated at the table would perhaps have provided a living image of "the condition of a knave": the state to which being covetous as a guest might bring the viewer. Above the table of gentlemen and *"armig^{er}or^{um}"* (perhaps "lay brothers") a displayed text advised on "*[h]onest maners*": gentlemen should speak

---

[111] Cf. ROBBINS, "Wall verses at Launceston Priory", p. 342; *DIMEV* 6621.5.

[112] Quoted from D.D. MOSSER, *A Digital Catalogue of the pre-1500 Manuscripts and Incunables of the Canterbury Tales*, 2nd, online edn. (2010), <http://mossercatalogue.net/index.html>, lightly edited. Robbins notes the parallel (ROBBINS,"Wall verses at Launceston Priory", p. 342) but the Naples manuscript example is not recorded in the *DIMEV* entry for 6621.5.

[113] *DIMEV* 6568; cf. ROBBINS, "Wall verses at Launceston Priory", p. 342.

[114] Cf. ROBBINS, "Wall verses at Launceston Priory", p. 342.

Graphic Display 257

well of those who are absent and tell the truth to those present. By looking at those assembled at the table, the viewer would know to whom he should speak frankly. At the end of the hall, a stanza in Latin advised giving to the poor and learning while young, for he who knows nothing and cares not to learn is "*stultus*" ("stupid", f. 268r). As the other displayed precepts were in English, the Latin of the "*stultus*" text is marked. Seemingly directed to everyone present in the hall, the text nonetheless represents social divisions. Paradoxically, those who cannot read the Latin text are identified as the foolish ones who had not cared to learn, while those who can read it can identify with the learned. The displayed texts at Launceston seem to have taken their meaning from their positioning in the hall which makes them serve to mark graphically the social differences manifested by the seating plan for the community that used the room. The texts were entered in a blank space after the final text on a page at the end of MS Bodley 315, an early fifteenth-century manuscript containing Latin texts by Rolle, John of Salisbury, etc., in a hand different from that of the text it follows. Judging from this manuscript's donation to Exeter Cathedral (just over forty miles from Launceston) by a former canon, it seems likely that the scribe of the Launceston precepts was local and used the displayed texts themselves as copy-texts, working either from memory or *in situ*, and that this act – and recording the place of display – signified some kind of identification of the scribe with a community of Anglophone literate practice at the priory.[115] The space is followed by a further copy-text, four lines of Latin verse concerning moral advice credited to Julius Caesar, in yet a different hand.[116]

---

[115] For the provenance of MS Bodley 315 see *MLGB3*. A Book of Hours, MS Birmingham, Cadbury Library, Little Malvern Court 1, on deposit at the University of Birmingham, survives from Launceston, its calendar at least possibly having been prepared there in the fourteenth century (F. WORMALD, 'The calendar of the Augustinian Priory of Launceston in Cornwall', *Journal of Theological Studies* 39, No. 153 (1938), pp. 1-21, at p. 1).

[116] "*Ite pares pariter parebus suadete medullis / Conuictus vestros non vincant oscula conche* [...]" ("Go forth together as peers and respect everyone; do not indulge in forbidden kisses [...]"). A side-note in the same hand says "*hoc illustris ille Iulius cesar*". Similar verses are quoted and credited to Apuleius in Book 3 of Higden's *Polychronicon*; see Ranulph Higden, *Polychronicon Ranulphi Monachi Cestrensis with English Translations of John Trevisa and of an Unknown Writer of the Fifteenth Century*, 9 vols., ed. C. BABINGTON (vols. 1-2), and J.R. LUMBY (vols. 3-9), (London, 1865-1886: *RS* 41), 3, p. 218.

258   *Chapter 4*

Civic Display: John Shirley's Records

So far we have examined the display of texts associated with the manifestation of the values and governance of noble, gentry, and religious households. Another social group associated with the display of improving Middle English texts is civic worthies. Our primary case study will be of the reconstructed graphic landscape of the chapel of the guild of the Holy Cross at Stratford-upon-Avon but first we will examine some schemes for which only a literary record survives. Lydgate's verse *Bycorne and Chychevache*, destined for display in a parlour, is a didactic piece about wifely waywardness and husbands' rule over their wives.[117] In the 1430s, the scribe John Shirley supplied a rubric to the text in MS Cambridge, Trinity College, R.3.20, "*Loo sirs the deuise of a peynted or desteyned clothe for an halle . a parlour . or a chaumbre deuysed by Johan Lidegate at þe request of a worthy citeseyn of londou*"" ("lo, sirs, the text for a painted or stained cloth for a hall, parlour, or chamber, devised by John Lydgate at the request of a worthy London citizen", p. 9). The rubric implies that the text was to be applied to a decorative fabric hanging and displayed in a room used for receiving guests ("a stained cloth" might refer to a painted hanging or possibly a tapestry).[118] Shirley records that the display text was commissioned "by a worthy London citizen", implying that an esteemed Londoner intended to display morally improving Middle English verse in his household, and / or perhaps the households of others. This suggests that displaying Middle English text is associated with those with social prestige in the city and that those who adopt the text for their own displays may signal belonging to groups of worthy citizens by imitatively adopting this marker. Shirley's rubric signals his own identity with such a community of Anglophone literate practice, for he has copied the text, and offers his esteemed audience ("*sirs*") the opportunity to belong to this group too. A colophon to the text in another manuscript of the poem, MS Cambridge, Trinity College, R.3.19, reads, "*Compylyd by John Ludgate monke of berye at the request of a worthye syttesyne of london to be paynted in a perler*" ("compiled by John Lydgate monk of Bury to be painted in a parlour, at the request of a worthy London citizen", f. 159r).

---

[117] John Lydgate, *Bycorne and Chychevache*, in: *John Lydgate, Mummings and Entertainments*, ed. C. SPONSLER (Kalamazoo, MI, 2010). *DIMEV* 4032.

[118] C. SPONSLER, "Text and textile: Lydgate's tapestry poems", in: *Medieval Fabrications: Dress, Textiles, Clothwork, and other Cultural Imaginings*, ed. E.J. BURNS (New York and Basingstoke, 2004), pp. 19-34, at pp. 26-27.

Graphic Display 259

This note has been added by a later hand.[119] It conveys information similar to that in Shirley's rubric, including the reference to the endorsement of display of the text by "a worthy London citizen", and perhaps was based on Shirley's rubric. Neither the rubric nor the colophon suggests that Shirley or the later hand had seen the text in a display setting, but both scribes clearly thought that this detail about the text having been commissioned by a high-prestige London citizen for display for a household and its guests was important to a reading of the text. John Shirley also recorded that Lydgate's *Legend of St. George* (*DIMEV* 4108) was made at the request of the armourers of London, for their "*steyned halle*", in honour of the brotherhood and their feast of St. George ("*þe devyse of a steyned halle of þe lyf of saint George ymagyned by daun Iohan þe Munk of Bery Lydegate and made with þe balades at þe request of þarmorieres of Londou*ⁿ *for þonour of þeyre broþerhoode and þeyre feest of saint George*", MS Cambridge, Trinity College, R.3.20, p. 74). This note is reflected by that in a later hand in MS Cambridge, Trinity College, R.3.21, which reads "*compyled by Iohn ludgate monke of bery at þe request of þe armerers of london to paynt about ther haulle*" (f. 315r). It has been pointed out that the annotator probably misunderstood Shirley's note, for, as mentioned above, in Shirley's day a 'stained hall' was a textile rather than a room whose walls bore a mural and there is evidence that such hangings sometimes bore inscriptions.[120] In theory, then, the armourers had an object available for display in whatever setting they chose to stage the feast of their saint as well as an item that displayed their status to anyone else who used the hall and that was usable on occasions other than their feast day.[121] These records relate to the commission of texts by civic worthies, apparently offering relatively little opportunity for them to demonstrate graphic ingenuity themselves through selecting and fitting of text to particular display settings. Further, in commissioning new text, they departed from the use of pedagogic material found in the gentry and aristocratic house-

---

[119] John Stow's hand also annotates this text but the note about authorship does not appear to be his.

[120] J. FLOYD, "St. George and the '*Steyned Halle*': Lydgate's verse for the London armourers", in: *Lydgate Matters: Poetry and Material Culture in the Fifteenth Century*, ed. L. COOPER and A. DENNY-BROWN (New York and Basingstoke, 2008), pp. 139-164, at pp. 145-152. Floyd states that the hand is that of John Stow (p. 145) but in my view it differs from Stow's hand in aspect and the forms of *r* and *e*. I am grateful to Linne Mooney for discussion of this question. This view however is my own.

[121] Discussing this point, Floyd states that the armourers' hall was rented by other groups (FLOYD, "St. George and the '*Steyned Halle*'", p. 157) and provides examples of the lending of decorative textiles among other London guilds.

260   *Chapter 4*

holds discussed above. These acts of commission for display, however, were clearly seen as offering models for imitation and adaptation in new settings and opportunities for others to express or experience feelings of shared taste and literate accomplishment. Shirley's rubrics extend these opportunities to himself and the readers of his manuscripts.

Civic Display: The Chapel of the Guild of Holy Cross, Stratford-upon-Avon

The association of the display of Middle English texts with esteemed citizens and their interest in imitating and adapting such material is further supported by lay patronage of displayed texts as part of the sponsorship of the construction and furnishing of guildhalls and chapels. One example is the display of Middle English moralising texts in the chapel of the guild of the Holy Cross at Stratford-upon-Avon. Some of this material was Lydgatean, and some of it belonged to the tradition of briefer pedagogic copy-texts displayed in gentry and religious households such as the Percy houses and Launceston Priory.

We know from surviving traces and various historic records that the Stratford chapel included an extensive programme of displayed text along with many images. Using these historical records, an attempt has recently been made to reconstruct the appearance of the medieval building in a three-dimensional interactive computer surrogate and painstaking restoration work of the paintings is in progress.[122] The legend of the discovery of the True Cross was depicted in images and text on the north wall of the chapel. From drawings made by Thomas Fisher in the early eighteenth century it appears that *tituli* in Latin and English accompanied the scenes.[123] An image of the five wounds of Christ in the chancel was accompanied by Latin texts,[124] and a picture of the Doom in the chancel may have included figures of damned souls bearing scrolls with their sins named in Latin, for example, "*ira*" and "*avaricia*" ("wrath", "avarice").[125] On the north wall of the nave the Dance of Death was

[122] K. GILES, A. MASINTON, and G. ARNOTT, "Visualising the Guild Chapel, Stratford-upon-Avon: Digital models as research tools in buildings archaeology", *Internet Archaeology* 32 (2012), n.p., <https://intarch.ac.uk/journal/issue32/index.html>.

[123] C. DAVIDSON, *The Guild Chapel Wall Paintings at Stratford-upon-Avon* (New York, 1988), plates 3-9.

[124] DAVIDSON, *The Guild Chapel Wall Paintings at Stratford-upon-Avon*, plate 18.

[125] DAVIDSON, *The Guild Chapel Wall Paintings at Stratford-upon-Avon*, plate 17.

Graphic Display

Fig. 22. *Erthe upon erthe* and *Who-so him bethought* murals, Stratford-upon-Avon, Holy Cross Guild Chapel. Photo: © Stratford Town Trust.

depicted in text and image.[126] Arranged in two tiers across the wall under the window, the Dance of Death frieze had space above each image for a title and below each image for another inscription. It is believed that a stanza from Lydgate's *Danse Macabre* was displayed in the band below each image. Those who commissioned the Stratford frieze seem to have selected and adapted the material for the new location.

On the west wall of the nave appeared an image of the martyrdom of Thomas Becket, below which are two recently restored murals of short Middle English mortality verses, *Erthe upon erthe* and *Who-so him bethought* (see Figure 22). *Erthe upon erthe* (DIMEV 1170) engages with *littera* pedagogy through riddling. It challenges the reader to make sense of a text in which the word 'earth' appears numerous times. Appearing in various versions and nu-

---

[126] DAVIDSON, *The Guild Chapel Wall Paintings at Stratford-upon-Avon*, plates 19-20.

262   *Chapter 4*

merous witnesses, the text reproduces in English the knotty challenges of brief Latin mortality verses that are frequently found as copy-texts associated with *littera* pedagogy and in particular developing the wordplay in Gen 3: 19, "*in sudore vultus tui vesceris pane donec revertaris in terram de qua sumptus es quia pulvis es et in pulverem reverteris*".[127] In the Stratford version, four stanzas riddle on the terms 'earth upon earth', challenging the reader to decode their various meanings, while three further stanzas emphasise that this is a riddle whose solution applies to the viewer:

> *Why that erth loueth erth wondur me thynke*
> *Or why that erth wold for erth other swett or swynke*
> *When erth apon erth ys broght w^{ith}yn the brynke*
> *Then shall erth apon erth haue a fowll stynke*
> *[...]*
> *I c[oun]sell erth upon erth that ys wondurly wroght*
> *The w\h/yl þ^{at} erth ys opon erth to [...] hys thowght*
> *And pray to god upon erth þat all erth wroght*
> *That all crystyn sowllys to blys may be broght*

Why earth loves earth seems strange to me or why earth would work or sweat for earth. When earth on earth is brought to the brink [of death] then earth upon earth shall have a foul smell [...] I advise earth upon earth that is marvellously created, while earth is upon earth to [...] his thought and pray to God that created all earth upon earth that all Christian souls may be brought to bliss.

The *Erthe upon erthe* text in the chapel appears to have been adapted for display in this location. *Erthe upon erthe* is arranged on painted scrolls in a horseshoe shape with images of a shrouded cadaver that is accompanied by two skulls and several bones beneath.[128] The riddling challenge of the text is

---

[127] Cf. M. HARRINGTON, "Of earth you were made: Constructing the bilingual poem '*Erþ*' in British Library, MS Harley 913", *Florilegium* 31 (2014), pp. 105-137, at p. 106.

[128] I am grateful to Pippa Brook of the Stratford Town Trust for supplying me with images. See L.R. MOONEY, "Verses upon death and other wall paintings surviving in the Guild Hall, Stratford-upon-Avon", *Journal of the Early Book Society* 3 (2000), pp. 182-190; and W.P. REEVES, "Stray verse", *Modern Language Notes* 9.4 (1894), pp. 201-205. On the other side of the west wall of the nave were depicted St. George and the Dragon, and beneath that image an allegorical figure surrounded by angels and demons who bore Latin inscriptions (DAVIDSON, *The Guild Chapel Wall Paintings at Stratford-upon-Avon*, plates 15-16). On the south wall of the Holy Cross chapel nave may have been images of saints and a life of Adam. Cf. DAVIDSON, *The Guild Chapel Wall Paintings at Stratford-upon-Avon*, plates 13-14; and GILES, MASINTON, and ARNOTT, "Visualising the Guild Chapel, Stratford-upon-Avon", fig. 27.

Graphic Display 263

emphasised graphically by the layout of the stanzas. Each quatrain is inscribed on a background painted to give the illusion of an unfolding scroll that forms the horseshoe or *U* shape. Stanzas one to three are placed on folds of the scroll on its left-hand wing, while the fourth stanza is placed in the centre at the bottom. On reaching the fourth stanza, in order to read the stanzas in the correct order, the viewer must read in an upwards direction to reach each new stanza but in a downwards direction within each stanza. This challenge to puzzle out the correct order of the stanzas by modifying the direction of reading reflects the graphic puzzles with which pedagogic riddles are associated, as discussed in Chapter Three. The reader who solves this puzzle has to recognise that the layout of the stanzas symbolises visually the theological solution to the riddle of earth upon earth. His or her reading journey will be completed at the stanza with the prayer about being brought to bliss, which is aptly positioned at the top of the *U* shape on its right branch.

At Stratford, *Erthe upon erthe* has seven monorhymed quatrains, whereas in its numerous manuscript copies it has up to sixteen quatrains. Pope lists thirty-five texts in all, including the two displayed texts but excluding five texts that are only linked to them by an introductory couplet before the first "*erthe*" line, and views the poem "not as a single Middle English lyric in thirty-five copies but as a tradition within which a few poems have multiple witnesses but most texts are unique and to some extent original compositions".[129] Pope suggests that twenty-one of the thirty-five texts "indicate scribal authorship to some extent".[130] The existence of so many variant versions, I would add, suggests that *Erthe upon erthe* was a popular example of a poem used as a copytext for writing practice that invited skilful adaptation and reworking, like the *ABC of Aristotle*. It offered opportunities to play with the text, to make the most use of the multiple meaning possibilities of the word 'earth', and it challenged readers to draw on their *littera* skills and knowledge and apply them to English to solve the riddles.

Codicological evidence supports this claim: in Pope's count, nine of the texts are "unplanned addition[s]" to earlier material made by hands different from those of the main texts.[131] For our purposes the significance of this is that they have the characteristics of other copy-texts used for writing practice as

---

[129] N. POPE, "*Erthe upon erthe* revisited", *Journal of the Early Book Society* 21 (2018), pp. 53-95, quotation at p. 53.
[130] POPE, "*Erthe upon erthe* revisited", p. 72.
[131] POPE, "*Erthe upon erthe* revisited", p. 69.

264   *Chapter 4*

discussed in Chapters Two and Three. For example, in MS Philadelphia, University of Pennsylvania, Codex 721, the poem has been entered on a blank leaf that follows the end of the priest's manual *Pars oculi*, at the end of the codex (f. 91v). The hand is later and different from that of the main text while a still later hand has bracketed the quatrains with the refrains "*memento*" and "*nosce te ipsu^{m}*" ("remember"; "know yourself"). Below, the same hand has written some riddling Latin copy-texts on the theme of mortality, some lines of which, "*Post mortis morsum vertit dilectio dorsum / Finita vita finit amicus ita*" ("after the sting of death love turns its back; life ended, just so the friend ends"), also occur in a fifteenth-century hand with other writing practice texts on the final leaf of a twelfth-century copy of Priscian's *Institutiones grammaticae* that is possibly from Canterbury (MS Oxford, Exeter College, 4, f. 143v). In MS London, BL, Harley 4486, the text occurs in a blank space on the last leaf of the *Livre de Sydrak*, a pedagogic dialogue in French between a king who asks questions and Sydrak the philosopher who answers. The text is written in a wobbly hand that appears rather later than the main text and is associated with other riddling copy-texts in English and Latin, some on mortality, for example "*P^{er} nullam sortem poteris euadere morte^{m}*" ("there is no chance that you can evade death") and "*Mors ^{et} vita in ma[n]ib^{us} lingue*" ("death and life are in the power of the tongue", ff. 145r-146v, at 146v). In early sixteenth-century MS Bod. Lib., Holkham misc. 39, a version of the text in one quatrain is included with a Latin translation and other riddling and proverbial grammatical material at the end of a Latin-English dictionary (f. 438r). Here, a riddling, rhyming macaronic couplet on mortality is repeated twice in different spellings (ff. 438r, 446v, *DIMEV* 4086), clear evidence that this material is associated with *littera* pedagogy and informal writing practice.[132] Versions of the poem in English, French, and Latin in a later fourteenth- or early fifteenth-century hand are arranged in two columns on the dorse of MS Kew, TNA E175/11/16 (mem. d), an earlier fourteenth-century Exchequer roll, providing further evidence of the use of *Erthe upon erthe* as a copy-text for writing practice.[133] Making a

---

[132] Pope edits the English quatrain, Latin quatrain, and both versions of the macaronic couplet (POPE, "*Erthe upon erthe* revisited", pp. 62-63). She considers the couplet on f. 446v to be a "draft" (pp. 62-63) but for me the processes of experimentation, play, and repetition associated with writing practice using copy-texts better explain the relation between the two texts.

[133] For an edition see M. HARRINGTON, "A trilingual version of '*Erthe upon erthe*' in the National Archives of the United Kingdom, E 175/11/16", *Journal of the Early Book Society* 19 (2016), pp. 197-215. Harrington infers from scribally-corrected errors that "the scribe was not

Graphic Display 265

conjunction reminiscent of the display in the Stratford guild chapel, a hand later than that of the main text has added the poem after Lydgate's *Danse Macabre* in MS Oxford, Bod. Lib., Selden supra 53, along with another brief mortality poem (f. 159v). The poem has been crammed into a blank space on the front flyleaf of MS London, BL, Harley 1671, in a hand later and less formal than that of the main text, a copy of the *Weye of Paradys* of *c.* 1400 (f. 1ar). In MS London, BL, Harley 984, the poem has been added by a later hand at the end of a fifteenth-century copy of the Middle English Gospel of Matthew. The scribe has signed by working another proverbial text into a colophon: "*Though seyle sey ys sone foryetten / yett pray for hym þat þis haþ wretyn*" ("though seldom seen is soon forgotten, yet pray for him who has this written", f. 72r).[134]

Even where the text does not occur on flyleaves and blank spaces, there are often other indicators that copies of the poem are linked with *littera* pedagogy. According to Pope twenty-four versions of the text appear in a "scribe's own compilation", that is, in manuscripts where the scribe is engaged in compiling and arranging material.[135] The text in mid fourteenth-century manuscript miscellany MS London, BL, Harley 913, demonstrates clear links with *littera* pedagogy through inclusion of a Latin version after each stanza (ff. 62r-63v). The Latin text does not translate the English or vice versa; instead, each Latin stanza plays on a different Latin word for the references of 'earth' in the English text: '*terra*', '*vesta*', '*humus*', and so on. The Latin stanzas are like an exercise in inflecting these various synonyms for 'earth' and playing on their meanings. The Latin exercise is made more complex by the rhyme scheme: the Latin lines have internal as well as end rhymes. The layout of the poem also promotes it as a resource for teaching *littera*. The poem is laid out in such a way that the rhyming syllables are only written once. For example, the verb endings '-*atur*' and '-*abunt*' are displayed as rhymes (f. 63r). This has the effect of drawing attention to the inflections and perhaps aiding grammar learning.[136] A context for the poem in *littera* pedagogy is also suggested by marginal glossing of some Latin and English words, for example, "*muntid*" is glossed

---

their author" (p. 199). However, we have seen that writing practice with copy-texts involves improvisation.

[134] The colophon is not included in *DIMEV*. For the proverb see *MED, foryeten*, v., 1g; for the text see the British Library Catalogue.

[135] POPE, "*Erthe upon erthe* revisited", p. 69.

[136] By contrast, Harrington suggests that the point of the layout is to emphasise the poem as "an interwoven aural composition" since the inflections "have no intrinsic meaning" (HARRINGTON, "Of earth you were made", p. 121).

266   *Chapter 4*

"*metit^{ur}*" ("measured", f. 62v). Other manuscripts also suggest a context in
littera pedagogy for *Erthe upon erthe*. In MS Edinburgh, National Library of
Scotland, Advocates' 18.7.21 (John of Grimestone's preaching book), the text
occurs with other riddling *vulgaria* on the theme of death and their Latin equivalents (f. 87v). For example, "*Siker is det to alle maner men / To tellen of is
time neuere no man kan*" is an English version of "*Mors cunctis certa nil est
incertius hora*" ("death is a certainty for all; the time of death is more uncertain").[137] Similarly, in MS Cambridge, UL, Ii.4.9, *Erthe upon erthe* is followed
by another quatrain on mortality:

> *Wherefor in this vale of myserye do you abyde*
> *Wherefor haue yowe plaisur in this vnclene Ioye*
> *yow that dey all thyngys yowe leue*
> *Deth weche spare no man taketh away yower ioye*

Why do you dwell in this vale of misery, why do you take pleasure in this impure
joy? You will leave everything when you die. Death that spares no man will take
away your joy.

The quatrain translates a preceding Latin quatrain.[138]

In the Stratford scheme, below *Erthe upon erthe* appears *Who-so him bethought* (*DIMEV* 6610), a poem that describes the frighteningly quick journey
from the bed to the grave and thence to hell:

> *Whoo soo hym be thowgh[t]*
> *In wardly and ofte*
> *How harde hyt ys to flett*
> *From bede to peyt*
> *From peyt to peyne*
> *That neu^{er} schall seys serten*
> *He wolde not doo no syn*
> *\¶/ all þ^e world to wy^nne*

Whoever considered inwardly and often how hard it is to move from one's bed to
one's grave and from grave to everlasting pain: he would not sin, even for the
whole world.

---

[137] Quoted from *DIMEV* 4836.
[138] Inc. "*Cur in hac miseria miseri moramini* [...]". Quoted from *DIMEV* 6500.

Graphic Display 267

This poem is inscribed on another painted scroll that unfurls horizontally directly above the shrouded cadaver. Two adult male figures, one on either side, gesture to the text. Although the poem consists of four rhyming couplets, and although each new verse line is marked out with a red initial, the poem is laid out as prose on three lines, the final couplet being positioned at the bottom to the right, as if it were a run over piece of text that belongs with the line above. The layout challenges the viewer to find the rhymes, to detect the couplets and the alliteration, but also to recognise that the whole text is a relentless sentence whose last clause completes its chilling sense.

Its textual and codicological features suggest that *Who-so him bethought*, like *Erthe upon erthe*, was a popular copy-text for writing practice. Copyists may have been treating the text as an opportunity to engage with and amplify the Latin proverb, "*Si quis sentiret, quo tendit et unde venerit, nunquam gauderet, sed in omni tempore fleret*" ("if anyone were to think on where he was heading and from whence he had come, he would never have joy, but would weep at all times") which is echoed in the poem's opening lines.[139] This proverb is found MS Manchester, John Rylands Library, Lat. 394, a fifteenth-century pedagogic manuscript containing English and Latin proverbs that we encountered in Chapter Three, though this particular copy-text has no English equivalent here (f. 23v). In MS Cambridge, UL, Hh.3.15 the copy-text is used as part of an ownership inscription in a blank space at the end of a text, "*Iste liber constat Thome Bartoun / Si quis sentiret quo tendit et vnde*" (f. 54v).[140] The text is unfinished, suggesting that it was written for practice rather than simply for the sake of the sentiment itself and that the ownership inscription may also be practice writing (another indication of this is that it is neither prominent nor at the end of the codex). Above this inscription a different hand has carried out some more practice writing, imitating the closing two lines of the text above. In MS Cambridge, Trinity College, R.14.22, a copiously glossed text of Geoffrey de Vinsauf and later material, the proverb occurs with others in a wobbly, informal and unpractised hand in spare space on a flyleaf (f. 1r); other copy-text writing practice material occurs in the volume, for example. "*Amen dico vob*[*is*]" (f. 43v). Other writers engaged with the proverb in English. The Latin proverb is found with *two* English paraphrases in the *Prick of Conscience*.[141] In

[139] Cf. *English Lyrics of the XIIIth Century*, ed. C.F. BROWN (Oxford, 1932), p. 175.

[140] I am grateful to Frank Bowles of the Cambridge University Library Department of Archives and Modern Manuscripts for providing information about and images of this manuscript.

[141] *Prick of Conscience*: *Richard Morris's* Prick of Conscience: *A Corrected and Amplified Reading Text*, ed. R. HANNA and S. WOOD (Oxford, 2013: EETS, o.s. 342), lines 892-903.

268   *Chapter 4*

John of Grimestone's preaching book, the proverb is given in Latin and is also translated as a quatrain:

Woso þouthte of his birthe
& wider he sal wende
He sulde neuere maken mirthe
But sorwe withouten ende

(f. 98r)[142]

Likewise, in MS Windsor, St. George's Chapel, E.I.I, the Latin occurs with a translation in English:

Si quis sentiret, quo tendit, et vnde veniret,
Numquam gauderet, sed in omni tempore fleret.
Who would thynke of thynges two:
Wheyn[s] he came and whyther to go,
Neuer more ioye should [se],
Bot euer in gretynge be[143]

This instance of the proverb and English stanza occur in a sequence of thematically-grouped proverbs, this text being grouped with similar texts on death and the grave. A proverb and English stanza on the theme of pride later in the volume engage with the 'earth' conceit:

Vnde superbimus, quid ego, quid tu nisi limus?
Primus homo limus, sortem mutare nequimus.
Cum fex, cum limus, cum res vilissima simus,
Vnde superbimus? ad terram terra redimus.
Qwer of prowd þan may we be,
Qwat I, what þ°u, oght bot clay?
The fyrst man clay was he;
Chau^n*ge þat cut we ne may.*
Dregg^es ^and *clay sythen we are th*^u*s,*
Þe fowlest þinge þ^a*t we be may,*
Qwer of haue we p^ri*de in vs?*

[142] Quoted from *DIMEV* 6634.
[143] "Latin and Middle English proverbs in a manuscript at St. George's Chapel, Windsor Castle", ed. S.M. HORRALL, in: *Medieval Studies* 45 (1983), pp. 343-384, at p. 359, lines 252-257.

Graphic Display 269

Erthe to erthe we turne away.

What have we to be proud of, you and I who are nothing but clay? The first man was formed of clay. Why do we have pride? From earth, we revert to earth.[144]

The play on Latin "*limus*" and "*terra*" equate to the play on "*clay*" and "*erthe*". The texts of *Who-so him bethought* suggest experimentation on the part of copyists similar to that with *Erthe upon erthe* and typically associated with copy-texts generally. The texts are highly various, having different numbers of lines and many accreting with other mortality texts as we have observed in the Stratford chapel scheme. For example, in MS London, BL, Harley 7322 some of the lines of the poem (see *DIMEV* 5043) are written continuously with *DIMEV* 5216:

Strong it hus [?is] to flitte
Fro worldes blisse to pitte;
St'ᵉngore is to misse
Heuene riche blisse;
Strengest is to wende
To pine wit-outen ende
Þe blisse of ourᵉ hᵉʳte, al it is ago,
Al vrᵉ wele torned is to wo.
Þe croune of vrᵉ heued
Fallen is to grounde:
Þat we euer syngeden,
Weylawey þe stounde.

It is terrible to fall from worldly bliss to the grave. It is more terrible to go without the bliss of heaven. It is most terrible to suffer endlessly. Our heart's bliss is all gone, all of our prosperity is turned to sorrow. The crown has fallen from our head. Alas the time that we ever sinned![145]

Indeed, the text is not easily analysable as distinct versions or a stemma and this is reflected by its treatment in *DIMEV* where several index numbers are relevant: 6610, 5009, 5043, 5216, and 2377. Comparing various texts of the poem, Brown notes, "[a] detailed comparison of all the texts makes it certain

---

[144] "Latin and Middle English proverbs", p. 376, lines 744-755.
[145] F. 172v; cf. *Political, Religious, and Love Poems*, ed. F.J. FURNIVALL (London, 1866: *EETS*, o.s. 15), pp. 242-243.

270   *Chapter 4*

that these verses were not transmitted directly from scribe to scribe but must in most cases have been written down from memory".[146] My proposal that these texts were copy-texts used in writing practice provides a scenario which explains this textual variety.

Manuscript contexts for *Who-so him bethought* support the suggestion that the text gave material for writing practice. For example, in MS Cambridge, Trinity College, O.2.53 on f. 74r the poem appears in possibly the same hand as the *ABC of Aristotle* in the manuscript on a leaf which is the last in the volume and bears numerous other brief copy-texts in Latin and English (f. 74r). In MS London, BL, Harley 7322, the poem in its adapted format (*DIMEV* 5043 and *DIMEV* 5216) occurs on f. 172v in a fourteenth-century miscellany containing basic priest's material with many verses in English and French, including Latin and English verses laid out as equivalents, for example, a tightly rhyming Latin text with English equivalent that teaches '*pro-*' words and adjectives in '-*ax*' with a moral twist (*DIMEV* 36):

p*ro*missio fallax.	*A fals by-hety[n]g.*
p*ro*moc*i*o mendax. a*n*gl*ice*	*A lyeres auansyng.*
p*ro*lac*i*o Mordax.	*A bytande fondi[n]g.*

A false promise. A liar's advancement. A biting attempt. In English.[147]

The tradition of using *Who-so him bethought* as copy-text material was long-lasting and widespread. The poem appears as early as the early thirteenth century, in MS London, BL, Arundel 292, a trilingual manuscript containing basic religious material in English, French, and Latin (f. 3v).[148] It also occurs in MS Cambridge, UL, Gg.4.32, a fourteenth-century manuscript containing similar material: basic prayers and other elementary theological material, mostly in Latin but with the *Pater noster*, *Creed*, and so on in French and English (f. 21r).[149] Later copies include MS Oxford, Bod. Lib., Bodley 416 (*c.* 1400)

---

[146] *English Lyrics of the XIIIth Century*, p. 175.

[147] F. 185r; cf. *Political, Religious, and Love Poems*, p. 242.

[148] *DIMEV* 2377; *English Lyrics of the XIIIth Century*, pp. 19-20.

[149] *DIMEV* 5009; Reliquiae antiquae: *Scraps from Ancient Manuscripts, illustrating chiefly early English Literature and the English Language*, ed. T. WRIGHT and J.O. HALLIWELL, 2 vols. (London, 1845), 1, p. 160. The catalogue gives f. 12v but 21r is confirmed by K. MURCHISON, *Intercultural Dialogue and Multilingualism in Post-Conquest England: A Database of French Literary Manuscripts Produced Between 1100-1550* (n.d.), <https://leidenuniversitylibrary. github.io/manuscript-stats/>.

Graphic Display 271

where the text occurs written as prose with other brief copy-texts after the end of *Book to a Mother* (f. 109r);[150] a copy among several brief texts in margins and on flyleaves in a fourteenth-century manuscript of the *Legenda sanctorum*, MS Hereford Cathedral Library, O.iv.14 (f. 223r);[151] MS Cambridge, Magdalene College, 13 (F.4.13), f. 2r, written in 1518 by London Dominican Jasper Fyball;[152] an entry in the fifteenth- to early sixteenth-century commonplace-book of Norfolk official Robert Reynes, MS Oxford, Bod. Lib., Tanner 407 (f. 37v);[153] and a sixteenth-century hand-written annotation on a flyleaf of a printed copy of Arnold's Chronicle (Oxford, Bod. Lib., Douce A.314, sig. V verso).[154]

There is evidence that *display* of *Erthe upon erthe* and *Who-so him be-thought* and the Dance of Death frieze contributed to increasing the importance of these materials as resources for identity formation among communities of Anglophone literate practice.[155] It is believed that the Stratford Dance of Death frieze draws on the famous display in the Pardon churchyard at St. Paul's, London (sometimes called the *Daunce of Poulys*), where Lydgate's *Danse Macabre*, a text translated from French, was accompanied by images.[156] The Stratford text draws on the B version of the *Danse* (which may not be Lyd-

---

[150] *DIMEV* 6610; *English Lyrics of the XIIIth Century*, pp. 173-74.

[151] *DIMEV* 6610; *English Lyrics of the XIIIth Century*, p. 174.

[152] *DIMEV* 6610; *English Lyrics of the XIIIth Century*, p. 174.

[153] *DIMEV* 6610; cf. *English Lyrics of the XIIIth Century*, p. 175.

[154] Another copy of *DIMEV* 6610 is in MS Erfurt, Stadtbibliothek, Amplon O.58, f. 139r; cf. *English Lyrics of the XIIIth Century*, p. 175. I have not been able to ascertain its status in this codex.

[155] Discussing the chapel of the guild of the Holy Cross in Stratford-upon-Avon as an example, Giles *et al.* argue that patronage of "artistic media such as sculpture, glass, screens, reliquaries, vestments and altar cloths [...] crosses, chalices and pattens [...] demonstrates the significance of architecture and material culture as the medium through which these new communities constructed a sense of identity, status and power" (GILES, MASINTON, and ARNOTT, "Visualising the Guild Chapel, Stratford-upon-Avon", n.p.). These examples of Middle English copy-texts at Stratford suggest that the display of graphically-challenging Middle English texts in meaningful locations and contexts was an important additional component of the repertoire of resources for identity formation used by those with aspirations as civic worthies and governors.

[156] For the name *Daunce of Poulys* see S. OOSTERWIJK, "Death, memory, and commemoration: John Lydgate and '*Macabrees Daunce*' at Old St. Paul's Cathedral, London", in: *Memory and Commemoration in Medieval England*, ed. C.M. BARRON and C. BURGESS (Donington, UK, 2010: *Harlaxton Medieval Studies* 20), pp. 185-201, at p. 196. For the scheme more generally see also A. APPLEFORD, "The Dance of Death in London: John Carpenter, John Lydgate, and the *Daunce of Poulys*", *Journal of Medieval and Early Modern Studies* 38.2 (2008), pp. 285-314; BLATT, *Participatory Reading*, pp. 142-156; and EDWARDS, "Middle English inscriptional verse texts", p. 31.

272 *Chapter 4*

gate's adaptation),[157] and includes civic characters similar to those that appeared there.[158] The patron of the Stratford chapel scheme was Hugh Clopton (1440-1496).[159] Born in Clopton near Stratford, Hugh became a worthy in London civic society, becoming member of the Company of Mercers and holder of civic offices, including that of Mayor in 1491. In his will he bequeathed funds for the restoration of the guild chapel. His links with London may provide one conduit for the transmission of the Dance of Death tradition to Stratford. Of course, the Dance of Death was well-known across Europe, appearing in numerous iconographic schemes and manuscripts. However, in his London capacities, Clopton would have almost certainly been aware of its particular associations as an act of charitable patronage and civic self-fashioning carried out by John Carpenter, Common Clerk of the City and executor of the will of the mayor Richard Whittington. It seems likely that this famous display informed and gave authority to the Stratford scheme.

There is evidence that display of the famous scheme at St. Paul's impacted directly on the tradition of using *Erthe upon erthe* and related mortality texts as copy-texts. In MS Oxford, Balliol College 354 (Richard Hill's commonplace book), *Erthe upon erthe* follows an excerpt from the *Vado mori*, a Latin Dance of Death text. In this text each stanza is spoken by a different estate, from pope to pauper.[160] Richard Hill's text is selective and adapted, having only the lines in the voices of the king, knight, doctor, and logician, and notably includes a reference to the display of the *Daunce of Poulys* at St. Paul's:

Now ye folk y^at be here ye may not lang endure
but y^at ye shall torn to erth I do you ensure
^And yf ye lyst of ye trewth to se a playn f[i]gure
Go to seynt powlis ^and se ye the portratowr

[157] OOSTERWIJK, "Death, memory, and commemoration", p. 197.

[158] Cf. GILES, MASINTON, and ARNOTT, "Visualising the Guild Chapel, Stratford-upon-Avon", n.p.

[159] Hugh Clopton was apparently no relation of the benefactor of displayed Lydgate texts in a chantry chapel at Long Melford Church, Suffolk. Here Lydgate's *Testament*, "*Quis dabit meo capiti fontem lacrimarum*", and part of a stanza from "*Balade at the reverence of our Lady*" were displayed in versions specially adapted to their location and audience with funds from the will of John Clopton († 1497); see *DIMEV* 176 and 4383, and M.E. DAVIS, "Lydgate at Long Melford: Reassessing the *Testament* and '*Quis dabit meo capiti fontem lacrimarum*' in their local context", *Journal of Medieval Religious Cultures* 43.1 (2017), pp. 77-114.

[160] For the *Vado mori* see E.P. HAMMOND, "Latin texts of the Dance of Death", *Modern Philology* 8.3 (1911), pp. 399-410.

Graphic Display   273

Now you folk that may not last long here, I assure you that you will become earth. And if you wish to see a clear representation of this, go to St. Paul's and see the painting.[161]

The scribe has adapted the text to credit its dependence on a displayed source. The displayed text and images at St. Paul's are cited as an authority for the claim in *Erthe upon erthe* that the reader must return to earth.

The display of *Erthe upon erthe* and *Who-so him bethought* at Stratford was not unique. There is one additional record of the use of *Erthe upon erthe* as a displayed text. At Edmonton Church, London, a quatrain from the poem was inscribed on a tomb:

Erth goyth vpon erth as mold vpon mold
Erth goyth vpon erth al glysteryng in gold,
As thogh erth to erth ner turne shold,
And yet must erth to erth soner then he wold.[162]

Here the *display* of the text gives authority to the claim that earth must turn to earth: the tomb bears witness to this truth. *Who-so him bethought* is recorded as a tombstone inscription in Saffron Walden, Essex, at Faversham, Kent, where it was displayed on the tomb of Richard Colwell, former mayor of the town († 1533), and at Diss, Norfolk.[163] Perhaps the display of the texts and their evident commissioning by civic worthies gave impetus to the tradition of using them as copy-texts in manuscripts to test accomplishment as a reader and writer of English. Those who commissioned their use for display or recognised them in the busy graphic landscape of the London parish churches or the Stratford guild chapel may have experienced feelings of belonging to elite communities of Anglophone literate practice.[164] Those who recognised the English texts as elegant vernacular plays on familiar Latin copy-texts even though – especially as, perhaps – the Latin was not displayed with them perhaps experienced feelings of belonging to select communities of Anglophone literate practice that could apply the pedagogy of *littera* to English as well as Latin. View-

[161] MS Balliol College, 354, p. 435.

[162] *Ancient Funerall Monuments*, p. 534.

[163] *Ancient Funerall Monuments*, pp. 625, 276-277. However, *DIMEV* 6610 describes the first and last of these as "bibliographic ghosts".

[164] Possibly the early-modern enthusiasm for copying epitaphs also arose from a desire for copy-text material. For early-modern collecting of epitaphs see S. NEWSTOK, *Quoting Death in Early Modern England: The Poetics of Epitaphs beyond the Tomb* (Basingstoke, 2009).

274   *Chapter 4*

ing these texts in the guild chapel or parish church might have given opportunities to see the display alongside people who did not recognise these associations and this collective but differentiated experience may perhaps have enhanced the power of the display to erect boundaries between belonging and difference.

Discussion

We have seen that, in religious and secular settings, the display of alphabets, proverbs, and other moralising or instructive copy-texts associated with *littera* pedagogy represented the discharge of responsibilities for moral governance and education on the part of the lord, householder, or other person or body with control over the fabric of the building, and signalled to members of the household or civic body and others the values of the community, making a link between graphic ingenuity and accomplishment and moral conduct. Those who commissioned these displays could exhibit their literate accomplishments and associate them with their civic or household authority and responsibilities. Audiences for these inscriptions could identify with these values and experience belonging to elite communities through recognition, appreciation, and understanding of them and through awareness that their taste and accomplishments were not shared by all who might view these materials. Displays of pedagogic copy-texts in English invited imitation of the behaviours enjoined and respect for the knowledge communicated, and they also provided graphic resources for individuals' identification with the households and other groups in whose presence the texts were displayed. We have seen that manuscript records of such texts, including rubrics and notes about their display, suggest the meanings of these gestures of display for wider publics and indeed that they are traces of the wider impact of these practices on identity formation through graphic means. While display was informed by and amplified the tradition of using copy-texts as part of *littera* pedagogy, display in turn influenced the use of texts as copy-texts in writing practice in manuscripts. Selecting, reproducing, and perhaps rearranging texts found in the graphic landscape of an influential or powerful household or other social group – and recording the place of display in some cases – may have been experienced as an act of belonging to a given community of Anglophone literate practice.

Graphic Display 275

The Pre-Conquest Epigraphic Landscape

In the final section of this chapter we turn to display in pre-Conquest graphic landscapes, with some brief remarks about how we might use the frameworks of *littera* pedagogy and identity formation as perspectives on this material. The corpus of pre-Conquest inscriptions provides data for the pre-Conquest graphic landscape but this material is of course scanty and problematic in many ways. Some of the material predates the introduction of Christian pedagogy. Although it sometimes appears to share some of the features we have identified in later display spaces, as pre-Christian material it necessarily eludes our attempts to interpret them in the terms of literacy pedagogy and identity construction used in the present study. An example is supplied by what has been claimed to be the earliest written English (also classified as pre-Old English), a word inscribed in runes on an ankle-bone (astragalus), dated 425-475.[165] This object was found in an urn in a burial ground in Caistor near Norwich and is now in Norwich Castle Museum.[166] Its spidery runes read "ᚱᚨᛁᚺᚨᚾ", transliterated as "*raihan*", and perhaps meaning 'roe', or 'roe's'.[167] The bone may be from a roe-deer and, if the interpretation of the runes is correct, we can say that the inscription identifies the object that bears it. Thus the object draws attention to itself as written: the inscribed word "*raihan*" labels the object while the object glosses the word. From a graphic landscape perspective this is a challenging and complex object. It is thought to be a piece for use in a game. Its inscription is also playful: for those who can solve the puzzle of its runes, it both names and figures, by means of material synecdoche (the part standing for the whole), the forest habitat of the hunt, and the convivial landscape of the hall where the deer would be eaten and games played with its bones. Surviving in a cremation urn, the object is connected with other locations. Perhaps those who buried it in the urn imagined that the object would be

---

[165] R.I. PAGE, *An Introduction to English Runes*, pp. 12, 19, and fig. 6; for discussion of the date see J. HINES, "The runic inscriptions of early Anglo-Saxon England", in: *Britain 400-600: Language and History*, ed. A. BAMMESBERGER and A. WOLLMANN (Heidelberg, 1990), pp. 437-455, at p. 442. For the pre-Old English classification see the entry for PreOE-GB-13 in *RuneSDB*, beta version (Göttingen, 2022), <https//www.runesdb.eu/>.

[166] Urn N59. See HINES, "The runic inscriptions of early Anglo-Saxon England", pp. 441-442; R.M. HOGG, "Introduction", in: *The Cambridge History of the English Language: Volume I: The Beginnings to 1066*, ed. R.M. HOGG (Cambridge, 1992), pp. 1-25, at p. 14; and PAGE, *An Introduction to English Runes*, pp. 179-180.

[167] For the transcription see HINES, "The runic inscriptions of early Anglo-Saxon England", p. 441.

276   *Chapter 4*

meaningful in some such location in the afterlife. The object and its playful
inscription *may* have been resources for signifying belonging and identity in
this world and the next for the individual committed to burial and for the community who buried him or her. Page points out that it could have been brought
from elsewhere, perhaps Scandinavia (its runes predate the Anglo-Saxon futhorc), and may have been old when buried.[168] Perhaps the presence of variant
runes was meaningful to the community that buried it. The inscription on this
object appears to represent the association between puzzling, gaming, letter-
symbolism, and perhaps writing practice that we have observed in previous
chapters, amplified in the context of its locations. But the object is pre-Christian, and therefore we can only speculate about the pedagogic traditions and
understanding of graphic practice that informed its production and use both as
a gaming-piece and as an object associated with cremation.

    Christian pre-Conquest material that was available in some kind of public
display and which can sometimes be located in a given environment or associated with a known provenance mainly comprises inscribed stone sculpture,
some of which we encountered in Chapter One. The Ruthwell Cross is perhaps
the most intriguing of these inscribed artefacts for the purposes of the present
study. As noted in the introduction to this chapter, the cross presents many
formidable difficulties of interpretation and any new proposition must remain
speculative. In this final section of this chapter the English inscription on the
cross will be considered in relation to ideas and processes of literacy training
and graphic identity-formation and their modification and amplification in
public display environments.

    The runic inscriptions on the Ruthwell Cross repay consideration as both
copy-text and graphic puzzle. Whether the text is extracts from the *Dream of
the Rood* is impossible to determine finally, but there is an intriguing parallel
for the display in runes of a fragment from a longer Old English verse text. At
least three lines of alliterative verse extracted from the *Benedicite* canticle form
an inscription on the Honington clip, a silver object with two arms of unknown
function. Corresponding lines also occur in the Old English poems *Daniel* and
Azarias. The poems are some one to two centuries later than the clip of *c.* 725-
825, but Hines infers that they all point to "an early witness" to an Old English
version of the canticle.[169]

---

[168] PAGE, *An Introduction to English Runes*, p. 21; see also R. DEROLEZ, "Runic literacy among
the Anglo-Saxons", in: *Britain 400-600: Language and History*, pp. 397-436, at pp. 415-416.
    [169] For the Honington clip see J. HINES, "New insights into early Old English from recent

Graphic Display 277

Whether its runic inscriptions comprise extracts from the *Dream of the Rood* or a standalone text, the Ruthwell Cross runic poem engages with riddling and graphic puzzling. Like the Old English pedagogic riddles discussed in Chapter Three, its text challenges the reader to identify the first-person speaker:

> + Almighty God bared his body as he prepared to climb the gallows, valiant in men's sight [...] bow [...]
> I [...] a mighty king, lord of heaven, I dared not bend down. Men mocked the pair of us together. I was stained with blood [...]
> + Christ was on the cross. Yet to this solitary one there came men from afar, eager and noble. I beheld it all. I was bitterly distressed with griefs [...] bowed down [...] Wounded with arrows. Down they set the man weary of limb. They stood at the corpse's head. There they beheld [...][170]

The poem's location amplifies its runic text's riddling challenge, inviting the reader to link the object on which it is displayed with the 'I' of the text. Graphically, the inscription also engages in the traditions of riddle pedagogy, for it challenges the viewer to play around with its letters and to use different strategies to decode them from those for the other text on the monument. First, and most obviously, it presents this challenge by encoding its text in runes. In display this challenge is amplified, for, while the ravages of time, erosion, and restoration have contributed to the illegibility of the poem text, it was probably always difficult for viewers to read. Whereas the Latin inscriptions align with the orientation of the image borders, the text of the English poem is written in lines that are always horizontal for the viewer. This means that on the vertical sides of the border they form very short lines of, at most, four characters per line in the narrow framing space, and words and phrases are broken up over the lines, compounding the difficulty of lack of word division usual in runic inscriptions. Even if they could decode runes, viewers probably would always have found the text hard to decode *in situ* owing to its height on the monument (it was perhaps some two or three metres above head height for a standing adult viewer), the size of the runes, and their awkward disposition in many lines and small groups of runes. Other material properties may have emphasised the exceptional decoding challenge presented by the English text. If runic

---

Anglo-Saxon runic finds", *NOWELE: North-Western European Language Evolution* 73.1 (2020), pp. 69-90, at pp. 71-76, quotation at p. 72.

[170] Trans. PAGE, *An Introduction to English Runes*, pp. 147-148.

278   *Chapter 4*

inscriptions like the one on the Ruthwell Cross were painted, as Scandinavian ones are known to have been,[171] this would have increased the salience of the legends and perhaps drawn the eye to the linguistic contrasts between them. Discussing the cross in relation to literacy, and observing the difficulties presented by the text, Elizabeth Okasha surmises that "the commissioner of the cross and the drafter of the texts had other motives in mind than the conveying of information to a reading public".[172] Perhaps these motives relate to identity-formation. By offering a graphic challenge that is amplified by the mode and place of its display, the inscription provides opportunities for the creation of boundaries between belonging and difference. Those who can overcome these formidable challenges of playing around with runes and decoding them are offered membership of an elite group of literates, a group distinguished from those who could not solve the riddle and decode the runes.

A graphic landscape approach offers a lens through which we might view the English text on the Ruthwell Cross. Conner argues provocatively that the English text was not part of the original plan for the cross when it was made in the eighth century but was added later, in the late tenth or even eleventh century.[173] He explains the addition of the runic text in relation to the *Adoratio Crucis* and the *Despositio Crucis*, ceremonies that were part of Good Friday devotions associated with the tenth-century Benedictine Revival. Both monastics and laity participated in this ceremony and English-language glosses of its prayers survive.[174] The poem on the Ruthwell Cross, an analogous text on the Brussels reliquary, and the *Dream of the Rood* may all, Conner suggests, echo this devotional tradition. From the perspective of linguistic landscape studies, the addition of text in a cryptic language and script could contribute to the negotiation and expression of identity. *Some* of the viewers for whom the poem text was added – the target audience – were presumably expected to be able to rise to its graphic challenge. Perhaps the community provided this knowledge, or perhaps viewers were expected to bring with them prior knowledge of the

---

[171] PAGE, *An Introduction to English Runes*, p. 155.

[172] E. OKASHA, "Literacy in Anglo-Saxon England: The evidence from inscriptions", in: *Medieval Europe, 1992: Art and Symbolism Pre-printed Papers* 7 (York, 1992), pp. 85-89, at p. 88.

[173] P.W. CONNER, "The Ruthwell monument runic poem in a tenth-century context", *Review of English Studies* 59 (2008), pp. 25-51. Conner's dating, however, is not accepted by the *RuneS-DB*; see the entry for OE-GB-69 where the inscription is dated 700-800, contemporary with the iconographical scheme. Kerstin Majewski is preparing a new study that concurs with this eighth-century dating (personal communication).

[174] CONNER, "The Ruthwell monument runic poem", pp. 45-48.

Graphic Display   279

Adoratio Crucis and *Depositio Crucis* traditions. Perhaps being able to decode the text reinforced a sense of membership of a group associated with these traditions.[175]

When receiving the runic English text, the Ruthwell Cross became bilingual, joining a corpus of monuments that bear inscriptions in two or more languages (and further possibly bilingual monuments whose language is not easy to decide).[176] In such contexts, however, English often appears to have the specialised function of recording the names of makers and patrons, often via the trope of the first-person speaking object.[177] But compared with examples of other bilingual inscriptions, the Ruthwell Cross stands out because it uses English for an extensive, non-formulaic text. As a first-person address to the viewer that announces the history of the object viewed, the Ruthwell poem

[175] Stancliffe suggests that one sector of the original audience for the Ruthwell Cross – including the runes – may have been British Christians. However, she does not mention Conner's proposal that the runes were applied later (C. STANCLIFFE, "The riddle of the Ruthwell Cross: Audience, intention, and originator reconsidered", in: *Crossing Boundaries: Interdisciplinary Approaches to the Art, Material Culture, Language, and Literature of the Early Medieval World: Essays presented to Professor Emeritus Richard N. Bailey*, ed. E. CAMBRIDGE and J. HAWKES (Oxford, 2017), pp. 3-14).

[176] E. OKASHA, "Vernacular or Latin? The languages of Insular inscriptions, AD 500-1100", in: *Epigrafik 1988: Fachtagung für mittelalterliche und neuzeitliche Epigrafik, Graz, Mai 1988*, ed. W. KOCH (Vienna, 1990), pp. 139-150, at p. 141. Okasha's corpus gives us a sense of the salience of English in the pre-Conquest monumental landscape on a broader scale. Of the 144 stone monuments that bear inscriptions, 108 are legible enough for their language to be identified. Of these, sixty-four, just over sixty-nine percent, bear some writing in English.

[177] A sundial set in the south wall of a church in East Yorkshire (Great Edstone 01), probably of the eleventh century, carries a maker's inscription that reads "+ *LOĐAN ME ÞROHTEA*" or "+ *LOĐAN ME ÞROHTE A*", while at the top of the sundial is an inscription in Latin; it may have read "*orologium viatorum*" ("travellers' clock"); similarly, York St. Mary Castlegate 07, a foundation stone of the tenth or eleventh century inscribed in Latin and Old English records in English the building of the church by Grim and Æse; the part in Latin records the names of the saints to whom it is dedicated (*The Corpus of Anglo-Saxon Stone Sculpture III: York and Eastern Yorkshire*, ed. J. LANG (London, 1991), <http://www.ascorpus.ac.uk/catvol3.php>). This bilingual moment possibly reflects, Lang suggests, differences of concern: "[p]atronage, a secular concern, is recorded in Old English, but the details of the dedication lapse into Latin, perhaps influenced by an official ecclesiastical record of the dedication in Latin" (cf. OKASHA, "Vernacular or Latin?", pp. 145-146). The runic inscription on the upper panel of the east face of the Ruthwell Cross seems to record the fragment ᛗᚫᚷᛁᛋᚷᚫᚠ ("*dægisgæf*"), perhaps a personal name in this tradition. I am grateful to Jeremy Smith for the transcription, transliteration, and suggestion that this may be a name. One wonders, however, if "*gæf*" could be part of a donation formula. Swanton, by contrast, sees this text as a fragment of the *Dream of the Rood* line "[*wæp*]*dæ giscæft*[*t*]" ("creation wept"); see *The Dream of the Rood*, ed. M. SWANTON, rev. edn. (Exeter, 1987), p. 31.

280   *Chapter 4*

chimes rather closely with formulaic inscriptions such as "Loðan made me", but it also differs challengingly and puzzlingly from this tradition.

The Ruthwell Cross stands out in relation to some other monuments in the area in ways that may signal links with communities in the south. Although standing stone crosses were common (over 1500 survive), and although many examples of pre-Conquest stone sculpture survive from the Dumfries region, with particular densities at Whithorn, the Ruthwell Cross is in many ways exceptional.[178] Discussing the styles of decoration associated with this material, Craig concludes that the Ruthwell Cross and other major works from the area show awareness of traditions to the south and east and suggest that "these monuments are the product of centres with a widespread network of contacts".[179] Conner acknowledges that the home of the Benedictine Reform was in Wessex, "[w]hile Dumfriesshire is far enough from Winchester, the networks of English monasticism during the reform period may well have reached there".[180] If Conner's later dating is correct, by means of its visible co-opting of linguistic markers of the Benedictine revival, and by contrasting them with the usual formulaic maker's and other memorial inscriptions, the addition of the runic text to the Ruthwell Cross may have signified new forms of belonging and identity. Possibly the modification to the graphic landscape made by the Ruthwell Cross rune-carver and his patron expressed identification with southern Benedictine traditions. Perhaps its target audience was not only the local community but also visitors from the south and wider monastic networks. It is not clear what community the Ruthwell Cross was associated with, but *some* of the pilgrims headed to St. Ninian's shrine and Whithorn Priory from the south may well have seen it and recognised its meanings as they passed by.[181]

---

[178] For numbers see *The Dream of the Rood*, p. 47; for densities see D.J. CRAIG, "The distribution of pre-Norman sculpture in South-West Scotland: Provenance, ornament, and regional groups", 4 vols. (unpublished PhD thesis, Durham University, 1992), <http://etheses.dur.ac.uk/1553>, 1, p. 304, fig. 20.

[179] CRAIG, "The distribution of pre-Norman sculpture in South-West Scotland", 1, p. 267.

[180] CONNER, "The Ruthwell monument runic poem", p. 43.

[181] St. Ninian, reputedly a bishop of the late fourth century, is mentioned by Bede in his *Historia Ecclesiastica* (731) and there is evidence for a cult at Whithorn from the seventh century. Unfortunately, CRAIG, "The distribution of pre-Norman sculpture in South-West Scotland", 1, p. 296, only shows routes from the north.

Conclusion

This chapter has argued that the understanding and functions of graphic practice cultivated and transmitted by basic literacy training and transferred to the writing and reading of English were amplified and modified by public display. The medieval parish church was a graphic landscape in which English-language graffiti participated in the conventions of graphic practice taught formally and informally and stood out as an exceptional resource for identity construction in a busy graphic landscape. The study of displayed English literary texts in domestic and civic spaces identifies a number of social groups for whom often similar material was a resource in the construction of identities: aristocratic and gentry households, and citizen households and civic bodies. Displaying English literary texts and graphic practice to public view signified the distinctive cultural, moral, and aesthetic leadership of these groups and associated it with graphic accomplishment. Imitation and other forms of participation in or appreciation of these text display traditions provided resources for identity-making. The amplification of the basics of understanding of graphic culture by the display of English pedagogic models and materials in these later medieval places may have had a long history. The runic poem on the Ruthwell Cross, this chapter has argued, could be seen as an intervention that, charged with graphic challenge, changed the ways in which the monument spoke of belonging and identity.

Chapter 5: Reprographics

For per chaunse, aftir my manere of writyng, sum word stondiþ in sum place, which same word, aftir þi maner of writyng, shulde stonde in anoþir place. If it plese to ony man to write þis concordaunce, & him þenkiþ þat summe wordis ben not set in ordre aftir his con-seit & his manere of writyng, it is not hard, if he take keep wiþ good avisement in his owne writyng, to sette suche wordis in such an ordre as his owne conseit acordiþ wel to.

It might be that, according to my way of writing, a word is in a certain place [in the alphabetical sequence] which in your way of writing should be in a different place. If it please any man to copy this concordance and it seems to him that some words are not ordered correctly according to his understanding [of the alphabet] and manner of writing, it is not difficult, if he takes good care in his own copying, to arrange such words in such an order that accords with his own understanding.

(*Preface to the Wycliffite Biblical Concordance*)[1]

The technique or practice of copying and reproducing documents or graphic material in facsimile form by means other than conventional printing (e.g. photocopying, microfilm, or by digitalization).

(*Reprography*, n., *OED*)

Previous chapters have argued that the understanding of graphic culture taught by elementary literacy pedagogy – teaching about the alphabet, the use of models, the development of graphic ingenuity through graphic play, and the pedagogies of graphic display – framed the production and reception of written English and contributed to the formation of identity among communities of Anglophone literate practice. This chapter explores some of the ways in which this framework informed the reprographic practices of

---

[1] *Preface to the Wycliffite Biblical Concordance*, ed. S.M. KUHN, in: "The preface to a fifteenth-century concordance", *Speculum*, 43 (1968), pp. 258-273.

284   *Chapter 5*

scribes and their understanding of what they were doing when they copied exemplars of English-language texts.

The *OED* examples of 'reprography', quoted in the epigraph to this chapter, exclude printing and do not even mention copying by hand. Yet scribal copying too is a technology of text reproduction and like other such technologies is associated with culturally-contingent philosophies and practices of text and copy. While *OED* restricts the definition of reprography to copying "in facsimile form", what counts as a facsimile is dependent on both available technologies and concepts of the copy.[2] We begin our consideration of attitudes to reprography among scribes of medieval English by returning to the text with which Chapter One opened, the *Preface to the Wycliffite Biblical Concordance*. In the passage quoted in the epigraph to the present chapter, the author offers guidance to scribes who may copy his text in future. He recognises the problems faced by scribes of English and in particular that the alpha-

---

[2]   What we would understand as facsimile reproduction is clearly a phenomenon in manuscript culture (see examples in A. HIATT, *The Making of Medieval Forgeries: False Documents in Fifteenth-Century England* (London, 2004), pp. 52-57; M. HUNTER, "The facsimiles in Thomas Elmham's history of St. Augustine's Canterbury", *The Library* series 5, 28.3 (1973), pp. 215-220; and M.B. PARKES, "Archaizing hands in English manuscripts", repr. in: M.B. Parkes, *Pages from the Past: Medieval Writing Skills and Manuscript Books*, ed. P.R. ROBINSON and R. ZIM (Farnham, 2012), pp. 101-141, at pp. 102-103). Medieval concepts however were different: see M. BOON, *In Praise of Copying* (Cambridge, MA, 2010) for classical and medieval philosophies of the copy. Many print historians perceive a rupture between scribal reproduction of text and print. For example McLuhan states that the "invention of typography [... provided] the first uniformly repeatable commodity" (M. MCLUHAN, *The Gutenberg Galaxy* (Toronto, 1962), p. 124). Eisenstein states "[u]niformity and synchronization have become so common since the advent of printing, that we have to remind ourselves repeatedly that they were usually absent in the age of scribes"; "it seems misguided to suggest that 'the multiplication of identical copies' was merely 'intensified' by the press" (E. EISENSTEIN, *The Printing Press as an Agent of Change*, 2 vols. (Cambridge, 1979), 1, pp. 16, 41, quoting J.H. HARRINGTON, "The production and distribution of books in Western Europe to the year 1500" (PhD thesis, Columbia University, 1956), p. 3). However, Johns points out that the printing press did not produce identical copies (A. JOHNS, "How to acknowledge a revolution", *The American Historical Review* 107.1 (2002), pp. 106-125). Writing a decade before the launch of the first phone-camera, Burrow presciently draws attention to some parallels between electronic reprography and scribal copying and their implications for ideas of authorship, "one may imagine that in the future, as reprographic devices become lighter and cheaper, individual readers will behave more and more like scribes – copying texts without regard to the author's rights, or even his or her identity, and assembling their own personal compilations of the documents which happen to interest them" (J.A. BURROW, "The sinking island and the dying author: R.W. Chambers fifty years on", *Essays in Criticism* 40.1 (1990), pp. 1-23, at p. 14). Compare the reflections on readers' responses to digital texts by Richard Lanham and others discussed in Chapter Three.

Reprographics 285

bet that he has used to organise his concordance (*"my manere of writyng"*) may not be shared by some other scribes (*"þi maner of writyng"*). He advises that any scribe whose *"maner of writyng"* differs from his own may reorder the concordance and the contents of the letter sections. This will pose a graphic challenge, he admits, but *"it is not hard, if he take keep wiþ good avisement in his owne writyng"*: he may meet the challenge if he pays attention (*MED, kep*, n., 1) giving due consideration (*MED, avisement*, n., 2b) to the order of letters and arrangement of entries in his copy. Basic literacy pedagogy, this chapter argues, gave scribes of medieval English ways of developing and thinking about modes of copying and the special challenges of transmitting texts in the English language. Scribes who were engaged in copying English texts such as those addressed by the author of the Wycliffite *Preface* might find themselves confronted with conflicting models: their exemplars might not conform with the alphabetical and spelling practices modelled in their education or training, with what 'we' do. For the Wycliffite author, these circumstances gave opportunities for the application of the graphic virtuosity developed in literacy training to solve the problems that arose and for the development of modified pedagogies for the purposes of facilitating copying and giving that practice meaning. Others, we shall see, applied *littera* pedagogy differently to such problems.

The analysis of reprography devised by Angus McIntosh and followed and developed by the scholars associated with the *LALME* and *LAEME* projects is summarised as follows:

A mediaeval scribe copying an English manuscript which is in a dialect other than his own may do one of three things:

A. He may leave it more or less unchanged, like a modern scholar transcribing such a manuscript. This appears to happen only somewhat rarely.

B. He may convert it into his own kind of language, making innumerable modifications to the orthography, the morphology, and the vocabulary. This happens commonly.

C. He may do something somewhere between A and B. This also happens commonly.[3]

---

[3] A. MᴄINTOSH, "Word geography in the lexicography of medieval English", repr. in: *Middle English Dialectology: Essays on some Principles and Problems by Angus McIntosh, M.L. Samuels, and M. Laing*, ed. M. LAING (Aberdeen, 1989), pp. 86-97, at p. 92.

286   *Chapter 5*

The practice with regard to copying an exemplar that the author of the *Preface to the Wycliffite Biblical Concordance* enjoins on future scribes would fall into type B. McIntosh first described three types of source text for dialect study in his 1963 essay "A new approach to Middle English dialectology". Here he gave descriptive labels to two of the three types of scribal practice: type B scribes are said to "translate", and type C scribes produce "*Mischsprachen*" ("mixed languages").[4] Texts in the third category of practice, type C, having elements of both methods, can also be "pseudo-*Mischsprachen*", the latter term being used by Benskin and Laing for a mixed text with layers of dialect that can be separated out.[5] In the typology as developed by Margaret Laing and Michael Benskin, McIntosh's Type A, Luick's "*getreu*" transcription, is called "literatim" copying, or sometimes "mirror copying".[6] On this basis, McIntosh and his colleagues proposed that scribal texts, although transmitted over many scribal copies, could represent coherent writing systems, either because they reproduce their exemplar exactly, being literatim copies, or because they represent new coherent writing systems (translated copies), or because they present a structured mix of the two (pseudo-*Mischsprachen*). This move was important to the project because it allowed scribally-transmitted texts to be used as a source of data whereas previously only authors' holographs were thought to be reliable evidence for dialect.

From time to time, McIntosh and his colleagues offered some explanations for the existence of three broad categories of copying practice. Observing that there might be a correlation between translation copying and didactic Middle

---

[4]   A. McINTOSH, "A new approach to Middle English dialectology", repr. in: *Middle English Dialectology*, pp. 22-31, at pp. 27-28.

[5]   M. BENSKIN and M. LAING, "Translations and *Mischsprachen* in Middle English manuscripts", in: *So meny people longages and tonges: Philological Essays presented to Angus McIntosh*, ed. M. BENSKIN and M.L. SAMUELS (Edinburgh, 1981), pp. 55-106.

[6]   The *LALME* methodology builds on the work of the Austrian philologist Karl Luick (1865-1935). Luick stated that Old English manuscripts were "as far as possible faithfully ["*getreu*"] transcribed", whereas, from the first half of the twelfth century, writings began to be copied as the scribe spoke ("*man schrieb wie man sprach*") and this practice prevailed "until well into the fourteenth century" (quoted and translated by M. LAING, "The Middle English scribe: *Sprach er wie er schrieb?*", in: *English Historical Linguistics 2006, Volume 3, Geo-Historical Variation in English: Selected Papers from the Fourteenth International Conference on Historical Linguistics (ICEHL 14), Bergamo, 21-26 August 2006*, ed. M. DOSSENA, R. DURY, and M. GOTTI (Amsterdam, 2008), pp. 1-44, at p. 1 and n. 2). Literatim copying can also produce texts of mixed language, when a scribe copies faithfully exemplars in different dialects, but in these cases the elements of the mixture occur in sections rather than layers. Our Carthusian case study below is of this kind.

Reprographics 287

English verse texts, McIntosh suggests that translations might have been "made for reading aloud to a strictly local audience".[7] He also suggests that variation between literatim and translation copying might be explained in terms of the development of the latter practice over time, literatim copying being the earlier practice that yields to translation as the numbers of scribes able to copy in local vernaculars grew and conventions for local writing became "well-established".[8] Benskin and Laing agree, finding that translation is more common in the later period but also noting that the phenomenon is associated with some earlier Middle English material that is "designed for reading aloud to local audiences"; these "show signs of having been translated as a matter of policy".[9] Another, rather different explanation for translation is that it is a product of the script used by scribes. Scribes who executed a fast cursive script could not copy letter for letter because in cursive script clusters of letters were traced in a single stroke; they must have memorised units of their exemplar and copied them in a kind of process of internal dictation.[10] In the view of McIntosh and his associates, therefore, scribal translation of lengthy didactic verse texts is a practice of graphisation of local spoken languages motivated by both communicative needs and practical considerations.

The vocabulary used by the Middle English Dialect Project to analyse types of copying is not, with one exception, claimed by scholars associated with the project to be based on medieval sources. According to *OED*, 'literatim' is a post-classical Latin word first used by Erasmus in 1532.[11] The earliest English example is 1623. The same source for the first instance of 'literatim', a text by Thomas Powell († *c.* 1635), also uses the term 'punctuatim': "The Originall must [...] be so exactly set downe and drawn, that all the following Processe and proceeding, may be tyed to agree with it punctuatim". '*Mischsprache*' ('mixed language') borrows a German linguistics term itself first attested in 1847 (*OED, Mischsprache*, n.). The one exception is 'translation'. McIntosh suggests that translation was a term scribes themselves used to think about the act of copying a text from one dialect to another: "I use the term 'translated' advisedly and it is used at least once in Middle English this way".[12]

---

[7] McIntosh, "Word geography", p. 93.

[8] McIntosh, "Word geography", p. 93.

[9] Benskin and Laing, "Translations and *Mischsprachen*", p. 88.

[10] See for example, Benskin and Laing, "Translations and *Mischsprachen*", pp. 90-91; D. Wakelin, *Scribal Correction and Literary Craft* (Cambridge, 2014), p. 165.

[11] *OED, literatim,* adv. and adj.

[12] McIntosh, "A new approach to Middle English dialectology", p. 27.

288   *Chapter 5*

LALME cites two statements that use the term as "contemporary evidence for translation".[13] The first statement cited comes from the introduction to the *Assumption of Our Lady* in the *Cursor mundi*. It refers to an indulgence issued and in the hand of St. Edmund of Pontigny or Pontenay (Edmund Rich, archbishop of Canterbury, † 1240), granting twenty days' pardon (forty days in some manuscripts) to anyone who hears or reads the text. It records that the text has been "turned" into northern English for the benefit of northern people who can read no other English:

> *In a writt þis ilk i fand,*
> *He-self it wrogh[t] ic vnderstand.*
> *In sotherin englis was it draun,*
> *And turnd it i till our aun*
> *Langage o nothrin lede,*
> *Þat can non oiþer englis rede*

In an indulgence I found this [*Assumption of our Lady*]. I understand that he [Edmund Rich] composed it himself. It was expressed in southern English and I turned it into our own language of northern people who can read no other variety of English.

(*Cursor mundi*, lines 20,059-20,064)[14]

The second statement quoted in *LALME* occurs in MS Cambridge, UL, Ii.4.9, a fifteenth-century religious miscellany, where a colophon records that the *Informacion of Richard the Ermyte* has been "*translate oute of Northarn tunge into Sutharne that it shulde the bettir be vndirstondyn of men that be of the Selve Countre*" ("translated out of northern dialect into southern so that it may be better understood by people of that same region"; f. 197v).[15]

It is important to note for the purposes of our present enquiry into scribes' reprographic processes and how they thought about them that these cited texts do not necessarily refer to *scribal* practice. In the first place, the cited statements are both apparently authorial rather than scribal statements and they relate to authorship rather than copying. While they provide evidence that

---

[13] *LALME*, General Introduction, 1.3.3.

[14] *Cursor mundi (The Cursor o the World): A Northumbrian Poem of the XIVth Century in Four Versions*, ed. R. MORRIS, 7 vols. (London, 1874-1893: EETS, o.s. 57, 59, 62, 66, 68, 99, 101), 3, p. 1148.

[15] Cf. MCINTOSH, "A new approach to Middle English dialectology", p. 27.

Reprographics 289

substitution of one dialect spelling or form for another was termed 'translation', they do not show that such an activity was associated with the *scribal reprographic process*. Compare the authorial voice's account of his choice of language for the entire work in the preface to the *Cursor mundi*. The authorial voice explains that he has "translated" the text into English for the sake of English people. When was English praised in France? Each to his own language:

> Þis ilk bok is es translate
> In to Inglis tong to rede
> For the loue of Inglis lede,
> Inglis lede of Ingland,
> For the commun at understand.
> [...]
> Mast es it wroght for frankis man
> Quat is for him na frankis can?
> [...]
> Giue we ilkan þare langage

This book has been translated to be read in the English language, for love of the English people of England, for the common people to understand [...] Much is available for French speakers. What is there for him that doesn't know any French? [...] Let us give to each their own language.

(*Cursor mundi*, 1, p. 20, lines 232-236, 239-240, 247).

Arguably, then, *none* of the typological labels used by the Middle English Dialect Project relates to medieval concepts of copying.[16] Attempting to supplement the analysis of the reprographic practices of scribes of Middle English offered by McIntosh and the Middle English Dialect Project, this chapter will propose that *littera* pedagogy provided a framework within which medieval scribes of English-language texts reflected on their practices and made sense of them in relation to the practices of other scribes.

---

[16] For consideration of some medieval terms used for the transmission of text broadly see the essays in *Vocabulaire du livre et de l'écriture au Moyen Age: Actes de la table ronde, Paris 24-26 septembre 1987*, ed. O. WEIJERS (Turnhout, 1989: *Etudes sur le vocabulaire intellectuel du Moyen Age* 2), especially O. GUYOTJEANNIN, "Le vocabulaire de la diplomatique en Latin médiéval", pp. 120-134 (on originals and copies); J. HAMESSE, "Le vocabulaire de la transmission orale des textes", pp. 168-194 (on oral dictation); and L.J. BATAILLON, "'*Exemplar*', '*pecia*', '*quaternus*'", pp. 206-219 (on terms related to the *pecia* system).

290   *Chapter 5*

Focusing on the Middle English manuscript corpus, where evidence for variation in practice is most plentiful and tractable, this chapter will identify and examine applications of *littera* pedagogy to the problems associated with copying English. In previous chapters we have encountered the identity-forming potential of basic graphic pedagogy and the resources it provided for drawing boundaries between belonging and difference. Our case studies of Middle English scribes in this chapter will give us the opportunity to observe identity boundaries being drawn within and among scribal communities of copying practice. By developing variant practices, ascribing meaning to them, and transmitting these practices and meanings to others, scribes may be seen as identifying as members of communities of Anglophone literate practice. The following sections of this chapter will offer case studies of various scribal communities of practice that are distinguished by their applications of elementary graphic pedagogy to the challenges of copying English. First we will examine how copyists of lengthy verse texts tackled the problems of copying poetry, with case studies of the transmission of texts in syllabic and rhymed metres. Next we will examine a scribe whom we encountered briefly in Chapter One, whose distinctive responses to his prose exemplars may be associated with precepts and understandings of practice transmitted by the Carthusian order. Finally, turning to the specific issues confronted by the author of the *Preface to the Wycliffite Bible Concordance*, we will examine how early scribes of the Middle English translation of the Latin *Polychronicon* tackled the problems of copying alphabetical indexes and how their practices interfaced with those of the decorators of initials.

Littera *and the Copying of Verse*

Basic *littera* pedagogy taught that spellings were essential to the correct analysis of metre in quantitative Latin poetry. We saw in Chapters Two and Three that the pronunciation of syllables was important in elementary *littera* pedagogy. Basic pedagogy also taught how syllables functioned in metre. Spellings were crucial to determining whether syllables – the building blocks of metrical feet – were long or short and hence how the words they made up could be scanned and placed in a line of verse; spellings were therefore also crucial to reading verse aloud. Donatus's *Ars maior* explains how syllables

Reprographics 291

combine to form words and how they combine to form metrical feet.[17] Donatus explains that if a short vowel is followed by two consonants, then the syllable is long, having the value of two beats, whereas a short syllable has only one beat. This was part of a complex of rules for determining syllable length in his *Ars maior*.[18] Different metres had different numbers of feet and arrangements for their deployment across the line.

This framework was taken up by Christian grammarians such as Bede, who in his long-lived and extremely influential *De Arte metrica* explains long and short syllables and how they combine to form the various feet. In chapter four of this work, Bede recommends that inexperienced students study long syllables by examining the first foot of every line of verse in any book of hexameter or pentameter verse, for the first syllable in these forms would always be long.[19] Aldhelm's pedagogic riddles, encountered in Chapter Three, were preceded by *De Metris,* a treatise on metre that begins with syllables.[20] In the early fifteenth century, the London grammar-school master John Seward (Seguarde) includes Bede among his authorities in his elementary metrical treatise *Hisigoga metrica*, introducing the concept of the foot as a metrical structure composed of two, three, or even four syllables (*"Pes est collatio duarum aut trium aut etiam quatuor sillabarum"*).[21] It followed that close attention to spelling and to accurate reproduction of Latin quantitative poetry was essential if metre was to be undamaged and able to be read correctly. Medieval English poetry, of course, had different metres from Latin, most forms, whether rhymed or unrhymed, being accentual, relying on some kind of stress pattern. But reproduction of poetry was still problematic. Variation in morphology and sound across time and space could affect syllable counts, stress patterns, and

[17] Donatus, *Ars maior*, in: "*Donati* Ars grammatica", ed. H. KEIL, in: *Grammatici Latini*, ed. H. KEIL, 8 vols. (Leipzig, 1864), 4, pp. 367-402, at pp. 369-370 ("*De pedibus*").

[18] Donatus, *Ars maior*, pp. 368-369.

[19] Bede, *De Arte metrica*, in: *Bede, Libri II* De Arte metrica *et* De Schematibus et tropis, ed. and trans. C.B. KENDALL (Saarbrücken, 1991). See C. RUFF, "The place of metrics in Anglo-Saxon Latin education: Aldhelm and Bede", *Journal of English and Germanic Philology* 104.2 (2005), pp. 149-170, at pp. 165-166. Ruff describes *De Arte metrica* as "the model for metrical instruction for centuries to come" (p. 149).

[20] RUFF, "The place of metrics in Anglo-Saxon Latin education", pp. 155-156.

[21] V.H. GALBRAITH, "John Seward and his circle", *Medieval and Renaissance Studies* 1 (1941), pp. 85-104, at p. 88 from MS Edinburgh, UL, 136, ff. 11r-30r. The *Hisigoga metrica* refers to the Council of Constance (1414-1418) as in session; a dedication to Robert Hallam, Bishop of Salisbury, suggests a date 1414-1417 (GALBRAITH, "John Seward", p. 92). Works on metre by Seward also occur in MS Oxford, Merton College, 299. Seward lived 1364-1435 (p. 96). He engaged in good-hearted debates on metre with other contemporary London school-masters.

292   *Chapter 5*

rhymes.[22] This section will examine how scribes deployed *littera* pedagogy to develop reprographic practices for the transmission of English verse. It will identify distinctive varieties of practice and propose that these variations could signify identity for communities of Anglophone scribal practice.

The Ormulum

> *Nu, broþerr Wallterr, broþerr min*
> *Affter þe flæshess kinde;*
> *And broþer min i Crisstenndom*
> *Þurrh fulluht and þurrh trowwþe;*
> *And broþer min i Godess hus [...]*
> *Icc hafe don swa summ þu badd,*
> *And forþedd te þin wille,*
> *Icc hafe wennd inntill Ennglissh*
> *Goddspelless hallȝhe lare [...]*
> *And whase wilenn shall þiss boc*
> *Efft oþerr siþe writenn,*
> *Himm bidde icc þatt het write rihht*
> *Swa summ þiss boc himm tæcheþþ,*
> *All þwerrt ut affterr þatt itt iss*
> *Uppo þiss firrste bisne.*

Now brother Walter, my sibling, my brother in Christianity, and my brother in the house of God [...] I have done as you asked and fulfilled your wish and turned the holy teaching of the gospels into English [...] And whoever shall wish to copy this book another time, I bid him that he write it correctly, just as this book shows him, all absolutely[23] after the way it is in this first exemplar.

(*The Ormulum*, Dedication, lines 1-5, 11-14, 95-100)[24]

The *Ormulum* provides, arguably, a record of how an early author, one Orm, Orrm, or Ormin, thought about the problems of recording verse in English and how he developed a pedagogy for its transmission by scribes. A set of homilies

---

[22] For further discussion see W. SCASE, "John Gower's scribes and literatim copying", in: *John Gower in Manuscripts and Early Printed Books*, ed. M. DRIVER, D. PEARSALL, and R.F. YEAGER (Cambridge, 2020), pp. 13-31.

[23] For "absolutely" see *MED, thwert-out*, adv.

[24] *The Ormulum*, ed. R.M. WHITE and R. HOLT, 2 vols. (Oxford, 1878). (Lightly edited.)

Reprographics 293

on the gospel texts for the Mass, the *Ormulum* is written in metre that has been described as having "a perfectly strict syllable count" which is "unparalleled in Middle English".[25] The line, a septenary, divides into two halves, the first half containing eight syllables with a final stressed syllable and the second containing seven syllables where the penultimate syllable is stressed and the final syllable is unstressed.[26] The last word before the caesura must be a monosyllable, and a line cannot end with a bisyllabic word in which the first syllable is open (e.g., '*sune*', 'son'). In this metre, syllable count, quality, and accent are therefore key. Quantitative metres, as already mentioned, were familiar to anyone trained in basic *littera* pedagogy. That the regularity of Orm's metre is unparalleled in Middle English is not surprising: with so many variant spellings and scribal transmission, the language was hugely problematic as a medium for such a metre. Orm, I argue, drew on basic *littera* pedagogy when devising schemes for encoding his metre in writing and for teaching future scribes to transmit it accurately.[27]

The manuscript of the *Ormulum*, MS Oxford, Bod. Lib., Junius 1, copied by the author himself and perhaps completed by the 1180s, is one of the most outlandish examples of written English from the medieval period.[28] The manuscript may disorientate the modern reader because of its untidy appearance, its over-sized letters, its numerous corrections, and above all its relentlessly systematic and idiosyncratic spelling of English. In Burchfield's view, "[n]o other surviving medieval English manuscript with comparable subject matter [...] is written [...] with so little regard for its appearance".[29] But from the perspective

---

[25] E. SOLOPOVA, "The metre of the *Ormulum*", in: *Studies in English Language and Literature: "Doubt Wisely": Papers in Honour of E.G. Stanley*, ed. M.J. TOSWELL and E.J. TOSWELL (London, 1996), pp. 423-439, at p. 423.

[26] Solopova suggests that Orm's verse may be based on the Latin heptameter (SOLOPOVA, "The metre of the *Ormulum*", pp. 428-431).

[27] Tony Hunt summarises the tradition of grammar available in the twelfth century and examines the supplementary texts produced towards the end of the century, the most important being the *Doctrinale* by Alexander of Villa Dei (T. HUNT, *Teaching and Learning Latin in Thirteenth-Century England*, 3 vols. (Cambridge, 1991), 1, pp. 83-98). Completed *c.* 1199, however, this work was likely slightly too late to have influenced Orm.

[28] For the scribe and date of the manuscript see M.B. PARKES, "On the presumed date and possible origin of the manuscript of the *Orrmulum*: Oxford, Bod. Lib., MS Junius 1", in: *Five Hundred Years of Words and Sounds: A Festschrift for Eric Dobson*, ed. E.G. STANLEY and D. GRAY (Cambridge, 1983), pp. 115-127, at pp. 115, 120.

[29] R. BURCHFIELD, "The Language and Orthography of the *Ormulum* MS", *Transactions of the Philological Society* 55.1 (1956), pp. 56-87, at p. 57.

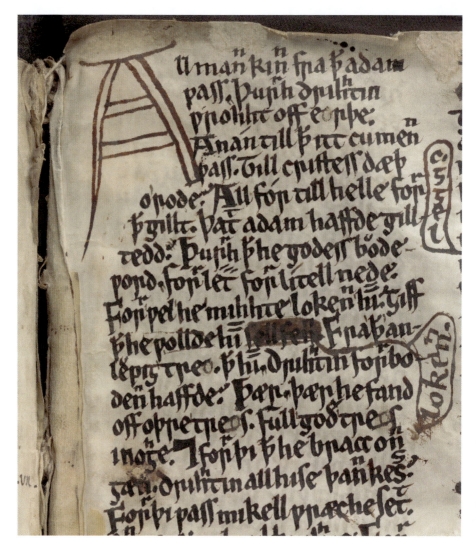

Fig. 23. Orthography and hand of the *Ormulum*, MS Oxford, Bod. Lib., Junius 1, f. 10ra (detail). Photo: © Bodleian Libraries, University of Oxford. Creative Commons licence CC-BY-NC 4.0.

Reprographics   295

of graphic practice, quite the opposite is arguably true: the manuscript displays an *extraordinary* regard for the appearance of English and intense attention in particular to features of orthography.

The first seventeen lines of column a on f. 10r provide examples of many of the features of Orm's manuscript (see Figure 23). As has often been remarked, in the *Ormulum*, every consonant that falls after a short vowel in a closed syllable is doubled. Sometimes the second consonant is stacked vertically on top of the first. Thus for example, "*mann*" and "*kinn*" ("mankind") in column a, line 1, have doubled final *n* stacked above the line of the text. This doubling policy extends to abbreviations. Where a word is abbreviated with a final macron, for example "*hi^m*" ("him") in column a, lines 10, 11, and 12, two macrons are used, one stacked above the other over the *i* like the modern equals sign. But doubling is only one among many graphic conventions used systematically in the manuscript. Liberal punctuation and diacritics are used. Each line of verse begins with a bold *littera notabilior* and the caesura between the first half of the line and the second is indicated with a punctus and a majuscule.[30] Accents are used, perhaps to indicate vowel quantity, for example "*Anán till*" ("until", col. a, line 4) and "*Fórr*" ("for", col. a, line 6).[31] A faint symbol that looks like a modern apostrophe indicates word division where it might be ambiguous in "*o'rode*" ("on the cross", col. a, line 6).[32] Orm appears to use all of the various allographs of *g* available to him for distinctive and systematic purposes.[33] Sometimes allographs are stacked one above the other. In column a, lines 8 and 9, Caroline *r* is placed above Insular long *r* in "*forr*". Perhaps this stacking is for reasons of space but it could relate to the process of ongoing revision evident from other features, such as the crossings out and marginal substitutions and the erasure of *o* after *e*, for example in "*tre<o>s*" ("trees", col. a, line 14) and "*e<o>rþe*" ("earth", col. a, line 3).[34] Perhaps more obvi-

---

[30] Cf. *The Orrmulum Project*, ed. N.-L. JOHANNSEN (Stockholm, 1993-2019), <http://www.orrmulum.net>, last accessed 2019, *Text Structure and Punctuation*, n.p.

[31] On the diacritics see J. ANDERSON and D. BRITTON, "The orthography and phonology of the *Ormulum*", *English Language and Linguistics* 3.2 (1999), pp. 299-334, at p. 308; and R.W. MURRAY, "Syllable cut prosody in early Middle English", *Language* 76.3 (2000), pp. 617-654, at pp. 645-648.

[32] However, some of these marks are possibly post-medieval; see BURCHFIELD, "The language and orthography of the *Ormulum* MS", p. 66; and J. ROBERTS, *Guide to Scripts Used in English Writings up to 1500* (London, 2005), p. 127.

[33] BURCHFIELD, "The Language and Orthography of the *Ormulum* MS", pp. 64-65.

[34] Angled brackets indicate erased material. For emendation in MS Junius 1 see C. CANNON,

296   *Chapter 5*

ously than many manuscripts, MS Junius 1 carries the traces of the scribal process of selecting from and deploying graphic resources, in this case to develop a systematic scribal practice for encoding English verse.

Modern analysis views Orm's output as a phonic representation of the spoken language of his locality of south Lincolnshire.[35] Because the work is an autograph and thought to be phonographic, it has been held to be a particularly valuable guide to the spoken English of the East Midlands. According to Milroy, the *Ormulum* is the "nearest we have" to "a Middle English text with a perfect 'fit' between the orthography and the phonology".[36] Anderson and Britton state that Orm's spelling was "designed to reflect" the phonology of "the late twelfth-century south Lincolnshire dialect".[37] Richard Hogg states that Orm, "employed a writing system of his own devising from which we can glean a considerable amount of information about his pronunciation", while Roberts states that "his spellings have much to tell us about the English of his time".[38] The *Ormulum* is also regarded as a textbook example of an early attempt to standardise written English.[39]

Orm's systematic approach to orthography and punctuation may be a boon to modern phonologists and to students of language standardisation, but viewed from the perspectives of himself and his community, his practice must have

---

"Spelling practice: The *Ormulum* and the word", *Forum for Modern Language Studies* 33.3 (1997), pp. 229-244, at pp. 240-241.

[35] Orm's manuscript has been located on linguistic and external grounds to south Lincolnshire (*LAEME*). The *Ormulum* was at first localised by 'fitting' (comparison with the spelling and form profiles of 'anchor texts', i.e. texts for whose provenance external evidence survives), and Parkes argued that Orm may have been a brother of the Arrouasian house in Bourne, south Lincolnshire (PARKES, "On the presumed date and possible origin of the manuscript of the *Orrmulum*"). Other scribal texts localised in Lincolnshire by *LAEME* are a brief set of verses in MS Cambridge, UL, Ff.6.15; a roll, MS London, BL Addit. 23986; a text of the *Euangelie* in MS London, Dulwich College 22; a song in MS London, Lincoln's Inn, Hale 135; some couplets in MS Oxford, Bod. Lib., Digby 55; *Dame Sirith* in MS Oxford, Bod. Lib., Digby 86; a lyric fragment in MS Oxford, Bod. Lib., Rawl. C. 510; and lyrics and other brief texts in MS Oxford, Merton College, 248. Two are of these are anchor texts. The others are localised to Lincolnshire on the basis of fitting.

[36] J. MILROY, "Middle English dialectology", in: *The Cambridge History of the English Language, Volume 2, 1066-1476*, ed. N. BLAKE (Cambridge, 1992), pp. 156-206, at p. 162.

[37] ANDERSON and BRITTON, "The orthography and phonology of the *Ormulum*", p. 299.

[38] R.M. HOGG, "Phonology and morphology", in: *The Cambridge History of the English Language: Volume 1: The Beginnings to 1066*, ed. R.M. HOGG (Cambridge, 1992), pp. 67-167, at p. 67; ROBERTS, *Guide to Scripts*, p. 127.

[39] For example, Cannon describes it as "an early type of the kind of reform" proposed in the sixteenth century (CANNON, "Spelling practice", p. 237).

Reprographics 297

looked rather different. For example, explaining the spelling of the word 'Adam', Orm engages with the basics of *littera* pedagogy. He describes the word in terms of the shapes and names of its letters first in Greek, "*An staff Allfa ʒehatenn*" ("a letter called alpha"; lines 16403, 16415), and then giving the letters and their names, "in *our* Latin language" (line 16435, my emphasis):

> *Þe firrste staff iss nemmnedd A*
> *Onn ure Latin spæche;*
> *Þatt oþerr staff iss nemmndd DE;*
> *Þe þridde iss A ʒehatenn;*
> *Þe ferþe staff iss nemmnedd EMM*
> *Onn ure Latin spæche,*
> *And ʒiff þatt tu cannst spelldren hemm.*
> *Adam þu findesst spelldredd*

The first letter [of the word 'Adam'] is called 'A' in our Latin language, the second is called 'de', the third is called 'A'; the fourth letter is called 'em' in our Latin language. And if you can put them together, you find the word 'Adam' spelt.

(*The Ormulum*, lines 16434-16441)

He then moves to the basic pedagogy of the syllable, observing that spelling the letters leads to reading the name *Adam*: if you can "spell" these letters, he teaches, you find the name of the father of all.[40] Orm's close attention to syllables, to both length and their quality, transfers to English some of the concerns of elementary Latin grammar pedagogy. He uses the language of *littera* pedagogy: the exercise of combining letters into syllables; '*syllabicare*' (*DMLBS*) was '*speldren*' in Middle English (*MED*). 'Spelling' involved the pronunciation of syllables, the basic units of sound from which words were composed.[41]

The passage discussed above illustrates how Orm's strict spelling system focuses attention on the syllable, both on recording vowel length and encoding syllable count and quality. No vowel is superfluous, even final -*e*. The precise linkage between his orthography and his metre remains to be elucidated, but the focus of both on the syllable is plain.[42] In particular, his use of doubled

---

[40] For "*spelldredd*", "voiced", cf. "[w]*iþþ tunge shollde spellen itt*", Dedication, line 311.

[41] Cf. N. ORME, *Medieval Children* (New Haven, 2001), pp. 249-251, 261-263.

[42] Murray (MURRAY, "Syllable cut prosody in early Middle English") pays some attention to metre but his main aim is to offer a new account of Orm's orthography and its implications for studying sound changes.

298 *Chapter 5*

consonants for indicating the length of the preceding vowel seems to adapt the principles of Latin metre where two consonants are a sign of a syllable with two beats. Arguably, Orm was attempting to devise a systematic spelling system to encode vowel length and syllable count and quality unambiguously, adapting basic *littera* concepts of syllable spelling to his English verse.

Just as Latin *littera* pedagogy taught that spellings were essential to the correct reading and transmission of verse, so Orm enjoins on future scribes a strict copying method and pedagogy. Orm states explicitly that this is the first exemplar of the work and anyone who copies it after him should copy it exactly, "[a]*ll þwerrt ut affterr þatt itt iss / Uppo þiss firrste bisne*" ("all absolutely after the way it is in this first exemplar"; Dedication, lines 99-100). Each future scribe should make sure that he includes all of the words and attends to the metre:

> *Wiþþ all swillc rime alls her iss sett,*
> *Wiþþ all se fele wordess;*
> *And tatt he loke wel þatt he*
> *An bocstaff write twiȝȝess,*
> *Eȝȝwhær þær itt uppo þiss boc*
> *Iss writenn o þatt wise.*
> *Loke he will þatt het write swa,*
> *Forr he ne maȝȝ nohht elless*
> *Onn Ennglissh writtenn rihht te word,*
> *Þatt wite he wel to soþe.*

[He must copy] with all such metre[43] as here is, with all the many words [all of the words in each line]; and may he look well that he writes a letter twice wherever it is written in that way in this book. May he look well that he writes it so for he may not otherwise write the word in English correctly; let him know that for a truth.

(*The Ormulum*, Dedication, lines 101-110)

Future scribes should copy all of the metre ("*rime*") and all of the words (i.e. in each verse line) carefully. They should attend in particular to the doubling of letters in certain places, and replicate this in their copy. Orm presents his exemplar as definitive: there is no other way "[o]*nn Ennglissh writtenn rihht te word*". "[*W*]*ritten rihht*" makes a verb from Latin '*orthographia*'. Orthography

---

[43] For the translation of 'rime' as 'metre' see *AND*, *rime*[1].

Reprographics 299

taught the correct use of letters to encode *potestates* graphically, drawing on examples from Latin literature. Etymologically meaning 'right, correct, proper' writing (*OED, ortho-; riht gewrit* in *Old English, ortografie* in Middle English), '*orthographia*' carried with it a sense that there were correct ways to spell, authorised by models valued by the community. Commenting on the etymology of '*orthographia*', Isidore explained that it meant "*recta scriptura*", from '*orto*' ('correct') and '*graphia*' ('writing').[44] Bede drew on classical orthographies and on Isidore for his own treatise *De Orthographia* and later Alcuin drew on Bede's work and other sources for his late eighth-century treatise on orthography.[45] Establishing a standard orthography for Latin "became a central concern" for Christian textual communities from the fourth to the eighth centuries; both of these works were guides to scribal practice.[46] From the later medieval period too there are treatises on orthography which provide guides for writers in the school books. For example, the Latin orthographic treatise in MS London, BL, Harley 1002, ff. 31r-81r, provides an account of each letter in alphabetical order. Each section gives an account of how a letter may be used and where it should not be used in writing. For example, under *z* is discussed the alternative spellings "*zmirna*" and "*smirna*" (f. 80v), using authorities as models.[47] The explicit norms for scribal copying in Orm's community are those associated with the study and copying of Latin texts and there is clear evidence that Orm is applying those basic pedagogic principles to the copying of English verse.[48]

[44] Isidore of Seville, *Etymologiae: Isidori Hispalensis Episcopi,* Etymologiarum *sive* Originum, ed. W.M. LINDSAY, 2 vols. (Oxford, 1911), 1, Book 1, ch. 27, section 1; cf. M. IRVINE, *The Making of Textual Culture:* 'Grammatica' *and Literary Theory, 350-1100* (Cambridge, 1994), p. 224.

[45] Bede, *De Orthographia*, in: *Bedae venerabilis Opera, Part VI, Opera didascalica*, ed. C.W. JONES, 3 vols. (Turnhout, 1975: *Corpus Christianorum, Series Latina* 123), 1, pp. 1-57; Alcuin, *Alcuini* Orthographia, ed. A. MARSILI (Pisa, 1952). On these relationships see Isidore of Seville, *The* Etymologies *of Isidore of Seville*, trans. S. BARNEY, W. LEWIS, J. BEACH, and O. BERGHOF (Cambridge, 2006), p. 24; and IRVINE, *The Making of Textual Culture*, pp. 74, 288, 327.

[46] IRVINE, *The Making of Textual Culture*, p. 74.

[47] Unfortunately this category of pedagogic literature has not been mapped in any detail; Vivien Law notes that many pre-Conquest grammatical texts are unedited and unstudied (V. LAW, *Grammar and Grammarians in the Early Middle Ages* (London, 1997), p. 113). The position seems to be rather worse, even, for the orthographic treatises from Britain in the later medieval period.

[48] These principles meant that "[c]opying Latin demand[ed] that in all essentials the spelling of the copy-text be replicated" (*LALME*, General Introduction, Appendix I: 1.3).

300   *Chapter 5*

The *Ormulum* demonstrates that the application of *littera* pedagogy to the practice of copying English may contribute to the formation of identity among communities of scribal practice. In his dedication, Orm tells us quite a lot about who he is, the community in which he lives, and why he has carried out his work. Orm is a brother in a house of Augustinian Canons (Dedication, lines 7-10). He has copied and authored (*"wrat and wrohhte"*, Dedication, line 333) a version of the gospels in English so that lay people can hear the gospels and follow them in "thought, word, and deed" – a phrase that recurs several times in his dedication (Dedication, lines 22, 94, 120, 125-140, 309-312). He has carried out this work on the instruction of Brother Walter, who is both his natural sibling and a brother in the same religious house (Dedication, lines 1-5, 11-14). He is making a first exemplar for future scribes to copy. And just as the lay audience that hear the text are to follow it in thought, word, and deed, so future scribes are to follow it precisely too with close attention to its graphic forms.

Given that Orm has been commissioned to produce the exemplar and that it has a purpose envisaged by Brother Walter, as part of the discharge of pastoral responsibilities by the religious house of which they are members, it appears that his literate practice, output, and strategy derive from his participation in the shared enterprise of his community.[49] Orm's instructions for the copying process and his standards for scribal output are made meaningful in relation to *his community's* shared enterprise, their rule, and their shared graphic resources. Orm's imagined community of practice is textually mediated: it is not clear that Orm knows precisely who the later scribes that he envisages might be. He develops elementary literacy pedagogy to suit these circumstances: he includes instruction to scribes in the body of his text, rather than (or perhaps as well as) relying on face-to-face instruction. And the framework in which he makes sense of his practice also extends far beyond the parameters of his immediate religious community. A "brother" of Orm's can be natural, a member of his order, or anyone else who has been baptised. Those who strive to reproduce the gospel as closely as possible can be himself, those future scribes who will copy his exemplar, and all of those who hear his text and follow holy lore. All are engaged in learning, reproducing, and transmitting by example / exem-

---

[49] The concept of "identity as mission", developed by Paul Gilbert in his study of contemporary identity politics, suits rather well Orm's circumstances: "a group may find itself having to ask itself what it is doing and find its shared identity in specifying a common purpose [... t]his is what I shall call identity as mission" (P. GILBERT, *Cultural Identity and Political Ethics* (Edinburgh, 2010), p. 87, and cf. p. 89 on religious missions).

Reprographics 301

plar. Orm creates a scribal practice that involves close attention to the graphic substance of the text, and associates it with the tenets of his community that the gospel should be followed closely in thought, word, and deed.

The South English Legendary

There is no evidence that anyone ever made a copy of Orm's exemplar. For an example of a kind of exact, *littera*-based copying method in practice we will turn to selected manuscripts of the *South English Legendary*, a lengthy compilation of saints' lives and other religious material written in rhyming couplets. Several early fourteenth-century manuscripts of this text have been recognised as closely similar by Manfred Görlach.[50] MS London, BL, Egerton 2891 and MS Cambridge, Corpus Christi College 145 are particularly closely related. For example, comparison of the *South English Legendary Life of St. Agnes* in MS Egerton 2891 and MS Corpus Christi College 145 (both first quarter of the fourteenth century) shows that textually these two witnesses are remarkably close and that the similarities between the manuscripts extend to layout, paratext, and decoration. Pages share the same number of lines (forty to a page), the same first and last lines, the same rubrication, running heads, decoration, some paraphs, placing of the caesura, and very similar letter-forms. Word division, abbreviations, letter-forms, and spellings are mostly identical. When MS Egerton 2891 omits a line on f. 4v, inserting it in the margin, the defective page has only thirty-nine lines; the first and last lines on the page are the same as in MS Corpus Christi College 145, so the scribe must have been copying by page. Probably the Egerton scribe was copying line by line. This is suggested by the occasional omission of whole lines as in this example. We have no reason to believe that either manuscript is an exemplar for the other, therefore it is likely that both scribes are copying in a fashion that exactly reproduces their exemplar. Fragments of two other *South English Legendary* manuscripts, the bifolium MS Wigston, Record Office for Leicestershire, Leicester, and Rutland, 18 D 59 (formerly located at Leicester City Museum) and the fragmentary leaf MS Nottingham, UL, Wollaton WLC/LM 38, may belong to this group. Görlach

---

[50] M. GÖRLACH, *The Textual Tradition of the* South English Legendary (Leeds, 1974: *Leeds Texts and Monographs* 6).

302   *Chapter 5*

describes the scribes of these four manuscripts as "meticulous, if mechanical, copyists".[51]

A particular and perhaps surprising focus for the scribes' attention is rhyme words. This relates to an important mode of encoding metre in these manuscripts that I shall call 'graphic rhyme'. Graphic rhymes always work for the eye and usually for the ear also. Graphic rhyme requires the scribe to identify rhyming syllables and to match the spelling of those syllables. Graphic rhyme is distinct from the phenomenon sometimes called eye-rhyme, visual rhyme, or sight rhyme, since the latter terms denote rhymes that work for the eye but not for the ear. To my knowledge, the only previous discussion of what I am calling graphic rhyme is in an essay by Burnley on motivations for standardisation in English. Burnley detects a habit among certain scribes of some early manuscripts of the *Canterbury Tales*, of "matching spellings" of rhyme words, displaying "a tendency to emphasise the correspondence between phonic and written modes of language", calling this "eye-rhyme".[52] As we shall see, graphic rhyme catches the eye when it travels down the end words of rhyming couplet lines or is drawn by brackets to the grouping of rhyming couplets.[53]

In MS Corpus Christi College 145 the majority of rhyme is graphic. Of the twenty rhymes on f. 4r, a page from the life of St. Wulstan, nearly all corre-

---

[51] GÖRLACH, *The Textual Tradition of the* South English Legendary, p. 93. In Görlach's view all four manuscripts could have been copied in the same "scriptorium" (pp. 78, 92, 113 (quotation), 117). There are similarities between the hands but also subtle differences. Round *w* is formed differently in MS Egerton 2891 and MS CCCC 145; *h* sometimes has a forked ascender in Egerton; *y* in Egerton has short descender that curls to right; MS CCCC 145 has a more sweeping leftward travelling descender on *y*. The Wollaton scribe sometimes has a forked ascender on *h* and encloses *w* in a circle. The scribe of MS 18 D 59 has a distinctive form and position of minuscule *r* (v-shaped and sitting on the line) and the form of minuscule *y* is also distinctive (contrast the dotted *y* with the distinctively straight, angled descender in MS CCCC 145). The Wollaton scribes's *r* and *y* are different again: *r* descends prominently below the line and *y* bears a curly descender.

[52] J.D. BURNLEY, "Sources of standardisation in later Middle English", in: *Standardizing English: Essays in the History of Language Change*, ed. J.B. TRAHERN (Knoxville, 1989), pp. 23-41, at pp. 29-30. For Burnley, this practice is particularly marked in the work of the scribe of the Ellesmere and Hengwrt manuscripts of the *Canterbury Tales*, and it is a sign that the scribe "might have been sympathetic to the development of a standardised writing system" (p. 30).

[53] Rhiannon Purdie describes a comparable phenomenon in the specific stanza layouts found in manuscripts of tail-rhyme romance, where couplets are entered on the left and tail-rhyme lines on the right, calling this kind of layout "graphic tail-rhyme" (R. PURDIE, *Anglicising Romance: Tail-Rhyme and Genre in Medieval English Literature* (Cambridge, 2008), pp. 66-85). But 'graphic rhyme' in the sense in which I am using the term involves both orthographic matching and layout.

Reprographics 303

spond graphically.[54] Graphic correspondence extends to abbreviations, for example, "*ky^ng*" ("king") rhymes with "*ry^ng*" ("ring"). There are signs of correction to improve the graphic rhyme; "*fyue*" ("five") has been corrected to "*fiue*" to rhyme graphically with "*liue*" ("live") with the addition of a jot over the first stroke of *y*, and a jot above the *y* in "*felonye*" ("felony") appears to mark a correction to rhyme graphically with "*normandie*" ("Normandy"). These corrections make no difference to the *sounds* of the words, confirming that it is visual rhyming that is important: the scribe is focusing on the *figurae*.[55] In MS Egerton 2891, the practice is broadly consistently in favour of graphically matched rhymes. All of the first ten rhymes on f. 152v match graphically except for "*þ^ere*" / "*nere*" ("there" / "were not") and all of the first ten on f. 153r are graphically equivalent. There is not much sign of *correction* to make the rhyme words match orthographically, suggesting perhaps that the exemplar had been prepared already and the scribe's responsibility was to copy it exactly. The rhyming words in MS Egerton 2891 do not *always* look alike. For example, in the life of St. Agnes, while "*þreu*" ("threw") rhymes with "*Ikneu*" ("knew") and "*side*" with "*abide*" ("side" / "abide"); unalike spellings of rhyme words include "*place*" / "*g^ace*" ("place" / "grace", with an abbreviation making a visual difference), and "*lye*" / "*deie*" ("fire" / "die") (f. 1r). In the *Life of St. Agatha*, several folios further in to the volume, we find that unmatched spellings continue, for example, "*lysse*" / "*misse*" ("relieve" / "miss"), "*st^ange*" / "*anonge*" ("strange" / "anon"), and "*stonde*" / "*wounde*" ("instant" / "wounds", f. 13r). In the *Life of St. Laurence*, much further in, we find "tresour" / "*emp^eror*" ("treasure" / "emperor", ff. 129v, 130r) and "*seide*" / "*wende*" ("said" / "wend", 133r). Attention to graphic rhyme in the 18 D 59 fragment is punctilious. On the opening page of the fragment the rhyme "come" / "*nome*" is enhanced with graphic matching twice ("came" / "took", f. 1r; the lines are repeated in error). Above and on the verso of this leaf, the

---

[54] Exceptions are "*lere*" / "*þ^ere*" ("unoccupied" / "there"), "*arere*" / "*aferde*" ("raise" / "frightened"), and possibly "*stonde*" / "*g^ende*" ("hour" / "ground"); however, it could be that the scribe is looking to match, not the spelling of the rhyme *syllable*, but the spelling of the last few letters of each word. If this is the case, it may be that attention to syllables in his case had degenerated into rather minimal application of the exact copying rule.

[55] Graphic rhyme supplements other forms of text mark-up as a guide to metre. In both MS London, BL, Egerton 2891 and MS CCCC 145 the metre is encoded visually with lineation and mid-line pointing, and in the Corpus manuscript the tipping of the first letter of each half line in red. Each line begins with a *littera notabilior*. These devices cue the reader as to how to scan the couplet on the journey to the closing rhyme. If they were marked likewise in the exemplar, these prosodic units might have helped the scribe too, if copying was by metrically meaningful unit.

304 Chapter 5

same words are rhymed *"com"* / *"nom"*. Some deviations do occur, for example on f. 2r: *"ney"* / *"ysay"*; *"wy^{n}ne"* / *"su^{n}ne"*; and *"londe"* / *"vndersto^{n}de"* ("nay" / "saw", "joy" / "sin", "land" / "understand"). In the latter case the abbreviation is inserted to reduce the length of the line; other examples are *"þinge"* / *"bri^{n}ge"* ("thing" / "bring", f. 2v) and *"wende"* / *"he^{n}de"* ("go" / "courteous"); below, where the lines are shorter, this rhyme pair is written in full. But the general punctiliousness of the letter for letter practice here is underlined by the repeated lines (f. 1r) where every feature is identical.

Arguably, the variety of copying practice used in these *South English Legendary* manuscripts was designed to facilitate fast production. Page-by-page, line-by-line, word-by-word replication would have allowed for easy checking against an exemplar (it would be easy to find corresponding passages). The Wollaton *South English Legendary* scribe adds another helpful strategy: he positions the first letter of each line at a distance from the body of the line. The positioning of the first letter of the line before a space in Wollaton might have supported its use as a finding aid to help match up text and exemplar. Indeed, it is possible that all of the letters in line-initial position were written first, very carefully, before the rest of the text was copied, so that omission of lines owing to eye-skip or repetition of lines was avoided.[56] Possibly he used this strategy as an alternative to maintaining a strict forty-line page layout.[57] This kind of layout with a wide space between the initial and second letters of lines is even found in later *South English Legendary* manuscripts such as MS Oxford, Bod. Lib., Addit. C. 220, where a narrow vertical column has been ruled to the left of the writing space and the initial letter of each line is placed before it, the second letter after it.[58] The use of graphic rhyme would also have provided a

---

[56] Jacob Thaisen has proposed on the basis of a statistical analysis of letters in line-initial position in ten Middle English verse manuscripts that the first letters of lines were copied literatim to aid a scribe's finding his place in the exemplar (J. THAISEN, "Initial position in the Middle English verse line", *English Studies* 95.5 (2014), pp. 1-14).

[57] The Wollaton manuscript is half a folio on which only the top twenty-one lines remain (from the *Life of St. Bridget*). Judging by the text that is missing between the last extant line on the recto and the first on the verso, it appears that the pages may originally have borne only thirty-four lines, fewer than the standard forty in MS BL, Egerton 2891, MS CCCC 145 and MS Wigston, Record Office for Leicestershire, Leicester, and Rutland, 18 D 59.

[58] Wide spacing of the first letter of verse lines is also found in many other manuscripts, for example, in the Auchinleck manuscript (MS Edinburgh, National Library of Scotland, Advocates' 19.2.1). For early, continental examples of verse with this layout see M.B. PARKES, *Pause and Effect: An Introduction to the History of Punctuation in the West* (Aldershot, 1992), pp. 232-233 and 294-295. I am grateful to Marco Mostert for drawing my attention to the examples in Parkes.

Reprographics 305

means of checking that no line was missing. Page-by-page copying would also have sped up work by relieving the scribe from calculating how many pages to rule, enabling him to concentrate on copying while leaving planning to others.

We might say that these *South English Legendary* scribes constitute a kind of community of practice. Their close attention to graphic production manifested itself in fairly uniform, distinctive products. They share with Orm an investment in faithful reproduction of their model and attention to the spellings of syllables, notably, in their case, to rhymed syllables, applying *littera* teaching on the syllable and metrics to rhyme. But their practice – their ways of expressing respect for their model – is associated with the development of strategies for promoting efficient, speedy, and accurate text production. We may infer that they were engaged in a shared enterprise of specialised, speedy, accurate reproduction of vernacular verse texts in rhyming couplets. Their work has a graphic identity and perhaps they too had identities as specialists in this particular graphic craft. But their outputs and practices are not completely alike: variations among them may have indexed different identities within the scribal community of practice engaged in the enterprise of transmitting vernacular rhymed didactic verse.

This analysis of some manuscripts of the *South English Legendary* taken with that of the *Ormulum* manuscript suggests that what has been categorised as literatim copying is not a uniform category. Where Orm enjoined scribes to attend to all of the words, and all of the metre, as well as to spellings, the *South English Legendary* scribes focused on matching rhyme words exactly, allowing the metrical shape of the rest of the line to vary. They also focused on the layout of the text on each page: on the number of lines, and in at least one case on the placing of the first letters of lines. Their application of the *littera* framework for orthography and metre permitted them to speed up copying. The close relationships between MS Egerton 2891, MS Corpus Christi College 145, and the Wollaton and Wigston fragments suggest, too, that these scribes must have had an understanding that this practice was shared: it was 'what we do'. It suggests that different communities' implementations of the basic *littera* pedagogy of verse may have marked identity among communities of Anglophone scribal practice.

306   *Chapter 5*

The Prick of Conscience

Our next case study concerns a text whose manuscripts are often cited as examples of translation copying: the *Prick of Conscience*. We have already seen that the term 'translation' may not correspond to what these scribes were actually doing as part of their reprographic process, or thought they were doing. This section will explore this possibility further by analysing the reprographic processes of examples of the *Prick of Conscience* scribes as distinctive implementations of the pedagogy of *littera*.

A lengthy didactic text in octosyllabic couplets thought to have originated in northern England perhaps in the mid fourteenth century and surviving in numerous copies, the *Prick of Conscience* has long been seen as a prime example of so-called translation copying.[59] Indeed this text provided the case study of translation copying used by Lewis and McIntosh as a foundation for their development of the *LALME* typology of scribal practice and their dialect mapping methodology. They were interested in the percentage of *Prick of Conscience* scribes whose output is of "sufficient dialect consistency for us to be able to say that it convincingly reflects the written-language conventions of some particular place or area" and about sixty-four (seventy-six percent) of the texts can be mapped.[60] Lewis and McIntosh therefore see some three-quarters of *Prick of Conscience* manuscripts as typifying local written language conventions and encoding the sounds and forms of local English.

Alternatively, I suggest here, we might approach the 'translated' texts of the *Prick of Conscience* as the products of a production process that shares the aims of speed and accuracy and the respect for the model exhibited by the *South English Legendary* scribes' process but achieves them differently and more efficiently. Arguably, the *Prick of Conscience* scribes whose language qualifies for 'mapping' as a local variety of written language together constitute a community of practice with its own shared enterprise and rules and its own resources. Evidence for this alternative view is provided by the treatment of rhyme. Lewis and McIntosh explain that scribes sometimes suspended translation into their own dialect "where the alteration of forms [...] would spoil

---

[59]   For the date and origins see *Prick of Conscience*: *Richard Morris's* Prick of Conscience: *A Corrected and Amplified Reading Text*, ed. R. HANNA and S. WOOD (Oxford, 2013: *EETS*, o.s. 342), p. XXXVI.

[60]   R.E. LEWIS and A. MCINTOSH, *A Descriptive Guide to the Manuscripts of the* Prick of Conscience (Oxford, 1982), quotation at p. 18.

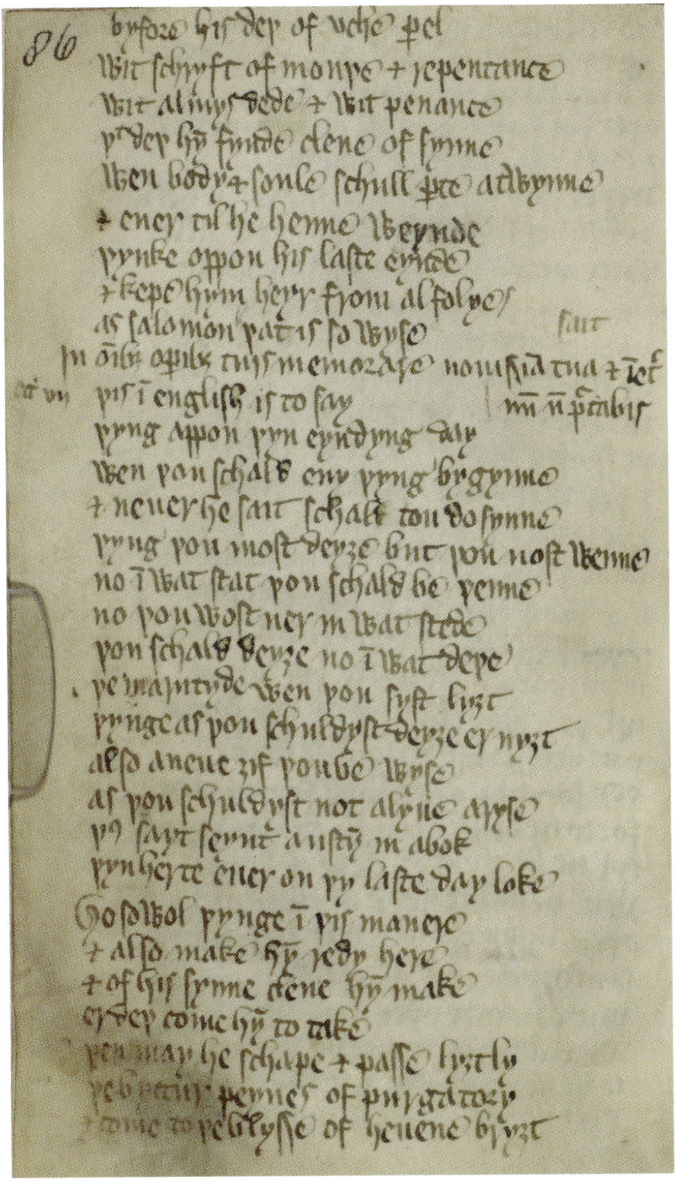

Fig. 24. Graphic rhyme in the *Prick of Conscience*, MS Leeds, UL, Brotherton 500, f. 43v. Reproduced with the permission of Special Collections, Leeds University Library.

308   *Chapter 5*

rhymes or alliteration".[61] In such environments scribal translation is constrained. However, here the practice of the *Prick of Conscience* scribes is like that of the *South English Legendary* scribes discussed above: they follow the convention of *graphic rhyme*. Below I shall present evidence for this argument. After providing evidence for graphic rhyme, I shall consider the implications for interpretation of 'translation' in non-rhyme positions. I shall argue that in these positions so-called translating scribes use learned sets of spellings as a novel means of speeding up copying. 'Translating' scribes negotiate between two graphic models: the model of the exemplar, especially when they replicate the spellings of rhyme syllables exactly, and the model forms and spellings they have learned.

There is clear evidence for graphic rhyme in the *Prick of Conscience* in MS Leeds, UL, Brotherton 500.[62] On f. 17r, the scribe at first wrote "*brode*" ("broad") in rhyme position, later correcting the spelling to northern "*brade*". The scribe's habitual spelling is "*brode*", but he corrects it for the rhyme. This could be seen as scribal constraint with the aim of preserving the rhyme with "*made*". But graphic rhyme *where no sound difference is at stake* seems to drive a strange correction on f. 43v (see Figure 24). Here a word that was perhaps spelled '*wende*' ('wend', the original middle letters are not visible) has been corrected to "*weynde*", a spelling that is distinctly odd but is explained by the need to match "*eynde*" ("end"), also an unusual spelling, below. Here the Brotherton scribe is obviously intent on making rhymes *look* the same, even when no sound difference is at stake. Indeed, that the graphic (the *figura*) takes priority over the phonic (the *potestas*) is suggested by the fact that many of his rhymes are a stretch to make work when reading aloud, for example "*folye*" and "*wyse*" ("folly" / "wise", f. 43v).[63] He clearly tries to match spellings as far as he can. He usually (but not always) checks that rhyming syllables correspond letter for letter, *even when no difference would be made to the sounds of the words*. For example, "*fal*" ("fall") rhymes with "*smal*" ("small"), but "*fall[e][cropped]*" rhymes with "*alle*" ("all", f. 15r). Again, "*settyt*" rhymes with "*lettyt*" ("set" / "let"), while "*callit*" rhymes with "*fallit*" ("call" / "fall",

[61] LEWIS and MCINTOSH, *A Descriptive Guide to the Manuscripts of the* Prick of Conscience, p. 17, n. 44.

[62] Folio references are to the pencil numbers at the bottom of recto pages.

[63] Rhyme of course is a matter of conventions of acceptability; for tolerance of half and imperfect rhymes in Middle English romance see J. JEFFERSON, D. MINKOVA, and A. PUTTER, "Perfect and imperfect rhyme: Romances in the *abab* tradition", *Studies in Philology* 111.4 (2014), pp. 631-651.

Reprographics 309

f. 17v). Similarly, "*knawe*" rhymes with "*gnawe*" ("known" / "gnaw", f. 16v) while "*knowe*" rhymes with "*lowe*" ("know" / "low", 18r). The scribe is not always consistent, for example, also on f. 17v "*fallyt*" rhymes with "*callit*". However, in general it seems clear that in rhyme position the scribe is focused on matching the *figurae* of rhyme syllables exactly.

There are a few examples of scribes who have been attributed with more than one copy of the *Prick of Conscience*. This gives us an opportunity to investigate what practices are common across their outputs. MS Manchester, John Rylands Library, Eng. 50 and MS London, BL, Harley 1205 are attributed to the same hand, located near Lichfield and dated later fourteenth century (*LALME*, LP 519).[64] The transition from Book 3 to Book 4, MS Harley 1205, f. 14v and MS Manchester, John Rylands Library, Eng. 50, page 72, provides a pair of parallel pages for comparison. In both, graphic rhyme is achieved consistently through use of the same spellings for rhyming syllables (though there are lapses). The spellings of rhyme words vary between the scribe's two manuscripts, but within each manuscript the scribe is careful to copy the spelling of the first rhyme word letter for letter when he writes the second rhyme word. For example, "*spedde*" ("finished") rhymes with "*redde*" ("read") in MS Harley, while "*sped*" rhymes with "*red*" in MS Eng. 50; likewise "*reden*" ("read") pairs with "*dreden*" ("dread") in Harley and "*rede*" with "*drede*" in MS Eng. 50. In MS Harley 1205, the scribe's rate of achieving graphic rhyme is high. For example, of the thirteen rhymes on f. 37v, only one does not rhyme graphically ("*þon*" / "*bygan*", "then" / "began"). Of the fourteen rhymes on f. 40v, three are not graphic ("*myȝt*" / "*siȝt*", "*reede*" / "*dede*", "*man^{er}e*" / "*sere*").[65] In MS Harley 1205, corrections improve the orthographic correspondence of rhymes; for example the penultimate vowels in "*hande*" ("hand") and "*lyuyande*" ("living") are both corrections (it is not clear what the original vowels were, f. 31r; cf. "*lyuyng*", f. 28v and "*honde*", f. 29r). In MS Eng. 50, rhyme is also enhanced visually by the use of a curly punctuation mark at the end of the first line of each couplet which indicates that the rhyme unit continues on the second line. On some pages of Harley 1205, red brackets visually indicate the rhyme units (presumably entered by the rubricator of the paraph in the running heading; these items may not be in the hand of the original scribe). Not all scribes attend

---

[64] For the attribution to the same hand see LEWIS and MCINTOSH, *A Descriptive Guide to the Manuscripts of the* Prick of Conscience, pp. 63, 87.

[65] "Might" / "sight", "read" / "deed", "manner" / "various". However it is possible that the scribe only aims to match the final two letters, in which case all of these would be graphic rhymes.

310   *Chapter 5*

to close matching of rhyme spellings. A late fourteenth-/ early fifteenth-century
northern copy of the *Prick of Conscience*, MS London, BL, Harley 4196, ff.
215v-258v, does not seem so scrupulous about graphic rhyme. For example,
rhymes include "*will*" / "*skyll*", "*thing*" / "*endyng*", and "*wytt*" / "*yhit*" ("will"
/ "reason", "thing" / "ending", "wit" / "yet", f. 215v). This copy does however
include brackets, apparently added later, perhaps to mitigate the deficiencies in
graphic rhyme. MS Oxford, Bod. Lib., Bodley 423, a *Prick of Conscience* dated
first half of the fifteenth century by Lewis and McIntosh, is on occasion somewhat variable: of nineteen rhymes on f. 271r, three are not graphic, "*lyght*" /
"*bright*", "*is*" / "*lesse*", "*Inne*" / "*syn*"; but on f. 272r only one of nineteen is
not graphic: "*þus*" / "*is*".[66]

These examples of *Prick of Conscience* manuscripts are evidence that so-
called translating scribes were perhaps instructed to copy rhyming syllables to
match visually rather than to copy the exemplar exactly only when the *sounds*
of rhymes were likely to be spoiled. Accurate copy is that in which rhyme
syllables have matching spellings. Rhyme syllables must be copied letter for
letter even when variations of spelling would make no difference to how the
words *sounded* when read aloud. In following this rule of strict reproduction of
the graphic model of the first rhyme word of a pair they shared practice with
the *South English Legendary* scribes discussed earlier. Where they part company with the *South English Legendary* scribes is in their practice with respect
to copying words in non-rhyme position. The term 'translation' is rather misleading if one deduces that every copyist of a translated text is involved in
word-by-word translation, that is, changing the spelling of his exemplar into his
own dialect spelling. An alternative scenario is that the 'translated' spellings
are in fact habitual, learned, spellings, producing writing in the way that many
of the writers of copy-texts did (as discussed in previous chapters), that is,
working from memory. That their spellings are habitual is shown by the fact
that scribes sometimes produce them in rhyme position and then have to correct them. When copying rhyming syllables, so-called translating scribes defer
to the model of the exemplar or the spelling of the first rhyme word of a pair,
whereas when copying the rest of the line scribes reproduce model or copy-text
spellings.

A practice of alternating between copy-text spelling and letter for letter
copying of rhyming syllables would have sped up copying of verse. Orm re-

---

[66] "Light" / "bright", "is" / "less", "in" / "sin", "thus" / "is". For the date see LEWIS and
MCINTOSH, *A Descriptive Guide to the Manuscripts of the* Prick of Conscience, p. 141.

Reprographics 311

quires that scribes attend closely to his fixed, invariant spellings for syllables but he does not propose that scribes learn those spellings. Not having a set of habitual spellings would have slowed progress. A scribe with a learned set of spellings could have retained more material for transfer, since he only needed to remember words, not spellings (the difference in time taken may have been similar to that experienced today between transcribing a Middle English quotation and transcribing a modern one). Using a learned repertoire of spellings would have cut down on the time spent consulting the exemplar. It would have been quicker to copy several words at a time using a habitual spelling system and then to go back and check for errors than to copy letter for letter. Telling evidence for this argument is provided by scribal corrections. Several scholars have noted that translating scribes do not 'translate' material when they correct their text.[67] Wakelin explains that scribes suspend the process of translation when they correct because correction "interrupts any reliance on internal dictation with a more visual scrutiny of the exemplar or copy".[68]

As mentioned earlier, Lewis and McIntosh explain the 'translated' manuscripts of the *Prick of Conscience* as copies that, in their view, were made to reflect the sounds of local speech in order to facilitate reading aloud to local audiences:

> [T]he nature and purpose of the poem [*Prick of Conscience*] is such that copies of it must often have been made by local scribes (e.g., by parish priests) for edificatory use in their own district. We may presume that a copy was often thus produced in a form which, when read aloud, was immediately familiar to its hearers in the sense that it reflected quite closely, e.g., in its vocabulary and morphology and in the sound-system which it symbolised the speech of the place where it was produced.[69]

The framework of *littera* teaching offers a rather different perspective: reading verse aloud correctly was certainly facilitated by careful attention to spelling,

---

[67] See citations in WAKELIN, *Scribal Correction and Literary Craft*, p. 164, n. 28.

[68] WAKELIN, *Scribal Correction and Literary Craft*, p. 165.

[69] LEWIS and McINTOSH, *A Descriptive Guide to the Manuscripts of the* Prick of Conscience, p. 17. In their view, translating scribes "purify" their texts; others "were either not competent to achieve this or were not interested in doing so" (p. 24). This suggests that Lewis and McIntosh view translation as an active process of replacing non-local forms and spellings in the exemplar with those of their locality rather than, as I am proposing, as a by-product of the reprographic process.

312   *Chapter 5*

but spelling unlocked metre not regional pronunciations.[70] In addition, if scribes were working with habitual spellings as I have proposed, those spellings may have been associated with a specialist community of practice whose relationships with local communities were more complex and dynamic than Lewis and McIntosh imply. As we have seen, scribes may have adopted the practice of combining model spellings with letter for letter copying primarily for reasons of speed and economy and their practice may have become associated with their identity. It is not safe to infer that when scribes share language this simply arises from their working in the same local area: the scribes are, I suggest, developing a sense of 'what we do' rather than simply all using a written language that is already available in their area and still less creating a written language from phonic first principles with every copy.[71]

---

[70] There are also difficulties with the argument that 'translated' texts would have facilitated reading aloud to local audiences and that this motive lies behind their production. First, pronunciation of words read aloud could and would have varied regionally whatever the spelling system used, as the reading aloud of standard spellings in varied accents attests today. Second, while familiarity with a spelling system might have sped up reading comprehension, unfamiliar or mixed systems clearly did not cause a problem, to judge from the survival of many such texts. Many of the *Prick of Conscience* manuscripts (around twenty) are "dialectally mixed" (LEWIS and MCINTOSH, *A Descriptive Guide to the Manuscripts of the* Prick of Conscience, p. 21). For example, Lewis and McIntosh state that MS Oxford, Bod. Lib., Digby 99, from the end of the fourteenth century, is written in one hand but in "at least three kinds of language" (p. 98). Likewise MS Oxford, Bod. Lib., Douce 157, in one hand from the end of the century, combines language of SW Lincs and SW Essex (p. 102). Presumably the fact that several languages were combined in these manuscripts did not trouble patrons unduly or interfere unacceptably with reading aloud.

[71] My view contrasts with that of Michael Johnston who interprets the sharing of dialect features among collaborating *Prick of Conscience* scribes as a sign that they lived locally to one another (M. JOHNSTON, "Copying and reading the *Prick of Conscience*", *Speculum* 95.3 (2020), pp. 742-801); I suggest that the shared features develop *because* they work together and share a distinctive reprographic practice that they associate with identity. It is worth remembering that many scribes in given local areas *do not* use forms and spellings associated with the region; such scribes are often dealt with perfunctorily or not at all in *LALME*; they are numbered 0 in the list of Linguistic Profiles where their language is often described as "colourless". The *Middle English Local Documents* (*MELD*) project led by Merja Stenroos (on which see M. STENROOS and K.V. THENGS, "Two Staffordshires: Real and linguistic space in the study of late Middle English dialects", in: *Studies in Variation, Contacts and Change in English, Volume 10, Outposts of Historical Corpus Linguistics: From the Helsinki Corpus to a Proliferation of Resources*, ed. J. TYRKKÖ, M. KILPIÖ, T. NEVALAINEN, and M. RISSANEN (Helsinki, 2012: *Research Unit for Variation, Contacts and Change in English (VARIENG)*), <https://varieng.helsinki.fi/series/volumes/10/stenroos_thengs/>) gives a valuable alternative approach. The makers of this corpus expect it to enable study of "the range of forms actually used in a particular area" (section 2, n.p.). The proposition that collaborating scribes develop shared spelling practices and the processes by which this occurs could be investigated further with the creation and use of large transcription corpora of collabora-

Reprographics 313

From the Ormulum *to Gower's* Confessio Amantis

Yet further applications of *littera* pedagogy to English-language verse are detectable among certain scribes of the major Middle English poets. I have dealt with the so-called literatim scribes of John Gower's *Confessio Amantis* elsewhere and will therefore simply summarise that work here, focusing on how it relates to the broader argument that I am proposing in the present chapter.[72] Gower's short verse lines have been shown to be exceptionally strict in terms of syllable count and metre: his lines all contain eight syllables and almost all of them are strictly iambic. The exceptional metrical regularity of Gower's ocosyllabic lines had not been matched in English since Orm's septenaries. The lengthy didactic poems discussed earlier in this section are in flexible accentual stress, observing end-rhyme but not regular metre or syllable counts. For example, the rhyming practice in the *Prick of Conscience* is not particularly impressive: it is repetitive and sometimes only the last syllable rhymes. The *Prick of Conscience* narrator himself says that he does not care if his rhymes (perhaps meaning his metre, not just the end rhymes) are "rude" provided that his *matter* is free of error.[73] The *South English Legendary* has been seen as similar. Görlach says the metre of the original texts must have been "rather irregular": "[t]here is much variation between the 'regular' line of fourteen syllables and seven stresses and all kinds of deviation [...] the original texts were probably never intended to conform with a strict metrical pattern,

---

tive products. For example, the two copies of the *Prick of Conscience* in MS Oxford, Bod. Lib., Eng. poet.a.1 (the Vernon manuscript) and MS London, BL, Addit. 22283 (the Simeon manuscript) are by the same scribe (the main Vernon hand) and are thought to have been copied from the same exemplar (R.E. LEWIS, "The relationship of the Vernon and Simeon texts of the *Pricke of Conscience*", in: *So Meny People Longages and Tonges: Philological Essays in Scots and Mediaeval English Presented to Angus McIntosh*, ed. M. BENSKIN and M.L. SAMUELS (Edinburgh, 1981), pp. 251-264). Yet their spelling varies; for instance, in Simeon – copied with some three or four other hands – the scribe doubles vowels before *-ld* and *-nd* whereas in Vernon he does not. Were we to have a full transcription of Simeon to use with the transcription of Vernon (*The Vernon Manuscript: A Facsimile Edition of Oxford, Bodleian Library, MS Eng. poet.a.1*, ed. W. SCASE (Oxford, 2012: *Bodleian Digital Texts* 3)), we might be able to determine if these spellings are characteristic of one or more of the other Simeon scribes and so test the proposition that collaboration affects spelling.

[72] SCASE, "John Gower's scribes and literatim copying".

[73] *Prick of Conscience*, lines 9580-9583: "*I pray yhou alle* [...] *Yhe haf me excused at þis tyme, / If yhe fynde defaut in þe ryme. / I rek noght, þogh þe ryme be rude, / If þe maters þar-of be gude*" ("I pray you all [...] excuse me if you find faults in the metre. I do not care if the rhyme is rough provided that the content is sound").

314   *Chapter 5*

and the later scribes did not care much about metre".[74] Some Gowerian scribes
adopted the practice of copying by column, with forty-six lines per column,
using a standard format and arguably adapting the practice that we observed
was used by the *South English Legendary* scribes to speed up copying and
improve accuracy.[75] But Gower's strict metre required a different method of
copying verse from those used by the scribes of the long didactic poems. As I
have argued elsewhere, the so-called literatim scribes of the *Confessio* modified the practice of the scribes of accentual verse in order to maintain the strict
syllable count and iambic metre of Gower's lines rather than out of respect for
Gower's idiosyncratic dialect as has previously been suggested.[76] The most
accomplished of these scribes copied literatim when variation would damage
the metre. While Orm taught scribes that exact replication of his exemplar was
a way that a scribe might follow and spread the gospel, we may infer that these
Gowerian scribes associated their practice with the innovative literary agendas
of the major poets. Some of them are indeed linked with other creative and
innovative scribal and literary activities as we shall see when we meet some of
these scribes again in the last section of this chapter.[77]

[74] GÖRLACH, *The Textual Tradition of the* South English Legendary, p. 11. Cf. "the original
pattern of the *SEL* line obviously permitted six or seven stresses with much freedom in the unstressed syllables [...] the 'A' redactor, though often smoothing out greater irregularities, was evidently far from consistent" (p. 64); "the surviving manuscripts show that some scribes thought
the rhyme more important than the sense, and sense more important than the metre, and thus irregularities in the metre were easily admitted" (p. 65); "[e]ven the most thorough experiment in
a different metre, the 'E' redaction, is neither consistent nor fully efficient [...] Scribes often took
in too much copy at a time, and then followed a word order which sounded more natural to them.
[...] If the transposition involved a rhyme word, some scribes apparently preferred supplying an
emergency rhyme to erasing their blunder" (p. 67).

[75] For the format see D. PEARSALL, "The manuscripts and illustrations of Gower's works",
in: *A Companion to Gower*, ed. S. ECHARD (Cambridge, 2004), pp. 73-97.

[76] SCASE, "John Gower's scribes and literatim copying".

[77] The alliterative long line also appears to have attracted the attention of reformers of
scribal reprography; for example, another example of an emphasis on exact replication of the
exemplar in the copying of the major Middle English poets appears to occur in three of the
manuscripts of *Piers Plowman*: MS London, BL Addit. 10574, MS Oxford, Bod. Lib., Bodley 814,
and MS London, BL, Cotton Caligula A.xi. Kane and Donaldson remark "their scribes seem to
have been under an injunction to copy slavishly rather than critically", recording examples of "the
acceptance of nonsense readings" (William Langland, Piers Plowman: *The B Version: Will's
Visions of Piers Plowman, Do-Well, Do-Better, and Do-Best*, ed. G. KANE and E.T. DONALDSON
(London, 1975), p. 42 and n. 63). Wakelin observes that two of these copies "have almost
identical spelling, letter for letter, even down to the choice of *i* or *y*" (WAKELIN, *Scribal Correction and Literary Craft*, p. 50).

Reprographics 315

This close examination of scribal product and practice in the manuscripts of the long Middle English didactic verse texts requires that we nuance the *LALME* typology of scribal practice. What McIntosh and the *LALME* scholars have seen as a practice of translation of texts into local dialect to promote reading aloud is called into question by the manuscript evidence. The examples from manuscripts of the *Ormulum*, the *South English Legendary*, and the *Prick of Conscience* reveal that their scribes pursued a shared enterprise of transmitting vernacular didactic text accurately and economically, but they developed distinctive varieties of practice. However, whereas Orm offers an ethical framework for his implementation of *littera* pedagogy for scribes – they must follow the exemplar exactly so that readers may follow the gospel in thought, word, and deed – we have only stray glimpses of how scribes of the *South English Legendary* and the *Prick of Conscience* may have been taught to rationalise their implementations of *littera* in their enterprises and must largely make inferences from their practice. Arguably the scribes of the long didactic verse texts belonged to a community of practice engaged in the common enterprise of producing religious texts quickly and (to judge from their materials and low levels of decoration) economically.[78] They had particular rules about

---

[78] The scanty evidence for who these scribes were suggests that many were connected with the Church's preaching and teaching mission. Of the scribes who signed their copies of the *Prick of Conscience*, John Bagby, scribe of MS London, BL, Addit. 24203, was a monk of Fountains Abbey (LEWIS and McINTOSH, *A Descriptive Guide to the Manuscripts of the* Prick of Conscience, pp. 74-75). John Farnley who signs MS London, BL, Addit. 32578 records that he is a chaplain living in Bolton and that he finished the work in 1405, praise be to God ("*ffini ffinito libro sit laus et Gloria Christo Amen*"); a later hand has added another name, perhaps Robert (LEWIS and McINTOSH, *A Descriptive Guide to the Manuscripts of the* Prick of Conscience, pp. 76-77); Johnston suggests that he must be associated with Bolton Priory, Yorkshire (JOHNSTON, "Copying and reading the *Prick of Conscience*", p. 788). The copy of the poem in MS Oxford, University College, 142 is attributed to Thomas Tilot, who was a vicar choral at Chichester Cathedral in 1415 (S. HOROBIN, "Manuscripts and readers of *Piers Plowman*", in: *The Cambridge Companion to* Piers Plowman, ed. A. COLE and A. GALLOWAY (Cambridge, 2014), pp. 179-197, at pp. 181-182). MS Manchester, John Rylands Library, Eng. 51 bears a book-marker that refers to Ulverscroft Augustinian Priory, Leicestershire, suggesting a later association at least with a religious house (LEWIS and McINTOSH, *A Descriptive Guide to the Manuscripts of the* Prick of Conscience, p. 115). John Appleton signed MS Oxford, Bod. Lib., Bodley 423, f. 351r and recorded ownership in the same hand; in his inscription, "*ecclesie beate marie*" ("church of Saint Mary") is legible, suggesting a parochial context. LEWIS and McINTOSH, *A Descriptive Guide to the Manuscripts of the* Prick of Conscience, p. 42) record "*de Suthwerk*" (Southwark) as well but this is not now visible. It seems possible therefore that some *Prick of Conscience* scribes made sense of their work in relation to the preaching and teaching mission with which the text and their ministry were associated. There are indications that the *South English Legendary,* although it may have started life as a "liturgical document" (GÖRLACH, *The Textual Tradition of the* South English

316 *Chapter 5*

what English verse should look like. In particular, where appropriate they aimed to produce graphic rhyme, in which rhyme syllables are encoded visually through coordinated spellings. Within this broad community of scribes who copied religious verse, some had at their disposal model or habitual spellings which meant that they could carry over a substantial amount of text at a time, perhaps often using transfer units of a line's length and working in the manner in which copy-texts were written but with considerably more material to handle. Others, instead of having a repertoire of learned spellings, were taught to follow an exemplar more rigidly. Some of these scribes sped up production by using systems where copying and checking were made more efficient by standard layouts and perhaps divisions of labour between those who did the copying and those who prepared the pages. The various groups shared a common aim and resources but deployed their resources differently. Certain scribes combined learned, habitual spellings and a process for attaining graphic rhyme while others were enjoined to copy an exemplar slavishly and yet others used physical layout to promote accuracy and economy of effort. The practices developed by the scribes of the long didactic poems required considerable further modification to meet the reprographic demands of Gower's strictly-counted verse.

To some extent, we might read these different practices and products as variant expressions of an identity of scribes who specialised in copying Middle English verse. Within the class that used learned spellings, the distinctive repertoire of model spellings would perhaps have been an additional identity marker: I have suggested that spelling habits developed within a community of practice as part of some form of collaborative scribal activity and may have come to signify belonging to that community. The statement about turning a text into "*our aun / Langage o northrin lede*" ("*our own* language of northern people") in the *Cursor Mundi* is evidence that model or habitual spellings such as might be used when writing copy-texts from memory might have come to

---

Legendary, p. 49, citing L.N. Braswell, University of Toronto PhD, 1964, p. 207), may similarly have been reproduced in connection with the Church's preaching and teaching missions. In the fifteenth century, John Kateryngton, canon, left MS CCCC 145 to the Augustinian Priory of Southwick (Hampshire), and the Premonstratensian house at Titchfield may have owned a copy (GÖRLACH, *The Textual Tradition of the* South English Legendary, pp. 45-46). Görlach's notes on the hands of the manuscripts frequently use the descriptor "professional" (for example, MSS Cambridge, Magdalene College, Pepys 2344; MS Cambridge, Trinity College, R.3.25 (James 605); MS Oxford, Bod. Lib., Tanner 17; and MS Oxford, Bod. Lib., Addit. C. 38 (GÖRLACH, *The Textual Tradition of the* South English Legendary, pp. 94, 97, 99, 106), which suggests that trained, possibly clerical, hands produced them.

Reprographics 317

signify identity: 'we' have "our own language". But the use of one's "own language" in copying from an exemplar in another dialect was a by-product or function of the reprographic process rather than the outcome of 'translation' into a local language that somehow existed independently of the communities of practice that produced it or the result of the application of phonic first principles.[79]

Littera *and the Copying of Prose*

Elementary *littera* pedagogy taught prose as a category of the study of grammar. In his *Etymologiae*, Isidore listed "*prosa*" as one of the thirty divisions of grammar, alongside tropes and metres.[80] He defined prose as "*productum*" ("extended"), "*rectum*" ("straightforward"), and free from the rules of metre ("*a lege metri soluta*").[81] 'Prose' sometimes referred to metres that did not rely on syllable quantity (*DMLBS*, *prosa*, 2). This meant that syllable count, quality, and rhyme were not features that the copyist had to take care not to damage in his writing. But *littera* pedagogy taught that prose too was structured into units, for all speech was analysable in its parts: the *colon* (clause), the *comma* (phrase), and the *periodus* (sentence or complete rhetorical unit). Isidore dealt with these divisions of the sentence in his book on rhetoric, for they relate to reading aloud: no sentence should be longer than what could be said in one breath.[82] Larger units were the *capitulum,* the *paragraphus*, and the book. Early grammarians aided pupils' analysis and correct reading by using punctuation marks to indicate divisions of the sentence and by laying out text '*per cola et commata*'.[83] The addition of punctuation marks, especially the paraph, the *punctus*, the *punctus elevatus*, and the *virgula*, and the use of *litte-*

---

[79] Some schools may have intersected with such communities. Investigating regional linguistic variation in late medieval England, Merja Stenroos examines Middle English copies of the school-text *Accedence*. Observing that "some of the most strongly dialectal written usages from the latter part of the fifteenth century are found in school texts", she infers that spelling of English may have been taught in school, "the retention and extension of marked regional spellings suggests a conscious learnt practice" (M. Stenroos, "Regional language and culture: The geography of Middle English linguistic variation", in: *Imagining Medieval English: Language Structures and Theories, 500-1500*, ed. T. Machan (Cambridge, 2016), pp. 100-125, at p. 120).

[80] Isidore of Seville, *Etymologiae*, Book 1, ch. 5, section 4.

[81] Isidore of Seville, *Etymologiae*, Book 1, ch. 38, section 1.

[82] Isidore of Seville, *Etymologiae*, Book 2, ch. 18, section 2.

[83] Parkes, *Pause and Effect*, pp. 11-16, 305.

318   *Chapter 5*

rae notabiliores also helped make the structure of sentences and larger units of prose visible. This meant that layout and punctuation were important features of the transmission of prose and copyists had a responsibility to reproduce them carefully. All of these features of layout and punctuation of prose were in principle readily transferable to prose written in English. This basic pedagogy of prose meant that the copyist of English prose could not rely so readily as his verse counterpart on transferring copy line by line even though paratextual features such as layout and punctuation may have served to help scribes divide their exemplar text into manageable units for copying. In addition, it meant that they had more purely visual features to reproduce. The scribe's pedagogical duties on occasion extended beyond preserving features of layout and punctuation accurately. In line with a tradition of pedagogy involving marking-up text to help pupils, some scribes might also add, change, or remove punctuation with the needs of new audiences in mind. Jeremy Smith's recent discussion of certain manuscripts of the *Ancrene Wisse* provides examples of what is arguably this process at work.[84]

The Amherst Scribe

It appears that scribes had a variety of ways of applying the framework of *littera* pedagogy to the reproduction of prose texts in English. This section will offer a case study of a copyist of later Middle English prose who has been called the Amherst scribe,[85] comparing his practice with that of other traditions of copying and considering how the differences might contribute to identity formation. The Amherst scribe is so named because he produced MS London, BL, Addit. 37790 (dated around the middle of the fifteenth century), known as the Amherst manuscript after its last private owner.[86] Here the scribe copied

---

[84] J.J. SMITH, *Transforming Early English: The Reinvention of Early English and Older Scots* (Cambridge, 2020), pp. 81-99.

[85] Cf. M. CRÉ, *Vernacular Mysticism in the Charterhouse: A Study of London, British Library, MS Additional 37790* (Turnhout, 2006: *The Medieval Translator* 9).

[86] Baron Amherst of Hackney, † 1909. I have elsewhere discussed this scribe's practice in relation to the McIntosh typology of scribal practice (W. SCASE, "The *LALME* typology of scribal practice: Some issues for manuscript studies", in: *Current Explorations in Middle English*, ed. M. STENROOS and K. THENGS (Berne, 2019), pp. 13-33. The present section summarises and extends the data presented there and develops its broader implications for investigating scribal reprographics and identities.

Reprographics 319

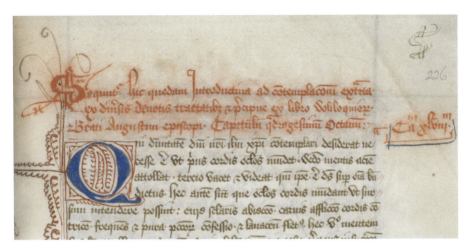

Fig. 25. Intertwined *SI* or *IS* in the hand of the Amherst scribe, in "*Sequitur*", line 1, and in top right corner, MS London, BL, Addit. 37790, f. 226r (detail). © The British Library Board, MS British Library, Addit. 37790, f. 226r.

Richard Misyn's Middle English prose translations of Richard Rolle's *Incendium amoris* and *Emendatio vitae,* the *Pistill of St. Bernard,* the *Perfection of the Sons of God*, *The Mirror of Simple Souls*, and the short text of the *Revelations of Divine Love* by Julian of Norwich. His hand has been found copying English prose texts in two other manuscripts: MS London, BL, Egerton 2006 (*Visions of St. Matilda*, a translation of Mechthild of Hackeborn's *Book of Ghostly Grace*) and MS Cambridge, St. John's College, 189 (G. 21), the *Pilgrimage of the Life of Manhood*. He copied substantial Latin texts as well as English ones (for example a compilation of extracts from Latin contemplative texts in Addit. 37790, ff. 226r-233v).

The Amherst scribe is careful and capable. He uses two scripts, deploying a display hand for biblical quotations, rubrics, and explicits and for the main text he uses a neat, regular Anglicana Formata, for example, Addit. 37790, f. 18r and f. 226r, where he is writing Latin (see Figure 25); and MS Cambridge, St. John's College, 189 (G.21), f. 1v (see Figure 26), where he is writing English. The Amherst scribe's practice is particularly apparent in his copies of the Rolle material in Addit. 37790 because his exemplars for those copies have

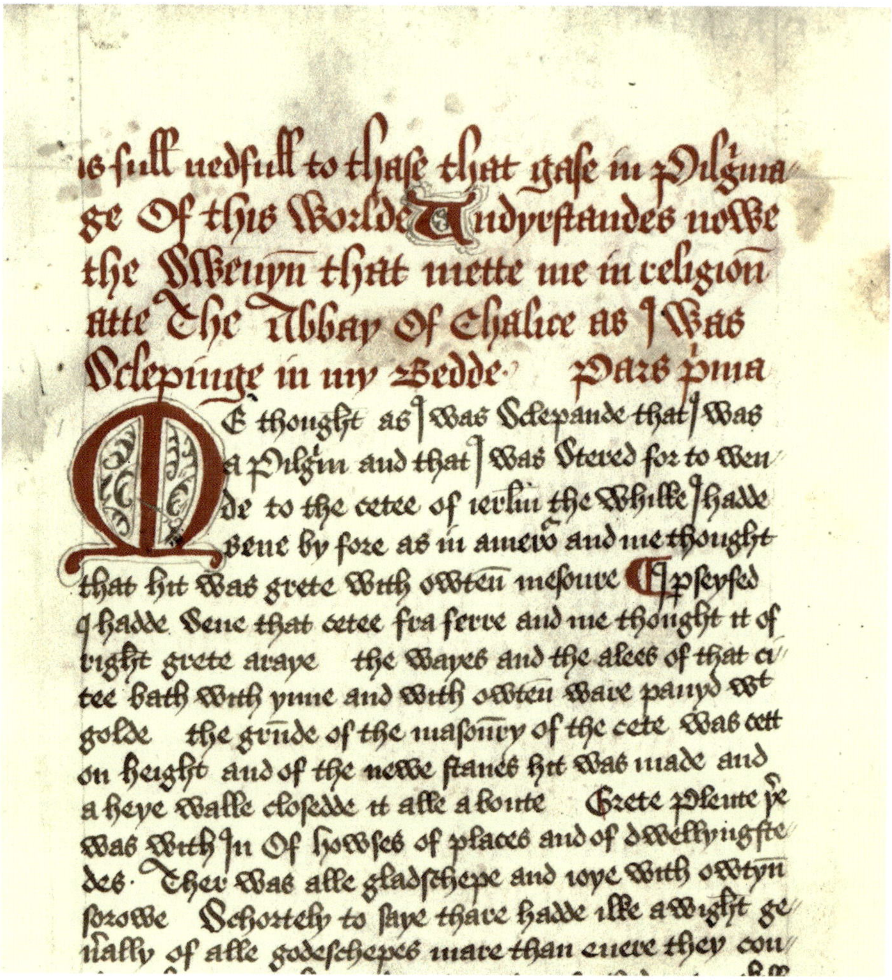

Fig. 26. The distinctive majuscule *I* in the hand of the Amherst scribe, e.g., "*as I was sclepande*", line 6, MS Cambridge, St. John's College, 189 (G.21), f. 1v. By permission of the Master and Fellows of St. John's College, Cambridge.

Reprographics 321

been identified in MS Oxford, Corpus Christi College, 236.[87] One characteristic of his hand is his range of majuscule letter-forms. See for example all of the different forms of majuscule *T* in Addit. 37790, ff. 15v, 16r. The scribe appears to be scrutinising closely the shapes and placing of such graphs in his exemplar. For example, he appears to replicate the *figurae* and positioning of the shapes of majuscule *I*. Examples include the phrase "*It is I nogh*" ("it is enough", Addit. 37790, f. 28r, lines 3-4 up) where the shapes and placings of these majuscules – the first *I* graph reaches to the line above and has a bowl at the top facing to the left, with a left-facing mark on the stem further down; the second majuscule *I* extends only to *x*-height and has no medial mark – reflect those in MS Corpus Christi College 236 (f. 6r, col. b, line 11 down). This focus on majuscules means that the start of new periods is eye-catching: the scribe implements basic *littera* pedagogy on the structure of prose and carries out his role as scribe in helping readers grasp the structure. Further evidence of the scribe's focus on the structure of the prose and his role in helping the reader is that he takes care to retain the punctuation of his exemplar. For example, copying the phrase, "*And we schalle be helyd ¶ many truly Truly ar nott helyd. / Bott rotys And þer Wondis festyr./*" ("and we shall be healed; many truly, truly are not healed, but become putrid and their wounds fester", Addit. 37790, f. 1r, bottom line, to f. 1v, top line), he carries over from his exemplar a paraph after "*helyd*" and a point and a virgule after a second "*helyd*", and also after "*festyr*" (MS Corpus Christi College 236, f. 45r, col. b, lines 14-16). Further evidence for his understanding of his pedagogic role as a careful transmitter of prose is that he has checked and corrected his work. For example, "*for*" is subpunctuated and "*fro*" inserted above ("for", "from", Addit. 37790, f. 2v, line 8); "*do*" is inserted with a caret mark (Addit. 37790, f. 5v, line 1); and dittography is corrected by crossing through (Addit. 37790, f. 14r, bottom two lines). Yet further evidence of his sense of pedagogic responsibility is that he routinely expands contractions found in the exemplar, even reading flourishes as *-e*; for example where MS Corpus Christi College 236 reads "*doand*" and "*turnand*" ("doing", "turning", f. 45r, col. b, lines 18, 19), he reads "*doande*", and

---

[87] M. LAING, "Linguistic profiles and textual criticism: The translations by Richard Misyn of Rolle's *Incendium amoris* and *Emendatio vitae*", in: *Middle English Dialectology: Essays on some Principles and Problems by Angus McIntosh, M.L. Samuels, and M. Laing*, ed. M. LAING (Aberdeen, 1989), pp. 188-223. According to Laing, Rolle's *Emendatio vitae* in MS Addit. 37790, ff. 1-18r is based on MS Oxford, Corpus Christi College, 236, ff. 45r-56v and the *Incendium amoris* in MS Addit. 37790, 18v-95r is based on MS Corpus Christi College 236, ff. 1r-44v (pp. 191-199).

322

Chapter 5

"turnande" (Addit. 37790, f. 1v, lines 1, 2). But occasionally, he retains contractions in cases where he may not be sure of their meaning. For example he retains the hook on *g* in *"chawng"* (MS Corpus Christi College 236, f. 45r, col. b, line 7 up) when copying the phrase *"with chawng of oure desyres"* ("with change of our desires", Addit. 37790, f. 1v, line 11). It is unclear whether *"chawng"* should be inflected in the plural and he allows the ambiguity to stand. Also in line with basic *littera* teaching, the Amherst scribe has a favoured orthography. Comparison of Addit. 37790 with the exemplar shows that he partially implements an alphabet that has *th* instead of thorn and has *y* for /j/.[88] He also replaces *q-* spellings found in the earlier part of the exemplar in 'when', 'where' etc., with *wh* and he introduces *ou* in words spelled with *oȝ* by the exemplar scribe (for example, replacing *"noȝt"* with *"nouȝt"* ("nought").

However, while the Amherst scribe carries out a 'search and replace' operation on certain letters and spellings, in all other respects he follows the spellings of his exemplar very closely. *LALME* analyses his texts as being in mixed and varied dialects, finding Lincolnshire forms together with more Northern, Southern, and Midlands forms.[89] He follows his exemplars rather than deploying model or habitual forms. For example, in a list of the scribe's usages compiled from all of his known copies, 'if' is spelt fifteen different ways: *"ȝif"*, *"if"*, *"ȝyf"*, *"yf"*, *"ȝiff"*, *"ȝyff"*, *"giff"*, *"gif"*, *"iff"*, *"gyf"*, *"yff"*, *"yif"*, *"ȝyffe"*, *"ȝiffe"*, and *"yiff"*. 'High' is also spelt fifteen ways: *"hye"*, *"hie"*, *"hey"*, *"heygh"*, *"he"*, *"hee"*, *"hegh"*, *"heghe"*, *"hyye"*, *"hy"*, *"hyȝe"*, *"heye"*, *"hiȝe"*, *"hiee"*, and *"hiegh"*.[90] Laing and Williamson classify him as a literatim copyist "to some extent" and state that as a result of copying a mix of dialects slavishly he produced a *Mischsprache* in Addit. 37790.[91]

---

[88] Replacement of thorn with *th* and word-initial yogh with *y* are among the "general changes" that he makes to his exemplar, as identified in M. LAING and K. WILLIAMSON, "The archaeology of medieval texts", in: *Categorization in the History of English*, ed. C.J. KAY and J.J. SMITH (Amsterdam, 2004), pp. 85-145, at p. 94.

[89] In the *LALME* entry for MS Addit. 37790, Misyn's translations of Rolle's *Incendium amoris* and *Emendatio vitae* are described as "S Lincs mixed with central Lincs"; the *Pistill of St. Bernard*, "S Lincs mixed with SE Central Lincs"; the short text of the *Revelations of Divine Love*, "S Lincs mixed with a more northerly element"; the *Perfection of the Sons of God*, "S Lincs mixed with SW Lincs"; and *The Mirror of Simple Souls*, "S Lincs mixed with Central W Worcs". The *Book of Ghostly Grace* in MS Egerton 2006 is analysed as "S Lincs, mixed with a more southerly component". The *Pilgrimage of the Life of Manhood* in MS Cambridge, St. John's College, 189 (G. 21) is described as "S Lincs, mixed with a more northerly component and a SW Midland component".

[90] LAING and WILLIAMSON, "The archaeology of medieval texts", pp. 117-19.

[91] LAING and WILLIAMSON, "The archaeology of medieval texts", pp. 92, 104; cf. LAING,

Reprographics 323

But how did the Amherst scribe think about and rationalise his reprographic practice? We have already seen that he appears to be aware of *littera* teaching on prose and to be paying close attention to its implications for his role as scribe. In what follows I will argue that he had available to him a number of varieties of practice and that his reprographic method represents a choice among them. This selection marked him out from other scribes of prose and may have constituted an identification with a particular community of scribal practice.

We may deduce a little more about the contours and meanings of his practice and his understanding of 'what we do' by following up the evidence for the milieu in which he was working. We do not know the name of the Amherst scribe (I will come back to the question of his name later in this section). We do, however, have some clues about the community or communities that he was serving. It appears from the work of Halligan, Cré, and Sargent that the manuscripts in which his hand appears were associated with a Carthusian milieu.[92] The evidence includes the appearance of a monogram and annotations in the hand of Carthusian James Grenehalgh in Addit. 37790.[93] A flyleaf in MS Cambridge, St. John's College, 189 (G.21) bears some names, including that of William Pole or Poole the hermit. Perhaps William was a Carthusian. Marleen Cré's study of Addit. 37790 offers some promising leads for us to develop a picture of the context of production and reception in which the scribe was working and which arguably might at least partly explain his practices and shed light on their meaning for him. Copying texts was part of the Carthusian vocation and the Carthusians continued to copy books themselves when other religious orders were commissioning copies from scribes beyond the cloister.[94] This means that, if he was a Carthusian or even was just associated with the order, the Amherst scribe belonged to a particular group of practitioners who were motivated by a distinct ideology. And if he was working in a Carthusian milieu, he may have been producing books for religious in his own or other

---

"Linguistic profiles and textual criticism".

[92] Building on work carried out by Theresa E. Halligan on MS Egerton 2006, Marleen Cré states, "it seems likely that the Amherst scribe was a Carthusian, and that he wrote Additional 37790, Egerton 2006, and St. John's College 189 in his cell in one of England's Charterhouses" (CRÉ, *Vernacular Mysticism in the Charterhouse*, p. 53). Michael Sargent also places MS Addit. 37790 among "Carthusian products" (M.G. SARGENT, "The transmission by the English Carthusians of some late medieval spiritual writings", *Journal of Ecclesiastical History* 27.3 (1976), pp. 225-240, at p. 230).

[93] CRÉ, *Vernacular Mysticism in the Charterhouse*, pp. 291-294.

[94] CRÉ, *Vernacular Mysticism in the Charterhouse*, p. 53.

324   *Chapter 5*

houses (a Carthusian made a copy of the *Speculum devotorum* for a woman and Carthusian texts found their way to Bridgettine and Dominican nuns), or he may have been copying for lay audiences.[95]

More light is shed on the meanings of the Amherst scribe's practice of careful, scrupulous attention to letter for letter accuracy and to punctuation and the shapes of graphs by the discussions of scribal activity in the founding documents of the Carthusian order. In his recent article about the foundations of the order, Bennett Gilbert emphasises that scribal copying of texts and the Carthusian rule of silence are intimately linked. Copying is a means of meditation. St. Bruno and other early Carthusian founders held that the text copied should not be vocalised.[96] The Middle English translation of Guigo II's *Scala claustralium* describes ascent to heaven as a four-runged ladder, the first step being "busy looking upon Holy Writ".[97] The process of "busy looking" and careful rumination would perhaps be enhanced if the text's variety of letter-forms and orthography slowed down reading. Perhaps the repertoire of majuscule graphs might also have aided the internalisation of fragments – an important part of the Carthusian process of reading – as the careful punctuation might have done.[98] The fine variety of majuscule letters might also have been held to enhance the experience of close rumination on the text. Putting effort into tidying up accidentals of the text such as orthography might have been considered a vain and unworthy distraction from the true book that lay beyond text.[99] Equally, the graphic ingenuity that texts in variable English language

[95] CRÉ, *Vernacular Mysticism in the Charterhouse*, pp. 53-54. Cf. discussion of the audiences for the work of Carthusians William Mede († 1473) and Stephen Dodesham († 1481/1482), and their "scribal networks" (L.S. McCLELLAND, "Studies in pre-Reformation Carthusian vernacular manuscripts: The cases of Dom William Mede and Dom Stephen Dodesham of Sheen" (unpublished PhD thesis, University of Glasgow, 2013), pp. 206-208, quotation at p. 208.

[96] B. GILBERT, "Cistercian script and silence", *Cistercian Studies Quarterly* 49.3 (2014), pp. 367-397, at p. 383.

[97] J. BRANTLEY, *Reading in the Wilderness: Private Devotion and Public Performance in Late Medieval England* (Chicago, 2007), p. 51.

[98] Cré argues that the choice and organisation of texts in the manuscripts resources the *lectio divina*, a practice of reading characterised by "the process of internalizing Scripture readings and other sacred texts" (CRÉ, *Vernacular Mysticism in the Charterhouse*, p. 252) involving committing text to memory for use in prayer and meditation. The reading process may have focused on fragments of text (p. 253) and may have been random rather than linear (p. 279).

[99] For the fundamental principle of Carthusian reading that the true book is Christ, who transcends text, see CRÉ, *Vernacular Mysticism in the Charterhouse*, p. 280. For Carthusian spiritual reading see also SARGENT, "The transmission by the English Carthusians of some late medieval spiritual writings", and BRANTLEY, *Reading in the Wilderness*, pp. 46-57.

Reprographics 325

demanded of scribe and reader might have been seen as enhancing the experience of rumination on the text.

Carthusian texts produced in the late fourteenth and early fifteenth centuries suggest that the Amherst scribe's close attention to the graphic level of his products and his lack of concern about spelling variation may have been informed by guidance, debate, and even anxieties in the order over scribal treatment of exemplars and adherence to other approved models.[100] His engagement with the marking-up of prose perhaps aligns with the emphasis on punctuation to facilitate correct pronunciation in the *Valdebonum*, a work emanating from a French Charterhouse, 1378-1402, which specifies rules of diphthongs and stress marking, "[t]he correct treatment of textual minutiae is essential [...] because 'dangerous' ('*periculosi*') errors of pronunciation destroy the power of speech to express meaning ('*virtutem significandi*')".[101] Yet the Amherst scribe's retention of his exemplar's varied spelling suggests that he did not accept all guidance on textual minutiae. His practice may reflect different positions and communities of practice in the order. The *Prima pars* of the *Statuta nova* of the Carthusians specified at the end of a chapter on diverse customs that the letter *x* was the preferred spelling in the order ("*in ordine*") for words such as "*exigo*", "*exhibeo*", and "*exaro*" (a long list is provided).[102] It further specifies that "among us" ("*apud nos*") one *s* (not two) is written between two vowels; examples include "*desolo*", "*designo*", "*desisto*", and "*resisto*".[103] But in his *Opus pacis* of 1417, German Carthusian Oswald de Corda took a differ-

---

[100] Before we pursue the question of whether the Amherst scribe may have fashioned his copying within a Carthusian community of practice, some alternative views must be acknowledged. Cré sees the Amherst scribe's "automatic and verbatim copying of his models" as being at odds with the design of Addit. 37790 as a Carthusian resource, "a model and also [...] an aid for the reader's spiritual ascent" (CRÉ, *Vernacular Mysticism in the Charterhouse*, p. 278). Malcolm Parkes's work on scribes of the Carthusian order suggests that perhaps Carthusian identity was not expressed through a shared scribal practice: Carthusian scribes display "a personal idiom" in their handwriting which is expressed in such features as "a similar range of variant letter shapes" and he found no evidence that the Carthusian order trained its scribes (M.B. PARKES, *Their Hands before our Eyes: A Closer Look at Scribes: The Lyell Lectures delivered in the University of Oxford 1999* (Aldershot, 2008), pp. 121-125). He also suggested that copying in the seclusion of a cell may have intensified the development of a personal idiom.

[101] WAKELIN, *Scribal Correction and Literary Craft*, p. 24; cf. G. OUY, "Le *Valdebonum* perdu et retrouvé", *Scriptorium*, 42 (1989), pp. 198-205, p. 203, lines 8-16 and 5-7.

[102] *Statuta nova ordinis Cartusiensis in tribus partibus*: *Evolution of the Carthusian Statutes from the* Consuetudines Guigonis *to the* Tertia compilatio, ed. J. HOGG, 25 vols. (Salzburg, 1989: *Analecta Cartusiana* 99), 2, p. 288.

[103] *Statuta nova ordinis Cartusiensis*, 2, p. 288.

326   *Chapter 5*

ent view. Here, evidently building on what basic *littera* pedagogy taught about alphabet variation, Oswald noted variations in practice across time and space. The prudent corrector is aware of many variations in language and expression of the rule of the order across communities and in different places as well as those caused by the errors of scribes. Some use *h* to denote aspiration, some do not. Some use *y* where others use *i*.[104] A name like "*Euila*" is spelt in different ways. Therefore, urges Oswald, it is better that variation be tolerated.[105] Oswald advises that as a general principle no kind of variation requires correction provided the sense is not impeded:

> *Generaliter igitur nouerunt correctores, quod ubicunque eadem dictio, latina, barbara, siue hebraica, in diuersis libris et capitulis, seu eciam in eodem libro aut capitulo, propter uicium scriptorum incertum, aut propter usum inueteratum, uel propter uarietates idiomatum et dissimiles habitudines hominum secundum suas linguas aliter et aliter pronunciancium, siue alio quocunque modo, uarie inunitur scripta, sensu tamen ac significacione propter huiusmodi uariacionem salua remanente, ibi pocius est tolerandum quam aliquid corrigendum [...]*

> In general, therefore, correctors know that wherever the same word, in Latin, other languages, or Hebrew, in various books and chapters, or even in the same book or chapter, on account of the uncertain succession of scribes or because of long-standing use, or because of varieties of idiom and differing habits of men according to their languages or pronunciations or anything else, is written in various ways, however with the sense or significance unchanged by this variation, it is more suitable to tolerate it rather than to correct anything [...][106]

Oswald's guidance demands that the scribe display graphic ingenuity and versatility by being able to tolerate variation and to judge when emendation should be made and when it should not. The Amherst scribe's practice aligns with that recommended by Oswald.

There is some evidence that the Amherst scribe's practice both engages with and differs from that of other scribes of English prose with Carthusian associations. A particular characteristic of his hand is his majuscule *I*. This letter extends above and below the height of the other letters and appears

---

[104] Oswald de Corda, *Opus pacis*, ed. B.A. EGAN (Turnhout: 2001: *Corpus Christianorum: Continuatio Mediaevalis* 179), lines 48, 52.

[105] Oswald de Corda, *Opus pacis*, line 111.

[106] Oswald de Corda, *Opus pacis*, line 115; cf. WAKELIN, *Scribal Correction and Literary Craft*, p. 24.

Reprographics 327

crammed into the horizontal space. Usually too it is topped with a small lobe that faces to the left; see for example, Addit. 37790, f. 4r, f. 226r, line 1 (see Figure 25) and MS Cambridge, St. John's College, 189 (G.21), f. 1v, lines 4, 6, 7 etc. (see Figure 26). Another characteristic of this scribe's hand is a version of the letter *s*. This is an exaggerated form that includes a second stroke that makes it appear that the letter-form continues from the base upwards to the left in parallel before re-joining the line. This letter-form occurs at the beginning of words but it is not a majuscule, just a distinctive form; for examples see MS Egerton 2006, f. 1r and MS Cambridge, St. John's College, 189 (G.21), f. 1v, lines 3, 5, 6, 7 (see Figure 26).

Similar interest in the visual forms of letters is displayed by the extraordinary graphic exuberance of the illustrated Carthusian manuscript, MS London, BL, Addit. 37049, encountered in Chapter Three, such as the rendition of "*Maria*" on f. 26r. Especially characteristic of this tendency in Carthusian manuscripts is an interest in the Holy Name. This and several other Carthusian manuscripts of around this date exhibit the Holy Name of Jesus in experimental monograms, such as the elaborate, coloured *IHC* monograms in Addit. 37049, ff. 36v, 37r, 46r, and 67r.[107] This tradition of graphic devotional attention to the Holy Name may explain the interest in the majuscules *I* and *S* in Addit. 37790 and the appearance of the intertwined letters *IS* or *SI* on ff. 1r, 96v, and 226r (see Figure 25). On f. 226r the intertwined *SI* or *IS* is part of an opening rubric, forming the first letter of "*Sequitur*". Also on f. 226r, a guide sketch of the monogram appears in the top right corner. A similar guide sketch occurs on f. 1r in the top right corner, though no fair copy of this graphic design appears on this page. On f. 96v the design appears to the right of a rubricated prayer that fills space at the end of the copy-text, "*Ih^{es}u : mercy : Lady : helpe*". Interpreting this feature has proved challenging. Marleen Cré believes that it is a monogram formed of the scribe's initials but finds no Carthusian monk with the initials *SI* or *IS* in the period when the scribe was at work.[108] She notes and dismisses the suggestion that the initials are those of Joanna Sewell,

---

[107] A monogram similar to the one in MS London, BL, Addit. 37049, f. 37r, appears in the fragmentary, five-leaf scribe's model book, MS Cambridge, Magdalene College, Pepys 2981, discussed in Chapter Two. Here the monogram precedes the criss-cross row. The two transepts and the foot of the cross are pierced with nails, while a spear and gall pierce all four vertical strokes (see B. WOLPE, "Florilegium alphabeticum", in: *Calligraphy and Palaeography: Essays Presented to Alfred Fairbank on his 70th Birthday*, ed. O.S. OSLEY (London, 1965), pp. 69-75, plate 22). Possibly this fragment is from a model book for a Carthusian scribe.

[108] CRÉ, *Vernacular Mysticism in the Charterhouse*, p. 50, n. 116.

328   *Chapter 5*

a nun of Syon Abbey, because "they are scribal" and antedate the time that Sewell could have used the book. However, telling against the notion that the mark is a personal monogram is its positioning. The *IS* monograms in Addit. 37790 appear in prominent places, in three cases on the opening pages of new texts, and never as part of an explicit or colophon where it would be more usual for scribes to position their signature. The placement of the examples in the rubric and as a guide figure on the opening page of Addit. 37790 is particularly curious. If this was the scribe's initials, he would presumably have no need to remind himself of them. Also telling against the personal monogram theory is that a desire for anonymity is precisely what Bennett Gilbert identifies as a central feature of early Carthusian ideas about scribal work.[109] A desire for anonymity is reflected in the rubric at the end of the Amherst scribe's *Pilgrimage of the Life of Manhood* in MS Cambridge, St. John's College, 189 (G.21) where prayer is requested for the author of the work, the patron of the manuscript, and the scribe, who is un-named ("*[p]raies for hym that made it, for hym þᵃᵗ garte it be made and also for hym that wrate it*", f. 136v). If the feature is not a personal monogram, how might it be explained? Could it, perhaps, be a version of the graphic engagement with the devotion of the Holy Name found in other Carthusian manuscripts such as Addit. 37049? In the context of the other manifestations of graphic devotional engagement with the holy monogram, perhaps the Amherst scribe's engagement with *i* and *s* illustrate the process of indexing of variables within a community as described by Drummond and Schleef:

> Indexicalities of variants are vague, complex and contestable. Once a variable has acquired social meanings, speakers can use associations of these social meanings to create new ones. [...] However, linguistic and non-linguistic practices can only create a link for both speaker and hearer if they share a belief system and recognise its relevance to a particular interaction.[110]

The holy monogram usually consists of the Latinised opening letters of the name *Jesus* in Greek, iota, eta, sigma (represented as '*IHS/C*'). Potentially the Amherst scribe is working with an abbreviation of the Middle English spelling *Iesus*. Contemporary English Carthusian manuscripts therefore provide sugges-

---

[109] B. GILBERT, "Cistercian script and silence".
[110] R. DRUMMOND and E. SCHLEEF, "Identity in variationist sociolinguistics", in: *The Routledge Handbook of Language and Identity*, ed. S. PREECE (London, 2016), pp. 50-65, at p. 55.

Reprographics 329

tive comparators for the Amherst scribe's process and practices, pointing to his membership of a community of practice.

While the Amherst scribe's possible engagement in his reprographic practice with the Carthusian devotion to the Holy Name may suggest some identification with Carthusian communities of Anglophone scribal practice, his slavish reproduction of variant spellings repays consideration in relation to the copying of Nicholas Love's *Mirror of the Blessed Life of Jesus Christ,* a text transmitted by Carthusians. An extreme respect for exemplars has been noted as characteristic of the manuscripts and prints of Nicholas Love's *Mirror*[111] and this seems to correspond with the debate in the order about how variation should be treated. In the manuscripts of the *Mirror* there are traces of concern with how attention to exemplars should be adapted in relation to spelling variation in English prose. In a manuscript of Nicholas Love's *Mirror*, MS Cambridge, UL, Addit. 6578, dated 1410-1420, below a famous memorandum that states that Archbishop Arundel has approved the text, in a different hand from those of the memorandum and the main text, appears the note, "*caue de ist^{is} verb^{is} 'gude' p^{ro} 'gode' It^{em} 'hir' p^{ro} 'heer^e' in plur^{al}i*" ("beware concerning these words, '*gude*' ['good'] for '*gode*', '*hir*' ['their'] for '*heere*' in the plural", f. 2v). The language of the volume is placed by *LALME* at the border of Northamptonshire and Oxfordshire. Sargent says of these instructions, "[t]he forms '*gude*' and '*hir*' do coincide in Warwickshire and southwestern Northamptonshire. Presumably the note on dialectal forms was placed there to instruct readers or, more probably, copyists who might find them misleading".[112] Perhaps, alternatively, the instruction concerns *favoured* spellings should the volume be copied again. The scribe for whom this book is intended as an exemplar is to look out for '*gude*' and '*hir*' and replace them with the forms mandated in the note, '*gode*' and '*heere*'. Some attempt has been made to do this through sporadic correction of the text, perhaps in the hand of the writer of the note.[113] Another

---

[111] L. HELLINGA, "Nicholas Love in print", in: *Nicholas Love at Waseda*, ed. S. ORURO, R. BEADLE, and M. SARGENT (Cambridge, 1997), pp. 143-162, at pp. 155, 156, 160; J.J. SMITH, "Dialect and standardisation in the Waseda manuscript of Nicholas Love's *Mirror of the Blessed Life of Jesus Christ*", in: *Nicholas Love at Waseda*, ed. S. ORURO, R. BEADLE, and M. SARGENT (Cambridge, 1997), pp. 129-141, at pp. 138-139.

[112] Nicholas Love, The Mirror of the Blessed Life of Jesus Christ: *A Full Critical Edition*, ed. M. SARGENT (Exeter, 2005), p. 87.

[113] For example, f. 5r: "*hir h^{er}tes*" ("their hearts", line 4), corrected to "*her^e*" in the margin, possibly in the hand of the note on f. 2v; f. 6r: "*godenes*" ("goodness"), possibly corrected from "*gudenes*" (line 2); "*godenesse*", corrected from "*gudenesse*" (line 3); "*gode lorde*" ("good lord"), possibly corrected from "*gude lorde*" (line 7). The *LALME* profile for MS Addit. 6578, LP 9340 (a

330   Chapter 5

manuscript of the *Mirror*, MS Cambridge, UL, Addit. 6686, shares the '*gude*' and '*hir*' forms of Addit. 6578. The author of the note is enjoining a policy of replacement of forms. But unlike the process used by the scribes of the didactic rhymed verse texts, that, I have argued, replaces 'their' forms with 'ours' as a by-product of rapid reprographic practice which only attends closely to exemplar forms in the rhymes, it appears that the annotator of Addit. 6578 expects a reprographic practice that involves close attention to the entire exemplar and imposition of mandated spellings. The page in Addit. 6578 with the note about '*gode*' and '*heere*' has a note which says that the book comes from Mount Grace Priory, and we may interpret the instruction in relation to the conflicting views of practice among Carthusian copyists.[114] The instruction in Addit. 6578 is on the side of the *Valdebonum* and the statutes, requiring strict adherence to prescribed spellings, and adapting those instructions to variation in spelling in English. By contrast, the scribe (or scribes) of the manuscript and of Addit. 6686 has adhered in some measure to Oswald's tolerance rule, admitting a variety of spellings. The Amherst scribe offers an extreme version of this philosophy. The Amherst scribe, the author of the note, and the scribes of the *Mirror* all demonstrate extreme attentiveness to the detail of their exemplars but differ in how they respond to the debate in the order about the transmission of texts and how they apply the conflicting positions to the reproduction of English prose.[115]

It appears from these materials that different groups had different ideas about the practice "*apud nos*", and that among Carthusian scribes, differentiation of practice may have become associated with the values and identities of sub-groups, of communities of practice who distinguished themselves by

joint profile that also covers MS Cambridge, UL, Addit. 6686, see further below), shows that the scribe uses all four forms but it does not mention the evidence for scribal correction. Doyle notes that the manuscript displays some corrections along these lines, observing that "this scrupulousness about minutiae only supplements that of the original scribe" (A.I. DOYLE, "Reflections on some manuscripts of Nicholas Love's *Myrrour of the Blessed Lyf of Jesu Christ*", *Leeds Studies in English* n.s. 1 (1983), pp. 82-93, at pp. 83-84).

[114] For the note see the entry in J.J. THOMPSON, I. JOHNSON, S. KELLY, R. PERRY, and A. WESTPHALL, *Geographies of Orthodoxy: Mapping English Pseudo-Bonaventuran Lives of Christ, 1350-1550* (Belfast and St. Andrews, n.d.), <https://geographies-of-orthodoxy.qub.ac.uk/ discuss/>.

[115] Also compare Carthusian scribes William Mede and Stephen Dodesham. McClelland characterises the language of Dodesham as largely "colourless", though she also notes that he retains "less-preferred forms" (MCCLELLAND, "Studies in pre-Reformation Carthusian vernacular manuscripts", pp. 128-130, quotation at p. 130). William Mede displays colourless language together with a variety of regional forms typical of southern Yorkshire, Lincolnshire, Norfolk, and Suffolk (p. 44).

Reprographics 331

means of their different ways of balancing precepts and models. The Amherst scribe's close attention to his exemplar and his careful negotiation between model spellings and the authority of the exemplar may be a practice developed in relation to those of these scribal communities. The strict guidance of the statutes perhaps informs the Amherst scribe's close attention to the minutiae of his exemplar and his conservative modification of it in line with certain rules – this is the practice "amongst us" (*"apud nos"*) urge the statutes – while Oswald's call for tolerance of spelling variation so long as the meaning is not unclear perhaps explains his retention of variant spellings and his care with the expansion of abbreviations.

Littera *and the Copying of Indexes*

In the passage from the *Preface to the Wycliffite Biblical Concordance* quoted in the epigraph to this chapter, the author acknowledges the problems that future scribes of his alphabetical work may face. Alphabetical organisation adds an additional level of structure to prose, challenging the scribe to attend not only to colons, commas, periods, and paragraphs but also to the display of material in a conventional order and using a set repertoire of letters. So far in the present chapter we have seen that scribes deployed elementary *littera* pedagogy to fashion reprographic practices for transmitting English texts. The theories and practices of Latin literacy pedagogy provided frameworks for developing practice and making sense of what they were doing. Drawing on understanding of the structure of verse and prose and how they might be represented graphically, they analysed the special requirements of copying English texts and developed practices that aligned with the objectives of their communities of practice. In this section we shall examine scribes who faced a very similar problem in copying the English index to John Trevisa's Middle English prose translation of Ranulph Higden's *Polychronicon*. The copyists of the English index had to negotiate between Latin and English model alphabets, the model of their exemplar, and in some cases the practices of decorators of the text.[116] When variant practices of scribe, decorator, and exemplar clashed it was not a

---

[116] For decoration in the manuscripts from an art-historical perspective see L. DENNISON and N. ROGERS, "A medieval best-seller: Some examples of decorated copies of Higden's *Polychronicon*", in: *The Church and Learning in Later Medieval Society, Essays in Honour of R.B. Dobson: Proceedings of the 1992 Harlaxton Symposium*, ed. C.M. BARRON and J. STRATFORD (Donington, 2002), pp. 80-99.

332   *Chapter 5*

simple matter of either following the exemplar or imposing another model: the utility and even integrity of the index were affected. This example gives us the opportunity to observe the ways in which several roughly contemporary scribes and decorators dealt with these complex reprographic problems. The most successful distinguish themselves with graphic flexibility and creativity. These scribes tackle a task comparable to that which the Wycliffite author invites future scribes to undertake when he invites them to refashion the *Concordance* according to their own manner of writing. Our survey of these scribes will reveal different approaches to this challenge and detect their association with different communities of practice, including a community of scribes that negotiates among practices to innovate in the reproduction of English literary texts.

Higden's original *Polychronicon* text, composed in the mid fourteenth century, included a Latin index, or *tabula*, which appears in various forms. Higden's autograph manuscript is MS San Marino, Huntington Library, HM 132, the index starting from f. 284r.[117] The Latin *tabula* runs from 'Abraham' to 'Zorobabel'. Another example of the Latin index to Higden in Latin occurs in MS London, BL, Royal 14 C.ix, ff. 3r-8r. Here it is laid out with decorated initials at the beginning of each letter section to support easy finding of a given letter. There is some evidence that the indexes facilitated further compilation and copying: John Benet, compiler of MS Dublin, Trinity College, 516, copied extracts from the *Polychronicon*, arranging them alphabetically with references and other material.[118]

In many manuscripts of Trevisa's translation of the *Polychronicon* (dated 1385-1387) an English index, or *tabula*, occurs, one attentive to the interests of later readers and probably the work of Trevisa himself.[119] Fifteen witnesses to

---

[117] J. FREEMAN, "'Towards acquaintance with the following table': The earliest indexes to Ranulph Higden's *Polychronicon*" (n.d.), <https://prezi.com/orlfwnhamvx4/the-earliest-indexes-to-ranulph-higdens-polychronicon/>. For indexes as part of paratexts to the work see A. LIIRA, *Paratextuality in Manuscript and Print: Verbal and Visual Presentation of the Middle English* Polychronicon (published PhD thesis, University of Turku, 2020); and K. TONRY, "Reading history in Caxton's *Polychronicon*", *Journal of English and Germanic Philology* 111.2 (2012), pp. 169-198, at pp. 174-181.

[118] John Benet, "John Benet's chronicle for the years 1400-1462", ed. G.L. HARRISS and M.A. HARRISS, in: *Camden Society*, 4th series, 9 (1972), pp. 151-233; cf. W. SCASE, "John Benet, scribe and compiler, and Dublin, Trinity College, MS 516", in: *Scribal Cultures in Late Medieval England: Festschrift for Linne R. Mooney*, ed. M. CONNOLLY, H. JAMES-MADDOCKS, and † D. PEARSALL (Woodbridge, 2022), pp. 241-258.

[119] R. WALDRON, "Dialect aspects of manuscripts of Trevisa's translation of the *Polychronicon*", in: *Regionalism in Late Medieval Manuscripts and Texts*, ed. F. RIDDY (Woodbridge, 1991), pp. 67-88, at pp. 76-77. Waldron (p. XVIII) lists manuscripts of the Latin text that he

Reprographics 333

the Trevisa translation of the *Polychronicon*, including Caxton's print (*STC* 13438), survive.[120] In Waldron's analysis, these manuscripts fall into three text groups, with one (MS Manchester, Chetham's Library, 11379 (Mun.A.6.90)) moving among the three groups. Waldron locates manuscripts C (MS London, BL, Cotton Tiberius D.vii) and M (the Chetham's manuscript) near Berkeley Castle, the seat of Trevisa's patron, and he associates another group with London production: ADLJPFR.[121] He notes that this London group share a "spelling norm", suggesting that they were subject to some kind of control that caused them to "overrid[e] their own local habits": "[t]he general picture [...] is of an initial translation from the Gloucestershire spelling of the earliest manuscripts into a more central South Midland form, and thereafter the preservation of this new form through something at times approaching literatim copying".[122] Nine of the manuscripts are dated by Waldron to the period from the end of the fourteenth century to 1425. Of these nine, Cotton Tiberius D.vii does not contain indexes. The present study focuses on six of the eight early fifteenth-century manuscripts that contain indexes, three of them belonging to Waldron's London group:[123] MS Manchester, Chetham's 11379 (Mun.A.6.90); MSS London, BL, Stowe 65, Harley 1900, and Addit. 24194; MS Cambridge, St. John's College, 204 (H.1); and MS Tokyo, Senshu UL, 1. This selection includes at least one representative of each text group and Chetham's. This set of roughly synchronous manuscripts displays diversity in scribes' and decorators' handling of the letters and ordering of the alphabet, enabling us to detect prob-

---

believes close to Trevisa's source: MSS Glasgow, UL, Hunter 223 (U.2.14) (fourteenth century, includes *tabula*, ff. 1-9v); MS Princeton, UL, Garrett 152 (early fifteenth century, includes *tabula*, ff. 1-8vb); and MS Oxford, New College 152 (fifteenth century, includes *tabula*, ff. 2ra-8va).

[120] *John Trevisa's Translation of the* Polychronicon *of Ranulph Higden, Book VI, an edition based on British Library, MS Cotton Tiberius D. VII*, ed. R. WALDRON (Heidelberg, 2004: *Middle English Texts* 35), pp. XXIII-XXXVIII; cf. WALDRON, "Dialect aspects". There are two other early prints. For paratext in all of the manuscripts and the three early prints see LIIRA, *Paratextuality in Manuscript and Print*. Liira includes a chapter on the indexes, relying on Waldron when discussing the alphabetical challenges they posed.

[121] WALDRON, "Dialect aspects", pp. 68, 76, 82 (decoration). Cf. *LALME*, LP 7052 and LP 7051. *Late Medieval English Scribes* attributes the Chetham's manuscript to the same hand as MS London, BL, Cotton Tiberius D.vii whom it calls the "*Polychronicon* Scribe". I use Waldron's sigils: A = MS London, BL, Addit. 24194; D = MS Aberdeen, UL, 21; L = MS Liverpool, Public Library, f909 HIG; J = MS Cambridge, St. John's College, 204 (H.1); P = MS Princeton, UL, Garrett 151; F = MS Tokyo, Senshu UL, 1 (formerly Schøyen Collection 194); R = MS CCCC 354. All of these except L and R are dated before 1425.

[122] WALDRON, "Dialect aspects", pp. 83-85, 87.

[123] I have not had access to MS Aberdeen, UL, 21 or MS Princeton, UL, Garrett 151.

334 *Chapter 5*

lems posed to scribes copying the index in English and to identify a range of their reprographic solutions, some less successful than others. Scribes and decorators were called upon to deploy their graphic virtuosity to solve problems posed by applying the conventions of the index to English.

The indexes to the early manuscripts of Trevisa's translation belong with the graphic apparatus developed to enhance access to the text by making its content findable and its structure visible.[124] We have become aware in recent years of the contribution of graphic organisation of the text to the display of text structure and to supporting reader navigation and interpretation through visual codes. The functions of features such as the layout of the page, running heads, rubrics, and the bracketing of rhymes have been well studied. A range of graphic resources was available to scribes to attract and guide the eye of the reader to particular letters and places in the text: decorated initials; majuscule letters (*litterae notabiliores*); and exaggerated ascenders and descenders. Most relevant to the indexing of the *Polychronicon*, letters could be made more 'noticeable' in a range of ways that ranged from majuscule forms to various grades of decoration and ornamentation. Decoration of the letters of the alphabet ranged from extravagant artwork to what Sandler terms "minor decoration", especially, in the period 1285-1385, small initials in one colour – red, blue or gold – flourished with pen-work of a contrasting colour, and perhaps on a ground and filled with motifs.[125] Such minor decoration was usually the work of the scribe, though painted initials might be executed by a specialist.[126] The index to the *Polychronicon* adds an extra level of graphic structure above that

[124] A. HIATT, "Worlds in books", in: *Taxonomies of Knowledge: Information and Order in Medieval Manuscripts*, ed. E. STEINER and L. RANSOM (Philadelphia, 2015), pp. 37-55, at pp. 46-50; M.B. PARKES, "The influence of the concepts of *ordinatio* and *compilatio* on the development of the book", repr. in: M.B. PARKES, *Scribes, Scripts, and Readers: Studies in the Communication, Presentation, and Dissemination of Medieval Texts* (London, 1991), pp. 55-74; R.H. ROUSE and M.A. ROUSE, "*Statim invenire*: Schools, preachers, and new attitudes to the page", in: *Renaissance and Renewal in the Twelfth Century*, ed. R.L. BENSON and G. CONSTABLE with C.D. LANHAM (Oxford, 1982); E. STEINER, *John Trevisa's Information Age: Knowledge and the Pursuit of Literature, c. 1400* (Oxford, 2021), pp. 106-117.

[125] L.F. SANDLER, *Gothic Manuscripts 1285-1385*, 2 vols. (London, 1986: *A Survey of Manuscripts Illuminated in the British Isles* 5), 1, p. 42.

[126] SANDLER, *Gothic Manuscripts 1285-1385*, 1, p. 43. Sandler distinguishes four types of initial: pen-flourished, often done by the scribe; small painted initials; and two- or three-line initials, normally painted and filled with decorative motifs but rarely historiated. A style of pen-work flourishing that uses foliate motifs for the centres and edges of initials appears in the mid-fourteenth century and is held to be typically English (pp. 43-45 and plate on p. 58).

Reprographics 335

of punctuation and on-page paratext, permitting non-linear navigation among the text's units of book and chapter.

Waldron draws attention to variations among the Middle English indexes as evidence for the early process of dialect translation.[127] He notes that the Berkeley manuscripts write initial *f* as *V*, indicating voicing. Trevisa listed many entries with word-initial voiced *f* under *V* in the index. Waldron deduces that this orthographic practice confronted scribes used to other spelling systems with a problem. MS Manchester, Chetham's Library, Mun. A.6.90 copies the exemplar. The scribe of MS Glasgow UL, Hunter 367 (V.1.4), a manuscript produced mid-century, also copies this entry even though he uses *f* in the text. MS London, BL, Harley 1900 changes *v* to *f* but does not move the new *f*-spellings to the *F* column. MS London, BL, Addit. 24194 omits the *v* entry but does not add the material to the *F* column.

The difference in spelling of initial voiced *f* is not the only problem the scribes faced, however, when engaging with their models. They faced problems like those noted by the author of *Preface to the Wycliffite Biblical Concordance* concerning the repertoire and order of letters in the alphabet that arose from the alphabet variation we discussed in Chapter One. And the problems were not restricted to the index scribe's engagement with his exemplar; additional complications potentially arose from the input of decorators whose work on initials and borders enhanced the visual structure of the prose text. For example, one scribe or decorator might use an alphabet in which thorn and yogh are conceptually merged with *y* and *z*, while another might view thorn and yogh as distinct characters. The letters *w*, *u*, and *v* also caused problems beyond that generated by the character used for voiced *f*. While *w* could be viewed as a digraph of double *u* or double *v*, it could also be recognised as being a letter in its own right with its own alphabetical position. The complex of inter-related problems illustrated in the scribal and decorator activity in the group of early Middle English *Polychronicon* manuscripts studied here includes the following possibilities for variation on behalf of scribes and decorators:

- Choice of thorn or *th* for initial unvoiced /θ/ (for example, in 'thin') and the voiced sound /ð/ (for example, in 'the');
- Choice of yogh or *y* for initial /j/;
- Choice of *i* or *y* for initial /i/;

---

[127] WALDRON, "Dialect aspects".

336   *Chapter 5*

- Whether yogh and *z* are different letters and if they are, whether the difference should be represented visually;
- Whether thorn and *y* are different letters and if they are, whether the difference should be represented visually;
- Whether *w* and *u* / *v* are different letters;
- Which of *y*, yogh, thorn, *z*, and *w* should appear in the repertoire of letters and where they should be positioned in the alphabetical sequence.

Adopting the scholastic alphabetical index as a way of providing easy visual organisation of and access to matter in the text was subject to disruption because of these problems. We shall see that some scribes create opacity, while others demonstrate awareness of and tolerance of variant practices and ingenuity in managing and mitigating the resultant problems. Lack of communication and misalignments in practice between the scribe of the text and the decorator may also cause difficulties, but some scribes demonstrate skills in anticipating and mitigating these issues.

MS Manchester, Chetham's Library, 11379 (Mun. A.6.90)[128]

The letters marking out each alphabetical entry in the English index in MS Manchester, Chetham's Library, 11379 (Mun. A.6.90) are decorated with blue initials with red pen-work. The sequence ends *U/V3Þ3W*. The first *3* heads a short list of words that begin with /z/, "*3oroastes*" to "*3eno*" ("Zoroastes", "Zeno", f. 33v; see Figure 27). The second *3* heads a list of words that begin with /j/, beginning with "*3ork ybuld*" ("York built", f. 34r; see Figure 28). All of the headwords under both entries are spelt with word-initial *3*. Both decorator and scribe (as the decoration is only pen-work, they may have been the same person)[129] use the same *figura* for yogh and *Z*, meaning that these letters

---

[128] Includes Latin and English indexes. Waldron's sigil M. *LALME* profiles the Chetham's scribe in Gloucestershire as LP 7052 and states that the language is "notably similar" to that of Hand A in MS London, BL Cotton Tiberius D.vii (LP 7051), which has "[t]wo hands in similar language" mapped in Gloucestershire. *Late Medieval English Scribes* attributes the Chetham's manuscript to the same hand as MS Cotton Tiberius D.vii, ff. 1-164: the "*Polychronicon* Scribe" (L.R. MOONEY, S. HOROBIN, and E. STUBBS, *Late Medieval English Scribes, Version 1.0* (2011), <https://www.medievalscribes.com/>).

[129] For responsibility for pen-work initials see A.I. DOYLE, "Penwork flourishing of initials in England from *c.* 1380", in: *Tributes to Kathleen L. Scott, English Medieval Manuscripts: Readers, Makers, and Illuminators*, ed. M. VILLALOBOS HENNESSY (Turnhout, 2009), pp. 65-72.

Reprographics 337

fall together in terms of shape while each has its own place in the alphabetical sequence. The helpfulness of the *litterae notabiliores* and the index is therefore reduced. By contrast, he / they distinguish thorn and *y* as separate letters.

MS London, BL, Stowe 65[130]

MS London, BL, Stowe 65 is an early fifteenth-century *Polychronicon* where missing text has been supplied later with pages copied from the Caxton print. The *Polychronicon* is followed by Trevisa's translations of William Ockham, *Dialogus inter clericum et militem*, and Richard Fitzralph's *Defensio curatorum*, Trevisa's preface to the *Polychronicon*, and his letter to Sir Thomas Berkeley. After this material, at the end of the codex, comes the *Tabula*, the English alphabetical index to the *Polychronicon* (ff. 218r-221v; no Latin index appears in this manuscript). The original text has received a programme of decoration with large initials set into borders designed to enhance navigation of the text and make visible its structure. Some of the initials incorporate creatures. For example, a six-line *A* in "*Aftir*" ("after") set in a full border marks the beginning of Book 2 (f. 37v), with fantasy creatures forming the corner pieces. The opening of Book 3 (f. 59r) is marked by a seven-line *T* in "*The*" in which the strokes of the letter comprise fantastic curling creatures painted in blue, rose, and orange with white highlights on a gold ground. This page too bears a four-sided border with central bar. Fantasy creatures inhabit the corner pieces and at the bottom of the central vertical bar is a creature with one head and two bodies. The creature in the top right corner piece has the head of a man with a beard, two-tone hat, and carefully tended hair.[131] Lesser text divisions are marked by pen-work initials, for example the two-line initial *D* in "*Dauid*" ("David", f. 53v) which is painted in blue and bears fine flourishing in red pen-work. The pen-work initials show variety and some bear human heads in profile, for example in the *P* in "*Ptholomeus*" ("Ptolemy") on f. 86v.[132]

---

[130] Sigil S; not in *LALME*.

[131] The decorative work in Stowe 65 is reminiscent of some of the decoration in the Vernon manuscript, MS Oxford, Bod. Lib., Eng. poet.a.1, but is of a higher quality. For inconsistencies between scribal and decorators' alphabets in Vernon see W. SCASE, "The artists of the Vernon initials", in: *The Making of the Vernon Manuscript: The Production and Contexts of Oxford, Bodleian Library, MS Eng. Poet. a. 1*, ed. W. SCASE (Turnhout, 2013: *Texts and Transitions* 6), pp. 207-226.

[132] Using phrases such as 'the pen-work artist', I do not mean to suggest any judgement about the number of artists contributing to any given codex.

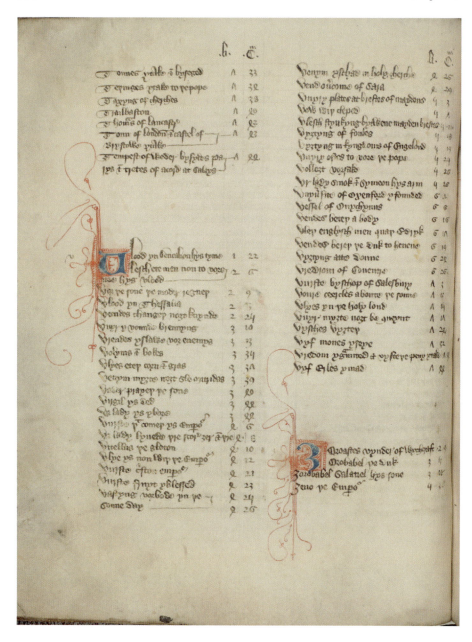

Fig. 27. The letter *3* (for '*Zoroastes*' etc.) in the English index to the *Polychronicon*, MS Manchester, Chetham's Library, 11379 (Mun.A.6.90), f. 33v. Photo: Chetham's Library.

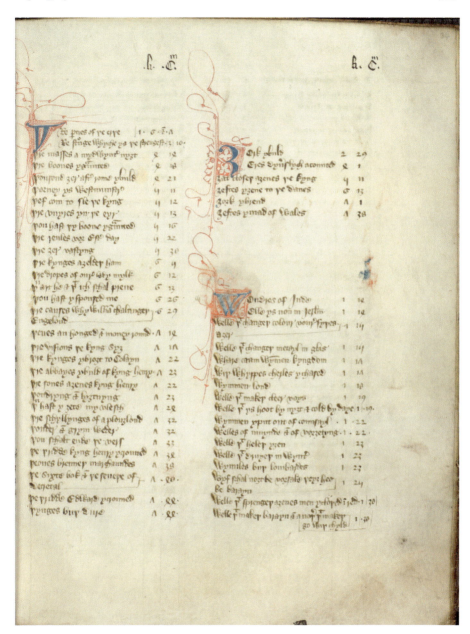

Fig. 28. The letter ʒ (for '*York*' etc.) in the English index to the *Polychronicon*, MS Manchester, Chetham's Library, 11379 (Mun.A.6.90), f. 34r. Photo: Chetham's Library.

340   *Chapter 5*

In the English *tabula* in Stowe 65, each entry starts with a *littera notabili-or*. Some letter sequences are marked by larger *litterae notabiliores*, for example *A* (f. 218r) and *B* (f. 218v) and some are signalled by large majuscules that serve as running heads, for example, *C* on f. 219r. Some of the sequence appears to be missing. The index runs *FG* (f. 220v), *Þ3* (f. 221r), and ends with *W* (f. 221v). Large *litterae notabiliores* head the columns for the letters *Þ* and *3*. *3* heads a list of headwords with word-initial /j/ and all of the entries begin with that letter (e.g., "*3iftes*", "*3ork y brend*", "gifts", "York burnt"). All of the entries under *Þ* begin with thorn. *Th* and *y* are not used as index headings (at least in the leaves of the index that survive). Insofar as one can tell from the fragmentary text of the index, the scribe of Stowe 65 has adopted a consistent practice in matching headwords to head letters.

In the main text, as in the index, words with initial /θ/ and /ð/ are spelled with thorn.[133] However, when these words are preceded by *litterae notabiliores* provided by a decorator, the illuminated initial is a *T*. The book is too tightly bound to see if there were a guide letters in such places, but the scribe left a square space for the initials and wrote the final two letters of the word, "*-he*", beside it, suggesting that he anticipated that the illuminator would paint *T* rather than thorn and planned for it. For example, *T* occurs in an 8-line painted initial that marks the opening of Book 7, "*Thanne*" ("then", f. 166r). The pen-work initials in the main text also use *T* rather than thorn, for example, "*The name*" (f. 64v), "*The puple*" ("the people", f. 65r), and "*The romayns*" ("the Romans", f. 66v). The scribe has prepared for these pen-work *T*s by leaving square spaces and writing "*-he*" after the gaps. However, he cannot mitigate the problem that the alphabetical system in the index does not match the diversity produced by the combinations of the decorator's and scribe's practices in the main text. The pen-work artist on occasion misinterprets guide letters. On f. 87v he supplies a *T* where the guide letter is *c*, writing "*Tleopatra*" for 'Cleopatra' (Book 3, ch. 41). On f. 84v he has erroneously supplied an *F* instead of a *P*. In Book 6, ch. 2, the pen-work artist supplies a 2-shaped *Z* for 'Young Edward', whereas the text uses yogh (or 3-shaped *z*) for initial /j/ (f. 151v). This suggests that *z* and *3* are allographs for the decorator.

The decorators of the text and the scribe of the text and index in Stowe 65 therefore have different repertoires of letters. The scribe is consistent in his use

---

[133] With the exception that *Th* spellings are used for Greek-derived names, for example, "*Thom*ᵃ*s of Caunt*ᵉʳ*bury*" and "*Thom*ᵃ*s of lancastr*ʳ" ("Thomas of Canterbury", "Thomas of Lancaster", f. 40r), as convention required.

Reprographics 341

of thorn and yogh and anticipates, tolerates, and accommodates differences between his own practice and that of the decorator(s) over these letters. The decorator(s) do not try to adapt their repertoire of initials to the alphabet of the text. Possibly they are working from model alphabets where thorn is replaced with *Th* and *ʒ* and *z* are allographs. The decorated initials are designed to display the structure of the text and improve finding and navigation, but mistakes and inconsistencies reduce their utility in that they are not keyed to the usage of the text or index: they become 'more noticeable' letters for the wrong reasons.

MS *London, BL, Harley 1900*[134]

The *Polychronicon* in MS London, BL, Harley 1900 has Latin and English indexes (ff. 21r-41v), the Latin being followed by the English. The beginning of each new letter sequence in the indexes is emphasised with alternating red and blue painted letters accompanied by red or violet pen-work. The violet pen-work includes motifs such as a bearded face in Latin *H* (f. 27v) and a different one in Latin *V* (f. 32r) and English *D* (fol 34r). The English alphabet ends *STF*[for /f/ and /v/]*ʒÞʒW*. The Latin alphabet ends *STU/VXʒ*. The same initial and guide letter *figura* (a yogh / ʒ-shaped *Z*) is used for Latin *Z* (f. 32v, heading the list of words that begin with /z/), English *Z* (f. 40v, /z/), and *ʒ* (f. 41r, heading the list of words that begin with /j/). This conflation of *ʒ* and *Z* under one *figura*, which is similar to that which we noted in MS Manchester, Chetham's 11379 (Mun.A.6.90), reduces the ease of use of the index, since one *figura* occurs in three positions across the two index alphabets.

MS *London, BL, Addit. 24194*[135]

MS London, BL, Addit. 24194, decorated in a style of borders and initials that recalls Stowe 65, includes both a Latin and an English index to the *Polychronicon* (ff. 21r-35v). Mooney, Horobin, and Stubbs attribute the manuscript to scribe Delta, who is also attributed with the early texts of the *Poly-*

---

[134] Sigil H; not in *LALME*. Decoration "probably not London work" (MOONEY, HOROBIN, and STUBBS, *Late Medieval English Scribes*).

[135] Sigil A; not in *LALME*. Decoration associated with London.

342   *Chapter 5*

chronicon in Princeton, UL, Garrett 151 (which does not include indexes), MS Cambridge, St. John's College, 204 (H.1), discussed below, and, possibly, part of MS Aberdeen, UL, 21.[136] Attributed with at least three *Polychronicon* manuscripts, Delta, like the "*Polychronicon* scribe" (the scribe attributed with MS Manchester, Chetham's Library, 11379 (Mun.A.6.90) and the first volume of MS London, BL, Cotton Tiberius D.vii by Mooney, Horobin, and Stubbs), appears to have been a specialist in copying this work. The Latin index (ff. 21r-28r) finishes *TU/VXZ* (headwords beginning with *w* such as "*De whiteby monast^{er}io*" ("about Whitby Abbey") are listed under *U/V*). The English index (ff. 28r-35v) ends *TZY/ÞY/ÞW* (there is no *U/V*). The letter sections are marked out at the beginning of the first headword by three-line gold initials on rose and blue grounds with gilded pen-work flourishing. The items listed under *Z* begin with /z/ (e.g., "*3orobabel*" ("Zorobabel"), "*3eno*"), written as the 3-shaped letter (that is to say, a letter indistinguishable from yogh). Items under *Y/Þ* begin with /j/, spelt *y* (e.g., "*York*"). In this index alphabet therefore, yogh does not appear as part of the organising alphabet either for the scribe or the decorator. Yogh does however occur in the *text* of the index (e.g., "*yeftes I 3eue*", "gifts given", under *Y*, f. 35r). The scribe therefore skilfully modifies his practice to maintain the principle that words beginning with /j/ are located under *Y/Þ* in the index, though he does not completely eliminate yogh as *figura* for /j/. Where word-initial /j/ is decorated in the main text, the letter falls together with the *figura* for /z/ ("*3ong Edward*", for 'Young Edward', f. 211r). Both the decorator and the scribe, therefore, have two ways of representing word-initial /j/: *Z* and *Y*. Perhaps for both scribe and decorator, yogh here conceptually falls in with *z* and the 2-shaped and 3-shaped *figurae* are allographs that can represent /j/ and /z/.

While we have met this falling together of *3* and *Z* in MSS London, BL, Stowe 65 and Harley 1900, in Addit. 24194 a different, further, related conflation occurs: the decorated initials *Y* and *Þ* in the English index and in the main text are identically shaped. Thus the first entry in the index for words that begin with /θ/ or /ð/ is "*Y/Þre parties of þe erþe*" ("three parts of the earth", f. 35r) and the first, decorated entry in the section for words beginning with /j/ is "*Y/Þork*" ("York", f. 35r). The *Y/Þ* shape is also used for decorated initial /θ/ or /ð/ in the main text, for example, 'This year' is written "*Y/Þis 3ere*" (f. 87r). For the decorator, therefore, the *figura Y/Þ* can represent either /j/ or /θ/ and /ð/. The scribe, however, maintains a clear distinction of shape between *y* and

---

[136] MOONEY, HOROBIN, and STUBBS, *Late Medieval English Scribes*.

Reprographics 343

thorn. His *y* is formed with a minim that sits on the line adjoined by a curvy stroke with a pronounced descender that flicks to the right. His thorn is formed from a long, straight, upright minim adjoined on the upper right by a curved stroke. This distinction of shape somewhat mitigates the confusion caused in the index by the decorator's use of the same *figura* for /j/, /θ/, and /ð/. The scribe also demonstrates awareness of the decorator's practice and modifies his own practice to accommodate the difference from his own practice. Clearly the scribe has anticipated decoration with a *Y/Þ* in places where this *figura* signifies /θ/ or /ð/ as there is no *h* following the decoration space. He anticipates a *different* practice where an initial falls in a *border* (often the responsibility of a more accomplished decorator) where initial *T* is used, for example at the beginning of Book 3, "*The fifte age*" ("the fifth age", f. 104v), where a six-line *T* is incorporated in a one-sided border that terminates in vines in the top and bottom margins, "*The name*", with an illuminated initial marking the beginning of Book 3, ch. 12 (f. 111r), and "*The peple*" ("the people", f. 111v). The scribe shows graphic tolerance and considerable ingenuity. He appears to have anticipated and accommodated the practices of the decorator. He also appears to have tried ingeniously to make his practice mitigate the confusions of the index alphabet, only using yogh in the index text when it is not the first letter of a headword and forming the graphs *y* and thorn distinctly (though this, a common feature of Southern and Midlands hands, was perhaps his usual practice rather than being his own initiative). Again, the conflation of letter-forms and the inconsistencies limit the utility of the index, creating opacity, but we see the scribe demonstrating tolerance of different alphabet practices and attempting to accommodate them by exercising his graphic skills.

MS *Cambridge, St. John's College, 204 (H.1)*[137]

Another manuscript attributed to the Delta scribe, MS Cambridge, St. John's 204 (H.1) includes a Latin and an English index (ff. 19r-34v). As in Delta's MS London, BL, Addit. 24194, the English index ends *ZY / ÞY / ÞW*. The beginning of each letter sequence is marked out visually by an illuminated initial that is decorated with sprays. Delta is arguably less successful here at mitigating the problems caused by the index than he was in MS Addit. 24194. As in MS Addit. 24194, the decorator conflates the shapes of the initials *Þ* and

---

[137] Sigil J; not in *LALME*. Decoration associated with London.

344   *Chapter 5*

Y. The decorated initial *Z* for words with initial /z/ has the 2-shaped form, while the entry words begin with the 3-shaped form that is indistinguishable from yogh (e.g., "*ʒeno*", f. 33r). In this *tabula*, the beginning of the list for words with initial /z/ is clearly distinguished from the beginning of the list of words that begin with /j/. But *Y* heads a lists of words that begin with both *y and* yogh ("*York*" and "*ʒiftes i ʒeue*", f. 33r) while the yogh *figura* also heads words in the *Z* list. Not only does the list that is headed with *Y* include both words with initial *y* and words with initial yogh, but the yogh *figura* is also used for the initial letter of words listed under *Z*. Once again, Delta is clearly comfortable with diversity of practice between his own alphabet and those of his exemplar and his decorator, but he is less ingenious here at mitigating its problematic impact on the utility of the index.

MS Tokyo, Senshu UL, 1[138]

MS Tokyo, Senshu UL, 1 includes both Latin and English indexes in its opening pages. The letter sections of the English index are clearly demarcated with three-line illuminated initials on cusped rose and blue grounds that are decorated with painted sprigs. The English letter sequence ends *TZTZW*. Under the first *T* occur words that begin with the spellings *t* or *th*. Under the first *Z* are listed words that begin with /z/; these words are spelt with both initial 2-shaped *Z* and 3-shaped yogh/*Z* ("*ʒeno*"). Under the second *T* are listed words that begin with /ð/ and /θ/. These are mostly spelt with thorn but there are two instances of *th* spellings. Under the second *Z* are words that begin with /j/. These are all spelt with yogh. Here, then, yogh and *z* fall together but in different ways from how they fall together in the manuscripts previously discussed. Thorn does not fall in with *Y*, but it is conflated with *T* in the practice of the decorator. The decorator has followed the practice that we noted in the text of MSS Stowe 65 and Addit. 24194 of spelling /ð/ and /θ/ as *Th*, but in also carrying this over to the index creates additional opacity. The scribe's practice conforms to the model of the index and its alphabetical practice, while the decorator has confused the system with his choice of *figurae*.

---

[138] Sigil F; not in *LALME*. Decoration associated with London; attributed to the Trevisa-Gower scribe; see below. Formerly Oslo / London, Schøyen Collection 194. I have used the online facsimile, where folio numbers are not visible, hence they are not supplied in references here.

Reprographics   345

Discussion

Three of these manuscripts, MS London, BL, Addit. 24194, MS Cambridge, St. John's College, 204 (H.1), and MS Tokyo, Senshu UL, 1, belong to Waldron's London group, which he argues display an association with professional London manuscript decorators and a shared language preserved "through something at times approaching literatim copying".[139] A rather different perspective emerges if we view these scribes as participants in a community of practice engaged in solving reprographic problems by applying *littera* pedagogy in distinctive ways. All of the early manuscripts are arguably the products of a scribal community of practice distinguished by skills in producing lavish copies of a lengthy prose work that are furnished with scholastic navigation aids whose *mise-en-page* is often enhanced by expensive decoration. Working close together in time and location and linked through networks of publication and patronage of the text, the scribes of these copies were perhaps distinguished by their attempts to replicate Latin alphabetical finding aids in English. The attempt to reproduce an English index required decisions to be made as to the nature of the alphabet. Clearly, notions of what 'we' do, of 'our' alphabet, had to be reviewed and adapted in such circumstances and tackling this challenge is one of the features that distinguishes this group of scribes. In the different kinds of opacity and different struggles to overcome the problems we can see scribes experimenting ingeniously with the resources available to them and engaging tolerantly with the work of decorators by deploying knowledge of their variant practices and conventions. The scribes' solutions to the problems varied in their success. But collectively these scribes are versatile in their pursuit of a scholastic English apparatus and tolerate diversity, and sometimes innovate, giving a new sense of what 'we' do.[140]

---

[139] WALDRON, "Dialect aspects", p. 83.

[140] Those who commissioned the manuscripts *may* have identified with this agenda but the evidence is inconclusive. MS London, BL, Addit. 24194 was apparently produced by Delta (and others) for aristocrat Richard Beauchamp († 1439), son-in-law of Trevisa's patron Sir Thomas Berkeley (R. HANNA, "Sir Thomas Berkeley and his patronage", *Speculum* 64.4 (1989), pp. 878-916, at p. 911; Beauchamp's arms appear on ff. 4r, 36r). Other copies share the deluxe appearance of this manuscript and also appear to have been made for wealthy, aristocratic clients and patrons and the production of at least some of these books seems to be associated with London. Evidently such clients had a taste for books that imitated and displayed the trappings of elite, scholastic literacy. Perhaps these audiences would have derived pleasure and pride from owning books that included the graphic challenges of inconsistent and opaque English indexes – they would be an opportunity for them to test their own literate skills and to show that they were equal to greater

346   *Chapter 5*

There was some overlap between the *Polychronicon* scribes of the early fifteenth century and members of another community of practice also associated with early fifteenth-century London book production: the scribes of John Gower's *Confessio Amantis* encountered above who were engaged in developing a reprographic practice adequate to the demands of copying Gower's strictly-counted octosyllabic verse. Scribe Delta, attributed with three or even four copies of the *Polychronicon* (MS London, BL, Addit. 24194, MS Cambridge, St. John's College 204 (H.1), MS Aberdeen, UL, 21, and MS Princeton UL, Garrett 151) is also attributed with a manuscript of the *Confessio* that is closely related to this group of so-called literatim Gower manuscripts: MS London, BL, Royal 18 C.xxii.[141] Jeremy Smith describes the language of this *Confessio* as "largely Gowerian",[142] while Delta's copies of the *Polychronicon* all fall into Waldron's text group A whose copying Waldron finds to be literatim. The scribe of MS Tokyo, Senshu UL, 1, the so-called "Trevisa-Gower scribe", is attributed with four manuscripts of the *Confessio*.[143] Jeremy Smith records that this scribe's *Confessio* copies in MSS Oxford, Bod. Lib., Bodley 693 and Laud Misc. 609 exhibit a "[m]ixture of Gowerian and colourless forms".[144] Both Delta and the Trevisa-Gower scribe worked in some kind of association with a London scribe known as Scribe D, now thought by many to be John Marchaunt. A specialist member of this so-called literatim Gower group, Scribe D is attributed with a copy of Trevisa's translation of *De Proprietatibus rerum* (MS London, BL, Addit. 27944) as well as with contributing

---

graphic challenges than, say, those offered by the lavish copies of Chaucer's *ABC* that we encountered in Chapter Three or the alphabet bowls that we encountered in Chapter Four. Alternatively, perhaps they regarded the indexes as for show and neither noticed nor cared about their ease of use. Evidence supporting this latter hypothesis is the presence of incomplete indexes in several of these codices. The scribes left gaps for the later addition of further entries as time and interest might dictate, but later owners and users rarely accepted the invitation to do some more indexing. For example, in MS London, BL Addit. 24194, "*William Waleys*" follows the last entry under *W* in a hand other than the scribe's. However there is no reference to the text given, suggesting that perhaps this is a signature, not an entry. Several centimetres below, William Shadwell signed his name, adding the date 1610. The Shadwell name does not follow directly after the last entry, and again there is no location reference, confirming that it is a signature rather than an addition to the *W* words.

[141] MOONEY, HOROBIN, and STUBBS, *Late Medieval English Scribes*.

[142] J.J. SMITH, "Spelling and tradition in fifteenth-century copies of Gower's *Confessio Amantis*", in: *The English of Chaucer and his Contemporaries*, ed. J.J. SMITH (Aberdeen, 1989), pp. 96-113, at p. 109.

[143] MOONEY, HOROBIN, and STUBBS, *Late Medieval English Scribes*.

[144] J.J. SMITH, "Spelling and tradition", p. 110.

Reprographics 347

to no fewer than eight copies of the *Confessio*.[145] The hands of both the Trevisa-Gower scribe *and* Scribe D appear in *Confessio* manuscript MS Oxford, Bod. Lib., Bodley 902.[146] Jeremy Smith finds the language of all three scribes of this manuscript to be "Gowerian".[147] The hands of Delta and Scribe D are very similar, and it has been suggested that they were competitors, Delta specialising in *Polychronicon* manuscripts and Scribe D in manuscripts of the *Confessio*, but both engaged in "a common or even competitive pursuit of an appropriate and distinctive mode of presentation, a 'look' for vernacular English poetry".[148] A centre for this activity may have been the London Guildhall.[149]

Like Orm, scribes in this *Confessio* group, I have argued, developed a reprographic practice that met the challenges of preserving metre, applying basic *littera* pedagogy to improve their copying. The best scribes in this group demonstrate immense ingenuity and flexibility when deploying this copying method. The *Polychronicon* scribes related to this group also apply *littera* pedagogy, demonstrating awareness of different alphabets and navigating among the practices of different communities in order to transmit an optimally navigable prose text. It is intriguing to speculate that such scribes developed their professional graphic identities in relation to the various innovative practices that were being developed in London at that period. Such scribes might arguably be thought of as members of a wider community of practice that was engaged in the common enterprise of improving copying of Middle English

---

[145] L.R. MOONEY and E. STUBBS, *Scribes and the City: London Guildhall Clerks and the Dissemination of Middle English Literature 1375-1425* (York, 2013), p. 38. For Scribe D as a literatim scribe see J.J. SMITH, "Spelling and tradition"; and J.J. SMITH, "The Trinity Gower D-scribe and his work on two early *Canterbury Tales* manuscripts", in: *The English of Chaucer and his Contemporaries*, ed. J.J. SMITH (Aberdeen, 1989), pp. 51-69. Stubbs has recently proposed that a copy of a Wycliffite petition should be added to Scribe D's oeuvre; see E. STUBBS, "Seeking scribal communities in medieval London", in: *Scribal Cultures in Late Medieval England*, ed. M. CONNOLLY, H. JAMES-MADDOCKS, and † D. PEARSALL (Woodbridge, 2022), pp. 125-145.

[146] MOONEY and STUBBS, *Scribes and the City*, p. 136.

[147] J.J. SMITH, "Spelling and tradition", p. 110.

[148] K. KERBY-FULTON and S. JUSTICE, "Scribe D and the marketing of Ricardian literature", in: *The Medieval Professional Reader at Work: Evidence from Manuscripts of Chaucer, Langland, Kempe, and Gower*, ed. K. KERBY-FULTON and M. HILMO (Victoria, BC, 2001: *English Literary Studies* 85), pp. 217-237, at p. 223.

[149] MOONEY and STUBBS, *Scribes and the City*. This suggestion has generated much debate; see for example L. WARNER, *Chaucer's Scribes: London Textual Production, 1384-1432* (Cambridge, 2018) and for further references see SCASE, "John Gower's scribes and literatim copying", p. 25 and n. 45.

348   *Chapter 5*

literature. Projects under the umbrella of this group included producing prose texts with scholastic finding aids, despite problems with alphabetical order, and finding a way of copying strictly syllabic rhymed verse. Perhaps scribes like the Trevisa-Gower scribe and Delta facilitated exchange and cross-fertilisation between these projects, enabling distinctions between 'what we do' and 'what they do' to develop as well as a sense of membership of a larger collective that recognised themselves as scribes that tolerated – indeed, handled with ingenuity and virtuosity – graphic diversity in pursuit of the transfer of Latin models of text presentation and reprography to English. The author of the *Preface to the Wycliffite Biblical Concordance* and his scribe (discussed in Chapter One) have much in common with these scribes and it is intriguing to speculate on whether their solutions for alphabetical organisation indicate some kind of association with – and distance from – this Wycliffite community of practice.

Conclusion

This chapter has examined scribes' reprographic practices in relation to elementary Latin literacy pedagogy about verse and prose and related training in paying attention to spellings, punctuation, and layout. We have seen that this pedagogy informed scribal practice and guidance and that it was adapted to the special demands of copying English verse and prose. We have found differences in the application of elementary pedagogy to the copying of English and have glimpsed the formation of communities of practice characterised by these differences. This chapter offers a rather different perspective on and approach to variation in scribal practice from that developed by Angus McIntosh and others associated with the Middle English Dialect Project. McIntosh's typology of literatim, translation, and mixed copying provides an analytical framework that makes non-localised, scribal copies of literary texts amenable to use in dialect analysis. The analysis in the present chapter has attempted to drill down into variations in practice within these categories as well as considering the relations between them. We have seen that what the Middle English Dialect Project calls literatim copying breaks down into a range of complex negotiations between models and that it involves the exercise of considerable graphic ingenuity and problem-solving skills. The term 'literatim copying' has been applied to the reprographic process taught by Orm, the process of some of the Gower scribes, the process adopted by the Amherst scribe, and that of the Lon-

Reprographics 349

don *Polychronicon* scribes, yet these processes have very different rationales. In principle the category of translation covers both many witnesses of the didactic long rhymed verse texts such as the *Prick of Conscience* and practices observable in copies of extended prose texts such as Nicholas Love's *Mirror*. Yet the reprographic process and its rationale was very different in each of these cases. This chapter has represented these differences of practice in terms that the scribes themselves would have recognised – those furnished by elementary literacy pedagogy – and has proposed that in fashioning different practices, scribes also fashioned understandings of their projects and their identities. Scribes were very aware of differences among communities of Anglophone scribal practice and negotiated among them to meet the special challenges of transmitting English texts. The witnesses to the *Polychronicon* indexes discussed here furnish examples of this process in action through collaboration and negotiation among scribes and decorators.

Conclusion: Medieval English Literacy

Visible English has attempted to recover and reconstruct the experience of reading and writing the language through the perspectives of *littera* pedagogy. It has argued that the graphic culture underpinned and transmitted by pedagogy provided frameworks for the development and understanding of English-language literacy practices and new ways of experiencing social belonging and difference. To be literate in English was to inhabit identities marked by Anglophone literate practices.

Key sources for this book have been labelled 'copy-texts': together with alphabets and pangrams, micro-texts such as prayer tags, dictaminal salutations, colophons, proverbs, and signatures, it has been argued, are traces of reading and writing practice. More complex versions of these genres, such as alphabet and riddling poems, it has been shown, also provided opportunities for the development, display, and appreciation of achievement in Anglophone literacy.

Reading and writing English was learned, practised, and given meaning in what this book calls 'communities of Anglophone literate practice'. Communities inflected *littera* pedagogy in particular ways and differences in practice contributed to the erection of boundaries between belonging and difference. Distinctions which were meaningful in the past may not be immediately obvious today. For example, we have seen that the same alphabet row might be analysed differently among different communities, and similar copying methods might have different meanings and rationales for the scribes who developed them.

In this conclusion, first, brief consideration will be given to some possible implications of this study for some deep-rooted and prevailing assumptions about medieval English literacy. In particular, questions arise about the relations between Latinity and reading and writing English, and about the implica-

352 *Conclusion*

tions of a communities of practice approach for broader linguistic and literary history. After that, the potential for studies that say more about multilingualism, for studies of other vernaculars, and for work on early printed materials will be considered.

A question raised by the arguments in this book concerns the relationship of English literacy to Latinity.[1] It is sometimes assumed that, for speakers of English, reading and writing the language were in principle independent of Latinity. Stephen Penn believes that there was a mode of English-only literacy; one could be "a reader of English alone", albeit that, "no reader of English alone would have been regarded as 'literate'".[2] *Visible English* has argued that basic *littera* pedagogy, the pedagogy of Latin grammar, was fundamental to reading and writing English. It was not necessary to acquire these basic skills and knowledges through formal education but it was necessary to have them. The assumption that some could read English who had not encountered *littera* pedagogy is questionable; even in very particular historical circumstances such as the Alfredian plans for literacy education in English before Latin, *littera* pedagogy must have been used.[3] The surviving corpus of books and documents provides evidence that English literacy was in practice as well as in pedagogy a specialised subset of Latin literacy. For every surviving medieval English codex, there are dozens in Latin, and similar ratios apply to documents.[4] And of course, it is often the case that English texts survive side-by-side with Latin ones. The fact that the paratext associated with texts in English is generally in Latin (rubrics, colophons, chapter headings, side notes and so on) also suggests that those who read from English books were expected to have some Latin.

Another question concerns whether anyone literate in Latin was automatically literate in English. For example, writing of the copying of Middle English

---

[1] Recent work has seen literacy in the medieval period as a spectrum of competence (for a survey of the secondary literature that charts this development see C.F. BRIGGS, "Literacy, reading, and writing in the medieval West", *Journal of Medieval History* 26.4 (2000), pp. 397-420, and for early medieval Europe see R. MCKITTERICK, "Introduction", in: *The Uses of Literacy in Early Medieval Europe*, ed. R. MCKITTERICK (Cambridge, 1990), pp. 1-10, at pp. 2-7. My comments here refer more narrowly to the processes of encoding and decoding script.

[2] S. PENN, "Literacy and literate production", in: *Chaucer: An Oxford Guide*, ed. S. ELLIS (Oxford, 2005), pp. 113-129, at pp. 115-116.

[3] For the text of the Alfredian educational prospectus see Alfred, *King Alfred's West-Saxon Version of Gregory's* Pastoral Care, ed. H. SWEET, 2 vols. (London, 1871: *EETS*, o.s. 45, 50).

[4] W. SCASE, "Reinventing the vernacular: Middle English language and its literature", in: *The Cambridge Companion to Medieval English Literature*, ed. L. SCANLON (Cambridge, 2009), pp. 11-23, at p. 16.

Conclusion 353

literature, Michael Johnston claims that "a scribe able to produce a charter or a manorial court roll could just as easily add 'literary codex' to his repertoire".[5] Our case studies offer a very different picture. *Visible English* has provided evidence that the encoding and decoding of English texts were not regarded or experienced as straightforward. We have seen that graphically-challenging texts in English were valued and sought-after. We have also seen that scribes' and readers' practices were associated with skill in encoding text and in solving letter puzzles. We have encountered evidence that scribes of medieval English were aware of the problems thrown up by the lack of standard alphabets and spellings and the difficulties of encoding metre and made ingenious attempts to solve them by drawing on and adapting their Latin literacy training. These transfers suggest that perhaps English was regarded as at least as challenging to read and write as Latin, if not more so, and that English literacy gave specially demanding opportunities for testing and displaying the competences taught by basic pedagogy.

A corollary of the association of reading and writing in medieval English with graphic challenge and accomplishment is that we should consider the possibility that the reading, and especially the writing, of English were rare and specialist skills for most of the period covered by this book. The difficulty evidently associated with reading and writing English, as well as, as has been demonstrated, the fact that literacy pedagogy was framed by Latinate traditions, in particular call into question prevailing assumptions about reading competences. What I am proposing runs very much counter to prevalent understandings of the extent to which and the rate at which literacy in English permeated medieval society. The emphasis on the politics of the vernacular in recent years and on English as a medium for widening lay access to learning has perhaps contributed to a sense that literate competence was more widespread than perhaps it was and increased faster than perhaps it did by leading us to elide *access* with *literacy*.[6] The provision of English translations of, for example, Latin or French didactic verse or devotional prose enabled *audience* numbers to expand, but the numbers with *reading* competence could have continued to be much lower. Competence in *writing* English was undoubtedly even rarer. Alongside rethinking the assumption that literacy in English was

[5] M. Johnston, "Copying and reading the *Prick of Conscience*", *Speculum* 95.3 (2020), pp. 742-801, at p. 768.

[6] See the useful literature survey *Vernacular Aesthetics in the Later Middle Ages: Politics, Performance, and Reception from Literature to Music*, ed. K.W. Jager (Basingstoke, 2019), pp. 1-8.

354   *Conclusion*

separable from Latin literacy, we necessarily need to rethink assumptions about how many people belonged to communities of Anglophone literate practice. We also need to revisit questions about the identities that belonging to one of those communities made available. If, as I am arguing, literacy in English was indeed a rare and specialised skill, this would have added to its value as a resource for drawing boundaries between belonging and difference.

Visible English also has implications for how we visualise the corpus of medieval English. This book has drawn a picture of Anglophone literate practice as a phenomenon – more accurately, a set of varied, multiple, and changing phenomena – grown in and dependant on communities of practice. We might want to try to visualise manuscripts, documents, and inscriptions that contain medieval English from this perspective. From this point of view, for example, the way the data in *LALME* is visualised could be reconsidered. Apparent clusters of dots (representing closely-related linguistic profiles) might indicate, not materials all emanating from a particular dialect *area*, but outputs distinctive of and developed within particular communities of practice. We already have pointers in this direction. Texts that display 'Central Midland' features in particular have been subject to reassessment. Noting that there are "no records of a scribal centre with an output of learned medical texts in the East Midland area", Taavitsainen calls into question McIntosh's proposal that texts in this dialect were produced at a scriptorium or centre in the East Midlands, identifying two different kinds of this language in groups of texts and proposing instead that the evidence points to "'house styles' of scriptoria with specialist book production", possibly located in London.[7] Hudson records that during her research questions arose regarding the geographical localisation of Wycliffite texts: "difficulties of various kinds began to emerge: the textual evidence simply did not add up to the conclusions drawn; in addition, substantial questions arose about the evidence that had been used in coming to those conclusions".[8]

---

[7]   I. TAAVITSAINEN, "Scriptorial 'house styles' and discourse communities", in: *Medical and Scientific Writing in Late Medieval English*, ed. I. TAAVITSAINEN and P. PAHTA (Cambridge, 2004), pp. 209-240, at p. 237.

[8]   A. HUDSON, "Observations on the 'Wycliffite orthography'", in: *Pursuing Middle English Manuscripts and their Texts: Essays in Honour of Ralph Hanna*, ed. S. HOROBIN and A. NAFDE (Turnhout, 2017), pp. 77-98, at p. 78, n. 4. The concept of the *scripta*, a term denoting a written form of a regional language that does not map simply onto local speech, might be usefully applied to some clusters of linguistically-alike Middle English texts. Serge Lusignan's investigation of Picard French of the thirteenth to fifteenth centuries models the kind of alternative historical narratives and perspectives that the idea of the *scripta* makes available. Lusignan presents evidence that although the *scripta* has a basis in regional spoken dialects, it is mistaken to localise

Conclusion 355

LALME's mapping of texts with convergent linguistic properties and its exclusion from maps and analysis of material that is not strongly marked by what it sees as regional dialect characteristics has perhaps contributed to creating the impression that the texts which are mapped, such as the lengthy didactic verse texts, reflect the spoken language and writing practices prevalent in local language communities. We could turn the proposition around: these clusters might represent the *creation* of a written language in a community, and a community's creation of its identity by means of that written language, rather than being examples of a pre-existing written language in a given area.

The examples discussed in *Visible English* have been drawn from manuscript and inscribed materials. Implications for printed materials must await another study. Aspects of print culture that could repay application of the framework developed in the present study include the reproduction of alphabets, writing models, and graphic puzzles; writing practice in the margins of printed books; reproduction of printed text in manuscript; and the display of printed materials in graphic landscapes.

Visible English also has implications for study of other medieval written languages and of multilingual materials. The focus here has been on English, but case studies could be made of other languages and societies where Latin pedagogy framed graphic culture. Study could also be broadened to consider more of the complexities of vernacular written multilingualisms, where alternative orthographies may have enriched the pool of resources for drawing boundaries between belonging and difference. We have encountered some examples of graphic pedagogy within multilingual communities of practice in this volume but much more work remains to be done. Old English was written by scribes who were evidently capable of reading and perhaps sometimes writing other Germanic languages. It has been proposed that the spellings of personal names in early Kentish documents may have been influenced by Frankish orthography. For example, the name particles '*Berht-*' and '*Bern-*' are not spelt

---

"*sans précaution un document écrit en picard à l'espace territorial situé au nord du pays d'oïl*" ("without caution a document written in Picard to the region situated in the north of the area where '*oil*' was the word for 'yes'"; S. Lusignan, *Essai d'histoire sociolinguistique: Le français picard au Moyen Age* (Paris, 2012: *Recherches littéraires médiévales* 13). p. 20). Furthermore, not every document written in this area is necessarily Picard: the use of the Picard *scripta* conveys identity rather than strict locality (p. 157). On the term and field see also J. Kabatek, "*Koinés and Scriptae*", in: *The Cambridge History of the Romance Languages: Volume II: Contexts*, ed. J.C. Smith and M. Maiden (Cambridge, 2013), pp. 143-86. The analysis in Chapter Five points towards similar communities of practice and even sub-communities in the Middle English context.

356   *Conclusion*

'*Beorht-*' or '*Beorn-*' as might be expected.[9] A complication when considering such scenarios is that modern language categories do not always clearly map onto the medieval material. The Saxon language of northern Germany was known and copied in pre-Conquest England, and although we today separate Old Saxon and Old English, it is a moot point how far the two languages were, rather, experienced by the speakers themselves as dialects of the same language. This question is raised, for example, by the use of the Saxon *Heliand* as a source for the Old English poem *Genesis B*, and the survival of a copy of the *Heliand* in a later-tenth century manuscript thought to have been made in southern England: MS London, BL, Cotton Caligula A.vii (ff. 11r-175v).[10] Did the Cotton scribe consider that he was copying a text in a language other than English? And did the author of *Genesis B* consider that he was translating from one *dialect* to another, or translating from one *language* to another? Other problems attend on the interpretation of glosses and other fragmentary texts created once copying of French had started to flourish in England. Laing notes that there is ambiguity concerning glosses comprised of French words that are known to have been borrowed into later Middle English and that the glossators themselves were sometimes not sure about the linguistic origins of the words they used, sometimes mis-labelling words of Old English origin as French ("*gallice*").[11]

The nexus between orthography and script could also be brought into consideration. For example, in relation to later medieval multilingual Anglophone and other communities, a complex strategy informs the orthography and script of the main scribe of the Trentham manuscript of literary works in English, French, and Latin by Gower, MS London, BL, Addit. 59495 (the Trentham scribe).[12] Ralph Hanna observes that this scribe uses different script variants for the three languages in the manuscript, but this point could be refined when

---

[9] J. HINES, "The writing of English in Kent: Contexts and influences from the sixth to the ninth century", *NOWELE: North-Western European Language Evolution* 50-51 (2007), pp. 63-92, at pp. 77-78.

[10] H. GNEUSS, *Handlist of Anglo-Saxon Manuscripts: A List of Manuscripts and Manuscript Fragments Written or Owned in England up to 1100* (Tempe, AZ, 2001), No. 308.

[11] M. LAING, *Catalogue of Sources for a Linguistic Atlas of Early Medieval English* (Cambridge, 1993), p. 7.

[12] Referred to as Scribe 5 in M.B. PARKES, "Patterns of scribal activity and revisions of the text in early copies of works by John Gower", in: *New Science out of Old Books, Manuscripts, and Early Printed Books: Essays in Honour of A.I. Doyle*, ed. R. BEADLE and A.J. PIPER (London, 1995), pp. 81-121, at pp. 90-91.

Conclusion 357

orthography is considered.[13] The visual difference between the Latin and the English arguably relates to the different distributions and frequencies of letters in Latin and English. The opposite is true of the graphic distinctions between the French and the English. Here the differences in script between the English (in Anglicana) and the French (in a mixture of Anglicana and Secretary) are specially marked, while orthographically the two languages are closely related since many of the words in the English text are French loans spelt using French orthography. Sebastian Sobecki suggests that, "it is possible to read the entire manuscript as an attempt to balance not only English and French, but also England and France".[14] Possibly this balance of identities and language is being worked out at a graphic level also. It appears that the Trentham scribe draws boundaries between belonging and difference through a complex deployment of orthographies *and* scripts. Complex multilingual literacies must lie behind such examples. The acquisition of literacy in English alongside one or more other vernaculars is a dimension of graphic culture that requires further study.

While asking and attempting to address new questions about medieval English, *Visible English* has confined its focus to the all-pervasive, basic, and foundational elements of graphic culture and their framing of English literate practice in manuscript and other hand-made materials. The many ramifying complexities of the subject such as those indicated in this Conclusion remain to be investigated in detail. It is hoped that this study may provide a framework for future work that will address these and other problems concerning medieval graphic culture, scribal practice, and identity.

[13] R. HANNA, *London Literature, 1300-1380* (Cambridge, 2005), p. 227.

[14] S. SOBECKI, "'*Ecce patet tensus*': The Trentham manuscript, 'In Praise of Peace', and John Gower's autograph hand", *Speculum* 90.4 (2015), pp. 925-959, at p. 947.

Bibliography

For medieval manuscript materials, see the Index of Medieval Manuscripts, at pp. 395-399.

Primary Sources: Printed and Electronic

ABC of Aristotle, "Das stabreimende *ABC des Aristoteles*", ed. M. FÖRSTER, in: *Archiv für das Studium der neueren Sprachen und Literaturen* 105 (1900), pp. 296-310.

Adam Murimuth, *Adami Murimuthensis, Chronica sui temporis*, ed. T. HOG (London, 1846).

Ælfric, *Grammar: Ælfrics* Grammatik *und* Glossar, ed. J. ZUPITZA (Berlin, 1880).

Ælfric Bata, *Colloquies: Anglo-Saxon Conversations: The* Colloquies *of Ælfric Bata*, ed. and trans. S. GWARA and D. PORTER (Woodbridge, 1997).

Albertus Magnus, *Compendium totius theologicae veritatis, septem libris digestum*, ed. J. DE COMBIS (Lyon, 1602).

Alcuin, *Alcuini* Orthographia, ed. A. MARSILI (Pisa, 1952).

Aldhelm, *Aenigmata*, ed. F. GLORIE, in: *Tatvini Opera Omnia, Variae collectiones aenigmatum Merovingicae aetatis*, ed. M. DE MARCO *et al.* (Turnhout, 1968: *Corpus Christianorum, Series Latina* 133), pp. 382-540.

Alfred, *King Alfred's West-Saxon Version of Gregory's* Pastoral Care, ed. H. SWEET, 2 vols. (London, 1871: *EETS*, o.s. 45, 50).

Ancient Funerall Monuments of Great Britaine, Ireland, and the Islands adjacent, ed. J. WEEVER, 2nd edn. (London, 1631) [*STC* 25223].

Ancrene Wisse: The English Text of the Ancrene Riwle*: BM MS Cotton Cleopatra C.vi*, ed. E.J. DOBSON (London, 1972: *EETS*, o.s. 267).

Andreas *and the* Fates of the Apostles, ed. K.R. BROOKS (Oxford, 1961).

Anglo-Saxon Poetic Records: A Collective Edition, ed. G.P. KRAPP and E.V.K. DOBBIE, 6 vols. (New York, 1931-1942).

360   *Bibliography*

An Anthology of Chancery English, ed. J.H. FISHER, M. RICHARDSON, and J.L. FISHER (Knoxville, 1984).

Antiente Epitaphes (from A.D. 1250 to A.D. 1800) collected [and] sett forth in chronologicall order, ed. T.A. RAVENSHAW (London, 1878).

Asser, *Life of King Alfred*, in: *Alfred the Great: Asser's* Life of King Alfred *and Other Contemporary Sources*, trans. S. KEYNES and M. LAPIDGE (Harmondsworth, 1983), pp. 66-110.

The Auchinleck Manuscript, ed. D. BURNLEY and A. WIGGINS (Edinburgh, 2003), <http://auchinleck.nls.uk/>.

Bartholomaeus Anglicus, *On the Properties of Things: John Trevisa's Translation of Bartholomaeus Anglicus* De Proprietatibus rerum, ed. M.C. SEYMOUR *et al.*, 3 vols. (Oxford, 1975-1988).

Bede, *De Arte metrica*, in: *Bede, Libri II* De Arte metrica *et* De Schematibus et tropis, ed. and trans. C.B. KENDALL (Saarbrücken, 1991).

Bede, *De Orthographia*, in: *Bedae venerabilis Opera, Part VI, Opera didascalica*, ed. C.W. JONES, 3 vols. (Turnhout, 1975: *Corpus Christianorum, Series Latina* 123), 1, pp. 1-57.

Bede, *De Temporum ratione*, in: *PL* 90.

Benedict Burgh, *Cato major*, "*Die Burghsche Cato-Paraphrase*", ed. M. FÖRSTER, in: *Archiv für das Studium der neueren Sprachen und Literaturen* 115 (1905), pp. 298-323 and 116 (1906), pp. 25-40, 304-323, 325-334.

Bernard of Clairvaux, *De Consideratione*, in: *PL* 182.

Byrhtferth, *Byrhtferth's* Enchiridion, ed. P. BAKER and M. LAPIDGE (Oxford, 1995: *EETS*, s.s. 15).

The Calendar and the Cloister: Oxford, St. John's College, MS 17, ed. F. WALLIS (n.d.), <https://digital.library.mcgill.ca/ms-17/index.htm>.

Chronicles of London, ed. C.L. KINGSFORD (Cambridge, 1905).

"A collection of proverbs in Rawlinson MS D. 328", ed. S.B. MEECH, in: *Modern Philology*, 38 (1940-1941), pp. 113-132.

The Complete Harley 2253 Manuscript: Volume 2, ed. S.G. FEIN with D. RAYBIN and J. ZIOLKOWSKI (Kalamazoo, MI, 2014: *TEAMS Middle English Texts Series*).

The Corpus of Anglo-Saxon Stone Sculpture I: County Durham and Northumberland, ed. R. CRAMP (London, 1977), <http://www.ascorpus.ac.uk/catvol1.php>.

The Corpus of Anglo-Saxon Stone Sculpture III: York and Eastern Yorkshire, ed. J. LANG (London, 1991), <http://www.ascorpus.ac.uk/catvol3.php>.

The Corpus of Anglo-Saxon Stone Sculpture VII: South-West England, ed. R. CRAMP (London, 2006).

Cursor mundi: Cursor mundi (The Cursor o the World): *A Northumbrian Poem of the XIVth Century in Four Versions*, ed. R. MORRIS, 7 vols. (London, 1874-1893: *EETS*, o.s. 57, 59, 62, 66, 68, 99, 101).

Cynewulf, *Elene*, ed. P.O.E. GRADON (Exeter, 1977).

Bibliography 361

Donatus, *Ars maior*, in: "*Donati* Ars grammatica", ed. H. KEIL, in: *Grammatici Latini*, ed. H. KEIL, 8 vols. (Leipzig, 1864), 4, pp. 367-402.

The Dream of the Rood, ed. M. SWANTON, rev. edn. (Exeter, 1987).

"An early treatise in English concerning Latin grammar [Cam. Trin. Coll. O.5.4]", ed. S.B. MEECH, in: *Essays and Studies in English and Comparative Literature: University of Michigan Publications, Language and Literature*, 13 (1935), pp. 81-125.

An Edition of the Middle English Grammatical Texts, ed. D. THOMSON (New York, 1984).

"An edition of the Ten Commandments commentary in BL Harley 2398 and the related version in Trinity College Dublin 245, York Minster XVI.L.12, and Harvard English 738, together with discussion of related commentaries", ed. J.A. JEFFERSON (unpublished Ph.D. thesis, University of Bristol, 1995).

English Lyrics of the XIIIth Century, ed. C.F. BROWN (Oxford, 1932).

Eusebius, *Aenigmata*, ed. F. GLORIE, in: *Tatvini Opera Omnia, Variae collectiones aenigmatum Merovingicae aetatis*, ed. M. DE MARCO *et al.* (Turnhout, 1968: *Corpus Christianorum, Series Latina* 133), pp. 209-271.

Everyman and Medieval Miracle Plays, ed. A.C. CAWLEY (London, 1974).

The Exeter Book of Old English Poetry with Introductory Chapters by R.W. Chambers, Max Förster, and Robin Flower, ed. R.W. CHAMBERS, M. FÖRSTER, and R. FLOWER (London, 1933).

A Fifteenth-Century School Book: From a Manuscript in the British Museum (MS Arundel 249), ed. W. NELSON (Oxford, 1956).

Geoffrey Chaucer, *ABC Hymn to the Virgin*, in: *The Riverside Chaucer*, ed. L.D. BENSON, 3rd edn. (Oxford, 1988), pp. 637-640 (text) and pp. 1076-1177 and 1185 (notes).

Geoffrey Chaucer, *Canterbury Tales*, in: *The Riverside Chaucer*, ed. L.D. BENSON, 3rd edn. (Oxford, 1988).

Historical Poems of the XIVth and XVth Centuries, ed. R.H. ROBBINS (New York, 1959).

Hugh of St. Victor, *De Grammatica*, in: *Hugonis de Sancto Victore Opera Propaedeutica*, ed. R. BARON (Notre Dame, IN, 1966), pp. 67-163.

Isidore of Seville, *Etymologiae*: *Isidori Hispalensis Episcopi, Etymologiarum sive Originum*, ed. W.M. LINDSAY, 2 vols. (Oxford, 1911).

Isidore of Seville, *The Etymologies of Isidore of Seville*, trans. S. BARNEY, W. LEWIS, J. BEACH, and O. BERGHOF (Cambridge, 2006).

Jerome, "Praefatio Hieronymi Presbiteri de omnibus libris de Veteris Testamenti", in: *Sancti Eusebii Hieronymi Stridonensis Presbyteri Divina Bibliotheca antehac inedita, studio et labore monachorum ordinis S. Benedicti è Congregatione S. Mauri*, ed. CONGREGATION OF ST. MAUR (Paris, 1693), cols. 318-322.

John Benet, "John Benet's chronicle for the years 1400-1462", ed. G.L. HARRISS and M.A. HARRISS, in: *Camden Society*, 4th series, 9 (1972), pp. 151-233.

362   *Bibliography*

John Lydgate, *Bycorne and Chychevache*, in: *John Lydgate, Mummings and Entertainments*, ed. C. SPONSLER (Kalamazoo, MI, 2010).

John Trevisa, *De Proprietatibus rerum*, see: Bartholomaeus Anglicus, *On the Properties of Things*.

John Trevisa, *Polychronicon*, see: Ranulph Higden, *Polychronicon*.

John Trevisa's Translation of the Polychronicon *of Ranulph Higden, Book VI, An Edition Based on British Library, MS Cotton Tiberiius D. VII*, ed. R. WALDRON (Heidelberg, 2004: *Middle English Texts* 35).

Juliana, ed. R. WOOLF, 2nd edn. (London, 1966).

Juliana Berner, The Boke of Saint Albans: *Containing Treatises on Hawking, Hunting, and Cote Armour by Dame Juliana Berner, printed at Saint Albans by the School-Master Printer in 1486, Reproduced in Facsimile*, ed. W. BLADES (London, 1901).

"Latin and Middle English proverbs in a manuscript at St. George's Chapel, Windsor Castle", ed. S.M. HORRALL, in: *Medieval Studies* 45 (1983), pp. 343-484.

Latin Vulgate Bible, <http://www.drbo.org>.

Mandeville's Travels, ed. M.C. SEYMOUR (Oxford, 1967).

Martianus Capella, *De Nuptiis Philologiae et Mercurii*, ed. J. WILLIS (Leipzig, 1983: *Bibliothecae Teubnerianae Scriptorum Graecorum et Romanorum*).

Medieval Grammar and Rhetoric: Language Arts and Literary Theory, AD 300-1475, ed. R. COPELAND and I. SLUITER (Oxford, 2009).

The Middle English Physiologus, ed. H. WIRTJES (Oxford, 1991: *EETS* o.s. 299).

Nicholas Love, The Mirror of the Blessed Life of Jesus Christ*: A Full Critical Edition*, ed. M. SARGENT (Exeter, 2005).

Norfolk Medieval Graffiti Survey (2010-), <http://www.medieval-graffiti.co.uk/index.html>.

Novus Thesaurus Adagiorum Latinorum: Lateinischer Sprichwörterschatz, ed. W. BINDER (Stuttgart, 1861).

The Old English Riddles of the Exeter Book, ed. C. WILLIAMSON (Chapel Hill, 1977).

The Old English Rune Poem, in: *Linguarum vett. septentrionalium thesaurus grammatico-criticus et archaeologicus*, ed. G. HICKES, 2 vols. (Oxford, 1705), 1, p. 135.

The Old English Rune Poem: A Critical Edition, ed. M. HALSALL (Toronto, 1981).

The Ormulum, ed. R.M. WHITE and R. HOLT, 2 vols. (Oxford, 1878).

The Orrmulum Project, ed. N.-L. JOHANNSEN (Stockholm, 1993-2019), <https://web.archive.org/web/20180518025014/http://www.orrmulum.net/orrmulum_site.html>, last accessed 2019.

Oswald de Corda, *Opus pacis*, ed. B.A. EGAN (Turnhout: 2001: *Corpus Christianorum, Continuatio Mediaevalis* 179).

Political, Religious, and Love Poems, ed. F.J. FURNIVALL (London, 1866: *EETS*, o.s. 15).

Preface to the Wycliffite Biblical Concordance, ed. S.M. KUHN, in: "The preface to a fifteenth-century concordance", *Speculum*, 43 (1968), pp. 258-273.

Bibliography 363

Prick of Conscience: *Richard Morris's* Prick of Conscience*: A Corrected and Amplified Reading Text*, ed. R. HANNA and S. WOOD (Oxford, 2013: *EETS*, o.s. 342).

Priscian, *Institutiones grammaticae*: "*Prisciani,* Institutionum grammaticarum *Libri I-XII*", ed. M. HERTZIUS, in: *Grammatici Latini*, ed. H. KEIL, 8 vols. (Leipzig, 1855), 2.

The Proverbs of Alfred *Re-edited from the Manuscripts*, ed. W.W. SKEAT (Oxford, 1907).

Ranulph Higden, Polychronicon *Ranulphi Monachi Cestrensis with English Translations of John Trevisa and of an Unknown Writer of the Fifteenth Century*, ed. C. BABINGTON (vols. 1-2), and J.R. LUMBY (vols. 3-9), (London, 1865-1886: *RS* 41).

Reliquiae Antiquae: *Scraps from Ancient Manuscripts, Illustrating Chiefly early English Literature and the English Language*, ed. T. WRIGHT and J.O. HALLIWELL, 2 vols. (London, 1845).

Le Roman de Renart, ed. E. MARTIN, 4 vols. (Strasbourg, 1882-1887).

Rotuli Parliamentorum; Ut Et Petitiones, Et Placita in Parliamento Tempore Edwardi R.I., 7 vols. (London, 1767-1777).

Runes-DB, beta version (Göttingen, 2022), <https://www.runesdb.eu/>.

Selections from English Wycliffite Writings, ed. A. HUDSON (Cambridge, 1978).

The Shepherds (2), in: *The Towneley Plays*, ed. G.P.J. EPP (Kalamazoo, MI, 2018).

Statuta nova ordinis Cartusiensis in tribus partibus: *Evolution of the Carthusian Statutes from the* Consuetudines Guigonis *to the* Tertia compilatio, ed. J. HOGG, 25 vols. (Salzburg, 1989: *Analecta Cartusiana* 99).

Suffolk Medieval Graffiti Survey (2014-), <http://www.medieval-graffiti-suffolk.co.uk>.

Surrey Medieval Graffiti Survey (2011-2014), <https://web.archive.org/web/2020081511 3317/http://www.medievalgraffitisurrey.org/the-project.html>, last accessed 2019.

Tatwine, *Aenigmata*, ed. F. GLORIE, in: *Tatvini Opera Omnia Variae collectiones aenigmatum Merovingicae aetatis*, ed. M. DE MARCO *et al.* (Turnhout, 1968: *Corpus Christianorum, Series Latina* 133), pp. 165-208.

The Teaching of Grammar in Late Medieval England: An Edition, with Commentary, of Oxford, Lincoln College, MS Lat. 130, ed. C.R. BLAND (East Lansing, 1992).

The Thornton Manuscript (Lincoln Cathedral MS 91), ed. D.S. BREWER and A.E.B. OWEN (London, 1977).

The Vercelli Book: A Late Tenth-Century Manuscript Containing Prose and Verse, Vercelli Biblioteca Capitolare CXVII, ed. C. SISAM (Copenhagen, 1976: *Early English Manuscripts in Facsimile* 19).

The Vernon Manuscript: *A Facsimile Edition of Oxford, Bodleian Library, MS Eng. poet.a.1*, ed. W. SCASE (Oxford, 2012: *Bodleian Digital Texts* 3).

Wessex Parallel WebTexts, ed. B. MILLETT (Southampton, 2003), <https://ota.bodleian. ox.ac.uk/repository/xmlui/bitstream/handle/20.500.12024/2463/AW-font-pref.html>.

364   *Bibliography*

William Langland, Piers Plowman: *The B Version: Will's Visions of Piers Plowman, Do-Well, Do-Better, and Do-Best*, ed. G. KANE and E.T. DONALDSON (London, 1975).

William Langland, The Vision of Piers Plowman: *A Complete Edition of the B-Text*, ed. A.V.C. SCHMIDT, new edn. (London, 1987).

The Winchester Anthology: A Facsimile of British Library Additional Manuscript 60577, ed. E.M. WILSON and I. FENLON (Cambridge, 1981).

Secondary Sources: Printed and Electronic

ABERCROMBIE, D., "What is a 'letter'?", *Lingua* 2 (1949), pp. 54-63.

ACKER, P., "A schoolchild's primer (Plimpton MS 258)", in: *Medieval Literature for Children*, ed. D.T. KLINE (London, 2003), pp. 143-154.

AHEARN, L., *Living Language: An Introduction to Linguistic Anthropology* (Oxford, 2012).

ALEXANDER, J.G., and P. BINSKI, *Age of Chivalry: Art in Plantagenet England 1200-1400* (London, 1987).

ALEXANDER, J.S., "Masons' marks and the working practices of medieval stone masons", in: *Who Built Beverley Minster?*, ed. P.S. BARNWELL and A. PACEY (Reading, 2008), pp. 21-40.

ALEXANDRE-BIDON, D., "La lettre volée: Apprendre à lire à l'enfant au Moyen Age", *Annales. Economies, Sociétés, Civilisations* 44.4 (1989), pp. 953-992.

ANDERSON, J., and D. BRITTON, "The orthography and phonology of the *Ormulum*", *English Language and Linguistics* 3.2 (1999), pp. 299-334.

ANON., [Untitled Proceedings of 3 February 1910], *Proceedings of the Society of Antiquaries*, 2nd series, 23 (1910), pp. 46-49.

APPLEFORD, A., "The Dance of Death in London: John Carpenter, John Lydgate, and the *Daunce of Poulys*", *Journal of Medieval and Early Modern Studies* 38.2 (2008), pp. 285-314.

ARONIN, L., and M. Ó LAOIRE, "The material culture of multilingualism: Moving beyond the linguistic landscape", *International Journal of Multilingualism* 10.3 (2013), pp. 225-235.

BACKHOUSE, J., "An illuminator's sketchbook", *The British Library Journal* 1.1 (1975), pp. 3-14.

BAHR, A., "Miscellaneity and variance in the medieval book", in: *The Medieval Manuscript Book: Cultural Approaches*, ed. M. JOHNSTON and M. VAN DUSSEN (Cambridge, 2015), pp. 181-198.

BAILEY, D., "Introducing Reith – the new face of the BBC", *GEL: Global Experience Language* (16 Jan. 2018), <http://www.bbc.co.uk/gel/articles/introducing-bbc-reith>.

Bibliography 365

BALE, A., "Belligerent literacy, bookplates, and graffiti: Dorothy Helbarton's book", in: *Book Destruction from the Medieval to the Contemporary*, ed. G. PARTINGTON and A. SMYTH (Basingstoke, 2014), pp. 89-111.

BALE, A., "Late medieval book-owners named John Leche", *Bodleian Library Record* 25.1 (2012), pp. 105-112.

BATAILLON, L.J., "'*Exemplar*', '*pecia*', '*quaternus*'", in: *Vocabulaire du livre et de l'écriture au Moyen Age: Actes de la table ronde, Paris 24-26 septembre 1987*, ed. O. WEIJERS (Turnhout, 1989: *Etudes sur le vocabulaire intellectuel du Moyen Age* 2), pp. 206-219.

BEDOS-REZAK, B.M., and J. HAMBURGER, "Introduction", in: *Sign and Design: Script as Image in Cross-Cultural Perspective (300-1600 CE)*, ed. B.M. BEDOS-REZAK and J. HAMBURGER (Washington, 2016), pp. 1-16.

BEIT-ARIE, M., "Why comparative codicology?", *Gazette du livre médiévale* 23 (1993), pp. 1-5.

BELLIS, J., and V. BRIDGES, "'What shalt thou do when thou hast an English to make into Latin?': The proverb collection of Cambridge, St. John's College F.26", *Studies in Philology* 112 (2015), pp. 68-92.

BENEDICTINS DU BOUVERET, *Colophons de manuscrits occidentaux des origines au XVf siècle* (Fribourg, 1965-1982).

BENSKIN, M., "The letters þ and y in later Middle English, and some related matters", *Journal of the Society of Archivists* 1 (1982), pp. 13-30.

BENSKIN, M., and M. LAING, "Translations and *Mischsprachen* in Middle English manuscripts", in: *So meny people longages and tonges: Philological Essays presented to Angus McIntosh*, ed. M. BENSKIN and M.L. SAMUELS (Edinburgh, 1981), pp. 55-106.

BERGS, A., "The uniformitarian principle and the risk of anachronisms in language and social history", in: *The Handbook of Historical Sociolinguistics*, ed. J.C. CONDE-SILVESTRE and J. HERNÁNDEZ-CAMPOY (Malden, 2012), pp. 80-99.

BERGS, A., "Writing, reading, language change – A sociohistorical perspective on scribes, readers, and networks in medieval Britain", in: *Scribes as Agents of Language Change*, ed. E.-M. WAGNER, B. OUTHWAITE, and B. BEINHOFF (Berlin, 2013: *Studies in Language Change* 10), pp. 241-258.

BERTRAND, P., *Les écritures ordinaires: Sociologie d'un temps de révolution documentaire (entre royaume de France et empire, 1250-1350)* (Paris, 2015).

BISCHOFF, B., "Elementarunterricht und *probationes pennae* in der ersten Hälfte des Mittelalters", in: ID., *Mittelalterliche Studien: Ausgewählte Aufsätze zur Schriftkunde und Literaturgeschichte*, 1 (Stuttgart, 1966), pp. 74-87.

BISCHOFF, B., *Latin Palaeography: Antiquity and the Middle Ages*, trans. D. Ó CRÓINÍN and D. GANZ (Cambridge, 1990).

366   *Bibliography*

BISCHOFF, B., "Übersicht über die nichtdiplomatischen Geheimschriften des Mittelalters", *Institut für Österreichische Geschichtsforschung, Mitteilungen* 62 (1954), pp. 1-27.

BITTERLI, D., *Say What I Am Called: The Old English Riddles of the Exeter Book and the Anglo-Latin Riddle Tradition* (Toronto, 2009).

BLATT, H., *Participatory Reading in Late Medieval England* (Manchester, 2018).

BLOMMAERT, J., *Discourse: A Critical Introduction* (Cambridge, 2005).

BODLEIAN LIBRARY, *Digital Bodleian* (2020), <https://digital.bodleian.ox.ac.uk/>.

BODLEIAN LIBRARY, *Medieval Manuscripts in Oxford Libraries* (2017-), <https://medieval.bodleian.ox.ac.uk/>.

BOFFEY, J., and J.J. THOMPSON, "Anthologies and miscellanies: Production and choice of texts", in: *Book Production and Publishing in Britain 1375-1475*, ed. J. GRIFFITHS and D. PEARSALL (Cambridge, 1989), pp. 279-315.

BONNER, S., *Education in Ancient Rome: From the Elder Cato to the Younger Pliny* (London, 1977).

BOON, M., *In Praise of Copying* (Cambridge, MA, 2010).

BRANTLEY, J., *Reading in the Wilderness: Private Devotion and Public Performance in Late Medieval England* (Chicago, 2007).

BRIGGS, C.F., "Literacy, reading, and writing in the medieval West", *Journal of Medieval History* 26.4 (2000), pp. 397-420.

BROWN, C.F., "The Maidstone text of the *Proverbs of Alfred*", *Modern Language Review* 21.3 (1926), pp. 249-260.

BROWN, C.F., "A thirteenth-century manuscript at Maidstone", *Modern Language Review* 21.1 (1926), pp. 1-12.

BROWN, G.H., "The dynamics of literacy in Anglo-Saxon England", *Bulletin of the John Rylands Library* 77.1 (1995), pp. 109-142.

BROWN, M.P., "The role of the wax tablet in medieval literacy: A reconsideration in light of a recent find from York", *British Library Journal* 29 (1994), pp. 1-16.

BROWN, M.P., and E. OKASHA, "The inscribed objects", in: *Life and Economy at Early Medieval Flixborough, c. AD 600-1000,* ed. D.H. Evans and C. Loveluck (Oxford, 2009), ch. 3.3 (n.p.).

BROWN, P.J., "'*Ventus vehemens et terribilis per totam Angliam*': Responses and reactions to a short-term crisis in the British Isles", in: *Waiting for the End of the World? New Perspectives on Natural Disasters in Medieval Europe,* ed. C.M. GERRARD, P. FORLIN, and P.J. BROWN (Abingdon, 2021), pp. 24-42.

BRUBAKER, R., and F. COOPER, "Beyond 'identity'", *Theory and Society* 29.1 (2000), pp. 1-47.

BUCHOLTZ, K., and K. HALL, "Identity and interaction: A sociocultural linguistic approach", *Discourse Studies* 7.4 (2005), pp. 585-614.

BUCHOLTZ, K., and K. HALL, "Locating identity in language", in: *Language and Identities,* ed. C. LLAMAS and D. WATT (Edinburgh, 2010), pp. 18-28.

Bibliography   367

BUNČIĆ, D., *et al.*, *Biscriptality* (n.d.), <http://biscriptality.org>.

BURCHFIELD, R., "The language and orthography of the *Ormulum* MS", *Transactions of the Philological Society* 55.1 (1956), pp. 56-87.

BURNLEY, J.D., "Sources of standardisation in later Middle English", in: *Standardizing English: Essays in the History of Language Change*, ed. J.B. TRAHERN (Knoxville, 1989), pp. 23-41.

BURROW, J.A., "The sinking island and the dying author: R.W. Chambers fifty years on", *Essays in Criticism* 40.1 (1990), pp. 1-23.

BUTCHER, A., "The functions of script in the speech community of a late medieval town, *c.* 1300-1550", in: *The Uses of Script and Print, 1300-1700*, ed. J. CRICK and A. WALSHAM (Cambridge, 2004), pp. 157-170.

BYNUM, C.W., *Metamorphosis and Identity* (New York, 2001).

CALVET, J.-L., *Les voix de la ville: Introduction à la sociolinguistique urbaine* (Paris, 1994).

CAMARGO, M., and M. CURRY WOODS, "Writing instruction in late medieval Europe", in: *A Short History of Writing Instruction: From Ancient Greece to Modern America*, ed. J.J. MURPHY, 3rd edn. (New York, 2012), pp. 114-147.

CAMILLE, M., "Seeing as reading: Some visual implications of medieval literacy and illiteracy", *Art History* 8.1 (1985), pp. 26-49.

CAMPBELL, C.I., "A study of Glasgow University Library MS Hunter 232: John Lydgate's 'Life of Our Lady'" (unpublished M. Phil. thesis, University of Glasgow, 2009).

CANNON, C., *From Literacy to Literature: England, 1300-1400* (Oxford, 2016).

CANNON, C., "Spelling practice: The *Ormulum* and the word", *Forum for Modern Language Studies* 33.3 (1997), pp. 229-244.

CARROLL, R., M. PEIKOLA, H. SALMI, M.-L. VARILA, J. SKAFFARI, and R. HILTUNEN, "Pragmatics on the page", *European Journal of English Studies* 17.1 (2013), pp. 54-71.

CARRUTHERS, M., *The Book of Memory: A Study of Memory in Medieval Culture* (Cambridge, 1990).

CECCHERINI, I., "Teaching, function, and social diffusion of writing in thirteenth- and fourteenth-century Florence', in: *Teaching Writing, Learning to Write: Proceedings of the XVIth Colloquium of the Comité International de Paléographie Latine*, ed. P.R. ROBINSON (London, 2010), pp. 177-192.

CENOZ, J., and D. GORTER, "Linguistic landscape and minority languages", in: *Linguistic Landscape: A New Approach to Multilingualism*, ed. D. GORTER (Clevedon, 2006), pp. 67-80.

CHAMPION, M.J., *Medieval Graffiti: The Lost Voices of England's Churches* (London, 2015).

CHAMPION, M.J., "Writing on the wall: workshop on historic graffiti", unpublished paper (University of Birmingham, 18 July 2019).

368 *Bibliography*

CHAMPION, P., *Le manuscrit autographe des poésies de Charles D'Orléans* (Paris, 1907).

CHRISTIE, E.J., "The cryptographic imagination: revealing and concealing in Anglo-Saxon literature", in: *Material History of Medieval and Early Modern Ciphers: Cryptography and the History of Literacy*, ed. K. ELLISON and S. KIM (New York, 2018: *Material Readings in Early Modern Culture*), n.p. (e-book).

CLANCHY, M.T., *From Memory to Written Record: England 1066-1307*, 3rd edn. (Malden, Oxford, and Chichester, 2013).

CLANCHY, M.T., *Looking back from the Invention of Printing: Mothers and the Teaching of Reading in the Middle Ages* (Turnhout, 2018: *Utrecht Studies in Medieval Literacy* 40).

CLARK, C., "The myth of the Anglo-Norman scribe", in: *History of Englishes: New Methods and Interpretations in Historical Linguistics*, ed. M. RISSANEN, O. IHALAINEN, T. NEVALAINEN, and I. TAAVITSAINEN (Berlin, 1992: *Topics in English Linguistics* 10), pp. 117-129.

CLARK, C., "Onomastics", in: *The Cambridge History of the English Language: Volume Two: 1066-1476*, ed. N. BLAKE (Cambridge, 1992), pp. 542-606.

CLEAVER, L., "Grammar and her children: Learning to read in the art of the twelfth century", *Marginalia* 19 (2015), n.p., <https://merg.soc.srcf.net/journal/09education/cleaver.php>.

COHEN, N., "Scratches and story-telling: Graffiti recording and interpretation at National Trust sites", unpublished paper (University of Southampton, 5 October 2019: *Making Your Mark: The First National Symposium for the Study of Historic Graffiti*).

COHEN-MUSHLIN, A., "A school for scribes", in: *Teaching Writing, Learning to Write: Proceedings of the XVIth Colloquium of the Comité International de Paléographie Latine*, ed. P.R. ROBINSON (London, 2010), pp. 61-87.

COLBOURN, B., and M. YNYS-MON, *Cambridgeshire Churches*, <http://druidic.org/camchurch/>.

Communities of Practice in the History of English, ed. J. KOPACZYK and A.H. JUCKER (Amsterdam, 2013).

CONDE-SILVESTRE, J.C., and J. HERNÁNDEZ-CAMPOY, "A sociolinguistic approach to the diffusion of chancery written practices in late fifteenth-century private correspondence", *Neuphilologische Mitteilungen* 105.2 (2004), pp. 133-152.

CONNER, P.W., "The Ruthwell monument runic poem in a tenth-century context", *Review of English Studies* 59 (2008), pp. 25-51.

CONNOLLY, M., "Books for the '*helpe of euery persoone þat þenkiþ to be saued*': Six devotional anthologies from fifteenth-century London", *The Yearbook of English Studies* 33 (2003), pp. 170-181.

CONNOLLY, M., "Compiling the book", in: *Book Production and Publishing in England 1350-1500*, ed. A. GILLESPIE and D. WAKELIN (Cambridge, 2011), pp. 129-149.

Bibliography 369

CONNOLLY, M., *John Shirley: Book Production and the Noble Household in Fifteenth-Century England* (Aldershot, 1998).

COOTE, L.A., *Prophecy and Public Affairs in Later Medieval England* (Woodbridge, 2000).

COPELAND, R., *Pedagogy, Intellectuals, and Dissent in the Later Middle Ages: Lollardy and Ideas of Learning* (Cambridge, 2004).

CORNELIUS, I., "The text of the *ABC of Aristotle* in the 'Winchester Anthology'", *Anglia* 139.2 (2021), pp. 400-418.

COULMAS, F., "Linguistic landscaping and the seed of the public sphere", in: *Linguistic Landscape: Expanding the Scenery*, ed. E. SHOHAMY and D. GORTER (London, 2009), pp. 13-24.

COULMAS, F., *Sociolinguistics: The Study of Speakers' Choices*, 2nd edn. (Cambridge, 2013).

COULMAS, F., *Writing and Society* (Cambridge, 2013).

COULTON, G.G., "Medieval graffiti, especially in the eastern counties", in: *Medieval Studies*, 2nd ser. 12 (London, 1915), pp. 53-62 and plates 1-16.

CRAIG, D.J., "The distribution of pre-Norman sculpture in South-West Scotland: Provenance, ornament, and regional groups", 4 vols. (unpublished PhD thesis, Durham University, 1992), <http://etheses.dur.ac.uk/1553>.

CRAMPTON, G.R., "Chaucer's singular prayer", *Medium Ævum* 59 (1990), pp. 191-213.

CRÉ, M., *Vernacular Mysticism in the Charterhouse: A Study of London, British Library, MS Additional 37790* (Turnhout, 2006: *The Medieval Translator* 9).

CRICK, J., "The art of writing: Scripts and scribal production", in: *The Cambridge History of Early Medieval English Literature*, ed. C. LEES (Cambridge, 2012), pp. 50-72.

CRICK, J., "English vernacular script", in: *The Cambridge History of the Book in Britain: Volume I: c. 400-1100*, ed. R. GAMESON (Cambridge, 2011), pp. 174-186.

CRICK, J., "Historical literacy in the archive: Post-Conquest imitative copies of pre-Conquest charters and some French comparanda", in: *The Long Twelfth-Century View of the Anglo-Saxon Past*, ed. M. BRETT and D. WOODMAN (Aldershot, 2015), pp. 159-190.

CRICK, J., "Learning and training", in: *A Social History of England 900-1200*, ed. J. CRICK and E. VAN HOUTS (Cambridge, 2011), pp. 352-372.

CRYSTAL, D., *Language Play* (Harmondsworth, 1998).

CUTLER, J.L., "A Middle English acrostic", *Modern Language Notes* 70.2 (1995), pp. 87-89.

DA ROLD, O., T. KATO, M. SWAN, and E. TREHARNE, *The Production and Use of English Manuscripts 1060 to 1220* (Stanford, 2018), <https://em1060.stanford.edu/>.

DALBELLO, M., "Introduction", in: *Visible Writings: Cultures, Forms, Readings*, ed. M. DALBELLO and M. SHAW (New Brunswick, 2011), pp. 3-11.

370   *Bibliography*

DALLACHY, F.J., "A study of the manuscript contexts of Benedict Burgh's Middle English *Distichs of Cato*" (unpublished PhD thesis, University of Glasgow, 2013).

DANET, B., *Cyberpl@y: Communicating Online* (Oxford, 2001).

DAVIDSON, C., *The Guild Chapel Wall Paintings at Stratford-upon-Avon* (New York, 1988).

DAVIS, M.E., "Lydgate at Long Melford: Reassessing the *Testament* and '*Quis dabit meo capiti fontem lacrimarum*' in their Local Context", *Journal of Medieval Religious Cultures* 43.1 (2017), pp. 77-114.

DE HAMEL, C., "Friar Baldry's pattern book", in: *Tributes to Kathleen L. Scott, English Medieval Manuscripts: Readers, Makers, and Illuminators*, ed. M. VILLALOBOS HENNESSY (Turnhout, 2009), pp. 21-30.

DE HAMEL, C., and P. LOVETT, "Introduction", in: *The Macclesfield Alphabet Book: A Facsimile*, introduced by C. DE HAMEL and P. LOVETT (London, 2010), pp. 7-21.

DEBIAIS, V., *Messages de pierre: La lecture des inscriptions dans la communication médiévale (XIIIe-XIVe siècle)* (Turnhout, 2009).

DENLEY, M., "Elementary teaching techniques and Middle English religious didactic writing", in: *Langland, The Mystics, and the Medieval English Religious Tradition: Essays in Honour of S. S. Hussey*, ed. H. PHILLIPS (Cambridge, 1990), pp. 223-241.

DENNISON, L., and N. ROGERS, "A medieval best-seller: Some examples of decorated copies of Higden's *Polychronicon*", in: *The Church and Learning in Later Medieval Society, Essays in Honour of R.B. Dobson: Proceedings of the 1992 Harlaxton Symposium*, ed. C.M. BARRON and J. STRATFORD (Donington, 2002), pp. 80-99.

DEROLEZ, A., *The Palaeography of Gothic Manuscript Books from the Twelfth to the Early Sixteenth Century* (Cambridge, 2003).

DEROLEZ, R., "Runic literacy among the Anglo-Saxons", in: *Britain 400-600: Language and History*, ed. A. BAMMESBERGER and A. WOLLMANN (Heidelberg, 1990), pp. 397-436.

DEUMERT, A., "Mimesis and mimicry in language – Creativity and aesthetics as the performance of (dis-)semblances", *Language Sciences* 65 (2018), pp. 9-17.

DEWA, R.J., "The runic riddles of the Exeter Book: Language games and Anglo-Saxon scholarship", *Nottingham Medieval Studies* 39 (1995), pp. 26-36.

DigiPal: Digital Resource and Database of Manuscripts, Palaeography, and Diplomatic (2011-2014), <http://www.digipal.eu/>.

DOLEŽALOVÁ, L., "On mistake and meaning: *Scinderationes fonorum* in medieval *artes memoriae*, mnemonic verses, and manuscripts", *Language & History* 52.1 (2009), pp. 26-40.

DOVE, M., "Evading textual intimacy: The French secular verse", in: *Studies in the Harley Manuscript: The Scribes, Contents, and Social Contexts of British Library MS Harley 2253*, ed. S.G. FEIN (Kalamazoo, MI, 2000), pp. 329-349.

Bibliography

DOYLE, A.I., "Penwork flourishing of initials in England from *c.* 1380", in: *Tributes to Kathleen L. Scott, English Medieval Manuscripts: Readers, Makers, and Illuminators*, ed. M. VILLALOBOS HENNESSY (Turnhout, 2009), pp. 65-72.

DOYLE, A.I., "Reflections on some manuscripts of Nicholas Love's *Myrrour of the Blessed Lyf of Jesu Christ*", *Leeds Studies in English*, n.s. 1 (1983), pp. 82-93.

DRIMMER, S., *The Art of Allusion: Illuminators and the Making of English Literature, 1403-1476* (Philadelphia, 2019).

DRIVER, M., "'*Me Fault Faire*': French makers of manuscripts for English patrons", in: *Language and Culture in Medieval Britain: The French of England c. 1100-c. 1500*, ed. J. WOGAN-BROWNE with C. COLLETTE, M. KOWALESKI, L.R. MOONEY, A. PUTTER, and D. TROTTER (York, 2009), pp. 420-443.

DROUT, M.D.C., "Instructional effects of the Exeter Book 'Wisdom Poems'", in: *Form and Content of Instruction in Anglo-Saxon England in the Light of Contemporary Manuscript Evidence*, ed. P. LENDINARA, L. LAZZARI, and M.A. D'ARONCO (Turnhout, 2007: *Fédération Internationale des Instituts d'Etudes Médiévales, Textes et Etudes du Moyen Age* 39), pp. 447-466.

DROUT, M.D.C., and E. CHAUVET, "Tracking the moving ratio of *þ* to *ð* in Anglo-Saxon texts: A new method, and evidence for a lost Old English version of the 'Song of the Three Youths'", *Anglia* 133.2 (2015), pp. 278-319.

DRUMMOND, R., and E. SCHLEEF, "Identity in variationist sociolinguistics", in: *The Routledge Handbook of Language and Identity*, ed. S. PREECE (London, 2016), pp. 50-65.

DUMITRESCU, I., *The Experience of Education in Anglo-Saxon England* (Cambridge, 2018).

DUMVILLE, D.N., *English Caroline Script and Monastic History: Studies in Benedictinism, AD 950-1030* (Woodbridge, 1993).

ECKERT, P., *Language Variation as Social Practice: The Linguistic Construction of Identity in Belten High* (Oxford, 1999).

ECKERT, P., and E. WENGER, "Dialogue: Communities of practice in sociolinguistics", *Journal of Sociolinguistics* 9.4 (2005), pp. 582-589.

EDWARDS, A.S.G., "Middle English inscriptional verse texts", in: *Texts and their Contexts: Papers from the Early Book Society*, ed. J. SCATTERGOOD and J. BOFFEY (Dublin, 1997), pp. 26-43.

EISENSTEIN, E., *The Printing Press as an Agent of Change*, 2 vols. (Cambridge, 1979).

ELDREDGE, L.M., *Index of Middle English Prose, Handlist IX: Manuscripts in the Ashmole Collection, Bodleian Library, Oxford* (Cambridge, 2007).

ELWORTHY, F.T., "Canonsleigh", *Reports and Transactions of the Devonshire Association* 24 (1892), pp. 359-376.

ETHERTON, J., "Cok [Coke], John (c. 1393-c. 1468), Augustinian canon and compiler of the cartulary of St. Bartholomew's Hospital, London", *Oxford Dictionary of National Biography* (Oxford, 2004), <https://www.oxforddnb.com/>.

372   *Bibliography*

FAVREAU, R., *Epigraphe Médiévale* (Turnhout, 1997: *L'atelier du médiéviste* 5).

FEIN, S.G., "The contents of Robert Thornton's manuscripts", in: *Robert Thornton and his Books*, ed. S.G. FEIN and M. JOHNSTON (Woodbridge, 2014), pp. 13-65.

FEIN, S.G., "Introduction", in: *Interpreting MS Digby 86: A Tri-lingual Book from Thirteenth-Century Worcestershire*, ed. S.G. FEIN (Woodbridge, 2019), pp. 1-9.

FIORETTI, P., "Ink writing and '*A sgraffio*' writing in ancient Rome: From learning to practical use", in: *Teaching Writing, Learning to Write: Proceedings of the XVIth Colloquium of the Comité International de Paléographie Latine*, ed. P.R. ROBINSON (London, 2010), pp. 3-16.

FLEMING, J., *Graffiti and the Writing Arts of Early Modern England* (London, 2001).

FLOYD, J., "St. George and the '*Steyned Halle*': Lydgate's verse for the London armourers", in: *Lydgate Matters: Poetry and Material Culture in the Fifteenth Century*, ed. L. COOPER and A. DENNY-BROWN (New York and Basingstoke, 2008), pp. 139-164.

FRAENKEL, B., "Rebus-Signatures", in: *Sign and Design: Script as Image in Cross-Cultural Perspective (300-1600 CE)*, ed. B.M. BEDOS-REZAK and J. HAMBURGER (Washington, 2016), pp. 71-84.

FREDELL, J., "The Thornton anuscripts and book production in York", in: *Robert Thornton and his Books*, ed. S.G. FEIN and M. JOHNSTON (Woodbridge, 2014), pp. 109-130.

FREEMAN, J., "'Towards acquaintance with the following table': The earliest indexes to Ranulph Higden's *Polychronicon*" (n.d.), <https://prezi.com/orlfwnhamvx4/the-earliest-indexes-to-ranulph-higdens-polychronicon/>.

FRIEDMAN, J.B., *Northern English Books, Owners, and Makers in the Late Middle Ages* (Syracuse, NY, 1995).

GALBRAITH, V.H., "John Seward and his circle", *Medieval and Renaissance Studies* 1 (1941), pp. 85-104.

GAMESON, R., *The Scribe Speaks? Colophons in Early English Manuscripts* (Cambridge, 2002: *H.M. Chadwick Memorial Lectures* 12).

GANZ, D., "Early medieval display scripts and the problems of how we see them", in: *Graphic Signs of Identity, Faith, and Power in Late Antiquity and the Early Middle Ages*, ed. I. GARIPZANOV, C. GOODSON, and H. MAGUIRE (Turnhout, 2017), pp. 125-143.

GANZ, D., "Risk and fluidity in script: An Insular instance", in: *Teaching Writing, Learning to Write: Proceedings of the XVIth Colloquium of the Comité International de Paléographie Latine*, ed. P.R. ROBINSON (London, 2010), pp. 17-24.

GARDHAM, J., *The World of Chaucer: Medieval Books and Manuscripts* (Glasgow, 2004), <https://www.gla.ac.uk/myglasgow/library/files/special/exhibns/chaucer/index.html>.

Bibliography 373

GARIPZANOV, I., "Introduction", in: *Graphic Signs of Identity, Faith, and Power in Late Antiquity and the Early Middle Ages*, ed. I. GARIPZANOV, C. GOODSON, and H. MAGUIRE (Turnhout, 2017), pp. 1-22.

GARIPZANOV, I., "The rise of graphicacy in late Antiquity and the early Middle Ages", *Viator* 46.2 (2015), pp. 1-21.

GILBERT, B., "Cistercian script and silence", *Cistercian Studies Quarterly* 49.3 (2014), pp. 367-397.

GILBERT, P., *Cultural Identity and Political Ethics* (Edinburgh, 2010).

GILES, K., A. MASINTON, and G. ARNOTT, "Visualising the Guild Chapel, Stratford-upon-Avon: Digital models as research tools in buildings archaeology", *Internet Archaeology* 32 (2012), n.p., <https://intarch.ac.uk/journal/issue32/index.html>.

GLORIEUX-DE GAND, T., with A. KELDERS, *Formules de copiste: Les colophons des manuscrits datés* (Brussels, 1991).

GNEUSS, H., *Handlist of Anglo-Saxon Manuscripts: A List of Manuscripts and Manuscript Fragments Written or Owned in England up to 1100* (Tempe, AZ, 2001).

GNEUSS, H., "The origin of standard Old English and Æthelwold's school at Winchester", *Anglo-Saxon England* 1 (1972), pp. 63-83.

GNEUSS, H., "The study of language in Anglo-Saxon England", in: *Textual and Material Culture in Anglo-Saxon England: Thomas Northcote Toller and the Toller Memorial Lectures*, ed. D. SCRAGG (Cambridge, 2003), pp. 75-105.

GODDEN, M., "King Alfred's *Preface* and the teaching of Latin in Anglo-Saxon England", *English Historical Review* 117 (2002), pp. 596-604.

GÖRLACH, M., *The Textual Tradition of the* South English Legendary (Leeds, 1974: *Leeds Texts and Monographs* 6).

GORTER, D., "Introduction: The study of the linguistic landscape as a new approach to multilingualism", in: *Linguistic Landscape: A New Approach to Multilingualism*, ed. D. GORTER (Clevedon, 2006), pp. 1-6.

Gothic: Art for England 1400-1547, ed. R. MARKS and P. WILLIAMSON (London, 2003).

GRAY, D., "A Middle English epitaph", *Notes and Queries* n.s. 8.4 (1961), pp. 132-135.

GRAY, D., "A Middle English verse at Warkworth", *Notes and Queries* n.s. 14.4 (1967), pp. 131-132.

GRAY, N., *Lettering as Drawing* (London, 1971).

GREEN, J., "The mystery of the medieval doodle" (BBC Radio 4, 2016: *Today Programme*), <https://www.bbc.co.uk/programmes/p04jq01b>.

GREG, W.W., "The troubles of a Norman scribe", *The Modern Language Review* 5.3 (1910), pp. 282-285.

GRETSCH, M., "Literacy and the uses of the vernacular", in: *The Cambridge Companion to Old English Literature*, ed. M. GODDEN and M. LAPIDGE (Cambridge, 2013), pp. 273-294.

374 *Bibliography*

GRIFFITH, D., "English commemorative inscriptions: Some literary dimensions", in: *Memory and Commemoration in Medieval England*, ed. C.M. BARRON and C. BURGESS (Donington, 2010: *Harlaxton Medieval Studies* 20), pp. 251-270.

GRIFFITH, M., "Riddle 19 of the Exeter Book: '*Snac*', an Old English acronym", *Notes and Queries* n.s. 39.1 (1992), pp. 15-16.

GRIVELET, S., "Introduction", *International Journal of the Sociology of Language* (Special issue: *Digraphia: Writing Systems and Society*) 150 (2001), pp. 1-10.

GUYOTJEANNIN, O., "Le vocabulaire de la diplomatique en latin médiéval", in: *Vocabulaire du livre et de l'écriture au Moyen Age: Actes de la table ronde, Paris 24-26 septembre 1987*, ed. O. WEIJERS (Turnhout, 1989: *Etudes sur le vocabulaire intellectuel du Moyen Age* 2), pp. 120-134.

GWARA, S., "Anglo-Saxon schoolbooks", in: *The Cambridge History of the Book in Britain: Volume I: c. 400-1100*, ed. R. GAMESON (Cambridge, 2011), pp. 507-524.

HAHN, C., "Letter and spirit: The power of the letter, the enlivenment of the word in medieval art", in: *Visible Writings: Cultures, Forms, Readings*, ed. M. DALBELLO and M. SHAW (New Brunswick, NJ, 2011), pp. 55-76.

HALL, S., "Who needs 'identity'?", in: *Questions of Cultural Identity*, ed. S. HALL and P. DU GAY (London, 1996), pp. 1-17.

HALSALL, M., "Runes and the mortal condition in Old English poetry", *The Journal of English and Germanic Philology* 88.4 (1989), pp. 477-486.

HAMBURGER, J., "The iconicity of script", *Word & Image* 27.3 (2011), pp. 249-261.

HAMER, R.F.S., "Spellings of the fifteenth-century scribe Ricardus Franciscus", in: *Five Hundred Years of Words and Sounds*, ed. E.G. STANLEY and D. GRAY (Cambridge, 1983), pp. 353-365.

HAMESSE, J., "Le vocabulaire de la transmission orale des textes", in: *Vocabulaire du livre et de l'écriture au Moyen Age: Actes de la table ronde, Paris 24-26 septembre 1987*, ed. O. WEIJERS (Turnhout, 1989: *Etudes sur le vocabulaire intellectuel du Moyen Age* 2), pp. 168-194.

HAMMOND, E.P., "Latin texts of the Dance of Death", *Modern Philology* 8.3 (1911), pp. 399-410.

HANNA, R., "Humphrey Newton and Bodleian Library MS Lat. Misc. c. 66", *Medium Aevum* 69.2 (2000), pp. 279-291.

HANNA, R., *London Literature, 1300-1380* (Cambridge, 2005).

HANNA, R., "Sir Thomas Berkeley and his patronage", *Speculum* 64.4 (1989), pp. 878-916.

HARRINGTON, M., "Of earth you were made: Constructing the bilingual poem '*Erþ*' in British Library, MS Harley 913", *Florilegium* 31 (2014), pp. 105-137.

HARRINGTON, M., "A trilingual version of '*Erthe upon erthe*' in the National Archives of the United Kingdom, E 175/11/16", *Journal of the Early Book Society* 19 (2016), pp. 197-215.

Bibliography 375

HARRIS, K., "The origins and bibliographical make-up of Cambridge University Library MS Ff.1.6", *Transactions of the Cambridge Bibliographical Society* 8.3 (1983), pp. 299-333.

HARRIS, R., *Rethinking Writing* (London, 2000).

HARRIS, S., *The Linguistic Past in Twelfth-Century Britain* (Cambridge, 2017).

HARRIS, S.J., "Anglo-Saxon ciphers", in: *Material History of Medieval and Early Modern Ciphers: Cryptography and the History of Literacy*, ed. K. ELLISON and S. KIM (New York, 2018), n.p. (e-book).

HEFFERNAN, T., "The use of the phrase '*plenus amoris*' in scribal colophons", *Notes and Queries* n.s. 28.6 (1981), pp. 493-494.

HELLINGA, L., "Nicholas Love in print", in: *Nicholas Love at Waseda*, ed. S. ORURO, R. BEADLE, and M. SARGENT (Cambridge, 1997), pp. 143-162.

HERNÁNDEZ-CAMPOY, J., "Overt and covert prestige in late Middle English: A case study in East Anglia", *Folia Linguistica Historica* 42 (2009), pp. 1-26.

HIATT, A., *The Making of Medieval Forgeries: False Documents in Fifteenth-Century England* (London, 2004).

HIATT, A., "Worlds in books", in: *Taxonomies of Knowledge: Information and Order in Medieval Manuscripts*, ed. E. STEINER and L. RANSOM (Philadelphia, 2015), pp. 37-55.

HILL, B., "Cambridge, Fitzwilliam Museum, MS McClean 123", *Notes and Queries* n.s. 12.3 (1965), pp. 87-90.

HILL, B., "A manuscript from Nuneaton: Cambridge Fitzwilliam Museum MS McClean 123", *Transactions of the Cambridge Bibliographical Society* 12.3 (2002), pp. 191-205.

HILL, J., "Ælfric's grammatical triad", in: *Form and Content of Instruction in Anglo-Saxon England in the Light of Contemporary Manuscript Evidence*, ed. P. LENDINARA, L. LAZZARI, and M.A. D'ARONCO (Turnhout, 2007: *Fédération Internationale des Instituts d'Etudes Médiévales, Textes et Etudes du Moyen Age* 39), pp. 285-307.

HILL, J., "Learning Latin in Anglo-Saxon England: Traditions, texts, and techniques", in: *Learning and Literacy in Medieval England and Abroad*, ed. S. REES JONES (Turnhout, 2003: *Utrecht Studies in Medieval Literacy* 3), pp. 7-30.

HINES, J., "New insights into early Old English from recent Anglo-Saxon runic finds", *NOWELE: North-Western European Language Evolution* 73.1 (2020), pp. 69-90.

HINES, J., "The runic inscriptions of early Anglo-Saxon England", in: *Britain 400-600: Language and History*, ed. A. BAMMESBERGER and A. WOLLMANN (Heidelberg, 1990), pp. 437-455.

HINES, J., "The writing of English in Kent: Contexts and influences from the sixth to the ninth century", *NOWELE: North-Western European Language Evolution* 50-51 (2007), pp. 63-92.

HINES, J., and M. JULIAN-JONES, "Below Malvern: MS Digby 86, the Grimhills and the Underhills and their regional and social context", in: *Interpreting MS Digby 86: A Tri-lingual Book from Thirteenth-Century Worcestershire*, ed. S.G. FEIN (Woodbridge, 2019), pp. 255-273.

HOGG, R.M., "Introduction", in: *The Cambridge History of the English Language: Volume I: The Beginnings to 1066*, ed. R.M. HOGG (Cambridge, 1992), pp. 1-25.

HOGG, R.M., "Phonology and morphology", in: *The Cambridge History of the English Language: Volume I: The Beginnings to 1066*, ed. R.M. HOGG (Cambridge, 1992), pp. 67-167.

HOLE, C., *English Custom and Usage*, 3rd edn. (London, 1950).

HOROBIN, S., *Does Spelling Matter?* (Oxford, 2013).

HOROBIN, S., "Manuscripts and readers of *Piers Plowman*", in: *The Cambridge Companion to* Piers Plowman, ed. A. COLE and A. GALLOWAY (Cambridge, 2014), pp. 179-197.

HUDSON, A., "Observations on the 'Wycliffite orthography'", in: *Pursuing Middle English Manuscripts and their Texts: Essays in Honour of Ralph Hanna*, ed. S. HOROBIN and A. NAFDE (Turnhout, 2017), pp. 77-98.

HUDSON, A., *The Premature Reformation: Wycliffite Texts and Lollard History* (Oxford, 1988).

HUEBNER, T., "Bankok's linguistic landscapes: Environmental print, codemixing, and language change", in: *Linguistic Landscape: A New Approach to Multilingualism*, ed. D. GORTER (Clevedon, 2006), pp. 31-51.

HULT, F.M., "Language ecology and linguistic landscape analysis", in: *Linguistic Landscape: Expanding the Scenery*, ed. E. SHOHAMY and D. GORTER (London, 2009), pp. 88-104.

HUNT, R.W., "Oxford grammar masters in the Middle Ages", repr. in: R.W. HUNT, *The History of Grammar in the Middle Ages: Collected Papers*, ed. G.L. BURSILL-HALL (Amsterdam, 1980: *Studies in the History of the Language Sciences* 5), pp. 167-197.

HUNT, T., *Teaching and Learning Latin in Thirteenth-Century England*, 3 vols. (Cambridge, 1991).

HUNTER, M., "The facsimiles in Thomas Elmham's history of St. Augustine's Canterbury", *The Library* series 5, 28.3 (1973), pp. 215-220.

IRVINE, J.T., and S. GAL, "Language ideology and linguistic differentiation", in: *Regimes of Language: Ideologies, Polities, and Identities*, ed. P. KROSKRITY (Santa Fe, 2000), pp. 35-83.

IRVINE, M., "Bede the grammarian and the scope of grammatical studies in eighth-century Northumbria", *Anglo-Saxon England* 15 (1986), pp. 15-44.

IRVINE, M., *The Making of Textual Culture: 'Grammatica' and Literary Theory, 350-1100* (Cambridge, 1994).

Bibliography 377

IRVINE, M., and D. THOMSON, "*Grammatica* and literary theory", in: *The Cambridge History of Literary Criticism, Vol. 2, The Middle Ages*, ed. A. MINNIS and I. JOHNSON (Cambridge, 2005), pp. 13-41.

JAMES, M.R., *A Descriptive Catalogue of the Manuscripts in the Library of Gonville and Caius College*, 2 vols. (Cambridge, 1914).

JAMES, M.R., *A Descriptive Catalogue of the Manuscripts in the Library of St. John's College Cambridge* (Cambridge, 1913).

JAMES, M.R., *A Descriptive Catalogue of the Western Manuscripts in the Library of Trinity College Cambridge*, 4 vols. (Cambridge, 1900-1904).

JAMES, M.R., *Supplement to a Descriptive Catalogue of the Manuscripts in the Library of Gonville and Caius College* (Cambridge, 1914).

JEFFERSON, J., D. MINKOVA, and A. PUTTER, "Perfect and imperfect rhyme: Romances in the *abab* tradition", *Studies in Philology* 111.4 (2014), pp. 631-651.

JENSEN, V., "The consonantal element *th* in some late Middle English Yorkshire texts", in: *Studies in Variation, Contacts and Change in English, Volume 10, Outposts of Historical Corpus Linguistics: From the Helsinki Corpus to a Proliferation of Resources*, ed. J. TYRKKÖ, M. KILPIÖ, T. NEVALAINEN, and M. RISSANEN (Helsinki, 2012: *Research Unit for Variation, Contacts and Change in English (VARIENG)*), n.p., <https://varieng.helsinki.fi/series/volumes/10/jensen/>.

JOHNS, A., "How to acknowledge a revolution", *The American Historical Review* 107.1 (2002), pp. 106-125.

JOHNSTON, M., "Copying and reading the *Prick of Conscience*", *Speculum* 95.3 (2020), pp. 742-801.

JONES, C., "Discourse communities and medical texts", in: *Medical and Scientific Writing in Late Medieval English*, ed. I. TAAVITSAINEN and P. PAHTA (Cambridge, 2004), pp. 22-36.

JOSEPH, J.E., "Historical perspectives on language and identity", in: *The Routledge Handbook of Language and Identity*, ed. S. PREECE (London, 2016), pp. 19-33.

JUCKER, A.H., and J. KOPACZYK, "Communities of practice as a locus of language change", in: *Communities of Practice in the History of English*, ed. J. KOPACZYK and A.H. JUCKER (Amsterdam, 2013), pp. 1-16.

KABATEK, J., "*Koinés* and *scriptae*", in: *The Cambridge History of the Romance Languages: Volume II: Contexts*, ed. J.C. SMITH and M. MAIDEN (Cambridge, 2013), pp. 143-186.

KELLOGG, A.L., and E.W. TALBERT, "The Wycliffite *Pater noster* and Ten Commandments, with special reference to English MSS 85 and 90 in the John Rylands Library", *Bulletin of the John Rylands Library* 42.2 (1960), pp. 345-377.

KENNEDY, K.E., "Reintroducing the English Books of Hours or 'English Primers'", *Speculum* 89.3 (2014), pp. 693-723.

KENT, E.A., "Some heraldic glass in Norwich", *Journal of the British Society of Master Glass-Painters* 4.3 (1932), pp. 137-141.

378 *Bibliography*

KER, N.R., *Catalogue of Manuscripts containing Anglo-Saxon*, reissued with supplement (Oxford, 1990).

KER, N.R., *Medieval Manuscripts in British Libraries, II: Abbotsford to Keele* (Oxford, 1976).

KER, N.R., "Membra disiecta", *British Museum Quarterly* 12 (1938), pp. 130-135.

KERBY-FULTON, K., and S. JUSTICE, "Scribe D and the marketing of Ricardian literature", in: *The Medieval Professional Reader at Work: Evidence from Manuscripts of Chaucer, Langland, Kempe, and Gower*, ed. K. KERBY-FULTON and M. HILMO (Victoria, BC, 2001: *English Literary Studies* 85), pp. 217-237.

KIDD, P., "An unpublished medieval scribe's advertisement sheet" (10 January 2015), <https://mssprovenance.blogspot.co.uk/2015/01/an-unpublished-medieval-scribes.html>.

KING, A., "Old English ABCs", in: *History of Englishes: New Methods and Interpretations in Historical Linguistics*, ed. M. RISSANEN, O. IHALAINEN, T. NEVALAINEN, and I. TAAVITSAINEN (Berlin, 1992: *Topics in English Linguistics* 10), pp. 130-143.

LAING, M., *Catalogue of Sources for a Linguistic Atlas of Early Medieval English* (Cambridge, 1993).

LAING, M., "Confusion *wrs* confounded: Litteral substitution sets in early Middle English writing systems", *Neuphilologische Mitteilungen* 100 (1999), pp. 251-269.

LAING, M., "Linguistic profiles and textual criticism: The translations by Richard Misyn of Rolle's *Incendium amoris* and *Emendatio vitae*", in: *Middle English Dialectology: Essays on some Principles and Problems by Angus McIntosh, M.L. Samuels, and M. Laing*, ed. M. LAING (Aberdeen, 1989), pp. 188-223.

LAING, M., "The Middle English scribe: *Sprach er wie er schrieb?*", in: *English Historical Linguistics 2006, Volume 3, Geo-Historical Variation in English: Selected Papers from the Fourteenth International Conference on Historical Linguistics (ICEHL 14), Bergamo, 21-26 August 2006*, ed. M. DOSSENA, R. DURY, and M. GOTTI (Amsterdam, 2008), pp. 1-44.

LAING, M., and R. LASS, "Tales of the 1001 nists: The phonological implications of litteral substitution sets in thirteenth-century South-West-Midland texts", *English Language and Linguistics* 7.2 (2003), pp. 257-278.

LAING, M., and K. WILLIAMSON, "The archaeology of medieval texts", in: *Categorization in the History of English*, ed. C.J. KAY and J.J. SMITH (Amsterdam, 2004), pp. 85-145.

LALOU, E., "Les tablettes de cire médiévales", *Bibliothèque de L'Ecole des Chartes* 162 (1989), pp. 123-140.

LANDRY, R., and R.Y. BOURHIS, "Linguistic landscape and ethnolinguistic vitality: An empirical study", *Journal of Language and Social Psychology*, 16.1 (1997), pp. 23-49.

Bibliography 379

LÅNGFORS, A., "*Ky voet amer saunz pesaunce*: Musée Britannique Cotton Cleopatra C.v [*sic,* for C.vi]", *Romania* 55 (1929), pp. 551-552.

LANHAM, C.D., "Writing instruction from late Antiquity to the twelfth century", in: *A Short History of Writing Instruction: From Ancient Greece to Modern America*, ed. J.J. MURPHY, 3rd edn. (New York, 2012), pp. 77-113.

LANHAM, R., *The Electronic Word: Democracy, Technology, and the Arts* (Chicago, 1993).

LAW, V., *Grammar and Grammarians in the Early Middle Ages* (London, 1997).

LAW, V., *The History of Linguistics in Europe: From Plato to 1600* (Cambridge, 2003).

LAW, V., *The Insular Latin Grammarians in the Early Middle Ages* (Woodbridge, 1982).

LAW, V., "The study of grammar in eighth-century Southumbria", *Anglo-Saxon England* 12 (1983), pp. 43-71.

LAWRENCE, M., "The story-teller's verbal *jonglerie* in '*Renart Jongleur*'", in: *Telling the Story in the Middle Ages: Essays in Honor of Evelyn Birge Vitz*, ed. K.A. DUYS, E. EMERY, and L. POSTLETHWAITE (Cambridge, 2015), pp. 31-46.

LEDFORS, J., "St Dunstan in the East: An architectural history of a late medieval London parish church", *London and Middlesex Archaeological Society Transactions* 66 (2015), pp. 47-77.

LENDINARA, P., "The world of Anglo-Saxon learning", in: *The Cambridge Companion to Old English Literature*, ed. M. GODDEN and M. LAPIDGE, 2nd edn. (Cambridge, 2013), pp. 295-312.

LERER, S., *Literacy and Power in Anglo-Saxon Literature* (Lincoln, NE, 1991).

LEWIS, R.E., "The relationship of the Vernon and Simeon texts of the *Pricke of Conscience*", in: *So Meny People Longages and Tonges: Philological Essays in Scots and Mediaeval English Presented to Angus McIntosh*, ed. M. BENSKIN and M.L. SAMUELS (Edinburgh, 1981), pp. 251-264.

LEWIS, R.E., and A. MCINTOSH, *A Descriptive Guide to the Manuscripts of the* Prick of Conscience (Oxford, 1982).

LIIRA, A., *Paratextuality in Manuscript and Print: Verbal and Visual Presentation of the Middle English* Polychronicon (published PhD thesis, University of Turku, 2020).

LILLIS, T., *Sociolinguistics of Writing* (Edinburgh, 2013).

LODGE, R.A., *A Sociolinguistic History of Parisian French* (Cambridge, 2004).

LOWE, K., "Bury St. Edmunds and its Liberty: A charter-text and its afterlife", in: *English Manuscripts Before 1400,* ed. A.S.G. EDWARDS and O. DA ROLD (London, 2012: *English Manuscript Studies 1100-1700* 17), pp. 155-172.

LOUIS, C., "Authority in Middle English proverb literature", *Florilegium* 15 (1998), pp. 85-123.

LUSIGNAN, S., *Essai d'histoire sociolinguistique: Le français picard au Moyen Age* (Paris, 2012: *Recherches littéraires médiévales* 13).

LYOTARD, J.-F., *Discourse, Figure*, ed. and trans. J. MOWITT and A. HUDEK (Minneapolis, 2010).

MACHAN, T.W., *English in the Middle Ages* (Oxford, 2003).

MACRAY, W.D., *Bodleian Library Quarto Catalogues IX: Digby Manuscripts*, repr. with addenda by R.W. HUNT and A.G. WATSON (Oxford, 1999).

MARSDEN, R., "Latin in the ascendant: The interlinear gloss of Oxford, Bodleian Library, Laud Misc. 509", in: *Latin Learning and English Lore: Studies in Anglo-Saxon Literature for Michael Lapidge*, ed. K. O'BRIEN O'KEEFFE and A. ORCHARD, 2 vols. (Toronto, 2005), 2, pp. 132-152.

MARTIN, C.A., "The Middle English versions of the Ten Commandments, with special reference to Rylands English MS 85", *Bulletin of the John Rylands Library* 64.1 (1981), pp. 191-217.

MAY, V., *Connecting Self to Society: Belonging in a Changing World* (Basingstoke, 2013).

MCCARREN, V.P., and R.N. MORY, "The *Abecedarium* from British Museum Cotton Titus D.18", *Modern Philology* 87 (1990), pp. 266-271.

MCCLELLAND, L.S., "Studies in pre-Reformation Carthusian vernacular manuscripts: The cases of Dom William Mede and Dom Stephen Dodesham of Sheen" (unpublished PhD thesis, University of Glasgow, 2013).

MCCOMISH, J.M., *Archaeological Investigations at 12-18 Swinegate, 14 Little Stonegate, and 18 Back Swinegate* (York, 2015: *York Archaeological Trust Web-Based Report* 2015/44).

MCCOMISH, J.M., *The Wooden Writing Tablets from Excavations at 12-18 Swinegate: An Insight Report* (York, 2015).

MCDONALD, N., "A York primer and its alphabet: Reading women in a lay household", in: *The Oxford Handbook of Medieval Literature in English*, ed. E. TREHARNE and G. WALKER with W. GREEN (Oxford, 2010), pp. 181-199.

MCINTOSH, A., "The analysis of written Middle English", repr. in: *Middle English Dialectology: Essays on some Principles and Problems by Angus McIntosh, M.L. Samuels, and M. Laing*, ed. M. LAING (Aberdeen, 1989), pp. 1-21.

MCINTOSH, A., "A new approach to Middle English dialectology", repr. in: *Middle English Dialectology: Essays on some Principles and Problems by Angus McIntosh, M.L. Samuels, and M. Laing*, ed. M. LAING (Aberdeen, 1989), pp. 22-31.

MCINTOSH, A., "Scribal profiles from Middle English texts", repr. in: *Middle English Dialectology: Essays on some Principles and Problems by Angus McIntosh, M.L. Samuels, and M. Laing*, ed. M. LAING (Aberdeen, 1989), pp. 32-45.

MCINTOSH, A., "Some linguistic reflections of a Wycliffite", in: *Franciplegius: Medieval and Linguistic Studies in honor of Francis Peabody Magoun,* ed. J.B. BESSINGER and R.P. CREED (London, 1965), pp. 290-293.

Bibliography   381

MCINTOSH, A., "Towards an inventory of Middle English scribes", repr. in: *Middle English Dialectology: Essays on some Principles and Problems by Angus McIntosh, M.L. Samuels, and M. Laing*, ed. M. LAING (Aberdeen, 1989), pp. 46-63.

MCINTOSH, A., "Word geography in the lexicography of Medieval English", repr. in: *Middle English Dialectology: Essays on some Principles and Problems by Angus McIntosh, M.L. Samuels, and M. Laing*, ed. M. LAING (Aberdeen, 1989), pp. 86-97.

MCKITTERICK, R., "Introduction", in: *The Uses of Literacy in Early Medieval Europe*, ed. R. MCKITTERICK (Cambridge, 1990), pp. 1-10.

MCLUHAN, M., *The Gutenberg Galaxy* (Toronto, 1962).

MEECH, S.B., "Early application of Latin grammar to English", *Proceedings of the Modern Language Association* 50.4 (1935), pp. 1012-1032.

MEGGINSON, D., "The written language of Old English poetry" (unpublished PhD thesis, University of Toronto, 1993).

MEGGINSON, D., "The case against a 'general Old English poetic dialect'", in: *Prosody and Poetics: Essays in Honour of C.B. Hieatt*, ed. M.J. TOSWELL (Toronto, 1995), pp. 117-132.

MENZER, M.J. "Ælfric's English 'Grammar'", *Journal of English and Germanic Philology* 103.1 (2004), pp. 106-124.

MEYERHOFF, M., and A. STRYCHARZ, "Communities of practice", in: *The Handbook of Language Variation and Change*, ed. J.K. CHAMBERS, P. TRUDGILL, and N. SCHILLING-ESTES (Oxford, 2002), pp. 525-548.

MILROY, J., "Middle English dialectology", in: *The Cambridge History of the English Language, Volume 2, 1066-1476*, ed. N. BLAKE (Cambridge, 1992), pp. 156-206.

MOONEY, L.R., "Verses upon death and other wall paintings surviving in the Guild Hall, Stratford-upon-Avon", *Journal of the Early Book Society* 3 (2000), pp. 182-190.

MOONEY, L.R., S. HOROBIN, and E. STUBBS, *Late Medieval English Scribes, Version 1.0* (2011), <http://www.medievalscribes.com>.

MOONEY, L.R., and E. STUBBS, *Scribes and the City: London Guildhall Clerks and the Dissemination of Middle English Literature 1375-1425* (York, 2013).

MORAN, J.A.H., *The Growth of English Schooling: Learning, Literacy, and Laicization in Pre-Reformation York Diocese* (Princeton, 1985).

MOSSER, D.D., *A Digital Catalogue of the Pre-1500 Manuscripts and Incunables of the Canterbury Tales*, 2nd, online edn. (2010), <http://mossercatalogue.net/index.html>.

MOSTERT, M., "Some thoughts on urban schools, urban literacy, and the development of western civilisation", in: *Writing and the Administration of Medieval Towns: Medieval Urban Literacy I*, ed. M. MOSTERT and A. ADAMSKA (Turnhout, 2014: *Utrecht Studies in Medieval Literacy* 27), pp. 337-348.

MURCHISON, K., *Intercultural Dialogue and Multilingualism in Post-Conquest England: A Database of French Literary Manuscripts Produced Between 1100-1550* (n.d.), <https://leidenuniversitylibrary.github.io/manuscript-stats/>.

MURRAY, R.W., "Syllable cut prosody in early Middle English", *Language* 76.3 (2000), pp. 617-654.

NAFDE, A., "Hoccleve's hands: The *mise-en-page* of the autograph and non-autograph manuscripts", *Journal of the Early Book Society* 16 (2013), pp. 53-83.

NEWSTOK, S., *Quoting Death in Early Modern England: The Poetics of Epitaphs beyond the Tomb* (Basingstoke, 2009).

O'BRIEN O'KEEFFE, K., *Visible Song: Transitional Literacy in Old English Verse* (Cambridge, 1990).

OCHS, E., and B.B. SCHIEFFELIN, "The theory of language socialisation", in: *The Handbook of Language Socialisation*, ed. A. DURANTI, E. OCHS, and B.B. SCHIEFFELIN (Oxford, 2012), pp. 1-22.

OKASHA, E., "Literacy in Anglo-Saxon England: The evidence from inscriptions", in: *Medieval Europe, 1992: Art and Symbolism Pre-Printed Papers*, vol. 7 (York, 1992), pp. 85-89.

OKASHA, E., "A second supplement to *Hand-List of Anglo-Saxon Non-Runic Inscriptions*", *Anglo-Saxon England* 21 (1992), pp. 37-85.

OKASHA, E., "A supplement to *Hand-List of Anglo-Saxon Non-Runic Inscriptions*", *Anglo-Saxon England* 11 (1982), pp. 83-118.

OKASHA, E., "Vernacular or Latin? The languages of Insular inscriptions, AD 500-1100", in: *Epigrafik 1988: Fachtagung für mittelalterliche und neuzeitliche Epigrafik, Graz, Mai 1988*, ed. W. KOCH (Vienna, 1990), pp. 139-150.

OKASHA, E., "The Waltham alphabet: An Anglo-Saxon inscription", *Medieval Archaeology* 20 (1976), pp. 129-131.

OLIVER, J., and T. NEAL, "Wild signs: An introduction", in: *Wild Signs: Graffiti in Archaeology and History*, ed. J. OLIVER and T. NEAL (Oxford, 2010: *Studies in Contemporary and Historical Archaeology* 6), pp. 1-4.

OOSTERWIJK, S., "Death, memory, and commemoration: John Lydgate and '*Macabrees Daunce*' at Old St. Paul's Cathedral, London", in: *Memory and Commemoration in Medieval England*, ed. C.M. BARRON and C. BURGESS (Donington, UK, 2010: *Harlaxton Medieval Studies* 20), pp. 185-201.

ORCHARD, A., "Enigma variations: The Anglo-Saxon riddle-tradition", in: *Latin Learning and English Lore: Studies in Anglo-Saxon Literature for Michael Lapidge*, ed. K. O'BRIEN O'KEEFFE and A. ORCHARD, 2 vols. (Toronto, 2005), 1, pp. 284-304.

ORME, N., "An English grammar school, *c.* 1450: Latin exercises from Exeter (Caius College MS 417/447, Folios 16v-24v)", *Traditio* 50 (1995), pp. 261-294.

ORME, N., *English School Exercises, 1420-1530* (Toronto, 2013: *Pontifical Institute of Mediaeval Studies, Studies and Texts* 181).

ORME, N., *English Schools in the Middle Ages* (London, 1973).

Bibliography 383

ORME, N., "Games and education in medieval England", in: *Games and Gaming in Medieval Literature*, ed. S. PATTERSON (New York, 2015), pp. 45-60.

ORME, N., *Medieval Children* (New Haven, 2001).

ORME, N., *Medieval Schools: From Roman Britain to Renaissance England* (New Haven, 2006).

ORME, N., "School exercises from Canterbury, *c.* 1480", *Archaeologia Cantiana* 131 (2011), pp. 111-128.

ORTON, P., *Writing in a Speaking World: The Pragmatics of Literacy in Anglo-Saxon Inscriptions and Old English Poetry* (Tempe, AZ, 2014).

OUY, G., "Le *Valdebonum* perdu et retrouvé", *Scriptorium*, 42 (1989), pp. 198-205.

OWEN, K., "Traces of presence and pleading: Approaches to the study of graffiti at Tewkesbury Abbey", in: *Wild Signs: Graffiti in Archaeology and History*, ed. J. OLIVER and T. NEAL (Oxford, 2010: *Studies in Contemporary and Historical Archaeology* 6), pp. 35-46.

PACE, G.B., "The adorned initials of Chaucer's *ABC*", *Manuscripta* 23.2 (1979), pp. 88-98.

PÄCHT, O., and J.G. ALEXANDER, *Illuminated Manuscripts in the Bodleian Library, Oxford*, 4 vols. (Oxford, 1966-1974).

PAGE, R.I., "The Bewcastle Cross", *Nottingham Medieval Studies* 4 (1960), pp. 36-57.

PAGE, R.I., *An Introduction to English Runes*, 2nd edn. (Woodbridge, 1999).

PAGE, W., *A History of the County of Warwick: Volume 2* (London, 1908: *Victoria History of the Counties of England*).

PAGE, W., "Parishes: Ashwell", in: *A History of the County of Hertford: Volume 3*, ed. W. PAGE (London, 1912: *Victoria History of the Counties of England*), pp. 199-209.

PALMER, R., "Bede as a textbook writer: A study of his *De Arte metrica*", *Speculum* 34.4 (1959), pp. 573-584.

PANTIN, W.A., "A medieval English collection of proverbs and riddles from the Rylands Latin MS 394", *Bulletin of the John Rylands Library* 14 (1930), pp. 81-114.

PARKES, M.B., "Archaizing hands in English manuscripts", repr. in: M.B. PARKES, *Pages from the Past: Medieval Writing Skills and Manuscript Books*, ed. P.R. ROBINSON and R. ZIM (Farnham, 2012), pp. 101-141.

PARKES, M.B., "The contribution of Insular scribes of the seventh and eighth centuries to the 'grammar of legibility'", repr. in: M.B. PARKES, *Scribes, Scripts, and Readers: Studies in the Communication, Presentation, and Dissemination of Medieval Texts* (London, 1991), pp. 1-18.

PARKES, M.B., "The influence of the concepts of *ordinatio* and *compilatio* on the development of the book", repr. in: M.B. PARKES, *Scribes, Scripts, and Readers: Studies in the Communication, Presentation, and Dissemination of Medieval Texts* (London, 1991), pp. 55-74.

384   *Bibliography*

PARKES, M.B., "Introduction", in: M.B. Parkes, *Scribes, Scripts, and Readers: Studies in the Communication, Presentation, and Dissemination of Medieval Texts* (London, 1991), pp. XV-XXII.

PARKES, M.B., "On the presumed date and possible origin of the manuscript of the *Orrmulum*: Oxford, Bodleian Library, MS Junius 1", in: *Five Hundred Years of Words and Sounds: A Festschrift for Eric Dobson*, ed. E.G. STANLEY and D. GRAY (Cambridge, 1983), pp. 115-127.

PARKES, M.B., "Patterns of scribal activity and revisions of the text in early copies of works by John Gower", in: *New Science out of Old Books, Manuscripts, and Early Printed Books: Essays in Honour of A.I. Doyle*, ed. R. BEADLE and A.J. PIPER (London, 1995), pp. 81-121.

PARKES, M.B., *Pause and Effect: An Introduction to the History of Punctuation in the West* (Aldershot, 1992).

PARKES, M.B., "*Rædan, areccan, smeagan*: How the Anglo-Saxons read", *Anglo-Saxon England* 26 (1997), pp. 1-22.

PARKES, M. B., "Reading, copying, and interpreting a text in the early Middle Ages", in: *A History of Reading in the West*, ed. G. CAVALLO and R. CHARTIER, trans. L.G. COCHRANE (Cambridge, 1999), pp. 90-102.

PARKES, M.B., *Their Hands before our Eyes: A Closer Look at Scribes: The Lyell Lectures Delivered in the University of Oxford 1999* (Aldershot, 2008).

PARRY, L., "Contributions [to Historic England List No 1102715] Church of St. Mary Ashwell", (n.d.), <https://historicengland.org.uk/listing/the-list/list-entry/1102715#contributions-banner>.

PATTERSON, S., "Sexy, naughty, and lucky in love: Playing *Ragemon le Bon* in English gentry households", in: *Games and Gaming in Medieval Literature*, ed. S. PATTERSON (New York, 2015), chapter 4, n.p. (e-book).

PAUES, A., "The name of the letter ȝ", *The Modern Language Review* 6.4 (1911), pp. 441-454.

PAVLENKO, A., "Linguistic landscape of Kyiv, Ukraine: A diachronic study", in: *Linguistic Landscape in the City*, ed. E. SHOHAMY, E. BEN-RAFAEL, and M. BARNI (Bristol, 2010), pp. 133-150.

PEARSALL, D., "The manuscripts and illustrations of Gower's works", in: *A Companion to Gower*, ed. S. ECHARD (Cambridge, 2004), pp. 73-97.

PEIKOLA, M., "The Wycliffite Bible and 'Central Midland Standard': Assessing the manuscript evidence", *Nordic Journal of English Studies* 2.1 (2003), pp. 29-51.

PENN, S., "Literacy and literate production", in: *Chaucer: An Oxford Guide*, ed. S. ELLIS (Oxford, 2005), pp. 113-129.

Peregrinations: Journal of Medieval Art and Architecture (Special issue: *New Research in Medieval and Later Graffiti*) 6.1 (2017).

Bibliography 385

PERRY, R., "The Clopton manuscript and the Beachamp affinity", in: *Essays in Manuscript Geography: Vernacular Manuscripts of the English West Midlands from the Conquest to the Sixteenth Century*, ed. W. SCASE (Turnhout, 2007), pp. 131-160.

PEVSNER, N., *Worcestershire* (London, 1968: *The Buildings of England*).

PICKERING, O., "Stanzaic verse in the Auchinleck manuscript: *The Alphabetical Praise of Women*", in: *Studies in Late Medieval and Early Renaissance Texts in Honour of John Scattergood*, ed. A.M. D'ARCY and A.J. FLETCHER (Dublin, 2005), pp. 287-304.

PLESCH, V., "Memory on the wall: Graffiti on religious wall paintings", *Journal of Medieval and Early Modern Studies* 31.1 (2002), pp. 167-197.

POPE, N., "*Erthe upon erthe* revisited", *Journal of the Early Book Society* 21 (2018), pp. 53-95.

PORTER, D., "Isidore's *Etymologiae* at the school of Canterbury", *Anglo-Saxon England* 43 (2014), pp. 7-44.

PRITCHARD, V., *English Medieval Graffiti* (Cambridge, 1967).

PURDIE, R., *Anglicising Romance: Tail-Rhyme and Genre in Medieval English Literature* (Cambridge, 2008).

PUTTER, A., "The linguistic repertoire of medieval England, 1100-1500", in: *Imagining Medieval English: Language Structures and Theories, 500-1500*, ed. T.W. MACHAN (Cambridge, 2016), pp. 126-144.

RAMSAY, N., and J.M.W. WILLOUGHBY, *Corpus of British Medieval Library Catalogues XIV: Hospitals, Towns and the Professions* (London, 2009).

REEVES, W.P., "Stray verse", *Modern Language Notes* 9.4 (1894), pp. 201-205.

REYNHOUT, L., *Formules latines de colophons*, 2 vols. (Turnhout, 2006).

REYNOLDS, S., *Medieval Reading: Grammar, Rhetoric and the Classical Text* (Cambridge, 1996).

RIGG, G., *A History of Anglo-Latin Literature 1066-1422* (Cambridge, 1992).

ROBBINS, R.H., "The poems of Humfrey Newton, Esquire, 1466-1536", *Proceedings of the Modern Language Association* 65.2 (1950), pp. 249-281.

ROBBINS, R.H., "Wall verses at Launceston Priory", *Archiv für das Studium der neueren Sprachen und Literaturen* 200 (1964), pp. 338-343.

ROBERTS, J., *Guide to Scripts used in English Writings up to 1500* (London, 2005).

ROBINSON, F.C., "Syntactical glosses in Latin manuscripts of Anglo-Saxon provenance", *Speculum* 48.3 (1973), pp. 443-479.

ROGOS, J., "Crafting text languages: Spelling systems in manuscripts of the 'Man of Law's Tale' as a means of construing scribal community of practice", in: *Communities of Practice in the History of English*, ed. J. KOPACZYK and A.H. JUCKER (Amsterdam, 2013), pp. 105-121.

ROUSE, R.H., and M.A. ROUSE, "*Statim invenire*: Schools, preachers, and new attitudes to the page", in: *Renaissance and Renewal in the Twelfth Century*, ed. R.L. BENSON and G. CONSTABLE with C.D. LANHAM (Oxford, 1982).

386   *Bibliography*

ROUSE, R.H., and M.A. ROUSE, "Wax tablets", *Language and Communication* 9 (1989), pp. 175-191.

ROYAL COMMISSION ON HISTORICAL MONUMENTS OF ENGLAND, "Great Bardfield", in: *An Inventory of the Historical Monuments in Essex, Volume 1, North West* (London, 1916), pp. 105-113.

RUDOLF, W., "Riddling and reading: Iconicity and logogriphs in Exeter Book Riddles 23 and 45", *Anglia* 130.4 (2012), pp. 499-525.

RUFF, C., "The place of metrics in Anglo-Saxon Latin education: Aldhelm and Bede", *Journal of English and Germanic Philology* 104.2 (2005), pp. 149-170.

RUST, M.D., "The 'ABC of Aristotle'", in: *Medieval Literature for Children*, ed. D.T. KLINE (London, 2003), pp. 63-78.

RUST, M.D., *Imaginary Worlds in Medieval Books: Exploring the Manuscript Matrix* (Basingstoke, 2007).

RUTKOWSKA, H., and P. RÖSSLER, "Orthographic variables", in: *The Handbook of Historical Sociolinguistics*, ed. J. HERNÁNDEZ-CAMPOY and J.C. CONDE-SILVESTRE (Oxford, 2012), pp. 213-236.

SAFRAN, L., "Public textual cultures: A case study in Southern Italy", in: *Textual Cultures of Medieval Italy*, ed. W. ROBINS (Toronto, 2011), pp. 115-144.

SALTZMAN, B.A., "*Vt hkskdkxt*: Early medieval cryptography, textual errors, and scribal agency", *Speculum* 93.4 (2018), pp. 975-1009.

SALVADOR-BELLO, M., *Isidorean Perceptions of Order: The Exeter Book Riddles and Medieval Latin Enigmata* (Morgantown, WV, 2015).

SAMUELS, M.L., "Langland's dialect", repr. in: *The English of Chaucer and his Contemporaries*, ed. J.J. SMITH (Aberdeen, 1988), pp. 70-85.

SAMUELS, M.L., "Spelling and dialect in the Late- and Post-Middle-English periods", in: *So Meny People Longages and Tonges: Philological Essays in Scots and Mediaeval English Presented to Angus McIntosh*, ed. M. BENSKIN and M.L. SAMUELS (Edinburgh, 1981), pp. 43-54.

SANDLER, L.F., *Gothic Manuscripts 1285-1385*, 2 vols. (London, 1986: *A Survey of Manuscripts Illuminated in the British Isles* 5).

SARGENT, M.G., "The transmission by the English Carthusians of some late medieval spiritual writings", *Journal of Ecclesiastical History* 27.3 (1976), pp. 225-240.

SAWYER, P., S. KELLY, and R. RUSHFORTH, *The Electronic Sawyer: Online Catalogue of Anglo-Saxon Charters* (2016), <http://www.esawyer.org.uk/about/index.html>.

SCAHILL, J., "Prodigal early Middle English orthographies: Minds and manuscripts", in: *Language Change and Variation from Old English to Late Modern English: A Festschrift for Minoji Akimoto*, ed. M. KYTOE, J. SCAHILL, and H. TANABE (Bern, 2011), pp. 239-252.

SCALES, L., "Bread, cheese, and genocide: Imagining the destruction of peoples in western medieval Europe", *History* 92.3 (2007), pp. 284-300.

Bibliography 387

SCASE, W., "The artists of the Vernon initials", in: *The Making of the Vernon Manuscript: The Production and Contexts of Oxford, Bodleian Library, MS Eng. Poet. a. 1*, ed. W. SCASE (Turnhout, 2013: *Texts and Transitions* 6), pp. 207-226.

SCASE, W., "John Benet, scribe and compiler, and Dublin, Trinity College, MS 516", in: *Scribal Cultures in Late Medieval England: Festschrift for Linne R. Mooney*, ed. M. CONNOLLY, H. JAMES-MADDOCKS, and †D. PEARSALL (Woodbridge, 2022), pp. 241-258.

SCASE, W., "John Gower's scribes and literatim copying", in: *John Gower in Manuscripts and Early Printed Books*, ed. M. DRIVER, D. PEARSALL, and R.F. YEAGER (Cambridge, 2020), pp. 13-31.

SCASE, W., "The *LALME* typology of scribal practice: Some issues for manuscript studies", in: *Current Explorations in Middle English*, ed. M. STENROOS and K. THENGS (Bern, 2019), pp. 13-33.

SCASE, W., *Literature and Complaint in England, 1272-1553* (Oxford, 2007).

SCASE, W., "Parrot poet: Humphrey Newton and Bodleian Library, MS Lat. Misc. c. 66", in: *Medieval Literary Voices: Embodiment, Materiality and Performance, Essays in Honour of David A. Lawton*, ed. S. RÍKHARÐSDÓTTIR and L. D'ARCENS (Manchester, forthcoming), pp. 172-190.

SCASE, W., *Reginald Pecock* (Aldershot, 1996: *Authors of the Middle Ages* 8).

SCASE, W., "Reinventing the vernacular: Middle English language and its literature", in: *The Cambridge Companion to Medieval English Literature*, ed. L. SCANLON (Cambridge, 2009), pp. 11-23.

SCASE, W., "Threshold-switching: Paratextual functions of scribal colophons in Old and Middle English manuscripts", in: *The Dynamics of Text and Framing Phenomena in the History of English*, ed. B. BOS and M. PEIKOLA (Amsterdam, 2020), pp. 91-113.

SCASE, W., "Tolkien, philology, and the *Reeve's Tale*: Towards the cultural move in Middle English studies", *Studies in the Age of Chaucer* 24 (2002), pp. 325-334.

SCATTERGOOD, J., "The copying of medieval and renaissance manuscripts", in: J. SCATTERGOOD, *Manuscripts and Ghosts: Essays on the Transmission of Medieval and Early Renaissance Literature* (Dublin, 2006), pp. 21-82.

SCHELLER, R.W., *A Survey of Medieval Model Books* (Haarlem, 1963).

SCHIEGG, M., "[Review of] *Communities of Practice in the History of English* (*Pragmatics & Beyond* New Series 235), edited by J. KOPACZYK and A.H. JUCKER", *Journal of Historical Sociolinguistics* 1.1 (2015), pp. 135-138.

SCHOFIELD, J., "Saxon and medieval parish churches in the City of London: A review", *Transactions of the London and Middlesex Archaeological Society* 45 (1994), pp. 23-146.

SCHWYZER, P., "'A tomb once stood in this room': Memorials to memorials in early modern England", *Journal of Medieval and Early Modern Studies* 48.2 (2018), pp. 365-385.

388   *Bibliography*

SCOTTISH GOVERNMENT and EDUCATION SCOTLAND, *Scots Language Policy* (2015), <https://www.gov.scot/binaries/content/documents/govscot/publications/factshee t/2015/09/scots-language-policy-scots-version/documents/scots-language-policy- scots-pdf/scots-language-policy-scots-pdf/govscot3Adocument/scots%2Blanguage %2Bpolicy%2B-%2Bscots.pdf>.

SCRAGG, D., *A Conspectus of Scribal Hands Writing English, 960-1100* (Cambridge, 2012: *Publications of the Manchester Centre for Anglo-Saxon Studies* 11).

SEBBA, M., "Orthography and ideology: Issues in Sranan spelling", *Linguistics* 38.5 (2000), pp. 925-948.

SEBBA, M., "Orthography as literacy: How Manx was 'reduced to writing'", in: *Orthography as Social Action: Scripts, Spelling, Identity, and Power*, ed. A.M. JAFFE, J. ANDROUTSOPOULOS, S. JOHNSON, and M. SEBBA (Berlin, 2012), pp. 161-175.

SEBBA, M., "Phonology meets ideology: The meaning of orthographic practices in British Creole", *Language Problems and Language Planning* 22.1 (1998), pp. 19-47.

SEBBA, M., "Sociolinguistic approaches to writing systems research", *Writing Systems Research* 1.1 (2009), pp. 35-49.

SEBBA, M., *Spelling and Society: The Culture and Politics of Orthography around the World* (Cambridge, 2007).

SEILER, A., *The Scripting of the Germanic Languages: A Comparative Study of 'Spelling Difficulties' in Old English, Old High German, and Old Saxon* (Zurich, 2014).

SEILER, A., "The scripting of Old English: An analysis of Anglo-Saxon spellings for *w* and *þ*", *Sprachwissenschaft* 33.2 (2008), pp. 139-172.

SEILER, A., "Writing the Germanic languages: The early history of the digraphs *th, ch,* and *uu*", in: *Writing Europe, 500-1450*, ed. A. CONTI, O. DA ROLD, and P. SHAW (Cambridge, 2015: *Essays and Studies collected on behalf of the English Association* 68), pp. 101-121.

SERJEANTSON, R.M., and W.R.D. ADKINS, "Hospitals: St. John Baptist and St. John Evangelist, Northampton", in: *A History of the County of Northampton: Volume 2* (London, 1906: *Victoria History of the Counties of England*), pp. 156-159.

SHARIFI, A., "Orthography and calligraphic ideology in an Iranian-American heritage school", in: *Orthography as Social Action: Scripts, Spelling, Identity, and Power*, ed. M. JAFFE, J. ANDROUTSOPOULOS, S. JOHNSON, and M. SEBBA (Berlin, 2012), pp. 225-254.

SHEP, S.J., "Urban palimpsests and contending signs", *Social Semiotics* 25.2 (2015), pp. 209-216.

SHERLOCK, D., *Medieval Drawings and Writings in Ashwell Church, Hertfordshire* (1978).

SHOHAMY, E., E. BEN-RAFAEL, and M. BARNI, "Introduction: An approach to an 'ordered disorder'", in: *Linguistic Landscape in the City*, ed. E. SHOHAMY, E. BEN-RAFAEL, and M. BARNI (Bristol, 2010), pp. XI-XXVIII.

Bibliography   389

SMITH, J.J., "Dialect and standardisation in the Waseda manuscript of Nicholas Love's *Mirror of the Blessed Life of Jesus Christ*", in: *Nicholas Love at Waseda*, ed. S. ORURO, R. BEADLE, and M. SARGENT (Cambridge, 1997), pp. 129-141.

SMITH, J.J., "John Gower and London English", in: *A Companion to Gower*, ed. S. ECHARD (Cambridge, 2004), pp. 61-72.

SMITH, J.J., "Spelling and tradition in fifteenth-century copies of Gower's *Confessio Amantis*", in: *The English of Chaucer and his Contemporaries*, ed. J.J. SMITH (Aberdeen, 1989), pp. 96-113.

SMITH, J.J., "Standard language in early Middle English", in: *Placing Middle English in Context*, ed. I. TAAVITSAINEN, T. NEVALAINEN, P. PAHTA, and M. RISSANEN (Berlin, 2000: *Topics in English Linguistics* 35), pp. 125-139.

SMITH, J.J., *Transforming Early English: The Reinvention of Early English and Older Scots* (Cambridge, 2020).

SMITH, J.J., "The Trinity Gower D-scribe and his work on two early *Canterbury Tales* manuscripts", in: *The English of Chaucer and his Contemporaries*, ed. J.J. SMITH (Aberdeen, 1989), pp. 51-69.

SMITH, M., "Writing models and the formation of national scripts", unpublished First Lyell Lecture in the 2020 Series, University of Oxford, Bodleian Library, <http://podcasts.ox.ac.uk/writing-models-and-formation-national-scripts>.

SOBECKI, S., "'*Ecce patet tensus*': The Trentham manuscript, 'In Praise of Peace', and John Gower's autograph hand", *Speculum* 90.4 (2015), pp. 925-959.

SOLOPOVA, E., "The metre of the *Ormulum*", in: *Studies in English Language and Literature: "Doubt Wisely": Papers in Honour of E.G. Stanley*, ed. M.J. TOSWELL and E.J. TOSWELL (London, 1996), pp. 423-439.

SOPER, H., "Reading the Exeter Book riddles as life writing", *Review of English Studies* 68 (2017), pp. 841-865.

SPINDLER, E., "Flemings in the Peasants' Revolt", in: *Contact and Exchange in Later Medieval Europe: Essays in Honour of Malcolm Vale*, ed. H. SKODA, P. LANTSCHNER, and R.L.J. SHAW (Cambridge, 2012), pp. 59-78.

SPITZMÜLLER, J., "Floating ideologies: Metamorphoses of graphic 'Germanness'", in: *Orthography as Social Action: Scripts, Spelling, Identity, and Power*, ed. A.M. JAFFE, J. ANDROUTSOPOULOS, S. JOHNSON, and M. SEBBA (Berlin, 2012), pp. 255-288.

SPITZMÜLLER, J., "Graphic variation and graphic ideologies: A metapragmatic approach", *Social Semiotics* 25.2 (2015), pp. 126-141.

SPONSLER, C., "Text and textile: Lydgate's tapestry poems", in: *Medieval Fabrications: Dress, Textiles, Clothwork, and other Cultural Imaginings*, ed. E.J. BURNS (New York and Basingstoke, 2004), pp. 19-34.

SPURKLAND, T., "Literacy and 'runacy' in medieval Scandinavia", in: *Scandinavia and Europe 800-1350: Contact, Conflict, and Coexistence*, ed. J. ADAMS and K.

HOLMAN (Turnhout, 2004: *Medieval Texts and Culture of Northern Europe* 4), pp. 333-344.

St. Mary's Ashwell: History, <https://stmarysashwell.org.uk/history/>.

STANCLIFFE, C., "The riddle of the Ruthwell Cross: Audience, intention, and originator reconsidered", in: *Crossing Boundaries: Interdisciplinary Approaches to the Art, Material Culture, Language, and Literature of the Early Medieval World: Essays Presented to Professor Emeritus Richard N. Bailey*, ed. E. CAMBRIDGE and J. HAWKES (Oxford, 2017), pp. 3-14.

STEINBERG, S.H., "A hand-list of specimens of medieval writing-masters", *The Library* 23 (1942), pp. 191-194.

STEINBERG, S.H., "Medieval writing-masters", *The Library* 22 (1941), pp. 1-24.

STEINER, E., *John Trevisa's Information Age: Knowledge and the Pursuit of Literature, c. 1400* (Oxford, 2021).

STEINOVÁ, E., "*Notam superponere studui*: The use of technical signs in the early Middle Ages" (unpublished PhD thesis, Utrecht University, 2016).

STENROOS, M., "From scribal repertoire to text community: The challenge of variable writing systems", in: *Scribal Repertoires in Egypt from the New Kingdom to the Early Islamic Period*, ed. J. CROMWELL and E. GROSSMAN (Oxford, 2017), pp. 20-46.

STENROOS, M., "A Middle English mess of fricative spellings: Reflections on thorn, yogh, and their rivals", in: *To Make his Englissh Sweete upon his Tonge*, ed. M. KRYGIER and L. SIKORSKA (Frankfurt am Main, 2007), pp. 9-35.

STENROOS, M., "Regional dialects and spelling conventions in late Middle English: Searches for *th* in the *LALME* data", in: *Methods and Data in English Historical Dialectology*, ed. M. DOSSENA and R. LASS (Bern, 2004), pp. 257-285.

STENROOS, M., "Regional language and culture: The geography of Middle English linguistic variation", in: *Imagining Medieval English: Language Structures and Theories, 500-1500*, ed. T. MACHAN (Cambridge, 2016), pp. 100-125.

STENROOS, M., and K.V. THENGS, "Two Staffordshires: Real and linguistic space in the study of late Middle English dialects", in: *Studies in Variation, Contacts and Change in English, Volume 10, Outposts of Historical Corpus Linguistics: From the Helsinki Corpus to a Proliferation of Resources*, ed. J. TYRKKÖ, M. KILPIÖ, T. NEVALAINEN, and M. RISSANEN (Helsinki, 2012: *Research Unit for Variation, Contacts and Change in English (VARIENG)*), <https://varieng.helsinki.fi/series/volumes/10/stenroos_thengs/>.

STERPONI, L., "Literacy socialisation", in: *The Handbook of Language Socialisation*, ed. A. DURANTI, E. OCHS, and B.B. SCHIEFFELIN (Oxford, 2012), pp. 227-246.

STOKES, P.A., *English Vernacular Minuscule from Æthelred to Cnut c. 990-c. 1035* (Cambridge, 2014).

STUBBS, E., "Seeking scribal communities in medieval London", in: *Scribal Cultures in Late Medieval England: Essays in Honour of Linne R. Mooney*, ed. M. CONN-

Bibliography 391

OLLY, H. JAMES-MADDOCKS, and † D. PEARSALL (Woodbridge, 2022), pp. 125-145.

SUTTON, A., and L. VISSER-FUCHS, "'The making of a minor London chronicle in the household of Sir Thomas Frowyk (died 1485)", *The Ricardian* 10 (1994), pp. 86-103.

SYMONS, V., "Commentary for riddles 75 and 76", in: *The Riddle Ages: An Anglo-Saxon Riddle Blog*, ed. M. CAVELL, V. SYMONS, and M. AMMON, Blog Post 26 March 2018, <https://theriddleages.wordpress.com>.

SYMONS, V., *Runes and Roman Letters in Anglo-Saxon Manuscripts* (Berlin, 2016).

TAAVITSAINEN, I., "Scriptorial 'house styles' and discourse communities", in: *Medical and Scientific Writing in Late Medieval English*, ed. I. TAAVITSAINEN and P. PAHTA (Cambridge, 2004), pp. 209-240.

TABOURET-KELLER, A., "Language and Identity", in: *The Handbook of Sociolinguistics*, ed. F. COULMAS (Oxford, 1997), pp. 315-326.

Teaching Writing, Learning to Write: Proceedings of the XVIth Colloquium of the Comité Internationale de Paléographie Latine, ed. P.R. ROBINSON (London, 2010).

THAISEN, J., "Initial position in the Middle English verse line", *English Studies* 95.5 (2014), pp. 1-14.

THOMPSON, J.J., *Robert Thornton and the London Thornton Manuscript* (Cambridge, 1987).

THOMPSON, J.J., I. JOHNSON, S. KELLY, R. PERRY, and A. WESTPHALL, *Geographies of Orthodoxy: Mapping English Pseudo-Bonaventuran Lives of Christ, 1350-1550* (Belfast and St. Andrews, n.d.), <https://geographies-of-orthodoxy.qub.ac.uk/discuss/>.

THOMPSON, J.J., S. KELLY, and R. PERRY, *Imagining History: Perspectives on Late Medieval Vernacular Historiography, Database of Manuscript Descriptions* (Belfast, 2013-2017), <https://web.archive.org/web/*/http://www.qub.ac.uk/imagining-history/resources/wiki/index.php/Special:Allpages*>.

THOMSON, D., *A Descriptive Catalogue of Middle English Grammatical Texts* (New York, 1979).

THOMSON, R.M., "Monastic and cathedral book production", in: *The Cambridge History of the Book in Britain: Volume II: 1000-1400*, ed. N. MORGAN and R.M. THOMSON (Cambridge, 2008), pp. 136-167.

THORNDIKE, L., "More copyists' final jingles", *Speculum* 31.2 (1956), pp. 321-328.

THUILLIER, M., "The Welsh *Hymn to the Virgin*: Contexts and reception" (unpublished M. Phil. thesis, University of Glasgow, 2018).

TILGHMAN, B.C., "The shape of the word: Extralinguistic meaning in Insular display lettering", *Word & Image* 27.3 (2011), pp. 292-308.

TIMOFEEVA, O., "'*Of Ledene bocum to Engliscum gereorde*': Bilingual communities of practice in Anglo-Saxon England", in: *Communities of Practice in the History of English*, ed. J. KOPACZYK and A.H. JUCKER (Amsterdam, 2013), pp. 201-223.

TONRY, K., "Reading history in Caxton's *Polychronicon*", *Journal of English and Germanic Philology* 111.2 (2012), pp. 169-198.

TREHARNE, E., *Living Through Conquest: The Politics of Early English, 1020-1220* (Oxford, 2012).

TREIMAN, R., J. GORDON, R. BOADA, R.L. PETERSON, and B.F. PENNINGTON, "Statistical learning, letter reversals, and reading", *Scientific Studies of Reading* 18 (2014), pp. 383-394.

TWEDDLE, D., "Medieval love poem written in wax", *Minerva: The International Review of Ancient Art and Archaeology* 3.2 (1992), pp. 10-12.

TYRKKÖ, J., "Printing houses as communities of practice: Orthography in early modern medical books", in: *Communities of Practice in the History of English*, ed. J. KOPACZYK and A.H. JUCKER (Amsterdam, 2013), pp. 151-176.

ULLMAN, B.L., "*Abecedaria* and their purpose", *Transactions of the Cambridge Bibliographical Society* 3 (1961), pp. 181-186.

UNSETH, P., "Sociolinguistic parallels between choosing scripts and languages", *Written Language & Literacy* 8.1 (2005), pp. 19-42.

VAN DIJK, S.J.P., "An advertisement sheet of an early fourteenth-century writing master at Oxford", *Scriptorium* 1 (1956), pp. 47-64.

VAN MENSEN, L., H.F. MARTEN, and D. GORTER, "Minority languages through the lens of the linguistic landscape", in: *Minority Languages in the Linguistic Landscape*, ed. L. VAN MENSEN, H.F. MARTEN, and D. GORTER (Basingstoke, 2012), pp. 319-323.

Vernacular Aesthetics in the Later Middle Ages: Politics, Performance, and Reception from Literature to Music, ed. K.W. JAGER (Basingstoke, 2019).

Vernacular Manuscript Culture 1000-1500, ed. E. KWAKKEL (Leiden, 2018).

Viewing Inscriptions in the Late Antique and Medieval Worlds, ed. A.D. EASTMOND (Cambridge, 2015).

Vocabulaire du livre et de l'écriture au Moyen Age: Actes de la table ronde, Paris 24-26 septembre 1987, ed. O. WEIJERS (Turnhout, 1989: *Etudes sur le vocabulaire intellectuel du Moyen Age* 2).

VOSTERS, R., G. RUTTEN, M. VAN DER WAL, and W. WANDENBUSSCHE, "Spelling and identity in the Southern Netherlands (1750-1830)", in: *Orthography as Social Action: Scripts, Spelling, Identity, and Power*, ed. A.M. JAFFE, J. ANDROUTSOPOULOS, S. JOHNSON, and M. SEBBA (Berlin, 2012), pp. 135-159.

WAKELIN, D., *Designing English: Early Literature on the Page* (Oxford, 2017).

WAKELIN, D., *Scribal Correction and Literary Craft* (Cambridge, 2014).

WAKSMAN, S., and E. SHOHAMY, "Decorating the city of Tel Aviv-Jaffa for its centennial: Complementary narratives via linguistic landscape", in: *Linguistic Landscape*

Bibliography 393

in the City, ed. E. SHOHAMY, E. BEN-RAFAEL, and M. BARNI (Bristol, 2010), pp. 57-73.

WALDRON, R., "Dialect aspects of manuscripts of Trevisa's translation of the *Polychronicon*", in: *Regionalism in Late Medieval Manuscripts and Texts*, ed. F. RIDDY (Woodbridge, 1991), pp. 67-88.

WARNER, L., *Chaucer's Scribes: London Textual Production, 1384-1432* (Cambridge, 2018).

WARNER, L., *The Myth of* Piers Plowman*: Constructing a Medieval Literary Archive* (Cambridge, 2014).

WEISKOTT, E., "Puns and poetic style in Old English", in: *Etymology and Wordplay in Medieval Literature*, ed. M. MALES (Turnhout, 2018), pp. 191-211.

WENGER, E., *Communities of Practice: Learning, Meaning, and Identity* (Cambridge, 1998).

WHITMAN, F.H., "Ænigmata Tatwini", *Neuphilologische Mitteilungen* 88.1 (1987), pp. 8-17.

WHITMAN, F.H., "Medieval riddling: Factors underlying its development", *Neuphilologische Mitteilungen* 71.2 (1970), pp. 177-185.

WIELAND, G., "The glossed manuscript: Classbook or library book?", *Anglo-Saxon England* 14 (1985), pp. 153-173.

WILKIE, R., *The Digital Condition: Class and Culture in the Information Network* (New York, 2011).

WILLIAMS, B., "Monsters, masons, and markers: An overview of the graffiti at All Saints Church, Leighton Buzzard", *Peregrinations: Journal of Medieval Art and Architecture* (Special issue: *New Research on Medieval and Later Graffiti*) 6.1 (2017), pp. 38-64.

WILSON, E.M., "A newly identified copy of the *ABC of Aristotle* in the 'Winchester Anthology'", *Notes and Queries* n.s. 47.3 (2000), p. 296.

WILSON, E.M., "An unpublished alliterative poem on plant-names from Lincoln College, Oxford, MS Lat. 129 (E)", *Notes and Queries* n.s. 26.6 (1979), pp. 504-508.

WILSON, R.M., "More lost literature in Old and Middle English", *Leeds Studies in English* 5 (1936), pp. 1-49.

The Wollaton Medieval Manuscripts: Texts, Owners, and Readers, ed. R. HANNA and T. TURVILLE-PETRE (Woodbridge, 2010).

WOLPE, B., "Florilegium alphabeticum", in: *Calligraphy and Palaeography: Essays Presented to Alfred Fairbank on his 70th Birthday*, ed. O.S. OSLEY (London, 1965), pp. 69-75.

WOODHOUSE, L., "After 130 years, Coca-Cola has the typeface it deserves", *Campaign*, 16 Jan. 2018, <https://www.campaignlive.co.uk/article/130-years-coca-cola-typeface-deserves/1454619>.

WORMALD, C.P., "The uses of literacy in Anglo-Saxon England and its neighbours", *Transactions of the Royal Historical Society* 27 (1977), pp. 95-114.

WORMALD, F., "The Calendar of the Augustinian Priory of Launceston in Cornwall", *Journal of Theological Studies* 39, No. 153 (1938), pp. 1-21.

WRIGHT, C.E., "Late Middle English *parerga* in a school collection", *Review of English Studies* 2 (1951), pp. 114-120.

YOUNG, J., and P.H. AITKEN, *A Catalogue of the Manuscripts in the Library of the Hunterian Museum in the University of Glasgow* (Glasgow, 1908).

YOUNGS, D., "Entertainment networks, reading communities, and the early Tudor anthology: Oxford, Bodleian Library, MS Rawlinson C. 813", in: *Insular Books: Vernacular Manuscript Miscellanies in Late Medieval Britain*, ed. M. CONNOLLY and R. RADULESCU (Oxford, 2015), pp. 231-246.

YOUNGS, D., *Humphrey Newton (1466-1536): An Early Tudor Gentleman* (Woodbridge, 2008).

Indexes

Index of Medieval Manuscripts

Aberdeen, University Library
  21: 333 nn. 121 and 123, 342, 346
Aberystwyth, National Library of Wales
  733B: 128-129
  Brogyntyn ii.1 (Porkington 10): 126
  Peniarth 356B: 203 n. 104
  Peniarth 481: 66 n. 125
Bergamo, Biblioteca Civica
  cod. Δ VII.14: 152, 154
Berlin, Staatsbibliothek Preussischer Kultur-besitz
  lat. fol. 384: 139 n. 67
Birmingham, University of Birmingham, Cadbury Library
  Little Malvern Court 1 (deposit): 257 n. 115
Cambridge: Corpus Christi College
  145: 301, 302-303, 305, 316 n. 78
  354: 333 n. 121
Cambridge, Fitzwilliam Museum
  McClean 123: 61, 80-83
Cambridge, Gonville and Caius College
  249/277: 208
  417/447: 76 n. 140
  468/575: 112 n. 29
  669*/646: 207, 208
  791/827: 112 n. 29
Cambridge, Magdalene College
  13 (F.4.13): 271
  Pepys 1916: 151-152
  Pepys 2006: 184 n. 59

  Pepys 2344: 316 n. 78
  Pepys 2981: 140-141
Cambridge, St. John's College
  28 (B.6): 206, 209
  29 (B.7): 209
  137 (E.34): 204, 209
  163 (F.26): 76 n. 140
  189 (G.21): Figure 26, 319, 322 n. 89, 323, 327, 328
  204 (H.1): 333, 342, 343-344, 345, 346
Cambridge, Trinity College
  B.11.14: 207
  B.11.18: 193
  B.14.39-40: 61, 73-77, 78, 116, 203 n. 104
  O.1.57: 117 n. 33
  O.2.53: 168 n. 38, 172, 173, 175, 180, 242, 251, 270
  O.5.4: 108-109
  O.9.38: 254, 256
  R.3.19: 258
  R.3.20: 258, 259
  R.3.21: 259
  R.3.25: 316 n. 78
  R.14.22: 267
  R.17.1: 94 n. 192
Cambridge, University Library
  Additional 6578: 329-330
  Additional 6686: 329 n. 113, 330
  Ee.4.31: 180 n. 52
  Ff.1.6: 126-127, 135, 206-207, 208, 211-

212, 251
Ff.2.33: 34
Ff.5.30: 184 n. 60
Ff.5.48: 168 n. 38, 179
Ff.6.15: 296 n. 35
Gg.4.32: 270
Hh.1.5: 51 n. 91
Hh.3.15: 267
Ii.4.9: 266, 288
Nn.4.12: 55 n. 105
Chicago, Newberry Library
32.9: 208
Dublin, Trinity College
509: 168 n. 38, 169, 172, 173, 175, 227
516: Figure 16, 209, 212-213, 332
Durham, University Library
Cosin V.i.9: 183-184
Edinburgh, National Library of Scotland
Advocates' Library 18.7.21: 232, 266
Advocates' Library 19.2.1: 190-192, 304
n. 58
Advocates' Library 19.3.1: 208
Edinburgh, University Library
136: 133 n. 59, 291 n. 21
Exeter, Cathedral Library
3501: Figure 5, 87-94
Glasgow, University Library
Hunter 197 (U.1.1): 212
Hunter 223 (U.2.14): 332 n. 119
Hunter 232 (U.3.5): 125, 129, 242
Hunter 239 (U.3.12): 186
Hunter 367 (V.1.4): 335
Hunter 472 (V.6.22): 52-55, 57, 58
p.e.6 [early printed book]: 70 n. 130
Hereford, Cathedral Library
O.iv.14: 271
Kew, The National Archives
C47/34/13: 118
C65/86: 31 n. 8
C65/103/47: 31 n. 6
E175/11/16: 264
SC8/28/1373: 31 n. 6
SC8/135/6716: 31 n. 8
Leeds, University Library
Brotherton 500: Figure 24, 308-309
Lincoln, Cathedral Library

91: 204, 207, 215
Liverpool, Public Library
f909 HIG: 333 n. 121
London, British Library
Additional 10574: 314 n. 77
Additional 12195: 51
Additional 19046: 109-110, 137
Additional 22283: 313 n. 71
Additional 23986: 296 n. 35
Additional 24194: 333 and n. 121, 335,
341-343, 345 and n. 140, 346
Additional 24203: 205, 208, 315 n. 78
Additional 27592: 55 n. 105
Additional 27944: 346
Additional 29729: 214-215, 251 n. 100
Additional 31042: 205
Additional 32578: 205, 208, 315 n. 78
Additional 34186: 125 n. 11
Additional 36983: Figure 14, 168 n. 38,
169, 170, 172, 173, 175, 183, 184-186
Additional 37049: Figure 13, 168 n. 38,
169, 170, 171, 174, 175, 177, 180-
181, 327, 328
Additional 37075: 76 n. 140
Additional 37790: Figure 25, 32, 318-323,
325 n. 100, 327-328
Additional 43797: 51 n. 91
Additional 59495: 356-357
Additional 60577: 118-119, 168 n. 38,
170, 172, 174, 177, 179, 181
Additional 62080: 113-114, 116, 131
Additional 88887: 154
Arundel 140: 209
Arundel 249: 107-108, 118
Arundel 292: 270
Cotton Caligula A.vii: 356
Cotton Caligula A.xi: 314 n. 77
Cotton Cleopatra C.vi: 61, 83-85
Cotton Nero A.x: 37
Cotton Otho B.x [not extant]: 195
Cotton Tiberius D.vii: 333, 336 n. 128,
342
Cotton Titus D.xviii: Figure 4, 61, 62, 63,
67-71, 72, 73, 87
Cotton Vespasian D.xxi: 122-124
Cotton Vitellius A.xii: 71

Indexes 397

Egerton 2006: 319, 322 n. 89, 323 n. 92, 327

Egerton 2891: 301, 303-304, 305

Harley 53: 124-125

Harley 63: 124

Harley 116: 193-194

Harley 208: Figure 1, Figure 2, 34, 44-45, 48, 61, 121-122, 124

Harley 541: 168 n. 38, 169, 172, 173, 174, 175, 177, 178, 179, 181

Harley 913: 265-266

Harley 984: 265

Harley 1002: Figure 8, 51, 116-117, 299

Harley 1205: 309

Harley 1277: 51, 114-116

Harley 1304: 168 n. 38, 173, 175, 177-178, 179-180, 181

Harley 1587: 118

Harley 1671: 265

Harley 1706: 168 n. 38, 170, 171, 173, 175, 177, 181-182

Harley 1735: 134-135, 167

Harley 1900: 333, 335, 341, 342

Harley 2248: 127

Harley 2251: 186

Harley 2253: 157-158, 161-162, 190-192

Harley 3763: 61, 72-73, 74, 94 n. 192

Harley 4196: 310

Harley 4486: 264

Harley 4775: 31-32

Harley 5086: 168 n. 38, 170, 172, 173, 174, 175, 227

Harley 5751: 76 n. 140, 107

Harley 6041: 127, 130, 180 n. 51

Harley 7322: 269, 270

Harley 7578: 186

Lansdowne 762: 153 n. 95

Royal 14 C.ix: 332

Royal 15 C.xii: 210 n. 141

Royal 17 A.xxvii: 210 n. 144

Royal 17 B.i: 59-60

Royal 17 B.xlvii: 251

Royal 18 C.xxii: 346

Royal 18 D.ii: 250-252

Sloane 1448A: 152-154

Stowe 57: 61, 63-67, 69, 71, 72, 73, 87

Stowe 65: 333, 337-341, 342, 344

London, Dulwich College

22: 296 n. 35

24: 209

London, Lambeth Palace Library

223: 210 n. 144

419: 235

853: 168 n. 38, 170, 172, 173, 174-175, 179

Sion College, Arc. L. 10.2/E44: 184 n. 60

London, Lincoln's Inn

Hale 135: 296 n. 35

London, Society of Antiquaries

93: 125, 129, 135

Maidstone, Museum

A.13: 61, 77-80

Manchester, Chetham's Library

6709 (Mun.A.4.104): 205, 208

11379 (Mun.A.6.90): Figure 27, Figure 28, 333, 336-337, 341, 342

Manchester, John Rylands Library

Eng. 50: 128 n. 55, 129, 137, 309

Eng. 51: 203 n. 204, 315 n. 78

Eng. 75: 125

Eng. 78: 128, 130, 136, 137

Eng. 85: Figure 3, 57-59, 60, 127, 129-130, 137

Eng. 87: 126, 130

Eng. 102: 126

Eng. 105: 126, 135

Eng. 113: Figure 9, 126, 130-131, 135

Eng. 895: 126, 135, 242

Lat. 394: 166-167, 267

Naples, Biblioteca Nazionale Di Napoli

XIII.B.29: 206, 209

New Haven, Yale University, Beinecke Library

439: 140 n. 69

Takamiya 61: 168 n. 38, 172, 173, 174, 180

New York: Columbia University

Plimpton 258: 55-57, 58, 127

New York, Pierpont Morgan Library

M.537: 66 n. 125

Nottingham, University Library

Mi LM 2: 111 n. 26, 112 n. 28

Wollaton WLC/LM 38: 301 and n. 51, 304, 305

Oxford, Balliol College
354: 254-255, 272-273

Oxford, Bodleian Library
Addit. C. 38: 316 n. 78
Addit. C. 220: 304
Ashmole 50: 208
Ashmole 61: 207, 209, 241-242
Ashmole 789: Figure 10, 141-144, 150
Ashmole 1468: 127, 128, 134, 138
Bodley 85: 55 n. 105
Bodley 315: 255-257
Bodley 416: 270-271
Bodley 423: 310, 315 n. 78
Bodley 638: 187-188, 213 n. 151
Bodley 693: 346
Bodley 814: 314 n. 77
Bodley 902: 347
Digby 55: 296 n. 35
Digby 62: 70 n. 130
Digby 86: 77 n. 142, 127, 134, 135-136, 137, 188 n. 63, 296 n. 35
Digby 99: 312 n. 70
Douce 157: 312 n. 70
Douce 372: 32
Douce 384: 169 n. 38, 173 n. 42
Douce A.314 [early printed book]: 271
e. mus. 198: 140
Eng. poet. a. 1: 313 n. 71, 337 n. 131
Fairfax 16: 188-189, 203 n. 104
Holkham misc. 39: 264
Junius 1: Figure 23, 293-296
Lat. Misc. c. 66: Figure 11, Figure 12, 144-150, 168 n. 38, 169, 171, 172-174, 175 n. 44, 178, 194, 213-214, 242, 253-254
Laud Misc. 509: 122, 123
Laud Misc. 598: 208-209
Laud Misc. 609: 246
Laud Misc. 740: Figure 15, 186-187
Rawl. B. 196: 168 n. 38, 169, 170, 172, 173, 174, 179, 227
Rawl. C. 48: 180 n. 52
Rawl. C. 209: 57, 137
Rawl. C. 510: 296 n. 35

Rawl. C. 813: 215
Rawl. D. 328: 76 n. 140, 111 n. 27
Rawl. Poet. 149: 205, 206
Selden supra 53: 265
Tanner 17: 316 n. 78
Tanner 407: 215, 271

Oxford, Christ Church
145: 10

Oxford, Corpus Christi College
197: Figure 6, 94
236: 321-322

Oxford, Exeter College
4: 264

Oxford, Lincoln College
Lat. 129/130: 110-113

Oxford, Merton College
248: 296 n. 35
299: 291 n. 21

Oxford, New College
152: 333 n. 119

Oxford, St. John's College
17: 63, 71

Oxford, University College
142: 204, 315 n. 78

Paris, Archives Nationales
Musée des documents français, Ancien fonds, AE/II/258, Cote d'origine: J//1168: 238 n. 67

Paris, Bibliothèque Mazarine
latin 717: 62

Paris, Bibliothèque nationale de France
fonds anglais 39: 208
fr. 25458: 193
lat. 8685: 140 n. 70

Philadelphia, University of Pennsylvania
Codex 721: 264

Princeton University
Garrett 151: 333 n. 121 and n. 122, 342, 346
Garrett 152: 332 n. 119

San Marino, Huntington Library
HM 132: 332
HM 136: 131-133
HM 137: 135

Tokyo, Senshu University Library
1: 333 and n. 21, 344, 345, 346

Indexes 399

Vercelli, Biblioteca Capitolare
   CXVII: 87-94
Vienna, Österreichische Nationalbibliothek
   Cod. 507: 153-154
Wigston, Record Office for Leicestershire, Leicester, and Rutland
   18 D 59 [formerly at Leicester City Museum]: 301, 302 n. 51, 303-304

Windsor, St. George's Chapel Library
   E.I.I: 268
Worcester, Cathedral Library
   F. 61: 51 n. 91
   F. 123: 51 n. 91
   Q. 50: 210
York, Minster Library
   Add. 2: 52, 57, 58

General Index

ABC à Femmes: 190-192
ABC of Aristotle: Figure 13, Figure 19, 168-183, 184, 190, 201, 227-228, 229, 230, 235-236, 241, 251, 252-253, 263
Accedence: 111, 203 n. 104
Acrostics: 26, 88-90, 165-166, 168, 192-194, 196, 197, 198, 201, 229
Adam Murimuth, *Chronica*: 235
Adam of Nutzard: 167
Adoracio Crucis: 278, 279
Ælfric: 13, 122
   Grammar: 9, 45-46, 49, 61
   Sermones catholici: 205 n. 112
Ælfric Bata, *Colloquies*: 101-102, 106-107
Æthelberht, King of Kent, laws: 33
Æthelwold, school of: 13
Alanus de Insulis, *Anticlaudianus*: 70 n. 130
Albertus Magnus, *Compendium*: 233 n. 43
Alcuin: 44, 205 n. 112
   Orthographia: 299
Aldhelm, Abbot of Malmesbury: 162, 166
   De Metris: 291
   Riddles: 164, 165, 291
Alexander of Villa Dei, *Doctrinale*: 293 n. 27
Alfred, King of Wessex: 13, 250, 352
   See also: Asser, *Life of King Alfred*; *Proverbs of Alfred*
Alice Shenton: 82
Alphabets: 9, 25, 46-61, 63, 164-165, 218, 351, 353, 355
   Alphabet poems: Figure 13, Figure 14, 26, 118, 168-192, 195, 201, 351
   Alphabet rows and tables: Figure 1, Figure 2, Figure 3, Figure 11, Figure 20, 44,

45, 46, 48, 51-53, 55-58, 61, 63-64, 67-69, 70, 71, 79, 87, 121-124, 126, 127, 140, 141, 143, 144-146, 152, 154, 165, 170-171, 174-175, 177, 232, 244-246, 247 and nn. 92, 95, 274, 327 n. 107
   Alphabetical organisation: 167, 331-349
   Latin alphabet: 34 n. 26, 35-36, 44, 45, 50-51, 53-54, 62-64, 65, 69, 124, 246, 331
   See also: *ABC of Aristotle*; Practice letters and writing
Alphabetical Praise of Women: 190-192
Amherst manuscript, see: Index of Medieval Manuscripts, London, British Library, Addit. 37790
'Amherst scribe': Figure 25, Figure 26, 32, 318-331, 348
Ancrene Wisse: 83-84, 318
Andreas Davidsonus: 70 n. 130
Anglicana script: 319, 357
'*Anglice littere*' ('English letters'), texts about: 25, 43, 61-85, 100
"*Annot and John*": 157-158, 161-162, 191
Anstey, Hertfordshire, Church, graffiti: 234, 240 n. 74
Apostles' Creed: 208
Apotropaic marks: 239, 242, 243
Apuleius: 257 n. 116
Aristotle, 250, 251, 252
   See also: *ABC of Aristotle*
Armourers of London: 259
Arnold's Chronicle: 271
Ash (letter): 33, 45, 94, 123

Names of: 33, 72

Ashwell, St. Mary's Church, graffiti: 25, 223, 226, 230-233, 236-237, 238, 239, 240, 243

Asser, *Life of King Alfred*: 1-2, 6-7

Auchinleck manuscript, see: Index of Medieval Manuscripts, Edinburgh, National Library of Scotland, Advocates' 19.2.1

Ave Maria: 52, 57, 58, 118, 137

Azarias: 276

Banbury, Broughton Church, graffiti: 234
    Warkworth Church, graffiti: 234

Barrington, Cambridgeshire, Church, graffiti: 233

Bartholomaeus Anglicus, see: John Trevisa, *De Proprietatibus rerum* (trans.)

Bede: 33, 51 n. 91, 61
    De Arte metrica: 47-49, 50, 62, 64, 291
    De Orthographia: 299
    Historia Ecclestastica: 104
    See also: *Scutum Bede*

Belaugh, Norfolk, St. Peter's Church, graffiti: 242

Belchamp Walter, Essex, Church, graffiti: 240 n. 76

Benedicite canticle: 276

Benedict Anglus: 177 n. 46

Benedict Burgh: 66 n. 125, 177 n. 46
    Cato major: 180 n. 52, 250, 251-252

Benedictine Reform: 34, 46 n. 69, 195 n. 73, 280

Berkeley Castle: 333

Bernys (scribe): 209

Bewcastle Cross: 96 n. 193, 198

Biblical tags: 113, 117, 137-138, 180, 232-233

Billingham, grave-markers: 98

Blakeney, Norfolk, St. Nicholas's Church, graffiti: 242

Blickling Homily for Easter: 200

Blythburgh, tablet: 106

Boke of St. Albans: 242

Bokyngham, Bishop: 80

Bolton Hours, see: Index of Medieval Manuscripts, York, Minster Library, Add. 2

Boniface: 166

Book to a Mother: 271

Books of Hours: 193, 257 n. 115

Borough Green, Cambridgeshire, Church, graffiti: 240 n. 74

Bromsgrove, Grafton Manor: 253-254

Brussels reliquary: 278

Brut (Middle English prose): 124-125, 126, 127, 135

Byrhtferth, *Enchiridion*: 45, 48, 61, 71

Caistor, inscribed astragalus: 275-276

Azarias: 276

Canonsleigh, Devon, Convent: 84

Canterbury, St. Augustine's Abbey: 20

Capesthorne manuscript, see: Index of Medieval Manuscripts, Oxford, Bodleian Library, Lat. Misc. c. 66

Caroline Minuscule script: 20, 94
    Caroline *g* (letter): 34, 74, 78, 122

Carthusian scribal culture: 324-331
    Statuta nova: 325, 330
    See also: Oswald de Corda, *Opus pacis*; *Valdebonum*

Catchwords: 128

Cato: 66 n. 125, 250
    See also: *Disticha Catonis*

Charles Booth, Bishop of Hereford: 143

Charles d'Orléans: 193

"*Chaunce of the Dyse*": 187-188, 189, 229

Cirencester, books: 20

Colophons, scribal, see: Signatures, colophons, and names, scribal

Combe, M.J. (scribe): 208

Communities of practice, theories of: 14-18

Computus tradition: 61, 62-63, 71

Copying, theories of: 283-284
    See also: Middle English Dialect Project of Angus McIntosh *et al.*

Coveney, Cambridgeshire, Church, graffiti: 240 n. 74

Cowlinge, Suffolk, St. Margaret's Church, graffiti: 240 nn. 75, 77, 242

Creed: 57, 58, 118, 234, 270

Criss-cross rows, see: Alphabets, Alphabet rows and tables

Crowhurst, St. George's Church, graffiti: 239 n. 73

Cryptography: 159, 163-164, 166, 196, 199, 200, 202, 206-207, 211, 229

Cursor mundi: 288, 289, 316

Indexes

401

Cynewulf: 87-94, 194, 198
  Christ II: 87, 89, 91, 199
  Elene: 87, 88-89
  Fates of the Apostles: 87, 88
  Juliana: Figure 5, 87, 89-90, 91-92, 199
Dalham, Suffolk, Church, graffiti: 239, 240 n. 76
Dame Sirith: 296 n. 35
Dance of Death: 260-261, 271, 272
  See also: John Lydgate, *Dance Macabre*; London, St Paul's Cathedral, *Daunce of Poulys*
Daniel: 276
De Ordine creaturum: 76
Deformational writing: 22, 235-238
  See also: Drawings, Graffiti; Graffiti; Wax tablets
Depositio Crucis: 278, 279
Dice and fortune game poems: Figure 16, 169, 182-183, 187, 213, 228-229, 241
  See also: *"Chaunce of the Dyse"*; *Ever is Six the best Chance of the Dice*; *Ragemon le Bon*; *Ragmanys Rolle*
Dictaminal formulas: 25, 117, 135-136, 146-147, 180, 351
  See also: Petitions
DIMEV: 192, 254 n. 103, 256 n. 112
  DIMEV numbers (used in place of, or in default of, titles):
    560: 253, 254
    785: 194
    917: 177
    961: 193
    1112: 249
    1150: 250, 251
    1219: 194
    1220: 194
    1265: 232, 234
    1318: 213 n. 151
    1363: 255 n. 108
    1418: 251
    1651: 255 and n. 108
    1911: 249, 255 n. 107
    1938: 194
    2377: 269
    2643: 175

    2840: 234
    2994: 233
    3141: 231
    3144: 233
    3370: 79
    3414: 234
    3454: 193
    3561: 194
    4423: 250, 252
    4448A: 249
    4836: 266 n. 137
    4954: 254
    4963: 255 n. 108
    5009: 269
    5017: 249 n. 97, 255 n. 107
    5043: 269
    5216: 269
    5635: 234
    6500: 266 n. 138
    6568: 256 n. 113
    6574.5: 231-232
    6610: 269
    6621.5: 256 n. 111
    6634: 268 n. 142
    6757: 230
    See also titles of poems
Diss, Norfolk: 273
Disticha Catonis: 66, 250
Domesday Book: 36
Donatus: 51 n. 91
  Ars maior: 8, 46, 47, 290-291
Doodles: 125, 147 n. 86
Dorothy Helbarton (book owner): 131-133
Double-*u* (letter): 53, 65, 71, 74, 78, 171-172, 336
  Names of: 83
Drawings: Figure 12, 135 n. 64, 147-149, 151-154, 181
  Graffiti drawings: 239-243
Dream of the Rood: Figure 17, 217-218, 276, 277, 278
Drinking bowl, New York Metropolitan Museum: Figure 21, 249
Ductus: 105, 109, 149
Duke of Norfolk's House: 253, 255
Duxford, St. John's Church, graffiti: 230, 238

n. 68
Duxwurth (scribe): 208
Edward I, King of England, writs: 34
Edward Lyster (book owner): 113-114, 131
Elizabeth Beaumont (Oxenford): 182
Ellerker (scribe): 210 n. 141
Enigmata, see: Riddles and riddling
Epigraphy: 26, 218-220, 275-280
    See also: Graphic landscape, theory of
Epitaphs: 273-274
Erthe upon erthe: Figure 22, 261-266, 273
Eth (letter): 21, 33-34, 45, 49, 70, 71, 72, 73,
    94, 123
    Names of: 33, 64, 65, 69
Euangelie: 296 n. 35
Eusebius: 164
    Riddles: 164-165
Ever is Six the best Chance of the Dice: 213,
    229
Everyman: 147 n. 85
Evesham Abbey: 72
Exeter Book, see: Index of Medieval Manu-
    scripts, Exeter, Cathedral Library, 3051
Exeter Book Riddles: 196-200, 206
Exeter Cathedral: 257
Fabula de Philomela: 147
Faversham, Kent: 273
Felix, *Life of St Guthlac*: 122
Femina: 112, 203 n. 104
Figura, see: *Littera*
Findern manuscript, see: Index of Medieval
    Manuscripts, Cambridge, University Li-
    brary, Ff.1.6
Fishburn (scribe): 210 n. 141
Futhark: 33, 69, 87
    See also: Futhorc; Runes
Futhorc: 33, 98, 195, 196, 197, 276
Gawain and the Green Knight, pastiche: 149
Genesis B: 356
Geoffrey Chaucer, scribes of works by: 17, 21,
    205 n. 112
    ABC *Hymn to the Virgin*: Figure 14, 168,
        183-184, 188, 189, 201, 246, 346 n.
        140
    Canterbury Tales: Figure 9, 126, 206, 212,
        302

Canon's Yeoman's Tale: 212
Clerk's Tale: 206, 212
Reeve's Tale: 4
Second Nun's Tale: 205
Tale of Melibee: 255
Geoffrey de Penedok: 134
Geoffrey de Ufford (scribe): 63, 64, 66-67
Geoffrey de Vinsauf: 267
Geoffrey Spirleng (scribe): 212
Glastonbury Abbey Commonplace Book, see:
    Index of Medieval Manuscripts, Cam-
    bridge, Trinity College, O.9.38
Gloucester, St. Peter's Abbey: 20
Golden Legend: 31
Gospel of Nicodemus: 126, 242
Graffiti: 26, 121, 224-243, 244
    Theories of: 224-225
    See also: Ashwell, St. Mary's Church,
        graffiti; Deformational writing; Great
        Bardfield, St. Mary's Church, graffiti;
        and other locations under placenames
Grammar schools: 13-14, 106-107, 111 n. 27,
    117-118, 120, 159, 238, 291 n. 21
    See also: School-books
Graphic communities, theories of: 19-20
    See also: Text communities, theories of
Graphic landscape, theory of: 218-220
Great Bardfield, St. Mary's Church, graffiti:
    Figure 18, 179, 183, 223, 226-230, 232,
    235-236, 239-240, 243, 252
Great Edstone, East Yorkshire, Church: 279 n.
    177
Gregorius Bock (scribe): 140
Gregory of Tours: 35
Guigo II, *Scala claustralium*: 234
Guillaume de Deguilleville, *Le Pèlerinage de
    la Vie Humaine*: 183, 186
    See also: *Pilgrimage of the Life of Man-
        hood*
Hackness, gravemarkers: 98 n. 200
Hartlepool, grave-markers: 96 n. 194, 98
Heliand: 356
Henry de Gauchy, *Gouvernement des princes*:
    183
Heraldry: 150, 241, 242
Hereford books: 20, 143

Indexes 403

Herrysoun (scribe): 208
Holy Name: 124, 234, 327-328, 329
Honington clip: 276
How the Wyse Man Tawght his Son: 250
Hugh Clopton: 272
Hugh of St. Victor: 61
    De Grammatica: 62, 64
Hull (scribe): 208
Humfrey Welles (scribe): 215
Humphrey, Duke of Gloucester: 143
Humphrey Newton (scribe): Figure 11, Figure
    12, 144-154, 171, 173-174, 178, 194, 213-
    214, 215, 243, 252-253
Identity, theories of: 14-21, 23
    See also: Indexicality
Indexicality: 15-16, 203
Inscriptions: 22, 26, 224, 231, 233 n. 48, 244-
    263, 266-267, 271-274, 275-280
    See also: Epigraphy; Graffiti
Insular Minuscule script: 69, 72, 90, 94, 122
    Insular *g* (letter): 34, 70, 73, 74, 78, 122-
    123
    Names of Insular *g*: 78
Isidore of Seville, *Etymologiae*: 47, 61, 62, 64,
    67, 69, 163, 166, 195 n. 73, 299, 317
Isumbras: 241
James Grenehalgh: 323
Jasper Fyball (scribe): 271
Jean Sarrazin (scribe): 238 n. 67
Jerome: 61, 67
Joanna Sewell: 327-328
Johan vom Hagen (scribe): 139
John, Bishop of Hexham: 104
John Appleton (scribe): 315 n. 78
John Bagby (scribe): 205, 208, 315 n. 78
John Benet (scribe): Figure 16, 207, 209, 212-
    213, 215, 332
John Broughton (book owner): 213
John Carpenter: 272
John Clopton: 272 n. 159
John Cok (scribe): 79, 207, 208
John Crophill (scribe): 134, 135, 167
John de Penedok: 136
John de Vere, Earl of Oxford: 182 n. 54
John Farnley (scribe): 205, 208, 215, 315 n. 78
John Gower, *Confessio Amantis*: 313-314,

    316, 346, 347, 348
John Haughton (scribe): 215
John Hull (scribe): 131
John Jones (scribe): 109-110
John Kateryngton (book owner): 315 n. 78
John Leche (book owner): 132-133
John Leke (scribe): 51
John Lydgate, 258, 259, 260
    "*Balade at the reverence of Our Lady*":
    272 n. 159
    Bycorne and Chychevache: 258
    Danse Macabre: 261, 265, 271-272
    Legend of St. George: 259
    Life of Our Lady: 125, 177, 181, 242
    "*Quis dabit meo capiti fontem lacrima-
    rum*": 272 n. 159
    Testament: 272 n. 159
John Mandeville, see: *Mandeville's Travels*
John Marchaunt (scribe): 346-347
John Morton (book owner), will: 247 n. 94
John of Gaunt: 82
John of Grimestone: 232
    Preaching book of, see: Index of Medieval
    Manuscripts, Edinburgh, National Li-
    brary of Scotland, Advocates' 18.7.21
John of Salisbury: 257
John Seward: 291
    Hisigoga metrica: 291
John Shirley (scribe): 79, 214-215, 258-260
John Stow (scribe): 251 n. 100, 259 n. 120
John Trevisa: 331, 332, 333
    De Proprietatibus rerum (trans.): 49-50,
    104
    Defensio curatorum (trans.): 337
    Dialogus inter clericum et militem (trans.):
    337
    Letter to Sir Thomas Berkeley: 337
    Polychronicon (trans.): Figure 27, Figure
    28, 331-348, 349
    Preface to the *Polychronicon*: 337
Jugs, inscribed with proverbs, 249
    British Museum: 249, 255
    Victoria and Albert Museum: 249, 254
Julian of Norwich, *Revelations of Divine Love*,
    32, 319
Julius Caesar: 257

404   *Indexes*

Katherine Group: 70 n. 130
  See also: *Ancrene Wisse*; *Sawles Warde*
Kedington, Suffolk, Church, graffiti: 240 n. 76, 241 n. 79
LAEME, see: Middle English Dialect Project of Angus McIntosh *et al.*
LALME, see: Middle English Dialect Project of Angus McIntosh *et al.*
Landwade, Cambridgeshire, Cotton chapel, graffiti: 235 n. 61
Language play, theories of: 159-160
Lapidarye of Philippe of France: 208
Launceston Priory Hall: 255-257, 260
  Book of Hours: 257 n. 115
Lay of Commandments: 241
Leconfield, Percy house: 244, 250-252
Legenda sanctorum: 271
Leghrewell (scribe): 208-209
Leighton Buzzard, All Saints' Church, graffiti: 239 n. 70
Leweston (scribe): 206, 208, 211
Libeaus Desconus: 256
Libellus de nominibus naturalium rerum: 65-66
Lidgate, Suffolk, Church, graffiti: Figure 19, 229
Lindisfarne, grave-markers: Figure 7, 97-98
Lindsey, Suffolk, Church, graffiti: 240 n. 76
Linguistic landscape, theory of: 220-223
  See also: Graphic landscape, theory of
Litcham, Norfolk, All Saints' Church, graffiti: 242
Literacy socialisation, theory of: 102-103
Littera: 8-11, 106, 182
  See also: Pedagogy of *littera*
Lollards: 13, 20, 55, 58-59, 60
  See also: *Preface to the Wycliffite Biblical Concordance*; Wycliffite Bible
London, Edmonton Church: 273
  St. Bartholomew's Hospital: 79-80
  St. Olave's Church, Hart Street: 231-232
  St. Paul's Cathedral, *Daunce of Poulys*: 271-272
  See also: Armourers of London
Long Melford, Suffolk, Church: 272 n. 159
Ludham, Norfolk, St. Catherine's Church, graffiti: 242

Macclesfield Alphabet Book, see: Index of Medieval Manuscripts, London, British Library, Addit. 88887
Malvern Priory: 234
Mandeville's Travels: 50
Margaret Selman: 82
Martianus Capella, *De nuptiis Philologiae et Mercurii*: 46-47
Masons' marks: 239, 241, 242-243
Maud de Lacy, Duchess of Gloucester: 84
Mechthild of Hackeborn, *Book of Ghostly Grace*: 319, 322 n. 89
Metre: 9, 290-292, 293, 298, 312, 313-314, 317, 348, 353
  See also: Rhyme
Middle English Dialect Project of Angus McIntosh *et al.*: 5, 21, 27, 285-289, 306-307, 311, 315, 318 n. 86, 348, 354, 355
Middleton, Suffolk, Holy Trinity Church: 234
Mirror of Simple Souls: 319, 322 n. 89
Model books, see: Pattern books
Moral precepts, maxims, sayings, and tags: Figure 21, 112-113, 116-117, 167, 177, 180, 181, 192, 232, 233-234, 248-250, 255-257, 260-274
  See also: Proverbs
More (scribe): 206, 207, 209, 256
Morte Arthure: 215
Mount Grace Priory: 330
Names, see: Signatures, colophons, and names, scribal
Nicholas (scribe): 208, 211
Nicholas Love, *Mirror of the Blessed Life of Jesus Christ*: 329-330, 349
Nomen, see: *Littera*
Northampton, Hospital of St. John the Baptist and St. John the Evangelist: 79
Nuneaton Codex, see: Index of Medieval Manuscripts, Cambridge, Fitzwilliam College, McClean 123
Nuneaton Convent: 82
Ogham letters: 63
Old English Heptateuch: 123
Orm (scribe), see: *Ormulum*
Ormulum: Figure 23, 27, 292-301, 305, 314,

Indexes 405

315, 348

Orthography: Figure 23, 9, 13, 25, 36, 37, 49, 51, 59-60, 116, 293-299, 305, 311-312, 322, 324, 325-326, 330, 331, 333, 335, 353, 356-357

　Sociolinguistic theories of: 25, 38-43

　See also: Alphabets; Metre; Rhyme

Oswald de Corda, *Opus pacis*: 325-326, 330

Ownership inscriptions, in books: 25, 113-114, 129-133, 138, 267

Oxford Painted Room: 253, 254

Pangrams: 111, 127-128, 143, 351

Pars oculi: 264

Pater noster: 52, 57, 58, 69, 118, 121, 122, 123, 127, 210 n. 144, 270

　Treatises concerning: 59

Patience: 37

Pattern books: Figure 10, Figure 11, 25, 139-155

Pedagogy of *littera*: Figure 13, 12-14, 21-22, 23, 61-85, 101-119, 159, 162, 163, 164-165, 166, 167, 169-174, 175-178, 192, 194-200, 218, 223, 226, 231, 232, 235, 244, 246, 247, 249, 252, 255, 261-263, 265, 273, 274, 275, 277, 283, 285, 289-292, 293, 299-300, 305, 306, 315, 317-318, 321-322, 323, 326, 331, 345, 347, 348, 349, 351, 352, 353, 355, 357

Pen-trials: 25, 120 and n. 41, 121, 125, 136 n. 65, 138

Percy family: 244, 252, 253, 260

　See also: Leconfield, Percy house; Wressle, Percy house

Perfection of the Sons of God: 319, 322 n. 89

Peterborough Abbey: 66-67

Peterborough Chronicle: 36

Petitions: 31, 149

Piers Plowman: 4, 127-128, 134-135, 314 n. 77

Pilgrimage of the Life of Manhood: Figure 15, 186, 319, 328

Pistill of St. Bernard: 319

Poema morale: 78, 80, 81

'*Polychronicon* scribe': 342

Pore Caitiff: 126

Potestas, see: *Littera*

Practice letters and writing: Figure 8, Figure 9, 110, 111-117, 114, 116, 117, 118-119, 120-138, 141, 143, 146-147, 153, 180-182, 186, 229-230, 264, 265-266, 267, 270-271, 276

Prayers and prayer tags: 120, 136-137, 138, 180, 181, 186, 234, 241, 246, 270, 327, 351

　See also: *Ave Maria*; *Creed*; Holy Name; *Pater noster*

Preface to the Wycliffite Biblical Concordance: 29-31, 32, 38, 50-51, 58, 59-60, 283, 284-285, 290, 331-332, 335, 348

Prick of Conscience: Figure 24, 27, 137, 203 n. 104, 204, 205, 208, 267, 306-312, 313, 315, 345

Primers: Figure 3, 51-61, 127, 137, 140-141, 177, 246, 247

Priscian, *Institutiones grammaticae*: 8-9, 47, 51 and n. 91

Process of the Passion: 126

Prose: 317-318, 348

Proverbs: 26, 76, 120, 153, 232-234, 249, 250, 252-253, 254, 255, 267, 268, 274, 351

　See also: Moral precepts, maxims, sayings, and tags; *Proverbs of Alfred*

Proverbs of Alfred: 74, 75-76, 77-78, 79, 80

Punctuation: 317-318, 324, 334

Pyramus and Thisbe: 208

Ragemon le Bon: 182

Ragman roll: 179, 182

　See also: *Ragemon le Bon*; *Ragmanys Rolle*

Ragmanys Rolle: 182, 183, 184, 188-189

Ranulph Higden, *Polychronicon*: 257 n. 118, 331, 332

　See also: John Trevisa, *Polychronicon* (trans.)

Rate (scribe): 207, 209, 241-242, 243

Recipes: 150

Regeminia: 111

Reginald Pecock: 143

Rhyme: Figure 24, 265, 302-305, 308-311, 334, 348

Ricardus Franciscus (scribe): 31-32, 144

Richard Beauchamp (book owner): 345

Richard Colwell: 273

406   *Indexes*

Richard Fitzralph, *Defensio curatorum*: 337
Richard Heege (scribe): 208, 215
Richard Hill (scribe): 272-273
  Commonplace book of, see: Index of Medieval Manuscripts, Oxford, Balliol College, 354
Richard Misyn: 319
Richard Rolle: 257
  Emendatio vitae: 319, 322 n. 89
  Incendium amoris: 319, 322 n. 89
Richard Whittington: 272
Riddles and riddling: 12, 92, 159, 164-165, 166-167, 194-200, 201, 218, 235, 261-262, 264, 277-278, 351
  See also: Aldhelm, Abbot of Malmsbury; Eusebius; Exeter Book Riddles; Tatwine, Archbishop of Canterbury
Ridgewell Church, graffiti: 233
Robert (scribe): 209
Robert de Penedok: 134, 135
Robert Gatenby: 247
Robert Johnson: 153
Robert Lefydys (scribe): 209
Robert of Nantes (scribe): 140
  Liber de arte scripturali: 140
Robert Reynes (scribe): 215, 271
Robert Thornton: 204, 207, 215
Roger Baldry, Prior of St. Mary's Priory, Thetford: 154
Rolls of Parliament: 31
Roman de Renart: 11
Roman script: 33, 35 n. 26, 43, 90, 96-99, 111, 216, 218
Rose (scribe): 206, 207, 209
Royal Gold Cup (British Museum): 247
Rubrics: 59, 61, 128, 175-177, 180, 184, 193, 194, 212, 251, 258-259, 274, 319, 334, 352
Rule of St. Benedict: 94
Rune Poem: 195-196, 198
Runes: Figure 5, Figure 7, Figure 17, 25, 26, 33, 43, 63, 67, 69, 71, 86-99, 195-196, 197-200, 216, 218, 275-280
  See also: Futhark; Futhorc; *Rune Poem*; Ruthwell Cross
Ruthwell Cross: Figure 17, 96 n. 193, 217-

218, 223, 276-280, 281
Saffron Walden, Essex: 273
Sawles Warde: 210 n. 144
Sawley Abbey: 107
School-books: Figure 8, 101-102, 107-119, 120, 129, 131, 135, 136, 138, 166-167
Scribbles: 121, 122 n. 44
'Scribe D', see: John Marchaunt
'Scribe Delta': 341-342, 343-344, 345 n. 140, 346, 347, 348
Scripta, in language study: 20, 354 n. 8
Scutum Bede: 66
Second Shepherd's Play: 4
Secretary script: 146 n. 83, 179, 357
Sedgeford, Norfolk, St. Mary's Church, graffiti: 239 n. 73, 242
Shibboleths: 10-11, 27
Sible Hedingham, Essex, Church, graffiti: 240 n. 76
Signatures, colophons, and names, scribal: Figure 11, Figure 16, 25, 110, 113-114, 116, 117 and n. 34, 126, 127, 133-135, 138, 146 and n. 83, 147, 153, 180, 181, 182, 184, 201-212, 213-214, 229, 235, 241, 265, 315 n. 78, 323, 327-328, 351, 352
  See also: Ownership inscriptions, in books
Simeon manuscript, see: Index of Medieval Manuscripts, London, British Library, Addit. 22283
Skull caps: 66
Solomon: 253-254, 255
South English Legendary: 27, 206, 210 n. 144, 301-305, 306, 313, 315
Speculum devotorum: 324
St. Albans, St. Peter's Church, inscription: 231
Stapledon, Bishop: 84
Steeple Bumpstead, Essex, Church: 234
Stephen Dodesham (scribe): 324 n. 95, 330 n. 115
Stetchworth, Cambridgeshire, Church, graffiti: 240 n. 76
Stoke-by-Clare, Suffolk, Church, graffiti: 240 n. 76
Stone, Kent, St. Mary the Virgin Church, graffiti: 239

Indexes 407

Stratford-upon-Avon, Holy Cross Guild Chapel: Figure 22, 223, 244, 256, 260-274

Studley Bowl: Figure 20, 244, 245-247

Syllables, study of: 9, 134, 146, 165, 167, 192, 199, 290-292, 297-298, 313
    See also: *Littera*; Orthography

Tatwine, Archbishop of Canterbury: 164, 166
    Riddles: 164, 165-166

Ten Commandments, treatises on: 55, 58, 118, 127, 128

Text communities, theories of: 18-19
    See also: Graphic communities, theories of

Text transparency and opacity, theories of: 160-161, 188 n. 64

Textura script: 20, 137, 140, 152, 154, 236, 237

Thomas Barton (book owner): 267

Thomas Becket: 261

Thomas Bekynton, Bishop: 143

Thomas Berkeley: 345 n. 140
    See also: John Trevisa, Letter to Sir Thomas Berkeley

Thomas Dackomb (scribe): 118, 181

Thomas Frowyk (book owner): 181

Thomas of Wottoun (book owner): 210 n. 144

Thomas Scargill, petition of: 31

Thomas Short (scribe): 110

Thomas Spirleng (scribe): 212

Thomas Tilot (scribe): 315 n. 78

Thorn (letter): 21, 29, 31, 32, 33, 36-37, 38, 45, 49, 50, 53-54, 57, 58, 59-60, 65, 69, 70, 71, 72, 73, 80-81, 83, 94, 123, 137, 141, 146 n. 81, 190-191, 192, 199, 245-246, 248 n. 95, 322, 335-337, 340-344
    Names of: 61, 64, 69, 70, 71, 72, 73, 74, 78, 80, 83

Thorney Abbey: 63

Trentham manuscript, see: Index of Medieval Manuscripts, London, British Library, Addit. 59495

'Trentham scribe': 356

'Trevisa-Gower scribe': 346, 347, 348

Troston, Suffolk, St. Mary's Church, graffiti: 240 n. 76, 242

Uniformitarian principle: 3

Valdebonum: 325, 330

Vercelli Book, see: Index of Medieval Manuscripts, Vercelli, Bibliotheca Capitolare, CXVII

Vernon manuscript, see: Index of Medieval Manuscripts, Oxford, Bodleian Library, Eng. Poet. a. 1

Veronica, St., and veil: 149

Virgilius Maro Grammaticus: 163

Visions of St. Matilda, see: Mechthild of Hackeborn, *Book of Ghostly Grace*

Walter Map, *De Nugis curialium*: 77 n. 141

Wax tablets: 105-106, 237-238

Weye of Paradise: 265

Whithorn: 280

Who-so him bethought: Figure 22, 266-271, 273

William Calverley (scribe): 208, 211

William Caxton: 23, 333, 337

William Cotson (scribe): 205, 208

William de Penedok: 134, 135, 136

William Langland, see: *Piers Plowman*

William Law (scribe): 210 n. 141

William Mede (scribe): 324 n. 95, 330 n. 115

William of Ockham, *Dialogus inter clericum et militem*: 337

William Stevens (scribe): 206, 207

William Underhull: 134, 136

Winchcombe Abbey, books: 20

Winchester, schools at: 13, 108, 181
    St. Peter Colebrook: 118
    St. Swithun's Priory: 118

Winchester Anthology, see: Index of Medieval Manuscripts, London, British Library, Addit. 60577

Wiveton, Norfolk, St. Mary's Church, graffiti: 241-242

Worcester books: 20

Worlington, Suffolk, Church, graffiti: 240 nn. 76, 77

Wressle, Percy house: 244, 250-252

Wycliffite Bible: 10, 12, 128, 136
    See also: *Preface to the Wycliffite Biblical Concordance*

Wynn (letter): 33-34, 45, 49, 69, 70, 71, 72, 73, 80-81, 83, 90-92, 123, 248 n. 95
    Names of: 64, 69, 70, 71, 74, 78, 80, 199

Yogh (letter): Figure 27, Figure 28, 21, 30-31, 32, 34, 38, 50, 51, 53-54, 57, 58, 59, 70, 71, 72, 73, 74, 80-81, 83, 94, 141, 146 n. 81, 245-246, 322, 335-337, 340-344
Names of: 34, 61, 72, 73, 74, 78, 80-81

York, gravemarkers: 96 n. 194
St. Mary Castlegate foundation stone: 279 n. 177
Writing tablets: 237-238